"I wish there had been a music business 101 course I could have taken."

—*Kurt Cobain*[1]

"OFF THE RECORD"

(4th Edition)

What you REALLY need to know about the Music Business!

Larry E. Wacholtz

With

Mark Volman

Rush Hicks

Jennifer Wilgus

Edited by

Emily J. Ramey

Thumbs Up Publishing
991 Westhaven Blvd.
 # 33
Franklin, TN 37064

[1] Kurk Cobain, "Music Business Quotes," Barryrudolph.com. http://www.barryrudolph.com/utilities/quotes.html (accessed December 31, 2010).

Larry E. Wacholtz, PhD
Mark Volman
Rush Hicks – Contracts
Jennifer Wilgus – Economics of Entertainment

lwacholtz@mac.com
615-521-1711

ISBN-**978-0-9840572-4-5**

LCCN: 2011937365
Library of Congress

This text uses *Chicago Stylebook* citation recommendations as provided by Kate L. Turabian in her book, *A Manual for Writers of Research Papers, Theses, and Dissertations*, 7th edition.[3]
Printed in the United States & England, available in printed editions, ebooks, Kindle, and on the iTunes/ iBookstore/iCloud.

---

[2] U.S. Library of Congress, "Title 17, U.S. Code", http://www.copyright (accessed October 2, 2010).

[3] Kate L. Turabian, *A Manual for Writers of Research Papers, Theses, and Dissertations*, 7th ed. (Chicago: The University of Chicago Press, 2007), 133-215.

About the Authors

Dr. Larry Wacholtz is a tenured full Professor of Entertainment & Music Business at The Mike Curb College of Entertainment & Music Business at Belmont University in Nashville. Degrees include a PhD. in Communication, an M.A., in Speech Communication-Film and Television Production ,a B.A., Radio Managment & an A.A. in gereral education. Wacholtz currentlly co-manages a band with Ontourage Artist Managment in Nashville. He has provided psychographic image research to Musicnet.com, MCA and Word Records and was the Director of the Center for Entertainment Industry Entrepreneurship Education at Belmont for several years. Grants include The Coleman Foundation in Chicago, The Kauffman Foundation of Kansas City and the Donald and Geraldine Hedbert Foundation Scholarship. Books authored are *Off the Record (4th edition) How the Music Business Works, Star Tracks: and Inside Country Music (Billboard Books).* Intellectual contributions and memberships include NARAS (Grammy Awards), USASBE (United States Association for Small Business and Entrepreneurship), MEIEA (Music & Entertainment Industry Educators Associations), IFBPA (The International Family Business Program Association), and The Academy of Entrepreneurship where he won a Distinguished Research Award. Keynote speeches include The Tennessee Association of College Stores Convention, *Self-Employment in the Performance Arts* in Chicago, *You in Music Conferences* in the Bahamas and Fisk University, SCORE, The Center for Entrepreneurship in Santa Fe, New Mexico, The Gospel Music Association, and classes at Vanderbilt University. National TV appearances include The Nashville Network and the *You in Music Conference* in the Bahamas (2009).

Mark Volman is a founding member, vocalist, and manager of the musical group, *The Turtles* featuring Flo & Eddie. Recordings include *Happy Together, She'd Rather Be With Me, It Ain't Me Babe, You Showed Me* and *Elenore.* In the 70's, he joined and made 10 albums with *Frank Zappa & the Mother's of Invention*, as well as sang with other artists such as *John Lennon, Bruce Springsteen, T.Rex, Linda Ronstadt, Roger McGuinn* and many more. He's worked in television as a writer and performer for CBS, NBC and the CBC in Canada and has written songs for children's television shows, and records, such as the *Care Bears, G.I. Joe* and *Strawberry Shortcake*, receiving a Grammy nomination for these works. Mark is currently the Chair and Assistant Professor of Entertainment Industry Studies in the Mike Curb College of Entertainment & Music Business at Belmont University. He and *The Turtles* have sold over 60 million recordings worldwide and continue to tour as *The Turtles*, performing 50+ concerts every year.

Rush Hicks is a top entertainment attorney in Nashville and currently serves as the Chair and Assistant Professor of Entertainment & Music Business in the Mike Curb College of Entertainment & Music Business at Belmont University. Previous clients include many famous artists including *Hayley Williams/Paramour.*

Jennifer Wilgus Fowler is an Assistant Professor of Economics with an Entertainment Industry Focus in the School of Business and The Mike Curb College of Entertainment at Belmont University.

Table of Contents

Formats

The following icons have been placed into this publication.

Direct links to Sources active in ebook publications.

Notice of a *List of Items* related to a specific topic

Important items you may want to remember to help you understand the industry and how it operates.

A quick review of the chapter.

1

The Biz

The Creative and Business Systems
The Three Revenue Streams
Digital Music Industry

"I wish there had been a music business 101 course I could have taken."

—Kurt Cobain[4]

"If I were not a physicist, I would probably be a musician. I often think in music. I live my daydreams in music. I see my life in terms of music."

—Albert Einstein[5]

"Music is what feelings sound like."

—Author Unknown[6]

"If we do our job… Music's not black or white, it's green."

—Jim Caparro, PhD[7]

"The music business is a cruel and shallow money trench, a long plastic hallway where thieves and pimps run free and good men die like dogs. There's also a negative side."

—Hunter S. Thompson[8]

Introduction

A bunch of guys get together and start a band. From a legal/business perspective *what does that mean?* Maybe the guys are in high school and just hanging out and jamming. They get better and better and the next thing you know, they start performing in schools and small clubs. *What does that legally mean?* People start talking about them and all of a sudden wow, someone actually offers money for them to play at a private party. *Now*

---

[4] Kurk Cobain, "Music Business Quotes," Barryrudolph.com. http://www.barryrudolph.com/utilities/quotes.html (accessed December 31, 2010).

[5] Albert Einstein, "Favorite Quotes about Music & Songwriting" Songwriters Resource Network, http://www.songwritersresourcenetwork.com/quotes.html (accessed July 13, 2010).

[6] Author Unknown, "Quotations about Music, " The Quote Garden.com, http://www.quotegarden.com/music.html (accessed December 31, 2010).

[7] Jim Caparro, "Music Business Quotes," Barryrudolph.com. http://www.barryrudolph.com/utilities/quotes.html (accessed December 31, 2010).

[8] Hunter Thompson, "Music Business Quotes," Barryrudolph.com. http://www.barryrudolph.com/utilities/quotes.html (accessed December 31, 2010).

what is the world does that legally mean? It mean your legally in business, in fact, surprise, your in the *music business.* How much money you make, how big you become is determined by how many consumers enjoy or hate you (get emotionally and psychologically excited about your music, looks, backstory, blah, blah, blah), and how much they will PAY (to see, hear, and associate with the image/emotions they have of you in their heads) and the rest is history.

You may also want to remember that somehow a few of the 6, 7, or is it now 8 billion people(?) on the planet have to HEAR your music and usually SEE YOU(hello, youtube) and dig your image EMOTIONALLY CONNECT (psychological self-definition or self elaboration) BEFORE you've got a shot at turning this sometimes fun gig into an actual money making CAREER. Say hello to PRICE, PRODUCT, PLACE/ DISTRIBUTION and PROMOTION better known as the 4 P's of business marketing mix![9] And if you really take off (become a CULTURAL ICON) then your financial success will be based on how smart or uneducated you are (or the people you hire) with FINANCE and ECONOMICS. After all, the MUSIC BUSINESS is about rock & roll, drugs, fame, and women. NOT REALLY, it's about being able to make a decent living, playing great music consumers enjoy enough to pay you to hear and emotionally connecting with them.

Look at it as a business. It doesn't matter if you want to be a major super star, songwriter, label or music company employee, manager, road musician, whatever; it's a business FIRST! According to Greenberg (2011), "If you are performing, selling artwork or otherwise making money as an artist, you're engaged in business."[10]

Types of Businesses

In general, there are five legal types of businesses and "what you do" with your career will fit into one, two, three, four or five, as you may own or participate in more than one business or company at a time.

A Sole Proprietorship

The type of businesses owned by most independent contractors working as songwriters, musicians, vocalists, and music producers are sole proprietorships (you're working for yourself). In addition, great musicians usually work as independent contractors represented by a union such as the AF of M, (The American Federation of Musicians) and label artists working in media and recordings are represented by AFTRA (The American Federation of Television & Radio Artists). Yet both the musicians and singers are still in business for themselves as sole proprietors or freelance artists. Advantages of being a sole proprietor include you're the boss and you get to collect all the profits. You also write off business expenses (see an accountant) as income and expenses are considered the same as your personal IRS federal taxes.

---

[9] *Complete Business Startup*, http://www.completebusinessstartup.co.uk/starting-business/the-4ps.html (accessed May 19, 2013).

[10] Sue Greenberg, *Artist as a Bookkeeper*, 2nd ed. (St. Louis, MO: St. Louis Volunteer Lawyers and Accountants for the Arts, 2011), 14.

However, you are also personally responsible for all expenses billed to you and your "company"and you are not protected against lawsuits.[11] You'll also be required to file a DBA (Doing Business As) form if you use a different name (such as a stage name or a business name) other than your given name.

http://www.sba.gov/content/register-your-fictitious-or-doing-business-dba-name

You usually need an EIN number from the IRS if you use a business name to open a bank account to cash the checks paid to you in the businesses name (instead of your real name). According to the IRS.gov (2011):

> *An Employer Identification Number (EIN) is also known as a Federal Tax Identification Number, and is used to identify a business entity. Generally, businesses need an EIN. You may apply for an EIN in various ways, including apply online. This is a free service offered by the Internal Revenue Service.*[12]

http://www.irs.gov/Businesses/Small-Businesses-&-Self-Employed/How-to-Apply-for-an-EIN

Partnerships, Joint Ventures, and Limited Partnerships

These are defined as businesses owned by more than one person. Many bands, small entertainment companies, and publishing companies are legal partnerships. They can be created with a handshake or verbal commitment, yet it is always smart to "get it in writing." In a general partnership (such as a band) each member is required to contribute to the operation of the *business* of the band including creative input, decision-making, profits, payment of expenses, and each other's business liabilities. Ownership is considered equal unless specifically agreed to in a written partnership agreement. The big advantage is that more than one person can own the business and contribute financially and creativity. The negative is that people change and thus the reason for the "partnership" may unravel and each partner is responsible for each other business debts.[13]

http://www.irs.gov/Businesses/Small-Businesses-&-Self-Employed/Partnerships

Limited Liability Companies

LLCs are encouraged for artists and bands as they provide some protection against personal losses (home, cars, first born kid-only kidding) if the business fails to meet expenses. Owners are called "members" who may in some states range from an individual to many other people, investors, businesses, and even corporations. Management decisions are by the members or a hired business manager, the name of the company should be available and trademarked, members may invest silently, and taxes are considered person income (so you're only taxed once). The advantages include the tax advantages found in partnerships and sole

---

[11] Sue Greenberg, *Artist as a Bookkeeper*, 2nd ed. (St. Louis, MO: St. Louis Volunteer Lawyers and Accountants for the Arts, 2011), 17 & personal interviews with industry insiders (2000-2011).

[12] International Revenue Service (IRS), "Employee Id Numbers," IRS.gov, http://www.irs.gov/businesses/small/article/0,,id=98350,00.html, (accessed April 5, 2011).

[13] Sue Greenberg, *Artist as a Bookkeeper*, 2nd ed. (St. Louis, MO: St. Louis Volunteer Lawyers and Accountants for the Arts, 2011), 16.

proprietorships and the legal protections often found in corporations. LLC's are state registered and each state has their own rules. There may be a significant filing fee, and you may be taxed on distributions even if you're not paid.[14]

http://www.irs.gov/Businesses/Small-Businesses-&-Self-Employed/Limited-Liability-Company-(LLC)

Corporations & S Corporations

Corporations bind the artists and business people together and end to merge artifacts, perspectives, values, and assumptions together. Corporations are a separate entity apart from the owners and stockholders. Legal action can usually be filed only against the corporation's assets, not the owners' personal property, who are typically record labels, artists, and stockholders. Thus, the corporation's business structure gives successful recording artists and entertainers a way to protect their personal assets from financial claims against the company. However, there are different types of corporations, which make things more complex. They may seek financial investors (stock or ownership) and according to Greenberg (2011), "S Corporations may transfer profits and/or losses to the individual shareholders' tax return in proportion to stock ownership."[15]

http://www.irs.gov/Businesses/Small-Businesses-&-Self-Employed/S-Corporations

Non-Profit Corporations

Non-profits or 501(c)3's are often used by classic arts organizations such as orchestras, educational dance companies, and other types of entertainment entities as they usually need corporate donations and cash angles to survive. Non-profits are not investment opportunities for profit seeking individuals, as they do not sell stock, nor pay dividends. Formation of a nonprofit is somewhat difficult as they must file with and meet IRS standards. They usually seek grants from the government and other businesses, and donations from corporations (who may use the financial contributions as a tax write-off) to support community art programs. Officers, employees, and operation directors are usually protected from liability situations.[16]

http://www.investopedia.com/ask/answers/08/nonprofit-tax.asp

Entrepreneurship

Entrepreneurship appears to illustrate the business psychology of the music industry. There is often an entrepreneur behind the success of a star or public personality that helps keep the entertainment industry engine running. Entrepreneurs write the songs and screenplays, finance recordings, manage the images and careers of artists, promote, publicize, and market the products to consumers. It is often these individuals and their small businesses that make the industry's profits soar. Relying on their own creative and business

---

[14] Sue Greenberg, *Artist as a Bookkeeper*, 2nd ed. (St. Louis, MO: St. Louis Volunteer Lawyers and Accountants for the Arts, 2011), 16.

[15] Sue Greenberg, *Artist as a Bookkeeper*, 2nd ed. (St. Louis, MO: St. Louis Volunteer Lawyers and Accountants for the Arts, 2011), 18.

[16] Sue Greenberg, *Artist as a Bookkeeper*, 2nd ed. (St. Louis, MO: St. Louis Volunteer Lawyers and Accountants for the Arts, 2011), 18.

decisions they work within the industry without the security of a corporate net to fall back on during negative sales periods. Once you have worked your way into the industry, networking with other industry professionals and entrepreneurs enhances mutually profitable opportunities. Joining with others who have similar interests and talents is a common practice among industry professional entrepreneurs. As an example, if you are a songwriter, start a legitimate publishing company. This is a great way to introduce yourself to industry insiders who can help your career and your business, while at the same time, increase bottom lines.

It's an Art and a Business

There's something burning inside many of us – a dream of success, a desire for fame, money, or maybe just happiness. It's a driving force that's hard to explain or control and sometimes it's hard to live with. It's that thing called creativity – a desire to be successful, a need for self-expression, to share our talents with others, and of course, a desire to be rich and famous.

One summer, on a flight to Berlin, I sat next to a tall attractive woman in her late twenties. I was surprised to discover that she was flying to Germany to sing as the featured artist with the Berlin Opera. As we exchanged pleasantries, she was surprised to learn that I write and teach classes about the business of entertainment and music. It was one of those magical occasions when you meet someone from other part of the country and find out how much you have in common.

As I congratulated her on her success, she told me her college professors had taught her how to sing, but not how to make a living as an artist in the business; that she had to learn herself. Accordingly, she taught herself about the legal, marketing, promotion, management, and accounting aspects of the business, as well as the importance of networking. In the end, she found out that nobody was coming to "discover her," and she realized that to be a financially successful artist, she first had to become an entrepreneur, own her business, and learn how to manage and market herself. It was a hard lesson for her to learn and it took many years away from her singing career.

Music is what our minds are thinking, our hearts are feeling, and our souls are judging. Indeed, it may be the greatest form of creativity known. We often express our listening experiences by laughing or crying, feeling heartbreak, love, sadness, longing, and every other emotion possible. It's complicated! One person may experience a recording or a live performance as positive and exciting whereas another may find it revolting, and still another may not even notice it.

The *business of music and entertainment* is how creative people and businesses cash in on consumer's emotional connection to the recordings, shows, and other related products monetized by the business. It's the same for the artists and "suits" who create, own, and manage the acts, recordings, videos, and songs we love and hate. However, they also hear another sound they love – the sound of the money they've earned "caching" in their bank account.

Right Side of the Brain – Creativity

What do you need to be successful? What do you want to do? If you want to be an artist, songwriter, producer, musician, or vocalist, start with your creativity and figure out what makes you special. Having creative talent is the beginning, not the end to stardom or career success. If you don't have musical, acting, or other talents be weird, be yourself, but most importantly figure out what you can contribute to the industry to make it bigger and more successful. Are you able to create a new software for recordings, a new marketing process, or entertainment merchandising product? As an artist, producer, manager, or label executive, what makes you valuable to the industry? What makes you special? What unique knowledge or creative skills can you provide to help an artist become rich and famous and financially successful? As an artist or performer, what messages are you trying to convey through your lyrics, image, or essence that connect with the emotional needs of consumers? Can your image be turned into "branding" a product consumers will want to buy?

Left Side of the Brain – Business

If you are not the creative type, what can you provide to the business side of the industry that will help it generate sales and profits? Creativity is also required from "suits" as well as the songwriters and performers; it's just a different type of "creativity." While the "artists" use their creativity to generate artistic products (songs, live shows, recordings) to which consumers emotionally connect, the "suits" figure out how to make a profit from their financial investment in the artist's products. Not easy! Marketing, promotion, publicity, and all the legal stuff – copyrights, contracts, you name it – you better know it. How does knowledge of copyrights contribute to success in music publishing? Why should an artist understand the difference between a development deal and a 360 deal? How important is it for a promoter to understand difference consumer preferences (types of acts) before staging a live concert in a variety of markets? You get the picture, you need to understand the broad perspective of the industry before you can grasp the potential of each speciality or niche.

Opportunity

Opportunity is the strategic placement of an artist's talents and products to various types of consumers based on their perceived emotions of an artist's image. Opportunity can be measured through the level of sales of recordings and concert tickets, along with the public's use of live and recorded music through the mass media and digital "click or new media" (personal devices such as iPods, iPhones, mp3 players, cell phones, and ring/ master tones). How much money is being made from the recordings merchandise, concert ticket sales and corporate sponsors? These various outlets establish *revenue streams* and profits for the industry.

Still, it is hard to understand and accept the reality that the entertainment industry is not based on pure artistic talent but on the profit and loss statements generated from products. So if this industry is just like every other one based on money, how can you become successful? Be creative, and learn the business!

Talent

According to the *World Book* (2006), the present use of the word "talent," meaning special ability, may come symbolically from a Bible story found in Matthew 25:14-30:

> *Talent is a famous old unit of weight and value. The Hebrews, Babylonians, Greeks, and Romans used it. No coin of this denomination was ever struck (made), because such a coin would be too large. Instead, a certain number of other coins equaled a talent. The Hebrew silver talent equaled 3,000 shekels in silver. The gold talent had different weights and values in different places.*[17]

Artists in the music and entertainment business are responsible for their own success. Instead of waiting to be discovered, young artists need to proactively pursue their career. Being able to sing well, knowing someone in the business, and going to school is a good start. Developing creative and analytical skills is important; grasping an understanding of the serious and popular cultures of society is helpful; gaining business and industry specific knowledge is useful; networking is necessary; and having a personal passion for success is absolutely essential.

---

[17] *World Book Encyclopedia*, CD-ROM, Windows XP, Chicago: World Book Inc., 2006.

Creativity

Creativity is defined as the "talent" present in the products, i.e. recordings, concerts, songs, provided to consumers through the business system of the music and entertainment industry. Thus, it has many different meanings to various entities.

The Foundation

A great song is truly the foundation of the communicative link between the artists and consumers. The business is built on the shoulders of a great song; yet the writers who create the songs are often the last to be paid.[18] What's being sold is a package consisting of a great song, or a recording of that great song, which is tied to the image of the artists and helps consumers to get excited about what they are hearing, seeing, and feeling emotionally. It really does start with a great song!

The Creative System

The traditional music and entertainment business is a complex industry. It is a collection of artists, entrepreneurs, mega entertainment organizations, record labels, consumers, the mass media (radio, television, print), cell phone networks, and Internet portals that all together form the industry. The creative side, or creative system, is typically composed of songwriters, musicians, producers, recording artists, singers, audio engineers, graphic artists, actors, film directors, union members, and computer technicians. They create the digital downloads, albums, concerts, movies, videos, computer games, and other entertainment products we use, listen to, rent, or buy. The supporting business side, or business system, generally consists of the traditional and independent labels and companies who finance and manage the artists, their recordings, and other entertainment products. Others provide management, promotion, and distribution of images, products, events, and artists. Entrepreneurs and corporations create concert events and management opportunities that generate product-based income, such as tours, merchandise sales, and corporate sponsorships for various media and communication outlets.

Songwriters

Are customarily creative and energetic, as they appear to be consistently seeking a better way to express a catchy idea or hook. Webster's New World dictionary (1986) claims that "they are poets who use music to ingeniously combine words (lyrics) and music (chords and melody) to create emotionally charged messages (songs)."[19]

Langer (1951) suggests that concerns about the emotional power of music include the Greek philosophers:

> *Plato demanded "a strict censorship of modes and tunes, least citizens be tempted by weak or voluptuous aires to indulge demoralizing emotions" (Republic bk iii). "The legend of the sirens is based on a belief in the narcotic and toxic effects of music, as is Terpander's preventing civil war in Sparta, or of the Danish King Eric, committing murder as a result of the harpist's deliberate experiment in mood-production" (Die Music XXIX-Part II).*[20]

---

[18] M. William Krasilovsky, and Sydney Shemel, *This Business of Music*, 10th ed. (New York, NY: Billboard Books, 2007), 157. Plus, private industry interview with writers and publishers (1978-present).

[19] *Webster's New World Dictionary*, 11th ed., 894.

[20] Susanne Langer, *Philosophy in a New Key*, 2nd ed. (Cambridge: Harvard University Press, 1951), 625-630.

It's amazing how few things really change. In "Mobilizing Against Pop Music and Other Horrors," Chris Hedges (1993) states that in Iran, "the Bassij are an army of volunteers formed by Islamic clerics to monitor and seize western popular entertainment products in an attempt to prevent western entertainment from corrupting the youth of their nation."[21] Additional creative system careers include the following:

Artists and Vocalists

Breathe life into a song by conveying the song's emotional message to potential listeners. They infuse energy into the lyrics and vitality into the notes printed on the sheet music. Session musicians and vocalists are considered recording artists. Performances must be believable, sellable, and true to the communicative message in the song as well as the persona of the artists. *The music business is really the emotion business.* Great songs are the foundation of the business. However, it is the *marriage of the great song to the right recording artist* that allows consumers to emotionally connect with creative entertainment products. If the economics are right (and they don't steal it through P2P), their excitement and corresponding purchases and uses of it (listening and viewing) may generate profits for the business. Thus, it is the artist's total package of their image, sound, stage name, backstory, and persona (who and what they represent in the minds of the fans) that drive the industry's profits.

Background Singers (BGVs)

BGV's are the "oohs" and "ah" of the recording and performance industry. They provide the vocal supporting harmony parts for major recording artists, along with singing live at theme parks and nightclubs, on concert tours and cruise ships, and often becoming the voices on popular radio jingles and television commercials.

Musicians

Musicians are the great interpreters of songs. They reveal their emotions and personalities through their musical instruments and performances. They are the backbone of the recording process, supporting both the lyrics of the song and the performance of the vocalists. Working in the "arts" is often a part-time gig as there are fewer recording studio positions available than players. However, there are plenty of opportunities for musicians to work in bands, orchestras, churches, theaters, and other various types of venues.

Record Producers

Producers can intelligently and creatively combine artists, talented background singers, studio musicians, and audio engineers to create potential hit recordings. In preproduction, producers, recording artists, managers, and record companies search to find the types of songs that will best fit the images and vocal capabilities of the artists. In the studio, producers are in charge of the actual recording session and responsible for the budget of the final master recording. *Super producers* are the wave of the future as they wear several "hats" by using Pro Tools or Logic Pro for engineering, and by singing, playing the instruments, choosing the material (songs), take care of the budget, mix and even produce the sessions. The process saves labels thousands of dollars and lowers their financial break-even points.

Audio Engineers

Audio engineers are considered electronic creative artists because they use computers and the studio's acoustics, microphones, consoles, tape machines, computers, and special effects outboard equipment to

---

[21] Chris Hedges, "Mobilizing Against Pop Music and Other Horrors" The New York Times International, July 21, 1993.

enhance the qualities of the recording. Audio engineers are responsible for the technical quality of the recording, just as the producers are responsible for the creative quality of the recording. Their job is to make the artists and musicians sound as good as technically possible. Accordingly, they work with the recording artists, musicians, and producer to capture the artists' and musicians' best creative efforts on tape or computer hard disk. Additional professional opportunities for audio engineers include audio production for movies, videos, television shows, radio broadcasts, jingles, and commercials. Entry-level jobs are often found in nightclubs, hotels, amusement parks, on cruise ships, convention performance art centers, as well as government and military installations.

The Business System

The traditional business side (business system) consists of entrepreneurs and business-minded individuals who publish songs; fund the development of films; computer- and Internet programs and games; finance artists, their recordings, shows, and concerts; and distribute, promote, and market the entertainment products through traditional retail outlets, traditional media, and click media to various consumer markets. It is the buying of the recordings, DVDs, CDs, downloads, concert tickets, and merchandise and the public and private use of music by consumers that provide the revenues and profits required for the creative and business sides of the industry to exist.

Music Publishers

Music publishers bridge the creative and business systems. On the creative side, they screen new songs from independent songwriters, hire staff writers to write new songs, demo record accepted songs, print or have sheet music printed, and pitch the songs to artists, record labels, managers, and producers. They also operate as part of the business system by registering copyrights, issuing licenses, marketing songs, collecting song royalties, and paying writers.

Recording Studios

Studios are where the two industry systems (creative and business) meet, but they often cost more than a million dollars to own and operate. Indeed, some of the same instrument sounds can be created with a $5.00 application on an iPad, so the future of the "big budget studio" is highly in question. The performance studio and control room can easily account for a couple hundred thousand dollars when designed and constructed by the best consultants and contractors in the business. Consoles, digital tape machines, computers, special effects equipment, Pro Tools software, microphones, and monitor speakers quickly add up to big bucks. Add offices, operational personnel, and a cup of coffee, and you have a million-dollar business. Major studios used to rent for $1,000 to $1,500 a day to cover the cost of their initial investments. However, in the world of Pro Tools and digital software, recording studios are less important. In addition, music companies (labels) need to reduce budgets and financial break-even points to compete in a world of theft and free product distribution. They rented studios instead of owning them due to the expense. Now, because of their profit and loss statements and the industry's *economics of scale,* music companies, or labels (whatever you want to call them), are reducing the number of albums being released as well as *how* the albums are being recorded. Studios will always be around, just used differently. The old days of a studio with a mixing console (board), microphones, and console are almost obsolete.[22] Added to the traditional studio setup of acoustics, performance, and control rooms are the computer software programs *Logic Pro* and *Pro Tools* due to the labels restricted budgets.

---

[22] Personal interviews with label executives and many industry insiders, (2008-2010).

Now we'll find albums where only the basic tracks (rhythm instruments) or a few minor parts of the album are actually recorded with live musicians and background vocalists and the remaining tracks are all computer generated.

However, the creative human element can't be ignored. The creative artists still need to sing the songs and the great musicians still need to perform them. Producers still need to tell the artists and musicians how to sing and play their instruments and the audio engineers still need to be able to capture a great track on tape or computer hard drive. In addition, great engineers are still required for the growing concert business and movie sound effects and tracks. Computers may replace the equipment in the studio and even the studio, yet they can not provide the expert musicianship, singing, audio and production of real live human beings. Yeah!

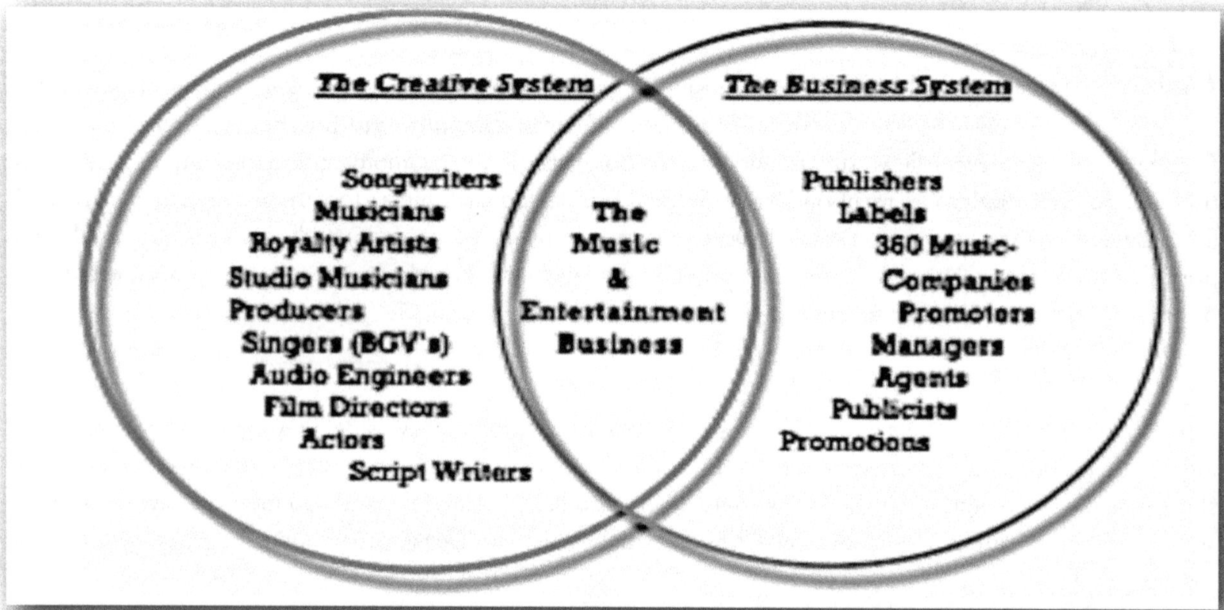

Figure 1.1. The industry consists of two systems (creative and business) that together make the industry work. Creative artists such as songwriters, musicians, singers, producers, audio engineers, actors, directors, and many others create the products the business system publishers, labels, music companies, promoters, managers, publicists, and others use to generate profits.

Digital Recording

Computer technology allows producers to create great tracks without the typical front-end costs of studios. Thus, studios are not as importance as *Pro Tools, Logic Pro* and even *GarageBand* provide quality recordings for a very limited price. Consumers usually do not care (and may not even realize) if the tracks they love are created by real musicians in a multimillion dollar studio or in a dorm room at the cost of a slice of pizza. This technology that may hurt the livelihood of many traditional studio musicians, BGVs, and other artists is providing wonderfully new opportunities for innovative creative artists and entrepreneurs to create new products at lower production cost.

Internet marketing, for example, can help unknown acts get their recordings "out there" to consumers for less money. Even the established traditional labels profit by using technology to reduce expenses in production, marketing, and promotion. CDs may very well be gone from traditional retail in about three years,[23] so if you want to be successful in the music business in the future, learn everything you can about the use of digital technology in the creative and business marketing and distribution system.

---

[23] Personal interviews with label executives and other industry sources, (2011).

Labels (Music Companies)

Labels and now music companies (labels which offer 360 deals) tend to define talent by the money and profits their recordings and image generate. An act with limited musical or vocal talent is as important to a label as any of its other acts if they can creatively connect with consumers and sell millions of units. A *unit* is the term labels use to describe one CD, digital download, or vinyl recording sold. A label's goal is to make the most profit for the least amount of investment. Thus, the need to use expensive recording studios and sessions that add hundreds of thousands of dollars to the debt of an artist's account is ending. Computer programs (discussed previously) provide quality recordings, lower the cost of recording, and quickly help make new artists more profitable. In addition, some labels are quickly moving away from the old business model of developing an act, funding all costs of recordings and tours, and then recouping their investments only from record sales. The newer 360 business model gives the labels (music companies) better returns on their investments by gaining a share to the artists other royalties from concert tours, merchandise, and corporate sponsorships. Still another model that is starting to develop is the partnership model, wherein the artist (and their management team) and the music company both contribute money to the act on the front end and then split the profits when the act becomes profitable.[24]

Promotion

Promotion is the processes used to alert the public to the artist's new products (which are for sale) and to create a buzz, a conversation or topic consumers get excited about and discuss. Giving consumers a *free sample* through radio station airplay, 30 second clips on internet such as iTunes, and cell phone downloads provide consumers a chance to discover an act and their recordings. The buzz is really *word-of-mouth*, which is commonly considered by the labels to be one of the best forms of promotion (new fans getting excited and talking about an act to their friends).

Younger consumers tend to hype each other about the artists and their recordings, which ultimately increase unit sales. *Radio stations* broadcast recordings to attract audiences to sell airtime to businesses., the larger the audience, the more stations charge for their commercial airtime. *Paid advertisements* in trade magazines, local newspapers, the popular press, and on the Internet (websites, blogs, news outlets, and chat rooms) provide visibility and increase the chances articles about the artists (publicity) being accepted and published. Thus, all forms of promotion generate record sale propensity for recording artists and labels. *Music videos* are not as important as in the past. To break a new artist labels may still hire *independent producers* and *production houses* to create the videos in an attempt to launch new acts. Sadly, expensive music videos do not necessary increase unit sales for the labels. They appear to stroke the artist's ego, but not generate any significant profit. Thus, some label executives have reduced video budgets and in some cases eliminated them altogether to make an artist's budget line profitable.

Publicists

Publicists provide consumers a *backstory* (hopefully real) about an artist's life that is tied to their image of a hero, rebel, lover, good guy, bad guy, cowboy, teen idol, or ideal partner. Television talk shows book celebrities to gain larger audiences to sell commercial airtime. Radio and television stations and businesses contract "star" appearances and even their voices to promote their products and stations. In addition, labels consider concert appearances as publicity as great shows may often increase unit sales. Lastly, live radio interviews, store signings, and Internet web pages are used to increase public awareness of the act. Labels provide tour

---

24 Personal interviews with label executives and many industry insiders, (2008-2010).

support money to encourage a successful concert tour because the *events* tend to increase the chances of radio station airplay, media publicity, unit sales and bottom-line profits.

Artist Managers

Mangers bring representation, administrative supervision, and surrogate control to a recording artist's complex image and long-term career. A *business plan* tied to a marketing plan for the business side of the artist's career is regularly developed. Career plans and goals are established based on the perceived commercialization of the artist's image and talents. Managers approve the artist's personal appearances and concert tours that are often booked through a booking agent (who are part of the manager's team). They use the albums distributed and marketed by record labels and promotion provided through radio station airplay to emphasize the image of the artist that, in turn, provides many opportunities to make money for the artist. In addition, new media (the click media) is becoming a vital outlet for both the artist managers and labels to connect with potential consumers. The younger generations (preteens - late 20s) have different consumer media preferences than the older generations when it comes to the music and entertainment business, thus labels and managers are quickly attempting to develop click media marketing strategies to connect artists and their sellable products to potential fans.

The Management Team

Managers build a team of *accountants* to balance the books, *financial advisors* to invest the profits in long-term investments, stocks and money markets, and attorneys to negotiate, draft and oversee the process of executing contractual agreements. *Event coordinators, security, merchandisers, union stagehands, road managers, roadies, arts managers,* and thousands of other niche occupations are available on the business side of the industry to anyone who has the knowledge and the desire to make positive and profitable things happen. The key is what can you (your company or you individually) contribute to the industry to make it better and more profitable? Working in the entertainment industry can be a great life, so how can you make it better so that others already in the business will also benefit? Remember, that knowledge, honesty, hard work, contacts and being creative and smart, are powerful in this business. They can quickly help you enter into the business by contributing to the financial success of others and as well as yourself.

Agents

Booking and talent agents encourage promoters to produce concerts in various markets. Agents with an *American Federation of Musicians* booking license generally book union musicians for concerts, nightclubs, and other types of personal appearances and tours. *The American Federation of Musicians,* (AF of M), contract provides protection to the union musicians who are playing the gig. Nonunion musicians and booking agents do not usually have the protection of union attorneys if the promoter or club owner fails to fulfill their contractual obligations. Agents work as part of the management team to generate revenues for the act based on the act's fame and consumers need to relate to the artist's image, essence, and the recordings the consumers "discovered" through promotion and publicity as defined and described previously.

Concert Promoters

Promoters provide the money required to fund concerts and tours. They are the industry's high rollers betting big money on the popularity of an act to sell seats in local venues and arenas. *Booking agents* representing specific acts call the promoters to set up concert tours. A retainer of 50% or more of the band's payment is customarily required to secure the date for the promoter. The promoter is also required to fulfill the obligations of *the rider*, which is the musician's or act's instructions to the promoter about their specific needs for the concert (staging, lighting, sound, load in and the load out, plus dressing room requirements and security). Accordingly, *the rider* is an addition to the contract between the management company booking agent and the concert promoter. It details specific additional requirements that must be satisfied before the artist will perform and thus becomes part of the contract. Examples of many artists' riders may be found at the website *www.thesmokinggun.com*. As an example, the size of the stage, lighting, sound requirements, dressing room, and dining preferences are listed. Promoters pay for radio advertisements, media promotion, the venue, security, and stagehands. They usually need 50-80% of all tickets sold to break even at an event depending on the fame of the act, size of the venue, and many other factors. Surprisingly, promotion companies are becoming labels, and labels are merging into concert promotion companies.

Tour Teams

Acts often include the *stage crews, lighting, sound, security, road manager*, and others who are required to put on a successful show on the road. Not an easy job, but a great experience for young people to break into the business. Most large venues productions are controlled by *The International Alliance of Theatrical Stage Employees, Moving Picture Technicians, Artists and Allied Crafts of the United States* (I.A.T.S.E.), which are the working crews behind most of the entertainment shows, films, and events created and staged in the United States, Canada, and other world locations.[25]

The Mass Media

The mass media consists of radio, broadcast television and cable, the print media, Internet, billboards and advertisement placed on everything from the side of trucks to shopping carts. Thus, success in the mass media is based on the number of *impressions* tied to the success of and amount of product(s) sold. A national number one hit recordings on radio is worth about one half million dollars split between the music publisher and songwriter(s). However, members of the younger generations appear to be listening less to local radio and more to their iPods and other streaming audio devices. This change in *consumer behavior* seems to be tied to consumer preferences for immediacy, digital technology devices, and music and entertainment products that are now more available, when consumers want them. The trick is getting them to pay for the entertainment products so that the creative system and business system workers and copyright owners are paid for their efforts.

The Digital & Social Media

New Media consists of interactive use of the Internet, cell phones, iPods, PDAs, and other devices that are used to download specific entertainment free promotional samples and to buy products. The mass media are dependent on free recordings from the labels to draw an audience such as radio airplay. Thus, the mass media are not in the music business or film business as they make their profits from selling airtime and space to advertisers. However, a distribution revolution is currently in progress as the beforehand "passive" mass media is now competing with the interactive digital entertainment media product sites such as iTunes, Google, Netflix, Amazon's MP3 Cloud drive and player, Spotify, MOG and other digital product suppliers. Unlike the traditional mass media, click media allows consumers to interact with their selected media sources to enjoy and buy entertainment products cheaper, quicker, and without having to pay for traditional retail markups or even visit traditional retail locations. Consumers save by paying a discount off the *suggested retail list price for digital downloads*. Labels make more money on digital products as they usually receive a 70/30 split of the

---

[25] I.A.T.S.E., "Welcome to IATSE," http://www.iatse-intl.org/about/about.html (accessed July 1, 2010).

revenues (70% to the label, 30% to the provider) as opposed to the traditional 40/20/40 splits (40% to the label, 20% to distribution, mega/local, and 40% to the retail outlet) for traditional retail.[26]

Associate Careers

There are many additional professional creative and business careers available in the music and entertainment industry. *Computer graphic artists* create computer generated movies, television shows, images, posters, computer games and album covers. *Music video scriptwriters, producers, directors, actors, and performers* are involved in music videos, commercials, advertisements and record labels to market, promote, and publicize artists and album releases.

As digital technology continues to inspire the ability of artists to create new forms of entertainment and as businesses evolve to meet the consumer's desire for click media products, many new careers will evolve and be created. *Corporate sponsors* often financially support artists, musicians, and orchestras in exchange for community service, product awareness, and increased product sales. *Retail outlets* sell and rent the industry's books, recordings, movies, and merchandise. Computer and software experts develop Internet-based web pages, movies, games, and music videos.

Consumers

Consumers, without whom the music and entertainment industry would not exist, support both the creative and business systems by buying and using traditional recorded and live presentations, plus the digital downloads and all the other wonderful products that use music (such as computer games). Consumer buying and use of music and entertainment products (made by the creative system and financed, marketed, and promoted by the business system) usually compensate the artists for their creative efforts and provide profits to the labels, entertainment production companies, networks, mass media, and click media for their financial and creative risks.

Revenue Streams

Learning the three revenue streams and all the corresponding business and creative opportunities (careers) will leapfrog you ahead of the millions of others who want a job or career in this business. It's how it works, even as it goes through the creative destruction caused by technology (peer to peer file sharing and the internet), and the introduction of *360 deals* that combine the revenue streams together. Today's industry is growing with new and better jobs and creative opportunities than the traditional businesses that are in the mist of transformation. Indeed, consumers want more entertainment products, not less. Getting them to pay for it, in some cases, may be a little tricky. Yet, even the consumers who illegally download music often find new acts to support through tours, merchandise, and actual album or single recording purchases.

Songwriting/Music Publishing Revenue Stream

Songs are the foundation of the music business. They bring the songwriters, producers, musicians, and the business world together. Once a song is written, it must be published, placed with an artist and recorded or performed publicly to make money. Businesses that use recordings or live performances of a song are usually required to pay for the use of the song through a performance license. Record labels pay mechanical license fees for the use of songs on their recordings. Visual production companies, including film and TV shows are

[26] Personal interviews with label executives and many industry insiders, (2008-2010).

required to pay for the use of a song in the production of the work through acquiring a sync license. In the end, consumers also pay for the use of the songs they hear in the purchase price of downloads, albums, and subscription rates for satellite radio and cable TV.

Label Revenue Stream

Record labels (now often called music companies) find and sign artists to their labels and songs to their publishing companies. They are the banks of the industry, providing hundreds of thousands of dollars to recording artists to pay for advances, producers, musicians, audio engineers, BGVs (background vocal singers), and studio rental time required to complete major album projects. Then they provide additional money to market the recordings to various types of consumers through promotion, publicity, and distribution to retail outlets. Labels range in size from worldwide distribution companies (mega entertainment organizations), such as *Disney, Sony, Universal, and EMI* to the one-person operations that offer digital downloads over the Internet. Favorite recording artists selected by different types of consumers usually reveal the personalities and lifestyles of the consumers through demographic and psychographic research.

Artist Management Revenue Stream

Managers provide advice and guidance to many established artists by *monetizing* consumers' perceptions and emotional connections to an artist through the perceived limited access of tour appearances, corporate sponsorships, endorsements, and merchandise sales. Labels use print media and the mass media of radio, television, cell phones, iPods, the Internet, and films to promote and circulate (publicize) their artists and available recordings. They use distribution outlets, Internet sites, PDAs, cell phones, and various types of retail outlets to promote and sell the recordings. It costs money, of course, which is then charged back to the artist's account at the label. The process of *recoupment* is the accounting method used by the labels to pay off the debt they have created in the artist's name through royalties that are supposed to be paid to the artist from record sales. The upside is that artists are given a shot at becoming a big star without having to use much of their own money. The downside is that most recording artists never receive any royalties from units sold as the labels do not sell enough for the artist to break even, even when the label is making millions. Artist royalties are only a small percentage of the money consumer's pay for a product. *Labels* who are risking their investment receive a much larger share of income and thus break even faster and often make money before the artist. However, the artist also wins as once they are famous, they can form management companies or hire a manager to run their businesses and make millions from touring, merchandise sales, and corporate sponsorship.

Promoters rent venues for concerts and then locally promote and advertise the event. *Facility managers* and their staff of event coordinators keep the arenas, theaters, and clubs in top shape for the concerts. *Stagehand union members* commonly provide the lighting and sound. *Publicists* and *marketing experts* provide artists' interviews to the mass and click media to promote concerts and the artists. Record labels provide free recordings to radio stations and in-store promotional items, called end caps and stand ups, to retail outlets. If you're not a signed recording artist yet, even non-label artists and musicians may attain a good living from personal performances as a member of an orchestra, nightclub band, or by playing in weddings, at parties and/or by providing the entertainment at a number of unique events. Others contributing to the management revenue stream include *business managers* who are hopefully financial experts and invest the artist's earnings into stock and bond markets, merchandise fulfillment providers who provide the merchandise, and corporate sponsors that provide financial support in exchange for icon and product identification.

Financials

Today's creative industries driven by music production and sales gross more than ever! According to the *International Federation of the Phonographic Industry* (2010), "Music is one of the leading creative industries driving the media and entertainment sector that is now worth an estimated *$1.4 trillion*, with experts predicting this figure will grow to *$1.8 trillion* by 2010."[27] They also state "music has a massive economic 'ripple effect,' helping generate a broader music sector, including live music, radio, publishing and audio equipment, estimated to be worth *$160 billion* annually."[28] Researcher Seek (2003-2007) claims "the United States Copyright Industry generates about *$1.52 trillion* annually"[29] and *The Recording Industry Association of America* (RIAA) reported, "Albums, singles, and digital downloads in the United States grossed *$8.7 billion* last year."[30]

[27] Gabriela Lopes, "The Broader Music Industry," International Federation of the Phonographic Industry, http://www.ifpi.org/content/library/the-broader-music-industry.pdf as reported from PriceWaterhouseCoppers (accessed July 8, 2010).

[28] I.F.P.I, "New Report Shows How Much Record Companies are 'Investing in Music,' http://www.ifpi.org/content/section_news/investing_in_music.html (accessed July 3, 2010).

[29] Stephen Siwek, "Copyright Industries in the U.S: Songwriters Resource Network, Economy: The 2003-2007 Report," Economists Incorporated, prepared for the International Intellectual Property Alliance (IIPA), June 2009, available at www.iipa.com. (accessed June 26, 2010).

[30] Recording Industry Association of America, "2008-2009 U.S. Shipment Numbers," "http://www.riaa.org/keystatistics.php?content_selector=2008-2009-U.S-Shipment-Numbers (accessed July 3, 2010).

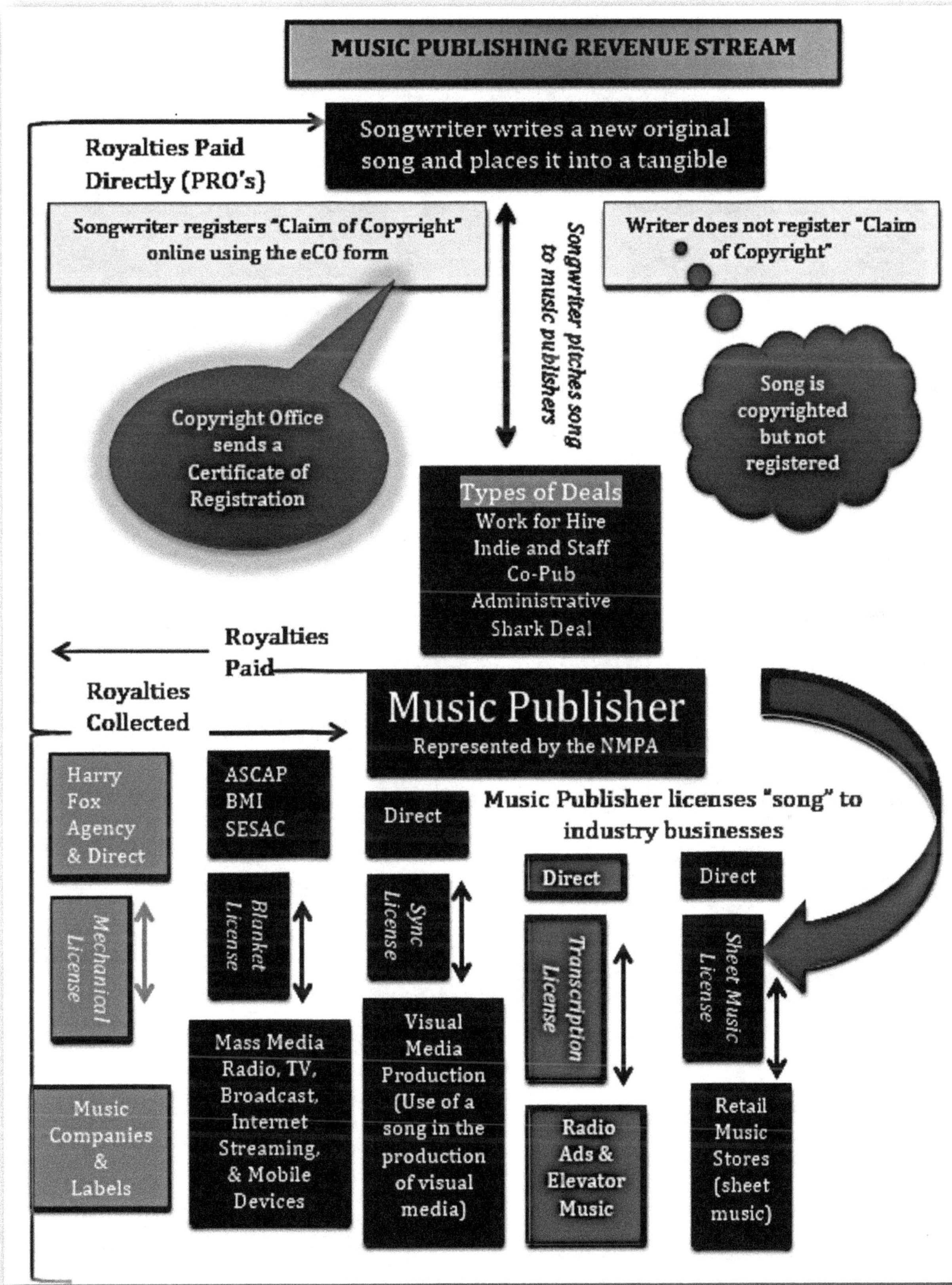

Figure 1.2. The Music Publishing Revenue Stream consists of songwriters making deals with publishers who exploit the songs to industry related companies for profits.

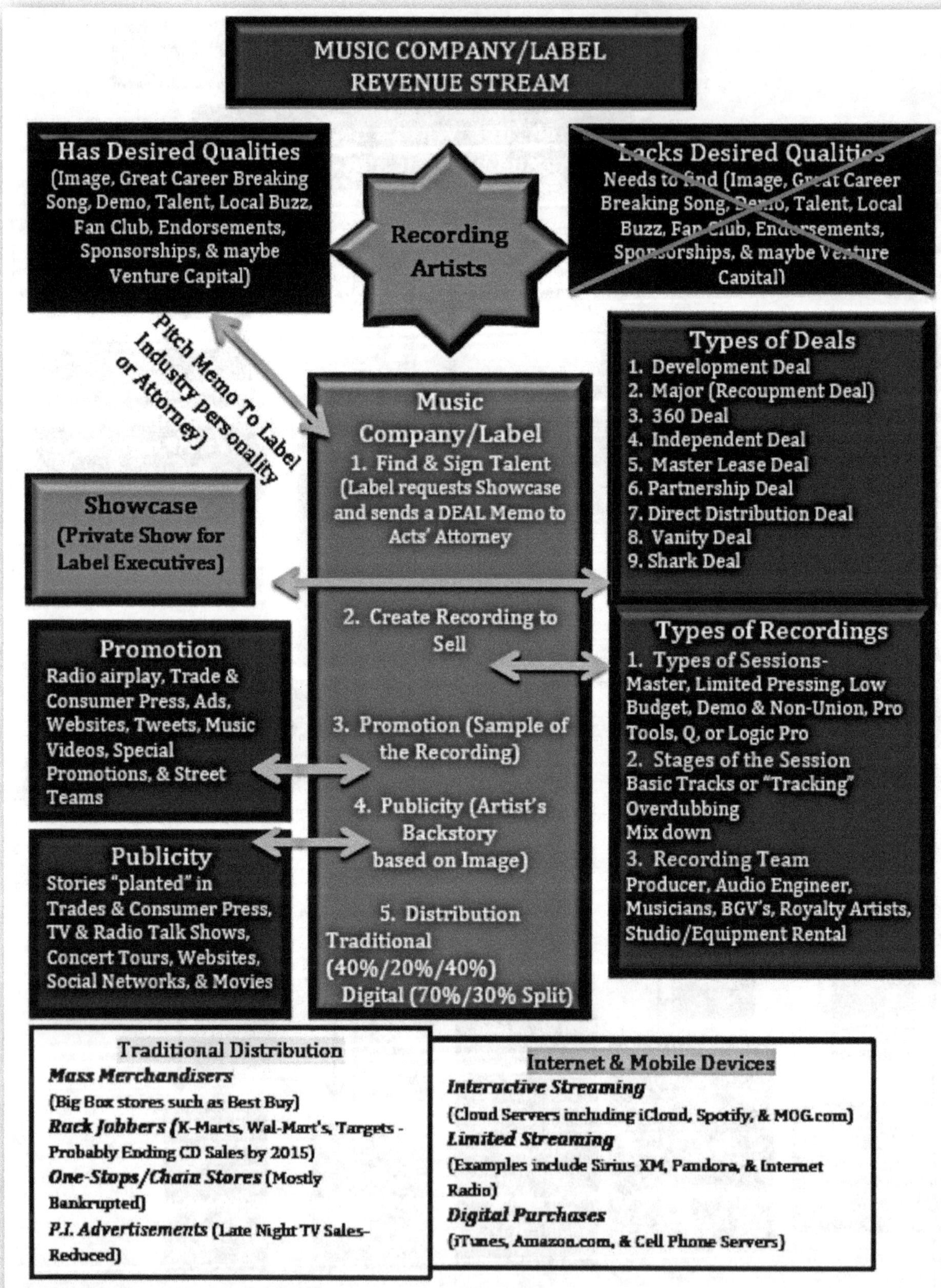

Figure 1.3 Labels sign talented artists, create recordings, promote, publicize, and distribute the recordings for profits. Music companies offer 360 deals that add tour and merchandise profits.

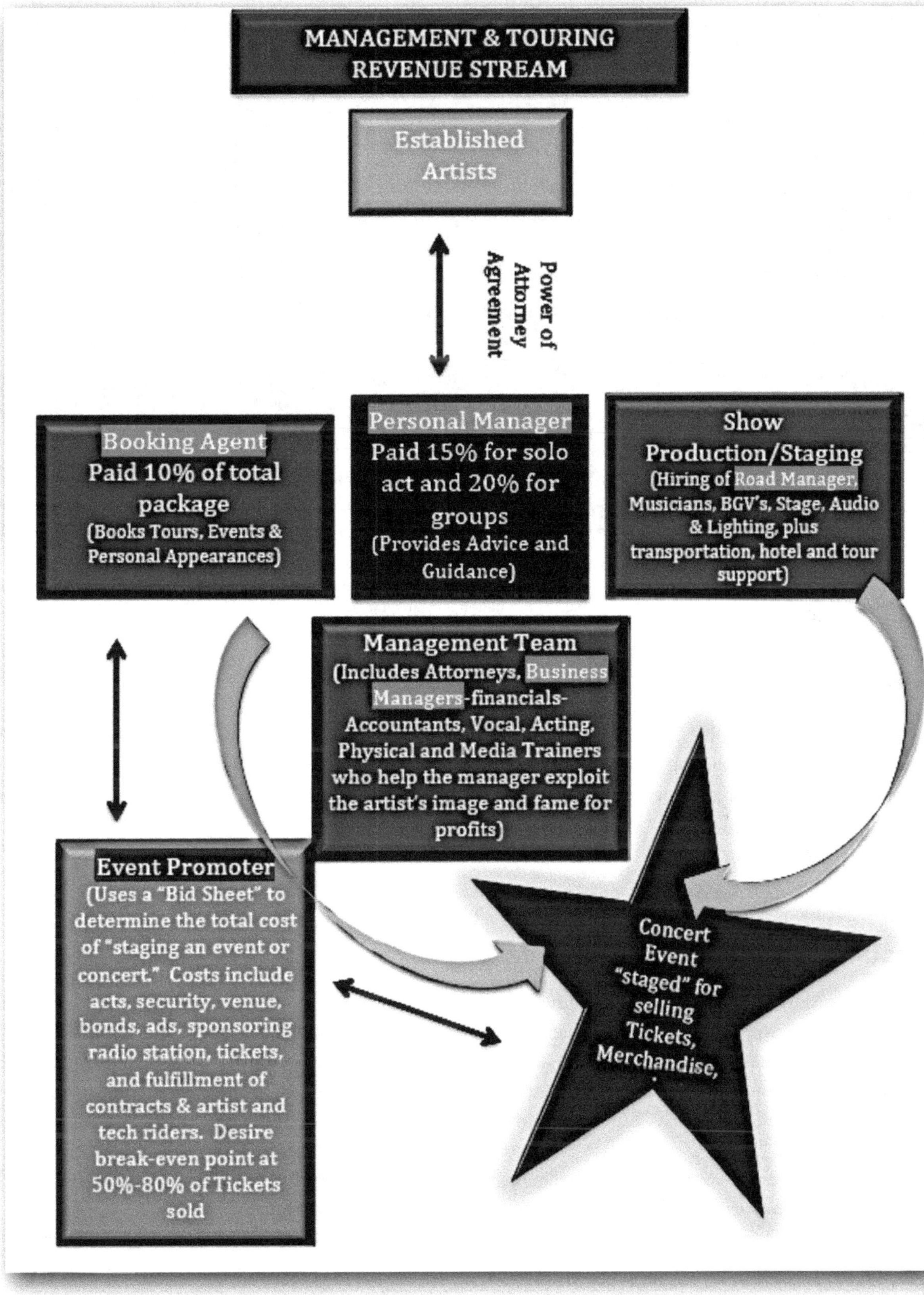

Figure 1.4. The Management/Touring "event" businesses add revenue opportunities from ticket sales, merchandise, endorsements, and sponsorships.

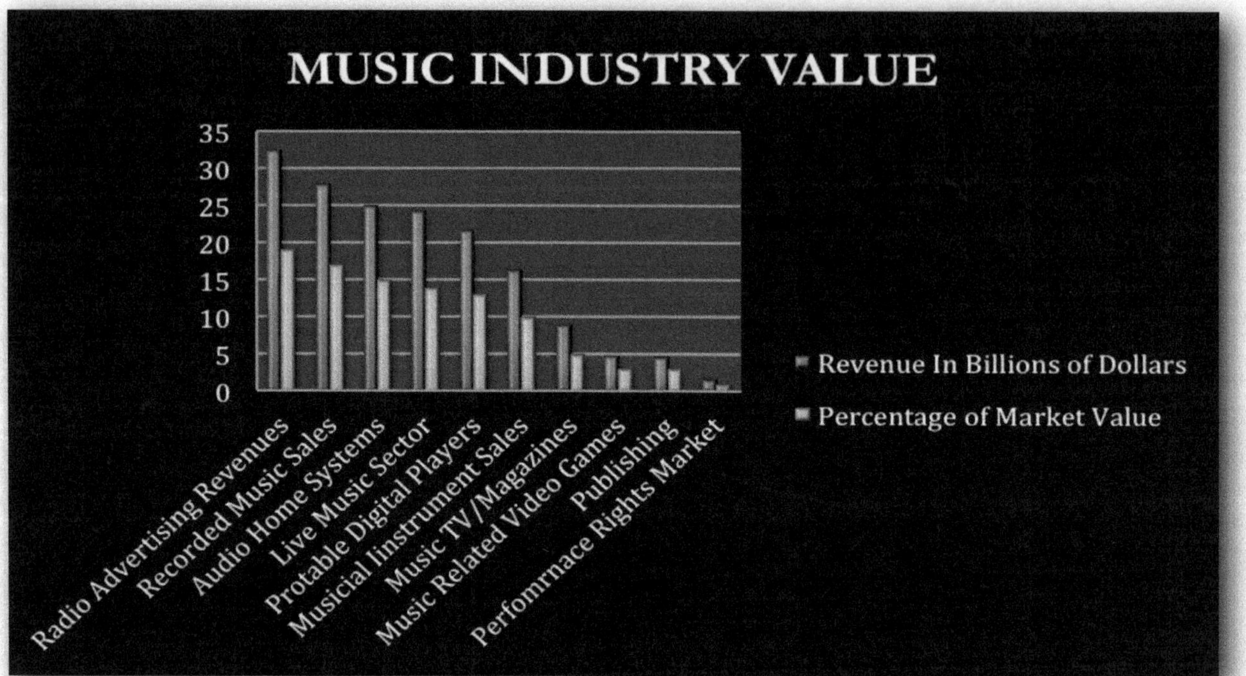

Figure/Table 1.5. Source: Data from the IFPI (International Federation of the Phonographic Industry), Recording Industry by the Numbers 2009. Music generates in the "broader" related industries about $160 billion annually, which includes radio advertising $32.5 billion, recorded music $27.8 billion, audio home systems $25 billion, portable digital players $24.2 billion, live music sector $21.6 billion, musician instruments sales $16.4 billion, music TV/magazine advertising $9 billion, music related video games $4.8 billion, publishing $4.6 billion, and performance rights $1.7 billion.[31]

Global Revenues

Global revenues of recorded music have turned upward for the first time since 1999. That's great news as changing consumers purchasing behavior is similar to turning the Titanic with too small of a rudder. Digital sales account for most of the upswing, which is a very slight increase, yet it's the first time in many years sales or recorded music have increased. According to *The Recording Industry in Numbers* published by the IFPI (2013);

> *Overall global recorded music trade revenues increased by 0.2% in 2012, the first year of growth since 1999. All the revenue streams IFPI tracks (physical, digital, performance rights and synchronization revenues), with the exception of physical sales, increased in 2012. A total of 21 countries saw market growth in 2012, including nine of the top 20 markets.*[32]

Consumers' Changing Preferences

The industry must provide the entertainment products consumers most want to use and buy. Public preferences often shift and businesses that stay in business often morph their business models into a structure to meet the new demands. Of course, digital technology is changing the entertainment world. Savvy digitally mobile consumers are driving the entertainment businesses to change in order to meet their new product demands and preferences. Entertainment and Music Businesses are struggling to survive in the digital world. New related business models are exploding! It is easy to understand how consumer's demand for instant and often "free" entertainment is changing the way the industry works. Even nightclub and dining experiences are enhanced with large flat screen TVs, great sound, and lighting.

---

[31] I.F.P.I., *Recording Industry in Numbers 2009*, International Federation of the Phonographic Industry: "The Broader Music Industry in 2008," (London: IFPI 2009) 23.

[32] I.F.P.I., *Recording Industry in Numbers 2013*, International Federation of the Phonographic Industry, http://www.ifpi.org/content/section_news/20130408.html (accessed July 3, 2013).

Creative Destruction

Joseph Schumpeter's original theory of creative destruction appears to describe the current state of the business of music and entertainment.[33] Clearly technology and consumer P2P file sharing is destroying the economic base of the music and film industry. However, at the same time, it is providing products to new consumers worldwide. It is only a matter of time before some entrepreneur develops a new business model that will safely support the financial investments of the industry in creative artists' products. Music and entertainment over the Internet is fundamentally changing the way artists, recording companies, retail channels, and end users, create, distribute, and buy music and entertainment products. The business of fame and all the corresponding sub-businesses (recordings, touring, cell phone distribution, merchandise, corporate sponsorships, and many more) are here to stay. They will just continue to grow into an even larger entertainment-based industry. The question is how.

Effects of Sound Recording Piracy[34]

Country/United States	What is Lost
U.S. Economy	$12.5 billion
Jobs	71,060
Salaries for U.S. Workers	$2.7 billion
Taxes (Federal, State, and Local)	$422 million

The Digital Revolution

More fans than ever are acquiring music, attending festivals, and buying merchandise. However, the traditional industry is struggling to get fans to pay for it! *The Berkman Center for Internet & Society* of Harvard University wrote in their publication *Rethinking Music: A Framing Paper* (2011),

> *Fans have little incentive to buy albums when they can instantaneously illegally download songs from peer-to-peer file sharing networks and other sources. …According to an NPD group study, in the third quarter of 2010, only 16.5% of American Internet users over the age of thirteen purchased music. When fans do purchase music, they would rather download individual tracks priced at $.99 than full-length albums at ten times the cost. As a result of all these factors and more, the value of the global recorded music industry has declined by one-third since 2004.*[35]

Nevertheless, the rebirth of the industry is continuing, thanks to digital technology, new media distribution, social network promotion and publicity, entrepreneurship, and actual creative talent. It's *back to the future*, similar to the 1950s when black artists and others, such as producer *Sam Phillips*, developed *Hillbilly* and *Rock & Roll* to turn a niche industry into an amazing cash machine. According to the *Rethinking Music* article (2011),

> *…The digital revolution brings new opportunities for growth and innovation in music distribution. There are now over 400 licensed digital music services worldwide, with thirteen million tracks licensed for digital use. Since 2004, the value of the US digital music market has increased by over 1,000% to around $4.6 billion. New companies, like* Radio *and* Mog*, give consumers an alternative to piracy by allowing them to stream the music of their choice on-demand. A large percentage of the subscription and advertising revenue*

---

[33] Joseph A. Schumpeter, "Creative Destruction" From the book, *Capitalism, Socialism and Democracy* (New York, NY: Harper, 1975) [orig. pub. 1942], 82-85 and found at http://transcriptions.english.ucsb.edu/archive/courses/liu/english25/materials/schumpeter.html, (accessed April 7, 2011).

[34] Stephen Siwek, "The True Cost of Sound Recording Piracy in the Uninted States," The United States Institute for Policy Innovation, http://www.ipi.org/IPI/IPIHome.nsf?OpenDatabase, (accessed May 13, 2011).

[35] The Berkman Center for Internet & Society at Harvard University, "Rethinking Music: A Framing Paper," Harvard University, http://cyber.law.harvard.edu/publications/2011/Rethinking_Music, (accessed May 2, 2011).

from these services goes directly into the pockets of artists, songwriters, labels, and publishers. Smaller artists, music's new middle class, are leveraging social networking platforms to reach out to a global fan base. Through do-it-yourself distribution tools, artists can cut out intermediaries and distribute music directly to their fans, earning more in royalties than they could have under traditional recording and publishing deals during the heyday of the compact disc. Some artists even raise money directly from their fans to support the production of new music. To survive the digital transformation, all players in the music industry are rethinking music. Labels are rethinking their business models. Digital companies are rethinking channels of distribution. Artists are rethinking their relationships with fans and traditional sources of revenue. And, lawyers, academics, and policymakers are rethinking the legal landscape in an effort to meet the needs of creators and consumers in the digital age.[36]

A natural business model cycle usually includes the beginning (invention or creation of a new service or product), the middle (the growth in sales and quality of the service or product), and the end (caused by a newer or better product or service consumers buy or use). In general, business cycles are unpredictable and vary in length and timing. Actually, the end of most business cycles is simply an evolution toward a new business model cycle with a newer and better product or service that often combines the best of the old with innovation for something new. Panay (2011) elaborates:

Amidst all the noise, we tend to forget that the modern music business has only existed for less than 60 years, propelled in earnest first by Frank Sinatra, taken to the next level by Elvis Presley and then the Beatles, and culminating in the mega stadium tours of the '70s and '80s and the blockbuster record sellers of the '90s. In most industries, it is rare that a new form of innovation and revenue generation will completely supplant the incumbents. In the transportation business, for example, ships, railroads, automobiles, and airlines all happily coexist. The same holds in the entertainment business with theater, radio, film, TV, and now the Internet all overlapping. In each of these examples, there have been clear losers (the horse and buggy for example, or the VCR and soon the DVD player), but the basic, underlying need for, respectively, movement and entertainment has ushered in new innovations by new breeds of entrepreneurs that led to the creation of new sub-industries and, very importantly, new ways of wealth creation. The music business is at a similar moment and has a similar opportunity for reinvention.[37]

Digital Production and Sales

The traditional music business model based on the three revenue streams is a very mature (dated) form of business compared to the new digital world of technology and the Internet. Indeed, the entertainment industry and the music business specifically are reeling with revenue losses based on Internet technology and consumers' peer-to-peer file sharing. It's hard to survive when more than 51-70 percent of the music acquired by consumers (in the United States) is not paid for or stolen through P2P.[38&39] The results are astounding. According to the RIAA (2011),

...The Institute for Policy Innovation concludes that global music piracy causes $12.5 billion of economic losses every year, 71,060 U.S. jobs lost, a loss of $2.7 billion in workers' earnings, and a loss of $422 million in tax revenues, $291 million in personal income tax and $131 million in lost corporate income and production taxes. For copies of the report, please visit www.ipi.org.[40]

In the last few years, the entertainment industry has slowly started to reinvent itself. Record labels are often seen as "stand alone" companies when in reality, they are generally just a small part of a global mega entertainment corporation. Corporate decisions made in Tokyo or Frankfurt may have serious repercussions

---

[36] The Berkman Center for Internet & Society at Harvard University, "Rethinking Music: A Framing Paper," Harvard University, http://cyber.law.harvard.edu/publications/2011/Rethinking_Music, (accessed May 2, 2011).

[37] Panos Panay, "Rethinking Music: The Future of Making Money as a Performing Musicians," The Berkman Center for Internet & Society at Harvard University, Harvard University, http://cyber.law.harvard.edu/publications/2011/Rethinking_Music, (accessed May 2, 2011).

[38] Digital Media Conference at Belmont University, 2007.

[39] Personal Interviews with industry leaders (2011).

[40] RIAA, "Piracy: Online and On the Streets," http://www.riaa.org/physicalpiracy.php, (accessed March 29, 2011).

for record labels, artists, and their employees as some of the mega entertainment companies (*Bertelsmann* and *Time Warner*) have sold their interest in labels. In addition, new technology and e-commerce are causing perilous cracks in the industry's skeletal foundation. Companies are merging and closing doors on many existing artist deals and industry employees. Thus, artists and others in the industry have fewer traditional major label options and more entrepreneurial opportunities. Examples are the tools we use every day: our iPods, cell phones, iPads, computers, and sites such as *MySpace, Facebook,* and *YouTube.* In addition, music companies are hiring employees for the new business models built around new media, lifestyle analysis, digital technology, licensing, and digital rights management.[41]

File Sharing

Sadly, consumers' continued "stealing" of copyrighted products with P2P file sharing is forcing most of the major record labels to sign all new artists to *360 deals*, which allow them to recoup their financial investment out of the artist's merchandise, corporate sponsorships, and concert ticket sales. Established artists and major superstars are reluctant to sign such deals unless they receive a huge financial advance. However, once an artist has established a fan base, they may pass on signing a major label deal and form their own labels, tours, and merchandise (using the same technology that has caused the creative destruction of the traditional business model) and sell it through their own entertainment-based companies.

Consumer Behavior

Therefore, digital music sales, cloud servers and the corresponding other products (such as concert tickets) sold over the Internet are fundamentally changing the way artists, recording companies, retail channels, and end users create, distribute, and buy music. According to Sir Howard Stringer, Chair & CEO of the Sony Corporation (2006),

> *Today, the relationship between content, technology and the consumer is being turned upside down. Or, more accurately, right side up. Content is no longer pushed at consumers. Content is pulled by them. Pulled when they want it. Pulled where they want it. How they want it. And often even in the precise format in which they want it. The whole world is essentially plugged in and turned on.*[42]

Major artists are already netting huge profits by selling products over iTunes and other sites. You'll see in later chapters how it cost the customer less and the labels make more money. It is a true win/win situation. Traditional sales of hard platforms such as CDs are fading quickly as digital downloads continue to increase quickly. Yet many consumers often buy singles instead of albums, which reduces the gross income labels make from unit sales. Traditional retail outlets are closing or dramatically reducing their inventory as the consumer buys, listens, or steals recorded products. So, labels have shifted toward the 360 deals. However, new technology may change consumer behavior again by offering recorded units for instant leasing (listen any time you want) on your own computer and cell phone clouds.[43] These digital sales are turning the industry around according to *The Recording Industry in Numbers* published by the IFPI (2013);

---

[41] Sony Corporation of America, "Jobs at Sony," Sony Corporation of America, http://www.sony.com/SCA/jobs.shtml & Warner Music Group, "Jobs," Warner Music Group, http://www.wmg.com/jobsoverview, (accessed April 3, 2011), & Personal interviews with industry insiders (2011).

[42] Sir Howard Stringer, "Entertaining the Future," (Speech presented at the 2006 International Consumer Electronics Show, Las Vegas, NV, January 5, 2006) and at http://www.sony.com/SCA/speeches/060105_stringer.shtml, (accessed April 3, 2011).

[43] R. NAKASHIMA, "MOG, Radio New Entrants to $10-a-Month Mobile Music," The Associated Press, http://www.rgj.com/article/20100704/BIZ15/7040316/MOG-Rdio-new-entrants-to-10-a-month-mobile-music (accessed 2010 July 5).

> *Digital channels now account for 35% of overall industry trade revenues, while physical sales now represent 57% of record companies' income. Downloads remain the biggest source of digital revenues, with combined unit sales of track and album downloads up by 11% in 2012.*[44]

Unknown artists and even formerly established label artists now own their own website, bypassing the established distribution and retail chains to retain a larger share of the profits for themselves. Some of the more famous artists record their own masters and arrange distribution deals with Wal-Mart stores. Clearly, the days of being a financial diva or a high maintenance label artist are mostly over unless you're an established super star. Even then, you're career skew lines better be in the up position (an increase in profits and sales) or your days are probably limited.

Summary

The music business is based on the fans' ability to emotionally connect with the music and iconic artists' communicative messages on recordings, in concerts, and played through the mass and social media. Artists creatively express their artistic talents in a "creative system," while a related "business system" of sole proprietorship, partnerships, and corporations exploit their products for profits. Non-profits businesses are formed to manage many orchestras, ballet, and other artistic operations.

It's the people behind the stars and public personalities that usually provide the "essence for success" in the creative and business systems. For every major star as many as 100 non-seen songwriters, musicians, producers, marketer, social media types, labels or music companies and their team of promoters, sales, distributors and others help create, promote and manage the act. Record labels and other entertainment-based companies often finance the recordings and entertainment products. Managers, publicists, and agents help develop images, career goals, and assist to promote, publicize, and market the music, images and merchandise of corresponding products to consumers. The mass and social media provide distribution of images, products, and in some cases, retail products.

The perception that all recording artists and stars have to do is sing, play their instrument, act, and provide shameless self-promotion is true, but they are also entrepreneurs, business owners, and employers. Realistic industry success involves passion, a unique world vision of humanity and society, street and learned knowledge, talent, an understanding of business principles, connections, money, and an excellent team of experts who are constantly searching for profits. Which is harder

---

[44] I.F.P.I., *Recording Industry in Numbers 2013*, International Federation of the Phonographic Industry, http://www.ifpi.org/content/section_news/20130408.html (accessed July 3, 2013).

to do now that most of the new music in the world is acquired without payment. All of this is based on a great song and the artist's ability to contribute artistically in some meaningful manner to a message of emotional importance to a various segment of consumers.

You have to make things happen yourself. Professional musicians, artists, and industry insiders have assertively earned their own success by having a positive attitude, meeting the right people, perfecting their artistic and business intellectual talents, obtaining a quality education, and by being in the right place at the right time. Successful industry related entrepreneurs provide products, startup businesses that solve problems, create win-win situations, and provide better entertainment products to various segments of the world's population. In the music business, there is a balance between the creative- and business minded men and women who own, operate, or work at industry related companies; this balance determines the companies' and industry's success.

Luck is important, but set personal goals, develop creative and analytical talents, have a positive attitude, find your niche, and educate yourself to turn your passion into a career. Entrepreneurship is becoming one of the main keys to success in the entertainment business. Industry professionals customarily associate with other colleagues for commonality, friendships, and to enhance career opportunities. Nobody can make it in this business by him or herself. It's too big of an industry. Work in teams! There are many opportunities to be found by working in teams with others who have similar interests, goals, and connections.

Key Website Resources

http://www.ifpi.org/

http://www.naras.org/

http://www.riaa.org/

2

Protecting Creativity

℗ ® © ™

Exclusive Rights
Copyright Duration
Intellectual Property Rights

"A form of protection provided by the laws of the United States for 'original works of authorship,' including literary, dramatic, musical, architectural, cartographic, choreographic, pantomimic, pictorial, graphic, sculptural, and audiovisual creations. 'Copyright' literally means the right to copy, but has come to mean that body of exclusive rights granted by law to copyright owners for protection of their work. Copyright protection does not extend to any idea, procedure, process, system, title, principle, or discovery. Similarly, names, titles, short phrases, slogans, familiar symbols, mere variations of typographic ornamentation, lettering, coloring, and listings of contents or ingredients are not subject to copyright."

—Definition of a Copyright, Copyright Office[45]

"Anyone who currently works in or aspires to work in the music industry including writers, artists, publishers, musicians or distributors should have a basic understanding of copyright law and how it applies to the music industry."

—Mike Curb, President of Curb Records[46]

"Copyright is the means by which a person or a business makes a living from creativity."

—IFPI[47]

"If you don't own the master, the master owns you."

—Rapper Chuck D[48]

Copyrights

We know what the word "copy" means and we know what the word "right" means, but the term "copyright" is a different matter. Why is it important to the music and entertainment industry? Better still, why is it important to the creative artist? Copyrights spring from a simple notion: the people who create, produce, or invest in original creative works should be the ones who own the works (examples being songs, recordings, films, and books). Copyright are about ownership as property with value. To simplify it, the word "right"

---

[45]U.S. Library of Congress, "U.S. Copyright Definitions", http://www.copyright (accessed July 12, 2010).

[46] Mike Curb, forward to *Moser on Music Copyright* (Boston, MA: Course Technology/Cenage Learning, 2006).

[47] International Federation of the Phonographic Industry, "What is a Copyright?" by the IFPI, ifpi.org, http://www.ifpi.org/content/section_views/what_is_copyright.html (accessed 07/06/2000).

[48] Chuck D. (Rapper), in an article by Richard Gehr, "Steal This Industry," Time Media Kit, http://www.time.com/time/digital/reports/mp3/artists.html (accessed 2010).

relates to the ownership rights called the *exclusive rights* of the copyright. The word "copy" relates to the owner's right to receive payment for each copy made, distributed, performed, digitally transmitted, or used by consumers. The other cool thing is that owning a copyright (let's say a great song) has value based on the *future royalties* it might generate. This is where the "value" comes into play. Look at it this way, if you buy a house or condo it's value may go up or down over time (because of consumer demand for housing) If the need for housing goes up, then you can sell it and make a profit. A great song (let's say *Silver Bells)* is played on radio world-wide every holiday season and its also recorded by new artists, placed into new movies and the money just keeps rolling in until it falls into public domain in about thirty years. Until then, the use of the song is tried to a payment or a license fee to the owner, writers (depending on the type of deal) and music publisher(s). That's how the songwriting and music publishing world work! The trick is to create such a wonderful piece of art, song, or entertainment product that consumers will pay for the use of it now and in the future.

There are two-forms of property: real property and personal property. According to Moser (2006),

> *Real property protects land or things that are built on land, such as houses and buildings. Personal property basically protects everything that can be owned other than real property... Intellectual property, on the other hand, cannot be possessed by anyone although this does not mean it cannot be owned. You cannot, for example, possess a song although you can certainly own one... it is easier to understand if you realize that property refers not the actual possession of a thing, but to the right to use it and control its use.*[49]

At its simplest, most basic level, the music and entertainment industry is really about the business of selling the same performances and recordings repeatedly. Labels sell recordings of a song created in a studio or by computers hopefully by the millions; radio plays the same copy of the recording trying to gain an audience in order to sell air time to advertisers; concerts are actually the basic same live performance of songs played in different venues before different audiences; film production companies sell movies to mega entertainment companies (*Sony, Time Warner, Bertelsmann AG,* or *Universal*) who sell viewings of a copy of the same film in theaters to millions and then later, copies on DVDs, digital streaming (Netflixs and Amazon.com) and downloads.

Thus, the entertainment business is really about the creation, marketing, promotion, and selling of "whatever" consumers find enjoyable. Only a few recordings are good enough to "hit" number one on the *Billboard* charts. So producers, songwriters, musicians, audio engineers, and recording artists are really trying to create a great recording (something that will sell) before anyone knows if consumers will even like it. Many won't.

Table/Figure 2.1 Units Sold "Less Than"

Units Sold Less Than Figures	Actual Sales
Sold at lease one copy	98,000
Less than 1,000 units	92,601
Less than 100 copies	81,000

Table/Figure 2.2 Units Sold "More Than"

Units Selling More Than Figures	Actual Sales
More than 5,000	2,058
More than 10,000	1,319
More than 250,000	85

[49] David Moser, *Moser on Music Copyrights*, (Boston, MA: Course Technology/Cenage Learning, 2006), 2.

So can you now see how important marketing and promotion is as consumers have to "hear it" before they buy it? Well, let's go another step. What is consumers just steal it over the Internet instead of buying it? Now, now body gets paid! Well, if it is a union gig the musician, producer, audio engineer and artist(s) will be paid for the recording time, but the label will not make any ROI or return on it's investment. Welcome to the reason record labels are becoming music companies and offering only 360 deals to new artist!

However, for consumers, it is still difficult to understand that you do not own the copyright of the song, recording, or artist's performance you just bought. All you own is the physical piece of plastic or digital download (codes of zeros and ones) that let you enjoy the song and recording (use of it) through the computer chip in the devices you own, such as a computer, iPod, or cell phone. According to Moser (2006),

> *To make it more confusing, although copyright law protects intangible property, copyrighted works are often embodied or contained in physical objects, which can be possessed (purchased)... A song can be embodied in a recording ... although you cannot possess the copyrighted work you can possess physical objects in which the copyrighted work is embodied.*[50]

Intellectual Properties

The business model of the mass media is all about gathering an audience by using, playing, or airing someone else's copyrighted entertainment products. The truth is that almost everything from sports teams to talk shows (Rush Limbaugh) is considered a *copyrighted entertainment product* owned by an individual or a company who sells it. With the success of the entertainment products come other cash-generating copyrighted opportunities in *endorsements, merchandise, and corporate sponsorships*. It's all based on the law of intellectual properties and who owns them. In the United States, the *legal protection of creativity* falls into definitions under the umbrella of *Intellectual Properties*, which includes:

Copyrights

Copyrights encourages artistic and creative people (often using the inventions and discoveries covered under patent laws) to make, among other things, musical recordings, paintings, photographs, literary works, choreographic works, computer-enhanced artwork, and films. Copyrights provided by the laws of the United States (title 17 U. S. Code) and many other countries provide protection to the authors of original works of authorship, including literary, dramatic, musical, artistic, and other intellectual works.[51] Additionally, the World Intellectual Property Organization, or WIPO (July 3, 2010), claims that international copyright law:

> *...Is above all one of the means of promoting, enriching and disseminating the national cultural heritage. A country's development depends to a very great extent on the creativity of its people, and encouragement of individual creativity and its dissemination is a sine qua non for progress.*[52]

Trademarks

Trademarks are tied to product and company identification. Company icons and logos identify a product as original and non-counterfeit merchandise.

---

[50] David Moser, *Moser on Music Copyrights*, (Boston, MA: Course Technology/Cenage Learning, 2006), 3.

[51] U.S. Library of Congress, "Title 17, U.S. Code", http://www.copyright (accessed October 2, 2010).

[52] W.I.P.O., *World Intellectual Property Organization Handbook*, W.I.P.O., http://www.wipo.int/export/sites/www/about-ip/en/iprm/pdf/ch2.pdf (accessed July 3, 2010).

Trade Secrets

Trade secrets are tied to valuable information a company may possess. Trade secrets provide a company with a competitive advantage over other businesses in an industry. Employees from one company are often required to sign a document stating that they will not share trade secrets with a competitor after they leave their employer.

Patents

Patents provide protection for useful inventions and discoveries such as CD players, CDs, computer chips, film cameras, recording tape, and film.

Industrial Designs and Integrated Circuits

Industrial Designs and Integrated Circuits are also protected by WIPO. They define industrial designs as

> *...The creative activity of achieving a formal or ornamental appearance for mass-produced items that, within the available cost constraints, satisfies both the need for the item to appeal visually to potential consumers, and the need for the item to perform its intended function efficiently.*[53]

In addition, the WIPO Treaty (2010) defines *integrated circuits* as "...another field in the protection of intellectual property" including "layout-designs (topographies) of integrated circuits."[54]

Converting "Ideas and Creative Talent" into Intellectual Property

How do you turn a great idea (which is not protected) or your creative talents into a form of intellectual property you own? Let's start with an "idea." Ideas are not protected. However, the corresponding products "created" from an "expression of an idea in a physical form" *may be* copyrightable *if* they meet certain legal definitions. The song, device, or logo may be protected as a trademark, trade secret, patent, or copyright if it meets specific qualifiers. As an example, an idea for a song has to be original and in a tangible (physical) form. Other copyrightable creative "works" include literary works (books), musical and dramatic (theater, plays) works, pantomimes, choreographic works, pictures, graphics, sculptures, films and other audiovisual works, and sound recordings! The songwriter owns the song only if it is original and placed it into a tangible form. A couple of songwriter have a great idea, make a copy of it by scoring it on paper, recording it on tape, flash drive, computer hard disc, and in doing so, create copyrighted "intellectual property" owned by the them. Ok, so you own your own song, now the question becomes, "Is it good enough to be recorded and used by the entertainment industry and, if it is, how much money will it make for you (the songwriters), the music publisher, the label or music company, the recording artists?"

Licenses

Consumers of entertainment products may understand the meaning of copyrights better by rearranging the roots, from "copyright" to "right to copy." The person who created the work now own it because it fits the definitions of property and copyright. Under copyrights, anyone who wants to use the work (by making or acquiring a copy of it) is required to pay for it (unless the creator wants to give it away for free). The artist

---

[53] W.I.P.O., *World Intellectual Property Organization Handbook*, W.I.P.O., http://www.wipo.int/export/sites/www/about-ip/en/iprm/pdf/ch2.pdf (accessed July 3, 2010).

[54] W.I.P.O., *World Intellectual Property Organization Handbook*, W.I.P.O., http://www.wipo.int/export/sites/www/about-ip/en/iprm/pdf/ch2.pdf (accessed July 3, 2010).

who created the work can now claim it as his or her own property (copyright) and attempt to sell it (music publisher) or allow another company or person to record and sell it (labels) or use it (film production companies and radio stations, as examples) through licensing processes. Now, because the entertainment and media industry are using it, the song is making money! How much they sell and use it, determines the amount of money your making. Knowing enough about the business of the business (administration, legal stuff like contracts) will help you make sure your getting paid what you are owned.

Copyrightable Works

Copyright protects original works of authorship that are fixed in a tangible form of expression. Copyright works include the following categories:

> **"Literary works,**
>
> **Musical works, including any accompanying words,**
>
> **Dramatic works, including any accompanying music,**
>
> **Pantomimes and choreographic works,**
>
> **Pictorial, graphic, and sculptural works,**
>
> **Motion pictures and other audiovisual works,**
>
> **Sound recordings, and**
>
> **Architectural works."**[55]

Historical Perspectives

The origin of copyright law is related to the invention of the printing press in 15th century England. This new ability to inform the masses threatened the image of the English government. To control the distribution of Protestant religious heresy and political upheaval, the government forced book publishers to obtain a *license to publish*.[56] This, of course, was a censorship law that allowed only the printing of books that were loyal or non-confrontational to the church and government.

Statute of Anne

The expiration of the *license to publish* law in 1695 initiated stiff competition between entrepreneurial book publishers who were seeking to profit from books expounding upon different perspectives and the established autocratic publishers.[57] In his book, *Understanding Copyright Law*, Leaffer (1989) suggests "…in defiance of the lobbying efforts of political leaders and the established book publishers, the *English Parliament* passed the first known copyright law in 1710, called the "*Statute of Anne*." He claims, "It established the ultimate purpose of modern copyright laws, which is to enhance public welfare by encouraging the dissemination of knowledge" (Leaffer, 1989).[58] The established book publishers lost their monopoly. The law encouraged the writing, printing, and distribution of useful works (books that were in some cases *critical* of the political establishment). It changed the world, as different levels of society were now able to

---

[55] U.S. Library of Congress, "Copyright Basics: What is a Copyright," http://www.copyright.gov/circs/circ1.pdf, (accessed June 25, 2010).

[56] William, Strong, *The Copyright Book: A Practical Guide*, 5th ed. (Cambridge, MA: The MIT Press, 1999), 2.

[57] Marshall Leaffer, *Understanding Copyright Law*, 4th ed. (New York, NY: Matthew Bender, 1989).

[58] Marshall Leaffer, *Understanding Copyright Law*, 4th ed. (New York, NY: Matthew Bender, 1989).

communicate, express their views, and make a profit all at the same time.[59] Thus, the *Statute of Anne*, caused with the new technology of the times (the printing press), shifted ownership, distribution rights, and potential profits to the creators of the original works. The act defined *ownership rights* and provided a method of gaining financial rewards to the artists, scientists, and investment companies who created the works.[60]

Think of all the political and social businesses that will grow and change in the next 20 years as a result of the inventions of the personal computer, the cell phone, and the Internet. Consider the impact that some political courage and the invention of the printing press have had on the on relationships, creativity, and business in the entertainment industry. And at the same time, consider the problems that technology (i.e. P2P digital downloads) creates for copyright holders and the freedom of conversation the Internet allows (Hint: so much that world political leaders are concerned about governmental control issues).

The United States Constitution

The authors of the United States Constitution did not miss the *Statute of Anne*'s inference. *Article 1, Section 8* "gives Congress the right to legislate copyright statute to promote the Progress of Science and Useful Arts, by securing for Limited Times to Authors and Inventors, the Exclusive Right to their respective Writings and Discoveries."[61] Now, let's break that down.

- "Promoting the Progress of Science and Useful Arts" is accomplished by providing legal ownership and therefore potential financial rewards to the individuals who invest their time and money into scientific discoveries (examples being inventions and medicines) and useful arts (such as the performing and creative arts including songs, scripts, recordings, movies and other entertainment products).[62] The word "useful" has not been challenged as removing it would lead to the censorship of creative products and ideas.
- Copyright protection subsists from the time the work is created in fixed form. The copyright in the work of authorship immediately becomes the *property of the author* who created the work. Only the author or those deriving their rights through the author can rightfully claim copyright.[63]
- Accordingly, the copyright is instant, and you do not need to apply for one. In reality, when you *register your claim of a copyright* with the Copyright Office, all you are doing is registering your right to claim what you've created (your *claim* is the copyright). The government only registers the time and date of your claim. Therefore, the Copyright Office does not issue a copyright; it only registers your claim of one.[64]
- The phrase "By securing for Limited Times" means ownership rights do not last forever but only for

---

[59] Marshall Leaffer, *Understanding Copyright Law*, 4th ed. (New York, NY: Matthew Bender, 1989).

[60] Marshall Leaffer, *Understanding Copyright Law*, 4th ed. (New York, NY: Matthew Bender, 1989).

[61] United States Constitution, "Art.1, sec.8" http://www.usconstitution.net/xconst_A1Sec8.html, (accessed June 25, 2010).

[62] United States Constitution, "Art.1, sec.8" http://www.usconstitution.net/xconst_A1Sec8.html, (accessed June 25, 2010).

[63] U.S. Library of Congress, "Copyright Basics: Who Can Claim a Copyright," http://www.copyright.gov/circs/circ1.pdf, (accessed July 4, 2010).

[64] U.S. Library of Congress, "Copyright Basics: How to Secure a Copyright," http://www.copyright.gov/circs/circ1.pdf, (accessed July 4, 2010).

a stated period of time. After that time, (currently, life of the author, plus 70 years), the copyright falls into public domain, meaning it can be used freely by the general public.[65]

- The "Exclusive Rights" bestow six rights to the copyright owners. Section 106 of the 1976 Copyright Act generally gives the owners of copyrights the exclusive rights to carry out for themselves or authorize others to accomplish them.[66]

Exclusive Rights

There are *six exclusive rights* authors of original works have to control the uses of their creative products (songs, recordings, films, books, and other forms of entertainment). These rights include the following:

To reproduce the © work in copies or phonorecords,

To prepare derivative works based upon the © work;

To distribute copies or phonorecords of the © work to the public by sale or other transfer of ownership, or by rental, lease, or lending;

To perform the © work publicly, in the case of literary, musical, dramatic, and choreographic works, pantomimes, motion pictures and other audiovisual works;

To display the © work publicly, in the case of literary, musical, dramatic, and choreographic works, pantomimes, and pictorial, graphic, or sculptural works, including the individual images of a motion picture or other audiovisual work, and;

To perform the © works publicly by means of a digital audio transmission, in the case of sound recordings.[67]

Copyright Notice

The Library of Congress suggests using a copyright notice on your songs or other creative products. The use of a notice was required until the Berne Convention of 1989.[68] At that time, the United States dropped its requirement of use and now "encourages" use; but it is not required. The *notice* is affixed "in a manner and location" that will provide "a reasonable notice of the claim of copyright."[69] The copyright notice consists of three elements:

> *The symbol ©, or the word "Copyright" or the abbreviated "Copr.,"… the year of creation (unpublished) or the year of first publication (if distributed),… and the name(s) of the owner of the copyright or an abbreviation by which the name(s) can be recognized.*[70]

Copyright Notice for a Recording

There are two copyrights on a typical recording, © for the song, usually owned by the music publisher and ℗ (Phonorecord), for the actual recording of the song usually owned by the label or music company who paid

---

[65]U.S. Library of Congress, "Copyright Basics: Duration of a Copyright," http://www.copyright (accessed July 4, 2010).

[66] U.S. Library of Congress, "Copyright Basics: What Works are Protected," http://www.copyright.gov/circs/circ1.pdf, (accessed June 25, 2010).

[67] U.S. Library of Congress, "Copyright Basics: What Works are Protected," http://www.copyright.gov/circs/circ1.pdf, (accessed June 25, 2010).

[68] Library of Congress, "Copyright Notice," http://www.copyright, (accessed January 1, 2011).

[69] Library of Congress, "Copyright Notice," http://www.copyright, (accessed January 1, 2011).

[70] Library of Congress, "Copyright Notice," http://www.copyright, (accessed January 1, 2011).

for the recording. The word copyright and the year of creation, if unpublished or the year of first publication, if distributed for sale are also required if you decide to use the notices.

Infringement

When someone uses or sells a copyrighted product (such as a song or a recording) without gaining permission from the owner (which is usually acquired though licenses), that person or company may have infringed on the copyright owners right to be paid for their creative works. According to the Copyright Office (2010), "As a general matter, copyright infringement occurs when a copyrighted work is reproduced, distributed, performed, publicly displayed, or made into a derivative work without the permission of the copyright owner."[71] This includes consumers who post major songs and recordings on *youtube.com* without first acquiring permission (a **sync license** for the song, a **master license** for the recording and the payment of **public performance royalties**). According to the BBC (2012):

> *A court in Hamburg ruled that YouTube is responsible for the content that users post to the video sharing site. It wants the video site to install filters that spot when users try to post music clips whose rights are held by royalty collection group, Gema. The German industry group said in court that YouTube had not done enough to stop copyrighted clips being posted. YouTube said it took no responsibility for what users did.... Currently, it is estimated that about 60 hours of video is uploaded to YouTube worldwide every minute.... Music streaming site Grooveshark pulled out of Germany claiming licensing rates set by Gema made it impossible to run a profitable business in the country.*[72]

Fair Use

Fair Use Rights are the exception to the exclusive rights of the copyright law. They allow for free use of copyrighted works in criticism or commentary, news reporting, teaching, academic scholarship, and research. No payment for the use of the materials in these situations is required. Fair Use can not be used to give away a few copies of your own "cover" of some major acts recording. You'll still own the few pennies through a mechanical you can obtain from the Harry Fox Agency. So, you may want to use some caution as specific standards to determine what may be used as a *fair use right* are based on *factors* including purpose, character, and the nature of the work, plus the amount used and its effect on the value of the original work.[73] Krasilosky and Shemel (2007) state that:

> *It is surprising how frequently songwriters and others in the music business think – incorrectly –that copying four bars or fewer of someone's music is legal. In most cases, this error stems from a misinterpretation of the doctrine of fair use, which recognizes the right of the public to make a reasonable use of copyrighted material in special instances without the copyright owner's consent.*[74]

Types/Stages of Ownership

There are several ways to own and transfer copyrights to others including when you first create something copyrightable (a song or a recording). Then you call sell it (the copyright or ownership of what your created) because it now property you own. Think of what you've created as a piece of "property" and it starts to make more sense. You build a house and own it, then someday you sell it and make a profit. Same thing with a

---

[71]U.S. Library of Congress, "Copyright: Stopping Copyright Infringements," http://www.copyright, (accessed January 1, 2011).

[72] "YouTube Looses Battle over Music Video Clips," http://www.bbc.co.uk/news/technology-17785613, (accessed April 21, 2012).

[73] U.S. Library of Congress, "Copyright: Fair Use Rights, http://www.copyright, (accessed January 1, 2011).

[74] M. William Krasilovsky, and Sydney Shemel, *This Business of Music*, 10th ed. (New York, NY: Billboard Books, 2007), 102.

song, recording and other copyrightable expressions of your creativity that have been "placed" into a tangible or physical form. You create a cool song in you head and then record it into your iPhone. You only "own it" when you've make a physical copy of it by recording it into your iPhone. Now it's yours (property you own) and if it's good enough then you can try to sell it to a music publisher.

Authorship ownership

You are the author "creator" of an original work and thus, the initial copyright is vested in you as the author and owner of the original work. The "creative work" you created is now considered your "property" and it can be sold, rented, leased, borrowed, handed down to whomever or given away.

Work-for-hire

Usually when an employer hires a creative artists to create a work of "art" the employer is considered the copyright owner. However, in a work-for-hire, the author may also be considered the owner, it just depends on how the "deal" is established.[75] There are two types of *work-for-hires* in copyright law, so who owns it (the copyright) depends on if the work is prepared by an employee "within the scope of his or her employment" (the employer owns the copyright) or if the work is "specially ordered or commissioned for use" and the artist has "a written agreement with the commissioning party that they are being hired as a work-for-hire" (the artist keeps their copyright).[76] According to Copyright Office (2013):

> *Only the author or those deriving rights from the author can rightfully claim copyright.There is, however, an exception to this principle: "works made for hire." If a work is made for hire, an employer is considered the author even if an employee actually created the work. The employer can be a firm, an organization, or an individual. The concept of "work made for hire" can be complicated. ...The Supreme Court's interpretation of it in Community for Creative Non-Violence v. Reid, decided in 1989 was ...The Court held that one must first ascertain whether a work was pre-pared by (a) an employee or (b) an independent contractor...*
>
> *If an employee created the work, (within the scope of his or her employment) ...the work will generally be considered a work made for hire. But note that the term "employee" in the definition differs from the common understanding of the term. For copyright purposes, "employee" means an employee under the general common law of agency. ... an "independent contractor" is someone who is not an employee under the general common law of agency. (which is) ...A work created by an independent contractor can be a work made for hire only if (a) it falls within one of the nine categories of works;*
>
> *(1) as a contribution to a collective work,*
> *(2) as a part of a motion picture or other audiovisual work,*
> *(3) as a translation,*
> *(4) as a supplementary work,*
> *(5) as a compilation,*
> *(6) as an instructional text,*
> *(7) as a test,*
> *(8) as an answer material for a test, or*
> *(9) as an atlas,*
>
> *... and (b) there is a written agreement between parties specifying that the work is a work made for hire.*[77]

Contribution to a collective work

When a songwriter creates a song and then contributes it to an album of many songs, the copyright of each song contributed remains with the original author/owner and is separate from the copyright of the collective work itself.

---

[75] M. William Krasilovsky, and Sydney Shemel, *This Business of Music*, 10th ed. (New York, NY: Billboard Books, 2007), 116.

[76] Library of Congress, "Works Made for Hire Under the 1976 Copyright Act," http://www.copyright, (accessed January 1, 2011).

[77] Copyright Office, Library of Congress "Works Made for Hire" Circular 9, http://www.copyright.gov/circs/circ09.pdf, (accessed July 15, 2013).

Transfer of copyright ownership

Songwriters usually transfer their ownership in whole or in part to a music publisher through the single song contracts in a typical songwriting/music publishing deal. Successful songwriters often form their own music publishing companies to retain all or part of the copyright ownership as they also accrue value and may be sold later. Copyright ownership can also be willed or passed as personal property to family or others. In addition, any of the rights specified by section 106 (exclusive rights) may be transferred… or owned separately.[78]

Duration and Public Domain

The current *duration of a copyright* (how long you or someone else owns what you've created) is currently your life plus 70 years. In addition, Beck and Tysver (2008) reveal that "for works made for hire, and for anonymous and pseudonymous works (unless the author's identity is revealed in Copyright Office records), the duration of copyright will be 95 years from publication or 120 years from creation, whichever is shorter."[79] If you write a great song and then sell it through some type of deal, the person or company who bought it will own it for the same amount of time: your life plus 70 years. However, once that time is up, then all your *property and ownership rights* fall into *public domain*, which simply means that you no longer own it, and according to Krasilosky and Shimel (2007), "Anyone can make full, unrestricted use of the material."[80]

There are a couple of exceptions. Krasilosky and Shimel (2007) state that "anything written and published by the United States government is in the public domain from the outset."[81] Also, many songs and other copyrighted materials are already in the *public domain* because they were originally protected under an earlier act, which provided a much shorter duration. However, there is one exception to the current life plus 70 years duration and it involves the play *Peter Pan*. Summarizing Allen's article (2007), it seems the stage play *Peter Pan* gained a very unique exception to the laws of public domain and copyrights (in England) when *Prime Minister Callaghan* was able to encourage the country's lawmakers to change the copyright act so that royalties from the play will continue to be given to the *Great Ormond Street Children Hospital* forever. As many of us know, the play's author, J.M. Barrie, gave ownership of the play and thus the royalties, to the hospital in 1929. The hospital has been receiving all royalties since the author died in 1937. England is the only country that has granted this exception as *Peter Pan* is now in the public domain in the rest of the world.[82]

---

[78] Library of Congress, "Copyright Law: Chapter One: 106A. Rights of certain authors to attribution and integrity," http://www.copyright, (accessed January 1, 2011).

[79] Robert Beck and Darwin Tysver, "Welcome to Bitlaw: Copyright Duration" http://www.bitlaw.com/copyright (accessed July 12, 2010).

[80] M. William Krasilovsky, and Sydney Shemel, *This Business of Music*, 10th ed. (New York, NY: Billboard Books, 2007), 123.

[81] M. William Krasilovsky, and Sydney Shemel, *This Business of Music*, 10th ed. (New York, NY: Billboard Books, 2007), 123.

[82] Katie Allen, "Never Ends for Peter Pan: JM Barrie bequeathed all rights to Peter Pan to Great Ormond Street hospital. Its imminent expiry is set to revive the debate over copyright term," *The Guardian*, http://www.guardian.co.uk/business/2007/dec/28/gtormondst (accessed January 1, 2011).

Phonorecords

Phonorecords are the actual signals recorded on any storage device and are therefore defined by the copyright law as

> *...Objects in which sounds, other than those accompanying a motion picture or other audiovisual work, are fixed by any method now known or later developed and from which sounds can be perceived, reproduced or otherwise communicated, either directly or with the aid of a machine or device.*[83]

Sound/Audio Recordings

Sound recordings are defined as;

> *...Works that result from the fixations of a series of musical, spoken, or other sounds, but not including the sounds accompanying a motion picture or other audiovisual work, regardless of the nature of the material objects such as disks, tapes, or other phonorecords in which they are embodied.*[84]

Major Copyright Acts

Following the instructions in the Constitution, Congress passed many copyright acts. Some of the most important acts affecting the entertainment and music business (the length of the copyright duration and various registration and other processes) are the laws of 1790, 1831, 1909, 1976, 1992, 1993, 1995, 1997, 1998, 2004, and 2006.[85]

Colonial Congress of 1783

Even at the time of the birth of our nation, Rudd (2007) claims that we were considering the importance of copyrights as

> *...The Continental Congress resolved that a committee be appointed to consider the most proper means of cherishing genius and useful arts through the United States by securing to authors or publishers their property in such new works. The committee chosen consisted of Hugh Williamson, Ralph Izard, and James Madison.*[86]

Recommendation of 1787

The founders of our Constitution knew of the importance of owning what you create. According to the Library of Congress (2010), "James Madison submitted to the framers of the Constitution a provision 'to secure to literary authors their copyrights for a limited time.'"[87]

---

[83] Library of Congress, "Copyright Basic: What is a Copyright," http://www.copyright.gov/circs/circ1.pdf, (accessed June 25, 2010).

[84] Library of Congress, "Copyright Basic: What is a Copyright," http://www.copyright.gov/circs/circ1.pdf, (accessed June 25, 2010).

[85] Library of Congress, "Notable Dates in United States Copyrights," http://www.copyright.gov/circs/circ1a.html, (accessed June 25, 2010).

[86] Benjamin Rudd, at the Library of Congress, "Notable Dates in American Copyrights 1783-1969" http://www.copyright, (accessed January 1, 2011).

[87] Library of Congress, "The United States Copyright Office: A Brief Introduction and History," http://www.copyright.gov/circs/circ1a.html, (accessed June 25, 2010).

Act of 1790

The Copyright Act of 1790 was the first copyright law of the United States. It was entitled "An Act for the Encouragement of Learning, by Securing the Copies of Maps, Charts, and Books to the Authors and Proprietors of such Copies during the Times Therein Mentioned."[88] It gave authors (for a limited time) monopoly ownership rights of approval for the copying and displaying of their creative works which were defined as books, maps, and charts. It also specified by statute that writing was a particular form of expression. The monopoly ownership rights, later called Exclusive Rights, were granted for one 14-year term, plus an additional 14-year renewal term (if applied) for a total of 28 years.[89] The act also required the following formalities to be accomplished in order for the copyright registration to be secured:

> *(a) The deposit of a printed title before publication in the clerk's office of the local U.S. district court; (b) The deposit of a copy of the work with the Secretary of State within six months after publication; and (c) The giving of a notice of the copyright by four advertisements in some newspaper.*[90]

Act of 1831

With the Act of 1831, Congress specified *music compositions as a useful art* that allowed for copyright protection and exclusive ownership rights.[91] *Welcome to the business of music and entertainment!* Now, the songs (if you lived back then), you wrote were your property, copyrightable, and therefore, something from which you could use to turn a profit. In addition, the Act extended the initial term of the duration to 28 years, doubling the Act of 1790.[92]

Act of 1909

What was going through the lawmakers' minds regarding copyright laws and the development of mass media back in 1909? They may have had a clue about the future of technology; *Thomas Edison* was in the process of inventing prototypes for the phonograph, film camera, telephone, and other related devices. Indeed, the inventions of the entertainment industry developed until the 1970s fell mostly within relevant copyright laws fixed under the 1909 act.

The 1909 act was the third general revision of the copyright law. The act expanded the monopoly ownership to a total of 56 years (original and renewal period). It also allowed protection for unpublished works and stated that a copyright notice on the work (© date and owner's name) was secured by publication, thus ending the need for newspaper copyright related advertisements. The works of foreign origin in foreign languages were exempted from the requirement of American manufacturing.[93] Additionally, the owners of musical

---

[88] Library of Congress, "The United States Copyright Office: A Brief Introduction and History," http://www.copyright.gov/circs/circ1a.html, (accessed June 25, 2010).

[89] Library of Congress, "The United States Copyright Office: A Brief Introduction and History," http://www.copyright.gov/circs/circ1a.html, (accessed June 25, 2010).

[90] Library of Congress, "The United States Copyright Office: A Brief Introduction and History," http://www.copyright.gov/circs/circ1a.html, (accessed June 25, 2010).

[91] Richard Schulenberg, *Legal Aspects of the Music Industry: An Insider's View of the Legal and Practical Aspects of the Music Business* (New York, NY: Billboard Books 1999).

[92] David Moser, *Moser on Music Copyrights*, (Boston, MA: Course Technology/Cenage Learning, 2006), 15.

[93] Library of Congress, "Copyright Act of 1909," http://www.copyright, (accessed January 1, 2011).

compositions were granted mechanical recording rights under the *compulsory licensing provisions*.[94] According to Moser (2006),

> *This provision created a compulsory mandatory mechanical license to reproduce and distribute sound recordings of musical compositions. It provided a two-cent royalty to be paid to the copyright owner of a song for each record distributed... provided that the copyright owner had previously authorized the first recording and distribution of the song.*[95]

Act of 1976

The problem facing the emerging music and entertainment industry became how to adapt the law of 1909 to the discoveries of the modern mass media and entertainment business. It was more than 60 years after the law of 1909 passed that Congress addressed many of these issues in the 1976 Copyright Act. Some of the country's greatest songwriters, including the late Irving Berlin, were outliving their copyrights, so the 1976 act extended the term of a copyright to life of the author plus 50 years. Joint authorship works were provided copyright protection for 50 years after the longest surviving author's death. Pseudonymous, anonymous, and works-for-hire were protected for 75 years from the date of first publication or 100 years from the date of creation, whichever expired first.[96]

Transitional Copyrights

The 1976 law retained the renewal system for works still under protection of the 1909 law. The shift from the 1909 Act with its 56 years of duration to the 1976 Act's "life plus 50" was a dramatic step toward awarding protection after the death of the author to the author's family members or others. To narrow the difference in duration between the two acts, an additional 19 years were added to the duration of copyrights (that had not already fallen into public domain) under the 1909 act. The original 28 years and 28 renewal years, plus 19 additional years provided for a total copyright term of 75 years for songs and copyrights that had not yet dropped into public domain at the time of the 1976 act.[97]

Amendment of 1984

Two events in 1984 have significantly affected the current business of music and entertainment. According to Moser (2006), "*The Record Rental Amendment* granted the copyright owner of a sound recording (the labels) the right to authorize or prohibit the rental, lease, or lending of phonorecords for direct or indirect commercial purposes."[98] This amendment should provide momentous benefit to the labels since distribution companies are currently beginning to offer instant listening to specific recordings by leasing the recording for a simple monthly fee through home computers and cell phone clouds.[99]

---

[94] Library of Congress, "Copyright Act of 1909," http://www.copyright, (accessed January 1, 2011).

[95] David Moser, *Moser on Music Copyrights*, (Boston, MA: Course Technology/Cenage Learning, 2006), 15.

[96] David Moser, *Moser on Music Copyrights*, (Boston, MA: Course Technology/Cenage Learning, 2006), 16-17.

[97] Library of Congress, "Duration of a Copyright: Effect of 1976 Act on Length of Subsisting Copyrights," http://www.copyright, (accessed January 1, 2011).

[98] David Moser, *Moser on Music Copyrights*, (Boston, MA: Course Technology/Cenage Learning, 2006), 19.

[99] R. NAKASHIMA, "MOG, Radio New Entrants to $10-a-Month Mobile Music," The Associated Press, http://www.rgj.com/article/20100704/BIZ15/7040316/MOG-Rdio-new-entrants-to-10-a-month-mobile-music (accessed 2010 July 5).

The Supreme Court Decision in Sony v. Universal Studios

The second major event in 1984 was the Supreme Court's decision in Sony v. Universal Studios. According to the case, SONY CORP. v. UNIVERSAL CITY STUDIOS, INC., 464 U.S. 417 (1984) pp. 428-456,

> *Respondents brought an action against petitioners in Federal District Court, alleging that VTR consumers had been recording some of respondents' copyrighted works that had been exhibited on commercially sponsored television and thereby infringed respondents' copyrights, and further that petitioners were liable for such copyright infringement because of their marketing of the VTRs.*[100]

The court held "the sale of the VTRs (by Sony) to the general public does not constitute contributory infringement of respondents' (Universal Studios) copyrights."[101] This decision established the idea of *time-shifting* as a valid consumer use of *fair use rights*.[102] In other words, consumers have the right to buy devices (i.e. video tape recorders) (and Sony has the right to sell them) so that they can record a TV show and watch it at more suitable time. This decision, in conjunction with the *Digital Millennium Copyright Act* (DMCA) of 1998, later became the *failed defense* of the lawyers representing P2P companies, as in the *Napster* copyright infringement case in 2000 and the Supreme Court decision in *MGM Studio*, Inc. v. *Grokster, LTD* in 2005.[103]

The Berne Convention

The Berne Convention for the Protection of Literary and Creative Works was first signed in Berne, Switzerland, on September 9, 1886, and completed in Paris in 1896. It is recognized as a primary international copyright agreement.[104] It ensures international copyright protection for American citizens' creative works in the 184-plus member countries. In return, international members' creative works are protected in America.[105] The effective date in the United States was March 1, 1989.[106] However the Act of 1976 had to be modified in order for the United States to become a member. Previously, a copyright notice had to be placed on all

---

[100] U.S. Supreme Court, "Sony Corp. v. Universal City Studios, Inc., 464 U.S. 417,"http://caselaw.lp.findlaw.com/scripts/getcase.pl?court=us&vol=464&invol=417 (accessed July 7, 2010)

[101] U.S. Supreme Court, "Sony Corp. v. Universal City Studios, Inc., 464 U.S. 417,"http://caselaw.lp.findlaw.com/scripts/getcase.pl?court=us&vol=464&invol=417 (accessed July 7, 2010)

[102] Electronic Frontier Foundation, "Fair Use Frequently Asked Questions (and Answers)," http://w2.eff.org/IP/eff_fair_use_faq.php, (January 1, 2011).

[103] United States Supreme Court, "GM Studios, Inc. v. Grokster, Ltd.," http://lawschool.courtroomview.com/acf_cases/9263-mgm-studios-inc-v-grokster-ltd- (accessed July 7, 2010).

[104] Samuel Ricketson, "The Birth of the Berne Union, 11 Colum-VLAJ.L. & Arts," http://www.peteryu.com/intip/class2.pdf, (January 1, 2011).

[105] Berne Convention, "Berne Convention for the Protection of Literary and Creative Works," http://www.wipo.int/treaties/en/ip/berne/trtdocs_wo001.html, (accessed January 1, 2011).

[106] Library of Congress, "Copyright Law of the United States of America and Related Laws Contained in Title 17 of the United States Code: 405 Notice of Copyright: Omission of Notice on Certain Copies and Phonorecords," http://www.copyright, (accessed January 1, 2011).

published works, but the U.S. had to drop this requirement to join the convention.[107] Therefore, a notice is no longer required in the United States, just recommended. In addition, the *Coalition for Networked Information* (2010) states that a song is considered a *Berne Convention* work if

> *...In the case of an unpublished work, one or more of the authors is a native of a nation adhering to the Berne Convention; or, if the work is published, one or more of the authors is a national of a nation adhering to the Berne Convention on the date of the first publication, or (b) if the work is first published in a nation adhering to the Berne Convention.*[108]

Additional Major Copyright Acts

Here is where things start to get really interesting. As an example, in 1992 most people where buying blank CD's and making copies of their "purchased recordings" to use in their cars and other devices in other places. Surprisingly, it was against the law until the !992 Home Recording Act.

Act of 1992

The *1992 Audio Home Recording Act* (commonly known as the Digital Audio Recording Technology Act or DART Act) provides royalties to songwriters, publishers, producers, recording artists, and record companies to compensate for their loss of royalties due to consumer copying or dubbing of their CDs and other media.[109] In effect, this made it legal for consumers to make copies of their purchased entertainment sound recordings for their own personal use. Obringer (2010) states,

> *...The Audio Home Recording Act of 1992 caused yet another royalty payment for songwriters and performers. This act requires that the manufacturers of digital audio recording devices and the manufacturers of blank recording media (blank cassette tapes, blank CDs, blank DVDs, etc.) pay some of their sales price to the Register of Copyrights to make up for loss of sales due to the possible unauthorized copying of music. There are two funds set up where this money is funneled. One is the Sound Recording Fund, which receives two-thirds of the money. This money goes to the recording artist and record company. The other fund is the Musical Works Fund, which receives the remaining one-third of the money to split 50/50 between the publisher and the songwriter.*[110]

Also, in the late 1980s, the concern was that digital recorders would lower revenues because sound quality of digital copies is perfect as opposed to analog copies that decrease the audio quality with noise and distortion on each generation (copy make). This, along with the combination of burnable CDs and the Internet, provided consumers with a way to illegally "share" music with the world, cutting record label profits and future financial investments in songwriters, publishers, and recording artists. The concern was real. An article by Tia Hall in the *Duke Law and Technology Review* (2002) explains that

> *...According to various newspaper articles, approximately 3.6 billion songs are illegally downloaded each month in the United States. In 1999, the music industry estimated that one in four compact discs of new music was an unauthorized copy. By the end of 2001, it was estimated that as many CDs were burned and copied as were bought. In Europe, blank CDs are outselling recorded CDs (although these blank CDs might have also been purchased for legitimate reasons, such as to back-up personal computer files). And*

---

107 Library of Congress, "Copyright Law of the United States of America and Related Laws Contained in Title 17 of the United States Code: 405 Notice of Copyright: Omission of Notice on Certain Copies and Phonorecords," http://www.copyright, (accessed January 1, 2011).

108 Berne Convention Implementation Act of 1988, ""Section 4, Subject Matter and Scope of Copyrights," The Coalition for Networked Information, http://www.cni.org/docs/infopols/US.Berne.Convention.html, (January 1, 2011).

109 Library of Congress, "United States Public Laws 102-563-The Home Recording Act of 1992," http://www.brouhaha.com/~eric/bad_laws/ahra.html (accessed January 1, 2011).

110 Lee Ann Obringer, "How Music royalties Work," http://entertainment.howstuffworks.com/music-royalties4.htm (accessed July, 20, 2010).

> *since 1999, ownership of CD burners has nearly tripled. This trend of consumers sharing their music rather than purchasing it may be attributable to many factors, including the slow economy. However, the music industry seems to believe that the most likely culprit in this trend is the rise of digital music, i.e., free online file sharing, and the growing popularity of CD burners.*[111]

Thus, besides applying a tax on recorders and tapes (the DART fund)[112] to compensate for the expected loss of revenues, the act also required *serial copying management systems* on digital recorders to limit the number of copies consumers could make.[113] According to the Library of Congress Copyright Office (2010), the DART Act is the "first statutory license to grant royalties to copyright owners for home copying."[114] It was the first time songwriters, music publishers, and labels were allowed to make money from consumers making copies for their own personal use within their homes. Currently the fees are collected by *The Alliance of Artists and Recording Companies* (AARC).[115]

Act of 1993

The *Copyright Royalty Tribunal Reform Act of 1993* eliminated the *Copyright Royalty Tribunal* (CRT) and replaced it with the *Copyright Arbitration Royalty Panel* (CARP) administered by the Library of Congress (Librarian).[116] The panel's job was to set *statutory rates* for the various *compulsory licenses*, including the mechanical license record labels must acquire for the use of preexisting songs their artists choose to record. The original purpose of replacing the *Tribunal* with *CARP* was to save money. It did not work, as the appointed industry leaders (the members of CARP) could not agree on rates (publishers wanted rates to be higher, labels lower), and a three-federal-judge panel replaced CARP in 2004.[117]

Act of 1995 – The "DPRA" or The Sixth Exclusive Right

The Digital Performance Right in Sound Recordings Act of 1995 authorizes copyright owners to be paid for digital transmissions of their recordings, including interactive digital audio transmissions.[118] Thus, the 1995 Digital Transmission Act expands the previous *compulsory licenses* by including *digital audio transmissions* as the sixth

---

[111] Tia Hall, "Music Piracy and the Audio Home Recording Act," Duke law and Technology Review, http://www.law.duke.edu/journals/dltr/articles/2002dltr0023.html (accessed July 20, 2010).

[112] Tia Hall, "Music Piracy and the Audio Home Recording Act," Duke law and Technology Review, http://www.law.duke.edu/journals/dltr/articles/2002dltr0023.html (accessed July 20, 2010), & http://everything2.com/title/Audio+Home+Recording+Act, (accessed June 26, 2010).

[113] Tia Hall, "Music Piracy and the Audio Home Recording Act," Duke law and Technology Review, http://www.law.duke.edu/journals/dltr/articles/2002dltr0023.html (accessed July 20, 2010), & http://everything2.com/title/Audio+Home+Recording+Act, (accessed June 26, 2010).http://www.copyright (accessed July 12, 2010)

[114] Library of Congress, "Announcements: Notice with Requests for Comments as Containment for Controversy for 1992 and 1993 Digital Audio Recording Royalty Funds http://www.copyright.gov/history/mls/ML-475.pdf (accessed July 8, 2010).

[115] The Alliance of Artist and Recording Companies (AARC), "What is AARC?," aarecroyalties.com, https://www.aarcroyalties.com/2008/home.php?nav=whatis, (accessed March 26, 2011).

[116] Library of Congress, "Copyright Arbitration Royalty Panels (CARP)," http://www.copyright (accessed July 7, 2010)

[117] Library of Congress, Copyright Law of the United States of America, The Copyright Royalty and Distribution Reform Act of 2004," http://www.copyright, (accessed January 2, 2011)

[118] Library of Congress, "Digital Performance Right in Sound Recording Act of 1995," http://www.google.com/#hl=en&expIds=17259,17315,23628,23670, (accessed January 2, 2011).

exclusive right.[119] According to the following statement from Marybeth Peters, Register of Copyrights, Library of Congress, to the Subcommittee on Courts, the Internet, and Intellectual Property of the House Committee on the Judiciary (2007), Congress needed to address the difference between physical phonorecords and digital streaming and downloads:

> *Congress made changes to Section 115 to meet the challenges of providing music in a digital format when it enacted the Digital Performance Right in Sound Recordings Act of 1995 ("DPRA"), Pub. L. 104-39, 109 Stat. 336, which also granted copyright owners of sound recordings an exclusive right to perform their works publicly by means of a digital audio transmission… The amendments to Section 115 clarified the reproduction and distribution rights of music copyright owners and producers and distributors of sound recordings, especially with respect to what the amended Section 115 termed "digital phonorecord deliveries."*[120]

The real question therefore "is streaming of music over the Internet a mechanical license fee requirement or a performance license requirement? The problem gets even more complex when we consider the type of streaming (passive or interactive). Marybeth Peter's letter to Congress (2007) continues:

> *During the 1990s, it became apparent that music services could offer options for the enjoyment of music in digital formats either by providing the public an opportunity to hear any sound recording it wanted on-demand or by delivering a digital version of the work directly to a consumer's computer. In either case, there was the possibility that the new offerings would obviate the need for mechanical reproductions in the forms heretofore used to distribute musical works and sound recordings in a physical format, e.g., vinyl records, cassette tapes and most recently audio compact discs. Moreover, it was clear that digital transmissions were substantially superior to analog transmissions.*[121]

What a mess digital technology has created within the legal side of the industry. What is a digital transmission? At its simplest levels, the 6th Exclusive Right appears to have expanded the copyright law to include public performances of audio (recorded songs) by means of digital transmissions for subscription and interactive providers. Thus, the DPRA and its DPD (digital phonorecord delivery) are the foundation of the *digital mechanical license,* which is required for digital downloads. Royalties are collected by The Harry Fox Agency and paid directly to music publishers who then pay the songwriters according to their deals. Marybeth Peters, Register of Copyrights, explains in detail (2007):

> *By 1995, Congress recognized that "digital transmission of sound recordings [was] likely to become a very important outlet for the performance of recorded music." S. Rep. No. 104-128, at 14 (1995). Moreover, it realized that "these new technologies also may lead to new systems for the electronic distribution of phonorecords with the authorization of the affected copyright owners." Id. For these reasons, Congress made changes to Section 115 to meet the challenges of providing music in a digital format when it enacted the Digital Performance Right in Sound Recordings Act of 1995 ("DPRA"), Pub. L. 104-39, 109 Stat. 336, which also granted copyright owners of sound recordings an exclusive right to perform their works publicly by means of a digital audio transmission, 17 U.S.C. §106(6), subject to certain limitations. See 17 U.S.C. §114. The amendments to Section 115 clarified the reproduction and distribution rights of music copyright owners and producers and distributors of sound recordings, especially with respect to what the amended Section 115 termed "digital phonorecord deliveries."*[122]

---

119 Library of Congress, "Digital Performance Right in Sound Recording Act of 1995," http://www.copyright (accessed July 7, 2010).

120 Marybeth Peters, "Statement of Marybeth Peters, The Register of Copyrights before the Subcommittee on Courts, The International and Intellectual Property of the House Committee on the Judiciary," http://www.copyright (accessed September 5, 2010).

121 Marybeth Peters, "Statement of Marybeth Peters, The Register of Copyrights before the Subcommittee on Courts, The International and Intellectual Property of the House Committee on the Judiciary," http://www.copyright (accessed September 5, 2010).

122 Marybeth Peters, "Statement of Marybeth Peters,The Register of Copyrights before the Subcommittee on Courts,The Internet and Intellectual Propertyof the House Committee on the Judiciary," http://www.copyright, (accessed July 18, 2010).

According to her letter to Congress in 2001, Peters stated that the industry itself had provided suggestions for the use of the DPD:

> *In 2001, the RIAA, the National Music Publishers' Association, Inc. ("NMPA"), and the Harry Fox Agency, Inc. ("HFA") entered into an agreement concerning the mechanical licensing of musical works for new subscription services on the Internet. Licenses issued under the RIAA/NMPA/HFA agreement are nonexclusive and cover all reproduction and distribution rights for delivery of on-demand streams and limited downloads and include the right to make server copies, buffer copies and other related copies used in the operation of a covered service. The license also provides at no additional cost for "On-Demand Streams of Promotional Excerpts," which are defined as a stream consisting of no more that thirty (30) seconds of playing time of the sound recording of a musical work or no more than the lesser of ten percent (10%) or sixty (60) seconds of playing time of a sound recording of a musical work longer than five minutes...*[123]

Sadly, it gets even more complicated as Congress tried to figure out the definition of interactive streaming. According to Peters' letter to Congress (2009),

> *The CRJs accurately noted that the statute does not define or mention the term "interactive streaming" and that there is no agreement among the participants as to the precise meaning of the term... The regulations ultimately contained in the CRJs' final determination establishing rates and terms of royalty payments for the activities under section 115, i.e. "making and distributing phonorecords, including by means of digital phonorecord deliveries," are divided into two subparts. The first portion, Subpart A, is the product of the findings and deliberations of the CRJs and delineates the rates and terms for three distinct categories of phonorecords under the section 115 license. These particular categories identify phonorecords made under specific conditions and are categorized as "Physical phonorecord deliveries," "Permanent digital downloads," and "ringtones." See 37 CFR 385.1-385.4. The second portion, Subpart B, is the product of settlement negotiations among the participants and delineates the rates and terms for two additional distinct categories identifying phonorecords made under the section 115 license. These particular categories identify phonorecords made under specific conditions and are identified as "Interactive Streaming" and "Limited Downloads." Subpart B also indicates specific conditions under which "promotional royalty rates" are applicable to "Interactive Streaming" and "Limited Downloads."*[124]

Thus, the mechanical license required by labels for the use of a song sold as a recording through the distribution of CDs, flash drives, old vinyl records, etc., is still required. The DPD is different, as it used for digital downloads and also provides third party distribution of original phonorecords, provided the service is licensed by the original copyright holders. Peters continues (2007),

> *Under the expanded license, a service providing DPDs can in effect become a virtual record store if it is able to clear the rights to the sound recordings. More importantly, the DPRA allows a copyright owner of a sound recording to license the right to make DPDs of both the sound recording and the underlying musical work to third parties if it has obtained the right to make DPDs from the copyright owner of the musical work. See 17 U.S.C. §115(c)(3)(I), S. Rep. No. 104-128, at 43 (1995).*[125]

As stated previously, a *compulsory license* gives artists the right to record and sell their own version of a song as a cover tune. It is not legal to make copies of the actual original recording and then distribute or sell them. However, the DPD appears to have changed the rule by allowing third parties [internet website providers] the right to make and sell copies of the original recordings as long as they have been licenses by the original copyright owners.

The "DPD" or Digital Phonorecord Delivery

The streaming of music over the Internet has caused some legal hurdles, as Ms. Peters states in her letter to Congress. She explains that although the *compulsory license* has worked well with physical product distribution, it is limited and may need to be eliminated (repealed) for digital streaming (2007):

---

123 Marybeth Peters, "Statement of Marybeth Peters, The Register of Copyrights before the Subcommittee on Courts, The Internet and Intellectual Propertyof the House Committee on the Judiciary," http://www.copyright, (accessed July 18, 2010).

124 Marybeth Peters, "Statement of Marybeth Peters,The Register of Copyrights before the Subcommittee on Courts, The Internet and Intellectual Property of the House Committee on the Judiciary," http://www.copyright, (accessed July 18, 2010).

125 Marybeth Peters, "Statement of Marybeth Peters, The Register of Copyrights before the Subcommittee on Courts, The Internet and Intellectual Property of the House Committee on the Judiciary," http://www.copyright, (accessed July 18, 2010).

The Section 115 compulsory license worked well for the next two decades, but the use of new digital technology to deliver music to the public required a second look at the license to determine whether it continued to meet the needs of the music industry.

First, Congress expanded the scope of the compulsory license to include the making and distribution of a digital phonorecord and, in doing so, adopted a new term of art, the "digital phonorecord delivery" ("DPD"), to describe the process whereby a consumer receives a phonorecord by means of a digital transmission, the delivery of which requires the payment of a statutory royalty under Section 115. The precise definition of this new term reads as follows:

> *A "digital phonorecord delivery" is each individual delivery of a phonorecord by digital transmission of a sound recording which results in a specifically identifiable reproduction by or for any transmission recipient of a phonorecord of that sound recording, regardless of whether the digital transmission is also a public performance of the sound recording or any nondramatic musical work embodied therein. A digital phonorecord delivery does not result from a real-time, nonintegrated subscription transmission of a sound recording where no reproduction of the sound recording or the musical work embodied therein is made from the inception of the transmission through to its receipt by the transmission recipient in order to make the sound recording audible.*[126]

Act of 1997

The *No Electronic Theft Act* (NET ACT) is significant because individuals or companies that do not make a monetary profit or commercial gain but create software that others can use to infringe on sound recording copyrights can be criminally prosecuted. Individuals are in violation of this act if they are sharing recorded music through P2P services *for financial gain* and may also be prosecuted. The NET Act amended the definition of commercial advantage or private financial gain to include the receipt (or expected receipt) of anything of value, including receipt of other copyrighted works.[127, 128] According to the U.S. Department of Justice (1998), fines for violation of *17 U.S.C.* and *18 U.S.C.* range from "180 days in jail and a $1,000 fine to 20 years in jail and $15 million in fines for trafficking in counterfeit goods or services."[129]

Act of 1998 – The Digital Millennium Copyright Act

The Digital Millennium Copyright Act in 1998 implemented the 1996 *World Intellectual Property Organization* (WIPO) treaties for the protection of copyrights, performances, and *phonorecords* in the United States. The treaty significantly helped protect digital creative works by addressing copyright issues concerning the Internet, online service providers, computer programs, web casting, digital movies, digital music transmission, and downloads.[130] According to Oxenford (2006),

---

126 Marybeth Peters, "Statement of Marybeth Peters, The Register of Copyrights before the Subcommittee on Courts, The International and Intellectual Property of the House Committee on the Judiciary," http://www.copyright (accessed September 5, 2010).

127 Library of Congress, "No Electronic Theft Act (NET ACT)," "http://www.copyright (accessed September 5, 2010)

128 Library of Congress, "The Digital Millennium Copyright Act of 1998," http://cryptome.org/dmca/dmca-index.htm#DMCA, (accessed January, 2, 2011)

129 Library of Congress, "No Electronic Theft Act (NET ACT), http://www.justice.gov/criminal/cybercrime/17-18red.htm (accessed January 2, 2011)

130 Marybeth Peters, "Statement of Marybeth Peters, The Register of Copyrights before the Subcommittee on Courts, The International and Intellectual Property of the House Committee on the Judiciary," http://www.copyright (accessed September 5, 2010).

> *The Digital Millennium Copyright Act (DMCA) required that royalties be paid to the performers for all digital uses of music except those in an over-the-air digital transmission by a broadcast station, e.g. through the Iniquity digital radio system or as part of a Digital Television stream.*[131]

The acceptance of the treaties into the DMCA was an attempt by Congress to protect both the copyright owners and businesses that use new technologies to create, distribute, and sell creative products. The conflict between the two seems to be always ongoing (you may remember the conflict cause by the new technology of the day (1600s and printing press) and the legislative solution (the Statute of Anne). Moser (2006) illustrates,

> *Although the media often like to portray the copyright industry as anti-technology, disputes involving copyright and technology are really just disputes between businesses. When new technologies are invented, businesses develop that intend to profit from the use of these technologies. Almost invariable, businesses based on new technologies believe they should not have to pay copyright owners of the content they use or make available. On the other hand, businesses based on ownership of copyrights (music, movies, books, computer software, video games) tend to believe that their rights apply regardless of innovative new technologies.*[132]

The American Federation of Radio and Television Artists (AFTRA) and The American Federation of Musicians (AF of M) together formed The AFM & AFTRA Intellectual Property Rights Distribution Fund to collect and distribute royalties to non-featured singers and musicians for the rental, home copying, and digital broadcasting of sound recordings in foreign countries required by the Digital Millennium Copyright Act.[133]

Act of 1998 – Fairness in Music Licensing Act

The *Fairness in Music Licensing Act* is considered one of the most damaging laws ever passed by Congress concerning music performance copyrights. Indeed, some music copyright holders consider it to be the *Non-*Fairness in Music Licensing Act because it exempted many "establishments," defined as food service and drinking establishments, with less than 3,750 square feet of gross space and other types of small businesses of less than 2,000 gross square feet, from paying a *performance license* fee for music played in their establishments. According to a report from ASCAP (2009),

> *...Businesses that perform music only from licensed radio, television, cable and satellite sources, that do not retransmit beyond their establishments, and do not charge admission, are exempted as follows: 1. All restaurants, bars and grills that are smaller than 3,750 gross square feet, and all other retail establishments that are smaller than 2,000 gross square feet, are exempt from paying license fees to songwriters, composers and music publishers, but only for their use of radio and TV music. 2. Businesses whose square footage exceeds the amounts listed also qualify for the exemption if they use six or fewer speakers with no more than four speakers in any one room or use audiovisual equipment consisting of no more than four TV's, with no more than one TV in each room, and no TV having a diagonal screen size greater than 55 inches, together with the same speaker restrictions.*[134]

Act of 1998 – Sonny Bono

The *Sonny Bono Copyright Term Extension Act of 1998* added an additional 20 years to the term of a copyright. Thus, the life plus 50 years that was granted in the 1976 Act became the current "life plus 70 years." The 1976 Act gave copyrights still under duration and created before the 1976 act an additional 19 years to extend the

---

131 David Oxenford, "Department of Commerce Seeks Comments on The Relationship of Protecting Copyrighted Content and Innovation in the Internet Economy," http://www.broadcastlawblog.com/tags/digital-millennium-copyright (accessed January 2, 2011).

132 David Moser, *Moser on Music Copyrights*, (Boston, MA: Course Technology/Cenage Learning, 2006), 192-3.

133 The AFM & AFTRA Intellectual Property Rights Distribution Fund, "About Us," RARoyalties.org, http://www.ahra.org/aboutus.html, (accessed March 26, 2011).

134 ASCAP, "Fairness in Music Licensing Legislation," http://www.ascap.com/legislation/legis_qa.aspx, (accessed January 2, 2011).

56 years granted under the 1909 act to 75 years. The Sonny Bono Act extended those copyrights an additional 20 years for a total of 95 years.[135]

Act of 2004

The *Copyright Royalty and Distribution Reform Act of 2004* replaced the *Copyright Arbitration Royalty Panels* (CARP) with three federal judges. The judges serve scattered six-year terms and send all compulsory license fee recommendations to Congress.[136]

Neighboring Rights

Recording artists and musicians public performance (mass media) broadcasts and digital transmissions and their respective royalties and payments are often different in various countries and territories.[137] Regretfully, there is not an automatic worldwide copyright protection registering system available for creative works. Thus, international copyright treaties negotiated to provide copyright protection in varies countries may or may not provide protection and royalty collections. The treaties are often named after the city in which they were held. Important treaties include Geneva in 1952 and 1972, Paris in 1974, and Brussels in 1974 and 1985.[138]

WTO & WIPO 1994 to Present

The *World Trade Organization* and the *World Intellectual Property Organization* have passed legislation in support of worldwide copyright protection. WTO ratified the *Marrakech Agreement* of April 15, 1994, that supports intangible property and copyrights of the *Uruguay Round Agreements*.[139] The *WIPO Performances and Phonograms Treaty* was concluded in *Geneva, Switzerland*, on December 20, 1996.[140] It protects *rights management information* (RMI), or *electronic watermarks* that are placed in copyrighted products. RMI is used to electronically label and thereby protect music and entertainment products from consumers who want to use or copy them for free through P2P. Copyright owners and representing organizations, such as the Recording Industry Association of America (RIAA), use software to detect the sequence of codes on personal hard drives.[141]

---

135 Library of Congress, "Sonny Bono Copyright Term Extension Act of 1998: Chapter 3, Duration of Copyright," http://www.copyright, (accessed January 2, 2011).

136 Library of Congress (accessed July 8, 2010) & Statement of Marybeth Peters, Register of the Copyrights, before the Sub Committee on the Courts and the Internet, and Intellectual Property Committee on the Judiciary," http://www.copyright.gov/docs/regstat040103.html, (accessed January 3, 2011)

137 Personal interviews with label executives and many industry insiders, 2008-2010.

138 M. William Krasilovsky, and Sydney Shemel, *This Business of Music*, 10th ed. (New York, NY: Billboard Books, 207), 211-216 & Library of Congress, "http://www.copyright.gov/wipo/, (accessed January 3, 2011).

139 World Trade Organization, "Marrakech Agreement." http://www.wipo.int/treaties/en/ip/wppt/trtdocs_wo034.html (accessed July 9, 2010)

140 World Intellectual Property Organization, "WIPO Performances and Phonograms Treaty," International Copyrights Relations of the United States, Circular 38A, http://www.copyright.gov/circs/circ38a.pdf (accessed 07/26/2000).

141 Recording Industry Association of America (RIAA), "Piracy Online and on the Street," http://www.riaa.org/physicalpiracy.php, (accessed January 2, 2011).

Publicity Rights

People often think that when a famous person dies everything about them falls into public domain. Not true! Sometime artists (estates) make more money after death than when they were alive. According to Edelman (2010),

> *Just because a celebrity is dead, doesn't mean she can't try and earn a living. Take, for example, Marilyn Monroe. Since the blonde bombshell's estate teamed up with the talent giant CMG Worldwide, Inc. ("CMG") in 1996, the licensing of Marilyn Monroe's name and image has pulled in over $30 million in revenues.* Forbes Magazine *routinely ranks Monroe as one of the top grossing dead celebrities; in fact, she earned a cool $8 million just last year alone. Not bad for someone who has been dead almost 45 years. Thanks to CMG's efforts, Monroe's name, voice and likeness are used to sell a vast array of products, including refillable lighters, vodka, cars, wine, leather furniture and jeans.*[142]

Many famous artists make more money dead than alive because of the youthful, positive, emotional memories consumers tie to the iconic image of the passed artists. The artist may have died, but the consumers' memories are still alive in their heads and hearts. The entertainment industry often monetizes these emotional connections to the passed artist by marketing products such as pictures, voices, images, and even signatures directly to consumers. Publicity rights are different in various states, so where the artist lived is important when trying to determine specific estate rights. O. Yale LewisJr.,2008) state "A right of publicity is the right of each person to control the commercial use of his or her identity and persona, such as name, voice, signature, photograph, and likeness."[143] Thus, even when the artist has passed, an opportunity for their estate to make money is still very much alive.

"Published"

The word *published* in copyright language is defined as *distributed for sale* to the public, whereas in the music industry terminology, it often refers to a songwriter deal with a music publisher. Same word, yet two different meanings! In this case, we are discussing the legal definition tied to copyrights, not the music business lingo. The 1976 law eliminated the dual registration copyright system of national registration for *published works* (distributed for sale) and state protection for *unpublished works* (not distributed for sale). Thus, according to Moser (2006), "copyright (protection) begins automatically when a copyrightable work is fixed in a tangible form without any registration requirement."[144]

Copyrights are instant (as long as the work meets the qualifiers of originality and placement into a tangible form), and both published and unpublished works are protected. Registration of a work is voluntary, yet required if you wish to file a lawsuit for infringement.[145]

The copyright owner (through the exclusive rights) determines who may use their creative works the first time they are "published" (distributed for sale). However, there is an exception in the music business: a copyright owner has to *grant permission* to cable television stations, jukebox owners, public broadcasting (including PBS-TV and PBS Radio), satellite retransmission operators, and music producers (i.e. for a cover song) for the use

---

[142] Sara Edelman, "Death Pays: The Fight Over Marilyn Monroe's Publicity Rights," http://www.metrocorpcounsel.com/current.php?artType=view&artMonth=July&artYear=2007&EntryNo=6903, (accessed January 3, 2011).

[143] O. Yale Lewis, Jr. for Hendricks & Lewis PLLC, "Publicity Rights Revisited," http://hllaw.com/images/78222PublicityRights.pdf, (accessed January 3, 2011).

[144] David Moser, *Moser on Music Copyrights*, (Boston, MA: Course Technology/Cenage Learning, 2006), 23.

[145] Library of Congress, "Copyright in General: When is My Work Protected?" http://www.copyright, (accessed January 1, 2011).

of their work.[146] *Compulsory licenses* are only available *after* the initial release (publication) of a composition or creative work. Thus, music publishers control who can record and use a new song for the first time. Music publishers use *song casting* to determine which songs to pitch to specific artists and *song pluggers* to deliver the songs to the artist through their producer, manager, or label. The goal is to get the song recorded by the biggest artist on the planet. Once the song has been "published" (in this case, recorded and distributed by a major artist), then under the *compulsory license*, anyone can record a cover of the song and release it for sale. The owner or music publishing company is required to grant permission. A "notice of intent form" must be filed and a mechanical acquired (a license that is typically paid for by the cover artist's label and usually offered through *The Harry Fox Agency* in New York City).[147]

Notice of Intent to Obtain a Compulsory License

If you decide to record a song that has already has been published (distributed for sale), you'll need to file a *Notice of Intent to Obtain a Compulsory License* with the music publisher of the song.[148] According to the Library of Congress (2010),

> *A "Notice of Intention" is a Notice identified in section 115(b) of title 17 of the United States Code, and required by that section to be served on a copyright owner or, in certain cases, to be filed in the Copyright Office, before or within thirty days after making, and before distributing any phonorecords of the work, in order to obtain a compulsory license to make and distribute phonorecords of non dramatic musical works.*[149]

Termination/Recapturing of Rights

The 1976 Act provides a new right to the original authors of copyrighted works by allowing them to *eliminate deals of ownership transfers* (as an example a songwriter publishing deal).[150] Thus, the author(s), surviving spouse, surviving children or grandchildren may recapture their assigned copyrights usually at any time during a five-year period beginning at the end of the 35th year of publication. The notice must state the effective date of termination (which must fall within the five-year period), and it must be served to the music publisher, etc., not less than two or more than ten years before the date of termination.[151] A copy of the notice must be filed and recorded with the Copyright Office before the date of termination.[152]

Non-Copyrightable Products

Copyrightable works must be an *expression* of an idea, not just the idea in your mind. It also needs to be "your expression of an idea in a tangible or physical form. Just having a great idea in your head does not make it legally yours. It is an old truism in copyright law that you cannot copyright an idea but only your expression

---

146 Harry Fox Agency, "Mechanical Licensing," http://www.harryfox.com/public/MechanicalLicenseslic.jsp, (accessed January 1, 2011).

147 Library of Congress, "United States Copyright Office: Compulsory License for Making and Distributing Phonorecords," http://www.copyright.gov/circs/circ73.pdf (accessed July 6, 2010).

148 David Moser, *Moser on Music Copyrights*, (Boston, MA: Course Technology/Cenage Learning, 2006), 66.

149 Library of Congress, Title 37: Patents, Trademarks, and Copyrights, "The Code of Federal Regulations: 201.18 Notice of Intent to Obtain a Compulsory License for Making and Distributing Records of Nondramatic Musical Works," http://www.loc.gov/cgi-bin/formprocessor/copyright (accessed July 6, 2010).

150 Library of Congress, "Copyright Basics: Termination of Transfers," http://www.copyright (accessed July 6, 2010).

151 Library of Congress, "Notice of Termination," http://www.copyright (accessed July 6, 2010).

152 Library of Congress, "Notice of Termination," http://www.copyright (accessed July 6, 2010).

of it; ideas are considered to be in the public domain.[153] Thousands of songs use the same title and slogans that have been used in many books, films, and commercials, without the need to gain permission from anyone. In some cases, titles and slogans can be protected by federal trademark law and by state laws against unfair competition and misappropriation. However this is rare, and copyright law does not protect unique ideas, titles, and slogans.[154]

Summary

If you want to be a part of the entertainment and music business, be grateful that the United States Congress and many other countries around the world have provided copyright protection for the songs, music, books, films, and other entertainment products you've created. The copyright law provides the legal foundation for ownership and justifies the corresponding financial rewards. Songwriters initially own the songs they write, record companies own the recordings they financially produce, scriptwriters own their scripts, and production companies own the films and television shows they have paid millions to create. Without strong American and international copyright laws, conventions, and treaties, the ownership of creative products would be almost meaningless. The music business, indeed the entire entertainment industry as we currently know it, would cease to exist without the copyright law.

Sadly, new technology has provided ways for many consumers to acquire entertainment products without payment. In addition, legislators have been very slow in providing the laws required to allow for legal action to stop the massive thief. From a historical perspective, it has taken legal action from the 1710 *Statute of Anne* in England to the current *WIPO Treaty* to build a legislative foundation that can protect creativity in our digital world. Thus, laws including the Acts of 1790, 1831, 1909, 1976, 1992, 1993, 1995, 1998, and 2004 have defined ownership rights, cost, and duration of a copyright, which is currently life of the creator plus 70 years. The *Berne Convention* provided international protection.

Lastly, lawsuits and the Supreme Court decisions on P2P file sharing have defined digital transmission rights for copyright owners and consumers. Younger consumers appear to use P2P to discover new acts as opposed to listening to their local radio stations. Peer-to-peer file sharing has provided both a marketing boom and a copyright protection nightmare to the music and entertainment industry. The industry has struggled to embrace the opportunities of digital technology because copyright laws are hard to enforce. This is a talent-driven, creative industry and as such, it is totally dependent on copyright protection and enforcement.[155] Past lawsuits by *Metallica* and the *Recording Industry Association of America* (RIAA) against *Napster* and various infringing consumers have not really curbed the illegal circulation and use of copyrighted music and recordings. The first major case concerning P2P file sharing was the case of *A&M Records v. Napster* in 2001. Judge Beezer (2001) summarized by stating,

> *"The district court correctly recognized that a preliminary injunction against Napster's participation in copyright infringement is not only warranted but required. We believe, however, that the scope of the injunction needs modification in light of our opinion. Specifically, we reiterate that contributory liability may potentially be imposed only to the extent that Napster: (1) receives reasonable knowledge of specific infringing files with copyrighted musical compositions and sound recordings; (2) knows or should know that such files are available on the Napster system; and (3) fails to act to prevent viral distribution of the works. The mere existence of the*

---

[153] Library of Congress, "What Does Copyright Protect?" http://www.copyright, (accessed January 3, 2011).

[154] Library of Congress, "What Does Copyright Protect?" http://www.copyright, (accessed January 3, 2011).

[155] Personal interviews with label executives and many industry insiders, 2008-2010.

> *Napster system, absent actual notice and Napster's demonstrated failure to remove the offending material, is insufficient to impose contributory liability."*[156]

The truth is that profits can only be gained from artistry and creativity financed by the promotion, publicity, and distribution of sellable entertainment products that satisfy consumers' emotional wants and needs. However, it costs money (usually in the million of dollars) to find, develop, create, market, and sell products to consumers. Thus, it is a sad comment on society when the majority of recorded music acquired by consumers is not paid for. Various studies state that up to 95% of all recorded music *acquired* is not paid for (approximately 40 billion files in 2008)![157] The labels have a much more difficult time breaking even and profiting on their investments in recording artists, and the creative songwriters, music publishers, and singers are simply not paid mechanicals and recording artist royalties. No wonder labels have moved toward a *360-degree fulfillment business model* where they can recoup their investment out of the artist tours and merchandise. *Marybeth Peters*, The Register of the Copyright Office (2003), states,

> *...Mr. Chairman, make no mistake. The law is unambiguous. Using peer-to-peer networks to copy or distribute copyrighted works without permission is infringement and copyright owners have every right to invoke the power of the courts to combat such activity. Every court that has addressed the issue has agreed that this activity is infringement. It can also be a crime and the perpetrators of such a crime are subject to fines and jail time.*[158]

In 2004, the *United States Supreme Court* issued its decision in the *Metro-Goldwyn-Mayer Studios v. Grokster Ltd.* Lawsuit, clearly stating that failure to pay for copyrighted products obtained free over the Internet is illegal.[159] The decision was not against the use of downloading of entertainment digital products over the Internet, just the *failure to pay the copyright holders' royalties and license fees.* Justice Souter (2003) delivered the opinion of the Court:

> *The question is under what circumstances the distributor of a product capable of both lawful and unlawful use is liable for acts of copyright infringement by third parties using the product. We hold that one who distributes a device with the object of promoting its use to infringe copyright, as shown by clear expression or other affirmative steps taken to foster infringement, is liable for the resulting acts of infringement by third parties.*[160]

Unlike Napster and Grokster, labels and copyright holders have allowed YouTube to exist by charging them money (a percentage of their advertisement royalties), even though copyrights are clearing being violated.[161] The perception is that some money is better than none. Mark Cuban, in the book *Fortune's Fool* (2010), claims:

> *"Considering the RIAA will sue your grandma or a twelve-year old at the drop of a hat, the fact that You Tube is building a traffic juggernaut around copyrighted audio and video without being sued is like... well, Napster at the beginning as the labels were trying*

---

156 A&M Records v. Napster, "The Ninth Circuit Decision, February 9, 2001," http://gseis.ucla.edu/iclp/napster.htm, (accessed January 3, 2011).

157 A&M Records v. Napster, "The Ninth Circuit Decision, February 9, 2001," http://gseis.ucla.edu/iclp/napster.htm, (accessed January 3, 2011)

158 Marybeth Peters, "Statement of Marybeth Peters, The Register of Copyrights before the Subcommittee on Courts, The International and Intellectual Property of the House Committee on the Judiciary," http://www.copyright (accessed September 5, 2010).

159 United States Supreme Court, "Metro-Goldwyn-Mayer Studios v. Grokster Ltd," http://www.oyez.org/cases/2000-2009/2004/2004_04_480, & http://scholar.google.com/scholar_case?case=8647956476676426155&hl=en&as sdt=2&as_vis=1&oi=scholarr (accessed January 3, 2011).

160 United States Supreme Court, "Metro-Goldwyn-Mayer Studios v. Grokster Ltd," http://www.oyez.org/cases/2000-2009/2004/2004_04_480, & http://scholar.google.com/scholar_case?case=8647956476676426155&hl=en&as sdt=2&as_vis=1&oi=scholarr (accessed January 3, 2011).

161 Personal interviews with label executives and many industry insiders, 2008-2010.

> *to figure out what it meant to them," he said. "With the Grokster ruling, it's just a question of when YouTube will be hit with a charge of inducing millions of people to break copyright laws, not if."*[162]

However, letting YouTube survive may not have been a good decision. According to Goodman (2010),

> *The most deeply troubling development..., is the growing realization that YouTube and the streaming and free-to-consumer music websites... ...are generating very little in the way of additional sales and royalties and no meaningful advertising income. The biggest problem with YouTube is it's microscopic payments. According to Tube Mogul, which measured Internet traffic, music and videos featuring music had been played 8 billion times on YouTube by the end of 2008. Yet of the $639 million digital revenues that WMB (Warner Music Group) reported for the fiscal year, YouTube accounted for less than 1 percent.*[163]

The task for the future will be getting digital users to pay for their entertainment products. The men and women who invest so much of their time and effort into creating the songs, recordings, and all the other entertainment products we enjoy deserve to be paid for their endeavors. Music makes life so much more enjoyable. It is important that the individuals who create the music and entertainment products that enrich our lives be financially rewarded for their efforts.

Key Website Resources

http://www.caselaw.lp.findlaw.com/

http://www.copyrights.gov/

http://www.ifpi.org/

http://www.law.duke.edu/

http://www.loc.gov/

http://www.riaa.org/

http://www.wipo.org/

---

162 Mark Cuban, as referenced in Fred Goodman's book *Fortune's Fool, Edgar Bronfman Jr., Warner Music, and an Industry in Crisis*, (New York, NY: Simon & Schuster, 2010), p.231.

163 Fred Goodman, *Fortune's Fool, Edgar Bronfman Jr., Warner Music, and an Industry in Crisis*, (New York, NY: Simon & Schuster, 2010), p247.

3
Action Pack: Registration

How to Register your claim of Copyright

"I don't think anybody steals anything; all of us borrow."

— BB King[164]

"If people want to steal our music, why don't they go into Tower and put the album under their shirts instead of hiding behind their computers."

— Lars Ulrich of Metallica[165]

Poor Man's Copyright

It doesn't work! Sending yourself a copy of your creative work (sheet music for a song, for example) through the mail does not protect your claim of a copyright. It does not copyright it, protect it, or validate your claim of ownership. According to the Copyright Office (July 10, 2010),

> *The practice of sending a copy of your own work to yourself is sometimes called a "poor man's copyright." There is no provision in the copyright law regarding any such type of protection, and it is not a substitute for registration.*[166]

Fixation Process

The copyright law provides copyright protection at the moment an original work is "fixed" into a tangible medium. The work must be original (not a copy or derived from another source), and it must be placed into a tangible (physical) form such as written onto a piece of paper or recorded onto a CD, DVD, computer hard drive, film, or cell phone.[167] Performing a song live does not protect the song, as it has not

---

[164] B.B. King, "Brainy Quotes," Brainyquotes.com. http://www.brainyquote.com/quotes/quotes/b/bbking173521.html, (accessed January 7, 2011).

[165] Lars Ulrich, (as quoted by Fred Goodman), *Fortune's Fool: Edgar Bronfman Jr., Warner Music and an Industry in Crisis*, (New York: Simon & Schuster, 2010) 133.

[166] U.S. Library of Congress, "United States Copyright Office, Copyrights in General," http://www.copyright.gov/help/faq/faq-general.html, (accessed January 7, 2011).

[167] U.S. Library of Congress, "Copyright in General: When is my Work Protected," http://www.copyright, (July 12, 2010).

been placed into a tangible form, it has just been played and heard but not fixed. Thus, works are not regarded as copyrighted until they are recorded into a tangible form.

Proof of Ownership

The U.S. Copyright Office was established in the Library of Congress in 1870. The office registers more than 500,000 claims to copyright annually. If you plan to commercially exploit your songs, recordings, books, music videos, movie scripts, etc., you should register your copyright (claim of ownership). The government recognizes the person or company who registers a claim as the copyright owner. It does not analyze the authenticity of the claim, but it is a crime to claim copyright (ownership) of a copyrightable work that you did not create or do not legally own. If you need to file a lawsuit, registration is required as proof of your ownership. It is also important to understand that the Copyright Office does not issue copyrights. It records only the date and time of your claim. If there is a conflict, legal action in court is usually required to determine the actual author or owner.

Pre-Registration

Very few creative works need to be pre-registered for copyright protection. However, if there is a concern about infringement before the work is completed or if you have a work that has not been finished or may not be finished for a long period of time, then a preregistration process is available. It cost more money (currently $115) compared to an actual electronic registration ($35). A preregistration is not an actual registration so you'll also need file an actual registration when the work is finished.[168]

Digital Registration – eCO Form

It is very easy to register your creative work (a song, for example) for a claim of a copyright. In July of 2007, the Copyright Office set in motion testing that lead to the new electronic registration process by using the eCO forms. Everyone is now encouraged to use the new online forms and submit copies digitally. The office also uses barcodes to automate the processing, if you want to snail mail the registration.[169] To use the eCO forms, you'll need to register once with the Copyright Office. Then, just remember your password, and you're in. The website also offers a tutorial that shows you how to step-by-step register your claim of copyright and upload your creative works.

Barcode Registration – CO Form

The downloadable CO form with a 2-D barcode replaces the traditional TX, VA, PA, SE, and SR snail mail forms (which are still available). You simply download the form and complete it on your computer, then print it and mail it to the Library of Congress with a copy of your work (a song you've written, for example) and the registration fee.[170]

---

[168] Library of Congress, "Copyright Office: eCO online system," http://www.copyright, (accessed July 12. 2-10).

[169] Library of Congress, "Copyright Office: eCO online system," http://www.copyright, (accessed July 12. 2-10).

[170] Library of Congress, "Copyright Office: eCO online system," http://www.copyright, (accessed July 12. 2-10).

Snail Mail Registration

You may still register your claim of copyright with the older "snail mail" forms: TX (literary works), VA (visual arts works), PA (performing artist works), SE (single serials works), and SR (sound recording works).[171] However, the forms are not available for download, so you'll have to request them by mailing the Copyright Office. Once you've received the forms, fill them out, submit either one or two copies of your work (one if not published, two if published), and then pay the current registration fee. Copyright protection begins at the date and time the registration forms are received, so the "snail mail" forms are very late in registration compared to the eCO and CO forms. Time of registration can be very important in lawsuits, so it is advised to register by either the eCO or CO forms. In addition, you may register everything that the older traditional forms registered under the new forms.[172]

Collaborations

Collaborative works are songs that are created by lyricists and music composers working together. The lyricists provide the words, the composers the musical notations. Collaborations allow lyricists to work with composers who are better at creating the music than the lyrics, and vice versa. Successful collaboration teams include Rodgers and Hammerstein, the Gershwin, Jay Livingston and Ray Evans, and many of today's famous songwriters. Copyright ownership and royalties are usually divided 50/50, which is negotiated in legal written agreements before the collaboration work begins.

Co-Writing/Joint Work

Co-writing is simply another form of collaboration in which more than one writer is involved in the creative process. All the contributing authors of the work should be listed on the copyright registration form. According to Beck & Tysver (2008), "when several people work together to create a single work, a joint work may be created under the Copyright Act."[173] They also claim a joint work is defined by the Copyright Act as

> *…A work prepared by two or more authors with the intention that their contributions be merged into inseparable or interdependent parts of a unitary whole. Under this definition, both authors must intend that their contributions be combined, and this intention must exist at the time the contribution is created. It is not necessary, however, that the contributions be equal in effort or value. Nor is it necessary that the joint authors work in the same physical area or at the same time. As defined in the statute, the only requirement is that both authors have the intention that the works are to be "merged into inseparable or interdependent parts of a unitary whole."*[174]

The current copyright duration of joint work is life of the surviving author plus 70 years.[175] Thus, because each author is listed as equal on the registration form, the corresponding royalties are usually divided equally

---

[171] Library of Congress, "Copyright Office: eCO online system," http://www.copyright, (accessed July 12. 2-10).

[172] Library of Congress, "Copyright Office: eCO online system," http://www.copyright, (accessed July 12. 2-10).

[173] Robert Beck and Dan Trysver, "Welcome to Bitlaw: Joint Ownership" http://www.bitlaw.com/copyright, (accessed July 12, 2010).

[174] Robert Beck and Dan Trysver, "Welcome to Bitlaw: Joint Ownership" http://www.bitlaw.com/copyright, (accessed July 12, 2010).

[175] Library of Congress, "Copyright Office: Copyright Basics-How Long Copyright Protections Endures," http://www.copyright, (accessed July 12, 2010).

or paid according to any previous agreements by the music publishers and/or performance rights organizations.[176]

Type of Copyrightable Entertainment or other Product	Defined As
Literary works	(Books/Poems/Writings)
Musical works	(Songwriting) Music & Lyrics
Dramatic works	(Theater/Plays) Including Music & Lyrics
Pantomimes & Choreographic works	(Dances for Theater)
Pictorial, graphic, & sculptural works	(Photos, Graphic Arts)
Motion Pictures & Audiovisual Works	(Films, Videos)
Sound recordings	(Audio Recordings of songs/acts/shows)
Architecture	Buildings & Other Structures

Registration of Sound Recordings

The copyright law usually addresses musical arrangements, orchestrations, etc., as a work-for-hire recording when a business or musical enterprise commissions the work (such as a record label signing an act and paying for the recordings). An arrangement of a previously public domain musical work may be considered a derivative of an original work and the actual recording and arrangement is copyrightable.

[176] Library of Congress, "Copyright Office: Copyright Basics-How Long Copyright Protections Endures," http://www.copyright, (accessed July 12, 2010).

Type of Registration	Process & Forms	Fee
[] On-Line Preregistration	Register at http://www.copyright.gov/prereg/	$115
[] Online Registration eCO Internet Registration	Register at http://www.copyright.gov/eco/ Login at http://www.copyright.gov/eco/notice.html	$35
[] Online Registration CO 2d bar code	Instructions at http://www.copyright.gov/forms/formco2d-ins.pdf Forms at http://www.copyright.gov/forms/formco2d.pdf	$50
[] Mail in Forms	[] TX (literary works) Form http://www.copyright.gov/forms/formtx.pdf	$65
[] Mail in Forms	[] VA (visual arts works) http://www.copyright.gov/forms/formva.pdf	$65
[] Mail in Forms	[] PA (performing arts works, including motion pictures) http://www.copyright.gov/forms/formpa.pdf	$65
[] Mail in Forms	[] SR (sound recordings) http://www.copyright.gov/forms/formsr.pdf	$65
[] Mail in Forms	[] SE (serials-newspapers) http://www.copyright.gov/forms/formse.pdf	$65

Sampling

Sampling is the process of using a portion of an already existing recording in a new recording or performance. The recording artist, act, or author will usually integrate newly recorded material with previously recorded, marketed, and what is more important, copyrighted material. Unauthorized sampling *is considered* a violation of the original copyright owner's exclusive rights. Permission is required from both the sampled song's music publisher (for use of the song) and the original artist's record label (for the recording), as they hold the copyrights for the material sampled. Any agreement to clear the use of sampling is often difficult to arrange, due to whom the major artist(s) and sampling artist are and the potential income and royalties splits, which are also difficult to negotiate. Recent court action has indicated that the use of even *one note* or part of one recorded note is a copyright violation.[177]

---

[177] Michael McCready, "Copyright Law, Treaties and Advice: The Law Regarding Music Sampling ," http://www.copynot.org/Pages/Music%20sampling.htm, (accessed January 17, 2011).

Certificate of Registration

If the copyright is not registered by the original songwriter(s), then the publishing company may register the song with the company as owner of the copyright and the songwriter as the author of the song (once the single song contract is signed).[178] They will receive (through traditional snail mail or email) a copy of the registration form with the registration number added, along with the date and time of registration. According to a release from the Copyright Office (August 14, 2009),

> *You will now receive an automated email notification once the deposit files you have uploaded have been received inside the eCO system's network firewall. Notifications will include the corresponding case number, and will list each file, along with its name, size, and date/time submitted.*[179]

Certificate of Recordation

If the song has been registered by the original songwriter(s), then the publishing company is required to notify the Copyright Office that they are the new owners of the copyright. The *notice of the transfer* must be in writing and signed by you (the original author of the song) and by a representative of the music publisher.[180] Once the Copyright Office has received the fees, transfer of ownership, and other documents, the Register of Copyrights will review the paperwork and return the original documents as a *Certificate of Recordation* under the same registration number as the original registration.[181]

Pre Registration	**First Registration (Not Distributed)** **Certificate of Registration**	**First Registration (Distributed) Certificate of Registration**	**Re-registration Certificate of Recordation**
[] Pre-Registration (Rare) Note: To be eligible for preregistration, a work must be unpublished and must be in the process of being prepared for commercial distribution. It must also fall within a class of works determined by the Register of Copyrights to have had a history of infringement prior to authorized commercial distribution. (60 days)	[]) Fixed (Original and Completed) Registration is at time the work (song or recording) being finished into a tangible or physical form.	[] Published Date work (song or recording, etc.,) is distributed for sale or to the media/Internet	[] Published Notice of transfer required to change the name of the owners of the copyright

Work-for-Hire

Always be aware of the different types of deals that are available between creative writers, vocalist, musicians, creative artists and an employer. As an example, if a label asks you to record a song as a work-for-hire, they will own your performance. According to the Copyright Office (July 10, 2010),

---

[178] Library of Congress, "Transfer of Copyright," http://www.copyright, (accessed January 30, 2011).

[179] Library of Congress, "Welcome to the eCO tutorial," http://www.copyright, (accessed January 30, 2011).

[180] Library of Congress, "Transfer of Copyright," http://www.copyright, (accessed January 30, 2011).

[181] Library of Congress, "Copyright Law Revision, Section 19: Certificate of Recordation," http://www.copyright, (accessed, January 30, 2011).

> *Although the general rule is that the person who creates the work is its author, there is an exception to that principle; the exception is a work made for hire, which is a work prepared by an employee within the scope of his or her employment; or a work specially ordered or commissioned in certain specified circumstances. When a work qualifies as a work made for hire, the employer, or commissioning party, is considered to be the author.*[182]

If you decide to work as a work-for-hire, a written agreement between the creative artist and the employer is required. Also, according to Beck and Tysver (2008), the Copyright Act limits the work-for-hire doctrine to two specific situations, one where the creative artist retains ownership of the copyright of their "works" and the other where the company hiring the artist gains ownership of the creative work:

> *...A work prepared by an employee within the scope of his or her employment; or a work specially ordered or commissioned for use as a contribution to a collective work, as a part of a motion picture or other audiovisual work, as a translation, as a supplementary work, as a compilation, as an instructional text, as a test, as answer material for a test, or as an atlas, but even then only if the parties agree in writing that the work is a work made for hire.*[183]

Authorship

Songwriters are the authors of the songs they create unless the work is a work-for-hire (also called a work-make-for-hire).[184] It is wise to negotiate to determine who the writer(s) of the work (and their shares) and owner(s) of the copyright (and their shares) before starting the creative process (writing the song). There are many stories of writers and music publishers who disagree about who should own what percentage of the copyright and what share of the songwriting and music publishing royalties they should receive after a song becomes a hit. Ownership of the song and the percentage of royalties depend on the type of deal you negotiate (See *Chapter 8. The Song Business* for more information on types of songwriter publishing deals). However, you'll need to know the answers to most of these questions before you register your work with the Library of Congress.

Key Website Resources

http://www.bitlaw.com/

http://www.copyright.gov/register/

http://www.copyrights.gov/

http://www.iamusic.com/

http://www.loc.gov/

http://www.music-law.com/

---

182 Marybeth Peters, The Register of Copyrights before theSubcommittee on Courts and Intellectual Property Committee on the Judiciary," "Sound Recordings as Works Made for Hire," http://www.copyright, (accessed January 7, 2011).

183 Robert Beck and Dan Tysver, "Works Made for Hire-the Standard," BitLaw, http://www.bitlaw.com/copyright, (accessed July 12, 2010).

184 Robert Beck and Dan Trysver, "Welcome to Bitlaw: Works Made for Hire, Why is it Important," http://www.bitlaw.com/copyright, (accessed July 12, 2011).

4

The Perfect Song

Professional Songwriting
The Psychology of Entertainment
Writing Great Songs
What Makes a Song "Great"

"Songwriting is my gift from God."

— Smokey Robinson[185]

"Music is a higher revelation than philosophy."

— Ludwig van Beethoven[186]

"Music and rhythm find their way into the secret places of the soul."

— Plato[187]

"Each song has its own secret that's different from another song, and each has its own life. Sometimes it has to be teased out, whereas other times it might come fast. There are no laws about songwriting or producing. It depends on what you're doing, not just who you're doing."

— Mark Knopfler[188]

Great Songs

Many successful songwriters are first known as 20-year overnight wonders. It's a saying in the industry to describe someone who has seemingly achieved success quickly, but has been working at it for many years. Thousands of potential songwriters each year send CDs and attachments in emails to music publishers. Most are rejected or returned with a "not soliciting new material" or "not what we are looking for" rejection letter. However, every so often, an unknown writer pens a great song, gets it picked up by a publisher who then places it with a major artist who records it, and before you know it – BAM – smash hit.

---

185 Smokey Robinson, "Great-Quotes.com." Gledhill Enterprises, 2011, http://www.great-quotes.com/quote/1460494, (accessed July 16, 2010).

186 Ludwig Van Beethoven, "Favorite Quotes About Music & Songwriting," http://www.songwritersresourcenetwork.com/quotes.html, (accessed July 13, 2010).

187 Plato, "Favorite Quotes About Music & Songwriting," http://www.songwritersresourcenetwork.com/quotes.html, (accessed July 13, 2010).

188 Mark Knopfler, "Brainy Quotes: Songwriting Quotes," http://www.brainyquote.com/quotes/keywords/songwriting.html, (accessed July 13, 2010).

The music industry is desperate for great songs to invest their money and creative talents into through recordings, live performances, movies, computer games, etc., etc. This business is based on the great song over the good song because artists, musicians, labels, concert promoters, etc., monetize on the consumers' emotional connection. Great songs are also the foundation of artist images, recordings, film soundtracks, commercials, radio, the mass media, computer games, and tours. Thus, it is the song's communicative success that drives the business system to financial success. However, the creative system's definition of "great" is rarely the same as the business system's, which is based on gross income. A great song from the label's perspective is anything that makes money, including many of those really lousy recordings on your local radio station. The values between the creative system and business systems are like oil and water – sometimes they just do not mix. However, when the creative system creates a great song and the industry invests money into its recordings, videos, movies, computer games, promotion, and publicity, huge money can be generated for everyone.

Imagination (Emotional Communication)

Why are songs and other entertainment products important to consumers? One theory is that consumers use music to express their own wants and needs, to live a more satisfying life by using the emotional, communicative message encapsulated in the complexity of the recording of a song, artist image, and performance. Songs allows consumers to celebrate their emotions and understand themselves better. Thus, music and other entertainment events and products are complex forms of communication sold to consumers to help them subconsciously define and express their constructed ethos and pathos. According to Kosslyn and Lindsay (2006),

> *...Imagination is the capacity to consider objects or events in their absence or as they might be. Imagination may refer to many things, such as fantasy, ingenuity, daydreaming, and make-believe. But it often involves the use of mental imagery, which is the ability to call to mind the sensations of sights, sounds, tastes, smells, and touches that have been experienced. Through mental imagery, people can also create mental sensations of situations or conditions they have not actually experienced. Imagination plays an important role in creativity, including the formation of abstract ideas. Mental images can substitute for the real thing allowing a person to plan how to paint a picture, compose a song, and so on.*[189]

The Emotion Business

Demographic research is an analysis of comparison based on gender, age, and education. Psychographic research is a deeper analysis that groups individuals by their lifestyles tied to zip codes. The results are for marketing of tours, corporate sponsorships, and merchandise. Thus the music business is really *the emotion business* based on enjoyment as perceived by various types of consumers who attend the concerts and listen to and buy the recordings. Clusters of consumer creative emotions often define various genres of music and the images of the artists themselves. As an example, record labels may niche market some of their artist's recordings to hip-hop fans that may have a different lifestyle or musical preference than jazz, country, or classical fans. Artists, publishers and songwriters also pay for non-label recordings, and thus a sub-revenue stream may include musicians, singers, producers, audio engineers, and the studio and digital recording business.

Recordings

If songs are the foundation of the business, then the recording process is the method used to build a sellable product. It is similar to building a house for sale. Think of the plans for the building as the song, the workers

[189] Stephen Kosslyn, "Imagination" as stated in the *World Book*, and at http://www.scribd.com/doc/15745675/Academic-Readings-Ok-2, (accessed July1 2006) and January 17, 2011).

who put the nails in the studs, floors, and ceilings as the musicians, artists, audio engineers, and producer. At the end of the process, in the home building business we have a house to sell. In the music industry, we have a recording to sell. Thus, studios and their recording software are integral parts of the music business – the places where dreams are made and sometimes broken. Mixing a great song with the creativity of recording artists, background vocalists, musicians, producers, and audio engineers makes a successful recording. Equipment ranges from multimillion dollar consoles and soundproof rooms to digital tape recorders and Pro Tools software linked to home computers. Budgets range from million dollar star-driven sessions to friends who agree to record some tracks for you. The payoff is based on money, how many units are downloaded or sold, and how many additional tours, corporate sponsorships, and merchandise purchases occur. And in the end, nobody really knows which recording will become the next number one *Billboard Magazine*-charted hit; the million dollar artists with the huge budget or the kid in the basement with access to the Internet.

Communication Theories

To summarize (Horowitz, et al., 1999-2002) one theory about wants and needs and how we appear to fall into three categories,

> *Stimulus-response relationships claim that learning is the forming of habits by connecting a stimulus and a response that did not exist (to us) before. Thus, psychologists believe that we use past experiences to solve new problems and thus we change our behavior (behavior modification).*[190]

A second group of psychologists believes that cognition or the act of knowing is more important than the stimulus-response relationships quoted previously. They believe and emphasize the importance of the learners' need to discover and perceive new relationships to achieve insights and understanding.

A third group of psychologists believe that human learning is based on our needs to express creativity. Thus, they claim that almost any activity including athletics, business dealings, and homemaking can serve as a creative outlet. The psychologists also believe that a person must become involved in challenging activities and must do reasonably well to have a satisfying life.[191]

There is little doubt that the quality of a song's message, the performance of the vocalists, and the musicians must all come together to touch the emotions of various types of listeners. Music affects the pulse rate, respiration, and concentration. However, the emotions being created by listeners seem to last only as long as the music is being heard or replayed in our minds. Suzanne Langer's classic book, *Philosophy in a New Key* (1951) suggests that

> *...Music is known to affect the pulse rate and respiration, to facilitate or disturb concentration, to excite or relax the organism, while the stimulus last. But beyond evoking impulses to sing, tap, adjust one's step to musical rhythm, perhaps to stare, hold one's breath or take a tense attitude, ...music does not ordinarily influence behavior.*[192]

---

[190] Leonard M. Horowitz, James Banner, and H.C. Cannon, *The Elements of Learning*, (New Haven: Yale, 1999), & John Bransford, *How People Learn*, (reprint, National Academy Press, 2000), and at http://www.nap.edu/openbook.php?isbn=0309070368, & Malvin Levin, *Mind at a Time* (New York: Simon & Schuster, 2002).

[191] Leonard M. Horowitz, James Banner, and H.C. Cannon, *The Elements of Learning*, (New Haven: Yale, 1999), & John Bransford, *How People Learn*, (reprint, National Academy Press, 2000), and at http://www.nap.edu/openbook.php?isbn=0309070368, & Malvin Levin, *Mind at a Time* (New York: Simon & Schuster, 2002).

[192] Susanne Langer, *Philosophy in a New Key*, 2nd ed. (Cambridge: Harvard University Press, 1951), 625-630.

Research appears to suggest consumers create for themselves the following emotions when they hear various forms of music. How the emotions are turned into meanings specific to an individual is not understood.[193] Examples suggested by Langer[194] (1951) include:

Sadness	Seriousness	Excitement	Happiness
Relaxation	Amusement	Sentiment	Longing
Patriotism	Devotion	Irritation	Wanting to Dance

There are many psychologists that support the humanistic theory, including Horowitz and his associates (1999-2002), who state that

> *...Each person must become involved in challenging activities-and must do reasonably well at them-to have a satisfying life. The individual gains a sense of control, growth, and knowledge from such activities. For learning to occur, people must feel free to make their own decisions. They also must feel worthy, relatively free from anxiety, self-respecting, and respected by others. Under these conditions, their own inner drives will lead them to learn... to increase people's awareness of their own thoughts and of the world around them.*[195]

Music and Intelligence

Research also appears to indicate some forms of human intelligence are enhanced by music. According to Begley's article that appeared in *Newsweek Magazine* (2000),

> *There is an indication that our brains may even be pre-wired for it! Scientists have interspersed PET scans and MRIs with snatches of Celine Dion and Stravinsky to show a correlation for the biological foundations of music... Music affects the mind in powerful ways: it not only incites passion, belligerence, serenity or fear but does so even in people who do not know from experience, for instance, that a particular crescendo means the killer is about to pop out on the movie screen.*[196]

Begley (2000) also writes that

> *Research at the University of California and the University of Wisconsin recently found a connection between the use of music and young people's improved math skills. They found that the neurons connecting the two sides of the brain in young musicians are larger which appears to help planning and foresight skills."*[197]

Construct Theory

This brings us to a very important question. Why do consumers enjoy songs and music? In other words, how and why do consumers use entertainment psychologically (emotionally)? George Kelly's *Theory of Personality* (1955) appears to provide us with some clues about how it might work. Kelly (1995) claims, "A person's

---

[193] Susanne Langer, *Philosophy in a New Key*, 2nd ed. (Cambridge: Harvard University Press, 1951), 212-213 & Charles Disserens, *Influences of Music on Behavior* (1926) as quoted in Langer on pages 212-213.

[194] Susanne Langer, *Philosophy in a New Key*, 2nd ed. (Cambridge: Harvard University Press, 1951), 201-215.

[195] Leonard M. Horowitz, James Banner, and H.C. Cannon, *The Elements of Learning*, (New Haven: Yale, 1999), & John Bransford, *How People Learn*, (reprint, National Academy Press, 2000), and at http://www.nap.edu/openbook.php?isbn=0309070368, & Malvin Levin, *Mind at a Time* (New York: Simon & Schuster, 2002).

[196] Sharon Begley, "Music on the Mind," Newsweek, July 24, 2000, & "Science and Technology." Newsweek.msnbc.com, http://www.brams.umontreal.ca/plab/research/dossiers_vulgarisation/newsweek_musicmind/newsweek_musicmind. (accessed July, 2010).

[197] Sharon Begley, "Music on the Mind," Newsweek, July 24, 2000, & "Science and Technology." Newsweek.msnbc.com, http://www.brams.umontreal.ca/plab/research/dossiers_vulgarisation/newsweek_musicmind/newsweek_musicmind. (accessed July, 2010).

processes are psychologically channeled by the ways in which he anticipates events."[198&199] Stewart (2010) adds,

> *Kelly's theory of personality is predicated on one axiom: that, as he put it, Man is a Scientist. In other words, from the dawn of consciousness each of us tries to make sense of the world as we experience it, and we do this by constantly forming and testing hypotheses about the world. By the time we are adults, we will have developed a very complex model of the world and our place in it: this model is, according to Kelly, our personality. Kelly's theory of personal constructs develops this principle further – for example, by considering whether and how we modify our constructs when faced with contradictory information, what are our "core constructs" – that is, the deeply-held values and principles which are unlikely to change, etc.*[200]

Could it be that consumers use entertainment products for cognitive emotional experiences to figure out who they are, at the speed of light and often at a subconscious level? Why do consumers connect with an act or a song at such a high level of personal connection or emotion that they pay to listen, see the act, download, steal or buy a CD, film, or computer game? What is the connection?

One theory is that consumers tend to select the types of music and acts that help them understand, define, or celebrate their subconscious self. After many replications called impressions, the selections may tend to help them shape the pathways in their mind (pathways that become their belief system and personality). Therefore, if we buy into Kelly and Construct Theory (and many people do), music is one of the many events we may use to help us understand and celebrate our personality and position in life.

The Choice Corollary

Kelly's Choice Corollary is "A person chooses for himself that alternative in a dichotomized construct through which he anticipates the greater possibility for extension and definition of his system."[201] Stewart (2010) claims that

> *The term construct is particularly well chosen, because it reflects the concept's dual role. On the one hand, your constructs represent the view you have constructed about the world as you experienced it. On the other hand, your constructs indicate how you are likely to construe the world as you continue to experience it. Your construct system is your history and your predisposition to perceive.*[202]

According to Boeree (2006),

> *...Kelly says that we will choose to do what we anticipate will most likely elaborate our construction system, that is, improve our understanding, our ability to anticipate. Reality places limits on what we can experience or do, but we choose how to construe, or interpret, that reality. And we choose to interpret that reality in whatever way we believe will help us the most.*[203]

Trevor Butt provides the following illustration in the Internet Encyclopedia of *Personal Contract Psychology* (2004):

---

198 George Kelly, "Personality Synopsis: Cognitive Theory-The Beginning of Cognitivism," http://allpsych.com/personalitysynopsis/kelly.html (accessed July 13, 2010).

199 Personal Construct Psychology, found at Learning and Teaching info," http://www.learningandteaching.info/learning/personal.htm (accessed July 14, 2010).

200 Valerie Stewart, "Enquire Within, Understanding Personal Construct Theory and George Kelly: Man is a Scientist," http://www.enquirewithin.co.nz/HINTS/skills2.htm, (accessed July 15, 2010).

201 Valerie Stewart, "Enquire Within, Understanding Personal Construct Theory and George Kelly: Man is a Scientist," http://www.enquirewithin.co.nz/HINTS/skills2.htm, (accessed July 15, 2010).

202 Valerie Stewart, "Enquire Within, Understanding Personal Construct Theory and George Kelly: Man is a Scientist," http://www.enquirewithin.co.nz/HINTS/skills2.htm, (accessed July 15, 2010).

203 George Boerre, "Personality Theories, George Kelly," http://webspace.ship.edu/cgboer/kelly.html, (accessed July 14, 2010).

…This corollary replaces the concept of motivation in PCP. In orthodox psychology there is an assumption of Cartesian dualism: it is assumed that a person is constituted by a mind (or set of personal cognitions) inside a body. There is then a problem of how mind, or psychological states, 'kick-start' the body into action. The person is seen as normally at rest and inert. Theories of motivation were designed to deal with this issue, and deal with factors that are said to energize and direct behavior. Kelly however, saw the person "as a form of motion" (1955, p. 48) and claimed that PCP was a thoroughgoing dynamic theory in that it "does not need any special system of dynamics to keep it running" (1969, p. 89). By this he meant that people are always doing something. He used the example of a child labeled lazy by a teacher to point out that the child cannot be doing nothing. It might be doing something other than is required, or it might be apparently doing nothing so as to annoy the teacher.[204]

"Wired" Like the Internet

Many researchers still think the brain works in a hierarchical structure like the administrative structure in a large business. The CEO gives orders to the President, who gives the orders to the Vice Presidents, who give the orders to supervisors, who tell the workers what to do. When there are suggestions from the workers, then the direction of communication is back up the chain of command to the top where the actual decisions are made. For many years, the common assumption is that our brains work the same way, with one part directing signals to other parts for feedback so that a decision can be made. However, more recent research appears to support a different view. Jason Palmer, a science and technology reporter for the *BBC News* (August 10, 2010), states that new research indicates the brain is wired and works more like the Internet. According to the article,

If the brain has a hierarchical structure like a large company, as neurology has long held, the "to" and "from" diagram would show straight lines from independent regions up towards a central processing unit: the company's boss. But instead, the researchers saw loops between differing regions, feeding back to and directly linking regions that were not known to communicate with one another. This is a better fit with the model of vast networks such as the Internet.[205]

Our Brains on Music

A review of the previous communication and psychological theories should help us understand the value of music in our daily life. However, Daniel Levitin takes it a few steps farther by claiming that music over the last 10,000 years has help us shape our brains and evolve in six ways, including knowledge, friendship, religion, joy, comfort, and love.[206] According to Levitin, in his book *The World in Six Songs* (2008), the importance of our connection to music…

…Explains, at least in part, the evolution of music and brains over tens of thousands of years and across the six inhabited continents. Music, I argue, is not simply a distraction or a pastime, but a core element of our identity as a species, an activity that paved the way for more complex behaviors such as language, large-scale cooperative undertakings, and the passing down of important information from one generation to the next. This book explains how I came to the (some might say) radical notion that that there are basically six kinds of songs that do all of this. They are songs of friendship, joy, comfort, knowledge, religion, and love.[207]

Professional Songwriting

Songwriting is tough profession and a difficult business because it's the consumers' use of the songs (in recordings, movies, live show, etc.) that makes songwriting financially rewarding. It is up to the business side

---

[204] Trevor Butt, "The Choice Corollary," The Internet Encyclopedia of Personal Construct Psychology. http://www.pcp-net.org/encyclopaedia/choice.html, (accessed July 15, 2010).

[205] James Palmer, "Brain Works More Like Internet than 'Top Down' Company," BBC, News Science & Environment. http://www.bbc.co.uk/news/science-environment-10925841, (accessed August, 10, 2010).

[206] Daniel Levitin, *The World in Six Songs: How the Musical Brain Created Human Nature*. (New York: Penguin Books: 2008).

[207] Daniel Levitin, *The World in Six Songs: How the Musical Brain Created Human Nature*. (New York: Penguin Books: 2008), 3-4.

of the industry to find and exploit (in a positive, profitable way) the talented individuals who can create sale able songs and corresponding entertainment products. The truth is that success for songwriters (as a career) depends on how well consumers connect emotionally to the music products and iconic acts using their songs. It also depends on how well the business system delivers their entertainment products to consumer eyes and ears so that they can discover the song's messages for their own psychological and emotional satisfaction, get excited about it, and use it or buy it. Almost anyone can sit on top of a mountain and write songs. However, if you want to make a living at it, you'll need the industry (producers, artists, labels, promoters, etc.) to invest their time, money, careers, and images to select *your song* for their next project, event, film, game, whatever. Just remember, even the greatest songs never make any money until consumers know they exist and get excited about them.

It customarily takes many years to achieve the competencies and industry contacts required to be successful. So how can you become a professional songwriter, composer, or arranger? If you are not a writer, what are some of the things you should understand about the mindset of creative writers?

Have Talent

Some type of natural talent is essential to being a successful songwriter. The ability to observe social and personal situations and the ability to interpret the social consciousness artistically is important. The ability to convey thoughts and observations emotionally through music and lyrics is paramount. Being able to play an instrument in tune is one thing; being able to create and convey emotional messages is clearly another.

Become an Educated Person

Formal education in music, literature, business, psychology, sociology, and world history is enriching. Great songwriters often write their best songs about their own life experiences or passions. Research the great philosophers, writers, poets, and leaders whose works you admire and find out what inspired their passions.

Become a Professional Songwriter

Join professional songwriters organizations. There are many such organizations across the country where songwriters encourage each other, co-write, and get advice from the experts. Network, network, network! Build friendships and acquaintances through the local and national songwriter organizations and attend national seminars in New York, Los Angeles, and Nashville. Co-write with someone who is better than you. Writing with others helps you see a lyric and hear music from a different perspective and often improves songwriting.

Have a Professional in the Business Listen to Your Songs

Performing Rights Organizations such as ASCAP, BMI, and SESAC will usually take a few minutes to listen to new writers. They have a staff whose job is to find and help new writers. Let them listen to your work, and if they like what they hear, they will often refer you to established music publishers. The door is now open for you to pitch your songs and seek a deal. Once a writer is signed with a music publisher, one of the PROs will become their exclusive performance license representative. A referral by an established writer who is a member of ASCAP, BMI, or SESAC will also increase your chances for a quick appointment and the possibility of being offered a contract.

Select the Right Publisher

Select the type of publisher who has a successful track record in your musical genre. If you're writing rock music, find a publisher who has been successful in casting rock songs. Successful publishers know the right people, have the right contacts, and can successfully place your songs.

Career Songs

Record producers and smart recording artists search for great songs that will establish their careers. Indeed, all artists are on a constant search for new songs that will sustain, enhance, and grow their fame and careers. It's usually a song that becomes so popular that the artist is always associated with it, like Bing Crosby and "White Christmas," Carl Perkins and "Blue Suede Shoes," or "Take This Job and Shove It," by Johnny Paycheck. Others include:[208]

"Stairway to Heaven"	**Led Zeppelin**
"Like a Rolling Stone"	**Bob Dylan**
"Hotel California"	**The Eagles**
"Imagine"	**John Lennon**
"Free Bird"	**Lynyrd Skynyrd**
"Let's Get It On"	**Marvin Gaye**
"Billie Jean"	**Michael Jackson**
"I Can't Get No Satisfaction"	**The Rolling Stones**
"All Along the Watchtower"	**Jimi Hendrix Experience**
"Bohemian Rhapsody"	**Queen**
"Johnny B. Goode"	**Chuck Berry**

What Songwriters Should Look for in Music Publishers

Find a music publisher who is well connected to the most successful people in the industry and who can place your songs with those individuals. They should be a progressive agent between the songwriter (you) and the record labels, producers, artist managers, and recording artists who are looking for songs from your genre. Find a publisher who will help you become a better songwriter by offering you constructive criticism and positive, creative, and financial support. Make sure they are honest business people who have a good reputation and passion for your success, besides their own.

Professional Songwriting Organizations

The Songwriters Guild of America (SGA) was formed in 1931 by songwriters Billy Rose, George M. Meyer, and Edgar Leslie.[209] As a voluntary songwriter association run by and for its members, it provides services and activities songwriters may need to be successful in the business. The SGA offers workshops, critique sessions, pitch opportunities, access to catalogs, award events, publishing company audits, catalog administration, financial evaluations, medical and life insurance, and legislative and legal support. The guild's support provided several important legal provisions in the 1976 Copyright Act.[210]

The Nashville Songwriters Association International (NSAI) sponsors regional workshops in various locations in the U.S. and Europe. The workshops provide opportunities for writers to improve their knowledge and craft. The NSAI also offers a song evaluation service to its members. Songs submitted are evaluated for their commercial appeal based on the theme, lyrics, melody, and overall impact. Once a year, the

---

[208] The 100 Greatest Songs of All Times, Squidoo, http://www.squidoo.com/100songs, (accessed July 15, 2010).

[209] Songwriter's Guild of America, "SGA Provides 75 Years of Advocacy, Education to Songwriters," http://www.songwritersguild.com/history.htm, (accessed July 15, 2010).

[210] Songwriter's Guild of America, "SGA Provides 75 Years of Advocacy, Education to Songwriters," http://www.songwritersguild.com/history.htm, (accessed July 15, 2010).

NSAI also sponsors Tin Pan Alley South, which is a series of shows, workshops, and opportunities for songwriting members to network and write with professional and successful writers.[211]

Ten Writing Principles

Mark Volman (2008) of the superstar group The Turtles suggests the following ten principles for writing great songs: "simplicity, clarity, compression, emphasis, consistency, coherence, specificity, reputation, unity, and genuine feeling."[212] His themes of love include "feeling the need, I think I've just found her or him, the big come on, this is it, I'm in love, the honeymoon is over, cheating, leaving, remember how it use to be." His shape and form of a hit song goes "verse, pre-chorus, chorus (the hook), and the bridge."[213]

Summary

Music publishers search for hit writers. You have to be more than a songwriter with passion and a great work ethic. What's most important is the ability to write great songs. If you can consistently deliver potential hit songs that turn into profitable recordings, you've got a great life and career waiting. Songwriting is a craft – talent supplemented by hard work, and you can live a blessed life if you're smart enough to learn the business of monetizing the great songs you've created. The value of great songs is huge, not only for the royalties they generate now, but also for the value of the royalties they may generate in the future.

"I learned very early in life that, 'without a song, the day would never end; without a song, a man ain't got a friend; without a song, the road would never bend – without a song.' So I keep singing a song…."

— Elvis Presley[214]

A great artist is nothing without a great song. Recording artists are really package deals of voice, image, persona, sound and stage production, promotion, publicity, and many other things (held together by a great song) that provide consumers with the opportunity to emotionally and psychologically connect with themselves or some meaningful event in their life. However, as they say in the business, it all starts with a great song.

Key Website Resources

http://sdsongwriters.org/

http://www.austinsongwritersgroup.com/

http://www.coloradomusic.org/fr_news.cfm/

http://www.fromnowherewithnothing.com/songwriting.htm/

http://www.gmia.org/index2.htm/

---

211 NSAI (The Nashville Songwriters Association International), "It all Begins with a Song," http://members.nashvillesongwriters.com/news.php?NewsSectionId=87, (accessed July 15, 2010).

212 Mark Volman, *All Access Pass* (Course Pack-Belmont University, 2008).

213 Mark Volman, *All Access Pass* (Course Pack-Belmont University, 2008).

214 Elvis Presley, "Elvis Presley Quotes," How Stuff Works, A Discovery Company, http://entertainment.howstuffworks.com/elvis-presley-quotes.htm, (accessed July 13, 2010).

http://www.musesmuse.com/

http://www.nashvillesongwriters.com/

http://www.portlandsongwriters.org/

http://www.songwriter.co.uk/

http://www.songwriters-guild.co.uk/

http://www.songwriters.ca/

http://www.songwritersguild.com/

http://www.westcoastsongwriters.org/

5

Music Publishing

How to Make Money Selling the *Use of a Song*
How to Make Money Selling the *Ownership of a Song*

"Publishing is a business. Writing may be art, but publishing, when all is said and done, comes down to dollars."

— Nicholas Sparks[215]

"Hit songs make hit artists"

— Louis O'Reilly[216]

History

In the early days of our nation, songwriter made deals with book publishers to "print and sell" their latest songs. Printed copies of the lyric or sheet music were the only method of mass distribution available to songwriters. Book publishers, knowing a good thing, hired sales representatives to sell the sheet music wholesale to local five-and-dime stores, who in turn sold them to the public (Poe, 1997).[217] In 1892, the song "After the Ball" sold over one million copies of sheet music (Baskerville, 1990).[218]

Seeing the profits in music publishing, many of the book publishers became entrepreneurial music publishers and moved to New York where they could place their new songs with the most popular Broadway shows and Vaudeville acts. They hired songwriters to write the songs and song pluggers to place the songs with leading artists (Baskerville, 1978).[219] World War II spread American music around the world. Global markets were created as different forms of recorded music were broadcast on American Armed Forces radio stations. In addition to the Allied soldiers, many Europeans and Asians enjoyed the broadcasts. Music publishers viewed radio airplay, concerts, and nightclub performances as promotion for record sales. A typical promotion cycle involved songs being performed by bands, then on radio, and then in films. Popular bands were used in films; their radio performances promoted the film, and the films promoted unit and print sales.

Many veteran Vaudeville performers became radio stars and later, television stars too. By the mid 1950s, Rock & Roll had evolved out of the Beale Street Blues, slave minstrels, country folk music, and Chicago's electric

---

215 Nicholas Sparks, "Publishing Quotes," Brainy Quote, http://www.brainyquote.com/quotes/keywords/publishing_3.html, (accessed July 17, 2010).

216 Louis O'Reilly, Personal Interview July 16, 2013.

217 Randy Poe, *Music Publishing: A Songwriters Guide*. Cincinnati, OH: Writers Digest Books, 1997.

218 David Baskerville, *The Music Business Handbook & Career Guide* 6th ed. Thousand Oaks: Sherwood Publication Partners, 1990.

219 David Baskerville, *The Music Business Handbook & Career Guide*. Thousand Oaks: Sherwood Publication Partners, 1979.

blues to become the language of independence for many teenagers. For one of the first times in history, teenagers had the time and money to spend, and they created a new rock & roll music industry (*The History of Rock & Roll Part One,* video tape, 1995).[220] Record sales exploded.

Things have changed with the Internet and peer-to-peer file sharing. Consumers' ability to acquire music and films without paying for them makes it tough on record labels and music publishers who are facing a much lower return on their investment. Yet, some artists are breaking through and still driving in much money from multiple sources. In some ways, it seems more difficult to make money in publishing until we think about all the new uses of music like computer games, cloud music services, branding, and other ways yet to be developed.

Serious Money

Thanks to consumers, fans, and businesses who continue to buy and use music, publishers with great copyrights (songs) own a very valuable asset. Publishers build their company's value or equity through the revenues generated from the songs they own and their potential future income. The wonderful thing about the music business is that great songs continue to make money long after the original recordings are released. They are bought by new generations, used in commercials, rerecorded as cover tunes, recorded in different languages, and performed over and over in different nations. *The Beatles'* songs have made more money since the band disbanded than when they were an actual group, recording and performing. According to the site *AskYahoo.com* (2003),

> *...Back in 1963, the Beatles gave their publishing rights to Northern Songs, a company created by their manager, Brian Epstein, and a music publisher, Dick James. Northern Songs went public in 1965, and John Lennon and Paul McCartney each had 15% of the company's shares, while Dick James and the company's chairman, Charles Silver, held a controlling 37.5% of shares. In 1969, James and Silver sold Northern Songs and its assets to the Associated Television Corporation (ATV). In 1985, ATV's music catalog was sold, and Michael Jackson was the high bidder. Jacko paid a reported $47 million for the publishing rights to somewhere between 159 to 260 Beatles songs.*[221]

Just twenty-one years later, in 2006, the value of the *ATV catalog* was estimated at about one billion dollars, and Jackson was in financial troubles. Jackson used his ownership in ATV (and The Beatles songs) as collateral to support about $270 million in bank loans. However, he was only able to cover the loans, according to Petrecca (2006),[222] by allowing *Sony Corporation of America* and *Fortress Investment Group LLC* to gain ownership of the copyrights in exchange for paying off the loans, thus,

> *A statement from Jackson representatives on Thursday announced that he "has restructured his finances with the assistance of Sony Corporation of America" and has "concluded refinancing with affiliates of Fortress Investment Group," his major creditor. Fortress bought Jackson's $270 million in loans from Bank of America last year.*[223]

Most of us have to work next week to pay the bills from last week. In the music business, great songs continue to generate money for the duration of the copyright and as long as it continues to be used. Remember that duration of a copyright, thanks to The Sonny Bono Act of 1998, is now life of the author plus 70 years. Buying The Beatles songs for $47 million and then being able to sell them for $270 million 21

---

[220] *The History of Rock & Roll* (Part One), Video Series: Warner Home Video, 1995.

[221] Ask Yahoo, "Does Michael Jackson Still Own the Publishing Rights to the Beatles Song Catalog?" Yahoo!, http://ask.yahoo.com/20031210.html, (accessed July16, 2010).

[222] Laura Petrecca, "Sony Nearer Control of Beatles' Songs," USA Today, http://www.usatoday.com/money/media, (accessed July 16, 2010).

[223] Laura Petrecca, "Sony Nearer Control of Beatles' Songs," USA Today, http://www.usatoday.com/money/media, (accessed July 16, 2010).

years later is a great example of the value of owning great songs. The real money in this business is in songwriting and music publishing. So, if you can write, publish, and record a great song that becomes part of the popular culture, you (and your children and grandchildren) will probably be very rich. That is of course, if you know what you're doing and understand the business.

Music Publishing

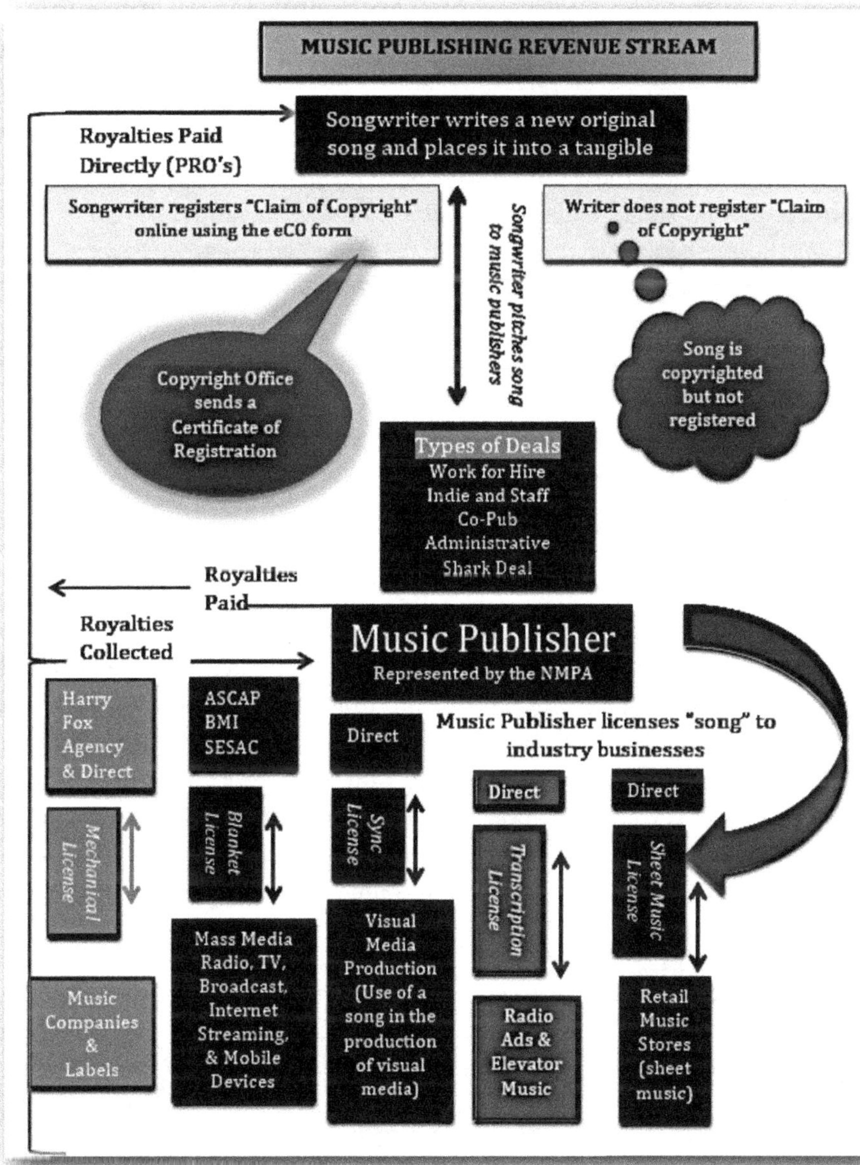

Although in many cases it is adversarial, music publishers appreciate songwriters who understand the business aspects of publishing. However, determining the "value" of a song is very difficult. If a song does not perform (generate money) as well as expected, the writer may blame the publisher, and the publisher may blame the writer. The *equity* (worth) of a song and its cumulative value are better judged over a period of years, as it takes time to determine the true financial value of a copyright. According to the Harry Fox Agency (2010),

> *A music publisher owns or administers works written by songwriters. Publishing companies range from large, multi-national corporations to individual, self-published songwriters. Publishers discover and promote songwriting talent, as well as provide important business services for their songwriters. These services include pitching their song catalog to music executives, recording artists, producers, managers and others to secure placement for the songs on appropriate commercial recordings. In addition, music publishers finance and produce demo recordings, pitch songs for television shows, movies, and commercials, collect royalties, and issue licenses. Music publishers also register and enforce the copyrights they administer.*[224]

What Publishers Look for in Staff Writers

any of today's great writers had to learn how to write songs from the master writers who came before them. Numerous music publishers still provide this mentoring process to young talented writers they feel have the

---

[224] Harry Fox Agency, "General Information," http://www.harryfox.com/public/FAQ.jsp#12, (accessed July 17, 2010).

potential to write the next hit song. Writers often offer their musical talents and vocal abilities to demo record their songs. Publishers appreciate writers who help place their own songs with industry insiders and major acts. Writers need to network, meet other writers, and insiders and in doing so, help the publishers and themselves connect their newest material (songs) with key managers, artists, producers, film production companies, and labels (through the A&R Department). Writers with great voices are seen as a bonus, as they have the potential to develop into recording artists. However, publishing companies usually want a few of the artist's royalty points for helping them secure the deal.

The Foundation of the Business

Music publishers usually know what types of songs artists, producers, labels and managers are seeking for their recordings, shows, and film products. They get emails, faxes, phone calls, personal contacts, and read the production schedules listed in some of the trade magazines (*Billboard, Variety, Aircheck*). Everyone wants the same thing: a career-breaking song that will make tons of money. The main reason, of course, is that a hit recording leads to tours, merchandise sales, and corporate sponsorships, which mean more money. It's a business that is very profitable *if* (a big "if") the act can find *the perfect song*, really nail it on the tracks, and sell the heck out of it through shameless self-promotion. It truly does all start with a song, and that is why a great song is the *foundation* for a recording artist's career. In addition, the great songs (recordings) give local acts material (and therefore, a living) for their live performances.

Thriving on Rejection

Music publisher's profits correspond directly with their ability to find and sign potential hit songwriters and songs. However they rarely have the extra time to listen to all the unsolicited tapes sent to their offices by amateurs. Publishers know that the most profitable songs originate from established professionals and well-known independent songwriters. However, professional songwriters were also amateurs themselves once. They had to learn to *thrive on rejection* and to perfect their ability to write great commercial songs. Assuming you've developed your songwriting as a craft, joined the professional songwriting organizations, learned the business, written some great songs, registered your copyrights, and networked in the business to the point where you know the right people, then it is time to pitch your songs to the right publisher.

Set Up an Appointment

Make sure the publishers are accepting demos. Publishers are much more likely to listen to your demos if they know who you are and are expecting the attached email, discs, or web address. Let them know that you are submitting material. Many publishers have web pages and use email more than snail mail. The copyright notation is not required, but it is a good idea to place it on the disc, along with your name and address. Write a brief cover letter detailing your association with the publisher, how you know them or who referred them to you. Many publishers will not see you unless referred by someone in the business or by someone at ASCAP, BMI, or SESAC.

Make Demo Recordings

Record a demo of three to four of your songs in an inexpensive yet "quality" recording studio or on your home computer. Don't waste money on a major recording studio production or overproducing the demo recording. In most cases, all you need is a couple of instruments (guitar, bass, etc.) and your vocals mixed louder than the instruments. Try to capture the "feel" or "emotion" in the demo that best displays the essence of your songs.

Provide Lyric Sheets

Provide lyric sheets (typed lyrics of the songs) or printed lead sheets (lyrics and the musical notations of melody, chords, and rhythm). Publishers usually read the lyrics as they are listening to the demo. Sometimes the voice is mixed too low or there is a word or two they can't understand without lyric sheets.

Keep a Journal

Keep a journal of where you have sent the email and demos. Send publishers *a thank you note* for reviewing the material. After a few days, email, call, or write to ask about the status of the review process. Most likely, if the music publisher knows you (established through your networking), they will listen to your material. If they hear positive talent in your songs, they may help you improve your skills, or better still, offer you a *single song contract*. They know that once you get good enough, you will come to them first with your potential hits. That's why they are in business: to make a profit by acquiring your copyrights, reworking the song (if it needs the work), exploiting and placing the song with major artists, film production companies, and other who need them, and then by issuing licenses and collecting the royalties.

Types of Publishers

Music publishers range in size from sole proprietorships (one-person) to partnerships (two or more owners) to fully staffed, multi-departmental, international corporations.

Major Publishers

Major publishers are part of or previously owned as a component of a mega entertainment corporation such as *Sony, EMI, Universal, Time Warner*, and *Bertelsmann*. However, consumer use of P2P has reduced profit levels, so Bertelsmann sold its label and music publishing to *Sony Music* and *Time Warner* sold Warner Music to an investment group headed by Edgar Bronfman, Jr.[225&226] Major music publishers are usually considered full-line, stand-alone operations (as they have many departments worldwide). Although they are typically within the major or affiliate record label structure, they may act and operate as a separate company.

Independent Publishers

Independent publishers are not affiliated with any one label or mega entertainment corporation. Even so, they frequently sign co- and sub-publishing deals with major entertainment corporations and other publishing companies for distribution and administrative assistance. Some independent publishers are full-line, others are one-person operations owned usually by a major writer or recording artist. Owning a music publishing company increases revenues to the songwriters and recording artists, as they retain control of their copyrights or at least a greater share of their copyrights and of the publishing revenues generated.

Specialty Publishers

Specialty publishers usually limit their catalogs to one or two genres of music. Examples include concert or classical music arrangements for ballet, opera, and symphony performances, gospel or Christian music for religious record labels and church performances, children music, jazz, big band, and other types of specialty niches.

---

[225] Sony Music Holdings, *Hoovers*, http://www.hoovers.com/company/Sony_Music_Holdings_Inc/ryhctsi-1.html, (accessed July 16, 2010).

[226] Edgar Bronfman, "Chairman of the Board and Chief Executive Officer, Warner Music Group Corporation," Forbes.com, http://people.forbes.com/profile/edgar-j-bronfman/42366, (accessed July 16, 2010).

Foreign Publishers

Foreign publishers may or may not be affiliated with a mega organization. Most are full-line companies doing business in their respective countries. Most have *cooperative agreements* with mega entertainment corporations and independent American music publishers. Foreign music publishers may act as agents for American publishing companies, conducting business, offering licenses, and collecting royalties in their home territories. The practice costs money though, as foreign publishers often retain between 20-50% of the royalties collected.

Vanity Publishers

Vanity publishers are songwriters who place their songs into their own companies. They may or may not be connected to powerful personalities in the industry. However, once they start to earn significant music publishing royalties they are considered independent publishers.

Administration

Full-line music publishers have many departments and industry connections. Whatever their size, some successful publishers may also use sub-or co-publisher deals to take care of these following tasks:

Acquisitions Department

Listens to songs pitched to find the next big hit. They are looking for needles in a haystack, as hundreds of songs are submitted to major music publishers and only a few are great enough to use. Submissions are also accepted as enclosures in email over the Internet as long as the publisher has agreed to accept the song for review. For legal purposes, most unsolicited songs are never listened to unless the publisher knows you or has agreed to listen to your material.

The Creative Department

In smaller publishing companies without an Acquisitions Department the Creative Department may also screen pitched songs. In most music publishing companies "creative" is the heart and soul of the company. Staff writers are hired to write their quota of acceptable songs. *Song casting* is when the Administrative and Creative departments work together to create or "find" from the company's catalog of songs (list of songs owned by the music publisher) material that may be pitched to producers, labels, artist mangers, artists, and film/video production companies.

Legal Department

May also be called Business Affairs and may be a part of Acquisitions in smaller music publishing companies. The legal department secures the song's copyright from the writer, registers the transaction with the Copyright Office in Washington, DC. It files and receives in return a *Certificate of Registration.* If the song has been previously registered with the LOC, then The Legal Department use the same registration number to have the ownership of the copyright changed into their name and they receive back a *Certificate of Recordation.*

Administration Department

If it is a small music publisher the Administration Department registers newly acquired songs and notifies corresponding organizations such *ASCAP, BMI, SESAC, Harry Fox, SoundExchange*, and *foreign administrative publishers* of recordings, film productions, and other entertainment based distribution of their copyrights.

Payroll, or Royalty Department

Every songwriters favorite place once their songs have "recouped" is the Payroll or Royalties person or department. They use computer programs to correlate the use and projected royalties due from various sources and payments to writers and copyright owners (co-publishers) often on a quarterly or semi-annual basis.

Song Casting

Hundreds of thousands of dollars and professional credentials are often made or forfeited based on the song casting process of trying to get the right song recorded by the perfect artist. Song casting (trying to figure out who to pitch songs to) is usually coupled with the song's message, the act's image and vocal capabilities, production for recording and film projects, and of course, the publisher's goal of making money by placing the song with the biggest possible artist. As already stated, recordings are communicative messages that have to emotionally connect with the public. If the recording fails, then the songwriter(s), music publisher, record company, recording artist, and record producer have also failed. It happens all the time, as consumers' emotional needs are so unpredictable that each effort (acts, films, entertainment products) has a considerable amount of risk. However, consumers have already invested their emotions, time, and money into superstars, and therefore song casting a new song to a known, famous artist (like casting a new movie with famous actors) reduces the industry's financial risk.

Recording Artists' Value to Publishers

New artists are considered a "risk" because their recordings have not yet been released to the public for sale. When artists have success and become better established, their worth is categorizes them into an "A," "B," or "C-line" artist group. It is very difficult to accurately estimate a song's potential earnings. However, music publishers have computerized the average previous earnings of their songs recorded by major artists. When a song is placed with a specific artist, the music publisher may glance at the average previous earnings to determine the song's potential income from performance and mechanical licenses. Artists are ranked as follows:

A-line artists are considered superstars with platinum recordings of one million units or more.

B-line artists have gold record sales of 500,000 units or more.

C-line artists are signed to a major label and have not sold gold or platinum.

Single Song Contracts

Single song contracts are provided on independent deals. Publishers require writers to complete and sign a single song contract for each song submitted and accepted. A *power of attorney clause* authorizes the music publisher to complete agreements with music users without the songwriter's signature. Staff writers often have a different situation as their year agreement cover all songs submitted and accepted although some additional paperwork or signatures from both parties may be required. It all depends on the small print negotiated in the original deal.[227] Independent songwriters may use a one-time single song agreement to develop a working relationship with a publisher. Publishers may also add a *right of first refusal clause* with their staff writers that stipulates that they will have the right to offer the writer a single song contract before any other publisher is allowed to hear the song. The truth is simple: no matter what type of deal a writer negotiates, a single song contract will often be used for each song being sold to the publisher. In a basic deal the publisher receives 100% ownership of the copyright and 100% of the publisher's share of the revenue

[227] Dan Keen, personal interview, (January 26, 2010).

stream, which is 50% of the total revenues generated from licenses. The songwriter receives 100% of the songwriter's share, which is the other 50% of the total revenues generated.

Splits and Shares

Splits are about *how much of the revenue stream* writers and publishers control. **Shares** are about how much of the total income is directed toward writers or publishers. Thus, 100% of the total song income in dollars (the revenue stream) is split 50/50, with half becoming 100% of the songwriter share and the other 50% becoming 100% of the publisher royalty share. To make it more difficult, there is a second level of splits and shares. In each side of the split is the share, or amount of the money, each writer or publisher in the revenue stream should receive. It is not always 50/50, however they are usually equal. Two writers might split their 100% of the songwriter part of the revenue stream (which is half of the money collected) 50/50, and three writers are usually paid 33 and 1/3 of half of the total money collected. When a songwriter also owns their own publishing company as in a co-pub or administrative deal, then the songwriter (who is also a publisher) can retain the songwriter's share (50% of the total money generated) and half of the publisher's share (25% of the total income). Therefore, in co-pub and administrative deals, the original songwriter(s), who is also a music publisher(s), retains 75% of the total money generated, and the co-pub or administrative music publisher receives the final 50% of the music publisher's share, or 25% of the total money generated.

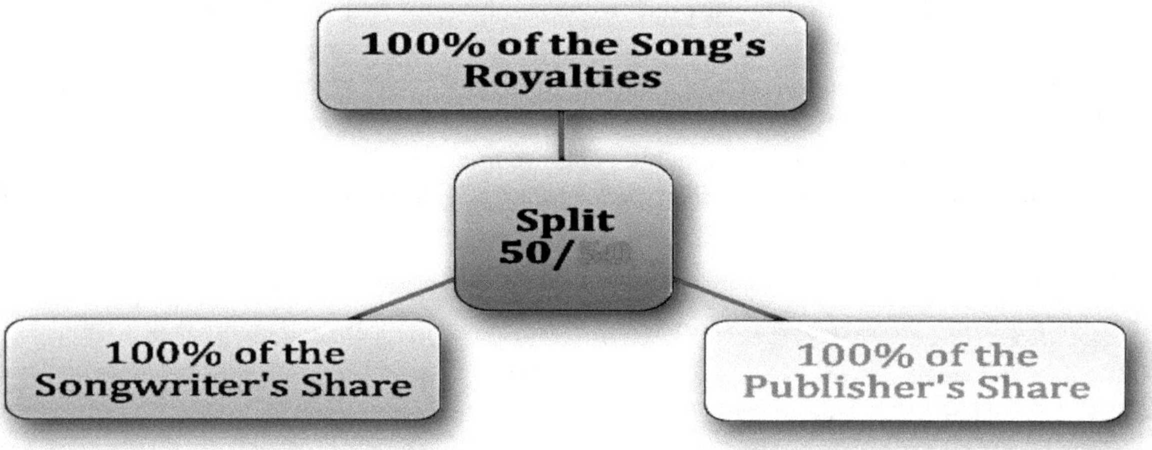

Typical Songwriter/Publisher Deal

When negotiating a deal what are most important issues to consider?

Ownership

Ownership of the copyright may also be shared if the writer is also a music publisher. Always remember that *three issues being determined on every deal* are the songwriter and music publisher splits and shares of the royalties and how much of the copyright each publisher owns (if more than one music publisher is involved). Keeping as much ownership in the copyright is important if the song becomes a hit as it will generate future royalties and is therefore a valuable piece of property.

Royalties

Royalties, such as the usual 50/50 split of the total revenues generated is usually divide into a *music publisher and songwriter share*, which are equal splits of the money the song's use has generated.

The "Catch-All" Phrase

A "Catch-All Phrase" is sometimes used at the end of a contract, according to Passman (2012), that "says that the writer gets 50% of 'all monies not referred to in this agreement.'"[228] This phrase covers new technology that may be developed in the future that generates new publishing and songwriter royalties. As an example, video games, the internet, Spotify, and many other revenue sources of today where not develop

ed in the 1950's. If your 1950 contract "listed" only mechanicals and performance rights royalties, then the publisher would pay the songwriter their share of only the mechanicals and performance rights royalties and keep all of the income generated from the newly developed technology. That does not happen if the "Catch-All Phrase" is included.

"Sweet Heart" Publishing Licensing

If you're a recording artist signed to a label or music company and you write your own material (songs), then the label will try to use the *Controlled Composition Clause* to reduce their payment to only 75% of the statutory rates. Also, they may cut a "Sweet Heart" licensing deal between the label and it's own music publishing company which often reduce the royalties to 50% or lower. Of course, they are paying less money from one hand to the other within same company. The writer(s) still receive 50% of the royalties but it's 50% of less money (the lower licensing fee) which means you make less money.[229]

Recapturing Copyrights

Writing a letter of termination to a publishing company requesting release from a single-song contract is the first step in recapturing your song's copyright due to a nonperformance default or reversion clause not being met by the music publisher. You are not blaming the publisher of failing to meet their obligation; you're simply requesting the return of your copyright. If the publisher has failed to successfully license your song with music users, they may agree to eliminate the contract. It must be a mutual agreement, or you'll end up in court. Writing a *Notice of Breach* to the publisher that states and defines a specific area of the contract that has not been satisfied is a more serious approach. Publishers are usually given a 60-day notice to alleviate the situation. If the notice is ignored, legal action may be required to conclude the contract. Publishers may negotiate some payment to help cover expenses. In either case, termination of the contract should state that all future rights are being assigned to another publisher or returned to you, the original copyright holder.[230] Additional exceptions include the following, according to Jassin (2010):

> *...To protect authors of older works from having to "live" with a bad deal they entered into when they had little negotiating skill or leverage, the Copyright Act provides that at the end of 56 years, the author (or if the author is dead, his wife and children or grandchildren), can recapture the last 39 years of copyright. For example, a publishing contract signed in 1948 can be terminated in 2004, provided timely notice of termination is given.*[231]

Section 203

The 1976 Copyright Act that became effective January 1, 1978, has a special section 203 that allows recording artists to reclaim their own actual recording performance copyrights from labels staring in 2013. Work-for-

---

[228] Donald S. Passman, *All You Need to Know About the Music Business,* (8th edition),New York: The Free Press, 2012.

[229] Donald S. Passman, *All You Need to Know About the Music Business,* (8th edition),New York: The Free Press, 2012.

[230] Mark Holloran, *The Musicians Business & Legal Guide*, (Prentice Hall Publishing, Upper Saddle River: NJ, 1991) 335.

[231] Lloyd Jassin, "Copyright Termination: How Authors (and their Heirs) can Recapture their Pre-1978 Copyrights," CopyLaw.com, (accessed March 9, 2011).

hires are exempt from the act and therefore labels for the past several years have placed into the recording contracts that the artists where "hired" or signed as a work-for-hire to create recording projects. According to *The Berkman Center for Internet & Society* of Harvard University's in their publication *Rethinking Music: A Framing Paper* (2011),

> *...When those provisions take effect in 2013, creative artists may force labels to relinquish copyrights they have owned and exploited for the past thirty-five years. Debate around Section 203 centers on two issues: (1) whether Section 203 applies to works created after January 1, 1978, the statutory starting date, by artists who entered licensing agreements prior to 1978; and (2) whether sound recordings are works-for-hire exempt from Section 203's termination requirement.*[232]

The National Music Publishers Association (NMPA)

The *National Music Publishers Association* is the largest U.S. music publishing trade association with over 3,000 members.[233] The NMPA claims (2010), "Its mission is to protect, promote, and advance the interests of music's creators."[234] They also claim to be the "voice of both small and large music publishers, the leading advocate for publishers and their songwriter partners in the nation's capital and in every area where publishers do business."[235] The goal of NMPA is to protect its members' property rights on the legislative, litigation, and regulatory fronts. In this vein, the NMPA continues to represent its members in negotiations to shape the future of the music industry by fostering a business environment that grows both creative and financial success.[236]

Selling a Publishing Company

Music publishers sell their business using a factor of between 5 and 15 times the average net revenues generated over several years to determine the value of their businesses. A music publishing company that averages an NPS (net publishers share) income of $10 million could be sold (if they can find the right buyer) for as much as $150 million ($10 million average net income multiplied by a factor of 15).[237] The idea is that even if the new publisher who buys the company leaves it alone, it will continue to generate enough income to pay for itself in 15 years. In addition, during those 15 years, the value of the songs may increase and the new company may be able to exploit the copyrights in a new innovative way that will again increase the value or equity of the purchased company. Even small publishing companies with a small average income are valuable assets. A company that has a few songs that average only $100,000 a year (for reference, a number one song on Top 40 radio will generate about $500,000), and a factor of 15 would bring the owner $1.5 million, plus continued songwriter's share royalties. Remember the Michael Jackson story! Some songwriters may also leverage their potential future royalty revenues for bank loans and stock market mutual funds. This is

---

[232] The Berkman Center for Internet & Society at Harvard University, "*Rethinking Music: A Framing Paper,*" Harvard University, http://cyber.law.harvard.edu/publications/2011/Rethinking_Music, (accessed May 2, 2011).

[233] National Music Publishers Association (NMPA), "About the NMPA,"http://www.nmpa.org/join/index.asp, (accessed June 10, 2013).

[234] National Music Publishers Association (NMPA), "About the NMPA," http://www.nmpa.org/home/index.asp, (accessed July 20, 2010).

[235] National Music Publishers Association (NMPA), "About the NMPA," http://www.nmpa.org/home/index.asp, (accessed July 20, 2010).

[236] National Music Publishers Association (NMPA), "About the NMPA," http://www.nmpa.org/home/index.asp, (accessed July 20, 2010).

[237] Dan Keen, former ASCAP Executive and Belmont University Instructor, personal interview, (January 27, 2011).

not advised as the bank may end up with your copyrights or songwriter's share of royalties if you cannot repay the loan.

6

Action Pack

Songwriting Deals

Negotiating Different Types of Deals

Ownership
Splits and Shares

"Music is spiritual. The Music Business is not."

— Van Morrison[238]

Types of Deals

There are several types of publishing deals and hundreds of variations that can be negotiated. Deals include a work-for-hire, staff writer deal, co-publishing and sub-publishing agreements, and the shark deal.

Work-for-Hire Deal

A work-for-hire deal returns us to the days of Tin Pan Alley when songwriters were paid a salary up front for their songs. Examples of a work-for-hire include specific "one-time jobs," such as writing jingles or commercials for radio or TV. The employer of the work-for-hire is considered the author and copyright holder of the song. Remember there are two types of work-for-hires: one within the scope of employment and the other when the work is specially commissioned. The disadvantage, if the "creative work" is part of your job, is that your employer will own everything you write as well as all future royalties paid on those works. However, if you are "commissioned" to create a copyrightable work, and you have a written

[238] Van Morrison, "Top 50 Music Quotations," John Pawlett, http://afgen.com/top50.html, (accessed January 7, 2011).

agreement stating that you're being employed as a *work-for-hire*, then the copyright remain with you, the author.[239] According to Marybeth Peters, United States Register of Copyrights (2000),

> *The work made for hire doctrine provides that under certain circumstances, the law will deem the employer of the person or persons who actually created a work to be the "author" of the work. The consequence of the work made for hire doctrine was and is that the employer can exercise all the rights of ownership of the work and avoid the consequences of other provisions of copyright law that have permitted the persons who actually created the work to recapture those rights. I will discuss those other provisions in a moment…*
>
> *…The 1909 Copyright Act stated that "the word 'author' shall include an employer in the case of works made for hire." The Act did not expressly address commissioned works, which left a broad scope for interpretation. In the cases regarding commissioned works decided under the 1909 Act, rights were generally held to vest with the hiring party….*
>
> *…The 1976 Act, however, made a clear distinction between works prepared by employees in the course of their employment and works prepared on commission, a distinction that is still maintained today. Works prepared by employees in the course of their employment are categorized as works made for hire, with authorship, and thus ownership as well, recognized in the employer. In contrast, commissioned works can only be considered works made for hire if they fall within certain specified categories, and even then, only if the person commissioning the work and the person or persons accepting the commission agree in writing that the work to be created will be considered a work made for hire.*[240]

In the music business, a work-for-hire songwriter is usually given a one-time payment and the employer receives the copyright (ownership of the song) and all revenues (both the songwriter and music publisher's shares). Just remember that songwriters can maintain their copyright if they satisfy the "type of employment" details in writing.

What's the Difference?

Let's take a look at *how* the different types of deals affect your overall income. Remember, three issues are being negotiated in every deal, (a) the songwriters royalties which are a percentage of the total income; (b) The music publisher's royalties that are a percentage of the overall income and; (c) The ownership of the copyright which may be a valuable and a sellable piece of personal property with the value based on how many companies what to use it and how many consumers want to buy or listen to it. You have written a song by yourself that generates $100,000 in revenues or royalties. In the Work-for-Hire deal you are paid $2000 to write the song and the company who hires you owns the copyright. In each deal the copyright owner later sells the copyright for an additional $500,000.

---

[239] Marybeth Peters, "Statement of Marybeth Peters: The Register of Copyrights Before the Subcommittee on Courts and Intellectual Property Committee on the Judiciary," Sound Recordings As Works Made for Hire. http://www.copyright, (accessed January 18, 2011).

[240] Marybeth Peters, "Statement of Marybeth Peters: The Register of Copyrights Before the Subcommittee on Courts and Intellectual Property Committee on the Judiciary," Sound Recordings As Works Made for Hire. http://www.copyright, (accessed January 18, 2011).

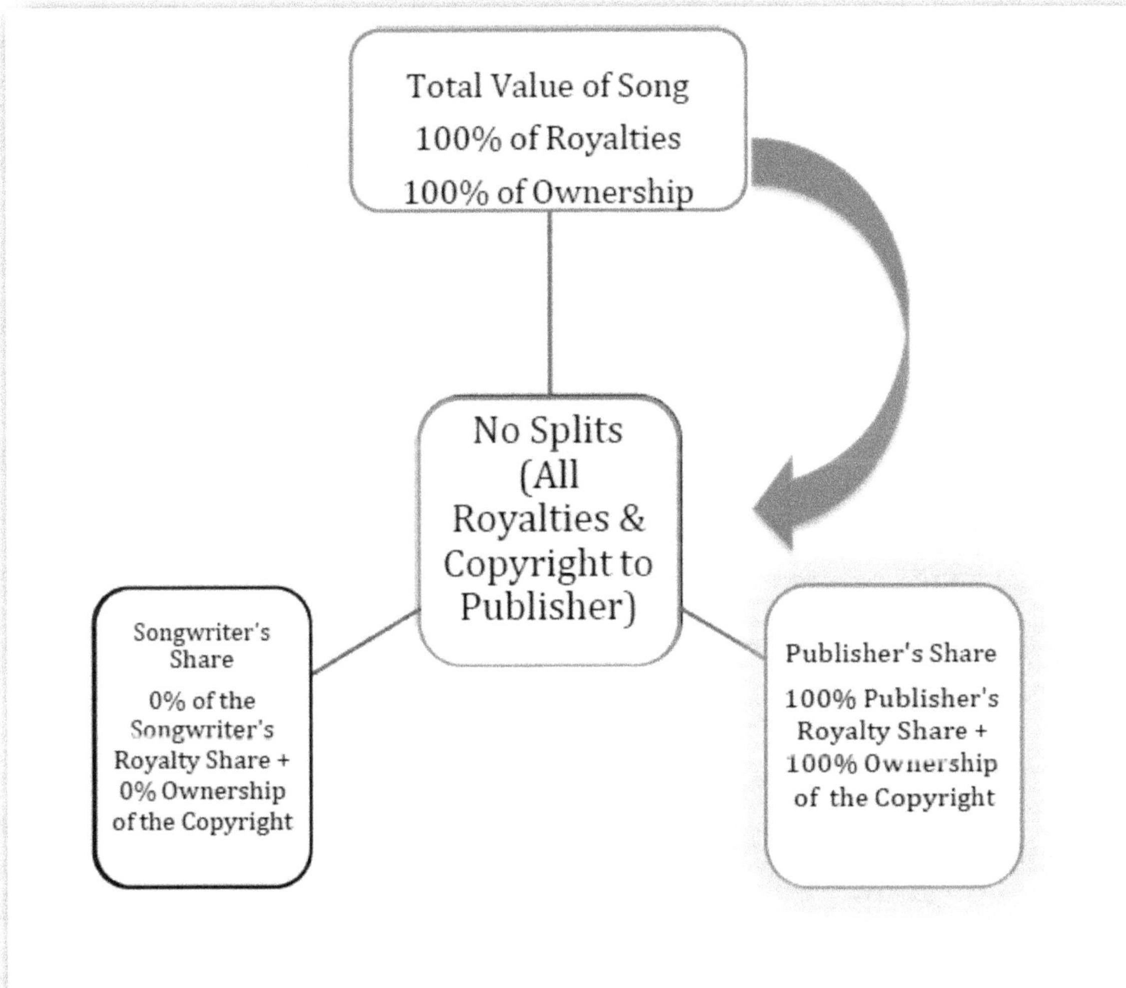

Type of Deal	Songwriters Share	Music Publishers Share	Copyright Ownership
Work-for Hire Deal	__________	__________	__________

Indie Deal

Independent writer deals are usually a *single song contract* offered to new writers who have written a great song a publisher wants to own. If the writer shows talent then they may be offered a staff writer deal where an advance is provided for a number of acceptable songs and yet the single song contract with the 50/50 split is still used.

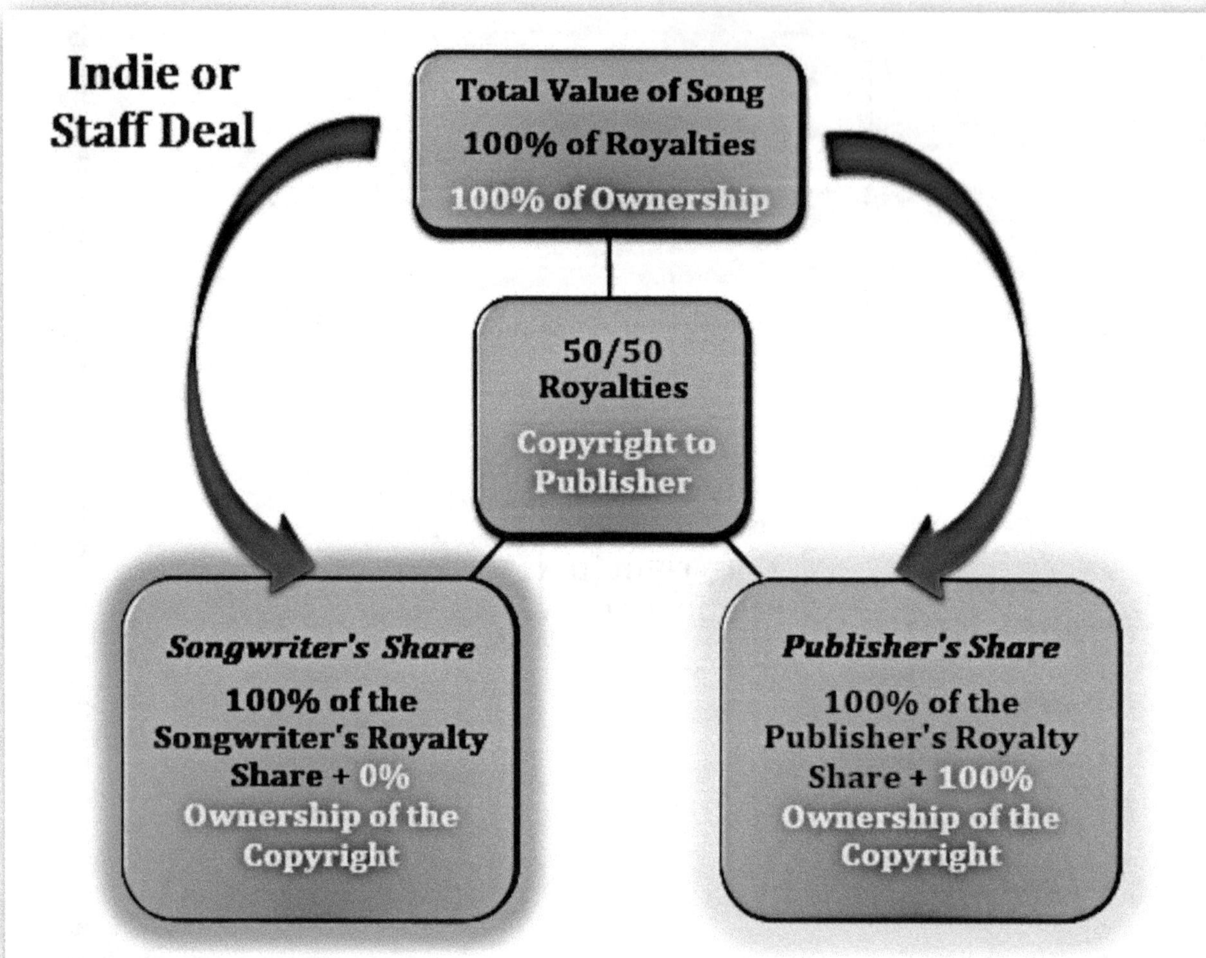

Now, let's say that you made an Indie or Staff Deal instead of a Work-for Hire. How much money do you receive out of the $100,000. How much money do you make with this type of deal?

Type of Deal	Songwriters Share	Music Publishers Share	Copyright Ownership
Indie or Staff Deal	__________	__________	__________

Staff Deals

Staff writer deals are positions at a music publishing company that are desirable because they provide songwriters with an opportunity to improve their songwriting skills, make industry contacts, network with other writers, co-write, and make a reasonable living all at the same time. Novice staff writers are often surprised to learn that the songs they write are owned by the music publisher who is paying them. However, from the music publisher's perspective, he or she is in effect, betting the advances (a draw of the money to be paid) that the writers will be able to create songs that will recoup the writer's advances, plus a profit. *Staff writers* are paid *a draw* in exchange for a quota of acceptable songs (usually 8-12 annually) and their royalty share *after* and *if* the advances are recoupment. They are usually considered *exclusive writers* for the music publisher.

The *advances or draw* are often paid semi-quarterly, which the music publisher hopes to recoup from royalties, if indeed there are any. Once the song's "royalties" repay the writer's advances, the remaining royalties are split into a songwriter's share and a publisher's share. The more successful the writer, the more the payment schedule favors the writer. A powerful publisher may have a contract that is skewed favorably toward the company. Beginning salaries often range from $18,000 to $30,000, while very successful writers can earn hundreds of thousands of dollars per year in advances, salaries, and royalties. In addition, if more than one writer or publisher is involved in the deal, the "share" is divided accordingly. Thus, 100 percent of the songwriters' share (which equals 50% of the total revenue income) is split 50/50 so in reality, each writer (or publisher) is really only receiving 25% of the total revenues generated. In other words, a 50% share of the songwriters' or publishers' share is only equal to 25% of the total revenues generated by the song. Crazy, yet it is the language often used in the industry so be careful to comprehend if you are talking about a "share" or "total income" when negotiating a deal.

Co-Pub Deal

Co-publishing agreements help songwriters capture more of their song's equity by establishing co-ownership of their song's copyright at the time of publishing. Co-publishing ordinarily occurs during the acquisition of a song when more than one publisher is involved. Songwriter, music producer, and recording artist-owned publishing companies need co-publishing deals with the major publishers for distribution around the world and in the entertainment centers of the United States, Asia, South America, and Europe. In addition, producers, recording artists (with their own publishing companies), and smaller independent music publishers generally make *co-publishing deals* with larger, better-connected publishers to take care of the administrative paperwork, such as licenses and royalty collections. In a *co-pub deal*, the songwriter, producer, label, or recording artist (whoever owns the song) gives up half of their copyright of the song (ownership). In addition, the total royalties are split 75/25, with 75% of the total generated revenues going to the original songwriter/publisher (100% of the songwriter's share and 50% of the publisher's share) and the remaining half of the music publisher's share of the revenue stream (25% of the total) going to the co-publisher.

This, of course, means that anyone can be a one-person music publishing company. All you need to be successful in the business is a great song and a co-publishing deal with a worldwide publishing company that can take care of all the paperwork in exchange for 50% ownership of the song and 50% of the publishing share of the revenue stream. Industry terminology and the practice of converting percentages to shares tend to make co-publishing agreements complex. Here is an example of what is really happening. The typical *single-song contract* has a 50/50 split of all royalties (except printed sheet music and folios where the writer(s) may be paid as much as 10% of the suggested retail price). The maximum percent of any whole is 100%. Yet, the music business splits the 100% of a song's potential collected revenue into 50% songwriter and 50% publisher shares, reconverts each 50% share into a 100% share for the writers and publishers. Co-publishing works to the advantage of both the songwriter (who is also a publisher) and established industry music publishers. The music publisher receives a share of the equity (copyright ownership) that can quickly increase the value of their catalog and the songwriter/publisher receives the major connections, distribution, and industry power of the major music publisher, plus more money as they now also receive half of the publishers share.

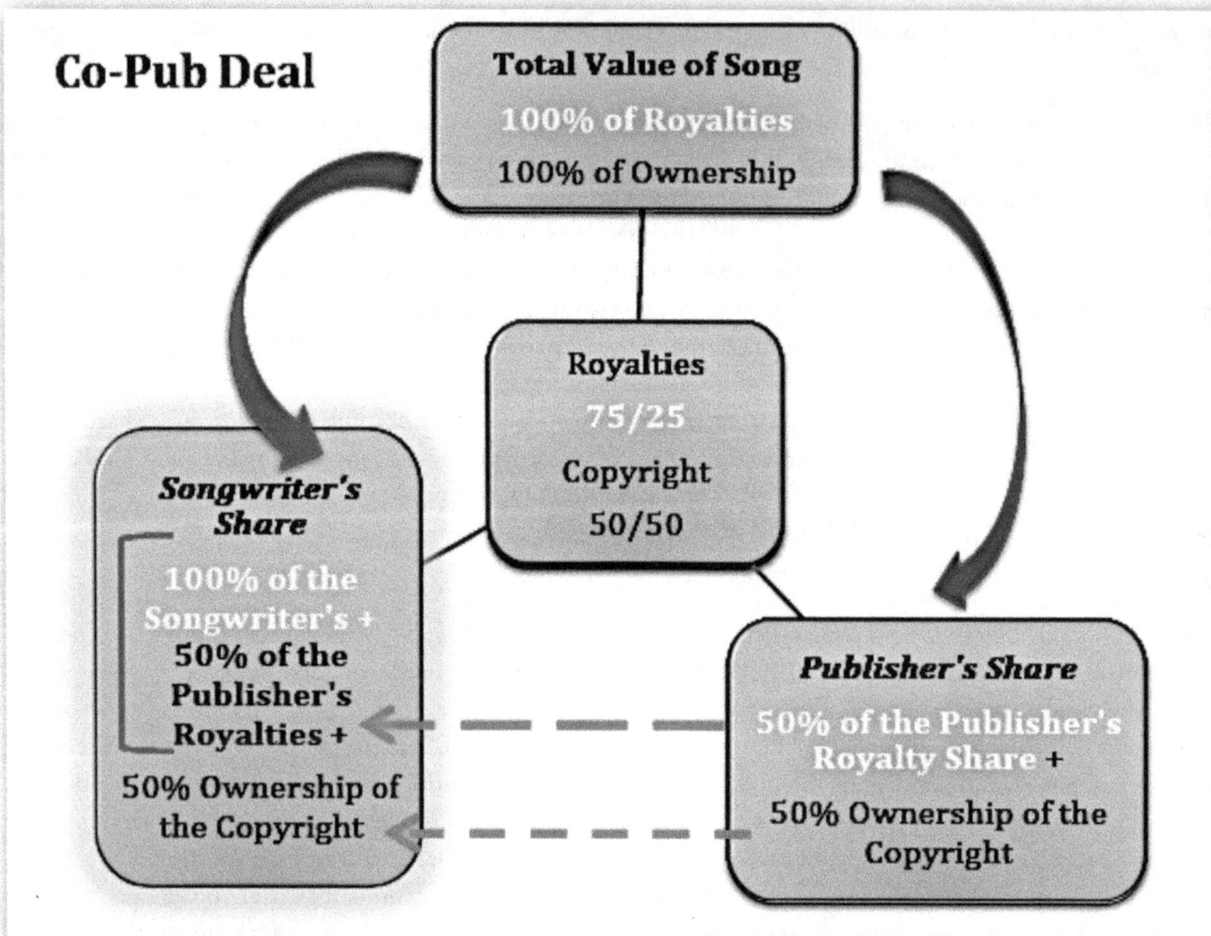

How much more money did you make under this deal?

Type of Deal	Songwriters Share	Music Publishers Share	Copyright Ownership
Co-Pub Deal	________	________	________

Administrative Deal

An Administrative Publishing Deal is the same as the co-pub except the songwriter (who is also publisher) retains 100% ownership of the copyright. It allows songwriters who own their own publishing companies to keep absolute ownership of their song's copyright. The royalty splits are the same as in the Co-Pub Deal. An administrative publisher or exclusive agent simply issues mechanical licenses, registers songs with the corresponding performance rights organizations, and commonly collects royalties in exchange for 50% percentage of the publisher's share of the revenues collected. Administrative agreements are advantageous to songwriters who demo record their own songs and have the networking contacts to place them with major recording artists themselves. These types of deals frequently occur between two or more publishers after the acquisition of a song by one publisher who then licenses a second or third publisher to administer and exploit the song's potential equity worldwide. Publishers seek administrative publisher deals to handle various aspects of the business, including the paper business (printing of sheet music and sales), legal, documentation, and demo recording. A sub-pub deal is the same as an administrative deal except with a foreign publisher (usually to collect foreign royalties).

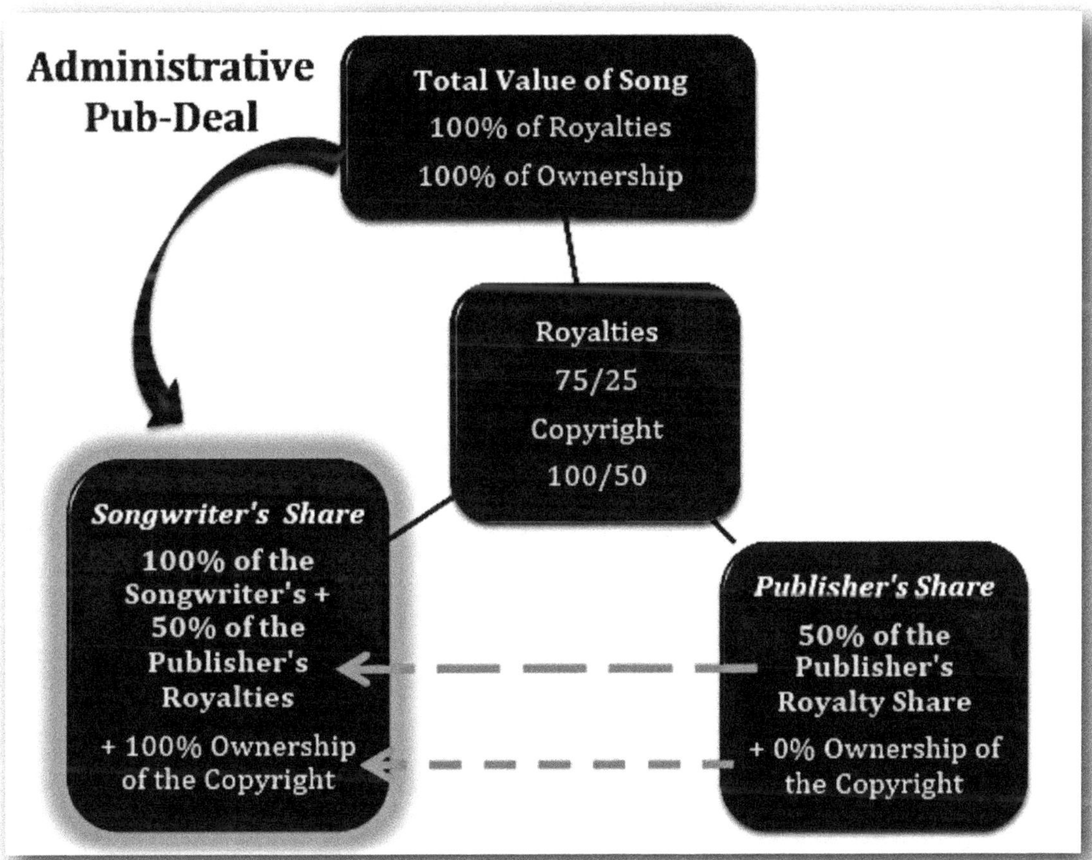

How much more money did you make out of an administrative deal?

Type of Deal	Songwriters Share	Music Publishers Share	Copyright Ownership
Administrative Deal	__________	__________	__________

Shark Deal

Avoid the Shark Deal. Whenever a publisher compliments your song and then asks you to put up some money to share the expenses, you are probably being cheated. Just remember, you don't pay them; they pay you! It is your song, *your* property, not theirs. Be careful! There have been many examples of songs sold to music publishers (mostly in the 1950s and early 60s) for a set fee of a few hundred dollars or less. Many of the songs became hits, but the writers did not receive any additional revenues as they had already sold all of their ownership. Unethical music publishers, who offer shark deals, are considered rip-off artists, as they are in the business of making money off of you, the songwriter. The only money shark publishers usually make is what you paid them to publish your song. In most cases, they do not have the industry contacts to place your song with a major artist, producer, or label, and correspondingly, you will almost certainly never receive any royalties.

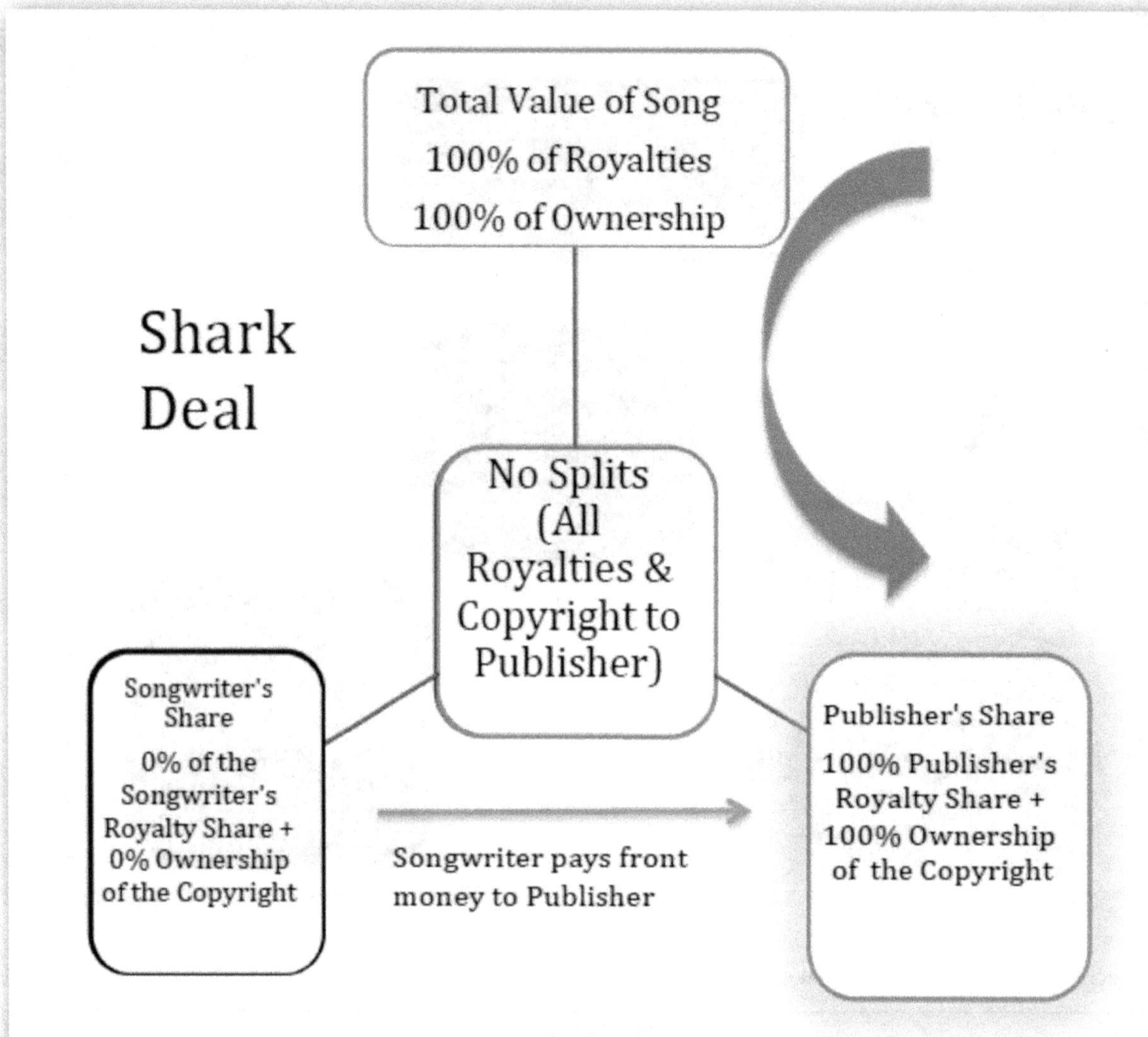

In the Shark Deal you pay a publisher to "publish" your song and they take all royalties and ownership of the copyright. The song is not usually distributed which means no royalties are generated. So, how much money will you make on this type of deal?

Type of Deal	Songwriters Share	Music Publishers Share	Copyright Ownership
Shark Deal	________	________	________

Best Effort

Publishers can only be proactive concerning a song's potential selection by an artist to record. Contracts customarily state that music publishers have satisfied their contractual obligations when they have, to the best of their ability, attempted to place a song with music users. It is very difficult for a songwriter (or their attorney) to define and prove that a music publisher did not attempt to place the song with various music users. In addition, publishers can usually provide a stack of invoices and paid statements as proof of their attempt to place the song with record labels, recording artists, and other types of music users.

Staff Writer Termination

Sometimes the marriage between the songwriter and music publisher fails. The quality of their agreement means very little unless both profit. Written contractual goals that are not fulfilled often lead to either side you and terminating the contract may be difficult. Legal action is customarily required to prove nonperformance of a contractual agreement. Publishers may default in their contractual obligation if they fail to provide licenses to music users; pay royalties in a timely manner; place the song with a major recording artist or an artist signed with a record label; provide sheet music (of the song) to music stores and other retail outlets; place the song in radio and TV commercials, advertisements, and movie soundtracks; or protect the copyright against infringement.

Summary-Do the Math

Many songwriters wonder how much money they should receive in a royalty check. It's complex as it all depends on; (a) the type of deal you struck with a publisher, (b) how successful the song is at generating money due to it use in recordings, films, commercials, etc., (c) Which performance rights organization do you below too (ASCAP, BMI, or SESAC in the United States or one of the hundreds around the world (d) the exchange rate on the value of different currencies compared to the dollar, (e) and many other factors.

Now compare the different types of deals and determine how much money you made in each. Remember, three issues are being negotiated in every deal, are; (a) the songwriters royalties which are usually 50 percent of the total income but are called 100 percent of the songwriters share; (b) The music publisher's royalties that are the remaining 50% percent of the total income but called 100% of the music publishers share, (c) the ownership of the copyright which may be valuable and a sellable piece of personal property with the value based on popularity (how many companies may what to use it in the future and how many consumers may want to buy or listen to it in the future).

Let's assume you've written a song by yourself that generates $100,000 in revenues or royalties. In the Work-for-Hire deal you are paid $2000 to write the song and the company who hires you owns the copyright. In each deal the copyright owner later sells the copyright for an additional $500,000.

Type of Deal	Songwriters Share of Royalties	Music Publishers Share Royalties	Copyright Ownership(s)	Totals
Work-for-Hire	$00.00 (Paid $2000 upfront)	$100,000	$00.00 to Songwriter	Songwriter $2,000
			$500,000 to Publisher	Publisher $600,000 (-$2,000 up front payment) $598,000
Indie/Staff Deal	$50,000	$50,000	$00.00 to Songwriter	Songwriter $50,000
			$500,000 to Publisher	Publisher $550,000
Co-Publishing	$75,000 (100 % of writers share plus 50% of publisher share)	$25,000 (50% of publisher's royalty share)	$250,000 to Songwriter as a publisher (50% of copyright ownership)	Songwriter acting also as a publisher $325,000
			$250,000 to Publisher (50% ownership)	Publisher $275,000
Administrative	$75,000 (100 % of writers share plus 50% of publisher share)	$25,000 (50% of publisher's royalty share)	$500,000 to Songwriter acting as also as a publisher 100% ownership)	Songwriter acting also as a publisher $575,000
			$00.00 to publisher	Publisher $25,000
Shark	**-$5000** **(You pay them to publish your song)**	**$100,000** **Plus $5,000 paid by writer or $100,5000**	**$00.00 to Songwriter**	**Songwriter loss of -$5,000**
				Publisher makes $605,000

7

Licensing Songs

Types of Licenses
The Harry Fox Agency
ASCAP, BMI, SESAC
SoundExchange

"People don't buy plastic and paper, they buy emotions."

— Scott Young, Wherehouse Entertainment[241]

"I'm a survivor in a business that constantly rejects you."

— Dick Clark[242]

"Publishing a volume of verse is like dropping a rose petal down the Grand Canyon and waiting for the echo."

— Don Marquis[243]

"It's intriguing that somebody at a computer across the world is playing my music, …Not only do I know I have access to a larger fan base, there seems to be more ways to sustain a living in the music business."

— Sandra McCracken[244]**, on receiving her first check from SoundExchange**

Revenues

The good news is that revenues from music publishing are up for both performance rights organizations and synchronization licenses. According to *The Recording Industry in Numbers* published by the IFPI (2013);

> *Performance rights revenues (from broadcasts and public performance) were the fastest growing sector in the recording industry in 2012, accounting for 6 per cent of recorded music revenues. Revenues grew by 9.4% globally, to US$943 million. Income from*

---

[241] Scott Young, "Music Industry Quotes to live by," The musicbizacademy.com., http://wwwmusicbizacademy.com/knab/articles/musicquotes.htm (accessed July 16, 2010).

[242] Dick Clark, "Music Industry Quotes to Live By," Christopher Knob-Fourfront Media & Music, http://www.musicbizacademy.com/knab/articles/musicquotes.htm, (accessed July 16,2010).

[243] Don Marquis, "Publishing Quotes," Brainy Quote, http://www.brainyquote.com/quotes/keywords/publishing_3.html, (accessed July 17, 2010).

[244] Sandra McCracken, "Music's Foreign Royalties bring Welcome Windfall," The Tennessean, http://www.tennessean.com/article/20100724/BUSINESS01/7240308/Music+s+foreign+royalties (accessed July 24, 2010).

synchronization deals - music used in TV adverts, films and brand partnerships - were also up. These grew by 2.1% to US$337 million in 2012.[245]

Types of Licenses

Permission to use a copyright (a song or a film, for example) is usually granted through the issuing of a license. Compensation for the use of the song is paid as a licensing fee either directly to the publisher or through agents like the *Harry Fox Agency, ASCAP, BMI*, and *SESAC*. Remember, music publishers and songwriters (and other creative artists) gain their ownership rights from the Copyright Law and control their corresponding six Exclusive Rights, (including reproduction, distribution, derivative, public performance, public display and digital transmission). Thus, licenses offered by the copyright owner (songwriter or music publisher, depending on the type of deal) in exchange for a fee (money) provides a legal clearance for the use of the song, by the company acquiring the license. There are different types of licenses for different types of song uses. Most notable are; (a) "Mechanicals" for audio recordings; (b) "Synchronization or Sync" audio recordings of a song used in a visual presentation such as a film or movie; (c) "Masters" use of the actual recording of a song by a major recording artist pulled from the *master recordings* owned by the label or music company; (d) "Blanket Licenses" provided by *Performance Rights Organizations* (such as ASCAP, BMI, and SESAC in the United States) for a "public performance" such as a radio station, business, or a song sung live in a concert; and (e) Digital licenses including "Digital Mechanicals", used for digital downloading of songs and "Digital Performances" used by digital radio stations for webcasting and terrestrial broadcast radio programs for simulcasting over the Internet. There are also "Print Licenses" required for selling sheet music ,"Dramatic Licenses" for songs in theater productions, and "Transcription Licenses" used for radio commercials and elevator music.

Mechanicals

Record labels must acquire the right to record and sell a song (the music publisher's copyright, and therefore, property) before the recording, distribution for sale, and promotion (release of the recording) to radio stations for airplay.

The Harry Fox Agency

Most American music publishers are represented by *The Harry Fox Agency* in New York City, who in turn collects the majority of mechanical royalties from labels who owe music publishers and songwriters "Royalties" for using their composition.[246] According to the *Harry Fox Agency* site (2010),

> *With over 80 years of experience, HFA is the premiere U.S. provider of licensing and rights administration services. They deliver copyright, licensing, royalty distribution, technology and consulting services to key music industry participants. They provide speed-to-market and cost-efficiencies that eliminate the need to invest in infrastructure and staff to handle back-office functions and… its database of publishing and sound recording data is the most accurate and comprehensive in the industry, unparalleled global relationships.*[247]

The NMPA (National Music Publishers Association) of which The Harry Fox Agency is a part of, represents music publishers. HFA collects mechanical license fee (paid as royalties) from businesses and labels who want to record and sell songs they do not own but want to have recorded by one of their major artists.

---

[245] I.F.P.I., *Recording Industry in Numbers 2013*, International Federation of the Phonographic Industry, http://www.ifpi.org/content/section_news/20130408.html (accessed July 3, 2013).

[246] Harry Fox Agency, "HFA Produces Industry's Highly Anticipated Publisher Airplay Charts," http://www.harryfox.com/public/userfiles/file/PressReleases/PublisherCharts3rdquarterFinal20101112.pdf, (accessed January 30, 2011).

[247] Harry Fox Agency, "General Information," https://www.harryfox.com/public/FAQ.jsp#12, (accessed July 18, 2010).

The Statutory Rate

Once an artist (in cooperation with their producer) decides to record a song, the label must acquire the legal right to record and distribute the song. A Mechanical License fee called the *Statutory Rate* is used to determine the total cost of the license. The fee is currently 9.1¢ per song ($.091) (for a song under 5 minutes in length) multiplied by the number of units pressed, shipped, downloaded, or sold. Therefore, if a label presses or downloads a combination of 1,000,000 units, the cost for the license is 9.1¢ * 1,000,000 or $91,000. A ten-song album will cost the label ten times that amount, as they owe the publishers 9.1¢ per song * 10 songs on the album, which equals 91¢ per album * the 1,000,000 units delivered or sold for a total mechanical fee of $910,000. If the song's recorded time is *over five minutes* then the *Statutory Rate* shifts to a *per-minute rate* of 1.75¢ per minute ($.0175) * the total minutes, with 1 second over being rounded up to another minute. As an example, a song with the recorded time of 8:01 is considered a nine-minute song, so the mechanical is figured as 1.75¢ * 9 minutes for a total of $0.1575 cents per unit pressed, ship, downloaded, or sold.

The Controlled Composition Clause

Labels, of course, want to save money on album projects, and one of the ways to do this is to pay only 75% of the statutory rate for mechanical licenses. As stated earlier, if the main artist owns, controls, or has written all or part of the composition, then the label can declare the song a controlled composition. *The American Society of Composers, Author, and Publishers* (2010) provides this explanation:

> *Many agreements – the majority, in fact – contain language which provides that if the recording artist or producer has written or co-written a song, has ownership or control of a song, or has any interest in any composition on the album or single, the mechanical royalty rate payable by the record company for that composition is reduced. Such compositions are referred to as* **controlled compositions**. *Most contracts attempt to establish a 75% rate (specifically, 6.825¢, which is three-quarters of the 9.1¢ full statutory rate) for all controlled compositions. The figures are computed at the mechanical rate in effect at either (a) the time the recording is produced, (b) the date of the recording contract with the artist, (c) the date that a particular album commenced recording (or should have commenced recording per the contract), or (d) the date the recording is originally released (regardless of whether the same recording is released again at a later date in another album).*[248]

Financial Changes Due to the Controlled Composition Clause

What happens to the music publisher's and songwriter's splits, shares, and royalties when the labels use the *Controlled Composition Clause* acquiring a mechanical license? Who wins and losses money? Of course, the label wins as it only has to pay 75% of the statutory rate. So at the current rate of .091 cents per-song on a ten song, platinum selling album, (all songs under five minutes), the label pays $682,500.00 in licensing fees instead of statutory rate of $910,000.00. In addition, if the royalty artist is declared the writer, co-writer, or owns a share of the music publishing, then they also receive some of the royalties, (even if they didn't really write or change the song). The publisher or writer may be linked with a major act, yet their royalties are reduced accordingly. As an example, if you write a song and the label demands the major artist changes a lyric or something else minor, than the label gets to pay the CCC rate saving them money and you have to split your songwriting share of royalties with the artists.

---

[248] ASACP, "Music and Money, The Controlled Composition Clause," http://.ascap.com/musicbiz/money-clauses.html, (July 18, 2010).

The Compulsory License – Hard Platforms

If you want to record a song that has been previously released for sale (a hit by Lady Gaga for example) and release it on a hard platform such as a CD, then obtain a *Compulsory (mechanical) License.* Contact the *Harry Fox Agency* (2010) as they have *songfile* system for licenses for anyone recording and releasing between 25 and 2,500 units:

> *Mechanical Licenses are required under U.S. Copyright Law if you want to record or distribute a song that you do not own. By properly licensing your recordings, you ensure that the publisher that represents the songwriter who wrote the composition gets paid. Reputable replicators and online music sites will require you to have these licenses before they duplicate your recording or offer it online. Royalties for Songfile licenses are set at the current U.S. statutory mechanical rate. In addition to royalty fees, there is a modest per-song processing fee of $13 to $15 charged by HFA, depending upon how many songs are licensed.*[249]

Notice of Intent

In addition, remember you'll need to file a *Notice of Intent to Obtain a Compulsory License* with the music publisher of the song mentioned in a previous chapter on copyrights.[250] According to the Library of Congress (2010),

> *A "Notice of Intention" is a Notice identified in section 115(b) of title 17 of the United States Code, and required by that section to be served on a copyright owner or, in certain cases, to be filed in the Copyright Office, before or within thirty days after making, and before distributing any phonorecords of the work, in order to obtain a compulsory license to make and distribute phonorecords of non dramatic musical works.*[251]

Foreign Mechanicals-Sub Publishing

Unlike the American practice of individual song mechanical licenses, most foreign countries require one mechanical license for all the songs on an album. Registration is mandatory. As an example, the European Union has declared 9.01% of the list price to dealer (per album) rate, with the United Kingdom and Ireland's rate at 8.5% per album.[252] Mechanicals are collected by government-owned agencies and turned over to the foreign music publishers. Part of the retail price is collected for the mechanicals that are split among all the songs on the album and between the foreign and American publishers. Therefore, other than in Europe, there is not a set international mechanical rate, and the amount of money collected varies from country to country and album to album. Total collected also depend on the number of songs on the album and how many albums were sold. Foreign administrative publishers often collect the mechanicals from the government or local agencies and split the royalties with American publishers by making payments directly to their American Publisher.[253&254]

---

[249] Harry Fox Agency, "Songfile Licensing," http://www.harryfox.com/public/moreSongfile.jsp, (accessed July 18, 2010).

[250] Library of Congress, "Copyright Office, Notice of Intent of Obtain a Compulsory License," http://www.copright.gov/circs/circ73.pdf, (accessed July 6, 2010).

[251] Library of Congress, "Code of Federal Regulations: section 201.18:Notice of intent to obtain a compulsory license for making and distributing phonorecords of non dramatic musical works," http://www.loc.gov/cgi-bin/formprocessor/copyright, (accessed September 18, 2010).

[252] M. William Krasilovsky, and Sydney Shemel, *This Business of Music*, 10th ed. (New York, NY: Billboard Books, 168).

[253] M. William Krasilovsky, and Sydney Shemel, *This Business of Music*, 10th ed. (New York, NY: Billboard Books, 168).

[254] Anthony Berman, "Multi-Media Law Online News: Foreign Publishing Royalties," http://beatblog.typepad.com/melon/2007/06/music-law-forei.html, (July 18, 2010).

SoundScan

Nielsen's *SoundScan* is an information system that tracks the sales of music and music video products (and therefore mechanicals) throughout the United States and Canada. Sales data from point-of-sale cash registers is collected weekly from over 14,000 retail and nontraditional stores.[255] Weekly data is compiled and made available every Wednesday. Nielsen SoundScan is the research sales source for the *Billboard* music charts. According to Nielsen (2010),

> *SoundScan clients include all major and most independent record companies, distribution companies, artist managers, booking agents, concert promoters, performing rights organizations, government agencies, venue owners, traditional retailers, online retailers and digital delivery companies. Since March 1, 1991, Billboard Magazine charts have been constructed directly from our data. MTV, VH1, CMT, MuchMusic and all major media regularly use SoundScan data as well.*[256]

Synchronization (Sync) License

Sync licenses are required for the use of music in the production of a visual presentation. Film, TV, and digital media production companies are required to obtain a sync license for the music and songs they plan to use in their productions. Most music publishers license their songs and music directly to the production companies. Live TV shows taped for delayed broadcasts, such as *Letterman* or *Leno*, must have all sync licenses in place before the productions are created and aired. Music videos are filmed only after the licenses are secure; however, movies are often being produced as the licenses are negotiated. Statutory rates are not required on sync licenses, so fees are negotiable. If the price for one song is too high, typically another is selected from a different publisher.[257]

Master License

Producers of a visual media production must acquire a *sync license* from the music publishers to use a song in their production. They must also secure a *master license* from a record label to use the actual recording of the song by a specific artist. In other words, if your want to use a recording by *Elton John* in a film you're producing, you'll need to negotiate two licenses: the sync license from the publisher for the actual use of the song and the master license from Elton John's label for his recording of the song. According to *wearelisting.com* (2010),

> *A Sync License pertains to the right to synchronize a composition to motion picture. Not to be confused with a Master Use License, which pertains to the use of the recording(s) of the composition, a Sync License encompasses only the intellectual property of the composition as opposed to its tangible manifestation. Although the two licenses are often grouped together into a single agreement for the purpose of music licensing, it is important to make the distinction in order to understand the authorities involved in a commercial music licensing relationship.*[258]

---

255 Nielsen, "Nielsen's U.S. Soundscan Venue Sales Procedures," http://www.nielsen.com/content/dam/corporate/us/en/public%20factsheets/Soundscan/SoundScan, (accessed March 9, 2011).

256 Nielsen, "Fact Sheet," http://en-us.nielsen.com/content/dam/nielsen/en_us/documents/pdf/Fact%20Sheets/Nielsen%20SoundScan%20One%20Sheet.pdf, (accessed July 18, 2010).

257 M. William Krasilovsky, and Sydney Shemel, *This Business of Music*, 10th ed. (New York, NY: Billboard Books, 238).

258 We Are Listening, "Expose Your Music: Sync Licensing," http://www.wearelistening.org/sync_license.php, (accessed July 18, 2010).

License Chart

Type of License	Exclusive Right Covered	Purchaser of License	Agency	Recipients of Royalties	Rates
Mechanicals	Reproduction Distribution	Labels- Music Companies	**Harry Fox Agency**	Copyright Owner- Music Publisher & Writers depending on the deal	1. Statutory Rate 2. Controlled Composition Clause Rate
Digital Mechanical	Downloading by transmission (DPD a Digital Phonorecord Delivery)	Providers of digital streaming and limited downloads.	**Harry Fox Agency**	Copyright Owner- Music Publisher & Writers depending on the deal	Digital Statutory Rate- Size of the payable royalty pool divided by the number of actual "plays" depending on interaction.
Synchronization "Sync"	Reproduction Distribution with a visual presentation	Film & Visual production companies	Direct	Copyright Owner- Music Publisher & Writers depending on the deal	Negotiated
Master	Reproduction Distribution	Film & Visual production companies	Direct & Fintage House	Copyright Owner- Record Label and Music Companies	Negotiated
Blanket	Public Performance	Mass Media radio, TV, clubs, restaurants, businesses and venues.	ASCAP BMI SESAC CCLI- Churches	Royalties collected and split paid directly to Music Publisher(s) & Songwriters	Analyzed by PRO's based on many factors such as audience size, number of plays (uses) size of venue
Digital Public Performance	Performance by means of digital transmission, webcasting and radio simulcasting	Satellite, Digital Providers & Broadcast radio, (passively transmitted)	Sound Exchange & Fintage House (non-traditional markets)	Recording Artist, Labels, Music Companies, Musicians	Statutory for Digital Passive song/music Streaming
Print	Reproduction Distribution	Book publishing companies	Direct	Music Publisher	Negotiated (usually 10-20% of revenues.
Transcription	Reproduction Distribution Public Performance	Audio Productions (resale to chain stores) & TV productions for audio commercials	Direct	Music Publisher	Negotiated
Dramatic	Stage Performance	Stage Production Company	Direct	Copyright Owner	Negotiated
Foreign	All	Foreign mass and digital media, plus foreign production companies	Harry Fox ASCAP, BMI, SESAC & Fintage House	Music publishing & in some cases songwriters	Usually 20% to 50% of collected royalties.

Blanket License

Although Congress authorized performance rights in 1897, royalties were not very significant until the formation of companies that could collect the royalties (ASCAP, and later SESAC and BMI) and the development of the mass media which uses music in much of its programming.[259] In the United States, the *public performance exclusive right* is usually covered by ASCAP, BMI, and SESAC, which offer a blanket licenses (as it "covers" all the publishers and writers of songs they represent) to radio, television, cable networks, live venues, bars, and others who are required by law to pay for the music they use in their businesses. According to *ASCAP* (2010), a blanket license is a license issued by them "a performing rights society" that authorizes the use of all the songs in their repertory for public performances (almost 8.5 million in their case).[260] *Bpi.co.uk* (2010) adds that a blanket license is "...(usually granted by a collecting society) the authorization to use all the recordings or songs that are owned or controlled by the collecting society in a specified way."[261] Their job is to find the businesses and collect licensing fees for their use of the songs. In the world, PROs license the mass media, hotels, motels, restaurants, nightclubs, concert halls, specific concert performances, airlines, trade shows, amusement parks, malls, and almost any other source of music performance venues they can find.[262]

Blanket License Royalties

Performance rights royalties (collected as *Blanket License Fees*) are split by ASCAP, BMI, and SESAC and sent separately to the writers and publishers. Fifty percent is equal to 100% of the writer's share and the remaining 50% is equal to 100% of the publisher's share. As stated earlier, mechanical fees are paid differently, as The Harry Fox Agency and other mechanical collection agents pay all the royalties to the publisher who splits the royalties (minus recoupment) with the writer. Until recently, both ASCAP and BMI used random sampling and statistical analysis to determine the number of performances, and therefore payments, to their writers and publishers. ASCAP recorded a random sample of local radio and television broadcasts and generalized the results to national performance figures. They sampled TV networks, PBS, and cable channels. BMI required a random sampling of radio stations to log (keep a list of each song's performance). BMI used producers' cue sheets to determine music performances for national and cable TV performances. All three used *TV Guide* to calculate TV local performances. However, today all three Pro's used digital monitoring of actual broadcasts to determine fee structures and royalty payments.

Blanket License Fees

Fees for blanket licenses are determined by weighing various factors, including the type of media (radio, TV, etc.), the size of the prospective broadcast audience (national, local, etc.), and the type of performance (music in movies, TV shows, theme music, etc.). None of the performance rights organizations sample hotels and concerts for violations. However, many business owners are not aware of the copyright law and their obligation to pay for the music they use in the daily operation of their businesses. Many become frustrated when confronted with a bill for the music they thought was free. However, once the law is explained, most understand why the copyright owner should be paid. License fees are estimated and issued on the size of the facility's potential occupancy rate and the use of the music (CDs being played, live band, etc.).[263]

---

[259] M. William Krasilovsky, and Sydney Shemel, *This Business of Music*, 10th ed. (New York, NY: Billboard Books, 142).

[260] ASCAP, "Common Licensing Terms," http://www.ascap.com/licensing/termsdefined.html, (accessed January 30, 2011).

[261] BPI, "About Us," http://www.bpi.co.uk/category/about-us.aspx, (accessed July 18, 2010).

[262] M. William Krasilovsky, and Sydney Shemel, *This Business of Music*, 10th ed. (New York, NY: Billboard Books, 143).

[263] ASACP, "Costumer Licenses," http://www.ascap.com/licensing/licensingfaq.html, (accessed July 19, 2010).

Payment Rates and Schedules

ASCAP and BMI pay competitively but not equally for the same chart placement. Different levels of payment are offered for different genres of music. To make it even more confusing, ASCAP and BMI do not pay the same amount of money for songs within the same genre. In other words, due to the way the charts are compiled by the PROs payment scheme methodology and competition from the other PROs, some records receive more airplay (performances, and therefore, money) than others.[264]

Performance Rights Organizations (PRO's)

Performance rights organizations collect *blanket licenses fees as performance royalties* from the users of music in a public performance for their affiliated writers and publishers. *The American Society of Composers, Authors, and Publishers (ASCAP), Broadcast Music, Incorporated (BMI),* and *SESAC* are the three American performance rights organizations. Over the last few years, ASCAP and BMI have each collected about $900 million from issuing blanket licenses (ASCAP reported $990 million collected in 2009[265] and BMI declared $917 million).[266] About 30% to 60% of the royalties collected are from foreign sources, depending on the types of media and catalog. A number one song on American Top 40 or country formatted radio stations is worth about $500,000 with half going to the publisher(s) and the other half sent to the writer(s), depending on how the original deal is structured (sometimes the publisher(s) request writers to allow the money to be sent to them and then they deduct expenses). Don't do that! ASCAP distributed $860.4 million to songwriters and music publishers out of the $990 million collected, spending the remaining 13.2% on operations and administrations.[267] BMI distributed $789 million out of the $917 collected.[268] Operation expenses for the PROs vary from about 12-16% depending on various annual advances in technology and business model structure. SESAC is more selective with its affiliation process for writers and music publishers; is a for-profit organization and collects much less money then ASCAP and BMI. However, because of the productivity of its writers and music publishers and because it has fewer of them to pay, SESAC's administrative expenses are much less and thus, it pays similar royalty rates as the other PROs.[269]

ASCAP

The American Society of Composers, Authors and Publishers was formed in 1914 to help music publishers and songwriters collect their public performance royalties. It is a nonprofit organization owned and operated by its 460,000 songwriters and music publisher members.[270] All three Performance Rights Organizations in the

---

[264] Personal interviews with industry leaders (1985-2010).

[265] ASCAP, "Annual Report 2009," http://www.ascap.com/about/annualReport/annual_2009.pdf, (accessed January 30, 2011).

[266] BMI, "Annual Report 2009-10," http://www.bmi.com/pdfs/publications/2010/annual_review_0910.pdf, (accessed January 30, 2011).

[267] ASCAP, "Annual Report 2009," http://www.ascap.com/about/annualReport/annual_2009.pdf, (accessed January 30, 2011).

[268] BMI, "Annual Report 2009-10," http://www.bmi.com/pdfs/publications/2010/annual_review_0910.pdf, (accessed January 30, 2011).

[269] Personal interviews with industry leaders (2005-2010).

[270] ASCAP, About, http://www.ascap.com, (accessed June 4, 2013).

United States represent songwriters and music publishers to collect public performance royalties owed the writers and copyright owners.[271]

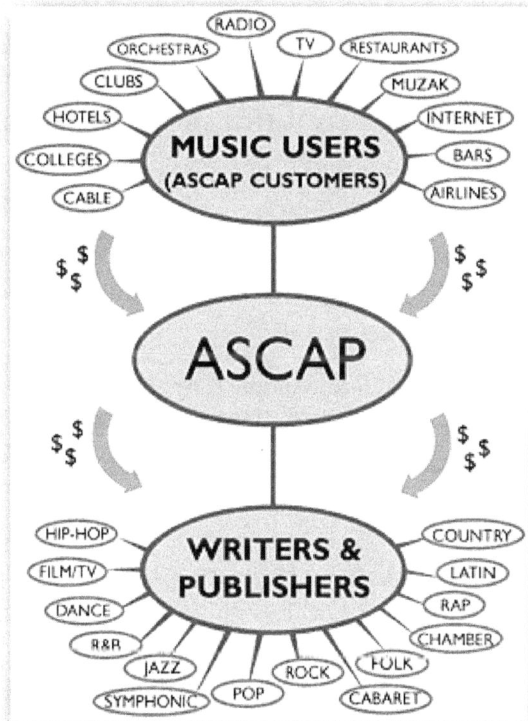

This includes songs used in businesses such as radio stations airplay, radio, TV and cable networks, websites, concert halls and venues, sports arenas, clubs, bars, malls, skating rinks, and many other types of businesses. All three PRO's use their own ways to analyze the value of a performance (which in this case means the use of a song).

The old methods of random samples of provided logs, recordings, and payments off of trade magazine chart placements have been updated to digital analysis of "captured" broadcast signals. The digital analysis is very accurate and thus payments are better than in the old days of estimated uses. Cue sheets are used for TV broadcast and other methods are used for night club song performances.

According to www.ascap.com 2013, ASCAP claims to collect the most money of the three PRO's and uses a "follow the dollar" principle payment system.[272] [273]

> *The annual rate depends on the type of business. Generally, rates are based on the manner in which music is performed (live, recorded or audio only or audio/visual) and the size of the establishment or potential audience for the music. For example, rates for restaurants, nightclubs, bars and similar establishments depend on whether the music is live or recorded, whether it's audio only or audio visual, the number of nights per week music is offered, whether admission is charged and several other factors.*
>
> *Concert rates are based on the ticket revenue and seating capacity of the facility. Rates for music used by corporations ("Music In Business") are based upon the number of employees. College and university rates are based upon the number of full time students; retail store rates depend on the number of speakers and square footage. Hotel rates are based on a percentage of entertainment expenses for live music and an additional charge if recorded music is used.*
>
> *Because ASCAP has over a hundred different licenses and rate schedules, one will likely fit your needs. ASCAP operates under the principle that similarly situated users should be treated similarly. This assures fairness and consistency in our licensing. For example, rates for restaurants of the same size, with the same use of music are the same regardless of whether the restaurant is in Oshkosh or New York City.*[274]

---

271 ASCAP, "Keeping Track of Performances." http://www.ascap.com/members/payment/keepingtrack.aspx, (Accessed June 6, 2013).

272 ASCAP, About, http://www.ascap.com, (accessed June 4, 2013).

273 ASCAP, ASCAP Payment System, "Identifying Sources," http://www.ascap.com/members/payment/identifying.aspx, (Accessed June 6, 2013).

274 ASCAP Licenses Help, http://www.ascap.com/licensing/licensingfaq.aspx#general, (accessed July 24, 2013).

Use Weight	X	Licensee Weight	X	"Follow the Dollar" Factor	X	Time of Day Weight	X	General Licensing Allocation

+

Radio Feature Premium Credits

(for radio performances only where applicable)

+

TV Premium Credits

(for performances in highly rated series, where applicable)

=

Credits

The "credits" are multiplied by the share which is multiplied by the credit value to equal the royalty. That number is divided into the total amount of royalties collected minus the cost of doing business to determine the amount of royalties paid to the writers and publishers.[275] [276]

BMI

In the late 1930s, ASCAP raised its fees for performance royalties for radio stations. According to *Answers.com* (2010),

> *...Three radio networks – National Broadcasting Company (NBC), Columbia Broadcasting System (CBS), and Mutual Broadcasting System – dominated the airwaves, and the music publishing business was increasingly controlled by movie studios, which needed music for their films. During the 1930s radio stations paid licensing fees based on a percentage of advertising time. This meant that ASCAP was collecting fees for any music being played but only paid those artists with whom it had agreements. ...The men and women who wrote or performed blues, ragtime, or jazz, and who did not belong to ASCAP, received no royalties even when their work was performed. ...In the fall of 1939, with the most recent ASCAP licensing agreement about to expire, leaders in the radio industry met in Chicago to discuss establishing a new licensing body for their music as a less expensive alternative to ASCAP. BMI was chartered as a nonprofit organization in October 1939 and began operating in New York City the following February. ... by the end of 1940, some 650 had signed licensing agreements with BMI.*[277]

The justice department filed a civil lawsuit alleging antitrust violations on the parts of ASCAP, BMI, NBC, and CBS. The performance rights organizations settled and radio stations returned to broadcasting music licensed by all the performance rights organizations.[278]

> *BMI was founded by radio executives to provide competition in the field of performing rights, to assure royalty payments to writers and publishers of music not represented by the existing performing right organization and to provide an alternative source of licensing for all music users.*[279]

---

[275] ASCAP, "ASCAP Payment System," http://www.ascap.com/members/payment/royalties.aspx, (Accessed June 6, 2013).

[276] ASCAP, ASCAP Payment System, "The ASCAP Surveys," http://www.ascap.com/members/payment/surveys.aspx, (Accessed June 6, 2013).

[277] Answers.com, "BMI: Some Industry Background," http://www.answers.com/topic/broadcast-music-inc, (accessed July 19, 2010).

[278] ASCAP, "The History of ASCAP: The Birth of BMI," http://www.fundinguniverse.com/company-histories/The-American-Society-of-Composers-Authors-and-Publishers-ASCAP-Company-History.html, (accessed January 30, 2011).

[279] BMI, "Tradition," http://www.bmi.com/about/entry/533105, (accessed July 19, 2011).

BMI has about 600,000 affiliate songwriters, composers, and music publisher.[280] They collects royalties from radio, TV stations, cable, new media, concerts, bars, clubs, the same places as ASCAP and SESAC. It also helps build songwriters' careers, gather licensing information, and host award shows, just as the other performance rights organizations.[281] Broadcast Music Incorporated is also a non-profit organization similar to ASCAP except it is owned by the radio stations who formed the company instead of the songwriters, publishers or composers who affiliate they businesses with it. Remember that ASCAP is owned by it's members.

BMI considers payment of a single "unit" or performance equal to 200% similar to the language found in some songwriter/music publishing deals.[282] Then, they divide the royalties into 100% to the music publishers and the other 100% to the songwriters and pay each directly.[283] They make quarterly payments in January, March, June, and September just as ASCAP and SESAC.[284] BMI's performance must be 60 seconds or longer, and they require radio stations to complete written logs in addition to digital recognition technology to assure accuracy. Royalties are based on the number of plays on the total number of stations. Songs that are played over 95,000 times in one quarter qualify for a "hit song bonus." Songs that are played over 2.5 million times and have at least 15,000 plays in one quarter receive the "standard hit bonus."[285] Theme credits are given to songs that are identified with a TV show and are used in the opening and closing credits.[286]

SESAC

SESAC is a different story. Much smaller than ASCAP or BMI, it is a privately owned for-profit business. Paul Heinecke formed SESAC in 1930 to represent European publishers and religious works. According to *SESAC.com* (2010), "SESAC was founded in New York in 1930 by German immigrant Paul Heinecke, who, to help European publishers with their American performance royalties, established SESAC as the Society of European Stage Authors and Composers."[287] It has dropped the formal name and is now known as simply SESAC. Until 1970, when they signed their first songwriters, SESAC represented only music publishers. In 1993, the family owned company was sold to Stephen Swid, Freddie Gershon, and Ira Smith, and they signed Bob Dylan and Neil Diamond as writers.[288] In addition, during the last several years, SESAC has been the

---

280 BMI, About BMI, http://www.bmi.com/about/entry/about_bmi, (accessed June 4, 2013).

281 BMI, Tradition, http://www.bmi.com/about/entry/bmi_history, (Accessed June 4, 2013).

282 BMI, U.S. Radio Royalties, http://www.bmi.com/creators/royalty/us_radio_royalties/detail, (Accessed June 4, 2013).

283 BMI, U.S. Radio Royalties, http://www.bmi.com/creators/royalty/us_radio_royalties/detail, (Accessed June 4, 2013).

284 BMI, U.S. Radio Royalties, http://www.bmi.com/creators/royalty/us_radio_royalties/detail, (Accessed June 4, 2013).

285 BMI, General Royalty Information, http://www.bmi.com/creators/royalty/general_information/detail, (accessed June 4, 2013).

286 BMI, U.S. Television Royalties, http://www.bmi.com/creators/royalty/us_television_royalties/detail, (Accessed June 4, 2013).

287 SESAC, "About SESAC: SESAC was Established in 1930, Built on Tradition, Service and Innovation," http://www.sesac.com/About/History.aspx, (Accessed July 19, 2010).

288 SESAC, "About SESAC: SESAC was Established in 1930, Built on Tradition, Service and Innovation," http://www.sesac.com/About/History.aspx, (Accessed July 19, 2010).

leading technology innovator of the performance rights organizations by using *BDS (Broadcast Data Systems)* and watermark technology for performance tracking and royalty distribution.[289]

SESAC has about 20,000 affiliate songwriters, composers, and music publisher.[290] They collects royalties from radio, TV stations, cable, new media, concerts, bars, clubs, the same places as ASCAP and BMI.[291] It also helps build songwriters' careers, gather licensing information, and host award shows, just as the other performance rights organizations. SESAC prides itself on being small and powerful as they focus on the success of their affiliate writers and music publishers.[292] In other words, while they pay similar amounts of royalties to their affiliate writers and publishers they have the highest standards for membership. Therefore, the majority of their writers and publishers are making money while only a small percent of ASCAP and BMI's are financially successful.

According to the SESAC website (2013) Their royalty formula is:

> *Performance x Affiliate Share x Bonus Factor (if their is one) equals Credits. The License Fees Available for Distribution are divided by the total Credits which equals the Value Factor Credits X Value Factor which equals the Royalty Payment.*[293]

CCLI

The *Christian Copyright Licensing International* organization was formed in 1998 to help churches comply with the requirements of the copyright law. CCLI assists religious organizations by licensing printed copies of songs and music used in over 200,000 churches worldwide with clearances for printed songs in bulletins, programs, recorded and used in visual overhead projectors for congregational singing.[294]

Monitoring

SESAC was the first to use a digital analysis system called *Broadcast Data Systems* (BDS) to calculate radio performances. The BDS monitors and digitizes an airplay performance by comparing the radio station's broadcast to a digital fingerprint of the recording stored in its data bank. If there is a correlation, the monitor tallies an airplay performance. Tuch (1997-2006) reports in *Music Media*:

> *BDS was started in 1980 in the United States. It was the brainchild of a country music writer who spent $25,000 producing and promoting a single in Florida. When making his tracking calls to a number of stations, he was told by music directors that they loved the song and were playing it in a solid rotation. However, not one copy of his album had sold. He found this somewhat odd and after doing some checking, he discovered that the stations were not telling the truth. The artist hooked up with a former defense industry*

---

[289] SESAC, "About SESAC: How Does SESAC Differ from ASCAP and BMI," http://www.sesac.com/EDU/faqs.aspx, (July 19, 2010).

[290] SESAC, About SESAC, "Writers/Publishers," http://www.sesac.com/WritersPublishers/faq.aspx, (Accessed June 6, 2013).

[291] SESAC, About SESAC "Writers/Publishers," http://www.sesac.com/WritersPublishers/HowWePay/LivePerformances.aspx, (Accessed June 6, 2013).

[292] SESAC, About SESAC, "Radio," http://www.sesac.com/WritersPublishers/HowWePay/Radio.aspx, (Accessed June, 6, 2013).

[293] About SESAC, "Other Sources, New Media," http://www.sesac.com/WritersPublishers/HowWePay/Other.aspx, (Accessed June 6, 2013).

[294] CCLI, "Who We Are," http://www.ccli.com/WhoWeAre/CompanyProfile.aspx, (accessed January 27, 2011).

> *scientist and came up with an idea to track radio stations electronically. The company was eventually purchased by the parent company of Billboard magazine.*[295]

BMI followed with its digital analysis system in 2004. In a new release, President and CEO Frances W. Preston stated that BMI's Digital Initiative

> *...Is now adding new census data for hundreds of radio stations to its existing nationwide sample of radio airplay on more than 10,000 stations which is the industry's most comprehensive. The census data will be provided through new strategic partnerships with two companies who will offer BMI complementary data: Nielsen Broadcast Data Systems (Nielsen BDS) and MediaBase. Data from these new sources will be streaming into BMI's radio performance analysis system where it will be used to enhance the scope and detail of BMI's radio royalty distributions.*[296]

ASCAP started its digital fingerprint system monitoring in 2006 with *Mediaguide*. In a news release ASCAP (2006) claimed that

> *Mediaguide provides the world's most comprehensive, accurate, timely, and reliable airplay data products. The company's information products, which span all media types, provide performers, publishers and the recording, advertising, radio, and television industries deep insight into what is being broadcast across America, in order to deliver better products that create broader consumer demand among audiences. Mediaguide, based in Berwyn, Pa., is a joint venture of the American Society of Composers, Authors and Publishers (ASCAP) and ConneXus Corporation.*[297]

Cue Sheets

The visual mass media (producers and TV networks, for example) provide the PROs with a listing of all the songs (prerecorded and live, as in award shows) in each of their productions, films, commercials, and other genres of broadcast. According to *ASCAP's Cue & A* (2007), "*RapidCue*, is a state-of-the-art application that allow production companies to enter, manage and electronically submit cue sheet data to ASCAP and BMI."[298] SESAC monitors the actual networks, local TV stations, and other broadcast providers by digitally monitoring their broadcasts with *TuneSat*.[299] It allows SESAC to drop the analysis of song performances by written cue sheets that were supplied by media producers. A SESAC news release (May 18, 2010), reported that

> *"...After a decade of industry attempts to streamline the process, tracking performances on TV is still a largely manual endeavor," said Hunter Williams, Senior Vice-President, Strategic Development with SESAC. "Cue sheets are notorious for being filed incorrectly, late, and in some cases, not at all, which adversely affects payments to songwriters and composers. We are very excited about the impact we believe TuneSat will have on improving the process and thereby increasing the accuracy in royalty reporting to rights holders."*[300]

Membership & Affiliation

---

295 Paul Tuck, "Broadcast Data Systems," Music Media, http://www.musicmedianetwork.com/diy-bds.html, (accessed July 19,2010).

296 BMI, "BMI Digital Initiatives' Project to Set Benchmarks for 21st Century Copyright Administration," http://www.bmi.com/news/entry/234045, (accessed July 19, 2010).

297 ASCAP, "ASCAP News: ASCAP"s MediaGuide has Become the New Standard in Broadcast Monitoring," http://www.ascap.com/press/2005/090705_mediaguide.html, (accessed July 19, 2010).

298 ASCAP, "Playback: Rapidcue," http://www.ascap.com/playback/2007/summer/action/rapidcue.html, (accessed July 20, 2010).

299 SESAC, "SESAC Selects TuneSet to Monitor Performance in Television Broadcasts," http://www.sesac.com/News/News_Details.aspx?id=1129, (accessed July 19, 2010).

300 SESAC, "SESAC Selects TuneSet to Monitor Performance in Television Broadcasts," http://www.sesac.com/News/News_Details.aspx?id=1129, (accessed July 19, 2010).

Songwriters and publishing companies may only affiliate with one performance rights organization at a time. Thus writers are often called ASCAP, BMI, or SESAC writers, while music publishers are ASCAP, BMI, or SESAC publishers. In reality, to get around the single affiliation situation, most publishers form three separate publishing companies with different names and affiliate each company with a different performance rights organization. BMI and SESAC writers and publishers are designated as *affiliates*, while ASCAP writers and publishers are considered *members*. ASCAP, BMI and SESAC participation requires slightly different professional writing standards of at least one song commercially published, recorded, or likely to be performed. All American PROs offer members or affiliates benefits, including career development, songwriting support, social networking, health insurance, financial advice, websites with many resources, newsletters, and awards shows for best songs and recordings.

Ringtone Statutory Rate

The *Copyright Royalty Board*, responding to a request by the RIAA (Recording Industry Association of America, Inc.), was asked two questions: (a) Does a ringtone, made available for use on a cell phone or similar device, constitute a delivery of a digital phonorecord (recording) that would require a statutory license (royalty payment), and (b) If so, what are the legal conditions and limitations on such licensing?[301] In general, the Board ruled in favor of the RIAA and declared ringtones and master tones to be excerpts of a preexisting sound that subsequently fall within the scope of the statutory license as derivative work. Music publishers and songwriters now receive a mechanical license statutory rate of $0.24 for master ringtones.[302]

Digital or Electronic Transmissions

In the past few years Congress has at last made some determinations about digital downloads and streaming and placed them under the heading of "Electronic Transmissions." The United States Copyright Royalty Judges made a final determination on Preexisting Subscription Services (PSS) and Satellite Digital Audio Radio Services (SDARS) with their "Final Determination" on February 14, 2013. According to the Final Determination (docket No. 2011-1 CRB) determined 2013; The standard for determining the rates for the "digital performance license" were calculated to achieve ;

- *To maximize the availability of creative works to the public*
- *To afford the copyright owner a fair return on his or her creative work and the copyright user a fair income under existing economic conditions.*
- *To reflect the relative roles of the copyright owner and the copyright use made available to the public with respect to relevant creative contribution, technical contribution, capital investment, cost, risk, and contribution to the opening of new markets for creative expression and media for communication.*
- *To Minimize any disruptive impact on the structure of the industries involved and generally prevailing industry parties.*[303]

Digital Royalty Rates

Royalties for *limited digital downloads* and *interactive streaming* (better known as *on-demand streams*) are difficult to determine as the royalty rates were usually paid as a percentage of the income minus various fees and other licenses and depend upon the date the companies started in business and the types of downloads or streams. It was also difficult to determine digital performance license rates, as the "fees" were really a part of a

---

[301] Library of Congress, "Copyright Office: Memorandum Opinion-In the Manner of Mechanical and Digital Phonorecords Delivery Rate Adjustment Proceedings," http://www.copyright, (accessed January 30, 2011).

[302] Library of Congress, "Copyright Office: Memorandum Opinion-In the Manner of Mechanical and Digital Phonorecords Delivery Rate Adjustment Proceedings," http://www.copyright, (accessed January 30, 2011).

[303] The United States Copyright Royalty Judges Final Determination, (Docket 2011-1), CRB (2012).

percentage as defined by different types of interactive streaming. Also, the fees are collected and paid by the company providing the digital service instead of the actual labels. The 2010 agreement complicated matter. ASCAP, BMI, and SESAC collected on passive streaming only.

UNITED STATES COPYRIGHT ROYALTY JUDGES

In the Matter of	)	
	)	
Determination of Rates and Terms for Preexisting Subscription Services and Satellite Digital Audio Radio Services	)	**Docket No. 2011-1 CRB PSS/Satellite II**
	)	

FINAL DETERMINATION

I. Introduction

The Copyright Royalty Judges ("Judges") convened this rate determination proceeding in accordance with 17 U.S.C. § 803(b) and 37 CFR § 351. On January 5, 2011, the Judges published in the *Federal Register* a notice announcing commencement of this proceeding with request for Petitions to Participate in this proceeding. The purpose of the proceeding is to determine the rates and terms of royalty payments payable by Preexisting Subscription Services ("PSS") and Satellite Digital Audio Radio Services ("SDARS") under the Copyright Act, 17 U.S.C. §§ 112 and 114. The rates and terms set in this proceeding apply to the period January 1, 2013, to December 31, 2017. Having carefully considered the relevant law and the evidence received in this proceeding, the Copyright Royalty Judges determine that the appropriate § 114(f)(1) rates for the PSS are 8% of *Gross Revenues* for 2013 and 8.5% for 2014 through 2017. The § 114(f)(1) rates for Sirius XM are 9% of *Gross Revenues* for 2013, 9.5% for 2014, 10.0% for 2015, 10.5% for 2016, and 11.0% for 2017.

Internet and Cell Phone Permanent Downloads

Sales from Amazon.com, iTunes and other providers are considered the same as buying a CD in a brick and mortar store. The music is licenses as a digital mechanical license and the rates are the same as the *Statutory Rates* or the *Controlled Composition Rates* of 75% of the *Statutory Rates.* Ring Tones are also considered a permanent download and the *Statutory Rate* is 24 cents.

Streaming on Demand

Spotify, Rhapsody, and many other *Streaming-on-Demand* providers are subscription services that require interactive streaming of recordings of songs. According to Passman (2012); it is a pretty complex set of formulas, as they cover (a) subscription streaming services, (b) subscription streaming services that are bundled with other services (c) portable services (such as cell phones), (d) non-portable services, and (e) non-subscription/advertiser-supported services.[304] The new rates from under the "Preexisting Subscription

---

304 Donald Passman, *All You Really Need to Know About the Music Business* (8th. Edition),(New York, Free Press 2012). 324.

Services" under the current final determination appear to be 8% of gross revenues for 2013 and 8.5% of gross from 2014-2017.

Non-Interactive Streaming

Satellite radio and non-interactive webcasting are collected by ASCAP, BMI, and SESAC with the royalties going to songwriters and music publishers. Payments are based on a minimum rate or a percentage of profits whichever is greater. Some of the larger companies by-pass the PRO's and negotiate their own deals with the providers.[305] Rates often vary for a number of complex political reasons, however, in general according to Passman (2012), they use to range from 10.5% of subscription fees, 10.5% of gross advertising or if the labels pays the publisher 17%-18% and 21%-22% if the provider pays a label for the master. [306] However under the 2013 "Final Determination" the rates under the "Preexisting Subscription Services" appear to be 8% of gross revenues for 2013 and 8.5% of gross from 2014-2017.

Bundled Providers/Services

When you purchase a music provider with your cell phone service then you're getting more than just the use of the cell phone for calls. The music services are part of what you're subscribing to when paying your phone bill. The companies offer the services "free" yet money still has to be paid (usually by them out of your payment) to the copyright owners. According to Passman (2012); a mixed service bundle is similar to a permanent usable song download and a music bundle is similar to two or music products together such as all the songs on a CD or music and a ringtone together. Rates use to vary from 11%-12% to 21%-22% depending on who's paying whom.[307] Under the 2013 "Final Determination" the rates under the "Preexisting Subscription Services" appear to be 8% of gross revenues for 2013 and 8.5% of gross from 2014-2017.

Clouds or "Locked" Services

The wave of the future are "cloud services" where you can get any song or movie, game, etc., you want at any time and place you want it on any device you own. Amazon.com, Apple with it's cloud store and others allow you to store (or backup) your previously purchased entertainment product on their servers. You pay a small fee for the storage space. They do not have to pay copyright royalties as you own it and are just leasing space or a place to save it. Full locker cloud servers provide access to entertainment products they own on their servers. This is similar to renting a CD from a red box machine in your local store or a video from Amazon.com or Netflixs. Now you have to pay a subscription or usage fee and they (the server or cloud company) have to pay the label of movie company for "leasing" the entertainment product. According to Passman, (2012) fees are roughly 17 cents per-subscriber per-month or 12%-20.65% of the amount the labels

---

[305] Donald Passman, *All You Really Need to Know About the Music Business* (8th. Edition),(New York, Free Press 2012). 254-256.

[306] Donald Passman, *All You Really Need to Know About the Music Business* (8th. Edition),(New York, Free Press 2012). 254-255.

[307] Donald Passman, *All You Really Need to Know About the Music Business* (8th. Edition),(New York, Free Press 2012). 257-258.

charge for the product whichever is greater.[308] Then, the labels or entertainment production companies have to pay a the publisher the lower or higher amount based on how much money it has grossed.

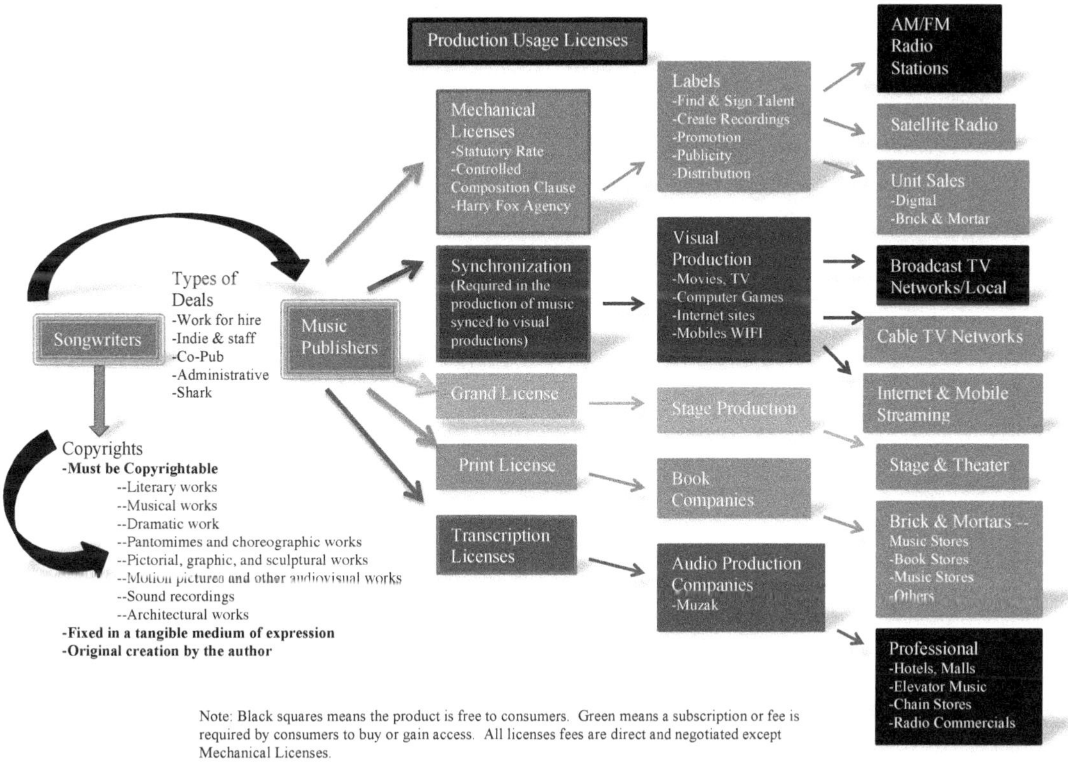

Video Streaming

Video streaming is a different matter as the Copyright Office doesn't control www.YouTube, Vevo or other video streaming services as they do not fit the definition of requiring a *compulsory licenses*. Therefore, the server companies (such as YouTube) have to strike a deal with each label or mega entertainment corporation. Now you know why sometimes video's are missing from YouTube. The label or music companies have demanded more royalties for their songs and recordings (which is usually a percentage of their income from advertisements) and if they do not pay, then they make them pull the videos.

---

[308] Donald Passman, *All You Really Need to Know About the Music Business* (8th. Edition),(New York, Free Press 2012). 258-259.

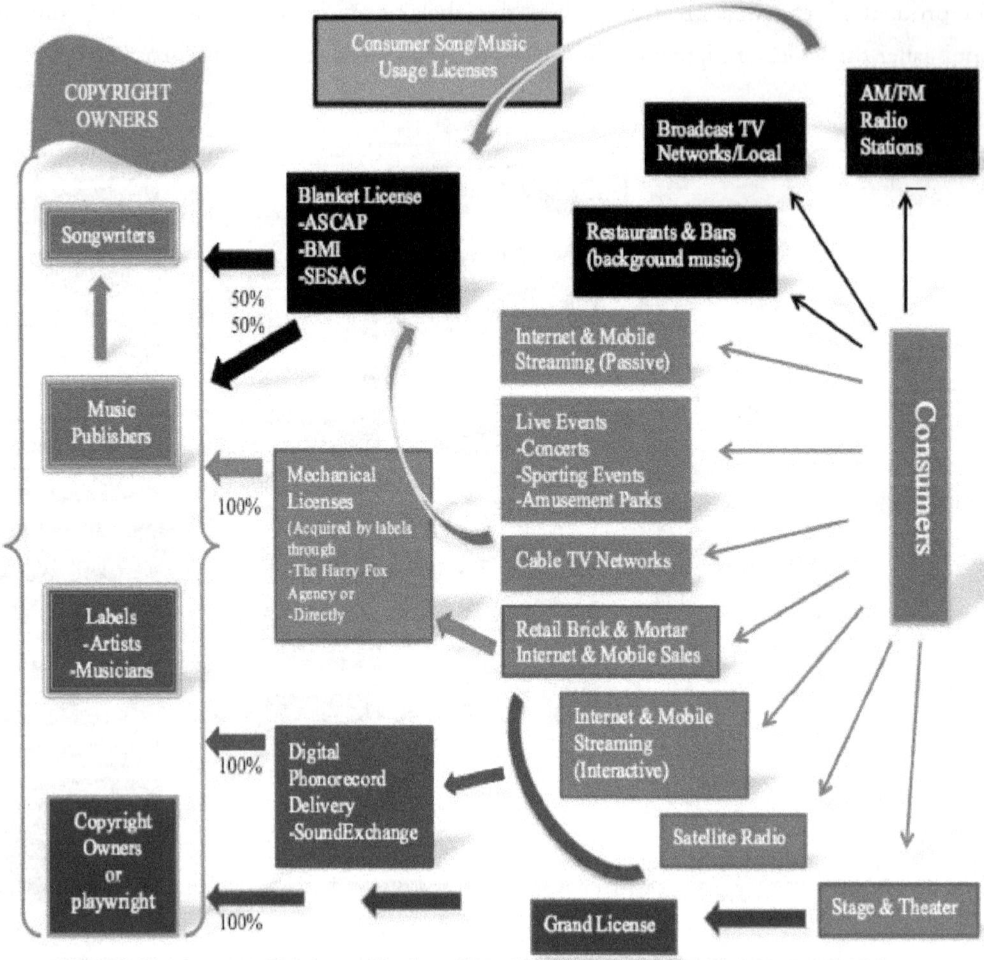

Note: A black arrow from the consumer means the product is free. Green means a subscription or fee is required to buy or gain access. Blanket license royalties are split 50/50 and checks are paid directly to the writers and publishers. All other royalties are paid directly to the copyright owner.

Apps & Podcasts

Here's where the money is pennies as, in most cases, it cost more to collect the penny royalties than its worth. Apps may offer recordings by the thousands, yet their deal with the music publishing companies is often a percentage of the income from the sale of the Apps times the number of plays, limited to only the first three months.[309] After that it's free. Podcasts usually limit their music or recordings to less then 30 seconds and then argue that the playing of the music is for promotional purposes and therefore free.

Satellite Digital Audio Services

Sirius XM satellite radio rates are now 9% of gross revenues for 2013, 9.5% for 2014, 10% for 2015, 10.5% for 2016 and 11% of gross revenues in 2017.[310]

---

[309] Donald Passman, *All You Really Need to Know About the Music Business* (8th. Edition),(New York, Free Press 2012). 258-262.

[310] The United States Copyright Royalty Judges Final Determination, (Docket 2011-1), CRB (2012).

Print License

A print license is used to secure payments to the music publishers and songwriters of sheet music, music books, arrangements, and folios. The songwriter usually receives about 10-15% of the money collected from the suggested retail list price of the material sold. Print or sheet music in most countries is often handled by a specialized administrative publisher who prints the sheet music, catalogs, and folios and distributes them to retail outlets.[311]

Transcription License

There are two types of Transcription Licenses: (a) background music providers such as *Muzak* who provide background (elevator) music to trade organizations and (b) radio stations that broadcast syndicated programs or use background music in radio commercials. Trade organizations license the use of the music to individual hotels, restaurants, malls, and retail stores. The trade organizations often contact companies to rerecord popular music in very mellow arrangements to sway consumer moods and encourage buying. Elevator music is suppose to help the riders maintain a pleasant mood even when they are packed tightly together in a very small space moving quickly up and down inside a building. The cost of the subscription service depends on the number of retail outlets, size, and consumer traffic in the stores. Muzak and 3M negotiate directly with the music publishers or through The Harry Fox Agency for the licenses and fee rates. After rerecording the songs, they negotiate a lease or purchase fee with the retail outlets and trade organizations.[312]

The use of music in radio background music, commercials, and syndicated shows hits us everything we turn on a radio. Sync licenses are required *in the production of* visual entertainment products before distribution for sale. Same thing applies in radio, except it's an *electronic transcription license* required *in the production of* a non-visual syndicated show, background music, or radio commercial before it is aired.[313]

Fintage House & Neighboring Rights

Fintage House is a foreign company that serves the entertainment industry for "rights exploitation and financial services." In the music industry, it collects royalties from all the existing foreign national agencies and royalties in non-represented territories. Besides music publishing and digital rights exploitation, it also directly represents artists in the collection of "master ownership and neighboring rights" which in the United

---

[311] Hillsidemusic.com, "License Types," http://www.hillsongmusic.com/publishing/types, (accessed March 9, 2011).

[312] Al Kohn & Bob Kohn, *Kohn on Music Licensing*, Google Books. Transcription Licensing, http://books.google.com/books?id=rMFSUTNWRzgC&pg=PT431&lpg=PT431&dq=TRANSCRIPTION+LICENSE&source=bl&ots=RIYsuflJlw&sig=0g0dBQGBvMtoAFQ4f6BJZnZUP88&hl=en&ei=YwJGTIizIcKqlAfsrvmPBA&sa=X&oi=book_result&ct=result&resnum=8&ved=0CDkQ6AEwBw%2522%20%255Cl%20%2522v=onepage&q=TRANSCRIPT#v=onepage&q=TRANSCRIPT&f=false, (accessed March 9, 2011).

[313] Al Kohn & Bob Kohn, *Kohn on Music Licensing*, Google Books: Radio Transcription Licensing, http://books.google.com/books?id=rMFSUTNWRzgC&pg=PT429&lpg=PT429&dq=radio+transcription+licenses&source=bl&ots=RIZktgfMmy&sig=bxyFiuAi1GlRSJ4Epkalai5I2iE&hl=en&ei=GxFjTN7ZJ8OclgeDrOStCg&sa=X&oi=book_result&ct=result&resnum=1&ved=0CBgQ6AEwAA%2522%20%255Cl%20%2522v=onepage&q=rad#v=onepage&q=rad&f=false, (accessed March 9, 2011).

States are usually collected by Sound Exchange.[314] According to *Fintage.com* and their American representative Bruce Lampcov (2011),

> *An owner of the master rights in a sound recording (record label or individual) are entitled to royalties for the primary use of the sound recording from sales, downloads and synchronization licenses. In addition the rights owner can be entitled to performance royalties for the secondary use of their sound recording, for instance when their sound recording is being broadcast on radio and TV or transmitted digitally. ... These rights in the copyright of a sound recording are called 'neighboring rights' as they are 'neighboring' to copyrights in a song. Royalties are collected and distributed pre dominantly in Europe by societies such as PPL, SENA and GVL and a digital counterpart in the USA (SoundExchange). Fintage has the infrastructure to collect neighboring rights directly at source from each territory worldwide. With these direct collections comes the ability to manage and control an artist's repertoire and to speed up the flow of money for our clients.*

Fintage House arranges and collects licenses fees for the film industry in international digital, secondary, and music publishing rights. They also directly represent talent (recording and movie stars) in international recording and publishing rights, image, merchandising, and digital rights. The financial services side of the company manages catalogs and connects venture capitalists to creative teams such as film producers, directors and others.

Summary

Music publishing is a gamble. While nobody knows which songs will become hit recordings, there are several "sources" of revenue for songwriters and music publishers in the music business. They include *Mechanical Licenses*, which are offered directly by music publishers or through a mechanical rights collection agency (such as The Harry Fox Agency) who represents the publishers. They collect royalties from record labels for the use of songs on albums, CDs, digital downloads, cell phone ringtones, and master ring tones. Royalties are paid to the publishers who recoup advances out of the songwriter's share. Royalties are split and paid (after commissions) separately to the songwriter (share) and a music publisher (share). Other revenue sources include;

Print Licenses, used for printing and selling sheet music in retail outlets;

Sync Licenses for songs used in the production of mass media TV, motion pictures, and Internet videos; *Transcription Licenses* for songs used in hotels, restaurants, and other business chains; Electronic Transcription Licenses for songs used in non-visual advertisements such as radio commercials; and

Blanket Licenses issued by ASCAP, BMI and SESAC in the United States for the public performance of songs in businesses such as bars, nightclubs, radio and TV broadcasts stations.

Major music publishers have their own departments to handle specific tasks or sub-out duties to administrative publishers and co-publishers in exchange for part of the royalties collected. Acquisitions Dept. is always searching for new songs and writers to sign. Attorneys or legal assistants work in Business Affairs, negotiating with writers the agreements in the single song contracts. Publishers file a Certificate of Registration or Recordation with the Copyright Office in the Library of Congress, depending on previous registrations. However, the most important part of a music publishing company is the Creative Department, consisting of staff writers who are paid a draw plus royalties to write a quota of acceptable songs. SoundExchange collects *digital license* royalties for the *recording of a song* transmitted interactively over digital

---

[314] Fintage House "Our Businesses," Fintage.com, http://www.fintagehouse.com/basic.php?sid=12&ptid=2, (accessed June 9, 2011), and personal interview with Bruce Lampcov, Los Angles, CA (June 1, 2011).

media such as the Internet and cell phones. Money is paid to performers, labels and artists instead of the music publishers and songwriters. The types of licenses include:

Mechanical – songs used in an audio reproduction and distribution for sale by labels.

Digital Mechanical – songs used in the interactive streaming of digital music over the Internet and mobile devices.

Sync (synchronization) – songs used in a visual production and distribution (as examples movies, TV shows, websites, computer animation games).

Master License – the recording of songs used in films, commercials and other visual media. A Sync License is obtained from the copyright owner (usually the publisher) for the use of the song in a visual media, whereas the Master License is the use of the recording of the song in a visual media. As an example, to use the original recording of a song in a movie two licenses are required, a Sync License from the publisher and a Master License from the Label or copyright holder of the recording.

Blanket (Analog Public Performance) – songs used in the operation of a business (radio station airplay, broadcast in a movie on network and local TV stations, live performance in bars, concerts).

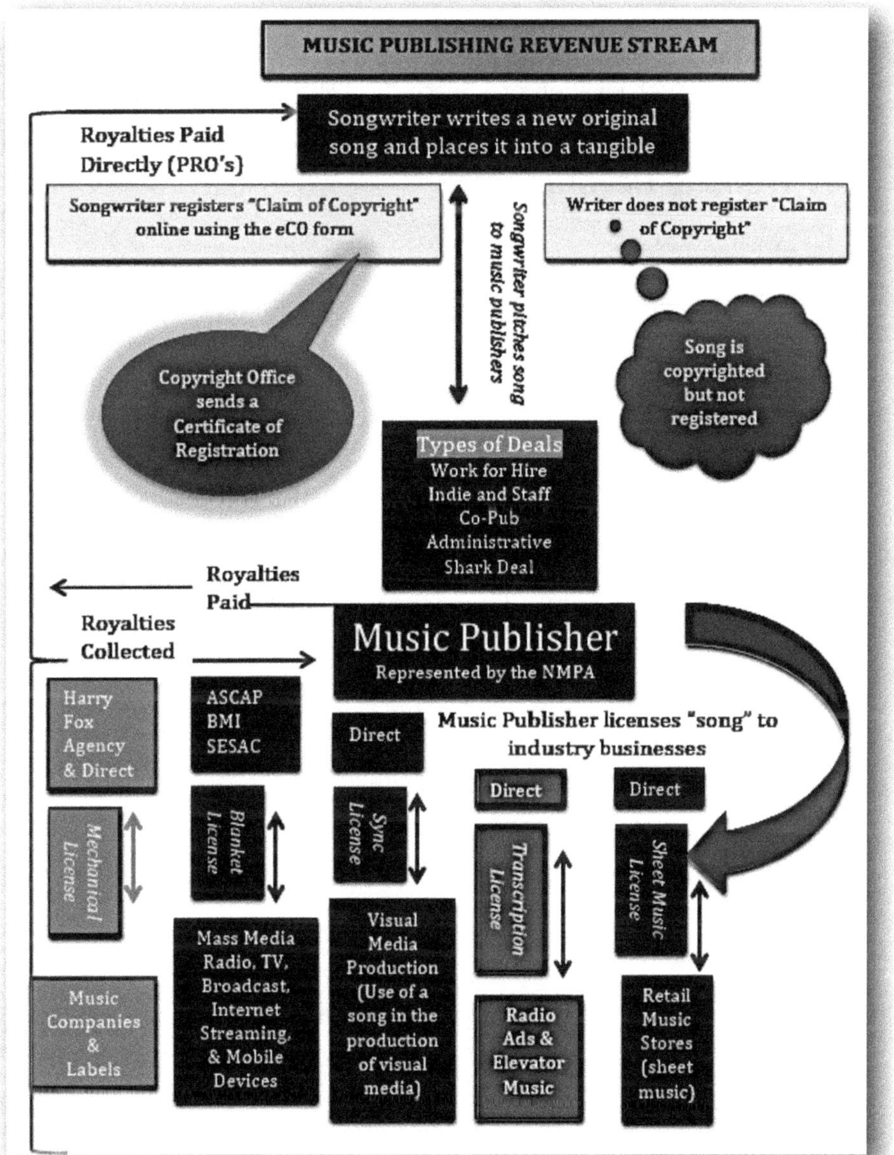

Digital Public Performance – (Satellite radio and Internet passive streaming) – songs used in the business of satellite broadcasting, (such as Sirius XM), cable TV music channels, and local radio stations being transmitted over the Internet and mobile devices qualify for this new license requirement.[315]

---

[315] Library of Congress, Mechanical and Digital Phonorecord Delivery Compulsory License," http://www.copyright, (accessed January 30, 2011).

The *Digital Performance License* shadows the worlds traditional standards of collecting royalties for radio station airplay of song recordings where the money collected is paid to the actual recording artists, musicians, labels and other. However, in the United States royalties are only collected from passive transmissions of radio station broadcast also being transmitted through the Internet and satellite radio. Traditional radio station analog broadcasts over the public airwaves are still exempt from this license requirement.

SoundExchange collects and pays the royalties to the labels, artists and musicians.[316]

Print – used for music sheets, books, arrangements, and folios.

Transcription – a combination of a mechanical and performance license used by companies to rerecord hits and then sell or transmit copies for in-store broadcast at hotel chains, malls, and retail stores.

Key Website Resources

http://www.ascap.com/

http://www.bmi.com/

http://www.harryfox.com/

http://www.nmpa.org/

http://www.sesac.com/

http://www.soundexchange.com/

---

[316] SoundExchange, "SoundExchange Is," http://www.soundexchange.com/, (accessed January 30, 2011).

8

The Single Song Agreement[317]

This Agreement is made as of this day of, 2010, by and between ______________, whose address is ______________, ("Writer") and ("Publisher") whose address is ______________________________.

1. Assignment of Copyright

1.1 With respect to the following musical composition(s) ("Original Works")

TITLE	WRITER(S)	PERCENTAGES

WRITER does hereby agree to and does assign and transfer to PUBLISHER all rights of whatsoever nature known, or which may hereafter come into existence, including, but not limited to the exclusive rights set forth in Title 17 U.S.C. section 106 (1977) in and to said Original Works invented, written, and conceived, arranged, composed, created or originated by WRITER and the right to secure copyrights thereon throughout the entire world in the name of PUBLISHER and all renewal and extension copyrights thereof and all right, title, and interest both legal and equitable in and to the same, it being understood and agreed that said Original Works and copyrights thereof and each and every right in said Original Works, whether now known or hereafter to become known covering the use or any manner or type of use of said Original Works, are and shall be the sole and exclusive property of PUBLISHER.

1.2 PUBLISHER shall have the right to grant licenses for the reproduction, printing, recording, arrangement, or performance of any Original Works without restriction.

1.3 PUBLISHER shall have the right, in its sole discretion, to re-title, translate, arrange and otherwise edit, review and adapt said Original Works created hereunder. In the event said Original Work is an instrumental composition, PUBLISHER shall have the right to have lyrics written for said Original Work by a writer or writers designated by PUBLISHER, said lyrics shall require only the approval of PUBLISHER.

1.4 WRITER agrees that WRITER shall deliver to PUBLISHER Original Works created hereunder in such a form as is deemed suitable by PUBLISHER. Unless otherwise specified by PUBLISHER, any form, as established by prior course of dealings between PUBLISHER and WRITER, or usual and customary industry practices shall be deemed suitable.

2. Grant of Exclusive Rights

At PUBLISHER's request, WRITER agrees to execute an Assignment of Copyright between WRITER and PUBLISHER for every Original Work created hereunder. WRITER agrees to execute any other documents as requested by PUBLISHER to effectuate such transfer of ownership. Upon WRITER's failure to do so, PUBLISHER shall have the right pursuant to the terms and conditions hereof, to execute such separate

---

[317] Rich Hicks, *The Single Song Agreement*, by (Rush Hicks Esq.,: TN, Nashville, 2009).

agreements on behalf of WRITER. Such separate agreements shall supplement and not supersede this Agreement. In the event of any conflict between the provisions of such separate agreement and this Agreement, the provisions of this Agreement shall govern. The failure of either party to execute such separate agreement shall not affect the rights of either party.

3. Power of Attorney

WRITER hereby irrevocably constitutes, authorizes, empowers and appoints PUBLISHER, and PUBLISHER's successors and assigns, WRITER's true and lawful attorney in WRITER's name, place and stead to execute and deliver any and all documents, which PUBLISHER may from time to time deem necessary to effectuate the intent and purpose of this Agreement, this power being coupled with an interest and irrevocable for any cause or in any event. Such power of attorney shall include, without limitation, such documents as PUBLISHER deems necessary to secure to PUBLISHER and PUBLISHER's successors and assigns the worldwide copyrights for the entire term of copyright and for any and all renewals and extensions under any present or future laws throughout the world.

4. Royalties

4.1 PUBLISHER, shall pay WRITER a royalty of fifty percent (50%) of any and all sums actually received by PUBLISHER, or its authorized agent, less the following:

(a) All outstanding recoupable advances between PUBLISHER and WRITER hereunder;

(b) any administration or collection fees, foreign taxes, etc. actually charged to PUBLISHER, its authorized agents, or foreign sub-publishers;

(c) royalties payable to co-writers; and

(d) any other sums or monies due PUBLISHER by WRITER of any nature.

4.2 Royalties on foreign sales shall be payable by PUBLISHER only after PUBLISHER, or an authorized agent of PUBLISHER, has received payment in the United States in United States currency, and shall be payable at the same rate of exchange as received by PUBLISHER.

4.3 Notwithstanding anything herein to the contrary, WRITER shall not be entitled to any portion of any sums received by PUBLISHER with respect to public performance of any Original Works from any performing rights society which pays a portion of performance fees directly to writers or composers and WRITER shall receive the writer's share of public performance royalties directly from the performing rights society.

4.4 Such royalties shall be paid in instances where WRITER is or was the sole author, composer, and arranger of the Original Works. With regard to Original Works where WRITER is or was only one of two or more authors, writers, or collaborators, WRITER shall be paid only the portion of such royalties equal to WRITER's percentage of authorship of said Original Work.

4.5 PUBLISHER or any of its affiliates, subsidiaries, or parent companies shall have the right to cross-collateralize this Agreement and any previous exclusive songwriter agreement, single song agreement, arranger's agreement or similar type of agreement between WRITER and PUBLISHER or any of its affiliates, subsidiaries, or parent companies. PUBLISHER or any of its affiliates, subsidiaries, or parent companies shall also have the right to cross-collateralize Original Works created hereunder.

4.6 In the event PUBLISHER creates or causes to be created a separately copyrighted arrangement or translation of any Original Work, or in the event PUBLISHER causes to be created lyrics for an instrumental composition, WRITER agrees that PUBLISHER may pay to the author or composer of such arrangement or translation, a portion, but not exceeding one-half (1/2), of the royalties due WRITER for said Original Work. In such event WRITER shall receive such royalties due WRITER for said Original Work less such portion.

4.7 No royalties will be earned or payable on Original Works contained in any uses pursuant to paragraphs 4.6 herein;

(a) given away or furnished on a "no charge" or "service charge" basis for promotional purposes or furnished as a sales inducement or otherwise to distributors, sub-distributors, dealers and others otherwise distributed as part of promotional activities; or

(b) sold as cutouts, scrap, salvage, overstock or closeout units.

5. Writer's Name and Likeness

PUBLISHER shall have the perpetual, nonexclusive worldwide right to use and to permit others to use: WRITER's name, both legal and professional and whether presently or hereafter used by WRITER; WRITER's approved likeness; WRITER's facsimile signature; and other identification and biographical material concerning WRITER. Such use shall be for purposes of trade and otherwise, without restriction, in connection with Original Works produced hereunder.

6. Writer's Warranties

6.1 WRITER represents and warrants that WRITER has the authority to enter into and perform all the terms of this Agreement and that WRITER is under no disability, restriction or prohibition, whether contractual or otherwise, with respect to WRITER's right to execute this Agreement, to grant the rights granted by WRITER to PUBLISHER hereunder and to perform each and every term and provision hereof.

6.2 WRITER warrants that all of the lyrics and music or Original Works delivered by WRITER to PUBLISHER hereunder shall be WRITER's own original compositions or arrangements and that no part thereof shall be an imitation or copy of any other copyrighted work.

6.3 WRITER further covenants and agrees to protect and defend the right, title, and interest of PUBLISHER in said Original Works hereby sold and assigned to PUBLISHER, to the fullest extent and to hold PUBLISHER free and harmless of and from all loss, liability, and damage in any action brought against PUBLISHER by reason of the inclusion in said works of material owned or copyrighted by others or on account of WRITER's violation of any warranties contained herein. All costs, fees, and expenses paid or incurred by PUBLISHER in defending, protecting, or perfecting its title to the Original Works, and the copyright thereon, shall be charged against WRITER and deducted from all sums due or becoming due from PUBLISHER to WRITER.

7. Royalty Payments

7.1 PUBLISHER, or an authorized agent, will compute royalties and payments due on or about forty-five (45) days after the end of a calendar quarter, for that quarter, and if royalties or other payments are due WRITER, PUBLISHER will make such payments less any then non-recouped advances paid to WRITER or on WRITER's behalf pursuant to this Agreement. If WRITER has accounts of any nature with PUBLISHER or PUBLISHER's affiliates and if WRITER owes PUBLISHER or PUBLISHER's affiliates money in such accounts(s), PUBLISHER may apply all royalties or payments which might be due and payable to WRITER to reduce the balance in WRITER's account(s).

7.2 WRITER, or a Certified Public Accountant representing WRITER, shall have the right, during PUBLISHER's normal business hours, and at WRITER's expense, after giving PUBLISHER, or an authorized agent of PUBLISHER, at least thirty (30) days advance notice in writing, to examine PUBLISHER's, or an authorized agent of PUBLISHER, books and records insofar as they pertain to the royalties or payments payable to WRITER.

7.3 Any payments to be made to WRITER hereunder shall be made to WRITER at the address set forth at the beginning of this Agreement. PUBLISHER shall make payment by a single check made payable to WRITER, or such agent as WRITER may designate in writing in accordance with the provisions of this Agreement governing notices.

7.4 All statements and all accounts rendered to WRITER hereunder shall be binding upon WRITER and not subject to any objection for any reason whatsoever unless specified objections in writing, setting forth the basis thereof, is given to PUBLISHER, or PUBLISHER's authorized agent, within two (2) years from the date the statement is rendered. No action, audit, or proceeding of any kind or nature may be instituted or maintained by WRITER with respect to any statements recorded hereunder unless such action or proceeding is commenced within one (1) year after delivery of such written objection by WRITER to PUBLISHER.

8. Suits and Actions Involving Original Works

PUBLISHER shall have the sole right to prosecute, defend, settle and compromise all suits and actions respecting the Original Works, and generally to do and perform all things necessary to prevent and restrain the infringement of copyrights therein or other rights with respect to the Original Works. If PUBLISHER recovers any moneys as a result of a judgment or settlement, the moneys shall be apportioned between PUBLISHER and WRITER fifty percent (50%) for PUBLISHER and fifty percent (50%) for WRITER pro-rated by WRITER's portion of ownership, if any, in the Original Works, after first deducting the expense of obtaining the moneys, including attorney's fees. WRITER shall have the right to obtain counsel for WRITER, but at WRITER's own expense, to assist in any such matter. Any judgments against PUBLISHER and any settlements by PUBLISHER of claims against it, respecting the Original Works, together with costs and expenses including attorney's fees, shall be covered by the indemnity provisions.

9. Indemnification

WRITER hereby agrees to and does hereby indemnify, save, and hold PUBLISHER harmless from any damages, liabilities, costs, losses and expenses including legal costs and attorney's fees arising out of or connected with any claim, demand, or action by a third party which is inconsistent with any of the warranties, representations, or covenants made by WRITER in this Agreement. WRITER agrees to reimburse PUBLISHER, on demand, for any payment made by PUBLISHER at any time with respect to any such damage, liability, cost, loss or expense to which WRITER's indemnity applies. PUBLISHER shall notify WRITER of any such claim, demand, or action promptly after PUBLISHER has been formally advised thereof. Pending the determination of any such claim, demand, or action, PUBLISHER shall have the right, at PUBLISHER's election, to withhold payment of any moneys otherwise payable to WRITER under this or any other Agreement between WRITER and any of PUBLISHER's affiliates.

10. Notices

All notices to be given to WRITER or PUBLISHER hereunder shall be addressed WRITER or PUBLISHER at the addresses set forth on page 1 or at such other address as WRITER or PUBLISHER shall designate in writing from time to time. All notices shall be in writing and shall either be served by personal delivery, mail, or telegraph, all charges prepaid. Except as otherwise provided herein, such notices shall be deemed given when personally delivered, mailed or delivered to a telegraph office, all charges prepaid, except that notices of change of address shall be effective only after actual receipt thereof.

11. Entire Agreement

This Agreement sets forth the entire understanding between WRITER and PUBLISHER concerning the subject matter hereof. No modification, amendment, waiver, termination or discharge of this Agreement or of any of the terms or provisions hereof shall be binding upon either party unless confirmed by a written instrument signed by WRITER and by a duly authorized officer of PUBLISHER. No waiver by WRITER or PUBLISHER of any term or provision of this Agreement or of any default shall affect WRITER's or PUBLISHER's respective rights thereafter to enforce such term or provision or to exercise any right to remedy in the event of any other default, whether or not similar.

If any portion of this Agreement shall be held void, voidable, invalid, or inoperative, no other provision of this Agreement shall be affected as a result thereof, and, accordingly, the remaining provisions of this Agreement shall remain in full force and effect as through such void, voidable, invalid, or inoperative provision had not been contained herein.

12. Notice of Breach

Before PUBLISHER or WRITER may assert that the other is in default in performing any obligation contained herein, the party alleging the default must advise the other in writing of the specific facts constituting default and the specific obligation breached. The other party shall be allowed a period of thirty, (30) days after receipt of such written notice to cure the default. No breach of any obligation shall be deemed to be incurable during such thirty, (30) day period.

13. Relationship of Parties

Nothing herein contained shall constitute a partnership or a joint venture between WRITER and PUBLISHER. Neither party here to shall hold itself out contrary to the terms of this paragraph and neither WRITER or PUBLISHER shall become liable for any representation, act, or omission of the other contrary to these provisions. This Agreement shall not be deemed to give any right or remedy to any third party whatsoever unless said right or remedy is specifically granted by PUBLISHER in writing to such third party.

14. Binding Effect and Benefit of Agreement

This Agreement shall be binding upon and shall inure to the benefit of PUBLISHER and its designees, successors, and assigns, as well as to WRITER or his heirs, executors, administrators, personal representatives and/or assigns.

15. Assignment

PUBLISHER may assign, license or otherwise transfer to any other entity any or all of PUBLISHER's rights, privileges and property under this Agreement including, without limitation, the right to WRITER's services. In the event of any assignment, the obligations of PUBLISHER shall be binding upon any such assignee or assignees for the express benefit of PUBLISHER and WRITER.

16. Controlling Law

This contract shall be deemed to have been made in the State of Tennessee, and its validity, construction, and effect shall be governed by the laws of said state. Any disputes arising between the parties shall be brought in the state and/or federal courts located in Nashville, Davidson County, Tennessee.

IN WITNESS WHEREOF, the parties hereto have executed this Agreement and the accompanying Schedules and Appendices as of the date first written above.

PUBLISHER: ____

WRITER: ____

Name:

Social Security No:

Date of Birth:

Copyright Assignment

For and in consideration of the mutual covenants, promises and undertakings set forth in separate publishing agreements between ________________ (WRITER) and ________________, with respect to the composition(s) described below, WRITER assigns, transfers, sets over and conveys to ________________, all WRITER's right, title, and interest in and to the following musical composition(s):

TITLE WRITER(S) PERCENTAGES

The within assignment, transfer and conveyance includes, without limitation, the lyrics, music and title of said composition(s) any and all works derived therefrom, the United States and worldwide copyright therein, and any renewals or extensions thereof, and any and all other rights that WRITER now has or to which WRITER may become entitled under existing or subsequently enacted federal, state or foreign laws, including, without limitation, the following rights: to reproduce the composition(s) in copies or phonorecords, to prepare derivative works based upon the composition(s), to distribute copies or phonorecords of the compositions, and to perform and display the compositions publicly. The within grant further includes any and all causes of action for infringement of the compositions, past, present, and future, and all proceeds from the foregoing accrued and unpaid and hereafter accruing.

THIS ASSIGNMENT IS EFFECTIVE THE ______ DAY OF ____________, _____.

WRITER: ____

STATE OF TENNESSEE

COUNTY OF DAVIDSON

Personally appeared before me, a Notary Public in and for said county and state, WRITER, the within named publisher, with whom I am personally acquainted, and who acknowledge execution of the foregoing Assignment of Copyright for the purposes therein contained.

Witness my hand and official seal at office on this ______ day of ____________, _____.

My commission expires: ____.

Notary Public

9

Action Pack

Analyzing Songwriter/Music Publishing Contracts

Music publishers offer several types of single song contracts depending on negotiating copyright ownership, and the royalty splits between the songwriter(s) and music publisher(s). Many songwriters give up their ownership rights (at first) until they become famous and have enough "power" to retain part of it through CO or Administrative deals. The following chart give us a summary of each of the "sections" in a typical single song contract.

Action Negotiation Point	**What it means**	**Type of Deal**	**What Happens (What each usually retain)** × **Songwriter** | √ **Music Publisher**
Assignment of Copyright	List names of writers and music publisher and the Percentage of the Songwriting Share they will receive. 1 States writers are transferring all ownership and exclusive rights (all 6 of them) to music publisher. 2 Gives music publisher the right to grant licenses for the reproduction, printing, recording, arrangement, or performance without restriction. 3 Publisher has sole discretion, to re-title, translate, arrange and otherwise edit, review and adapt or change the original work in order to licenses it without songwriters permission. 4 How the song is to be delivered correctly in form and media to the music publisher.	[] Work for HIre	[×] One time Payment [√] Songwriters Royalties (100% of share to publisher) [√] Music Publishers Royalties (100% of share to publisher) [√] Music Publisher (100% owner of Copyright)
		[] Staff or Indie Deal	[×]Songwriters Royalties (100% of share/50% of total income) [√] Music Publishers Royalties (100% of share/50% of total income) [√] Music Publisher (100% owner of Copyright)
		[] Co Pub Deal	[×]Songwriter Royalties (100% of share/50% of total) Plus, [×] Music Publishers Royalties (50% of share/25% of total to songwriter who is also a publisher) [√] Music Publishers Royalties (50% of share/25% of total) [×] Songwriter (50% owner of Copyright) [√] Music Publisher (50% owner of Copyright)
		[] Administrative Deal	[×]Songwriters Royalties (100% of share/50% of total) Plus, [×] Music Publishers Royalties (50% of share/25% of total) [√] Music Publisher Royalties (50% of share/25% of total) [×] Songwriter (100% owner of Copyright}
		[] Shark Deal	[√] Songwriter pays publisher and gives up all royalties and copyright ownership

<table>
<tr><th>Action
Negotiation Point</th><th>What it means</th><th>Type of Deal</th><th>What Happens
(What each usually retain)
× Songwriter | √ Music Publisher</th></tr>
<tr><td rowspan="5">Grant of Exclusive Rights</td><td rowspan="5">Songwriter gives music publisher all exclusive rights which are;

1 Reproduction (make copies)

2 Distribution (Distribute for sale and promotion)

3 Derivative (Made a new copyright such as a film or TV show based on the original copyrighted song)

4 Public Performance (song used in a recording played in a business such as a night club, arena, broadcast on radio or TV in a recording or in a movie, advertisement, etc.)

5 Public Display (song lyrics sold on a T-shirt as example)

6 Public Performance be means of digital transmission (Satellite radio, internet transmissions such as Pandora).

Music publishers then license the song to music users by issuing licenses in exchange for money (fee) which are called royalties when collected by the music publisher or collection agency such as ASCAP, BMI, SESAC, The Harry Fox AGENCY, or SoundExchange.</td><td>[] Work for HIre</td><td>[√] Reproduction
[√] Distribution
[√] Derivative
[√] Public Performance
[√] Public Display
[√] Public Performance by audio digital transmission
[] Mixture or limited rights</td></tr>
<tr><td>[] Staff or Indie Deal</td><td>[√] Reproduction
[√] Distribution
[√] Derivative
[√] Public Performance
[√] Public Display
[√] Public Performance by audio digital transmission
[] Mixture or limited rights</td></tr>
<tr><td>[] Co Pub Deal</td><td>[] Reproduction
[] Distribution
[] Derivative
[] Public Performance
[] Public Display
[] Public Performance by audio digital transmission
[×] [√] Mixture or limited rights to each (shared)</td></tr>
<tr><td>[] Administrative Deal</td><td>[] Reproduction
[] Distribution
[] Derivative
[] Public Performance
[] Public Display
[] Public Performance by audio digital transmission
[×] [√] Mixture or limited rights to each (shared)</td></tr>
<tr><td>[] Shark Deal</td><td>[√] Song is not usually distributed, all rights given to publisher if distributed</td></tr>
</table>

Action Negotiation Point	**What it means**	**Type of Deal**	**What Happens (What each usually retain)** × **Songwriter | √ Music Publisher**
Power of Attorney	Songwriter gives music publisher legal right to use his or her name to place, license, sell, and execute and deliver any and all documents needed to lease, license or sell compositions	[] Work for HIre	[] Limited Control [√] Total and irrevocable control of all required documents to music publisher
		[] Staff or Indie Deal	[] Limited Control [√] Total and irrevocable control of all required documents to music publisher
		[] Co Pub Deal	[×] Limited Control to Songwriter who is also a publisher Or [×] [√] Mixture or limited rights to each (shared)
		[] Administrative Deal	[√] Total and irrevocable Control of all required documents. [] Limited Control
		[] Shark Deal	[] Limited Control [√] Total and irrevocable control of all required documents to music publisher

Action Negotiation Point	**What it means**	**Type of Deal**	**What Happens** **(What each usually retain)** × **Songwriter | √ Music Publisher**
Royalties	Royalties are the monies earned from licensing the use of the song through Mechanical, Sync, Public Performance Blanket, Transcription, and other special licenses. The amount of money paid to the writer or shared with other writers and the publisher is often determined by the type of deal. Also the publisher may deduct certain expenses such as demo recordings, fees, exchange rates between countries, advances and legal fees. Some royalties are paid directly to the publisher, while others are split and paid directly to the writers (s) and publisher, such as money collected by ASCAP, BMI and SESAC	[] Work for HIre	[×] One time Payment [√] All Songwriters Royalties (100% of share/50% of total) [√] All Music Publishers Royalties (100% of share/ 50% of total) [√] Music Publisher (100% owner of Copyright unless writer has publisher sign a work-for-hire deal giving writer copyright)
		[] Staff or Indie Deal	[×] Songwriters Royalties (100% of share/50% of total income) [√] Music Publishers Royalties (100% of share/50% of income) [√] Music Publisher (100% owner of Copyright)
		[] Co Pub Deal	[×] Songwriters Royalties (100% of share/50% to total) Plus, [×] Music Publishers Royalties (50% of share/25% of total) to songwriters acting as a publisher [√] Music Publishers Royalties (50% of share/25% of total) [×] Songwriter (50% owner of Copyright) [√] Music Publisher (50% owner of Copyright)
		[] Administrative Deal	[×] Songwriters Royalties (100% of share/50% of total) Plus, [×] Music Publishers Royalties (50% of share/25% of total to songwriter acting as music publisher) [√] Music Publisher Royalties (50% of share or 25% of total) [×] Songwriter (100% owner of Copyright}
		[] Shark Deal	[√] You pay publisher and usually receive nothing in return

Action Negotiation Point	**What it means**	**Type of Deal**	**What Happens (What each usually retain)** × Songwriter | √ Music Publisher
Writer's Name and Likeness	The writer (s) gives a nonexclusive worldwide right for the music publisher to use and to permit others to use the writers' legal and professional name and approved likeness, facsimile signature, and and bio. All information should only be allowed for the purposes of business in connection with the original song. Writers may restrict certain commercial endorsements (such as smoking advertisement) but it must be in writing in this section.	Same in most types of deals	[√] Songwriter provides usage of name and likeness to music publisher. Same in most types of deals

Action Negotiation Point	**What it means**	**Type of Deal**	**What Happens (What each usually retain)** × **Songwriter | √ Music Publisher**
Writer's Warranties	The songwriter validates that he or she has the authority to make the deal; they are of legal age, the song is their own original material (lyrics, composition or arrangement), and they created and own the song/copyright. The songwriters also provide the authority to the music publisher to exploit the song as the music publisher determines and to support the music publishers against legal actions.	Same in most types of deals	[√] Songwriter provides usage of name and likeness to music publisher. Same in most types of deals

Action Negotiation Point	**What it means**	**Type of Deal**	**What Happens (What each usually retain) × Songwriter | √ Music Publisher**
Royalty Payments	The payment schedule for the songwriter to receive royalties collected by the music publisher through mechanical, sync, transcription, and other types of deals. Writers are often paid 45 days after the end of a quarter (every three months) if the song has earned royalties and if the music publishers cost of doing business have been repaid (recouped). Sometimes, writers are paid for the first year and then recoupment kicks in. Staff songwriters are usually paid an advance (quarterly) based on the music publisher assumptions the songs written by the writer will generate enough money to recoup the advances, pay minor obligations, and make a profit. Writers are often provided the opportunity to have an accountant audit the "books" once a year with a 30 day notice to make sure all royalties are correctly paid.	Same in most types of deals	[√] Songwriter provides usage of name and likeness to music publisher. Same in most types of deals

Action Negotiation Point	**What it means**	**Type of Deal**	**What Happens (What each usually retain)** × **Songwriter** | √ **Music Publisher**
Suits and Actions Involving Original Works	The music publisher has the right to prosecute, defend, settle and compromise all suits and actions when infringement of the copyright occurs. The publisher and writer will usually split any financial awards after payment of legal expenses.	Same in most types of deals	[√] Songwriter provides usage of name and likeness to music publisher. Same in most types of deals

Action Negotiation Point	**What it means**	**Type of Deal**	**What Happens (What each usually retain)** × **Songwriter** | √ **Music Publisher**
Indemnification	The writer agrees to indemnify, save, and hold PUBLISHER harmless from any damages, liabilities, costs, losses and expenses arising out of any legal actions connected with a third party action or lawsuits. Also the writer agrees to reimburse the music publisher for any costs due to claims against the publisher that are proven as an inconsistencies made by the writer in this agreement that cause financial damage, liability, loss or expense to the music publisher. (As an example a claim by another writer that you're not the sole owner of the copyright). The music publisher may withhold payments of any royalties due to the WRITER until the full amount of the legal action to correct the situation is recouped.	Same in most types of deals	[√] Songwriter provides usage of name and likeness to music publisher. Same in most types of deals

Action Negotiation Point	**What it means**	**Type of Deal**	**What Happens (What each usually retain) × Songwriter | √ Music Publisher**
10. Notices	All notices or correspondence regarding this agreement must be s in writing and delivered by personal delivery, mail, or telegraph, prepaid. Notices may also be personally delivered, mailed or delivered to a telegraph office, with all charges paid.	Same in most types of deals	[√] Songwriter provides usage of name and likeness to music publisher. Same in most types of deals
11. Entire Agreement	Whatever is written is the entire agreement and understanding between WRITER and PUBLISHER and no modification, amendment, waiver, termination or discharge (additions or changes to the agreement) will be allowed without a written amendment signed by WRITER and authorized by the PUBLISHER.	Same in most types of deals	[√] Songwriter provides usage of name and likeness to music publisher. Same in most types of deals

Action Negotiation Point	**What it means**	**Type of Deal**	**What Happens (What each usually retain)** × Songwriter | √ Music Publisher
12. Notice of Breach	*Before the PUBLISHER or WRITER* claim that the other is in default of performing any obligation contained in the contact, they must advise the other in writing of the specific facts constituting default claim and the specific obligation breached. The other party shall thirty days after receiving the written notice to cure the default.	Same in most types of deals	[√] Songwriter provides usage of name and likeness to music publisher. Same in most types of deals
13.Relationship of Parties	The writer and music publisher are not in business together as in a partnership or joint venture. This is simply a contract of a songwriter selling his copyright (ownership of the song) to a music publishing company. in exchange for a percentage of whatever is negotiated. Neither party is liable for any representation, act, or omission of the other contrary to whatever is agreed to in the contract.	Same in most types of deals	[√] Songwriter provides usage of name and likeness to music publisher. Same in most types of deals

Action Negotiation Point	**What it means**	**Type of Deal**	**What Happens (What each usually retain)** × Songwriter | √ Music Publisher
Binding Effect and Benefit of Agreement	Both the songwriter and music publisher agree that this contract is a legal binding agreement for the benefit of the songwriter and music publisher and their estates.	Same in most types of deals	[√] Songwriter provides usage of name and likeness to music publisher. Same in most types of deals
Assignment	The PUBLISHER may assign, license or otherwise transfer/sell (the song or songs or even his entire company) without limitation, plus the rights to the WRITER's services (if the writer is a staff writer). However the obligations stated in the contract shall continue with the new assignee or company.	Same in most types of deals	[√] Songwriter provides usage of name and likeness to music publisher. Same in most types of deals

Action Negotiation Point	**What it means**	**Type of Deal**	**What Happens (What each usually retain)** × **Songwriter** | √ **Music Publisher**
Controlling Law	This contract is considered to be made and signed by both parties in one of the states of the United States and its validity, construction, and effect shall be governed by the laws of that state. Any disputes between the parties shall be heard in the state and/or federal courts located in the home state.	Same in most types of deals	[√] Songwriter provides usage of name and likeness to music publisher. Same in most types of deals
Copyright Assignment	The actual place in the contact where both parties (songwriter and music publisher) sign the agreement (execute the agreement and any accompanying schedules, appendices) with the date, signature and legal Notary Public as a witness.	Same in most types of deals	[√] Songwriter provides usage of name and likeness to music publisher. Same in most types of deals

10

Mega Entertainment Conglomerates

Bertelsmann, Disney, Sony, Time Warner, & Universal

"The formula for success is straightforward enough: Produce something for a fixed cost and exploit the —— out of it, selling it over and over in different markets, venues, and formats. And if enough people see it (or hear it) the property becomes a cultural touchstone that can continue to draw in revenue for decades."

— Author Unknown, *Business Week* **Magazine**[318]

"...The music business is rapidly evolving. From the changing ways music is made, distributed and sold to the greater control demanded by artists, the industry of the next decade may hardly resemble that o the last one. Where the record labels once called the shots, now companies like Apple, Wal-Mart and Best Buy seem to have just as much say with their ability to promote individual songs or albums to dedicated audiences of buyers."

— Kelsey Swanekamp, *Forbes.com*[319]

Mega Conglomerates

In the past, *mega entertainment corporations* have controlled most of the world's entertainment consumer markets. They were and in some cases, still are, **Bertelsmann AG** of Germany, **The Walt Disney Company, Time Warner and MCA** of the United States, **Polygram** of the Netherlands, **EMI** of England, **Sony** of Japan, and **Vivendi Universal** of France. Things have changed over the last twenty years as **MCA** and **Polygram** merged into **Universal** owned by *Seagrams Liquor of Canada* which was then sold (in a somewhat shaky deal) to *Vivendi of Paris France.*[320] **Columbia Records,** films and music were sold in the late 1980's to **Sony** of Japan when *CBS TV* ran into financial trouble and *Coco-Cola* (which owned 49% of the film company) wanted out of the business.[321] Later, **Universal** sold Universal Film, etc., to **NBC-TV** in the United States (which then became known as **NBC/Universal** owned by General Electric) and then

---

318 Unknown Author, "The Entertainment Glut," Business Week Magazine, (09/11/1998).

319 Kelsey Swanekamp, "RealNetworks Spins off Rhapsody," http://www.forbes.com/2010/02/10/realnetworks-rhapsody-music-markets-equities-closer.html (July 25, 2010).

320 MCA, "MCA, Seagram and Universal Group," Ketupa.com, http://ketupa.net/universal.htm, (accessed July 22, 2010)

321 Geraldine Fabrikant, "Deal is Expected for Sony to buy Columbia Pictures," The New York Times, http://www.nytimes.com/1989/09/26/business/deal-is-expected-for-sony-to-buy-columbia-pictures.html, (accessed June 18, 2013)

Comcast bought it for $30 billion in 2009.[322] **EMI** (Electrical Musical Instruments) better know by its major label **Capitol Records** in the United States) filed for bankruptcy and was split in two with **Universal** purchasing the recording masters (including the Beatles) and **Sony** grabbing the music publishing rights. **EMI** is now used by **Sony** to collect intellectual property rights and is not considered a mega entertainment conglomerate. **Bertelsmann AG**, which is still one of the worlds largest entertainment companies, in 1998 sold all of it's music labels (including **RCA Records**) and music publishing (under the title Bertelsmann's Music Group or BMG) to **Sony**.[323] **Time Warner** (which is still a mega entertainment conglomerate) sold **Warner Music** which includes all of its labels and music publishing to a private investment group.[324] Confused yet? Don't be as mergers are common in the entertainment business. The other thing to remember is that entertainment products (copyright ownership of songs, recordings, movies, computer games) have a projected financial value based on their possible "future" royalties and revenues. So, do not give your copyright away.

New Business Models

Bertelsmann, Disney, Sony, Time Warner and Universal have the money, business structure, and distribution systems to create, produce, market, promote, publicize, distribute, and deliver music, movies, books, computer games, and other entertainment products consistently to the global markets. Historically, they were built on the *passive* consumer acceptance of various types of entertainment products created from the inventions and developments in audio recording, film production, popular print press, television, radio, photography, computers, and other forms of mass media innovation and technology. However, the times are changing and the technology they once used wisely to create their entertainment financial empires is now causing them to reinvent themselves because of a business phenomenon called *creative destruction*. Schumpeter (1942) defines it:

> *Capitalism, then, is by nature a form or method of economic change and not only never is but never can be stationary. And this evolutionary character of the capitalist process is not merely due to the fact that economic life goes on in a social and natural environment which changes and by its change alters the data of economic action; this fact is important and these changes (wars, revolutions and so on) often condition industrial change, but they are not its prime movers. Nor is this evolutionary character due to a quasi-automatic increase in population and capital or to the vagaries of monetary systems, of which exactly the same thing holds true.*

---

[322] TimArango, "G.E. Makes It Official: NBC Will Go to Comcast," The New York Times, Media & Advertising, http://www.nytimes.com/2009/12/04/business/media/04nbc.html?_r=0, (accessed June 18, 2013)

[323] Andrew Ross Sorkin, "Bertelsmann Sells Stake in Sony BMG," Deal B%K, The New York Times, http://dealbook.nytimes.com/2008/08/05/bertelsmann-sells-stake-in-sony-bmg/, (accessed June,18, 2013)

[324] David Kirkpatrick, "Time Warner Sells Music Unit for $2.6 Billion," New York Times, http://www.nytimes.com/2003/11/25/business, (July 22, 2010).

The fundamental impulse that sets and keeps the capitalist engine in motion comes from the new consumers, goods, the new methods of production or transportation, the new markets, the new forms of industrial organization that capitalist enterprise creates.[325]

Mega's and Labels

For the last 125 years, the conglomerates and their earlier enterprising business ventures have controlled between 80 and 90% of the audio recordings, films, and mass media entertainment products in various world markets. Now, due to consumer use of P2P and other forms of digital technology, (clouds) they have shifted their basic business models toward an *interactive consumer*. Some of the conglomerates have replaced their labels with intellectual property rights management. Instead of producing and selling recordings they simply management the use of their copyrights of songs and recordings for financial gain. Others, use 360 deals and other forms of contractual reversions to recoup their investments faster through revenue streams previously controlled by artists (such as merchandise sales, concert tickets, and corporate sponsorships). In other words, labels would help an artist become successful through funding and selling great recordings and the label would profit if they sold enough albums to break-even and then sold millions more. The artist would make most of their money from the "fame" launched by the recordings (airplay, distribution, marketing, promotion and publicity) which turned into concert ticket, sales, merchandise, and corporate sponsorship revenues. Now, new artists are usually required to sign a 360 deal which means they have to "share" a percentage of the profits from their concert ticket sales, merchandise, and corporate sponsorship revenues with the labels who "funded" their albums and corresponding marketing. Thus, the labels and their umbrella conglomerates have had to change toward a 360 business model or declare bankruptcy. The innovation of technology has forced the industry to change the way it makes money and its placed the power and future success of the industry into the consumer's fingers (social click media) who are able to interactively select almost any entertainment product, ranging from a deeply discounted priced digital album to a free download, whenever and wherever they want it! According to Time Warner's (2009) annual report,

> *Technology, particularly digital technology used in the entertainment industry, continues to evolve rapidly, and advances in that technology have led to alternative methods for the delivery and storage of digital content. These technological changes have driven and reinforced changes in consumer behavior, as consumers increasingly seek control over when, where and how they consume digital content. For example, content owners are increasingly delivering their content directly to consumers over the Internet, often without charge, and consumer electronics innovations have enabled consumers to view such Internet-delivered content on televisions and portable devices. Further, the current economic conditions could have the effect of accelerating the migration to digital technologies among both providers and consumers of content, with companies seeking greater efficiencies and consumers seeking more value and lower cost alternatives.*[326]

Everything is changing. The keys now are (a) interactive digital storage and distribution, (b) branding of the image, (c) building a fan base through local performances, self-promotion club tours, buy-on tours, and tours when the act is famous enough to draw an audience that promoters will buy, videos (youtube and others) fandoms (creating a following of fans, as an example, through tumbir) who write about the "meanings or provide a storyline" of the recordings video, etc., and (d) new business models such as 360 deals, where the money invested by labels is hopefully recaptured (recouped) through other non-album revenue sources. Bertelsmann, Disney, Sony, Time Warner and Universal are still divided into divisions that allow them to operate successfully by creating entertainment products, marketing through promotion and publicity their own media and popular press publications, distribute the entertainment products through their own

---

325 Joseph Schumpeter, "Creative Destruction," From the book, *Capitalism, Socialism and Democracy*, (Harper: New York: NY, 1942) 82-85.

326 Time Warner, "Corporate Report," http://phx.corporate-ir.net/External.File?item=UGFyZW50SUQ9MzkxNTR8Q2hpbGRJRD0tMXxUeXBlPTM=&t=1 (July 21, 2010)

worldwide distribution networks and clouds and in some cases, they even create the electronic devices and products consumers use to listen, watch (8k, 4k, LCD/Plasma TVs), and cell phones, and pad devices.

Bertelsmann AG

Carl Bertelsmann started Bertelsmann AG in 1835 as a lithographic printing company. Today, it is Europe's leading media company. One of Bertelsmann's first books, a hymnal, helped the company to grow despite the poverty and low literacy rate in the 1830s. The Nazis shut down the company during WWII, but its major growth was in the 1950s when it developed the "book club" marketing idea that created huge profits from the sale of print media distributed directly to consumer homes. At one time, Bertelsmann's book clubs had over 25 million members in 15 countries and BMG Direct (the direct music, book and record club) had over four million American record club members.[327] According to *Yahoo Finance* (2010),

> *This company is so big it takes up space on the bookshelf, the magazine stand, and on television. Bertelsmann is one of the world's leading media conglomerates with operations in publishing and TV. It owns about 90% of RTL Group, Europe's #1 TV broadcaster with more than 40 channels operating in a dozen countries. Bertelsmann also owns Random House, the world's top trade book publisher, as well as 75% of magazine publisher Gruner + Jahr. In addition, its arvato unit is a leading provider of distribution, manufacturing, and other business services to media companies. Carl Bertelsmann founded the company in 1835. His descendants, the Mohn family, control the business through the Bertelsmann Stiftung foundation.*[328]

The foundation of Bertelsmann's success is a corporate culture based on partnership, entrepreneurial spirit, creativity, and corporate responsibility. The company strives to bring creative new ideas to market and create value.[329] In their 2012 Annual Report (2013) they stated their business strategy as four cornerstones:

> **Strengthening the Core:** *Television, radio, books, magazines, digital businesses, service providers - Bertelsmann does business in a wide variety of fields. However, all of the company's businesses have one thing in common : they require creativity - artistic as well as entrepreneurial.*[330]

> **Digital Transformations:** *"...the use of digital media has now reached the bulk of consumers" ..."The transformation to digital not only affects all of our businesses, it is already contributing substantially to our core businesses."*[331] *... Bertelsmann publishes books - and has done so for more than 177 years. A look at how book content is created at Random House, Bertelsmann's book publishing division, reveals a nearly fully digitalized process - right through the actual print and electronic copies purchased and read by consumers. More than 47,000 ebooks in English Spanish and German are available form Random House and Bertelsmann's book publishers now generate over 20 percent of their global revenues from digital business.*[332]

---

[327] Bertelsmann, "Corporate Report 2009," Bertelsmann A.G. Carl-Bertelsmann-Strasse, 270, D-333111 Gutersloh, Germany Phone:+49-52-41-80-1362, http://www.bertelsmann.com and Yahoo.com, http://biz.yahoo.com/ic/40/40661.html (July 21, 2010).

[328] Bertelsmann, "Corporate Report 2009," Bertelsmann A.G. Carl-Bertelsmann-Strasse, 270, D-333111 Gutersloh, Germany Phone:+49-52-41-80-1362, http://www.bertelsmann.com and Yahoo.com, Company Profile, http://biz.yahoo.com/ic/40/40661.html (July 21, 2010).

[329] Bertelsmann, "Corporate Report 2009," Bertelsmann A.G. Carl-Bertelsmann-Strasse, 270, D-333111 Gutersloh, Germany Phone:+49-52-41-80-1362, http://www.bertelsmann.com and Yahoo.com, http://biz.yahoo.com/ic/40/40661.html (July 21, 2010).

[330]Bertelsman's 2013 Annual Report, Strengthening the Core, "The Power of Creativity," http://reports2.equitystory.com/reports/bertelsmann/annual/2012/gb/English/0.html, (accessed July 7, 2013).

[331] Thomas Hesse, Bertelsman's 2013 Annual Report, Strengthening the Core, "Shaping Change," http://reports2.equitystory.com/reports/bertelsmann/annual/2012/gb/English/0.html, (accessed July 7, 2013).

[332] Bertelsman's 2013 Annual Report, Digital Transformation, "Shaping Change," http://reports2.equitystory.com/reports/bertelsmann/annual/2012/gb/English/0.html, (accessed July 7, 2013).

Building Growth Platforms: *In just four and a half years, BMG Rights Management has become the world's fourth largest music publisher with rights to over one million songs - a true success story. At the same time, the music rights company established in 1998 is a prime example of how small promising businesses can quickly turn into supporting pillars at Bertelsmann. ...As different as the various growth platforms of Bertelsmann are - there are key similarities: All of them should meet binding investment criteria. Specifically, this means that among other things, they have an internationally proven and digitally established business model, operate in markets with high growth potential, are subject to only minor economic fluctuations, and are scaleable - i.e. they generate increasing returns as their size increases.*[333]

Expanding the Groups Presence in Growth Regions: *Bertelsmann operates in some 50 countries worldwide. Beyond the next few years, the core European markets and the United States, there will be an increased focus on three growth regions: Brazil, India and China. ...According to forecasts, by 2050 if not sooner, they will be the worlds biggest economic powers. Their populations largely consist of a growing middle class-young, urban, and digitally savvy. The level of media consumption is corresponding high as the media sector in the BIC (Brazil, India, and China), is expected to grow by an average 12 percent annually through 2015.*[334]

Disney

The Walt Disney Company is the leading teen entertainment company in the world. According to the Corporate Report (2009), "Since its founding in 1923, The Walt Disney Company and its affiliated companies have remained faithful to their commitment to produce unparalleled entertainment experiences based on the rich legacy of quality creative content and exceptional storytelling."[335] The report also states that it is divided into five business segments:

The Walt Disney Studios *distributes motion pictures under Walt Disney Pictures including Walt Disney Animation Studios, Pixar Animation Studios and DisneyToon Studios, Touchstone Pictures, Hollywood Pictures and Miramax Films. Walt Disney Studios Motion Pictures International serves as the studio's international distribution arm. Walt Disney Studios Home Entertainment distributes Disney and other film titles to the rental and sell-through home entertainment markets worldwide. Disney Theatrical Productions are the producers of Broadway musicals, and Disney Live Family Entertainment and Disney on Ice. Disney Music Group distributes original music and motion picture soundtracks under Walt Disney Records, and Hollywood Records.*[336]

Disney's Parks and Resorts *...traces its roots to 1952, when Walt Disney formed what is today known as Walt Disney Imagineering to build Disneyland Park in Anaheim, California. Since then, Parks and Resorts has grown to encompass the world-class Disney Cruise Line, eight Disney Vacation Club resorts (with more than 100,000 members), Adventures by Disney (immersive Disney-guided travel around the world), and five resort locations (encompassing 11 theme parks, including some owned or co-owned by independent entities) on three continents including Disneyland Resort, Anaheim, California; Walt Disney World Resort, Lake Buena Vista, Florida; Tokyo Disney Resort, Urayasu, Chiba; Disneyland Resort Paris, Marne La Valle, France; Hong Kong Disneyland, Penny's Bay, Lantau Island and a new park in Hawaii.*[337]

Disney Merchandising *began in 1929 when Walt Disney was approached by a businessman interested in placing Mickey Mouse on the cover of a children's writing tablet. Disney Consumer Products and affiliates (DCP) extend the Disney brand to merchandise ranging from apparel, toys, home décor and books and magazines to interactive games, foods and beverages, stationery,*

---

333 Bertelsman's 2013 Annual Report, Growth Platforms, "More than Promising Approaches," http://reports2.equitystory.com/reports/bertelsmann/annual/2012/gb/English/0.html, (accessed July 7, 2013).

334 Bertelsman's 2013 Annual Report, Growth Platforms, Growth Regions, "On the Way to Becoming a Global Network," http://reports2.equitystory.com/reports/bertelsmann/annual/2012/gb/English/0.html (accessed July 7, 2013).

335 The Walt Disney Company, "Corporate Report 2009" http://corporate.disney.go.com/corporate/overview.html (July 21, 2010).

336 The Walt Disney Company, "Corporate Report 2009" http://corporate.disney.go.com/corporate/overview.html (July 21, 2010).

337 The Walt Disney Company, "Corporate Report 2009" http://corporate.disney.go.com/corporate/overview.html (July 21, 2010).

electronics and fine art. …Disney Publishing Worldwide is the world's largest publisher of children's books and magazines, reaching more than 100 million readers each month in 75 countries.[338]

Media Networks *…include Disney-ABC Television Group, ESPN Inc., Walt Disney Internet Group, ABC owned television stations, and the supporting headquarters group. …The Disney-ABC Television Group is home to all of Disney's worldwide entertainment and news television properties. The Group includes the ABC Television Network (including ABC Daytime, ABC Entertainment Group and ABC News divisions); the Disney Channels Worldwide global kids' TV business, ABC Family and SOAPnet; as well as television distribution divisions Disney-ABC Domestic Television and Disney-ABC ESPN Television. The Disney-ABC Television Group also manages the Radio Disney Network, general interest and non-fiction book imprint Hyperion, as well the Company's equity interest in A&E Television Networks.*[339]

The Walt Disney Interactive Group *is both a developer of unique new media experiences specifically designed for Internet and mobile media and a developer of new platforms for distributing content selected from broad, existing entertainment divisions and libraries of The Walt Disney Company or its affiliated companies. …include Disney.com, Family.com, Movies.com and mDisney mobile entertainment. …Disney's Club Penguin, Disney's Toontown Online, Pirates of the Caribbean Online and Disney Fairies Pixie Hollow.*[340] *...Disney Interactive Games creates and publishes immersive interactive experiences across video game consoles, mobile devices, social networks and online virtual worlds. Interactive properties from the group include #1 kids' virtual world Club Penguin, hit mobile game Where's My Water?, popular social network game Gardens of Time, and the award-winning game Disney Epic Mickey.*[341]

Sony Global

Sony Entertainment is a wholly owned subsidiary of the Sony Corporation, a $50+ billion-a-year electronic software, entertainment, and hardware producer and manufacturer. Founder and Chief Advisor, Masaru Ibuka, and Founder and Honorary Chairperson, Akio Morita, founded Sony on the concept of "the establishment of an ideal factory, free, dynamic, and pleasant, where technical personnel of sincere motivation can exercise their technological skills to the highest levels."[342] The company has fostered a culture of curiosity in science tied to leading edge technologies, entrepreneurship, development, and the commercialization of fun and profits through the sale of consumer products.

Sony's 1998 Corporate Reports 1998 state:

> *…Content that originates from dreams should be enjoyed on hardware conceived from dreams, and that tools, which originate in dreams, should have creativity as well as offer a variety of elements such as superior sound and picture quality, easy operation and portability, and an innovative design and pleasing feeling.*[343]

Little has changed in Sony's fundamental believes, as the 2010 Corporate Report states:

> *…Make.believe (makedotbelieve) symbolizes the spirit of our brand.*[344]

---

338 The Walt Disney Company, "Corporate Report 2009" http://corporate.disney.go.com/corporate/overview.html (July 21, 2010).

339 The Walt Disney Company, "Corporate Report 2009" http://corporate.disney.go.com/corporate/overview.html (July 21, 2010).

340 The Walt Disney Company, "Corporate Report 2009" http://corporate.disney.go.com/corporate/overview.html (July 21, 2010).

341 The Walt Disney Company "Corporate Report 2011" http://thewaltdisneycompany.com/disney-companies/disney-interactive-media-group (accessed July 7, 2013).

342 Sony Corporation, "Remembering Masaru Ibuka," Sony Corporation Annual Report 1998, "Do You Dream in Sony?" http://www.sony.net/SonyInfo/IR/financial/ar/qfhh7c000000g7ry-att/ar_sony_1998.pdf, (accessed March 11, 2011).

343 Sony Corporation, "Remembering Masaru Ibuka," Sony Corporation Annual Report 1998, "Do You Dream in Sony?" http://www.sony.net/SonyInfo/IR/financial/ar/qfhh7c000000g7ry-att/ar_sony_1998.pdf, (accessed March 11, 2011).

344 Sony Corporation, "Make.Believe," Sony Corporation Annual Report 2011, http://www.sony.net/SonyInfo/IR/financial/ar/8ido18000003dkyy-att/8ido18000003dl0u.pdf, (accessed March 11, 2011).

> *...It stands for the power of our creativity, our ability to turn ideas into reality and the belief that anything we can imagine, we can make real. The Sony brand ranges from electronics to entertainment it reaches continents and cultures, and touches the lives of more people in more places and more ways than ever before. ...Through our unique combination of technology and content, Sony aims to inspire consumers around the world with innovation and joy.*[345]

Sony bought CBS Records in 1988 for $3.5 billion and the film division (Columbia and Tri-Star Pictures) in 1989 for $4.5 billion. Consolidated under Sony Pictures Entertainment (SPE) are subgroups of companies including Columbia Tri-Star Motion Picture Group (Columbia Pictures, Sony Pictures Classics, Sony Pictures Releasing, Columbia Tri-Star Film Distributors International); Columbia Tri-Star Television Group (Columbia Tri-Star Television, Columbia Tri-Star Television Distribution, Columbia Tri-Star International Television); Columbia Tri-Star Home Video, the Digital Studios Division; Sony Pictures Studios; and the Culver Studios in California. Sony makes both Sega and Nintendo video games and owns Merv Griffin's Enterprises, which produces the *Jeopardy* and *Wheel of Fortune,* TV shows.[346] Sony Corporation is a leading manufacturer of audio, video, game, communications, and key device and information technology products for the consumer and professional markets.

Sony recorded consolidated annual sales of approximately $70 billion for the fiscal year ended March 31, 2007. It appears that Sony will continue to provide consumers with the devices they need to create entertainment products. A summary of the Annual Report (2010) concludes that

> *...Sony will be offering a new live up of Bravia LCD TVs, ...3D Televisions, ...Vaio PC computers, ...ebook readers, ... another PlayStation3, ...smart phone by Sony Ericsson, ...digital projectors for 11,000 cinemas in the United States (including 3D), ...continued Sony/ATV music publishing and it's labels and film companies will continue to sign and product recording artists and films.*[347]

Sony Global has recently faced some difficult financial turns. Recent events have challenged it's business strategy and actual business models. Accordingly, Sony Global is refocusing its businesses and is ,evaluating each division to determine if they should be sold off, eliminated or expended into other markets. According to Kazuo Hirai, President and CEO of Sony Global, in a letter to Stakeholders (2012):

> ... *"During the fiscal year ended March 31, 2012 (fiscal year 2011), our operating results, particularly in our electronics business, were negatively affected by the Great East Japan Earthquake and the 2011 Thailand floods. Conditions were exacerbated by the economic downturn across the developed world, which caused other currencies to fall in comparison with the persistently strong yen. Owing to reduced sales in the Consumer Products & Services and Professional, Device & Solutions segments, our consolidated sales and operating revenue for the period declined 9.6%. We recorded an operating loss of 67.3 billion yen, compared to the 199.8 billion yen of operating income recorded in the previous fiscal year. This deterioration in operating income was due to a decline in net sales, and a significant deterioration in equity in net income (loss) of affiliated companies, despite the re-measurement gain associated with obtaining control of Sony Mobile Communications.*[348]

According to its' Corporate Report (2012) Sony is quickly refocusing the company toward five key initiatives:

- *Strengthening Core businesses: Digital Imaging, Game and Mobile*
- *Turn Around the Television Business*
- *Expand businesses in emerging markets*
- *Create new businesses and accelerate innovation*

---

345 Sony Corporation, "Make.Believe," Sony Corporation Annual Report 2011, http://www.sony.net/SonyInfo/IR/financial/ar/8ido18000003dkyy-att/8ido18000003dl0u.pdf, (accessed March 11, 2011).

346 Sony Corporation, "Remembering Masaru Ibuka," Sony Corporation Annual Report 1998, "Do You Dream in Sony?" http://www.sony.net/SonyInfo/IR/financial/ar/qfhh7c000000g7ry-att/ar_sony_1998.pdf, (accessed March 11, 2011).

347 Sony Corporation, "Make.Believe," Sony Corporation Annual Report 2011, http://www.sony.net/SonyInfo/IR/financial/ar/8ido18000003dkyy-att/8ido18000003dl0u.pdf, (accessed March 11, 2011).

348 Kazuo Hirai, Annual Report 2012, Letter to Stakeholders, "Operating Result in Fiscal Year 2011, http://www.sony.net/SonyInfo/IR/financial/ar/2012/message/page02.html, (accessed July 7, 2013).

- *Realign our business portfolio and optimize resources*[349]

Time Warner

Briton Hadden and Henry Luce created Time Publications in 1922. According to an analysis of its history provided by Kelly (2003), "*Time* was first published on March 3, 1923, as a newsmagazine which summarized and organized the news so busy men' could stay informed."[350] It published *Life* and other social and business periodicals for many years.

Warner Music was created in 1811 as Chappell & Co., a sheet music and musical instrument store in London.[351] In 1923, Harry, Jack, Albert, and Sam Warner founded Warner Bros. Films and in 1925 they purchased exclusive right to the invention of the "Vitaphone" which allowed them to turn silent films into "talkies."[352] Wayne states (2010) that;

> *Warner Brothers, one of Hollywood's most famous studios, was founded in 1923 by four actual brothers: Jack, Sam, Harry & Albert Warner. The siblings never seemed to get along with each other, but Warner Bros Studios managed to produce some of the most memorable movies in the history of Hollywood, including the world's first "talkie" with Al Jolson,* The Jazz Singer *(1927),* The Adventures or Robin Hood *(1938),* Casablanca *(1942),* Yankee Doodle Dandy *(1942),* Cool Hand Luke *(1967),* Deliverance *(1972),* The Exorcist *(1973),* Chariots of Fire *(1981),* Body Heat *(1981), and the current string of* Batman *films.*[353]

In 1989, Time Publications and Warner Communications International exchanged stock and money to merge into Time Warner Inc.[354] In 1995, Ted Turner became a 10% owner of Time Warner when he sold Turner Broadcasting, Inc. (TBS Superstation, TNT cable network, the Cartoon Network, New Line and Castle Rock movie production studios, Hanna-Barbera Cartoons, Headline News, plus the Atlanta Braves baseball franchise) for $8 billion.[355] Then, in a surprising move and an attempt to merge traditional media with new marketing opportunities created by the dot-COMs of the Internet, Time Warner approved a friendly takeover by America Online (AOL) in a swap and trade for $185 billion.[356] According to a report from *CNNMONEY* (January 10, 2000),

> *The merger, the largest deal in history, combines the nations top Internet service provider with the world's top media conglomerate. The deal also validates the Internet's role as a leader in the new world economy, while redefining what the next generation of digital-based leader will look like. "Together they represent an unprecedented powerhouse," said Scott Ehrens, a media analyst with Bear Stearns.*

---

349 Kazuo Hirai, Annual Report 2012, Letter to Stakeholders, "Operating Result in Fiscal Year 2011," Transforming our Electronics Business, http://www.sony.net/SonyInfo/IR/financial/ar/2012/message/page03.html, (accessed July 7, 2013).

350 Time Archive, "History of Time," http://www.time.com/time/archive/collections/0,21428,c_time_history,00.shtml (July 22, 2010).

351 Warner Music Group. "Time Line", http://www.wmg.com/timeline, (accessed June 18, 2013)

352 Warner Music Group. "Time Line", http://www.wmg.com/timeline, (accessed June 18, 2013)

353 Gary Wayne, "Seeing Stars: The Movie Studios," http://www.seeing-stars.com/Studios/warnerBrosStudios.shtml, (July 22, 2010).

354 Time Warner, "The CBS-Viacom Merger: World of the Media Giants," http://www.time.com/time/magazine/article/0,9171,992008,00.html, July 22, 2010).

355 Skip Wollenberg, "Dream Deal Still Faces Many Hurdles," The Associated Press, as reported in The Tennessean, "Business Section," (page IE, 9/23/1995).

356 Tom Johnson, "Internet Leader and Entertainment Firm to Join Forces; New Company worth $350 Billion," CNN Money, http://money.cnn.com/2000/01/10/deals/aol_warner/, (March 11, 2011).

> *"If their mantra is content, this alliance is unbeatable. Now they have this great platform they can cross-fertilize with content and redistribute."*[357]

Digital technology and P2P usage by consumers caused the marriage of the two to experience some serious financial problems. Many consumers decided that *free* is a great price to pay for music! Their illegal acquisition of Warner Music products appears to have scuttled the music business profits expected from the AOL/Time Warner merger. So in 2003, Time Warner sold all of its interest in recorded music and music publishing (Warner Music) to Edgar Bronfman, Jr. and an investment firm. Remember Bronfman from the days of MCA and Universal? Kirkpatrick wrote in the *New York Times* (2003),

> *Time Warner confirmed the sale of its Warner Music division yesterday for about $2.6 billion to an investor group led by the Seagrams heir Edgar Bronfman, Jr. and the investment firm Thomas H. Lee, ending an 18-month corporate garage sale to pay down debts. The sale is a pivotal point in Time Warner's recovery from the disappointing aftermath of its merger with America Online in 2001. With the proceeds from the sale, which is expected to close in two months, the company will have whittled its nearly $30 billion in debt down by about $10 billion. With that, Time Warner, already the largest media company in the world, can stop scrounging for miscellaneous parts of its far-flung holdings to sell and begin looking for opportunities to grow again.*[358]

Other problems arose with the AOL merger as it failed as to grow its membership, and many consumers moved to faster and less expensive services. Time Warner split with its AOL business. According to its 2009 Annual Report,

> *On March 12, 2009, the Company completed the legal and structural separation of Time Warner Cable Inc. ("TWC") from the Company (the "TWC Separation"), and, on December 9, 2009, the Company completed the legal and structural separation of AOL Inc. ("AOL") from the Company (the "AOL Separation"). With the completion of these separations, the Company disposed of its former Cable and AOL segments in their entirety.*[359]

Time Warner (without music labels, music publishing, or AOL) now operates in the following three content production classifications, according to its recent 2009 Annual Report:

> **Networks**, *consisting principally of cable television networks that provide programming (HOB, Cinemax and Turner Networks. Turner's networks in the U.S. consist of entertainment and news networks. Turner's entertainment networks include TBS, which reached approximately 100.1 million U.S. television households as reported by Nielsen Media Research ("U.S. television households") as of December 2009; TNT, which reached approximately 99.1 million U.S. television households as of December 2009; Cartoon Network (including adult swim, its overnight block of contemporary animation aimed at young adults), which reached approximately 98.3 million U.S. television households as of December 2009; truTV, which reached approximately 92.2 million U.S. television households as of December 2009; Turner Classic Movies, a commercial-free network; and Boomerang. Turner's CNN and HLN networks, 24-hour per day cable television news services, reached approximately 100.2 million and 99.3 million U.S. television households, respectively, as of December 2009.*[360]
>
> **Filmed Entertainment** *businesses produce and distribute theatrical motion pictures, television shows, animation and other programming and video games, distribute home video product, and license rights to the Company's feature films, television programming and characters. ...Warner Bros. distributes feature films for theatrical exhibition to more than 125 international territories. In 2009, Warner Bros. released internationally 11 English-language motion pictures and 33 local-language films that it either produced or acquired. After their theatrical exhibition, Warner Bros. licenses its newly produced films, as well as films from its*

---

357 Tom Johnson, "Internet Leader and Entertainment Firm to Join Forces; New Company worth $350 Billion," CNN Money, http://money.cnn.com/2000/01/10/deals/aol_warner/, (March 11, 2011).

358 David Kirkpatrick, "Time Warner Sells Music Unit for $2.6 Billion," New York Times, http://www.nytimes.com/2003/11/25/business, (July 22, 2010).

359 Time Warner, Annual Report 2009, http://phx.corporate-ir.net/External.File?item=UGFyZW50SUQ9MzkxNTR8Q2hpbGRJRD0tMXxUeXBlPTM=&t=1, (accessed July 22, 2010).

360 Time Warner, Annual Report 2009, http://phx.corporate-ir.net/External.File?item=UGFyZW50SUQ9MzkxNTR8Q2hpbGRJRD0tMXxUeXBlPTM=&t=1, (accessed July 22, 2010).

library, for distribution on broadcast, cable, satellite and pay television channels both domestically and internationally, and it also distributes its films on DVD and Blu-ray Discs and in various digital formats.[361]

Publishing, *consisting principally of magazine publishing is the largest magazine publisher in the U.S. based on advertising revenues, as measured by Publishers Information Bureau ("PIB"). As of December 31, 2009,* Time Inc. *published 21 magazines in the U.S., and over 90 magazines outside the U.S., primarily through IPC Media ("IPC") in the U.K. and Grupo Editorial Expansion ("GEE") in Mexico.* Time Inc. *licenses over 50 editions of its magazines for publication outside the U.S. to publishers in over 20 countries. In addition,* Time Inc. *operates almost 50 websites.* Time Inc. *also operates certain direct-marketing businesses.*[362]

Vivendi Universal

MCA (Music Corporation of America) is an interesting story. According to McDonald (2010), "Music Corporation of America (MCA) was founded in 1924 as a Chicago-based talent agency. Music Corporation of America became incorporated as MCA Inc. in 1958 and began public stock trading in 1959."[363] Matsushita Electrical Industrial of Japan bought the company in 1990 for $7.5 billion.[364] However, due to the exchange rate of the yen to the dollar, it became more difficult to achieve overseas profits. They also had a difficult time understanding Hollywood's business operations. According to media resource *Ketupa.com* (2010),

> *Performance by MCA was underwhelming and Matsushita appears to have faced difficulties coming to grips with the "creative" in Los Angeles. In 1995 it accordingly offloaded a controlling stake MCA to Seagram for $5.7 billion.*[365]

So, in 1995 Matsushita sold 80% of the company (and later, the remaining 20%) to The Seagram Company of Canada, which at the time was primarily a hard liquor company. Sam Bronfman had created it in 1916, as the Bonaventrue Liquor Store Company, and by the time of his death in 1971, he had become a billionaire.[366] Edgar Bronfman, Jr., who was the CEO of the Seagram Company and a direct relation to Sam Bronfman, bought MCA from Matsushita. In 1996, "MCA Inc. was renamed Universal Studios, Inc. and MCA Music Entertainment Group was renamed Universal Music Group."[367] In 1998, he bought Polygram (at the time, the world's leading entertainment company) from Philips Electronic of Holland for $10.1 billion.[368] He

---

[361] Time Warner, Annual Report 2009, http://phx.corporate-ir.net/External.File?item=UGFyZW50SUQ9MzkxNTR8Q2hpbGRJRD0tMXxUeXBlPTM=&t=1, (accessed July 22, 2010).

[362] Time Warner, Annual Report 2009, http://phx.corporate-ir.net/External.File?item=UGFyZW50SUQ9MzkxNTR8Q2hpbGRJRD0tMXxUeXBlPTM=&t=1, (accessed July 22, 2010).

[363] Macy McDonald, "History of MCA Records," Ehow.com, http://www.ehow.com/facts_5122069_history-mca-records.html, (accessed July 22, 2010).

[364] Paul Farhi, "Matsushita to Acquire MCA for $7.5 Billion; Deal is Largest Japanese Buyout of U.S. Firm," The Washington Post, accessed at HighBeam.com, http://www.highbeam.com/doc/1P2-1160780.html, (accessed July 22, 2010).

[365] MCA, "MCA, Seagram and Universal Group," Ketupa.com, http://ketupa.net/universal.htm, (accessed July 22, 2010).

[366] Stephen Schneider, *Iced: The Story of Organized Crime in Canada*, http://books.google.com/books?id=ZO8jKSn25DAC&pg=PA200&lpg=PA200&dq=Bonaventure+Liquor+Store+Company.&source=bl&ots=rZnXslgXrj&sig=nk3YfFaOmeVaP0JYxA9nYdA-ozM&hl=en&ei=SHpITMOoJIGClAfj0dnkDA&sa=X&oi=book_result&ct=result&resnum=2&ved=0CBYQ6AEwAQ#v=onepage&q=Bonaventure%20Liquor%20Store%20Company.&f=false (July 22, 2010).

[367] Universal Music Group, "History, Polygram and Universal," http://www.universalmusic.com/history#year1996, (July 22, 2010).

[368] Barry Willis, "Seagram Buys Polygram," Stereophile.com, http://www.stereophile.com/news/10176/, (accessed July 22, 2010).

merged the two entertainment giants under the name the Universal Music Group.[369] The combined company brought content from the world's largest music company, second largest film library, major film production studio, second largest destination theme park company, and global leader in reference, consumer, and PC-based software game publishing.[370]

Bronfman shocked the entertainment business again in June 2000 by selling all of Seagram Inc., including both the liquor and entertainment companies, to Vivendi of Paris, France. In 2005, Vivendi sold most of its old and worthy film and movie copyrights to NBC of the United States,[371] but according to a recent Vivendi news release (2010),

> *...A world leader in communications and entertainment, Vivendi controls Activision Blizzard (#1 in video games worldwide), Universal Music Group (#1 in music worldwide), SFR (#2 in mobile and fixed telecom in France), Maroc Telecom Group (#1 in mobile and fixed telecom in Morocco), Canal+ Group (#1 in pay-TV in France), GVT (#1 alternative operator in fixed telecom and internet in Brazil) and owns 20% of NBCU (leading U.S. media and entertainment group). In 2009, Vivendi achieved revenues of €27.1 billion and adjusted net income of €2.6 billion. With operations in 77 countries, the Group has over 49,000 employees.*[372]

EMI (Sold & Divided)

EMI Group, PLC of England was the world's leading music publisher with over one million titles in its publishing catalogs. It was started in 1898, as the Gramophone Company. It merged with Columbia Graphophone in 1931 to form Electric and Musical Industries, now better known as EMI. It has acquired many labels, including Capitol Records, United Artists Records, The Sparrow Corporation, Charisma Records, and Priority Records. EMI bought Richard Branson's Virgin Music Group in 1992 for $834 million. In 1962, EMI made history with The Beatles, and in 1998, EMI succeeded again with Garth Brooks, who has sold over 67 million albums worldwide.[373] It celebrated its first 100 years in business in 1997.

EMI was owned Terra Firma, a private investment company. In their 2009 Annual Review, they claim that

> *In short, Terra Firma is busy creating value in essential businesses throughout the world in an extremely difficult environment. ... EMI, earnings increased from approximately £165 million to nearly £300 million over the first full fiscal year of Terra firma's ownership. ...On the creative side, in the last 18 months, EMI has signed new agreements with over 200 artists and has continued to win numerous artistic accolades including 24 awards at the 2010 Grammys. While we are proud of our operational accomplishments at EMI, its capital structure has proven challenging.*[374]

However, in the spring of 2011 the financial walls caved in on Terra Firma and its £3.4 billion debt to Citi. EMI moved to Citi ownership to satisfy the majority of the debt. Sadly, P2P file sharing which allows consumers to obtain music free without paying the creators, songwriters, and music publishers destroyed the

---

369 Universal Music Group, "History, Polygram and Universal," http://www.universalmusic.com/history#year1996, (July 22, 2010).

370 Universal Music Group, "History, Polygram and Universal," http://www.universalmusic.com/history#year1996, (July 22, 2010).

371 Vevendi/Universal, "Corporate Information," Vivendi.com, 42, Avenue de Friedland, 75380 Paris Tel: 33 1 71 7110 00, Fax: 33 1 71 7111 79, www.vivendi.com

372 Vivendi, "Vivendi: Favorable US Supreme Court Judgement," http://www.vivendi.com/vivendi/Vivendi-Favorable-US-Supreme-Court (July 22, 2010).

373 EMI, "History of EMI," Emigroup.com, http://www.emimusic.com/, (accessed 1998).

374 Terrafirma, "Terrafirma Annual Review 2009," http://www.terrafirma.com/ar09/AR09.pdf, (accessed July 21, 2010).

financial structure of most important entertainment company. According to the letter Roger Faxon, head of EMI wrote to his employees (2011):

> *First off, I'd like to explain exactly what has happened. When a company's value is less than its debts, one solution is to go through an administration procedure which allows the sale of the business in partial satisfaction of those debts. In our case it is not hard to see that our parent company would never be able to repay the £3.4 billion it owed to Citi. With that being the case, it appointed an administrator empowered to sell EMI Group to Citi. This is sometimes called a 'pre-pack' because it can be done in a matter of hours – and that's exactly what happened here. This was followed by an immediate recapitalization of EMI, reducing the debt by 65% to £1.2 billion.*[375]

Sometimes in business, parts of the business or assess are worth more if sold separately. In a surprise move Sony Music and Universal both bought parts of EMI late in 2011. Universal paid about $1.9 billion for the master recordings (including the Beatles) and Universal paid about $2.2 billion for EMI's music publishing (including "Somewhere Over the Rainbow").[376] However, *Warner Bros. Music* is fighting the sale claiming that it would "reduce competition."[377] Brofmann stated in a speech at the *D: Dive Into Media Conference* hosted by the *Wall Street Journal*, January 2012 that;

> *...his company would oppose the sale of EMI Group to Warner's two biggest rivals, saying the deals would reduce competition. ...In a parting shot, Bronfman on Tuesday, his last day as chairman of Warner, told an audience at a media conference in Dana Point that EMI's sale was "dangerous" because the concentration of market share would stifle innovation and reduce payments to musicians they represent. Bronfman said Warner would "fight tooth and nail" to convince antitrust regulators to stop the deals.*[378]

Media Distribution Networks

There are several additional networks that are primarily focus only in one or two genres of entertainment. Some examples include:

Rupert Murdock's News Corp.'s focus is news, politics and business. It includes all the Fox network shows and productions, Blue Sky, Dow Jones, Harper Collins Publications, *The National Geographic*, *The Weekly Standard*, *The New York Post*, and outside the United States the BSkyB satellite network, The News Digital Media and STAR cable networks.[379]

Comcast Corporation's focus is a distribution system for cable programming, phone, and Internet providers. It is the nation's leading provider of cable, entertainment, and communication products and services, with 24.7 million cable customers, 14.1 million high-speed Internet customers and 5.2 million voice customers.

---

375 Roger Faxon as reported by David M. Ross, "Faxon's Note to EMI Staff," http://www.musicrow.com/2011/02/citigroup-acquires-emi/, (accessed February 4, 2011).

376 Andrew Edgecliffe-Johnson & Salamander Davoudi "EMI to be Split Between Universal and Sony," http://www.ft.com/intl/cms/s/0/f5721134-0c86-11e1-88c6-00144feabdc0.html#axzz1s1QmyXKS, Accessed April, (2012).

377 Company Town, "The Business Behind the Show" as reported in the Los Angeles Times, "Warner's Bronfman vows to 'fight' EMI sale to Universal and Sony." http://latimesblogs.latimes.com/entertainmentnewsbuzz/2012/01/warner-bronfman-to-fight-emi-sale-to-universal-and-sony-1.html (ccessed May 4, 2012).

378 Company Town, "The Business Behind the Show" as reported in the Los Angeles Times, "Warner's Bronfman vows to 'fight' EMI sale to Universal and Sony." http://latimesblogs.latimes.com/entertainmentnewsbuzz/2012/01/warner-bronfman-to-fight-emi-sale-to-universal-and-sony-1.html (ccessed May 4, 2012).

379 NewsCorp, "Executives and Contacts," http://www.newscorp.com/management/index.html, (accessed March 11, 2011).

Comcast is principally involved in the development, management, and operation of broadband cable networks and in the delivery of programming content.[380]

Viacom's focus is cable and TV show production to niche audiences. There former key to the music business was MTV and VH1 worldwide music networks. However, now they are following the Disney model with teen entertainment productions through its two businesses Media Networks and Filmed Entertainment. According to its 2009 Annual Report,

> *Media Networks provide entertainment content for consumers in key demographics attractive to advertisers, content distributors and retailers. ...video games and other content for distribution to our audiences how and where they want to view and interact with it: on television, the Internet, mobile devices, game consoles and through a variety of consumer products and themed entertainment. MTV Networks reaches over 640 million households in more than 160 countries worldwide via its approximately 170 channels and multi platform properties, which include MTV: Music Television®, VH1®, CMT®: Country Music Television™, Logo®, Nickelodeon®, Nick at Nite®, Nick Jr.®, TeenNick®, COMEDY CENTRAL®, Spike TV® and TV Land®, among others.*
>
> *Filmed Entertainment produces, finances and distributes motion pictures and other entertainment content under the Paramount Pictures®, Paramount Vantage®, Paramount Classics®, MTV Films® and Nickelodeon Movies® brands. The Filmed Entertainment segment also continues to release certain pictures under the DreamWorks® brand. Paramount Pictures has been a leading producer and distributor of motion pictures since 1912 and has a library consisting of approximately 3,300 motion pictures and a small number of television programs. It also acquires films for distribution and has distribution relationships with DreamWorks Animation and MVL Productions LLC ("Marvel"), a subsidiary of The Walt Disney Company.*[381]

RIAA Gold, Platinum, and Diamond

Unit sales reports are provide by labels and music companies to the *Recording Industry Association of American* (RIAA) who represent labels and maintain the sales statistics and awards Gold, Platinum, and Diamond certification to artists and labels who have achieved the corresponding success. According to the RIAA (2011),

> *...In the beginning, there was only a Gold album award for the sale of 500,000 copies. As the industry grew, other awards were developed. The Platinum award (1,000,000 sold) was created in 1976 and with the advent of the compact disc and the subsequent increase in sales, the Multi-Platinum award was created in 1984. On March 16, 1999, the RIAA launched the Diamond Awards, honoring sales of 10 million copies or more of an album or single. In 2004, the RIAA ...launched the Digital Sales award. ...In 2006, the RIAA added a Digital Ringtone Award, recognizing the success of Mobile Mastertones.*[382]

Summary

The recording business started with Edison's 1877 invention of a recording device. It was used by entrepreneurs to sell recordings to consumers, which led to the film business, show business, and the companies turning into mega entertainment corporations that have controlled most of the world's film and music industry for the past 50 years. After many years of mergers and buyouts, Time Warner, Sony, Disney, Bertelsmann and Universal are the current mega's remaining. Their business models are different, but they all control financial structures from the creation of entertainment products to the distribution, promotion, publicity, and unit sales figures. The mega have divisions in which the labels' financial and administrative

---

380 Comcast Corporation, "Corporate Report 2010" http://apps, (accessed March 11, 2011).

381 Viacom, "Viacom Annual Report 2009." http://www.viacom.com/news/Pages/newstext.aspx?RID=1312788, (accessed March 11, 2011).

382 Recording Industry Association of American (RIAA) "Gold and Platinum," RIAA.org, http://www.riaa.com/goldandplatinum.php?content_selector=digital_sales_award, (accessed April 2, 2011).

structures are divided into departments. The most successful labels in American history started as entrepreneurial ventures and grew to become a mega or to be bought out by one. Examples include Capital, Columbia, RCA, Warner Bros, Motown, and A&M Records.

The keys now are (a) interactive digital storage and distribution, (b) branding of the image, (c) building a fan base through local performances, self-promotion club tours, buy-on tours, and tours when the act is famous enough to draw an audience that promoters will buy, videos (youtube and others) and fandoms, and (d) new business models such as 360 deals, where the money invested by labels is hopefully recaptured (recouped) through other non-album revenue sources. Edgar Bronfman Jr., an important industry leader who has been involved with several deals including the MCA/Universal and Polygram merger and the sale of Universal to Vivendi of France. Bronfman currently heads the Warner Music Investor Group.

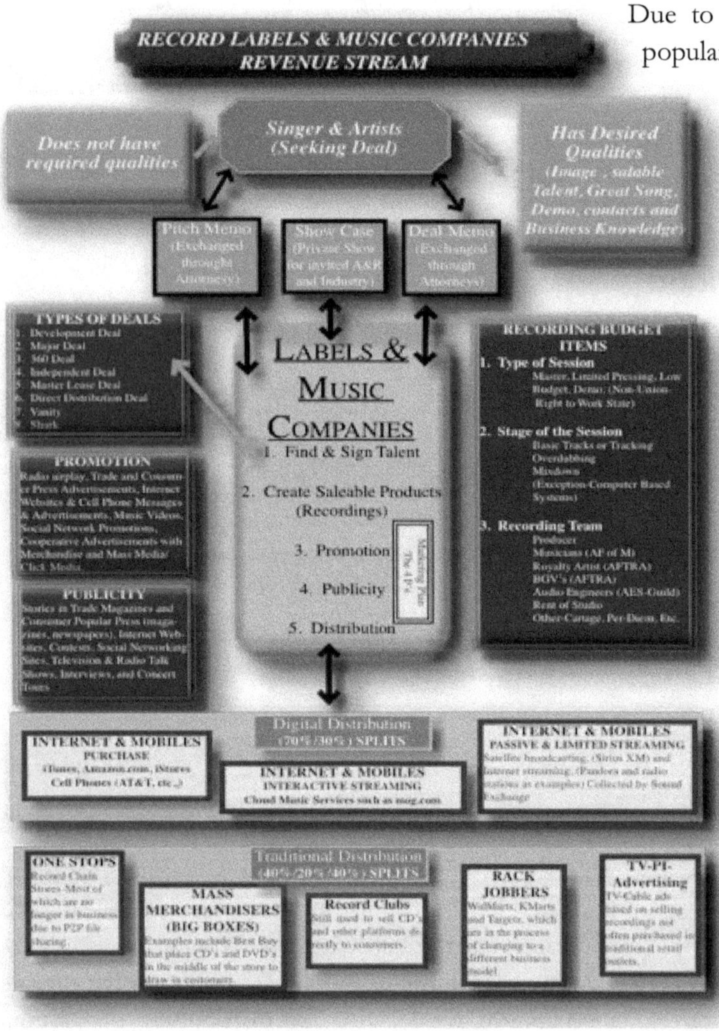

Due to the financial stress incurred through the popularity of consumer file sharing, most of the mega have sold or downsized their music business publishing companies and labels to individual investors or smaller companies. Warner Music, Universal, Sony, and Disney and their hundreds of worldwide labels are considered the only major record labels remaining. EMI which was one of the largest entertainment companies, was sold and split in two due to bankruptcy.

Key Website Resources

http://corporate.disney.go.com/investors/shareholder_faq.html/
http://home.disney.go.com/music/
http://ir.timewarner.com/phoenix.zhtml?c=70972&p=irol-annualmeeting/
http://www.disney.com/
http://www.emimusic.com/
http://www.facebook.com/
http://www.myspace.com/
http://www.netflix.com/WiHome/
http://www.sony.net/SonyInfo/IR/financial/ar/2010/index.html/
http://www.sonymusic.com/
http://www.terrafirma.com/annual-reviews.html/
http://www.universalmusic.com/
http://www.vivendi.com/vivendi/Annual-Reports,4975/
http://www.wmg.com/

11

Music Companies & Labels

Signing Acts and Creating Products
Promotion, Publicity, and Distribution

"Record companies, believe me, no matter what record company you're with, they're going to try to hype you, because, really, all record companies are interested in is making money."

— Elton John[383]

"This story is about a bidding-war band that gets a huge deal with a 20 percent royalty rate and a million-dollar advance. (No bidding-war band ever got a 20 percent royalty, but whatever.) This is my "funny" math based on some reality ...What happens to that million dollars? They spend half a million to record their album. That leaves the band with $500,000. They pay $100,000 to their manager for 20 percent commission. They pay $25,000 each to their lawyer and business manager. That leaves $350,000 for the four band members to split. After $170,000 in taxes, there's $180,000 left. That comes out to $45,000 per person. That's $45,000 to live on for a year until the record gets released. The record is a big hit and sells a million copies... So, this band releases two singles and makes two videos. The two videos cost a million dollars to make and 50 percent of the video production costs are recouped out of the band's royalties. The band gets $200,000 in tour support, which is 100 percent recoupable. The record company spends $300,000 on independent radio promotion. All of those independent promotion costs are charged to the band. Since the original million-dollar advance is also recoupable, the band owes $2 million to the record company. If all of the million records are sold at full price with no discounts or record clubs, the band earns $2 million in royalties, since their 20 percent royalty works out to $2 a record. Two million dollars in royalties minus $2 million in recoupable expenses equals ...zero!"

— Courtney Love, Recording Artist[384]

Historical Record Labels

The invention of the recording process by Thomas Edison in 1877, combined with some forward-thinking entrepreneurial wisdom, was the birth of what was to become the music business. However, this new technology was originally intended for a different purpose, as suggested in *The History of Recording Technology* (2010):

> *The story of the sound recording industry is mostly a story of musical entertainment on phonograph discs for the whole period from the invention of the phonograph in 1877 to about the 1950s, when new technologies emerged. The major players in the industry were Victor, Columbia and HMV (which originally stood for His Master's Voice) until the end of World War II, and are still important today. These three companies all got their start in the 1890s, when the phonograph was still young. Thomas Edison's 1877 invention of the phonograph was followed by many imitators, most notably the "graphophone," which became the basis of the Columbia company. Both inventions used a cylinder record which captured sound in a groove. Just as the graphophone of 1887*

[383] Elton John, "Elton John Quotes," Artquotes.net, http://www.artquotes.net/entertainment-quotes/famous-singers, (accessed March 15, 2011).

[384] Courtney Love, "Courtney Love does the Math," Salon.com, http://www.salon.com/technology/feature/2000/06/14/love, (accessed March 15, 2011).

> *borrowed many ideas from Edison, so too did Edison's "improved phonograph" of 1888 borrow back from the graphophone. Soon both machines were for sale or lease to the public. The primary market was intended to be businessman, lawyers, court reporters, and others who currently used stenography to capture important thoughts or compose letters. Although the sound recorder as a business machine has its own history, it is the entertainment uses of sound recording that made the biggest impact.*[385]

Several of the must successful labels in the early stages of the business were started by entrepreneurs who were either creative artist themselves or executives who visualized the profits of marketing live performance artist as "recording artists." Bill Damain in a *Performing Songwriter Magazine* article (2003) summarizes the most successful labels:

> **Columbia Records** *was the biggest of record labels dating from its start with the invention of the Graphophone in 1886 to its purchase by Sony in 1988. Marconi created an indestructible "Velvet Tone" disc that boosted sales for the label to an unheard of $150 million a year in 1919. In 1948, the now CBS owned label introduced the 33 & 1/3 LP (long play) album on a vinyl disc, which became the industry standard. In the 1960s, the label introduced Columbia House direct mail order record club (after the Bertelsmann A. G. model) to the public.*[386]
>
> **RCA Records** *(Recording Corporation of America) started as a by-product label from the establishment of the Victor Talking Machine Company in 1901 by Emile Berliner and Eldridge Johnson. The company label under the name Victor connected to HMV (the English label – His Master's Voice) and grew into a very successful label with recording artists Enrico Caruso, Al Jolson, and then later under the RCA label with Tommy Dorsey, Glenn Miller, Perry Como, Dinah Shore, Dolly Parton, David Bowie and Elvis Presley.*[387]
>
> **Capitol Records** *was founded in 1942 by songwriter Johnny Mercer, movie producer and songwriter Buddy Desylva and retail record storeowner Glenn Walichs. Capitol Records' major success came after it was purchased by EMI (Electrical Music Industries) in 1956 and its release of very successful albums by the Beach Boys and The Beatles.*[388]
>
> *Movie mogul Jack Warner founded* **Warner Bros. Records** *in 1958. He used many of Warner Bros.'s TV shows and movies to sell music by connecting the two in cross marketing efforts using artists in hit shows such as Kookie, Edd Byrnes in (77 Sunset Strip) and comedian Bob Newhart to sell recorded products. ...The Everly Brothers and Frank Sinatra joined the roster along with Dean Martin and Sammy Davis Jr. Other great acts who recorded for the label under the supervision of Mo Ostin including The Kinks, The Grateful Dead, Joni Mitchell, The Doobie Brothers and Fleetwood Mac.*[389]
>
> *"Hitsville, USA" was the sign in front of Berry Gordy Jr's house in Detroit when he started his label* **Motown Records** *in 1959. A songwriter himself ("Lonely Teardrops"), Gordy used $800.00 of borrowed family money to start his company. Within just a few years the label crossed over into top 40 radio with such acts as Smokey Robinson & The Miracles, The Temptations, Diana Ross, Marvin Gaye, The Commodores, the Jackson 5 (starring a very young Michael Jackson) and Stevie Wonder.*[390]
>
> *Herb Alpert and Jerry Moss started Carnival Records in 1962 with $200. Later, they found out the name Carnival was already being used so they changed the name of their label to* **A&M Records**. *Using their experience from viewing a bullfight in Tijuana, Mexico, Alpert and Moss recorded a brassy sounding instrumental titled "The Lonely Bull" in their garage. It sold over 700,000 copies, which they also packed and shipped from the same garage. Additional artists such as the Carpenters, Joe Cocker, Humble Pie, Cat Stevens, the Police, Janet Jackson, and Alpert's own album "Whipped Cream," with the hit "A Taste of Honey" made A&M one of the most successful independent labels ever launched. In 1989, Alpert and Moss sold their $200 investment label to PolyGram (owned at that time by Philips Electronic of Holland) for half a billion dollars.*[391]

---

385 Recording History, "The History of Recording," Recording-history.org, http://www.recording-history.org/HTML/musicbiz1.php, (accessed March 15, 2011).

386 Bill Damain, "The History of the Major Labels," Performing Songwriter Magazine, July/August, 2003.

387 Bill Damain, "The History of the Major Labels," Performing Songwriter Magazine, July/August, 2003.

388 Bill Damain, "The History of the Major Labels," Performing Songwriter Magazine, July/August, 2003.

389 Bill Damain, "The History of the Major Labels," Performing Songwriter Magazine, July/August, 2003.

390 Bill Damain, "The History of the Major Labels," Performing Songwriter Magazine, July/August, 2003.

391 Bill Damain, "The History of the Major Labels," Performing Songwriter Magazine, July/August, 2003.

What is a Label?

What is a major record label? The current business models are much different than the historical labels of the past. As an example, Warner Music, really consist of many labels all under the Warner Music Logo including: Asylum, Atlantic, East West, Elektra, Fueled By Ramen, Nonesuch, Reprise, Rhino, Roadrunner, Rykodisc, Sire, Warner Bros. and Word, as well as Warner/Chappell Music Publishing which controls over one million titles.[392]

Warner Music

In the late 1990s and early 2000s, consumers' use of P2P, the AOL merger, and a few questionable management decisions had caused serious financial problems for Time Warner. In 2003, they sold Warner Music to Edgar BronfmanJr., an investment firm. Bronfman had previously owned Universal Music and sold it to Vivendi.[393] According to *Forbes.com* (2010),

> *Mr. Bronfman was President and CEO of The Seagram Company Ltd., a post he held since June 1994. From 1989 until June 1994, Mr. Bronfman served as President and COO of Seagram. Between 1982 and 1989, he held a series of senior executive positions for The Seagram Company Ltd. in the U.S. and in Europe.*[394]

Edgar BronfmanJr., one of the top players in the business of music. Bronfman, despite having very little music business experience in his past, seems to be one of those rare executives that just *get it.* In the book *Fortune's Fool* (2010), he admits, "The days of the record industry dictating formats to the consumers are gone, and they're not coming back."[395] In the last couple of years, he and his management team have reestablished Warner Music as one of the most financially successful major labels, primarily by signing all new artists to 360 deals. Bronfman is the first to clearly explain why labels need them as they are tied to marketing, consumers stealing of copyrighted music and recordings, and label's projected returns on their financial investment in an act. Arrington (2008) reviews a speech by Bronfman:

> *...Warner Music Group CEO Edgar Bronfman told the Web 2.0 Summit audience that his label now requires all new artists to sign 360 Deals, and that about a third of their signed artists are under those contracts. Bronfman argued to a hostile crowd that it doesn't make sense for labels to pour money into artist development when CD sales, their primary source of revenue, continue to decline (although he did say that digital sales now make up 20% of their revenue). Without other ways to make money from an artist, he said, they wouldn't continue to promote artists.*[396]

Sony Music

The music business for Sony was directed through Sony Music Entertainment (Japan), and Sony Music Entertainment International (SMEI) in the rest of the world, until the Sony/BMG merger (Bertelsmann Music Group formerly owned by the mega Bertelsmann AG). Because of the lower profits in the business caused by P2P, Sony and Bertelsmann AG separated their music divisions from the parent companies and placed them into a new combined company titled Sony/BMG. However, in August 2008, Sony bought

---

[392] Warner Music Group, "Investor Relations", http://investors.wmg.com/phoenix.zhtml?c=182480&p=irol-newsArticle&ID=1819485&highlight=, (accessed June 18, 2013)

[393] David Kirkpatrick, "Time Warner Sell Music Unit for $2.6d Billion," *New York Times*, http://www.nytimes.com/2003/11/25/business, (accessed March 17, 2011).

[394] Edgar Bronfman, "Edgar Bronfman," Forbes.com, http://people.forbes.com/profile/edgar-j-bronfman/42366, (accessed March 17, 2011).

[395] Fred Goodman, *Fortune's Fool: Edgar Bronfman Jr., Warner Music and an Industry in Crisis*, (New York: Simon & Schuster, 2010) 7.

[396] Michael Arrington, "360 Music Deals Become Mandatory as Labels Prepare for Free Music," Techcrunch.com, http://techcrunch.com/2008/11/08/360-music-deals-become-mandatory-as-labels, (accessed March 17, 2011).

BMG's half of the music for $1.2 billion.[397] It's now called Sony Music. BMG is still a part of Bertelsmann's but operates as a property rights management company (exploiting copyright uses) as compared to a label.

Universal Music Group

Remember that in 1996 MCA Music Entertainment Group was renamed Universal Music Group as part of Edgar Bronfman's revitalization of MCA, which he had bought from Matsushita Electrical Industrial of Japan.[398] He had also bought Polygram in 1998 from Philips Electronic of Holland.[399] He merged the two entertainment giants under the name the Universal Music Group and then sold all of its holdings to Vivendi of Paris.[400] Universal Music Group is still owned by Vivendi of Paris and is now considered one of the most successful major labels in the world. It has, of course (just as the other major labels have), many affiliate labels in most countries and territories of the planet.[401] According to a Universal Music Group news release (2010), UMG

> *…Is the world's leading music company and is comprised of two core businesses: recorded music and music publishing. The company discovers, develops, markets and distributes recorded music through a network of subsidiaries, joint ventures and licensees in 77 countries, representing 98% of the music market. …Also sells and distributes music video and DVD products, and licenses recordings, encouraging the legal distribution of music online and over cellular, cable and satellite networks. …Includes Universal Music Latin Entertainment, the world's leading Latin music company. …Bravado, its merchandising company, and Twenty-First Artists, its full service management division; and Helter Skelter, its live music agency. Labels include: A&M/Octone, Barclay, Decca, Deutsche Gramophone, Disa, ECM, Emarcy, Fonovisa, Interscope, Geffen, A&M Records, Island Def Jam Music Group, Machete Music, Mercury Records, Polydor Records, Show Dog–Universal Music, Universal Motown Republic Group, Universal Music Latino, Universal Music Group Nashville (which includes Lost Highway, MCA Nashville and Mercury Nashville), and Verve Music Group.*[402]

---

[397] JCN Newswire, "Sony to Purchase Berteslmann's 50% Stake in Sony BG: Music Company to Become Wholly Owned Subsidiary of Sony Corporation of America," 50 BMG, http://wn.com/50_BMG, (accessed 2008).

[398] Universal Music Group, "History," http://new.umusic.com/history.aspx, (accessed March 17, 2011).

[399] Barry Willis, "Seagram Buys Polygram," Stereophile.com, http://www.stereophile.com/news/10176/, (accessed March 17, 2011).

[400] Universal Music Group, "History," http://new.umusic.com/history.aspx, (accessed March 17, 2011).

[401] Universal Music Group, "History," http://new.umusic.com/history.aspx, (accessed March 17, 2011).

[402] Universal Music Group, "Overview," http://new.umusic.com/Overview.aspx, (accessed March 17, 2011).

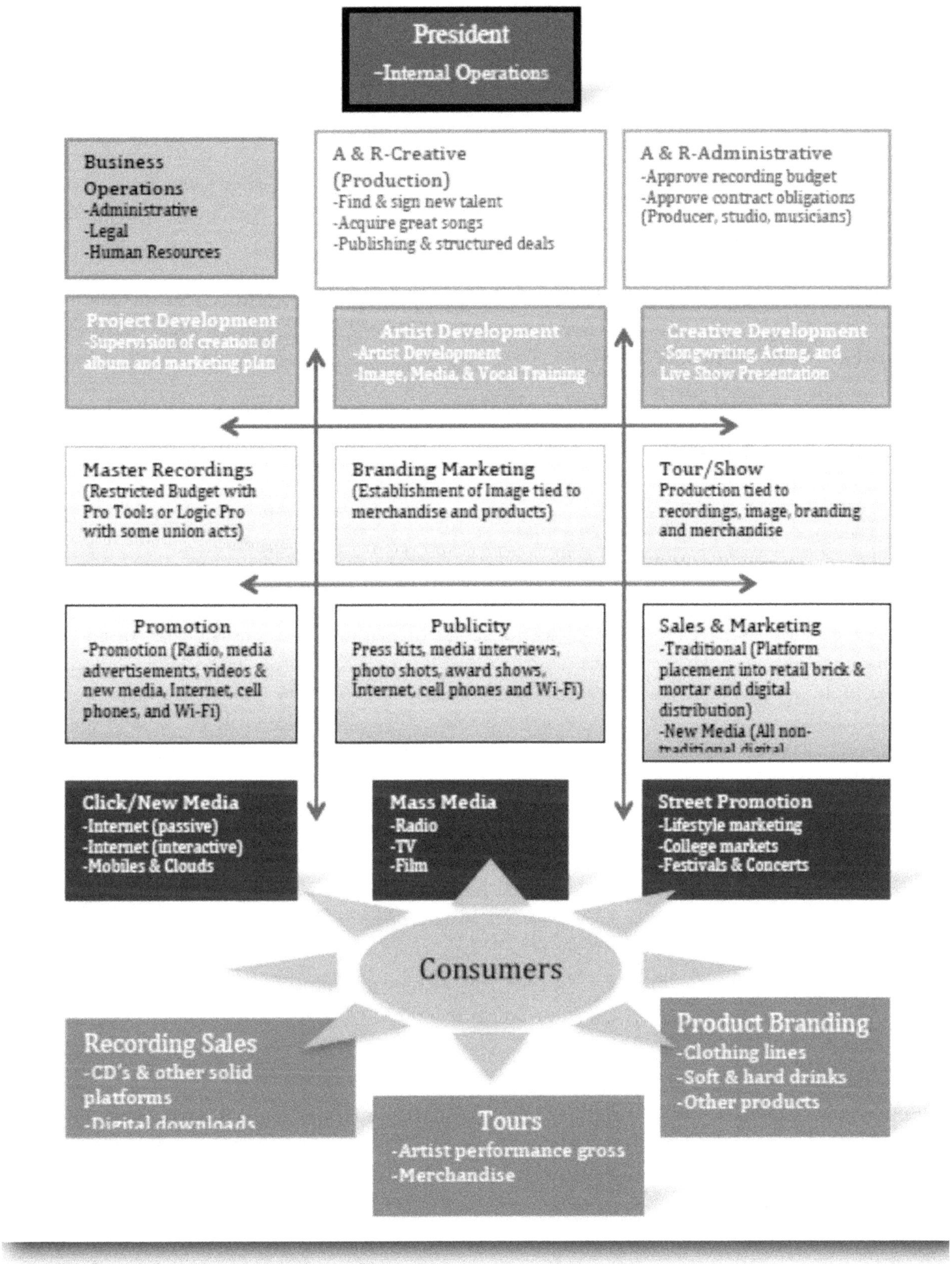
President
-Internal Operations
Business Operations
-Administrative
-Legal
-Human Resources
A & R-Creative (Production)
-Find & sign new talent
-Acquire great songs
-Publishing & structured deals
A & R-Administrative
-Approve recording budget
-Approve contract obligations (Producer, studio, musicians)
Project Development
-Supervision of creation of album and marketing plan
Artist Development
-Artist Development
-Image, Media, & Vocal Training
Creative Development
-Songwriting, Acting, and Live Show Presentation
Master Recordings
(Restricted Budget with Pro Tools or Logic Pro with some union acts)
Branding Marketing
(Establishment of Image tied to merchandise and products)
Tour/Show
Production tied to recordings, image, branding and merchandise
Promotion
-Promotion (Radio, media advertisements, videos & new media, Internet, cell phones, and Wi-Fi)
Publicity
Press kits, media interviews, photo shots, award shows, Internet, cell phones and Wi-Fi)
Sales & Marketing
-Traditional (Platform placement into retail brick & mortar and digital distribution)
-New Media (All non-
Click/New Media
-Internet (passive)
-Internet (interactive)
-Mobiles & Clouds
Mass Media
-Radio
-TV
-Film
Street Promotion
-Lifestyle marketing
-College markets
-Festivals & Concerts
Consumers
Recording Sales
-CD's & other solid platforms
Product Branding
-Clothing lines
-Soft & hard drinks
-Other products
Tours
-Artist performance gross
-Merchandise

The Traditional Business Model

Traditional labels and music companies use a five-step process to find, sign, create, promote, and sell an artist's recordings, image, tickets, merchandise, and corporate sponsorships.

1. Find & Sign Great, Sellable Talent.

Labels seek recording artists who are able to capture the imagination of the human spirit and of the current popular culture themes and beliefs. New artists who have an established a local image, a fan base, and a successful number of units sold (even in small numbers) are seen as having potential, as they may have already developed a meaningful image that communicates some emotional message to consumers. Labels view small successes in local markets as an indication that if the act is developed, recorded, and exploited (marketed), they may become very profitable. According to record producer Jimmy Bowen (Frank Sinatra, Dean Martin to Hank Williams, Jr.), (1984);

> *You should always strive to work with an artist who is a one-of-a-kind. They are the only ones that really, really break through. You can record an artist who's a copy of an artist, you can have success with them, but it's not really worth the effort. Anytime you have an artist who's like somebody else, you're starting off in second place, no matter how well you produce it. If you're producing a one-of-a-kind artist, you're doing something new. ...Sometimes a one-of-a-kind is not obvious when you first start with them. Usually, there will be a little something, you'll hear, just four bars somewhere, you'll see them in person, you'll hear them with a guitar or piano someplace, and you'll catch that little moment of magic. You've got to hunt it, look for it. You're always hunting that gold, that one-of-a-kind. And when you see it, it may be 4 years away; 6 month away; that your problem. You've got to figure out when it is, see if you can get it into a point where it's valuable before you lose the opportunity to work with it.*[403]

2. Creation

Labels/music companies have to create sellable product (recording) in major recording deals includes renting great studios, contracting AF of M musicians and AFTRA vocalists, hiring major producers and audio engineers, and the cost of the mechanical license at statutory rate (or at the controlled composition clause rate) multiplied by the number of units pressed and sold or digitally downloaded. The cost to the label is often $50,000-200,000, plus mechanicals, supervised by A&R administration. The recording cost plus mechanicals and advances are usually 100% recoupable and are considered the all-ins.

3. Promotion

Exposing the recordings is providing a sample of the recordings (made in the studio) through the mass media and click media including radio, music videos, the Internet, cell phones, and paid advertisements on the Internet and in trades such as *Billboard Magazine*. It costs money for advertisements and websites and to encourage radio to add recordings to their playlists. Budgets are usually between 100-200% of the all-ins. This may sound like tons of money (and it is), but remember that the public has to hear it before they can use it, buy it, or steal it.

4. Publicity

The artist's backstory is often used to develop an iconic image. The artist's job (once the album is completed and they are on tour) is to provide shameless self-promotion by appearing on talk shows, doing interviews and/or performing. Publicity is also the placement of stories (about the artist life or daily events) in trade magazines and the popular press and the use of in-store end caps, images on the Internet, concert tours, and even paparazzi photos placed in print, broadcast news, and digital media. These materials and placements cost

---

[403] Jimmy Bowen (as quoted by Larry Wacholtz) *Inside Country Music*, Billboard Books, (New York: Watson-Guptil Publishers, 1986) & Larry Wacholtz, *Lights, Glitter and Business Sense*, Thumbs Up Publishing, (Washington: Cheney, 1984) 184-198

money as well, and budgets are usually 50-100% of the all-ins. The good news is that great publicity tied to awesome promotion in a 2-4 week campaign will usually give consumers a chance to "discover" the act and their recordings. Accordingly, the label will examine the unit sales numbers to determine if the act is catching on and if they want to pour more money into the project or dump it in favor of another act.

5. Distribution

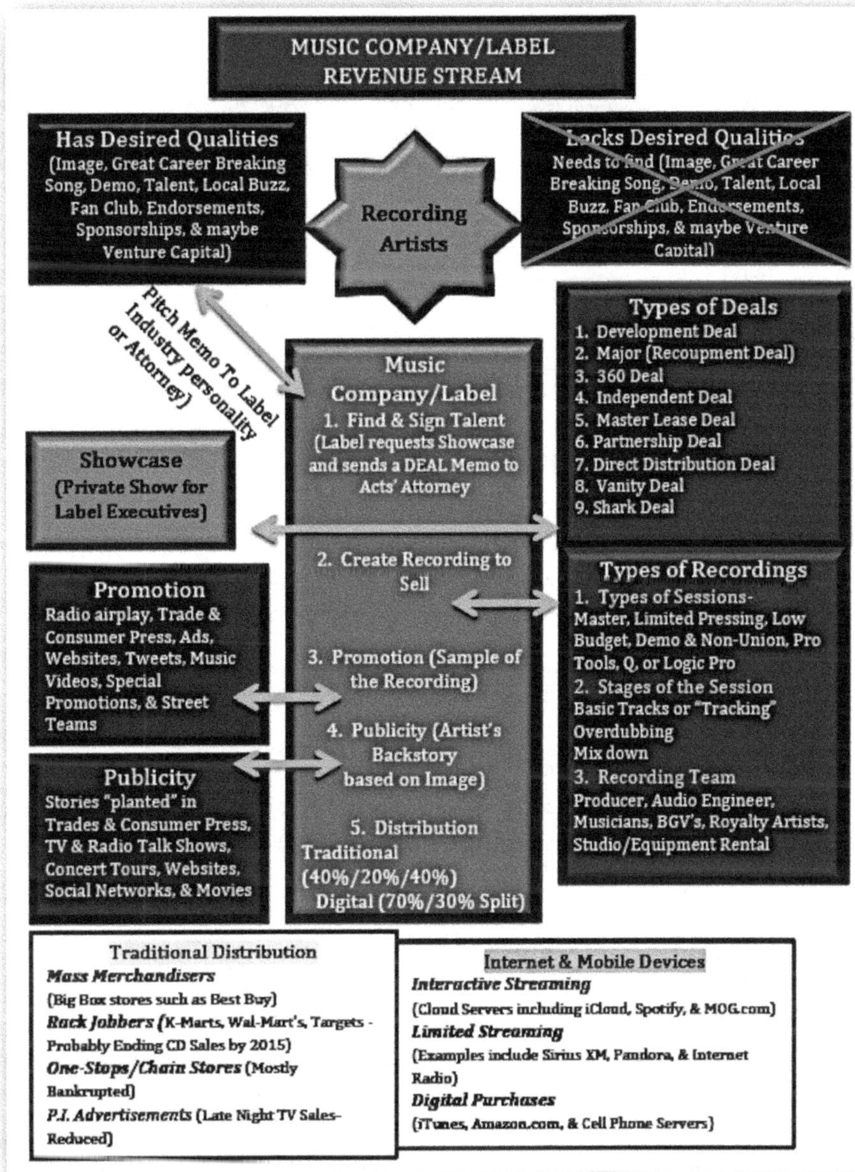

Delivery of the recordings to wholesale and retail outlets using worldwide mega entertainment distribution channels is vital. Timing is imperative, as labels want consumers to be able to easily buy, lease, or listen to the recordings they have just "discovered." Thus distributions of a recording to traditional retail outlets such as one-stops (record chain stores, most of which are now out of business), mass merchandisers (Best Buy), rack jobbers (Target, Wal-Mart, and Kmart), PI advertisements through local late night TV ads, and record clubs are made available for buying on a street date release. However, brick and mortar stores are quickly reducing CD and DVD products and it appears that within 3-5 years they will stop stocking and selling them.[404] Digital sales usually follow the same street date schedule, with buys available for digital download through cell phone providers and Internet websites such as iTunes and Amazon. *Leasing music* is now available (monthly rate of $5-10) through cloud music services such as MOG.com and Spotify.com, which connect computer servers to consumer mobile devices with binary codes to songs stored on the servers. The connection is almost instant so "why buy" when you can acquire anything you want to hear (or watch such as Netflix) instantly at a very low cost or free (if you want to listen to advertisements).

[404] Personal interviews with industry sources, (2010).

The good news for the artists and their labels is the money they make in the distribution process though consumers (hopefully) paying for hard copies (CDs), digital copies (downloads), and leases (cloud music services). However, because of the huge decrease in actual CD sales three of the four remaining major labels now use *Anderson Distribution* instead of the traditional methods and companies used in the past. According to Hypebot (2012);

> *Sony DADC which has acted as the U.S. CD distributor for three of the four major labels has transferred those rights to Knoxville, TN based Anderson Merchandisers. Anderson will now distribute Universal Music, Sony Music Entertainment and EMI CDs to every U.S. wholesaler and retailer.According to the announcement, the purchase "means the vast majority of physical music sold in America will soon reach customers through Anderson." Warner Music Group, the one distribution holdout, had a U.S. music market share of 18.6% at the end of October 2011, down from 20% at the end of 2010 and falling, according to Nielson SoundScan.*[405]

Departments

Record labels are usually divided into several departments, all of which have specific tasks to accomplish as they attempt to profit from the recordings of their artists. The departments have their own autonomous but interlinked responsibilities. They must accomplish their individual missions while working together with the other label departments to accomplish the overall strategic mission of the label, which is of course, to create and sell recorded music in this very difficult digital market. The Legal department and Royalties (Payroll) are part of the administration directly serving the President. They support the other departments including A&R, Development, Promotion and Publicity, and Sales and Marketing.

Legal Department

Legal is responsible for writing and negotiating contracts, as well as (a) signing songwriters or their songs, (b) signing co-publishing deals, (c) signing new and returning recording artists, (d) signing label employees' government forms, (e) negotiating mechanical, performance, sync, and other licenses with domestic and foreign agencies, and (f) representing the label in legal actions. Accordingly, attorneys negotiate the "terms of agreement" between the creative and business sub-system players of this creative business. Again, it is creativity battling business principles. Most labels have one or more attorneys on retainer, which means they are paid a monthly stipend for their part-time employment.

Royalty/Payroll Department

Payroll or the Royalty Department pay the bills and royalties, accepts sales payments, and reviews artists' recoupment. Financial experts control the flow of money in the label and artists' accounts. Most expenses are billed to the artists' accounts and are recouped through album sales. This concept called "recoupment" is a standard practice in the business that helps the label make millions before the average artist makes their first dollar in royalties. Accountants add the recording costs to the rest of the label expenses (artist development, photography, tour support, and most of the marketing, promotion, etc.) to the recording artist's ledger. Artist royalties are paid only *after* the negotiated label expenses for the recording, marketing of the album, and all additional expenses (tour support, etc.) have been repaid from unit sales. Artists are regularly supplied with quarterly or semiannual profit and loss statements through their manager.

---

[405] Indie Band Hub, Belmont University/Coursity of Hyperbot "82% Of U.S. CDs Are Now Distributed By One Company & It's Not Universal Music,"http://indiebandhub.com/industrynews.cfm?feature=2675543&postid=1782987 (accessed May 4, 2012),

Artists and Repertoire

Better known as A&R, the department of *Artists and Repertoire* is the communicative link between the label's creative and business subsystems. It brings the acts to the label and administers the paperwork of an album project. Accordingly, A&R is often divided into two sections, creative and administrative. Creative A&R is the "ears" of the label, always searching for a new act or song that will help make the label more profitable. It is not an easy job. Between a half million to 1.2 million dollars are spent on "breaking" a new recording artist; however, the actual cost generally depends on the type of artist, the genre of music, and the type and size of the target audience. The department may also act as an administrative facilitator between the creative and business subsystems. Songwriters create songs, musicians and vocalists record demos, and then writers pitch those tapes to music publishers. Publishers, in turn, pitch the songs to A&R. Songs selected by A&R are evaluated for album projects and pitched to the recording production team, consisting of the producer, artist, and artist's manager. In preproduction, the recording artist, producer, artist's manager, and A&R representative determine which songs, musicians, and recording studio to use. However, the producer makes the final decision about which songs to record. After the final master recording, the accepted master tapes are converted into consumer products, such as CDs and digital downloads, and distributed, marketed, and promoted through the mass media, cell phones and Internet sites to generate sales.

Development

Artist Development may be its own department or part of A&R or even Sales & Marketing within the label or music company. However, marketing is usually defined in the music business as distribution and unit sales whereas development is often divided into creative, artist, and product development.

> *Artist Development* concerns the artist's image including acting, speech, appearance, demeanor, and social manners. The artist's image frequently has to be enhanced. Trainers are hired to help the artist control a weight and/or drug problem, dentists to improve the smile, and stylists to suggest various types of cosmetics, clothing, and hairstyles for concert, stage, TV, and/or movie appearances. Image consultants are hired to suggest methods to help the act appear comfortable and confident on stage and with the media.
>
> *Creative Development* may control a few of the Artist Development issues at some labels; however, they often focus on songwriting, music publishing, and the ability to promote the artist through self-promotion. They may also supervise video script treatments, budgets, and production and provide the finished videos to the marketing department for promotion.
>
> *Product Development* supervises and coordinates the development of the label's actual album projects through each department and each stage of the marketing, promotion, publicity, and distribution process.

Promotion

Promotion or "exposure" of the artist and their recordings is vital to the financial success of the artists *and* their label or music company. It is usually handled as a "campaign," with most of the label's efforts being focused on breaking a new release to radio stations and Internet sites. In addition, the labels often hire independent promoters to motivate radio station airplay as well as retail sales. Publicity, which helps drive promotion, is often thought of as free promotion because the artists do not have to pay for the stories, pictures, and articles used in the mass media. Nevertheless, professional publicists who are paid by the label or artist's manager supply most stories to the mass media. The three levels of promotion are national, regional, and local, all of which have their advantages and disadvantages. National ads are expensive and targeted toward several demographic and psychographic types of consumers. Regional ads build support in only a section of the country, and the label may therefore miss its true market. Local ads (from free press to posters on local telephone poles) are usually poorly produced and sometimes do not generate an increase in consumer buys; however, they can start word-of-mouth conversations leading to a buzz about a new act. Labels also provide tour support through financial advances to place the act on the road. These shows are considered events that provide primary opportunities to create radio airplay, fan hype, and word-of-mouth publicity, all of which are tied to the artist's self-promotion. Of course, this is the label's effort to increase consumer excitement and bottom-line product profits by raising the level of consumer awareness and motivation to buy. Before 360 deals, labels would rarely receive any money from the merchandise bought by fans at the concert. Now, it is usually part of the recording deal and will probably soon include other event income sources like ticket sale profits and corporate sponsorship endorsements. Note that product distribution, promotion, and publicity are designed by the label's marketing plan and usually occur before or at the same time as the street release of the recording or album.

Publicity

Publicity is about telling consumers the story behind the artist and their image; plus it's very powerful when combined with a corresponding promotional campaign. While promotion provides a sample of what the labels or music companies have for sale (recordings, concert tickets, merchandise and corporate sponsorships), publicity tells consumers why they should enjoy the artist and their recordings. The hope is that consumers will see the artists as a hero, a villain, a good old boy, a sex icon, whatever, and use the images for their own self-enjoyment based on subconscious self-definition or self-elaboration. Publicity from the label's perspective includes stories and interviews planted in the trades, popular press, and click media. It also includes appearances on TV talk shows (i.e. *Leno*, *Letterman*, *Good Morning America*, etc.) and the stories, pictures, and articles publicists provide the click media, local newspapers, national trade and consumer magazines. All of these "impression" opportunities are maximized to communicate messages that the consumer can use to form a positive image of the artist.

Marketing and Sales Department

The weekly sales figures related to the marketing plan and may indicate the need for additional co-op ads and other materials such as retail end caps, radio, and tour support to increase profits. The Marketing and Sales department makes sure that CDs and digital albums are placed into retail stores and Internet websites and that point-of-purchase promotions are available. Free goods to the retail outlets are used to stimulate rack stocking and potential sales of new artists and releases. Promotional copies are different, as they are not sold (as free goods) and are used by the marketing and promotion departments to provide "samples" of the releases to radio stations and TV talk shows. They are used to encourage websites, local papers and magazines to print stories about the artist, their career, recordings, and tour dates.

Getting Noticed

Acts and bands are still discovered through local personalities: radio station DJs, local promoters, and record storeowners who inform regional label distribution and promotions about the "local buzz" an act is creating. Without the band's knowledge, labels have personalities, street promotion, or regional employees attend a live performance to determine the act's potential. Often the response of the audience is seen as just as important as the band's actual quality of performance. The band's originality, uniqueness, age, industry knowledge, and sellable image are also evaluated to determine if they can be molded or developed into a major recording act.

Websites

Acts may be first noticed on websites such as *Facebook, MySpace, YouTube*, or some other related site. Sadly, the odds are millions to one of being discovered, as most of the artists posted do not have the potential to develop into major recording acts. In addition, getting noticed on a social network is not enough to interest a label. However, it is a good first step to see if you can build a real fan base for your act. Label executives know that recordings made with the use of Pro Tools and other improvement software does not give an act the necessary talent and personality required to record for major labels and to perform live before huge audiences. Take a different approach. Develop a huge following on the Internet. Tie it to a local or a regional buzz based on your live performances and units sold. Get some local airplay and create your own fan base, and you have significantly put the odds of being "noticed" by a label in your favor.

Showcases

Live performances before a small invited group of guests (including music industry A&R personnel, managers, media, and concert promoters) can be a positive way to introduce your act to powerfully established industry personalities. Of course, we are assuming a certain level of success before you offer a showcase to the labels. However, if you've achieved a following on the Internet, a local or a regional buzz, airplay, and retail sales, it may be time to invite the industry to a performance.

Pitch Memo

If a showcase is well received and you've built a significant fan base, it may be time to send a pitch memo to the heads of A&R at various labels. At this point, there has usually been some conversation between someone who represents the label and the act. A "cold turkey" pitch (first time contact) is unusual unless investment money is also included, as in a master tape lease deal with a "no financial loss" guarantee for the label. Most of those deals are rejected, as the label does not usually want to be connected to self-financed acts (unless you're a proven success, like Garth Brooks). However, a pitch memo is a notice to the label that you are serious about pursuing a deal with them. In some cases, it is as simple as using legal representation to contact labels and other industry personalities to invite them to listen to demos or attend concerts. Internet website information and an electronic press kit consisting of a bio, recordings, videos of concerts, copies of any press articles and advertisements should be included in the pitch memos. If the label is interested, they will either send someone they know (who lives nearby) or someone from the label to check you out by calling or catching a show unannounced.

Deal Memo

The first stage of negotiation between a label interested in an act and the attorney who represents an act is covered in a three-to four-page deal memo. If the label, at its weekly meeting (President and all the departments' Vice Presidents), agrees to pursue signing an act, then a deal memo is drafted by the Legal Department or representing attorneys.

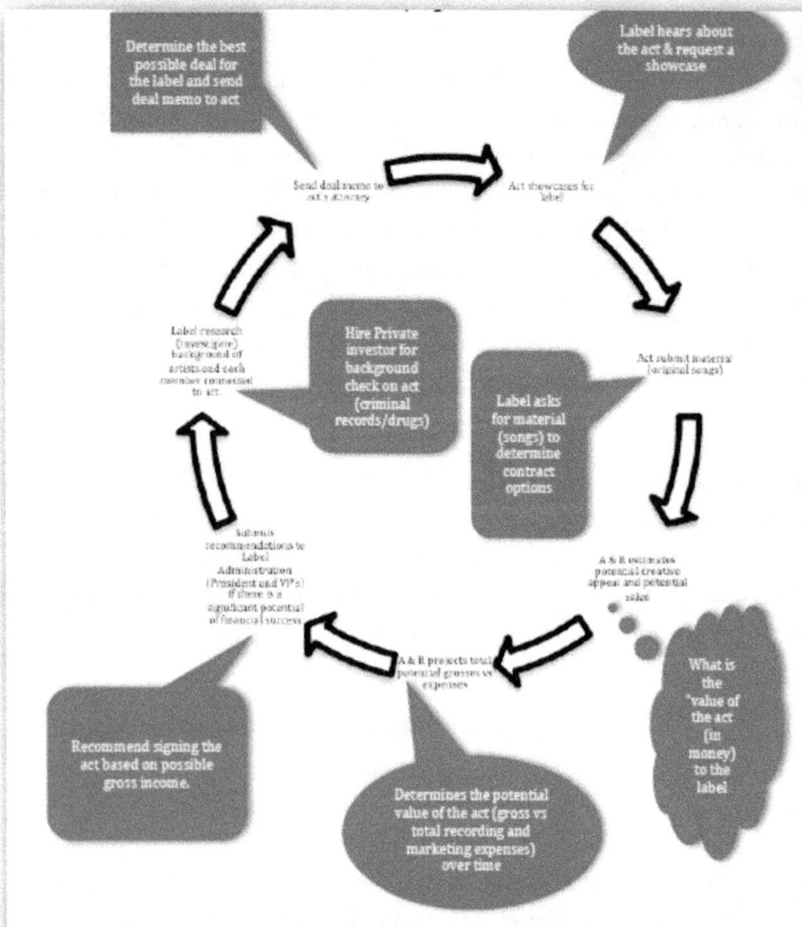

The basic points of the contract are detailed: royalty points for the artist, options, advances, number of recordings, tour advances, and other relevant issues. Deal memos allow each party to determine if and where there is common ground and to establish how close they are to an actual agreement. It is at this point that the label will often investigate your personal life for any negative deal-breakers like unknown crimes, drugs, or emotional problems. They do not want to invest half a million to a million dollars into an unstable artist without being aware of the risks. If they find out highly negative information and still want to pursue a deal, the issues will be addressed in the contract in a manner that will protect the financial investment and reputation of the label.

Types of Deals

The business of record labels starts with a great recording of a great song tied to a sellable artist. The business of artist management and the corresponding corporate sponsorships, concert tours, merchandise sales, TV roles, and film careers usually begins after the release of a sellable recording and the corresponding branding and fame. Therefore, having some type of label deal is extremely important for the ultimate success of most artists. Actual deals are very specific and often cover many legal points not discussed in the deal memo. Therefore, do not be surprised to find actual contracts to be 75-125 pages in length. It is also very important to read and understand what you are signing, as most contracts can tie up an artist's career for at least seven years.

During negotiations, the label should include all points verbally promised in writing. Budgets should be established for recording expenses, promotion, distribution, and publicity. Financial advances must include tour support and basic living expenses, as you are probably going to work-for-hire status while completing the recordings. A work-for-hire means that the label will own your performances of the master recordings. The deal will probably span seven years, with an album release required in the first year. The following six years will be options based on album sales. Thus, you want to make sure the deal from the label will give you an opportunity to successfully record, distribute, promote, and publicize your recordings and image so that the label will pick up the option for the next album. From the label's perspective, they are really signing you to a one-year minimum deal (with additional option years) to see if you can catch on, become popular, and make them money. After the label has found and signed a sellable talent and recorded them, then the marketing plan, consisting of distribution, promotion, and publicity, is launched.

Development Deals

Development deals are offered to talented vocalists, groups, and bands perceived as having the potential to develop into major recording acts. It's a chance for the artists to professionally develop their talent at the label's expense. The label pays for extra musicians, studio time, audio engineers, tapes, computers and effects equipment, and the producer. If the final master tape is accepted, the act is offered a recording contract. The cost of the recording is recouped through record sales. If it is rejected, the recording is routinely defined as a tax write-off. Some music publishers also offer promising vocalists development deals. Publishers pitch the demos to record labels in exchange for part of the artist's points when artist is signed.

Independent Deals

Indie labels range from the major personality-driven labels (Mike Curb/Curb Records, David Geffen/Geffen Records, as examples) to artist's labels (Madonna/Maverick Records) to novice recording artists and musicians. It is another opportunity for many niche artists to be recorded and distributed. Amateur recording artists, musicians, and producers often work together (and may or may not share the expenses) to record albums that can be used to promote a band, generate a local buzz, and sell off the bandstand at a live performance. Former major label artists usually retain the names and addresses of their fan club members and then use the lists to sell their self-produced CDs and digital downloads through iTunes, Amazon, CD Baby, or other outlets. Alternative music formats are frequently self-produced on computers and sold at conventions, festivals, church services, and concerts. Regional and genre independent record labels sign recording artists who may only have a niche client base in a specific region of the country or genre of music. Examples include Texas music, Latino music, or Carolina Beach music. Sometimes major labels offer successful regional and genre labels affiliate status (part ownership or part of the profits in exchange for worldwide distribution) or buy out the labels to gain their recording artists' contracts.

Major Deals

Exclusive recording agreements between artists and record labels are often complex, lengthy, and confusing. Traditional major deals offer high exposure and large budget agreements between artists and labels (that are either part of or formerly owned by a mega entertainment corporation) such as Sony Music, EMI, Warner Music, Disney (which is more of an artist development machine), or Universal. Each agreement is uniquely tailored to the specific requirements of the label and artists. Terms may vary from a single, one-time release to a multiple album, several-year obligation for both parties. *Most recording artists never make any money from their record deals and most labels fail to make any money on some of their acts.*[406] Thus, it's the few acts who really break through and become superstars that provide the labels (depending on the details of the deal) with their profits. However, major deals are usually very expensive, and most artists never make any royalties. Even the Beatles didn't make much money from their original deal. According to Courtney and Cassidy (2011),

> *George Martin (Producer and label executive) ...signed the Beatles to an unusually stingy contract, with only a penny royalty for every two-sided single sold. Of this one English penny, Brian Epstein (manager of the Beatles) and NEMS (Epestein's North End Music Store) took 25% off the top, leaving the Beatles with three-quarters of a penny, or three "farthings," to split four ways. So,*

[406] Personal interviews with industry sources, (2004-2011).

> *for every million records sold, the Beatles took home just 7,500 pounds or 1,875 pounds apiece. And this sum was their before-tax income.*[407]

Artists should look at a major deal as a shot to become famous, as a chance to see if your artistry and image can build a global fan base. It is also a way to see if the fan base you've already built can be expanded into millions of paying fans on the label's nickel. This is the emotion business, but it is built on the profit and loss statements at the labels.

Bob Donnelly, Esq., (who claims to have been affiliated with artists and managers who have sold over 300 million units, 2011), provides a different perspective. He describes traditional major record label deals as

> *… A profitable ATM for the multi-national entertainment companies, which control the major record labels. In general terms, the record label is entitled to receive 85% of net income, and the recording artist receives the remaining 15%. Any funds that the labels advanced to the artist are then repaid solely out of the artist's 15%. Now here's the best part of all from the label's perspective: in exchange for the advance paid to the artist, the label owns the copyrights to the master recordings in perpetuity. This is analogous to taking out a mortgage on a house, repaying the mortgage in full, but the bank winds up owning your house. …But wait, it gets better... for the record labels. The labels will insist that they will be able to deduct from the artist's share of income 50% of all independently contracted marketing, promotion, and publicity costs, 100% of the cost of making music videos (but the labels get to own the videos), and 50% of website costs (but the labels own the website).*[408]

360 Deals (Multiple Rights Deals)

Consumers' continuous use of P2P has reduced the labels economies of scale to a point at which it is difficult to break even financially, even with reduced budgets and limited artist rosters. Thus, most major labels are morphing into entertainment labels (that can be more appropriately referred to as music companies) by signing artists to 360 deals that reduce their risk of doing business. The negative shift in the traditional label's economics of scale is destroying the traditional business model of the music industry. It is very difficult for traditional labels to fund new artists (often at $500,000-1.2 million) when more than half of the new music and recordings acquired by consumers is not being bought. Labels break-even points have dramatically increased as a result, but a 360 deal allows the labels to repay their investments with a percentage of the artists other revenues, such as music publishing, concert tickets, and merchandise.

Some of the labels have even become full service suppliers of tour merchandise so they can take all the income as well until they have recouped their original investments. Others recoupable income included in 360 deals can be anything from song copyrights to ticket sales and corporate sponsorships. According to Chaffin in his article in the *Financial Times* (2008),

> *…The Pussycat Dolls, Paramore, and Korn have agreed to variations on the 360 theme. Disney, whose roster of stars includes the Jonas Brothers, employs multiple rights deals, as does American Idol. …Live Nation … inked a deal with Madonna in which (she was) paid more than $100m in exchange for the rights to just about everything she does. …Still, each deal differs from the next, depending in part on the composition of artists' business and their leverage in negotiations. In some 360s the record company provides merchandise sales, concert promotion and other activities while in others it takes a "passive" percentage of the revenues from these businesses without doing the work.*[409]

---

407 Richard Courtney & George Cassidy, *Come Together: The Business Wisdom of The Beatles*, (New York, NY: Turner Publishing, 2011) 71.

408 Bob Donnelly, Esq., "Why Artists Should "Do a 180" on "360 Deals," Lommen, Abdo, Cole, King & Stageberg, http://www.lommen.com/pdf/Bob-Donnelly-360-Article.aspx, (accessed April 23, 2011).

409 Joshua Chaffin, "By Promotion Gigs, Record Labels Get in on Bigger Acts," Financial Times, http://us.ft.com/ftgateway/superpage.ft?news_id=fto062420081450546621, (accessed March 17, 2011).

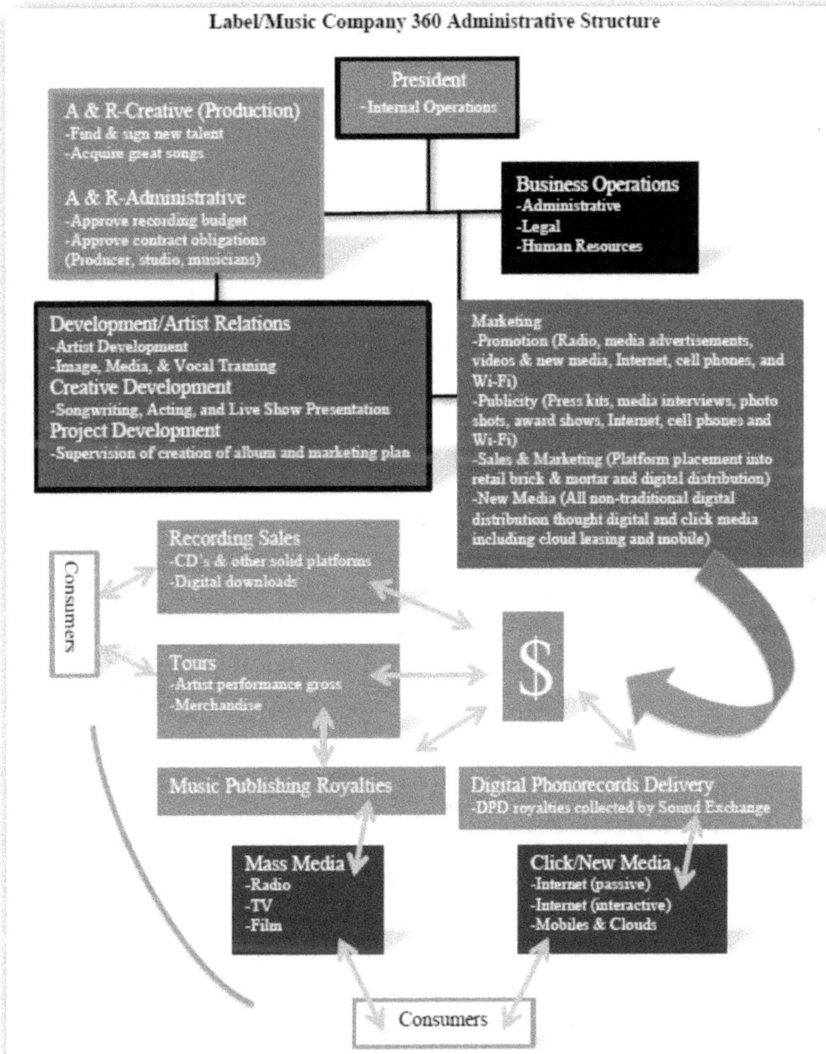

As negative as all this may sound, the creative destruction of the business is also leading to many new entrepreneurial business opportunities. Money invested in your recordings, promotion, publicity, and marketing is just the "shot in the arm" many acts need to get discovered by consumers. Without the label's money, most artists remain unknown or limited to local fame. In these digital times, 360, 270, and 180 deals (depending on the amount of touring, tickets, merchandise, endorsements, the artist company provides to the label) allow the artist a chance to widen their fan base and the label a quicker method to recoup their financial investment and both to share profits generated by an artist's success. Bob Donnelly, Esq., (2011) says,

> *The 360 deals that I've reviewed require the artist to relinquish between 5% and 50% of revenues from sources other than record sales. To illustrate this point, let's use 20% as the percentage that the record company is seeking from an artist's live touring income. If that artist is paying all of the traditional touring costs (e.g. hotels, transportation, etc.) as well as paying her manager a 20% commission, her booking agent a 15% commission, and her lawyer and business manager 5% each, then that could result in a record company receiving half of every net touring dollar which winds up in the artist's pocket. …Record companies love to cross-collateralize. This thirty-one-point Scrabble word refers to the practice of taking an artist's positive earnings from one category (e.g. publishing income) and applying it as a record company expense that affects the artist's unrecouped balance in another category (e.g. the record royalty account). …360 deals are also rife with conflicts of interests. For example, will an artist still be free to accept a sponsorship… Are the labels going to defer their commissions (as managers and artists often do) in one phase of their business (like merchandise) in order to ensure that there will be enough money for a tour to stay on the road? And how will record company's deal with fiduciary obligations to their artists (which they were previously able to avoid?) … And how do record companies think they are going to get around the booking agency laws in California and other states?*[410]

Partnership Deals

Music companies and labels are more aggressive seeking to structure partnership deals with independent, newly successful acts (with local and regional success). They can use their proven worldwide branding and marketing networks to quickly market, promote, and provide publicity of an act's products and tours thought new and traditional media. The artists who have build their own fan base, unit sales, merchandise, and

---

[410] Bob Donnelly, Esq., "Why Artists Should "Do a 180" on "360 Deals," Lommen, Abdo, Cole, King & Stageberg, http://www.lommen.com/pdf/Bob-Donnelly-360-Article.aspx, (accessed April 23, 2011).

sponsorships have a proven sellable product. In effect, the act has test marketed their "it" factor and found success with consumers. The music companies and labels (knowing the act is successful), can then very quickly "break" the act into national radio, touring, new media and traditional markets. Sometimes the deals involve venture capital (outside money matched with the labels), plus the recording masters and a variety of negotiated issues, however artist may be able to "recapture" their copyrights at the end of the deal.[411]

Master Lease Deals

Once you've become a superstar, why not do it all yourself? It is not hard today to record your own tracks, release a master tape with a major label. Let them do the distribution, promotion, publicity and sales and give them part of the profits in return. Of course, you'll need to have a high level of fame and platinum unit sales. However, the real advantage is that you as the artist maintain the copyrights to your songs and song performances on the recordings. Depending on their success, you can reissue them later (every ten years, perhaps) or sell them for an average income over several years compounded by a multiple between 5 and 15.

Direct Distribution Deals

Some acts have benefited from remaining in control of all aspects of the production, recording, marketing, and distribution of their products. Garth Brooks and the Eagles have profited from recording their own albums and marketing them directly to retail stores like Wal-Mart.[412] They've taken out the intermediary (label), reduced all expenses, and can therefore claim all current and future profits. Of course, you better be a business person if you plan this type of deal. You'll need to own or control your copyrights and be free of other commitments to industry entities.

Shark Deals

The recording label shark deal is a rip-off, just like the music publishing song shark deal. Recording artists should never pay money for a recording contract or deal unless the artist wants to continue to own their master recordings. In addition, if approached, you (the artist) should always confirm that the distribution is through a major label or mega entertainment company (Sony Red, for example) and that it has a budget for promotion (radio airplay) and publicity (trade and popular press publication). If not, pass on the deal, since all they really want is your money, and their business model will not provide profitable sales figures. Remember, it is the record label that pays the bills, takes the risks, and provides tour support money. A legitimate label will cover the cost of recordings, pressing of the CDs, digital downloads, as well as the marketing, promotion, and advertising of the artists and recordings.

Vanity Deals

Vanity labels run by are artists who have started their own label and pay all expenses or find an investor to pay for the studio musicians, audio engineer, and producer, as well as the mastering, marketing, promotion, and pressings and/or downloads. Most vanity recordings lose money because they fail to receive radio airplay and cannot generate enough sales to cover the production costs. In addition, most are of poor quality and lack promotion, publicity, and distribution. However, occasionally, a successful vanity label may become an independent label once consumers "discover" them and start to buy their recordings.

Financial Perspectives

Artists usually want to make a living doing what they love, which is of course, being an artist. However, another way to think about it is that the labels are in the business of making money, and the artist is in the

---

[411] Private interview with industry sources (2010).

[412] Private interview with industry sources (2010).

business of getting famous (so that they can also make money). Labels provide huge investment financing that they have to repay (to themselves) out of selling your recordings. They may make money (if they can sell enough of them); you may not. In fact, your probably won't. However, you're being given a shot at world fame, and it has not cost you any money. So, make the best deal you can, create a wonderful recording, let the label do its thing (promotion, publicity, and distribution), and then tour and make all the money you can while the fans still love you and your music. Once you have become famous, the power has shifted to you and your manager. Now, do you want to sign another 360 deal or start your own label and stand-alone business? Your job as a new artist is to become so successful that the choice is yours.

Traditional Recoupment Structure

Labels use artist's negotiated royalties (per unit sold) to pay the debt of the recording costs, advances, and mechanicals (the all-ins), which are 100% recoupable. In addition, the marketing plan bills (promotion and publicity) are charged to the artist's account at 50% of their total expenses. However, if the label declares the marketing expenses "tour support" (and they usually do), then the marketing bills are also 100% recoupable. The traditional business model has the label paying back the entire artist debt before the artist receives any royalties. Sadly, most artists never break even much less receive any royalties from their record deal. However, the label puts their money into an act's creativity (on the hope they will make a profit) and then they pay it all off themselves. On the average, it takes between 75,000 and 200,000 units sold (depending on the total debt) before the label breaks even and about 500,000 units or more sold (a gold record) before the artist breaks even.

Dan Hipgrave of the English band *The Toploaders* explains recoupment like this:

> *...When I was part of an international rock band, everything was given to me – all our travel, hotels, drinks, food and entertainment were laid on. It seemed to me that the more successful we were, the more was given, but the reality is we were paying for it all and didn't realize. The artist may receive a royalty of between 12pc and 13pc, but the promotional and travel costs all come out of the artist's side of the deal, not from the record company. I remember we were recording with a big LA producer once and he threw his cigar on the desk in front of us and said: "Look guys – take Sony for whatever you can – make them pay for the best hotels and travel. You're never going to get any money out of them in any other way." We took him literally. By the time Toploader split up in 2003 we had sold over 2million records, but we didn't walk away with a penny because we had been reckless.*[413]

Packaging Fees

In the old days, a certain percentage of the records would frequently break inside the packages when delivered to the retail outlets. Labels would tell the retail outlets to throw the broken records away and replace them. However, artists were "charged" for the broken records by taking a percentage off the *Suggested Retail List Price* used as a royalty base to determine actual royalties. The unscrupulous thing about all of this, of course, is that CDs and digital downloads almost never have "breakage" problems anymore, yet the labels still use this practice in contracts. Now they simply call it a "packaging fee." Fees can be as high as 15-25% of the SRLP (*Suggested Retail List Price*), which will reduce the artist royalties on each unit sold, and in turn, increase the time and number of units that must be sold before the label recoups its investment.

Artist Royalties (Points)

Let's say that an artist's royalties are established as 15% of the SRLP of $16.95. The artist would expect to receive about $2.54 for every unit sold. Yet, the breakage or packaging fee reduces that royalty by taking a

---

413 Dave Hipgrave, (by Mark Anstead), "Toploader's Dave Hipgrave: We Sold Over 2Million Records, But Didn't Walk Away with a Penny." Telegraph.com, http://www.telegraph.co.uk/finance/personalfinance/fameandfortune/8184741/Toploaders-Dan-Hipgrave-We-sold-over-2m-records-but-didnt-walk-away-with-a-penny.html, (accessed March 17, 2011).

percentage of between 10-25% off the SRLP. Let's say the packaging fee is 20%, so the label takes 20% off the SRLP of $16.95 or the SRLP of $16.95 minus $3.39. This determines the new royalty base of $13.56. Then, the label takes 15% (points determined in the contract) of the new adjusted royalty base of $13.56 to determine the actual artist's royalties, $2.03.

Wait! We are not done yet because most producers are paid producer royalties for producing the album out of the artist's royalties. So, let's say the producer receives 2% (usually between 1-3%) of the artist's royalties. That reduces the artist's royalty points from 15% to 13%. The adjusted artist's royalty points are now 13% of the adjusted royalty base of $13.56, which is just $1.76 per unit sold. The artist thought they would receive $2.54 per unit sold, but in reality, they really only receive $1.76 per unit sold (and that is after recoupment by the label). Also, labels still credit all royalty points to the artist until directed (by the artist) to pay the producer points out of their royalty points. In other words, the artist and producer will not receive royalties until the label pays all recoupable fees out of unit sales.

Accounting

The label's debt in the name of the artist account, say $1,000,000, is paid off by the artist's royalties (per-unit sold minus the packaging fee, as in our previous example of $1.76 per unit sold (the figure after the packaging fee and producer points have been subtracted)). By dividing the artist's royalties ($1.76) into the label's million-dollar debt, you can see that it will take approximately 568,181 units sold before the artist makes their first royalties. Record labels break even usually three times faster than their signed artists. The label receives about 40% of the SRLP from traditional brick-and-mortar distribution ($6.78 minus the artist's royalties of $1.76 for a total of $5.02). Divide the label's return of $5.02 into the million-dollar debt it created for the artist, and it only takes about 199,203 units sold before it breaks even.

How much money does the record label make (in our example) before the artist receives their first royalties? (This is where artists who do not understand how the business works go ballistic.) In our example, the number of units a label has to sell before the artist's account is paid is 568,181. Subtract the number of units the label has to sell before it breaks even (199,203) and the difference is 368,978 units. Take the 368,978 difference multiplied by the $5.02 the label makes on each unit sold, and you'll see that the label should make about $1,852,269 before the artist make their first dime. Labels keep the sales figures current as they usually report quarterly to the artists. Of course, the artist receives only their recoupable account debt totals or a check for units sold after recoupment is accomplished.

Summary

Having musical and vocal talent does not guarantee a hit recording. Consequently, A&R directors seek the types of acts who not only have talent, but who can also sell records through a clearly defined image. There *is* a difference, and record labels make and lose millions of dollars each year gambling on which acts connect with the music-buying public. Recordings are packages consisting of great songs that fit the image and persona of the artist, supported by an excellent vocal and musical performance by the artists and musicians. Successful acts establish the credibility of the A&R person who signed them. Failures can cost them their jobs. Successful signings provide additional record producing opportunities. Album productions enhance an A&R person's status as a record producer within the company and industry. Multiple successful deals and session productions (with the corresponding gold and platinum records) make the A&R producer a powerful, wealthy individual, often famous within the industry.

Of course, songs published by non-mega/major music companies are often accepted. Songs are first considered on their "potential hit qualities," not on who owns the copyright. However, most record labels apply "pressure" to the non-major label or non-mega-affiliated publishing company to accept the controlled composition clause. If accepted, the label saves money by paying only 75% of the statutory rate, but the writers or publishers are often faced with reduced royalties. It is a hard decision because a major recording artist may sell millions and spark performance royalties and radio airplay whereas the alternative is that the song is not recorded at all or recorded by a lesser known artist who will accept the full statutory rate per unit but won't generate as much money due to less airplay and fewer album sales.

After the master tape is recorded and accepted by the label, a marketing plan that coordinates publicity, promotion, distribution, and sales is made active. The Sales and Marketing department coordinates the label's efforts to ensure a successful launch of the product in retail markets. The Promotion and Publicity Department coordinates the label's promotion efforts for radio airplay, free 30-second clips on iTunes, and other websites and advertisements in the trade and popular press. At the same time, Publicity works on the placement of stories in the trades and popular press, scheduled TV and radio talk show appearances, an active presence on social networks like MySpace and Facebook, and co-op ads and stories in approved tour date media.

There are several types of deals depending on the label and where you are in you career as an artist: (a) Shark deals are for suckers who pay a label to get recorded, (b) Vanity records are for artist who record themselves and give them away, (c) Development deals are for new artists who show potential, (d) Major deals are usually a 7-year commitment by the artist (which really means a one-year deal with 6 options for the label, (e) Independent deals can be any type of deal by an indie label, (f) 360 deals are multiple rights deals where the artist is providing the label a percentage of their touring, merchandise, and corporate sponsorship revenues to compensate the label for monies lost due to the changing marketplace), (g) Master lease deals are when the artist pays for the recordings (they own the copyright) then strikes a distribution deal with a major label, and (h) Direct distribution deal is when the artist owns the label and the recordings, and they make a distribution deal with a retail outlet like Wal-Mart.

12

Label Revenue Sources

Album Sales, 360 Deals, YouTube, Digital Transmissions & Internet Radio

"We ultimately will become the fifth member of each band."

— Monte Lipman, President, Universal Republic Records, on 360 deals[414]

"'360 deals' have become the principal survival strategy for many music companies at a time when compact disc sales are grinding towards extinction."

— Joshua Chaffin, *The Financial Times*[415]

"If you look around, I don't know how much additional expertise has been added at various record companies to justify why they should be participating in all these other areas (360 deals)."

— Rick Dobbis, Business Manager, Rolling Stones[416]

"We have such crazy fans, and those are the ones that are going to stick with us forever."

— Josh Farro, Guitarist, Paramore[417]

Album Sales

Sadly, very few artists make any money from their recording deals and it's not always because of the deal structure based on recoupment. According to Silverman and Garland of Big Champagne and as reported on *digitalmusician.com* (2010), the total number of albums released in 2009 that sold at least one copy was about 98,000.[418] Sadly, only 85 of the 98,000 sold more than 250,000 units. Why? Clearly, many of the 98,000 albums are probably of great quality, so why did they not sell very well? Nobody knows they exist! Without major label support, promotion, publicity, and distribution, most albums fail to sell because consumers have

---

[414] Monte Lipman, (as quoted by Joshua Chaffin), "By Promoting Gigs, Record Labels Get in on Bigger Acts," The Financial Times, http://www.ft.com/cms/s/0/6e362eee-4204-11dd-a5e8-0000779fd2ac.html#axzz1GgKEQk46, (accessed March 15, 2011).

[415] Joshua Chaffin, "By Promoting Gigs, Record Labels Get in on Bigger Acts," The Financial Times, http://www.ft.com/cms/s/0/6e362eee-4204-11dd-a5e8-0000779fd2ac.html#axzz1GgKEQk46, (accessed March 15, 2011).

[416] Rick Dobbis, "By Promoting Gigs, Record Labels Get in on Bigger Acts," The Financial Times, http://www.ft.com/cms/s/0/6e362eee-4204-11dd-a5e8-0000779fd2ac.html#axzz1GgKEQk46, (accessed March 15, 2011).

[417] Josh Farro, (as quoted in) "The New Deal, Band as Brand," The New York Times, http://musicrowlawyer.typepad.com/music_row_lawyer/360, (accessed July 21, 2010).

[418] Tommy Silverman & Eric Garland, "Warning, Some of these Stats are really, really Scary," Digitalmusicnews.com, http://www.digitalmusicnews.com/stories/072110nmsstats#sm_FMtJUSBV5-9voXkkYLQ, (accessed March 17, 2011).

not yet "discovered" them through radio, iTunes, concert appearances, or other promotional and marketing methods. However, for the bands that make it, millions of dollars are created in tours, merchandise, endorsements, and other types of product sales. Exposure is the vital element to success, and labels and music companies are still the only solid way to achieve it. There are exceptions, of course, such as iTunes *Free Tuesday Download,* which provides consumers with a chance to discover new acts. Some acts pay promoters and nationally known acts to open on tours, again seeking the exposure of their music (and merchandise) to a new fan base.

The Good News

After years of gloom and doom the industry is starting to take off again. Yeah! According to Frances Moore of the IFPI (2013) "...today is different and we can afford to be more upbeat. This is a very exciting time in the music industry"[419] According to Moore (2013)

- *After a 13 year struggle, the recording industry has adapted to the Internet world and has learned to monetise the digital marketplace;*
- *More than 30% of revenues come from digital channels with that figure increasing to more than 50% in some leading markets;*
- *Subscription services were up more than 60% globally in 2012.*[420]

Billboard.Biz's Glenn Peoples reports that analyst Horace Dediu estimates (2013):

> *The total spending on iTunes accounts is $43 per-year across all media... At 575million iTunes accounts that works out to $24.7 billion of consumer spending at iTunes per-year... iTunes accounts for a large portion of all global spending on digital music. At the $12 per-account estimate (by Dediu), the 575 million accounts result in $6.9 billion of annual consumer spending on music. ...Trade value of the global digital music market was $6.9 billion in 2012 (35% of the $16.5 billion recorded music market), according to IFPI.*[421]

Partnership Royalty Structure

With the 360, 270, or 180 deals, anything is possible. On some of the newer deals, the artist or band may be allowed to provide the finished master recordings completed on Pro Tools to reduce the cost to the label. On the other end of the spectrum, some deals require venture capital infusion by the band or a third party. The *partnership deal* is when the band provides the talent and sometimes a part of the money up front, in exchange for the label's promotion, publicity, distribution services, and matching funds. Tours may be set up with the leverage of the major label instead of a typical booking agent or by partnering with agents and promoters. However, the label can't bring full management decisions into the deal unless the bands can manage themselves (which is rare). The purpose is to "launch the act" with a couple of marketing campaigns to see how successful the act might become and then to pay the debt and split the profits. Again, everything is negotiable, as revenue splits between the artist and label range from 50/50 on some to all income from all artist activities, merchandise, and sponsorships down to a 90/10 (artist/label) on all revenues, depending on the power of the artist to maintain as much control as possible. Last are the famous artists who just start their

---

[419] Lela Cobo,Frances Moore (Speech At FILAIE/IFPI meeting 2013) as reported in Billboard.Biz Bulletin 2013.

[420] Lela Cobo,Frances Moore (Speech At FILAIE/IFPI meeting 2013) as reported in Billboard.Biz Bulletin 2013.

[421] Glenn Peoples Business Matters, "Average iTunes Account Generates Just $12 in Music Revenue Per Year," Billboard.biz.bulletin (2013).

own label, production companies, and merge with an established major label or music company to distribute the product.[422]

Traditional Retail (Distribution)

Labels still make money from the sale of the recordings they place into retail, and while labels determine the suggested retail list price, the cost of creating, promoting and marketing recordings seldom determines the selling price of an album. Consumer demand and profit levels are more important. Album sales still bring in money as stated by *The Recording Industry in Numbers* published by the IFPI (2013);

> *Albums continue to hold their appeal, accounting for 56% of recorded music sales value. Digital album downloads grew faster than singles and vinyl sales hit their highest point since 1997. Consumer usage on streaming services shows that the album format remains very relevant. Many of the year's best-selling albums generated a large streaming volume across all tracks included on the album.*[423]

Wholesale and retail markups between retail outlets and distribution depends on (a) the type of distribution (retail, department stores/racks, or one-stops); (b) the type of platform on which the music is recorded (CDs, DVDs); and (c) the sales propensity of the artist (a hot superstar, a high-ticket item, known artist with current radio airplay, or title albums with recurrent radio airplay).

Retailers often ignore the suggested retail list price in favor of their own marketing strategies like offering discounts on some items and raising prices on hot-selling or hard-to-find recordings. However, the suggested retail list price is used to determine the wholesale price. Retail outlets use the range (difference) between wholesale (what they paid for the product) and retail (the price they quote to the public) to generate profits.

Accordingly, brick-and-mortar retail outlets that sell CDs for $16.95 more than likely paid about 60% or approximately $10.17 for that CD. The distributors are paid about 20% ($3.39, in this case), and the labels recoup the remaining 40% or around $6.78 per album.

Traditional retail outlets have suffered financially as consumers have more choices for their entertainment dollars. In addition, consumers know they can buy the same album for several dollars less at another store or online (which is instant and more convenient), and that's if they plan paying for it all. Traditional retail includes the following:

One-Stops

One stops are the brick-and-mortar stores and the Mom 'n' Pop places that are now mostly out of business or bankrupt. They simply cannot compete with the lower economies of scale of digital downloads.

Mass Merchandisers

Best Buy still place the CDs and DVDs in the front or middle of the store and price them low to draw in customers, then encourage them to buy a larger ticket item such as a computer, TV, or home appliance.

---

[422] Personal interview with industry sources, (2010-2011).

[423] I.F.P.I., *Recording Industry in Numbers 2013*, International Federation of the Phonographic Industry, http://www.ifpi.org/content/section_news/20130408.html (accessed July 3, 2013).

Rack Jobbers

Wal-Mart, K-Mart, and Target, place CDs in racks in their stores, rent the floor space, and pay a small commission on each unit sold. Unlike the one-stops with their large inventory and slow turnover (and therefore, higher prices), rack jobbers stock a smaller inventory of mostly hits that will sell quickly at a lower price. The racks keep getting smaller as most of these companies believe they will stop selling CD's within the next three to five years.[424]

Record Clubs

BMG Direct and Columbia House have been one of the best-kept secrets in the business as they have often been used to unload overstocked items for a huge profit. The CDs are sold at higher prices, (after the discounted membership units which are used as a tax write-off by the labels), the customer pays the distribution cost (shipping and handling) and artists usually only receive 50% of their royalties which is an industry standard. Columbia House and BMG Direct, which are owned by Sony Music, have quickly moved into digital downloads.

PI Advertising

"Per-inquire advertising," are those late night attempts to sell the overstocked albums through television. Older consumers who do not shop in record stores or online still buy old recordings that seem to stimulate fond memories of their youth. Television and cable systems play the advertisements for free when they have unsold air or broadcast time available. They are then paid a small percentage of the money consumers send in when they buy the products.

Free Goods

Labels provide free goods (free units that can be sold) to retail outlets to stimulate sales. Retail usually want some guarantee from distributors that they will not lose money or be stuck with albums they can't sell. Thus, the labels (through the distributors) usually give a certain amount of new and unknown artist releases to the retail outlet (as much as 25%) when they buy and stock a minimum inventory. Additionally, retail will usually demand 100% return on the unsold units. Thus, the retail store agrees to stock and sell the new release, it can sell or give away free units they did not pay for, and the label will accept returns on all the bought units that didn't sell.

Digital Distribution

The Internet has changed the rules of the game when it comes to the music business. Labels make more money per unit from digital downloads than CD sales. Labels make about 70¢ on every 99¢ download. In addition, they do not have to press CDs, ship them, or administrate traditional marketing. The downside is that they sell more singles than albums now, and therefore the industry is starting to appear much like the entrepreneurial singles businesses of the 1950s and early 60s. Labels have somehow survived in a market where 37% of their products are acquired without being paid for, while simultaneously adapting to new technology, unique delivery systems (iPods and cell phones), and consumer buying habits.[425]

---

424 Personal industry interviews, 2012-2013.

425 Personal industry interviews and Recording Industry Association of American (R.I.A.A.), (NPD Digital Music Study 2009 as Reported in "Let the Music Play," RIAA 2010) 11.

In the digital entertainment business, the customer gets the album for less money, but the label makes more money. A true win/win situation!

Digital Downloads

Digital Downloads are sold by providers iTunes, Amazon, and many others including phone services such as AT&T. Downloads are priced close to *wholesale* (60% of SRLP). As in our previous example, a $16.95 album is downloadable for about $9.95. In addition, digital downloads bypass the cost of brick-and-mortar retail outlets and of shipping and pressing, and (most importantly) the split is 70/30 (label/provider), as opposed to the 40/20/40 of retail outlets. Thus, the label receives slightly more money on digital downloads then on traditional sales. In the case of a digital download, the label receives about $6.96 (70%) on a $9.95 album instead of the $6.78 on the traditional brick-and-mortar unit that probably cost the consumer $16.95 at a one-stop or $12.95 at a rack jobber. The royalty points for the artist are a percentage of the digital sale price, but the packaging fees are usually dropped.

Applications- "Apps"

The future may be direct sales of recording, tickets, and merchandise, by recording artist through their own apps which provide a direct link to fans. Free or low-cost apps simply take out the intermediary and reduce the cost and time consumers need to acquire products. Apps also provide a direct marketing connection to the fan base. However, potential fans need to know who you are and have "discovered" your music before they buy the app. Thus, cell phone apps are great for known acts but not very useful for new acts until a marketing, promotion, and publicity program has been successful. Once an act and their recordings have been "discovered" by consumers, then label may need to increase the quality, speed, and value of the "discovery." The process is tied to the consumers' actual emotional connection(s) to the songs, recordings, and images of the acts. The label or music company is in the background, just trying to profit off its investments. Cell phone applications are a great way to provide a more personalized pathway to the act that will hopefully enhance the emotional connection and increase the buying of an act's products. As an example, ReverbNation's *band app* has been converted to *band profile* to include the *fan booster* function, which automatically helps acts grow their mailing lists and fan clubs.[426]

Digital Subscription Services

Labels are starting to make significant money from digital subscription services such as Napster, Rhapsody, MySpace, and Yahoo. The key terms to remember are *interactive* and *passive* when referring to customers and *tethered* or *untethered* when talking about labels.[427] Some of the digital music providers allow interactive streaming where consumers can choose what they want to listen to or download (such as Pandora for listening and iTunes for 30 second clips and buying). "Passive" means that the listener has to listen to whatever is offered, like traditional radio stations streaming their signal over the Internet. "Tethered" and "untethered" are label terms that define whether the label is giving up certain rights, allowing the purchaser to make unlimited copies (untethered), allowing the recording to be downloaded and used for a limited time, or allowing the consumer to make a limited number of copies on various devices (tethered).[428] According to Passman (2009),

---

[426] ReverbNation, (article posting by Ferol) "Reverbnations' Facebook app My Band gets a name (Band Profile) new features, and it's still 100% Free," ReverbNation & Digital Music News, http://blog.reverbnation.com/, (accessed April 2, 2011).

[427] Donald Passman, *All You Need to Know About the Music Business*, 7th ed. (New York: Freepress, 2009) 163.

[428] Donald Passman, *All You Need to Know About the Music Business*, 7th ed. (New York: Freepress, 2009) 163.

> *...To record companies everything that isn't a CD is an electronic transmission, which is the industry term for digital delivery (whether by download, streaming, or otherwise) ... A digital download, which is also called DPD (standing for digital phonorecord delivery) is a transmission to the consumer (via Internet, satellite, cell phone) ... tether ... is a fancy word for "leash," means the record company doesn't give you complete control over the download.*[429]

Digital Leasing (Cloud Music)

Why buy music or even steal it when you can lease it instantly for a few pennies on your computer, cell phone, or mobile device any time you want it? Consumer behavior trends (their use of cell phones and other devices) appear to indicate support for cloud music providers' growth. In an interview with Bruno of *Forbes.com* (July 22, 2010), Evan Schwartz of Thumbplay.com stated, "...we've seen the number of users with smart phones go from about 5% two-and-a-half years ago to over 70% now."[430]

Cloud music sites merge the idea of acquiring music over the Internet (Rhapsody) with social networking, tied to the labels' desire to make money and break new artists. Many companies are quickly merging the social networking model to their own digital retail websites. The relationship between *iTunes* and *PING* (recently introduced by Apple) is a great example of this trend. The *iCloud* syncs everything on to all devices. *Amazon.com* offers its MP3 digital store with its Cloud Player and corresponding phone app. *Spotify* is a European model that offers music for free with advertisement, for a low monthly fee without advertisements, and millions of songs your can listen to almost instantly. The common denominator is the music. It is the glue that connects the consumers to the acts, and the labels intend to profit from that connection, along with the owners and investors of the website provider. Cloud music has many advantages for everyone involved. Consumers can listen to anything they want (7.5 million recordings available) and discover new acts and music legally, and labels are making money (digital streaming performance royalties and storage or leasing fees) – only a penny and a half per song per listener, but even that is better than nothing.[431] According to David Hyman at *MOG.com* (2010),

> *"Our goal with MOG All Access was to build the best service for listening to and discovering music, period," explained MOG Founder and CEO David Hyman. "To accomplish this, we're providing access to millions of songs (just about everything), with a drop dead easy way to hear any song or album you like in an instant, from the convenience of your web browser. You'll get access to MOG radio, a revolutionary listening experience that will forever change how you discover music and truly redefines what radio is... And you get it all monthly for the price of a beer."*[432]

Internet Radio

There are thousands of internet radio stations and music subscription services transmitting around the world. According to *The Recording Industry in Numbers* published by the IFPI (2013);

> *Digital channels now account for 35% of overall industry trade revenues... Music subscription services are seeing rapid growth. Music subscription and ad-supported streaming services now account for 20% of digital revenues globally, up from 14% in 2011. Subscription and ad-supported revenues combined now account for almost one third (31%) of all digital music revenues in Europe.*[433]

---

[429] Donald Passman, *All You Need to Know About the Music Business*, 7th ed. (New York: Freepress, 2009) 163.

[430] Evan Schwartz (as quoted in an article by Ken Bruno), "Music in the Cloud," Forbes.com, http://www.forbes.com/2010/07/21/music-cloud-computing-technology-thumbplay.html?boxes=techchanneltopstories, (accessed March 17, 2011).

[431] Evan Schwartz (as quoted in an article by Ken Bruno), "Music in the Cloud," Forbes.com, http://www.forbes.com/2010/07/21/music-cloud-computing-technology-thumbplay.html?boxes=techchanneltopstories, (accessed March 17, 2011).

[432] David Hyman, "MOG Announces Premium digital Music Service Coming Soon," Reuters.com, http://www.reuters.com/article/2009/10/14/idUS109142+14-Oct-2009+PRN20091014, (accessed March 17, 2011).

[433] I.F.P.I., *Recording Industry in Numbers 2013*, International Federation of the Phonographic Industry, http://www.ifpi.org/content/section_news/20130408.html (accessed July 3, 2013).

The number of Americans (ages 12 and over), who are listening and watching entertainment online is nothing short of amazing. According to Edition Research (2013), the growth in consumer's ability to access entertainment programs per-week is increasing quickly for the owners of smart phones and tablets who have home broadband with WiFi. Quality and interactive programs are instantly available with the used of broadband, WiFi and mobil devices as more than half of consumers now own smart phones. The combined usage of all media is now 8:15 per day[434] Online radio is now very popular with AM and FM internet and audio content programming being selected by 120 million per-month and one out of every three people (83 million) per-week for an average of about 12 hours a week.[435] Eighty-two percent of people who listen to online radio also listen to broadcast radio. Pandora is listened to by about 181 million people per-week followed by iHeart radio with 119 million, and Spotify with 57 million.[436] According to Edison Research (2013), media usage is in the million for several hours ever day.[437]

Media	Millions of Users per Week
Broadcast TV	256
Radio	243
Internet	232
Home Broadband	182
Home WiFi	177
Smart Phones	139

SoundExchange

Most of the royalties being collected are for the "use of a song" and the money is usually paid directly to the copyright owner(s) and songwriter(s). However, if the songs are recorded and "transmitted digitally" over the Internet, then another fee is collected and paid to the performing artists, musicians and label (the owner of the copyright of the recording)! In most of the world this type of "recording performance fee" is collected from all media uses. But in the

---

434 Edison Research and Arbitron Research, The Infinite Dial 2013: "Navigating Digital Platforms," http://pdl.vimeocdn.com/36993/110/155378364.mp4?token=1372879771_fb76f84ebbc791c593159e86c0499fec,(accessed July 3, 2013).

435 Edison Research and Arbitron Research, The Infinite Dial 2013: "Navigating Digital Platforms," http://pdl.vimeocdn.com/36993/110/155378364.mp4?token=1372879771_fb76f84ebbc791c593159e86c0499fec,(accessed July 3, 2013).

436 Edison Research and Arbitron Research, The Infinite Dial 2013: "Navigating Digital Platforms," http://pdl.vimeocdn.com/36993/110/155378364.mp4?token=1372879771_fb76f84ebbc791c593159e86c0499fec,(accessed July 3, 2013).

437 Edison Research and Arbitron Research, The Infinite Dial 2013: "Navigating Digital Platforms," http://pdl.vimeocdn.com/36993/110/155378364.mp4?token=1372879771_fb76f84ebbc791c593159e86c0499fec,(accessed July 3, 2013).

United States its only for digitally transmitted signals over the internet as broadcast stations have been able to lobby Congress for an exception. SoundExchange collects royalties and fees (about half a billion a year) and pays them directly to the label, artists, and musicians.[438] According to the SoundExchange.com website (2013):

> *... it is a non-profit organization "they are the sole entity in the United States authorized by Congress to collect and distribute digital performance royalties on behalf of featured and non-featured recording artist, master rights owners (usually record labels), and independent artists who record and own their own masters.*[439]

SoundExchange collects statutory rates from Internet streaming providers such as Pandora and Spotify, satellite radio (SIRIUS XM) and cable television. Its administration fee is about 5.3%. The rates for licenses are statutory yet, SRCO's (a person who owns the master recording to a recorded artistic content can negotiate directly with web casters for different fees.[440]

Streaming Revenues

Millions may be listening but the streaming rates are shockingly low. As a result, there is some confusing blogs about rates. Rates depend on several variables including the type of passive or interactive connection, date the service originated and a basic rate compared to gross profits and revenues. Confusing, but here is an example of the older rate of $.005 per stream. According to an article by David Macias on Hypebolt.com (2013):

> *You want an example? Let's look at the Matisyahu "Sunshine" single. Over the last quarter, that song has been streamed 291,391 times on Spotify, generating a total of $1,569.11."*[441] *Divide the 291,391 into the $1,569.11 and you'll get $.005384 per stream. The new streaming rates are about $.0142 so they are much higher and will continue to increase slightly over the next few years.*[442]

According to Glenn Peoples of Billboard.biz (2013) "Pandora's revenue per-listener hour is 0.3 cents (3 tenths of 1 penny) based on 418 billion listener hours and revenues of $123.51 million for the first quarter of 2013 (three months)."[443] Peoples (2013) also claims:

> *... iTunes radio will pay slightly about the minimum royalty Of 0.142 cents... based on a royalty of 45% of net advertising revenues or $21.25 per 1,000 listener hours in the first year and $22.25 in subsequent years. In this case, $0.2125 per-listener hour works out to 0.142 cents per-stream, assuming iTunes Radio will stream 15 songs per-hour with an average of four-minute songs.*[444]

Promotion (Radio and Street Promotion)

Radio stations and networks are *not* in the music business; they are in the advertisement business, so they program whatever they think will draw an audience to charge for the airtime (advertisements). Companies buy advertising airtime based on the demographics and psychographics of cumulative audiences,

---

438 SoundExchange, About, "News and Views," http://www.soundexchange.com/about/, (Accessed June 7, 2013).

439 SoundExchange, http://www.soundexchange.com, (Accessed June 7, 2013).

440 SoundExchange, "General Questions," http://www.soundexchange.com/faq/, (Accessed June 7, 2013).

441 David Macias, "Making Dollars, Clearing Up Spotify's Payment Confusion," Hypebolt.com, http://www.hypebot.com/hypebot/2012/11/clearing-up-spotify-payment-confusion.html (accessed July 18, 2013).

442 David Macias, "Making Dollars, Clearing Up Spotify's Payment Confusion," Hypebolt.com, http://www.hypebot.com/hypebot/2012/11/clearing-up-spotify-payment-confusion.html (accessed July 18, 2013).

443 Glenn Peoples, "Business Matters" Billboard.biz Bulletin, 2013.

444 Glenn Peoples, "Business Matters" Billboard.biz Bulletin, 2013.

tying listening habits to lifestyles and the products or services they use. Radio is still important to labels as a method of breaking new artists as well as releases from established acts. However, most labels have downsized their Radio Promotion departments and increased the emphasis on Internet, cellphone, and cloud music sites.

Labels still have national radio promotion positions that control local and territorial promotion (street teams) whose job is to increase the buzz about an act and recording to drive radio airplay and increase sales. However, many stations are now owned by one of three conglomerates that control and program stations from a national broadcast location. As a result, it has become much more difficult to break new acts and place established acts on major radio station chains unless a certain amount of corresponding advertisements are bought. Just as the music and entertainment industry are changing drastically, so is radio. Automation of programming is now commonplace; however, stations are developing more Internet transmission options and cell phone delivery systems, along with the merger of Sirius XM satellite digital radio. Examples of radio chains include the following:

Clear Channel Radio

Clear Channel has more than 110 million listeners each week in all the nation's major radio markets though it's 850 stations. Its programming is available on AM and FM stations, HD digital radio channels, the Internet through iPods and cell phones, and is used by navigation systems in cars and global positioning systems (GPS), such as TomTom and Garmin. The company's operations include radio broadcasting, syndication, and independent media representation. Clear Channel Radio is a division of Clear Channel Communications, Inc. (NYSE: CCU), a leading global media and entertainment company.[445]

Cox Radio

Cox is one of the largest radio companies in the United States, based on revenues. Upon the completion of all announced transactions, Cox Radio will own, operate, or provide sales or marketing services for 86 stations (71 FM and 15 AM) clustered in 19 markets, including major markets like Atlanta, Houston, Miami, Orlando, San Antonio, and Tampa.[446]

NPR (National Public Radio)

NPR is an internationally acclaimed producer and distributor of noncommercial news, talk, and entertainment programming. A privately supported, not-for-profit membership organization, NPR serves a growing audience of 26 million Americans each week in partnership with more than 860 independently operated, noncommercial public radio stations. Each NPR Member Station serves local listeners with a distinctive combination of national and local programming.[447]

Social Networks

Social network sites allow consumers with common interests and preferences the opportunity to construct their own virtual reality tribes of friends and fans. The owners of the websites then use the membership totals to price and sell advertisement impressions (based on hits) to companies that market products correlated to the memberships' usage (click) patterns. Of course, the music and entertainment industry has many albums, films, TV shows, etc., that they want to sell to those social network members. Huge social

---

[445] Clear Channel, "Clear Chanel Fact Sheet," http://www.clearchannel.com/Corporate/PressRelease.aspx?PressReleaseID=1564&p=hidden, (accessed March 17, 2011).

[446] Cox Radio, "Company Overview," http://coxradio.com/company/profile.html, (accessed March 17, 2011).

[447] NPR (National Public Radio), "About." www.npr.org/about, (accessed March 17, 2011).

networks give established artists and labels another way to connect their products to consumers. According a *New York Times* article by Jenna Worthma (July 21, 2010),

> *Facebook, the social network created in the dormitories of Harvard six years ago… that it now has 500 million members. …Each month, Facebook says, more than 30 billion photographs, links to Web sites and news articles are shared through the site, and its members spend roughly 700 billion minutes there.*[448]

However, it's not as easy as it looks. New acts are rarely discovered on social networks. Consumers see the value of recorded music differently in today's P2P market. It's available for free (not legally, unless given away by the copyright owners), so how can artists and labels encourage consumers to use or buy it? Take a look at the bigger picture, and we'll see that social network members who build tribes and connect to specific acts may help the act (label) become more financially successful by connecting the act/recordings to the experience of the site members building their social network. Once a fan base is established, then the labels and independent artists seem to be able to sell their some recordings and additional products through the site. Yet, it is often the fan who "discovers" the act instead of the act finding the fan. Sites and artists that provide recordings that members can use to connect with other members have established the pathway that lets the artist and label make more money and the site members increase their enjoyment and site usage. According to Crum (July 21, 2010),

> *"The New Music Seminar convenes the architects of the next music business and Pandora is certainly one of them," said Tom Silverman, director of the New Music Seminar. "This milestone is a major building block in the foundation of the next music business. We congratulate Pandora on its achievement." Not only are Pandora's mobile apps popular, but the company was one of Facebook's launch partners for the Open Graph, which likely provided a nice boost. With the Open Graph, users can see music their Facebook friends like on the service, which can make it even more fun.*[449]

Some sites have tried to establish legal and free music downloads based on advertising hits (viewers/ impressions) per thousand. Advertisers pay an amount of money based on the number of viewers who use the site for music downloads. Sadly, most of the smaller ones are failing. Honestly, there are so technology-based business models and so many acts postings their recordings that only the very best may generate word-of-mouth advertising that *might* lead to some financial success. Sadly, *MySpace, Facebook, Twitter*, and others have failed to provide the unit sales labels expected, yet they are providing some pathways for consumers to connect and discover new acts and products.

Email and Social Network Membership

Most consumers find out about specific social networks through an email to their personal account. Others visit the website directly, and still more find them through mobile messaging.[450] According to *marketingcharts.com* (2010),

> *When participants in "Global Perspectives" were asked what prompts them to go to social networking sites, an email to their personal email address was the clearly the primary driver to social networking activity. Overall, 53% of respondents across borders stated that email to a personal account was the primary driver to social networking activity. While a large number of consumers also*

---

448 Jenna Wortham, "Facebook Tops 500 Million Users," New York Times, http://www.nytimes.com/2010/07/22/technology/22facebook.html?_r=1, (accessed July 22, 2010).

449 Chris Crum, "Pandora Reaches 69 Million Milestone," Webpronews.com, http://www.webpronews.com/pandora-reaches-60-million-user-milestone-2010-07, (accessed July 21, 2010).

450 MC Marketing Charts, "Email Drives Social Networking," Marketingcharts.com, http://www.marketingcharts.com/direct/email-drives-social-networking-13448/, (accessed August 1, 2010).

> *sign in directly to these social networking sites (35% overall), email topped all other forms of direct communication, including SMS mobile messaging (19% overall).*[451]

Promotional Copies

Promotional copies are different from free goods as they are not to be sold and are used by the Marketing and Promotion departments to provide copies of the releases to radio stations, Internet sites (30 second clips), trade magazines, TV talk shows, and to local papers and magazine editors along with stories about the artist's new albums, singles, tours, and other public events.

Trade Magazines

Labels use the industry trade magazines (*Billboard*, *Variety*, *Pollstar*) to alert key industry professionals about their acts, recordings, label news, and releases. They release publicity through articles "planted" in the trades and popular press (*People Magazine* and local newspapers) and their corresponding websites (*Billboard.com*, etc.), promoting the act's image (backstory) and their recordings. The trades also provide weekly insight into sales and airplay on charts like the "Hot 100," which ranks the top-selling radio singles (using Soundscan and BDS data) and the "*Billboard* 200" that ranks the top 200 bestselling albums (using Soundscan data).[452]

Billboard Magazine

Billboard Magazine and the corresponding *billboard.com* are the most important music business sources to the industry and consumers. According to its website (2011), Billboard is

> *The world's premier music publication, Billboard has served the entertainment business since 1894. Beginning as a weekly for the billposting and advertising business, Billboard and its popular music charts have evolved into the primary source of information on trends and innovation in music, serving music fans, artists, top executives, tour promoters, publishers, radio programmers, lawyers, retailers, digital entrepreneurs and many others. As Billboard's consumer-faced online home, Billboard.com features an extensive array of searchable, playable charts, breaking music news, artist interviews and exclusives, news, video and more. Launched in 1995 as Billboard Online, Billboard.com now attracts more than 4 million unique visitors each month in more than 100 countries and has become the de facto digital destination for popular music.*[453]

Pollstar

Pollstar and it's corresponding website *pollstar.com* are the *Billboard Magazine* of the concert business. Its offers daily updates on tours, venues, reviews, news and other vital information for industry insiders such as tour support schedules and information, plus directories for talent buyers, managers, labels, booking agents, venue and tour support.[454]

Big Champagne.com

Big Champagne analyzes and measures downloads (legal and illegal) to provide the industry with a more realistic perspective on actual media products acquired by consumers. Their website claims (2010) "...companies

---

451 MC Marketing Charts, "Email Drives Social Networking," Marketingcharts.com, http://www.marketingcharts.com/direct/email-drives-social-networking-13448/, (accessed August 1, 2010).

452 Billboard Magazine, "About Us," http://www.billboard.com/#/footer/about-us, (accessed March 17, 2011).

453 Billboard Magazine, "About Us," Billboard.com, http://www.billboard.com/#/footer/about-us, (accessed April 8, 2011).

454 Pollstar, "Store," Pollstar.com, http://www.pollstar.com/reviews.aspx, (accessed April 8, 2011).

collaborate with them to better understand their needs, develop simple, powerful, and scalable technologies and tools to inform strategic decision making with more timely relevant data and new insights."[455]

Tour Support

Labels provide their artists with front-end money (recoupable) with which to tour. The concerts or events provide radio stations, promotions, the mass media, and click media a chance to talk about the act and the tour, which tends to reinforce the word-of-mouth buzz (fans), which then results (hopefully) in increased record sales. When the label releases their recording, newly signed acts are often placed on a radio tour where they visit key radio stations to introduce themselves to programmers through interviews and airplay.

Digital Rights Management (DRM)

DRM is a copyright lock technology used on digital downloads by major record labels to restrict the use and copying of the recordings. CEO Steve Jobs comments in an Apple news release called *Thoughts on Music* (February 6, 2007),:

> *…To prevent illegal copies, DRM systems must allow only authorized devices to play the protected music. If a copy of a DRM protected song is posted on the Internet, it should not be able to play on a downloader's computer or portable music device. To achieve this, a DRM system employs secrets. There is no theory of protecting content other than keeping secrets. In other words, even if one uses the most sophisticated cryptographic locks to protect the actual music, one must still "hide" the keys which unlock the music on the user's computer or portable music player.*[456]

Apple has dropped DRM, and all the major labels are dropping it as well to offer recordings through all digital distributors.

Professional Organizations

Two organizations represent labels in the United States and the rest of the world. They support record label issues before Congress and other international governments.

The Recording Industry Association of America (RIAA) represents music companies and labels in the United States. According to *www.riaa.com* (2010), it

> *…Is the trade organization that supports and promotes the creative and financial vitality of the major music companies. Its members are the music labels that comprise the most vibrant record industry in the world. RIAA® members create, manufacture and/or distribute approximately 85% of all legitimate recorded music produced and sold in the United States.*[457]

The International Federation of the Phonographic Industry (IFPI) represents the recording industry around the globe. According to *www.ifpi.org* (2010), its mission is to

> *…Represent the recording industry worldwide with some 1400 members in 66 countries and affiliated industry associations in 45 countries. Its mission is to (a) promote the value of recorded music, (b) safeguard the rights of record producers, and (3) expand the commercial uses of record music.*[458]

---

[455] Big Champagne, "About," http://bcdash.bigchampagne.com/who, (accessed March 17, 2011).

[456] Steve Jobs, "Thoughts on Music," Apple.com, http://www.apple.com/hotnews/thoughsonmusic/, (accessed August 1, 2010).

[457] Recording Industry Association of America, (RIAA), "About Us," http://www.riaa.com/aboutus.php, (accessed March 17, 2011).

[458] International Federation of the Phonographic Industry, (IFPI), "IFPI's Mission," http://www.ifpi.org/content/section_about/index.html, (accessed March 17, 2011).

Major Labels with 360 Deals

Record labels have in the past been a vital part of their parent mega entertainment corporations' strategic business plan, method of operation, and bottom-line financial success. The mega conglomerates provide the annual budget to finance the label's operation and album projects. Once artists are signed and recorded the mega distribution system, mass media and print media promote and sell the albums worldwide to consumers through traditional and digital retail outlets.

Most major labels have the budgets, world distribution, promotion, and publicity to launch an act. In the past, they often signed, recorded, and distributed American artists and culture for profits. Now, they are also trying to develop territory markets by signing and exploiting (in a positive way) local acts such as Chinese and Japanese acts to the Asian markets, Eastern European acts to Europe, and so on. At the same time, P2P has cut the financial profits of the major labels because according to the RIAA (Recording Industry Association of America), 37% of all releases are stolen (acquired without being paid for), which makes it difficult for the labels to stay in business.[459]

It is amazing how quickly major labels are changing their business models toward music companies (instead of labels selling only recordings). Most take advantage of digital production, creative operations, promotion, publicity, and several forms of product distribution, including radio, TV, cable, satellite, Internet, social websites, and cell phones, to grow their consumer base and increase profits. They are bigger than record labels but smaller than mega entertainment corporations. All are signing new acts to 360 deals, which merge all industry revenue streams. Of course, there are many different types of 360 deals being developed; however, music entertainment umbrella companies are offering them to survive the creative destruction of the traditional industry. Established artists are safe in their current recoupable deals, but new artists are offered some type of 360 or partnership deal. Of course, once the superstar's deal expires, they will have to make the decision to either sign a 360 or start their own label. However, because they are famous, they may make more money owning and controlling their own label and businesses then allotting a percentage of all the revenues they generate through tours, merchandise and corporate sponsorships in the typical 360 or partnership (multiple rights) deals.

Artist Images and Branding

Music companies and labels sign artists to make money. What a concept! Having the "talent" to sing is not enough to get signed. Even artists who can't sing are signed because they still make money for the labels. Turn on the radio! So what are labels looking for in an artist? The answer is, of course, someone who generates emotions in consumers (really consumers use whatever their perceptions of the artists are to generate their own emotional responses). Hopefully, the consumers' responses can be monetized into several revenue streams such as recordings, tickets, merchandise, corporate sponsorships, and endorsement that will generate profits for the label and artists. Thus, being able to sing in tune is not enough to get you signed. Artists need a career-breaking hit song that is tied to their personal image, which is hopefully based on their personal passions and frame of reference (how they view the world). Promotion is tied to that song, giving consumers a sample of the essence of the act and a sample of their "talent." Publicity is tied to the backstory of the act, as illustrated by their image. Branding is the next step where the artist, manager, or label uses the

---

[459] Personal industry interviews and Recording Industry Association of American (R.I.A.A.), (NPD Digital Music Study 2009 as Reported in "Let the Music Play," RIAA 2010) 11.

image to "brand" merchandise and products consumers will also buy based on their emotional "connections" to the act.

Branding

Sean "Diddy" Combs	$475 million	Clothing line, label, Ciroc Vodka, acting
Shawn "Jay-Z" Carter	$450 million	Rocawear clothing label, Live Nation deal, New Jersey Nets, 40/40 club
Curtis "50 Cent" Jackson	$100 million	Vitamin Water, video games, books, clothes, headsets

Other Types of Labels

Other types of labels besides the 360s and majors are still around and may become powerful by the success of the acts they have signed. The keys to being a successful label include (a) the artists you sign, (b) world distribution (before the Internet), (c) promotion and (d) publicity (which only the majors can usually afford). However, with digital technologies almost anyone can create music on a computer. But can you sell it? Can you let consumers know that your recordings exist (giving them a sample of what you've got to sell)? And can you tell them why they might emotionally connect to it and the artist (publicity)?

On one side of this issue is the process of creation (quality of the recording of the perfect song married to the right artist and their image) and on the other side are the business operations – promotion (radio airplay, Internet clips, music videos), publicity (talk shows, articles, trades, and press), and distribution (brick-and-mortar retail, digital through cell phones and Internet). The merging of these two systems is foundation of a label. Other types of labels that exist include the following.

Affiliate Labels

Are connected financially and through distribution deals with the major labels that provide unit sales through traditional retail outlets and promotion and publicity through the labels' established media connections.

Independent Labels

Are usually controlled, owned, and established by major industry personalities, such as record producers like Sam Phillips (Sun Records) or artists such as Madonna (Maverick Records). Producers use their own labels to land distribution deals with major labels, and established artists often use their labels for tax write-offs and to record their friends and newly discovered talents.

Vanity Labels

Are created by unsigned artists to sell their own recordings or to provide additional revenues.

Specialty and Virtual Reality Labels

Focus on a genre niche, such as children's music or comedy albums, or a type of unique distribution such as digital downloads, cell phones, or websites like MySpace and Facebook. The virtual reality labels do not often press CDs; they keep expenses low by providing only digital downloads to the Internet users, cell phones, and PDAs.

Promotion Branding Labels (PBLs)

Have recently emerged as marketing tools for other products. Starbucks formed its own label and signed Sir Paul McCartney. Many companies are signing artists in an attempt to sell other products. Others form labels to support manufactured artists such as dolls, cartoons, or children and teenage stars on TV shows and movies.

Perspective on Music Companies

Recording artists rarely enter into a recording deal with any real understanding of how labels or music companies work. They are often on an ego trip dreaming of becoming rich and famous from the deal. Instead, artists need to consider what the label can and will do for them to launch their career. Most recording artists never received any royalties from their recordings. The truth is simple: the record labels are not in the business of making artists rich, they are in the business of selling discs and digital downloads that will make *them* rich. Thus talent, as defined by the labels, is related to the amount of money they can make from an artist's recordings. This is the merger of the creative system and business system where in the past neither could accomplish much in the worldwide market without the other. The creative system provides the songs, vocalists, musicians, audio engineers, and producers. The business system, consisting of labels, provides the money to fund the recordings, promotion, publicity, and distribution. On the front end, labels treat artists with great respect. On the back end, in closed meetings, it is the number of units moved, break-even points achieved, and the financial outcome that determines the respect the label has for an artist. This sounds harsh of course, but this is a business and who else would spend millions on an unknown artist for the promotion, publicity, and distribution of artistic products? According to the *International Federations of The Phonographic Industry's* release *Investing in Music* (2010),

> *...Investing in music begins with record labels funding the work and the livelihood of artists. Leading international music companies have artist rosters ranging from several hundred to more than 2,000 acts, while there are thousands of smaller independent labels with rosters ranging from a handful to over a hundred acts. Major companies alone have an active roster of more than 4,000 acts, with tens of thousands more on independent labels worldwide. All labels are continuously investing in new signings and renewing agreements with existing acts.*[460]

Administration

The Chairperson of the Board or Chief Executive Officer commonly heads the label, provides and meets with external business opportunities and contacts, and reports earnings figures and strategic management decisions to the parenting mega executive board (of which they are a member). The President generally provides a vision of operation to the label and oversees the internal daily operations of the label. Vice Presidents supervise their departments and are responsible for individual area employees and the successful completion of departmental tasks and goals.

Operations

The label CEO, President, and Vice Presidents work together, after the initial signing of an act, to suggest a producer, establish a budget, and develop a marketing plan for the act. A strategic allegiance is usually established with the artist's manager. It is notable that the manager must be careful not to let his or her associations with the label's executives become a conflict of interest with the recording artists they manage. Upper level administrators are responsible for the development and implementation of a strategic management plan. This includes the development of a vision and mission statement, short and long-term personal and financial goals, the organization's internal policies and objectives, and the responsibility of a continuous internal and external financial analysis (profit and loss statements).

---

460 John Kennedy & Alison Wenham, "Investing in Music," IFPI.org, http://www.ifpi.org/content/library/investing_in_music.pdf, (accessed March 17, 2011).

Signing Acts

Label decisions about which acts and songs to sign are often based on research, experiences, gut instincts, and consumer reaction. The profitability and survival of the label depends on their decisions. To avoid being a casualty of a poor decision, many labels make their "final" signing decision by committee consensus. The committee consists of the label Vice Presidents of each department, an A&R person presenting the act, and the label's President and/or Chairperson of the Board. The purpose is to involve everyone as a team to campaign for the signing of the artist, and then to work together for the successful selling of their respective recordings. Thus, the final decision to sign an act is generally a "company decision" with the final decision being made by the CEO, President, and Vice Presidents based on the recommendation of the committee and support from all the label employees.

Picking Up Options and Dropping Older Acts

Administrators review the sales projections and accomplishments of each of the labels' recording artists and personnel. Artists failing to achieve profitable unit sales are customarily dropped from the label after the first few poor-selling record releases. The label fulfills their contractual obligations for the commitment albums and then simply does not pick up the artist's option. Artists who are not satisfied with a label may, in rare cases, "buy out" of their contract by mutual agreement, in one lump sum payment, or future artist royalties generated from projected album sales. However, successful artists often find it very difficult to terminate a current agreement. Court action is often required and rarely approved. Obviously, major labels have spent millions to make an artist successful, and they do not appreciate an artist who wants to jump to another label after the hard work and money has been invested to make the artist famous. In addition, label employees who fail to sign or generate profitable products or sales are encouraged to improve or leave. After continued decline in profits, both productive and nonproductive employees are usually dismissed. It is not uncommon for the entire staff of a major label to be replaced for not producing profitable acts and recordings.

Course of Action/Distribution

In the past, labels were in the business of selling discs to wholesalers to create a profit. They worked on a 40/20/40 split of the suggested retail list price (SRLP), paying their bills and hopefully creating low financial break-even points based on unit sales figures. Digital distribution is a 70/30 split, with the label receiving the larger amount. Other than finding and signing talent, the functions of a successful label consist of the four "Ps" of marketing: product, placement (distribution), promotion/publicity, and price. Together these ideas allow the label to successfully bring the album to market to a specific demographic and psychographic consumer base at the right price for maximum profit levels. These four variables in the marketing mix are distributed thorough most of the labels' departments. Finding an artist and the songs that can satisfy the wants and needs of the typical music consumer is the job of the A&R Department. Delivering a master recording to the label that will satisfy consumers' emotional needs is the job of the recording team (headed by the producer). Retail is the selling of the recordings (product) to consumers so that the label may make a profit on its financial investments. The Marketing Plan includes the job of the marketing and sales department to expose the right product to the right demographic and psychographic consumer base.

Summary

Music companies (labels) create recordings they hope to sell to the public. Major labels use their own music publishing companies to promote and place their own songs with their signed artists. Most songs selected for album projects are funneled through the label's A&R department. Mechanical royalties are paid at the controlled composition rate of 75% of the statutory rate and are literally paid from one pocket of the company (label) to another pocket (publishing) keeping all expenses in-house. Foreign performance royalties are collected by internationally situated performance rights organizations and shared internally by patriarchal labels and music publishing companies. Sync rights are often reduced or paid between the TV and movie production companies within the same mega entertainment corporation, again keeping expenses within the same corporate organization and profits higher.

Digital music sold online to consumers is profitable for the music industry. Consumers can either buy a hard copy (CD), buy a digital download, (iTunes), listen to it on radio, stream audio from a website, or lease the music through monthly subscription providers *spotify.com, iTunes radio,* and *mog.com.* These distribution methods have added new and exciting ways for consumers to acquire music quickly. Record labels make more money from each songs or albums sold because they are cutting out the distribution and retail outlets, record stores, TV outlets, or record clubs' percentage of the purchasing price. Thus, consumers can now acquire their music at traditional retail outlets, or choose to get it in a quicker, less expensive, more convenient manner through the Internet or cell phones.

Key Website Resources

http://www.billboard.com/

http://www.ifpi.org/

http://www.pollstar.com/

http://www.riaa.com/

http://www.variety.com/

13

The Record Deal

Exclusive Recording Artist Agreement[461]

This EXCLUSIVE RECORDING ARTIST AGREEMENT (this "Agreement") is made and entered into as of ____________, by and between ___________, whose address is ____________ __________________________ ("Company") and __________ ("you"), whose address is _________________________________.

1. Exclusive Services

Company hereby engages your exclusive personal services as a recording artist in connection with the production of Records and you hereby accept such engagement and agree to exclusively render such services for Company in the Territory during the Term and all extensions and renewals thereof. (You are sometimes called "Artist" below).

2. Term

(a) The term of this Agreement shall consist of an "Initial Period" and the "Option Periods" set forth below as may be exercised by Company pursuant hereto.

(b) The "Initial Period" shall commence on the date hereof and shall end on the date that is twelve (12) months after Delivery and acceptance by Company of the Recording Commitment (as defined below) for the Initial Period.

(c)You hereby grant to us four (4) separate, consecutive and irrevocable options, each to extend the Term for additional contract periods (each herein called an "Option Period") upon the same terms and conditions applicable to the Initial Period, except as otherwise provided herein. Each such Option Period shall run consecutively beginning on the expiration of the Initial Period or the previous Option Period, as the case may be, and shall end on the date twelve (12) months after Delivery and acceptance by Company of the Recording Commitment for such Option Period. The Initial Period and the Option Periods are sometimes referred to herein as "Contract Periods", as the same may be suspended or extended as provided herein. Company shall exercise each such option by notice to you at any time prior to the expiration of the then current Contract Period.

(d) Notwithstanding anything to the contrary contained in paragraph 2(a)-(c), if, as of the date when the current Contract Period would otherwise have expired, Company has neither exercised its option to extend the Term for a further Contract Period nor notified you that Company does not wish to exercise such option, then: (i) you shall immediately notify Company that its option has not yet been exercised (an "Option Warning"); (ii) Company shall be entitled to exercise its option at any time before receiving the Option Warning or within ten (10) business days thereafter; and (iii) the current Contract Period shall be deemed to

---

[461] Rush Hicks, "The Recording Deal/Contract," provided by attorney Rush Hicks, Nashville, TN, (2010).

have continued until Company exercises its option or until the end of such ten business day period (whichever shall occur first).

3. Recording Commitment/Delivery

(a) During each Contract Period you shall record and Deliver to Company sufficient Masters to constitute the Record specified in the following schedule (the "Recording Commitment"):

CONTRACT PERIOD	RECORDING COMMITMENT
Initial Period	One Album (the "First Album")
First Option Period	One Album (the "Second Album")
Second Option Period	One Album (the "Third Album")
Third Option Period	One Album (the "Fourth Album")
Fourth Option Period	One Album (the "Fifth Album")

(b) (i) The First Album shall be Delivered to Company within ninety (90) days following commencement of the Initial Period; (ii) the Recording Commitment in respect of each Option Period shall be Delivered to Company within ninety (90) days following commencement of the applicable Option Period; and (iii) unless an authorized officer of Company shall otherwise agree in writing, and without limiting any of the other provisions herein, you shall not Deliver any Album within nine (9) months following the date of the initial commercial release of the immediately preceding Album in the United States. If any Recording Commitment is Delivered between October 15th and December 31st of a particular year, then Delivery of the Recording Commitment concerned will be deemed to have occurred on January 2nd of the succeeding year.

(c) No multiple Albums, "theme" Masters (e.g., Christmas Masters), "live" performances, instrumental Masters, joint recordings or spoken-word Masters shall be recorded or Delivered hereunder in satisfaction of the Recording Commitment without Company's prior written consent, which may be withheld in Company's sole discretion; provided however, if Company consents to the Delivery of a multiple Album hereunder, then such multiple Album shall be deemed a single Album for the purposes of Artist's Delivery obligations under this Agreement. If Artist Delivers and Company accepts Masters consisting of "theme", "live", instrumental, joint or spoken-word recordings, then such Masters shall not be deemed to be in partial or complete fulfillment of any of Artist's obligations hereunder.

(d) During the Term, Company shall have one (1) option ("Greatest Hits Sides Option"), to require Artist to record and Deliver up to two (2) Sides recorded after Company's exercise of such Greatest Hits Sides Option (the "New Greatest Hits Masters"). Each such New Greatest Hits Master shall embody a Composition not previously recorded by Artist and shall be intended for initial release on a "Greatest Hits" or "Best Of" Album (a "Greatest Hits Album"). Artist shall deliver such New Greatest Hits Masters no later than sixty (60) days after Company's exercise of the Greatest Hits Sides Option. New Greatest Hits Masters shall not be deemed to fulfill any of Artist's obligations hereunder with respect to Recording Commitments.

4. Recording Procedure

(a) Prior to the commencement of recording any Recording(s), you and Company shall mutually agree on each of the following, in order, before you proceed further: (i) selection of, and compensation for, individual producer(s) (including, without limitation any producer advance [or fee] and producer royalty, if any); (ii) selection of material, including the Compositions to be recorded; and (iii) the dates of recording and mixing and studios where recording and mixing are to take place. Artist shall be responsible for engaging and paying all producers of each Master ("Producer") (except that Company may engage Producer(s) at its election and deduct any sums paid to such Producer(s) from any sums payable hereunder). Company shall have the right to have a representative attend each recording session. For the first album, ------------ is approved as record producer.

Reversion clause: IF I WRITE THIS & YOU DON'T RELEASE IT, I GET IT BACK.

(b) Upon the reasonable request of Company, Artist shall re-record any selection until a Master commercially and technically satisfactory to Company has been obtained. Company may refuse to accept, and may require Artist to deliver substitute Masters for, compositions Company deems patently offensive or which, in its judgment, violates any law, violates the rights of any person, or subjects Company to material liability for any reason.

re coop ment

(c) It is of the essence of this Agreement that Artist timely supply Company with all of the information Company needs in order: (i) to make payments due or required in connection with the Masters; (ii) to comply with any and all other obligations Company may have in connection with recording the Masters, and (iii) to release Records embodying the Masters. Subject to the provisions of this Agreement, Company will pay Recording Costs incurred in connection with any Master(s) Delivered hereunder not to exceed the applicable Recording Fund with respect to such Master(s). Without limiting the foregoing, Artist shall deliver to Company within forty-eight hours after each recording session the following documents pertaining to such session: all union contract forms or report forms and all necessary payroll forms (including without limitation all I-9 forms and related documentation and all W-4 forms). Artist shall deliver all other invoices, receipts, vouchers and documents within one week after the related expense is incurred. Artist shall be solely responsible for and shall pay any penalties and/or interest charges incurred by Company for late payments by reason of Artist's failure to comply with the terms of this paragraph (or Company may deduct any resulting penalty or interest charges from any and all monies payable under this Agreement or any other agreement between you or Artist and Company or its affiliates). In addition, Artist shall deliver promptly complete label copy, any liner credits and any information required to be submitted to unions, guilds or other third parties.

(d) Your submission of Masters to Company shall constitute your representation and warranty that you have obtained all necessary licenses, approvals, consents and permissions including, without limitation, written clearance(s) from the copyright owner(s)/publisher(s) for any and all "first use" compositions, licenses for sampled material, etc.; provided that, unless Company has specifically requested that Artist do so, Company will secure the actual Mechanical Licenses for compositions recorded hereunder; provided that you are solely responsible for obtaining and you hereby represent, warrant and covenant that you will obtain written clearance(s) from the copyright owner(s)/publisher(s) for any and all "first use" compositions prior to recording any such composition and promptly provide Company with copies of all such clearances. You shall be solely responsible for and pay any and all costs, fees, and expenses in connection with any and all sample licensing and authorization, and all such sums (including, without limitation, royalties and any "rollover" payments) to the extent not paid by you, shall be deducted from any and all monies payable under this Agreement or any other agreement between you or Artist and Company or its affiliates. Company shall have the right to approve or disapprove (in its unrestricted discretion) all terms and conditions of any such sample license prior to embodiment on any Master. Notwithstanding the foregoing, Company may elect to arrange directly for such authorization and licensing in which event, you shall nevertheless be solely responsible for and pay any and all costs, fees and expenses in connection with such sample licensing and all such sums (including, without limitation, royalties and any "rollover" payments) to the extent not paid by you, shall be deducted from any and all monies payable under this Agreement or any other agreement between you or Artist and Company or its affiliates.

when you're makin' money, KEEP IT DUDE

manager TAKES CARE OF everything

(e) Nothing in this Agreement shall obligate Company to continue or permit the continuation of any recording session, even if previously approved hereunder, if Company reasonably anticipates that the Recording Costs attributable to the recording session shall exceed the Advances/Recording Fund for that Album or other applicable Recording Commitment or that the Recordings being produced will not be technically and commercially satisfactory in accordance with the provisions of this Agreement.

(f) Unless Company requests or approves otherwise, your performances hereunder shall be reasonably consistent in concept and style, and the Masters will be similar in general artistic concept and style, to Masters recorded and accepted by Company as satisfying your Recording Commitment for the Initial Period hereof. You will obtain Company's written consent prior to performing in any new concept or style.

5. Grant of Rights

(a) All Masters, Video Masters and other Recordings embodying Artist's performances made during the Term from the inception of the recording thereof and all reproductions derived there from, together with the performances embodied thereon (but excluding musical compositions embodied therein), shall be the property of Company, free from any claims whatsoever by Artist or any person deriving rights or interests from or through Artist. Without limiting the generality of the foregoing, Company shall have the exclusive and unlimited right to all the results and proceeds of Artist's recording services rendered during the Term, including, without limitation, the exclusive, unlimited and perpetual right throughout the Territory: (i) to manufacture, advertise, sell, lease, license, distribute or otherwise use or dispose of, in any or all fields of use by any method now or hereafter known (including but not limited to any form of digital or electronic transmissions as well as sales through Company's website), Records embodying Masters (including accompaniment tracks without the vocal tracks), or to refrain therefrom; (ii) to use and publish and to permit others to use and publish Artist's name (including any professional name currently utilized or hereafter adopted by Artist), approved photographs and likenesses, and approved biographical material concerning Artist for advertising and trade purposes in connection with the sale of Artist's Recordings and the exploitation, in accordance with the terms hereof, of all Masters and Video Masters produced during the Term. The materials approved by Artist that contain the Artist's name or likeness or photograph or biography may also be used by Company's foreign affiliates and licensees; (iii) to obtain copyrights and renewals thereof in sound Recordings and Video Masters (as distinguished from the musical compositions embodied thereon) recorded by Artist during the Term, in Company's name as owner and "employer-for-hire" of such sound recordings and Video Masters. Artist acknowledges that Artist's services hereunder are rendered as Company's employee-for hire for the purposes of copyright ownership of the sound Recordings and Video Masters and any related artwork made hereunder. If any such Recording or artwork is determined not to be a "work made for hire", it will be deemed transferred and assigned to Company by this Agreement, together with all rights in it, including without limitation the worldwide copyright therein and all renewals and extensions thereof. You and Artist hereby irrevocably and unconditionally waive any and all moral and like rights (including, droit morale) that you and Artist have in such Recordings and in the performances embodied therein and related artwork and hereby agree not to make any claim against Company or any party authorized by Company to exploit such Recordings or artwork based on such moral or like rights; (iv) to release Records derived from Masters recorded during the Term by Artist under any name, trademark or label which Company may from time to time elect; and (v) to perform such Records and to permit performances thereof by means of radio broadcast, television, Internet or any other method or medium now or hereafter known or devised.

(b) Company shall have the perpetual right, without any liability to any party, to use and to authorize others to use your name and the names (including any professional names heretofore or hereafter adopted), and any likenesses (including photographs, portraits, caricatures and stills from any Videos made hereunder) and biographical material relating to Artist and any producer of Masters hereunder, on and in the packaging of Records hereunder, for purposes of advertising, promotion and trade and in connection with the making, exploitation, promotion, marketing and publicity of Records hereunder, the writing and publishing of articles by Company or third parties, in general goodwill advertising (advertising designed to create goodwill and prestige for Company and not for the purpose of selling any specific product or service), and including, without limitation, purposes collateral to such permitted purposes (e.g., MTV's advertising and promotion), without payment of additional compensation to Artist or any other person. You warrant and represent that you own the exclusive right to so use such names, likenesses and biographical materials and that the use of same will not infringe upon the rights of any third party. If any third party challenges Artist's right to use a professional name, Company may, at its election and without limiting Company's rights, require Artist to adopt another professional name approved by Company without awaiting the determination of the validity of such challenge. During the Term, Artist will not change the name by which Artist is professionally known without Company's prior written approval.

(c) Company shall have the right to maintain an artist website (including the right to incorporate Artist's name, likeness, photographs and biographical material therein) in accordance with Company's standard policies (including, without limitation, incorporating links to other sites). Artist may also maintain his/her own website; provided that (i) during the Term of this Agreement, Company shall have approval rights regarding all aspects of such website and (ii) Artist may not sell recorded product on such website. No Person other than Company and Artist shall have the right to maintain an artist website regarding Artist during the Term hereof.

6. Marketing Restrictions

Company agrees that it will not release any Album delivered in fulfillment of the Recording Commitment as a Budget Record in less than twelve (12) months; or as a Mid-Price Record in less than six (6) months after initial release of the Album in the United States. If Company releases any such Album that is a Mid-Price Record or Budget Record, as applicable, prior to the expiration of the applicable time period without your consent, your sole remedy shall be that Company shall not reduce your royalty rate pursuant to paragraph 8(i) below for sales of such Album made during such period.

7. Advances/Recording Funds

Company shall pay to Artist the following sums as Advances:

(a) In connection with Artist's Delivery to Company of the applicable Album(s) hereunder, Company will pay Artist an Advance in the amount by which the applicable sum below (each herein called a "Recording Fund"), as reduced pursuant to paragraph (b) below, exceeds all Recording Costs paid or incurred by Company for such Album(s). Such Advance shall be payable to Artist promptly following the Delivery of the applicable Album(s). (i) With respect to the First Album, the Recording Fund shall be $____________, payable as follows:

(A) The sum of $____________________ shall be payable to the Artist upon the execution of this Agreement.

(B) The balance shall be payable upon Delivery of the Master Recordings. (ii) With respect to each of the Second Album through the Fifth Album, if any, the Recording Fund shall be an amount equal to sixty-six (66%) percent of the royalties earned by Artist under paragraph 8 hereof on paid Net Sales through United States normal retail distribution channels of the previously released Recording Commitment

Album for twelve (12) months from USA release of such previously released Recording Commitment Album. In no event shall any such Recording Fund be less than the "Minimum" or more than the "Maximum" set forth below for the Album in question:

(C)

Applicable Album/Recording Commitment

	MINIMUM	MAXIMUM
Second Album	$150,000	$250,000
Third Album	$200,000	$300,000
Fourth Album	$250,000	$400,000
Fifth Album	$300,000	$500,000

(iii) Any monies paid by Company to third parties for independent record promotion and marketing shall constitute an Advance to Artist.

(b) In calculating each Advance hereunder, the applicable Recording Fund shall be reduced by all Anticipated Costs, partial payments of such Recording Fund, and all charges and other Advances deductible therefrom (each such Recording Fund, as so reduced, is sometimes referred to herein as the "Available Fund"). As used herein, "Anticipated Costs" means any costs Company reasonably anticipates will be paid or incurred by Company for recording, mastering, mixing or re-mixing the Masters concerned and all costs which Company reasonably anticipates are necessary to clear "samples" on such Masters. Any Anticipated Costs which are deducted from a Recording Fund but are not paid or incurred by Company as set forth in the previous sentence shall be remitted to Artist. Artist agrees that the Recording Fund includes the prepayment of session union scale to Artist as provided in the applicable union codes and Artist shall complete any documentation required by the applicable union to implement this sentence. It is understood and agreed that Company shall not be responsible for paying any charges or fees for arrangements or orchestrations supplied by Artist.

(c) Each Recording Fund set forth in paragraph 7(a) above is inclusive of all Recording Costs for the production of the Masters comprising the applicable Album. All Recording Costs incurred by Company with your approval and/or all Recording Costs incurred by you or your representatives which are in excess of the aforementioned Recording Funds shall be your sole responsibility, and you hereby agree to forthwith pay and discharge all such excess Recording Costs. In the event Company elects to pay any such excess Recording Costs on your behalf (which Company shall have the right but not the obligation to do), you shall, upon demand, reimburse Company for such excess Recording Costs or, in lieu of requesting reimbursement: (i) with respect to excess Recording Costs incurred by Company (with your approval), Company shall have the right to deduct such excess Recording Costs from any monies otherwise due you under this Agreement except for Mechanical Royalties and (ii) with respect to excess Recording Costs incurred by you or your representatives, Company shall have the right to deduct such excess Recording Costs from any monies otherwise due you under this Agreement, including without limitation Mechanical Royalties.

(d) (i) All sums paid to you or Artist or on your or Artist's behalf, or at your written request to anyone on your or Artist's behalf, or to or on behalf of any person, firm or corporation representing you or Artist, other than royalties payable hereunder and (ii) any and all Recording Costs paid or incurred by Company hereunder, shall constitute Advances. Company may recoup Advances from any and all royalties (excluding Mechanical Royalties, except as otherwise specified herein) accruing hereunder.

(e) If any Album is not delivered within ninety (90) days following its due date, Artist shall, upon Company's written demand, repay Company any amounts previously paid by Company for or in connection with such Album.

8. Royalties

Company shall credit to your royalty account royalties as described below. Royalties shall be computed by applying the applicable royalty percentage rate specified below to the applicable Royalty Base Price in respect of top-line Net Sales of the Record concerned:

(a) (i) The royalty rate (the "Basic U.S. Rate") in respect of Net Sales of Records (other than Audiovisual Records) consisting entirely of Masters made hereunder during the respective Contract Periods specified below and sold by Company through Normal Retail Channels in the United States ("USNRC Net Sales") shall be as follows:

TYPE OF RECORD	BASIC U.S. RATES
First Album	12%
Second and Third Albums	13%
Fourth Album and Fifth Albums	14%
Singles, EPs and Twelve-Inch Singles	10%

(ii) Notwithstanding anything to the contrary, a sale of a Digital Download shall result in Company crediting to your royalty account a royalty rate of 10% prorated based upon the number of downloads. By way of example, should Company sell an Album via Digital Download and the retail price to the consumer is $9.99, you will receive 10% or 99.9 cents per album download.

(b) The Basic U.S. Rate will escalate prospectively solely in respect of Net Sales of any particular Album constituting your Recording Commitment in excess of the following number of units: 1% at 500,000 USA Soundscan units, and an additional 1% at 1,000,000 USA Soundscan units.

(c) The royalty rate on Records sold for distribution through normal retail distribution channels outside of the United States shall be the following percentages of the Basic U.S. Rate, applied to the applicable Royalty Base Price, and, if sold by a licensee not owned or controlled by Company, shall be paid to Artist upon the same number of Records for which Company is paid:

Territories	Percentage of Basic U.S. Rate
Canada	75%
EU, Australia, New Zealand, & Japan	66.67%
Rest of the World	50%

(d) With respect to Records sold by Company through mail order or a record club or in conjunction with a television advertising campaign, and for Records sold other than through normal retail distribution channels, Artist's royalties shall be computed at fifty percent (50%) of the applicable rate set forth above. With respect to Records licensed by Company for sale through mail order or a record club or licensed by Company for sale in conjunction with a television advertising campaign, and with respect to Company's licenses of the Masters or Video Masters, Company shall credit Artist's royalty account with fifty percent (50%) of Company's Net Royalty Receipts, or fifty percent (50%) of the Net Amount Received by Company, as applicable, from such sales and licenses. No royalties shall be payable with respect to Records received by members of any Club

Operation in an introductory offer in connection with joining it or as a result of the purchase of a required number of Records including, without limitation, Records distributed as "bonus" or "free" Records, or Records for which the Club Operation is not paid.

(e) On Records sold as premium merchandise, Artist's royalties shall be computed at fifty percent (50%) of the applicable rate and the Royalty Base Price shall be the price the distributing record company receives for the premium Record.

(f) Notwithstanding any provision to the contrary herein contained and without limiting any of Company's rights hereunder, Company shall have the right to license Masters for all types of use (visual and non-visual) on a flat fee or royalty basis, in Company's discretion, for any uses referred to in this subparagraph, and as to any such license Company may credit to Artist's royalty account, in lieu of any other royalty, fifty percent (50%) of the Net Royalty Receipts from that license.

(g) Notwithstanding anything to the contrary contained herein, the royalty rate on any Record in a New Technology Configuration shall be seventy-five percent (75%) of the otherwise applicable royalty rate. Audio-only compact discs are not a New Technology Configuration. It is specifically acknowledged that Company's actual out-of-pocket costs incurred directly in connection with the development and production (but not the manufacturing) of Records hereunder in any New Technology Configuration shall constitute Recording Costs.

(h) With respect to Records sold directly to consumers by Company in the United States or by a Principal Licensee outside the United States, other than by the methods described in subparagraph 8(d) (e.g., without limitation, telephone, satellite, cable, direct transmission over wire or through the air, and on-line computer sales) (collectively, "Direct Transmissions"), the royalty rate shall be seventy-five percent (75%) of the royalty rate that would otherwise apply if the Record concerned was sold through Normal Retail Channels. With respect to Records licensed by Company for sale directly to consumers by means of a Direct Transmission, Company shall credit Artist's royalty account with fifty percent (50%) of Company's Net Royalty Receipts, or fifty percent (50%) of the Net Amount Received by Company, as applicable, from such licenses.

(i) The royalty rate on a Budget Record or on any Record sold to the United States government, its subdivisions, departments or agencies, through military exchange channels, or to educational institutions or libraries shall be fifty percent (50%) of the applicable royalty rate set forth above; on a Mid-Price Record, seventy-five percent (75%) of the applicable royalty rate set forth above.

(j) No royalties shall be payable to Artist in respect of Records sold or distributed for promotional purposes; as surplus, overstock or scrap; as cutouts after the listing of such Records has been deleted from the catalog; as "free," "no charge" or "bonus" Records other than Albums; for Records distributed to radio stations; or for Records distributed for use on transportation carriers or for use in juke boxes. As to Records sold at a discount to "one-stops," rack jobbers, distributors or dealers, whether or not affiliated with Company, in lieu of the Records given away or furnished on a "no-charge" basis as provided above, the applicable royalty rate otherwise payable hereunder with respect to such Records shall be reduced in the proportion that said discount wholesale price bears to the usual stated wholesale price.

(k) If any Master is recorded by an Artists jointly with another artist or musician to whom Company is obligated to pay a royalty for the Master, Artist's applicable royalty rate therefor shall be divided by the number of persons (including Artist) to whom Company is obligated to pay a royalty in respect of the Master. For purposes of the immediately preceding sentence, a group of artists to whom Company is obligated to pay one "all-in" royalty shall constitute one person.

(l) The royalties provided for in this Agreement are inclusive of all royalties payable to producers and all third parties (other than Mechanical Royalties) for sale of Records and use of the Masters.

(m) As to a Record not consisting entirely of Recordings delivered hereunder, the royalty to be paid hereunder shall be prorated in the proportion the Masters (or Video Masters, as applicable) that are embodied on the Record bear to the total number of royalty-bearing master recordings (or Video Masters, as applicable) embodied on that Record.

9. Accounting

(a) Statements as to royalties payable hereunder shall be sent by Company to Artist on or before the September 30th and March 31st for the respective semi-annual period ending the preceding June 30th and December 31st, together with payment of accrued royalties due to Artist, if any, on sales and licenses for which Company has received payment by the end of the semi-annual accounting period involved. No statements need be rendered by Company for any accounting period after the expiration of the Term for which there are no sales, or other exploitations of Records derived from Masters hereunder. Company may withhold from Artist's royalty account a reasonable reserve against anticipated returns, rebates and credits. With respect to sales of singles and other Record configurations, such reserves shall be held in accordance with Company's reasonable business judgment. Company will liquidate such reserves within four (4) accounting periods following the period in which such reserves were initially established.

(b) Artist shall be deemed to have consented to all royalty statements rendered by Company to Artist, and they shall not be subject to any objection by Artist for any reason, unless specific objection in writing, stating the basis thereof, is given by Artist to Company within two (2) years from the date the statement is rendered to Artist (the "Objection Period"). Any action, suit or proceeding action relating to any royalty statement (rendered hereunder) must be commenced by the Artist within one (1) year after expiration of the Objection Period for that statement.

(c) Company shall maintain books of account concerning the sale, distribution and exploitation of Records and Masters made hereunder. A certified public accountant or attorney on Artist's behalf may, at Artist's expense, once per calendar year, examine Company's books as same pertain to the sale, distribution and other exploitation of Records hereunder, at Company's office, during usual business hours and upon no less than thirty (30) days prior written notice. Company's books relating to activities during any accounting period may only be examined as aforesaid during the Objection Period.

(d) Royalties hereunder for sales and licenses derived from sources outside the United States shall be computed in the national currency in which Company is paid therefor, shall be credited to Artist's royalty account hereunder at the same rate of exchange as Company is paid or credited, and shall be proportionately subject to any foreign income, withholding, added value, transfer or comparable taxes which may be imposed upon Company's royalties for those sales and licenses. If Company cannot collect payment in the United States in U.S. Dollars, Company shall not be required to account to you for the sale, except as provided in the next sentence. Company shall, at your request and at your expense, deduct from the monies so blocked, and deposit in a foreign depository, the equivalent in local currency of the royalties which would be payable to you on the foreign sales concerned, to the extent such monies are available for that purpose, and only to the extent to which your royalty account is then in a fully recouped position. All such deposits shall constitute royalty payments to you for accounting purposes. To the extent possible, Company will allow you to select the foreign depository referred to in this paragraph (d).

(e) Company shall have the right to deduct from any amounts payable to Artist hereunder (1) such portion thereof as may be required to be deducted by any governmental authority, and (2) any amount payable by

Company with respect to Artist's royalties under any union or guild agreement applicable to the Records and Masters hereunder. Artist agrees to execute and deliver promptly to Company such forms and other documents that may be required in connection with this paragraph.

(f) In the event Company makes any claim, or brings any action, suit or proceeding, that recovers any sums with respect to any Master, and in the event royalties are payable to Artist under this Agreement from such sums received by Company, all costs and expenses of such recovery (including, without limitation, reasonable attorneys', accounting and auditing fees and expenses) shall be deducted from the gross sums so recovered.

10. Notices

Except as otherwise specifically provided herein, all notices under this Agreement shall be in writing and shall be given by courier or other personal delivery, by overnight delivery by an established overnight delivery service (e.g., Federal Express, Airborne Express, DHL or United Parcel Service), or by registered or certified mail, return receipt requested, at the applicable address below, or at a substitute address designated by written notice by the party concerned,

TO YOU AT:

WITH A COURTESY COPY TO:

TO COMPANY AT:

WITH A COURTESY COPY TO:

Notices shall be deemed given when mailed or deposited into the custody of an overnight delivery service for overnight delivery, or, if personally delivered, when so delivered, except that a notice of change of address shall be effective only from the date of its receipt.

11. Licenses for Musical Compositions

(a) Artist hereby grants to Company an irrevocable license under copyright to reproduce each Controlled Composition for uses as contemplated hereunder. Company shall pay Mechanical Royalties on Controlled Compositions at 100% of the respective minimum statutory rates (without regard to playing time) for the United States and Canada, determined at the date effective on the earlier of (i) the date such Masters are Delivered to Company hereunder or (ii) the date such Masters are required to be Delivered to Company hereunder, as applicable.

(b) There shall be an aggregate Mechanical Royalty cap of twelve (12) times such rate per Album; two (2) times such rate per Single; three (3) times such rate per Twelve-inch Single; and five (5) times such rate per EP. To the extent that the aggregate Mechanical Royalty rate would exceed the cap in any Record, the excess will be deducted from any and all monies payable hereunder including without limitation, the Mechanical Royalties payable for the Controlled Compositions recorded under this Agreement. If a Composition recorded hereunder is embodied more than once on a particular Record, Company shall pay Mechanical Royalties in connection therewith at the applicable rate for such Composition as though the Composition were embodied thereon only once. All Mechanical Royalties payable hereunder shall be paid on the basis of Net Sales of Records hereunder for which royalties are payable pursuant to this Agreement. No Mechanical Royalties shall be paid on Records described in subparagraph 8(j). Company may maintain reasonable reserves with respect to payment of Mechanical Royalties. Notwithstanding anything to the contrary contained herein, Mechanical Royalties payable in respect of Controlled Compositions for sales of Records for any use described in subparagraphs 8(d), 8(e) and 8(i) shall be seventy-five percent (75%) of the otherwise applicable rate in the United States or Canada, as the case may be. Any assignment of the ownership or administration of copyright in any Controlled Composition shall be made subject to the provisions hereof and any inconsistencies between the terms of this Agreement and mechanical licenses issued to and accepted by Company shall be determined by the terms of this Agreement. If any Single, Maxi-Single, EP or Album contains Compositions which are not Controlled Compositions, you will obtain for Company's benefit mechanical licenses covering such Compositions on the same terms and conditions applicable to Controlled Compositions pursuant to this paragraph 11.

(c) In respect of all Controlled Compositions, Company is hereby granted the irrevocable perpetual worldwide right to reprint the lyrics on the jackets, sleeves and other packaging of Records derived from Masters hereunder. Company is hereby granted the irrevocable right throughout the Territory to recreate the title and/or lyrics to any Composition embodied in a Recording delivered hereunder in the so-called "text mode" of digital compact cassettes, interactive compact discs or any other New Technology Configuration embodying such Recording, without payment to any person or entity. If Company is required to pay any monies for the exercise of any of the rights granted to it under this subparagraph 11(c), then Company shall have the right to demand reimbursement, therefore from you and Artist (and you and/or Artist shall immediately make such reimbursement) and/or the right to deduct such costs from any monies payable under this Agreement or any other agreement for Artist's services.

(d) In respect of all Controlled Compositions performed in Videos, Company is hereby granted an irrevocable perpetual worldwide license to record, synchronize and reproduce such Compositions in such Videos and to distribute and perform such Videos including, without limitation, all Audiovisual Records thereof, and to authorize others to do so. In addition, in respect of all Controlled Compositions performed in Webcasts, Company is hereby granted an irrevocable perpetual worldwide license to record, synchronize and reproduce such Compositions in such Webcasts, and to distribute and perform such Webcasts and to authorize others to do so. Company will not be required to make any payment in connection with the uses referred to in the immediately preceding two sentences, and those licenses shall apply whether or not Company receives any payment in connection with those uses. Notwithstanding the immediately preceding sentence, following Company's full recoupment of all costs in connection with a Video, Company shall negotiate in good faith with you regarding a royalty to be paid prospectively with respect to Controlled Compositions embodied in such Video in connection with the commercial exploitation of such Video. Simultaneously with your and Company's selection of creative elements of each Video produced hereunder, you shall furnish Company with a written acknowledgment from the person(s) or entity(ies) controlling the copyright in each non-Controlled Composition to be embodied in any Video confirming the terms upon which said person(s) or entity(ies) shall issue licenses in respect thereof and in respect of Webcasts. Upon Company's request therefor, you shall cause said person(s) or entity(ies) to forthwith issue to Company (and its designees) licenses containing said terms and such other terms and conditions as Company (or its designees) may require. Royalties in connection with licenses for the use of non-Controlled Compositions pertaining to Videos and Audiovisual Records are included in the royalties set forth in paragraph 17 hereof. If the copyright in any Controlled Composition is owned or controlled by anyone else, you will cause that person, firm or corporation to grant Company the same rights described in this paragraph 11, on the same terms.

12. Events of Default

(a) In the event Artist fails to fulfill any of Artist's recording commitments hereunder in accordance with all of the material terms and conditions of this Agreement, then, in addition to any other rights or remedies available to Company, Company shall have the right, upon notice to Artist at any time prior to the expiration of the then current Contract Period (i) to terminate this Agreement without further obligation to Artist as to unrecorded or unfinished Masters or Video Masters, or (ii) to extend the then current

Contract Period for the duration of such default plus one hundred and fifty (150) days, with the times for the exercise by Company of its options to extend the Term and the dates of commencement of subsequent Option Periods deemed extended accordingly. Company's obligations hereunder, other than the obligation to pay earned royalties to Artist, shall be suspended for the duration of any such default. The provisions of this subparagraph shall not result in an extension of the Term for a period in excess of the period permitted by applicable law, if any, for the enforcement of personal service contracts.

(b) Company reserves the right, at its election, to suspend the operation of this Agreement for the duration of any of the following contingencies, if, by reason of any such contingency, Company is materially hampered in the performance of its obligations under this Agreement or its normal business operations are delayed or become impossible or commercially impracticable: Act of God, fire, catastrophe, labor disagreement, acts of government, its agencies or officers, any order, regulation, ruling or action of any labor union or association of artists, musicians, composers or employees affecting Company or the industry in which it is engaged, delays in the delivery of materials and supplies, or any other cause beyond Company's control. No suspension under this subparagraph shall exceed six (6) months during any Contract Period unless such contingency is industry-wide, in which event Company shall have the right to suspend the applicable Contract Period for the duration of such contingency.

(c) If Company refuses without cause to allow you to fulfill your Recording Commitment for any Contract Period and if, not later than sixty (60) days after that refusal takes place, you notify Company of your desire to fulfill such Recording Commitment, then Company shall permit you to fulfill said Recording Commitment by notice to you to such effect, such notice to be given, if at all, within forty-five (45) days of Company's receipt of your notice. Should Company fail to give such notice as aforesaid, you shall have the option to terminate the Term by notice given to Company within thirty (30) days after the expiration of the forty-five (45) day period; on receipt by Company of such notice, the Term shall terminate and all parties will be deemed to have fulfilled all of their obligations hereunder except those obligations that survive the end of the Term (e.g., warranties, Re-Recording Restrictions, rights of approval, and obligation to pay royalties), and you shall have no other remedy for such refusal without cause by Company to allow you to fulfill your Recording Commitment.

13. Injunctive Relief

Artist expressly acknowledges that Artist's services hereunder are of a special, unique and intellectual character which gives them a peculiar value, and that in the event of a breach or threatened breach by Artist of any term, condition or covenant hereof, Company shall incur immediate irreparable injury. Artist expressly agrees that Company shall be entitled to injunctive and other equitable relief, as permitted by law, to prevent a breach or threatened breach of this Agreement by Artist, which relief shall be in addition to any other rights or remedies, for damages or otherwise, available to Company.

14. Collective Bargaining Agreements

During the Term, Artist warrants and represents that, if Company so requests, Artist shall become and remain a member in good standing of any labor unions with which Company may have agreements lawfully requiring such union membership, including, but not limited to, the American Federation of Musicians and the American Federation of Television and Radio Artists.

15. Warranties and Representations; Indemnities

LIL PUMP agreement 12.

(a) You and Artist warrant and represent that: (i) Artist is over the age of eighteen (18) and neither you nor Artist is under any disability, restriction or prohibition, whether contractual or otherwise, with respect to your right to execute this Agreement or your and Artist's rights to perform its terms and conditions. Without limiting the foregoing, you specifically warrant and represent that no prior obligations, contracts or agreements of any kind undertaken or entered into by Artist, will interfere in any manner with the complete performance of this Agreement by Artist or with Artist's right to record any and all compositions hereunder.

You further warrant and represent that Company shall not be required to make any payments of any nature for, or in connection with, the rendition of your or Artist's services or the acquisition, exercise or exploitation of rights by Company pursuant to this Agreement, except as specifically provided herein. As of the date hereof, Artist is not a resident of the State of California. Artist shall notify Company immediately in the event that Artist becomes a resident of the State of California. (ii) (1) Artist shall enter into a valid and binding contract with each producer (each, a "Producer Contract") prior to the rendering of each such producer's services hereunder. Each Producer Contract shall grant to Artist all rights necessary for Artist to fulfill all of Artist's obligations hereunder. Artist will fully and promptly perform its obligations under the Producer Contracts. Without limitation of the foregoing, Artist shall cause each producer to execute and deliver a document in the form of Exhibit A prior to commencement of recording of the applicable Master. If Artist does not enforce any of Artist's rights under a Producer Contract, Company may without limitation of Company's rights enforce such rights in Artist's name and/or the name of Company. If Artist breaches any Producer Contract, then Company may cure such breach on Artist's behalf and at Artist's expense. No modification of or amendment to a Producer Contract will be made which would directly or indirectly diminish any of Company's rights hereunder. Artist will upon Company's request furnish Company with a complete copy of any or all Producer Contracts and/or any modification of the Producer Contracts.

(2) You shall be solely responsible for and shall pay promptly all monies becoming payable to Artist, each individual producer of Recordings hereunder and all other parties rendering services on or in connection with such Recordings, both in connection with such individuals' services and also the exploitation by Company and its designees of the results of such services; provided that Company shall, in accordance with all of the terms hereof, pay Mechanical Royalties becoming payable to the copyright proprietors of Compositions embodied on Masters and monies required to be paid to the A.F. of M. Music Performance Trust Fund and Phonograph Record Manufacturers Special Payments Fund in connection with the manufacture and sale of Records derived from Masters.

(iii) No materials, or any use thereof, will violate any law or infringe upon or violate the rights of any third party. "Material," as used herein, includes:

(i) all musical compositions and other intellectual property, embodied in the Masters,

(ii) the name ----------- as used in connection with the Masters, and

(iii) all other ideas, other intellectual property or elements contained in or used in connection with the Masters or the packaging, sale, distribution, advertising, publicizing or other exploitation of Records embodying the Masters.

(iv) No changes in the individuals comprising Artist will be made without Company's prior written consent. Neither you nor Artist shall have the right, so long as this Agreement is in effect, to assign Artist's professional name as mentioned on page 1 hereof or any other name(s) utilized by Artist in connection with Masters or to permit the use of said name(s) by any other individual or group of individuals without

Company's prior written consent, and any attempt to do so shall be null and void and shall convey no right or title. You hereby warrant and represent that you are and shall be the sole owner of all such professional name(s), and that no other person, firm or corporation has the right to use said name(s) or to permit said name(s) to be used in connection with Records, and that you have the authority to grant Company the exclusive right to use said name(s) in the Territory in accordance with all of the terms and conditions of this Agreement, and Company shall have the exclusive right to use said professional name as aforesaid.

(v) Except as otherwise specifically set forth in this Agreement, during the Term, Artist shall not perform for the purpose of making Records for anyone other than Company for use in the Territory and neither you nor Artist shall authorize the use of Artist's name, likeness, or other identification for the purpose of distributing, selling, advertising or exploiting Records for anyone other than Company in the Territory.

(vi) Artist shall not perform any Composition recorded hereunder for anyone other than Company for use in the Territory on Records for a period of (i) five (5) years after the initial date of release of the respective Record containing such selection or (ii) two (2) years after the expiration or other termination of the Term, whichever is later ("Re-recording Restriction").

(vii) The Masters made and/or Delivered hereunder shall be produced in accordance with the rules and regulations of the American Federation of Musicians, the American Federation of Television and Radio Artists and all other unions having jurisdiction. All persons rendering services in connection with such Masters shall fully comply with the provisions of the Immigration Reform Control Act of 1986 and any other applicable laws.

(viii) There exist no previously recorded Recordings embodying Artist's performances except those that have been sold, transferred or otherwise assigned to Company.

(b) (i) Artist agrees to and does hereby indemnify, save and hold Company harmless of and from any and all liability, loss, damage, cost or expense (including without limitation reasonable attorneys' fees) arising out of or connected with any breach, threatened breach or alleged breach of this Agreement or any claim which is inconsistent with any of the warranties or representations made by you or Artist in this Agreement, provided that such claim has been settled with Artist's consent, or has been reduced to final judgment. Artist agrees to reimburse Company on demand for any payment made or incurred by Company with respect to any liability or claim to which the foregoing indemnity applies. Pending final determination of any claim involving such alleged breach or failure, Company may withhold sums due Artist hereunder in an amount reasonably related to the amount of such claim.

If no action is filed within one (1) year following the date on which such claim was first received by Company, Company shall release all sums withheld in connection with such claim, unless Company, in its reasonable business judgment, believes an action will be filed thereafter. Notwithstanding the foregoing, if, after such release by Company of sums withheld in connection with a particular claim, such claim is reasserted, then Company's rights under this paragraph will apply in full force and effect. Artist shall have the right to participate in the defense of any action instituted on a claim for which Artist is responsible to indemnify Company, with counsel of Artist's choice and at Artist's expense; however, Company shall have the right at all times to maintain control of the conduct of the defense.

(ii) Notwithstanding anything to the contrary contained herein, Company shall have the right to settle without your consent any claim involving sums of Seven Thousand Five Hundred Dollars ($7,500) or less, and this indemnity shall apply in full to any claim so settled; if you do not consent to any settlement proposed by Company for an amount in excess of Seven Thousand Five Hundred Dollars ($7,500), Company shall have the right to settle such claim without your consent, and this indemnity shall apply in full to any claim so settled, unless you post a surety bond with a surety acceptable to Company in its sole discretion. The surety bond must name Company as the beneficiary and assure prompt, unconditional payment to Company of all expenses, losses and damages (including without limitation costs and reasonable attorneys' fees) that Company may incur in connection with said claim.

16. Approvals

Whenever in this Agreement Artist's approval is required, it shall not be unreasonably withheld or delayed. Artist must send written notice of approval or disapproval within five (5) days after Artist receives Company's request for the approval. Failure to give due notice of approval or disapproval shall be deemed to be approval.

17. Videos

(a) Company shall have the right to require Artist to perform at such reasonable times and places as Company designates for the production of Video Masters featuring Artist's performances of Compositions embodied in the Masters and Artist agrees to perform to the best of Artist's ability thereon. Company shall be the exclusive owner throughout the Territory in perpetuity of such Video Masters and all rights therein, including, without limitation, all copyrights and renewal of copyrights with respect thereto, and the right to use and exploit such Video Masters in any and all forms and media. Company will consult with Artist with respect to the budget, producer, director and storyboard for each Video Master produced hereunder, but Company shall make the final decisions thereon.

(b) Company shall pay all Video production costs incurred in connection with the Videos consistent with the approved production budget. All sums paid by Company in connection with the production of the Video Masters shall constitute Advances to be charged against and recouped from Artist's royalties (excluding Mechanical Royalties) under this Agreement, subject to the following sentence. Fifty percent (50%) of the aggregate amount of Video production costs shall not be recoupable from royalties payable pursuant to paragraph 8 above, but shall nevertheless be one hundred percent (100%) recoupable from Video royalties hereunder. All Video production costs in excess of the approved budget that have been incurred due to your or Artist's acts or omissions shall be your sole responsibility, and you hereby agree to forthwith pay and discharge all such excess costs. In the event that Company agrees to pay any such excess costs on your behalf, you shall, upon demand, reimburse Company for such excess costs or in lieu of requesting reimbursement, Company may deduct such excess costs from any monies otherwise due you under this Agreement or any other agreement between you or Artist and Company or its affiliates (including without limitation Mechanical Royalties). In the event that Artist fails to appear at locations and/or on dates which have been mutually approved by you and Company, without reasonable excuse, the costs of cancellation of the shoot shall be fully deductible from all monies payable to you under this or any other agreement between you or Artist and Company or its affiliates (including without limitation Mechanical Royalties).

(c) In the event that Company decides to commercially release any Video Masters produced hereunder for sale, Company and Artist shall negotiate in good faith an artist royalty payable to Artist hereunder in connection with such sales of such Video Masters. Any such artist royalty negotiated with respect to sales of Video Masters hereunder is inclusive of any third party payments (including without limitation any payments to music publishers with respect to non-Controlled Compositions) required to be made by Company in connection with the manufacture and commercial exploitation of Video Masters hereunder.

18. Marketing and Publicity

(a) Artist shall be available from time to time to appear for photography, poster, and cover art, and the like, under the direction of Company or its nominees and to appear for interviews with representatives of the communications media and Company's publicity personnel.

(b) Artist shall be available from time to time at Company's request to perform for the purpose of recording for promotional purposes by means of film, videotape, or other audiovisual media performances of Compositions embodied on Masters.

19. Group Provisions

Artist's obligations under this Agreement are joint and several. All references in this Agreement to "Artist" include all members of the Group, inclusively, and each member individually, unless otherwise specified. If any member of the Group ceases to perform as a member of the Group, that member will be deemed to be a "Leaving Member" and the following shall apply in that circumstance:

(a) The remaining members of Artist will notify Company within thirty (30) days after a member has left, that a member has left, and the Leaving Member will be replaced by a new member, if Artist and Company so agree, to be substituted as a party to this Agreement in the place and stead of the Leaving Member. Artist agrees to cause the new member (and any new member joining the Group after the date hereof, even if not replacing a Leaving Member) to execute and deliver to Company such instruments as Company may require to accomplish that substitution (hereinafter collectively referred to as the "Substitution Instruments"). Thereafter, the Leaving Member will have no further obligation to perform under this Agreement but will continue to be bound by the other provisions of this Agreement, and Company will continue to have the right to use the name of the Group (and any other name hereafter used for the Group) pursuant to this Agreement. Artist agrees that no person will be permitted to perform in place of the Leaving Member under this Agreement unless that performer has executed and delivered to Company his/her Substitution Instruments. Company will continue to have the right to use the name of the Group (and any other name hereafter used for the Group). No Leaving Member will make any use of the Group's name in any circumstances, nor authorize or permit anyone other than Company to use or trade upon the Group's name for any purpose. For the avoidance of doubt, it is specifically agreed that the Leaving Member shall not make or authorize any reference to the Group's name for or in connection with the Leaving Member's performances, live or recorded or taped or filmed, nor make or authorize any reference in any packaging of phonorecords or videograms, any artwork or stickers used in connection with phonorecords or videograms, or any advertising, marketing, promotion or publicity in connection with phonorecords or videograms.

(b) Company will have the right to terminate the Term with respect to the remaining members of the Group by notice to be given to Artist at any time before expiration of ninety, (90) days after Company's receipt of the notice referred to in sub-paragraph (a) above. In the event of such termination, all members of the Group will be deemed to be Leaving Members as of the date of such termination notice, and sub-paragraph (c) will apply to all of them, collectively or individually as Company may elect.

(c) Artist grants to Company an option to engage the exclusive recording services of each Leaving Member (hereinafter referred to as a "Leaving Member Option"). Each Leaving Member Option may be exercised by Company at any time within ninety (90) days after Company's receipt of notice under subparagraph (a), or within ninety (90) days after the date of Company's termination notice pursuant to subparagraph (b) above, whichever shall be later. If Company exercises a Leaving Member Option, the Leaving Member concerned will be deemed to have entered into a new agreement with Company containing the same provisions as this Agreement, except as follows:

(i) The new agreement will apply only to that Leaving Member, and all references to "Artist" in that new agreement will be deemed to refer to the Leaving Member;

(ii) The term of the new agreement will commence on the date Company exercises that Leaving Member Option and may be extended by Company (exercisable in the same manner as provided in paragraph 2 above) for the same number of Option Periods that remained under paragraph 2 hereof at the time Company exercises that Leaving Member Option (but Company shall have at least 2 such Option Periods in any event);

(iii) The Recording Commitment for each Contract Period of such Term shall be one (1) Album;

(iv) If Artist's royalty account under this Agreement in an unrecouped position at the date Company exercises a Leaving Member Option, a pro-rata portion of the amount of that unrecouped balance will be recoupable from the royalties payable by Company under the new agreement. That portion shall be determined by a fraction, the numerator being one and the denominator being the number of members constituting the Artist prior to Company's receipt of the notice referred to in subparagraph (a) above. (e.g. 25% of that unrecouped balance if there are 4 members of Artist and one of them becomes a Leaving Member for whom Company has exercised a Leaving Member Option.) To the extent that unrecouped portion is recouped under the new agreement, it shall be credited toward recoupment under this Agreement, and to the extent that unrecouped portion is recouped under this Agreement it shall be credited toward recoupment of charges against royalties under the new agreement.

(v) As to any Leaving Member who has a songwriter's agreement or copublishing agreement with Company or any of Company's affiliates, the term of that agreement shall be coterminous with the new recording agreement, as same shall be substituted for, extended and renewed.

20. Definitions

For the purposes of this Agreement, the following definitions and terms shall be:

(a) Advance – a prepayment of royalties. Company may recoup Advances from all royalties to be paid or accrued to or on behalf of Artist pursuant to this Agreement. Mechanical Royalties shall not be chargeable in recoupment of any Advances unless otherwise expressly provided.

(b) Album – one (1) or more audio-only Records, at least forty-five (45) minutes in playing time and embodying at least ten (10) Masters of different compositions sold in a single package.

Mid-Price Album or Record – a Record which is sold by Company or its Principal Licensee(s) at a price that is below Company's or the applicable Principal Licensee's then-prevailing top-line suggested retail list price, which price is consistently applied by Company to such Records and which Records are sold by Company or its Principal Licensee(s) as mid-priced Records.

Multiple Record Set – two or more Records packaged and/or marketed as a single unit.

Budget Album or Record – A Record which is sold by Company or its Principal Licensee(s) at a price which is below Company's or the applicable Principal Licensee's then-prevailing top-line suggested retail list price, which price is consistently applied by Company to such Records and which Records are sold by Company or its Principal Licensee(s) as budget Records.

Single – a vinyl, audio-only Record not more than seven (7) inches in diameter, or the equivalent in non-vinyl configurations.

Twelve-inch Single – an audio-only record, which contains not more than four (4) Recordings of different compositions.

Extended Play Record or EP – an audio-only Record embodying thereon either five (5) Masters or six (6) Masters, but does not constitute an Album.

Audiovisual Record – a record that embodies, reproduces, transmits or otherwise communicates visual images, whether or not the interaction of a consumer is possible or necessary for the visual images to be utilized or viewed.

(c) Base Price – for Records and Audiovisual Records, the Suggested Retail List Price. "Royalty Base Price" The Base Price less all excise, sales and similar taxes included in the Base Price and less the applicable Container Charges and less distributors' discounts and rebates, if any.

(d) Container Charge – the applicable percentages of the Base Price specified below for sales by Company:

(i) **Analog cassette Records** – twenty percent (20%);

(ii) **Compact disc Records and Records in all other configurations** – twenty-five percent (25%);

(iii) **Analog vinyl Records** – twenty-five percent (25%); and

(iv) **Electronic phonorecord delivery** – no deductions.

(e) "Controlled Composition" – a composition wholly or partly written, or directly or indirectly owned or controlled, by Artist or a producer of Masters or by any representative of Artist or a producer hereunder.

(f) "Digital Download" – a type of record by which a Master is transmitted or otherwise communicated to a consumer on demand via digital distribution over the internet which results in that particular Record being placed in storage on that consumer's computer or other device such that the consumer owns the Record in perpetuity (as opposed to a limited rental or license). Company will not deduct a Container Charge from your portion of Digital Download royalties.

(g) "Delivery," "deliver," or "Delivered" – the actual receipt by Company of completed, fully mixed, leadered and edited Masters comprising the applicable Recording Commitment, technically and commercially satisfactory in Company's opinion and ready for the manufacture of Records, together with all materials, consents, approvals, licenses, and permissions Artist is required to supply to Company hereunder.

(h) "Master" – an individual sound Recording recorded hereunder that embodies Artist's performance(s) as the featured recording artist(s).

"Video" or "Video Masters" – videocassettes, Videodiscs or any other devices, now or hereafter known or developed (including, without limitation, any visual and/or audiovisual work using digital technology), that enable motion pictures and other audiovisual works that have a soundtrack substantially featuring the performances of Artist to be perceived visually, with sound, when used in combination with or as part of a piece of electronic, mechanical or other apparatus.

(i) "Mechanical Royalties" – royalties payable to any person for the right to reproduce and distribute copyrighted compositions on Records, including, without limitation, Audiovisual Records.

(j) "Merchandise Rights" – any use, reproduction or other exploitation in any manner, media or formats of the name, photographs, likenesses, biographical material, trademarks and/or any other identification utilized by you (other than in connection with Records hereunder), including, without limitation "fan clubs", any products, endorsements, sponsorships and/or the sale of merchandise (i.e., t-shirts and other apparel, caps, posters, biographical books, etc).

(k) "Net Amount Received" – the gross, earned, non-returnable amount received by Company (excluding royalties that are based upon a percentage of a retail or wholesale or other price and excluding advances

against such royalties), less any out-of-pocket costs or expenses which Company is contractually required to make to third parties, including, but not limited to, payments to a trustee or fund to the extent required by any agreement between Company and any labor organization or trustee, and less Mechanical Royalty payments. An example of a Net Amount Received is an earned payment (not an advance) under a flat fee license or flat rate license.

(l) "Net Royalty Receipts" – company's gross, earned royalty receipts less any out-of-pocket costs or expenses which Company is contractually required to make to third parties, and less any amounts included in the receipts that are for payments to a trustee or fund required by any agreement between Company or Artist and any labor organization or trustee, and less Mechanical Royalty payments.

(m) "Net Sales" – eighty-five (85%) percent of Gross Sales of Albums, and seventy (70%) percent of Gross Sales of Singles and EPs, sold, paid for and not returned. "Free goods" that are given by Company or Company's distributor in lieu of discounts shall be included in "Gross Sales" under this paragraph, except for additional free goods given by Company or its distributor pursuant to special "impact" marketing programs of limited duration.

(n) "New Technology Configurations" – Records in the following configurations: mini-discs, digital compact cassettes, digital audio tapes, DVD, laser discs, CD-ROM and other Records embodying, employing or otherwise utilizing any non-analog technology (whether or not presently existing or hereafter created or developed), but specifically excluding audio-only compact discs.

(o) "Record" – any form of reproduction, transmission or communication of Recordings, now or hereafter known, manufactured, distributed, transmitted or communicated primarily for home use, school use, juke box use or use in means of transportation, including, without limitation, Records embodying or reproducing sound alone and Audiovisual Records.

(p) "Recording" – every recording of sound, whether or not coupled with a visual image, by any method and on any substance or material, or in any other form or format, whether now or hereafter known, which is used or useful in the recording, production and/or manufacture of Records or for any other commercial exploitation.

(q) "Recording Costs" – all amounts paid or incurred in connection with the production of Masters hereunder. Recording Costs include, without limitation, all union scale payments required to be made to the Artist in connection with Masters recorded hereunder, all costs of instrumental, vocal and other personnel in connection with the recording of the Masters, travel, rehearsal, and equipment rental expenses, per diems, advances to producers, studio and engineering charges and personnel, all other amounts required to be paid pursuant to any applicable law or any collective bargaining agreement between Company and any union representing persons who render services in connection with the Masters, and all costs of mixing, remixing, mastering and re-mastering. Recording Costs do not include the costs of producing metal parts, but include all studio and engineering charges or other costs incurred in preparing Masters for the production of metal parts and/or final production Masters. (Metal parts include lacquer, copper, and other equivalent masters.)

(r) "Suggested Retail List Price" – (i) with respect to Records sold for distribution in the United States, Company's suggested retail list price in the United States during the applicable accounting period for the computation of royalties to be made hereunder, it being understood that a separate calculation of the suggested retail list price shall be made for each price configuration of Phonograph Records manufactured and sold by Company; and (ii) with respect to Records sold hereunder for distribution outside the United States, Company's or its licensees' suggested or applicable retail price in the country of manufacture or sale, as Company is paid, or, in the absence in a particular country of such suggested retail list price, the price as

may be established by Company or its licensee(s) in conformity with the general practice of the recording industry in such country, provided that Company shall not be obligated to utilize the price adopted by the local mechanical copyright collection agency for the collection of Mechanical Royalties. Notwithstanding anything to the contrary contained herein, (A) the Suggested Retail List Price for premium Records shall be Company's actual sales price of such Records and (B) the Suggested Retail List Price with respect to Videos manufactured and distributed by Company shall be Company's published wholesale price as of the commencement of the accounting period in question.

(s) "Territory" – the Universe.

(t) Sales "through normal retail distribution channels" – sales made to retail stores, or for re-sale to retail stores, through Company's record distributors, or, outside the United States, through Company's foreign licensees, or by Company itself, to retail stores or for re-sale to retail stores.

21. Assignment

Company shall have the right to assign this Agreement in whole or in part to any subsidiary, parent company or affiliate of Company or to any third party acquiring all or a substantial portion of Company's assets or equity interests or pursuant to an initial public offering. Neither you nor Artist shall have the right to assign this Agreement.

22. Assignment of Publishing Interest in Recorded Songs

With respect to any and all musical compositions written in whole or in part by any or all members of Artist which is recorded and commercially released on any Master or Album recorded hereunder (a "Recorded Composition"), each such member of Artist hereby assigns and transfers to Company or its publishing designee, its successors and assigns, fifty percent (50%) of all of such Artist member's right, title and interest in and to each and every Recorded Composition, or portion thereof, as described above, for the entire Universe, including but not limited to such Artist member's interest in the copyrights therein and any renewals or extensions thereof. Each Artist member agrees, upon Company's request, to execute a publishing agreement with Company's affiliated publishing company with respect to each such Recorded Composition, promptly following the recording thereof by Artist and commercial release of same on any Master or Album hereunder. The parties agree that Company's affiliated publishing entity will administer and license 100% of such Recorded Composition.

23. Merchandising

In consideration for Company's development of your name, brand, identity and services as a recording and touring artist, you grant Company exclusive Merchandise Rights during the term of this Agreement. After deducting from gross income received from the sale of merchandise, the costs of manufacturing, shipping and fulfillment, costs associated with a merchandise salesperson (if required) such as per diems, salary, transportation and lodging, insurance, venue or hall fees, product design fees and other costs customarily associated with selling artist merchandise, the parties shall equally divide all net receipts. Company shall account to you monthly for your portion of net receipts, which shall not be subject to recoupment of Advances hereunder, other than advances that specifically constitute prepayment to you of a portion of your merchandise net receipts. Company, or its designee, shall maintain books and records for the purpose of verifying the accuracy of statements rendered by Company pursuant to this paragraph, which books and records are available for your examination upon reasonable notice and at Company's principal office.

24. Confidentiality

Each of Artist and Company agree to keep strictly confidential the monetary terms of this Agreement; provided however that this restriction shall not apply to information which:

(a) is required to be disclosed by law or by any order, rule or regulation of any court or governmental agency; or 25.

(b) is disclosed to Artist's or Company's attorney(s) or manager(s) in the ordinary course of business so long as such persons have agreed to be subject to restrictions identical to those imposed upon Company and Artist under this provision.

25. Miscellaneous

(a) This Agreement sets forth the entire agreement between the parties with respect to the subject matter hereof. No modification, amendment, waiver, termination or discharge of this Agreement shall be binding upon Artist or Company unless confirmed by a written instrument signed by an authorized person of Company and Artist. A waiver by either party of any term or condition of this Agreement in any instance shall not be deemed or construed as a waiver of such term or condition for the future, or of any subsequent breach thereof. All of Company and Artist's rights, options and remedies in this Agreement shall be cumulative and none of them shall be in limitation of any other remedy, option or right available to Company. Wherever possible, each provision hereof shall be interpreted in such manner as to be effective and valid under applicable law, but in case any one or more of the provisions of this Agreement shall, for any reason, be held to be invalid, illegal or unenforceable in any respect, that provision shall be ineffective to the extent, but only to the extent, of such invalidity, illegality or unenforceability without invalidating the remainder of that provision or any other provisions of this Agreement. It is agreed that all accountings and royalty payments required herein, and all grants made herein, shall survive and continue beyond the expiration or earlier termination of this Agreement. No breach of this Agreement by Company or Artist (except for Artist's breach of the exclusivity provisions hereof) shall be deemed material unless notice is given specifying the nature of the breach and the recipient of the notice fails to cure such breach, if any, within thirty (30) days after receipt of the notice; notwithstanding the foregoing, Artist expressly acknowledges that Company may obtain injunctive relief hereunder immediately, and Company is not required to delay for thirty (30) days or any other period.

(b) This Agreement is made in the State of Tennessee and its validity, construction and performance shall be governed by the laws of the State of Tennessee applicable to agreements made and to be entirely performed in Tennessee, without regard to any conflicts of laws principles. The Federal and State courts in Davidson County shall have exclusive jurisdiction of any dispute arising under or concerning this Agreement. Service of process pursuant to this paragraph may be made, among other methods, by delivering the same via overnight mail or mailing by certified air mail, return receipt requested, in the same manner as giving other notices under this Agreement, and shall be effective upon sending the process. Such service is deemed to have the same force and effect as personal service within the State of Tennessee.

(c)This Agreement has binding legal effect, and grants certain exclusive rights to Company for Artist's services. Artist acknowledges that Company has requested Artist to consult with and be represented by an attorney who is knowledgeable about the subject of this Agreement and the record and music and entertainment industries, to be advised about the content and effect of the provisions of this Agreement, and to follow Artist's attorney's advice about entering into this Agreement.

(d) This Agreement shall not become effective until it is executed by all parties.

IN WITNESS WHEREOF, the parties hereto have executed this Agreement on the day and year first above written.

COMPANY:

By: ______________________________

ARTIST:

By: ______________________________

Date:

14

The Recording Business

(Studios)
Stages of a Session, Types of Sessions
Recording Team Members
Unions, Guilds, and Budgets

"Basically, you're trying to bottle lightning all the time. There's no use putting a record out unless it's got some magic on it. And magic doesn't come easy."

— Quincy Jones, Record Producer[462]

"My music will go on forever. Maybe it's a fool to say that, but when me know facts me can say facts. My music will go on forever."

— Bob Marley[463]

"Music is your own experience, your own thoughts, your wisdom. If you don't live it, it won't come out of your horn. They teach you there's a boundary line to music. But, man, there's no boundary line to art."

— Charlie Parker[464]

"The intersection of music and law begins with the very creative process itself. That process is becoming increasingly individualized, particularly when it comes to recording and distributing music. It is now possible to produce professional-level music recordings using only an iPad and its GarageBand app at a total cost of $505. The rise of inexpensive recording tools and channels for self-distribution has led some to avoid producers, studios, and labels. There may be fewer recording professionals, but anyone can record. Even more can remix."

— The Berkman Center for Internet & Society, Harvard University[465]

The Creative Business Milieu

In the entertainment business, there is a constant underlying philosophical conflict between the creative and business sides of the industry. Successful industry professionals accept these philosophical differences and work together to interface the creative with the business. Nonetheless, when large sums of money are involved, attitudes often develop between the values of art v. the profits of business. Disagreements range

---

462 Quincy Jones, *The Recording Industry Career Handbook*, NARAS Foundations (NARAS: Los Angeles, CA) 1995.

463 Bob Marley, "Bob Marley Quotes," Artnotes.net, http://www.artquotes.net/entertainment-quotes/bob-marley.htm, (accessed March 19, 2011).

464 Charley Parker, "Charley Parker Quotes," Thinkexist.com, http://thinkexist.com/quotation/music_is_your_own_experience-your_own_thoughts/202273.html, (accessed March 19, 2011).

465 Berkman Center for Internet & Society at Harvard University, "*Rethinking Music: A Framing Paper,*" Harvard University, http://cyber.law.harvard.edu/publications/2011/Rethinking_Music, (accessed May 2, 2011).

from friendly discussions to lawsuits, which sometimes define the boundaries of the conversations and potential solutions to the personal and financial conflicts. As an example, in recording sessions, most artists want to control their own sound and performances, but at the same time, the labels want to control the costs. The solution is to bring in a third player, the producer, who has to bridge both the creative process and the financial aspects of creating an album. They've got to create great sellable tracks *and* hold the line on budgets. Therefore, during the recording of an album, the creative and financial control of the session and budget is the producer's responsibility. Still, no matter what issues are involved, labels and music companies still fund and invest in recording artists and their creativity. According to the *International Federation of the Phonographic Industry's Investing in Music* (2010),

> *...New signings, leading to new releases, are the lifeblood of record companies. Based on data received from its members, IFPI estimates that one in four of all the artists on a typical international record company's roster were signed in the previous 12 months. Continually investing in new talent is a hugely risky business, as only a minority of the artists developed will be commercially successful in a highly competitive market.*[466]

The Recording Team

Recording artists are idolized as superstars, but it is the very creative team of talented studio musicians, backup singers, audio engineers, and record producers that often create the recordings that lead to fame. Having the ability to sing well is one thing; getting it recorded with magic is quite another. Major artists usually need to reach iconic status before consumers buy (or steal) the recordings that pay for the distribution, promotion, and publicity required to launch careers.

Producers

The session producer is the captain of the ship, directing and stimulating the creative elements of the audio engineer, studio musicians, and recording artists. Suggested skills and knowledge include a passion for music, an understanding of music theory and sight-reading, and in some places knowledge of the "number system." Producers also need to know copyright laws, music publishing, business finance, and the music business subsystems. Musicianship skills are essential for music producers. Successful producers communicate well with others, are decisive leaders, understand basic accounting skills for controlling budgets, and have strategic management skills for administration. In addition, producers commonly have a consummate understanding of recording studio acoustics, basic electronics, equipment capabilities, and an almost magical ability to "marry" the right song to the right recording artist.

Producers know other industry professionals through networking, showcases, parties, meetings, professional organizations, industry events, award shows, etc., and *successful* producers know who the industry movers and shakers are (the insiders and personalities who manage and control the industry), as the majority of their work originates from those connections.[467]

Independent producers begin their careers learning the trade by producing demo sessions for publishers and custom or vanity albums that are commonly non-label productions paid for by the recording artist or band. Some are demo recordings that showcase the recording artists or songs, which are then "pitched" to a record

---

[466] John Kennedy and Alison Wenham, "Investing in Music: How Music Companies Discover Promote Talent," IFPI.org, http://www.ifpi.org/content/library/investing_in_music.pdf, (accessed March 19, 2011).

[467] Bruce Weber, "Jerry Wexler, A Behind-the-Scenes Force in Black Music is Dead at 91," New York Times, http://www.nytimes.com/2008/08/16/arts/music/16wexler.html?_r=2&hp=&pagewanted=all, (accessed March 19, 2011).

label. Great demo recordings often lead to the next step in the career of a producer: working for a label in the A&R department, recording development deals.

Record label staff producers are hired by labels to produce development deal acts. The label pays for all expenses, including the studio, musicians, and vocalists. The producer gains additional opportunities to work with better musicians, artists, and studio equipment. If the tracks are perceived as sellable, exciting, or quality, labels may sign the act and release a single. If a label passes on the act, the cost of the development deal is commonly used as a tax write-off.

Major independent producers are at the top of their profession and paid handsomely. Extremely successful producers earn $1,000-5,000 per side (per song) depending on the genre of music and the financial success of the acts they are producing. In addition, they receive producer points (usually 1-3%) of the artist's royalties on each unit sold. Major producers are highly respected for their abilities to produce hit records. Their success makes them behind-the-scenes stars within their own industry. Because major producers gain so much power and respect in the industry, they control their destiny as clever entrepreneurs by letting different labels and artists bid for their services. Major labels often hire very successful producers as executives to run a label and use and protect their talents instead of competing with them.[468]

Musicians

Musicians change our world; life would not be the same without them. All musicians are artists – it doesn't matter where they play or how much money they make. Although the recording artists usually get the fame, it is the musicians that create the tracks and "feel" in the studio who are the real heroes. Without them, singers are poets.

Garage/jam band musicians are usually the high school students who jam to learn cover tunes of popular acts. This often becomes their first step toward a professional career in the industry. Most musicians volunteer to perform in small clubs, coffeehouses, churches, and other types of local gigs to learn the business and improve their performance skills. Many continue to improve their performance skills and knowledge during college by jamming with others who share their interests and taking private lessons from classically trained musicians. Others simply learn how to make recordings on their computers using GarageBand, Pro Tools, and Logic software programs.

Working musicians receive money for their music performances. Serious musicians join unions and audition to become members of various levels of performance groups including orchestras, bands, and other types of entertainment ensembles. Many use their musical skills to supplement other types of occupations. Others continue to struggle either part-time or full-time to develop a "sound" and a "following" that may lead to greater financial opportunities through their creative musical performances.

Road musicians and event artists are the musicians and vocalists who are on tour as an opening act or as the musicians hired to perform with a recording artist. Others are often classically trained musicians who form smaller groups to perform at special social, political, or other types of events. It is very rare for the road musicians of a major recording artist to be on the actual hit recordings they are playing live. That is the job of studio musicians.

Studio musicians are most often heard on major recording artists' recordings, yet very few consumers know them by name. Great studio musicians can make thousands of dollars a day, charging double or triple scale for a three-hour session. They often become true stars known only by the best producers and recording artists. They are recording artists themselves, but are rarely known by the public. Studio musicians play their

---

468 Personal interviews with industry experts, (2005-2011).

instruments to highlight the marriage of the song to the vocal characteristics of the recording artist. Some of the best musicians in the world are studio session musicians, so of course, most record labels and recording artists use master session studio musicians for their album projects. Recording opportunities include music soundtracks for TV shows, movies, commercials, jingles, and major artists' recordings. Possessing musical talent is imperative if you want to be a recording artist or studio musician. In addition, a music education and an understanding of copyright law, music publishing, networking, and the music business, are important for success.

Audio Engineers

Audio engineers mix the creativity of music and the artistic capabilities of the artists, musicians, and BGVs to the logical physical and technological potential of the studio's acoustics and equipment to capture (record) the best performances. Suggested skills and knowledge include a basic understanding of the business of music and entertainment, music theory, copyright laws, music publishing, marketing, management and business finance. Knowledge of computer software programs Pro Tools, Logic Pro, and even GarageBand is important as the industry moves toward less expensive modes of recording to save money and improve the profit and loss statement. Basic electronic, acoustics, and recording equipment variables and having a continuous desire to learn the latest technical advances in recording equipment and audio production are fundamental. Communication skills and the ability to work with highly creative individuals are crucial. Business courses are also helpful, as most audio engineers often become producers, and both are entrepreneurs. They also need to be able to have fun, experiment, be a little crazy and bend the rules, and do whatever it takes to get the best creative performance possible out the artists. In their book *Come Together*, Courtney and Cassidy state:

> *George Martin (the Beatles' producer) brought a new engineer, Geoff Emerick, into the control room. …Emerick had raised thought the EMI ranks quickly and was young enough to have a healthy disregard for the "rule," a fact that endeared him to the Beatles. Emerick was not fazed when John Lennon told him that his voice should sound like the Dalai Lama singing from a mountaintop. Run the voice though a rotating speaker cabinet (normally used for an electronic organ). Problem solved. He thought nothing of flipping the tape around and recording a guitar solo with the tape reversed, so that when the song is played forward, the guitar solo is played backwards (this is a distinctive and now easily recognizable sound, in which each notes fades in and ends with the "attach" of the plectrum). He was willing to cut a tape into little pieces, glue it all back together in random pieces, and add it to the final mix if that was what the Beatles wanted.*[469]

Most will own or lease a recording studio, computer and software, a music publishing company, and *some* own independent record labels. The career of the most successful audio engineers starts with basic lessons in recording or on their own computer recording themselves and others. Careers often follow a similar path, including the following steps:

> *Entry-level Audio Engineers* are often college students who are working in a studio as an intern. At the same time, they are recording local musicians on the latest computer recording software. They are rarely paid for their efforts; however, they are given opportunities to learn the basics and to meet members of the creative team.
>
> *Second Engineers* are a step up in the process from entry-level engineers. They set up microphones, cables, headsets, the console, and alignment of the tape machines. Second engineers also run the tape machines, keep the log sheets during the sessions, and occasionally travel with artists on the road to hone audio and mixing skills.

---

469 Richard Courtney & George Cassidy, *Come Together: The Business Wisdom of The Beatles*, (New York, NY: Turner Publishing, 2011) 101.

Staff Engineers are sometimes employed at a recording studio. They accomplish any level of session, from demo to master, with major recording artists and triple scale musicians. Staff engineer positions are commonly found in non-music recording centers where great engineers are difficult to find. Annual salaries range from $50,000 plus, to huge sums for engineers with great track records.[470]

Major-Artist/Independent Engineers are at the top of their profession with a long list of hit records they helped create. They are "on-call" for and most often work on master sessions for label artists and known superstars. Their pay is negotiable, ranging between $1,000 a day, plus expenses, to huge per-side (whatever they want) salaries based on their track record. It is very rare for audio engineers to also receive points from the artist's points; however, in very special situations, it has happened. Most studios located in major music recording centers (Los Angeles, New York, and Nashville) have replaced staff audio engineers with independent engineers. The location for the production has become less important as many artists have studios in their homes or vacation homes, and many use computers and software to record all their tracks instead of renting a major studio.

Recording Artist

Royalty Artists are usually signed as *work-for-hire* deals for the specific purpose of creating recordings. However, in 360 deals the artist is also responsible for other revenue generating work such as concert tours, promotions and endorsements.[471] The label retains the copyright of the artists' musical and vocal performances in the work-for-hire deals and thus the artists give up ownership (the copyright) of their performances. Record deals are just weird when compared to a typical bank loan where you have to prove you can repay the debt or put up something of value to guarantee it. On the front end of a recording deal, the label acts as a bank, providing financial security to pay for the artists' recordings, tours, and advances. However, artists never owe the label any money! It is the label that pays off the loan (to itself) by applying the artists' royalties from each unit sold to the debt posted in the artists' names. Therefore, it is the label (who signs, finances the recording, and markets the act) that pays off its own debt by selling the recordings in the name of the artist. What does it cost the artist? Only their talent and "best efforts" to create recordings that the label can sell for a profit. Additional vocal opportunities include:

Virtuosos are celebrated as the best in the world based on their musical and vocal talents and fame. Examples of virtuosos are *Luciano Pavarotti*, *Itzhak Perlman*, and *Andrea Bocelli.*

BGVs (background vocalists) provide the harmony in recording sessions and live performances. It is amazing how often background vocalists are used to blend their voices with the main star to improve or "carry" the superstar act.

Professional singers are found everywhere: on recordings, in choirs, advertisements, jingles, and movie soundtracks – you name it; they are there. Professional singers (vocalists) frequently net more money than label artists, as they do not have to support an entourage of road musicians, managers, producers, and label marketing and promotion executives.

Demo singers find entry-level work at publishing companies singing demo recordings. Nonunion members and college interns may earn $10-$50 a song, which is not much money, but singing in a recording studio is different from performing in a choir or on stage. Demo sessions provide the

---

470 Personal interviews with industry experts, (1998-2011).

471 Personal interviews with industry experts, (2009-2011).

novice studio singer with some valuable studio experience. The acoustics, lighting, and monitoring are often quite complex. So, the more experience gained in the studio, the quicker an artist may become a professional recording artist. There is also another advantage, as producers, A&R, and artist managers often listen to the demo tapes hoping to find a great song. Sometimes, they also find a great voice! Therefore, singing on demos is a great way to gain studio experience and be heard by many industry insiders who are seeking the "next big thing."[472]

Studios

To make money, labels and music companies invest money into their signed artists and their hired recording team so that together they can create a sellable recording. Traditional studios tend to be earmarked by their acoustics (sound), equipment, cost, and reputation for making hits. In the past, these studios were an integral part of the music business: the place where dreams were made and sometimes broken. In general, traditional studios fall into five categories:

Master Studios – most master studios are solidly packed with the latest acoustic audio equipment and special effects toys producers use to create great tracks.

Project/Mini Studios – if you need a low-budget, limited pressing master tape or a movie soundtrack, project studios fill the gap between the very expensive master studios and the basic demo studios. They are often filled with dated equipment and minor acoustics.

Post-Production Studios – after overdubbing sessions, producers and artists often move to the special equipment in the post-production studio to mix the master tapes to computer flash drives.

Demo Studios – these studios are often the older analog studios with minor special effects equipment. They are used for demos as well as vanity and limited budget recordings.

Garage/Basement Studios – the bottom line basic studio often found in homes of young musicians and producers.

Dorm Rooms and Bedrooms – it's hard to believe that you can use a dorm room or bedroom as a "studio" but with *Logic Pro, Pro-Tools* and other computer software programs, the need for the acoustic and equipment of a major studio are diminished.

Design

Most music companies still use traditional studios on some or all of their artists' albums, probably because the talents of the recording artists, musicians, audio engineer, and producers combined are still only as good as the studio's equipment and acoustics. Poor acoustics can destroy the even best creative efforts of world-class artists. Floating walls, ceilings, and floors are used to isolated sound from room to room in performance studios and control rooms. Grooves are cut into the floors, walls are mounted on rubber tubes, and ceilings are often spring-loaded. Windows between the performance rooms and control room are often made of two thick double-or triple-pane pieces of glass separated by several inches of air space. Soundproof doors complete the package. Studios are usually divided into the following:

Performance rooms are where the royalty artists and musicians perform.

The control room is where the producer and audio engineers supervise and control the quality and amount of the recorded signal.

---

[472] Personal interviews with industry experts, (1998-2011).

Equipment room isolates the noise and heat generated by tape recorders, amps, computers, room equalizers, and most of the other electrical equipment needed in the traditional recording process.

Storage area is where microphones, music stands headsets, cords, direct boxes, and other recording gear are stored.

Aesthetics

While musicians and vocalists create the music in the performance studio, the audio engineer and producer enhance the quality of the sound in the control room. They may use tone controls (equalizers) on the console to improve the quality of the signal. Just as colors of paint help create emotions in a piece of art, engineers use acoustics, microphones, and consoles to emphasize and match the "feel" of the song to the image and vocal characteristics of the recording artist.

Microphones

Microphones, which according to answer.encyclopedia.com (2010), were "invented in 1877 in various forms by Emile Berliner, David E. Hughes, and Thomas A. Edison, and were first used as a telephone transmitter."[473] Mics convert sound waves into electronic signals. They all sound different, have different axis for picking up sounds and vary in sound quality. Thus, it is extremely important engineers knows which ones to select, where to place them in the performance room and in the correct proximity to the talent and instruments. Proper selection and usage is often the difference between a "great" sounding session and something less. Basic differences include:

Dynamic mics have a coil or wire in the element (top) of the mic. Sound waves vibrate a plastic diaphragm connected to a coil of wire, moving the coil in and out of a permanent magnetic field. Electricity is created anytime you pass a wire through a magnetic force field. Thus, the movement converts the sound waves (acoustic waves) into an electronic signal.[474]

Ribbon mics operate on the same principle as dynamic microphones, except they have flexible, metallic ribbons (or foal) that sound waves vibrate in and out of the permanent magnetic force field. Because the ribbon is flexible, the quality of the sound generated is often considered smoother and warmer.[475]

Condenser mics have two plates that hold a static electronic charge. One is a permanent plate and the other is moveable. Sound waves move the moveable plate, changing the distance between the two plates, which generates an electrical output. Condenser microphones need batteries or a phantom power source supplied through the microphone cable.[476]

Pick Up Patterns

Microphones have different pickup patterns or areas where they are most sensitive to sound. The patterns are used to acoustically isolate one instrument or vocal, excluding the leakage of sounds from other instruments

---

473 Answers.encyclopedia.com, "Who Invented Microphones," Answers.encyclopedia.com, http://answers.encyclopedia.com/question/do-dynamic-microphones, (accessed March 19, 2011).

474 Answers.encyclopedia.com, "How Dynamic Microphones Work," Answers.encyclopedia.com, http://answers.encyclopedia.com/question/do-dynamic-microphones, (accessed August 5, 2010).

475 Answers.encyclopedia.com, "How Dynamic Microphones Work," Answers.encyclopedia.com, http://answers.encyclopedia.com/question/do-dynamic-microphones, (accessed August 5, 2010).

476 Answers.encyclopedia.com, "What is an Electrostatic Microphones," Answers.encyclopedia.com, http://answers.encyclopedia.com/question/electret-microphones-96543.html, (accessed March 19, 2011).

or vocals into the microphone. Engineers also use pickup patterns to induce an acoustic mixture of "live" sound (omnidirectional) from a very isolated single sound source. Consumers often feel the quality of the mixture of the sound as an emotion when they hear the recording.[477] Examples include:

> *Omnidirectional pickup patterns* allow sound waves to enter from all directions into the mic at approximately the same loudness level (measured in dBs).
>
> *Cardioid pickup patterns* cancel the sound coming from the sides and rear of the mic. Most engineers use mics with cardioid patterns to limit and avoid leakage problems that usually occur when using omnidirectional mics.
>
> *Bidirectional pickup patterns* receive sound waves from the front and back of the mic and cancel out sound waves coming from the sides of the mic.

Consoles

Consoles often appear to be straight from the bridge of the starship *Enterprise.* Consoles act as traffic cops, dividing and directing the microphone signals and connecting instruments to various destinations, all at about 186,000 miles per second. Each microphone plugged in is one signal controlled through one module in the console.

Recorders/Software

Analog tape machines record a magnetic copy of both the amplitude (loudness) and frequency (number of vibrations per second) sent through the console to the tape recorder.[478] The advantages of analog tape recordings are a "warmer sound" at a lower price. However, there is also distortion of the signal and unwanted noises like tape hiss. Digital machines, on the other hand, convert the microphone electronic signals into binary codes of 0s and 1s (pulse or no pulse). They only use recording tape to store the binary code.[479] When the codes are played back, the computer inside the tape machine converts the binary code into the music previously recorded. The advantages of digital recording include the lack of noise and distortion that are usually found in analog recordings. However, digital machines cost much more than analog machines (although great analog machines are becoming a rare commodity). Nowadays, computer software programs such as *Pro Tools, Logic Pro*, and even *GarageBand* are replacing analog and even older digital machines. These software programs sound great and cost very little compared to an actual physical studios (GarageBand is often free when you buy a Mac computer). However, it is surprising to discover that the first digital musical recording was in 1951. According to a posting on *NoiseAddicts.com* (August 4, 2008),

> *The University of Manchester housed the Ferranti Mark 1 computer, the successor to the famous "Baby" computer in 1948. The Ferranti computer had a subroutine that emitted a short tone when an application finished running. (They called it the "Hoot"). This "Hoot" subroutine was modified… to actually produce pitched notes that could be played successively to play songs. Thus, the first computer music was born.*[480]

---

[477] Personal interviews with industry sources (1984-2011).

[478] Answers.encyclopedia.com, "How is Sound Recorded on an Audio Recorder," Answers.encyclopedia.com, http://answers.encyclopedia.com/question/sound-recorded-audio-recorder-105145.html, (accessed March 19, 2011).

[479] Answers.encyclopedia.com, "What is the Definition of a Binary Code," Answers.encyclopedia.com, http://answers.encyclopedia.com/question/definition-binary-code-747599.html, (accessed March 19, 2011).

[480] Noiseaddicts.com, "First Ever Recording of Digital Music," Noiseaddicts.com, http://www.noiseaddicts.com/2008/08/first-ever-recording-of-digital-music/, (accessed August 5, 2010).

Speakers

In the control room, the electronic signals (from the microphones to the console) are converted back into acoustic sound waves by monitors (speakers). To make sure they are providing a correct sound (flat frequency response), room equalizers are used to compensate for the "hype of the sound" created by the speakers and control room acoustics. As an example, control rooms are shot with "pink noise" which measures the frequency response to determine how to use the room equalizers to compensate for the acoustical problems.[481] The electronic signals coming into the console from the microphones, tape machines, effects, and computer software programs are amplified and divided into different frequencies (bass, mid-range, and treble) by a crossover network (often in the speakers) and then sent to the corresponding bass, mid-range, and treble speakers. Large speaker cones vibrate slowly and move a significant amount of air to reproduce bass frequencies. Smaller cones vibrating faster generate higher tones (frequencies). Tweeters reproduce the highest frequencies adding clarity to the quality of the music or sounds you're hearing. The bass or lower frequencies have longer and more powerful wavelengths, while the highest tones are shorter and much more directional. Thus, room acoustic need to be correct in order for the audio engineer and producer to hear the signal correctly as they mix the tracks.

Effects

Effects equipment called "outboard gear," are devices used to improve, change, or fake the quality of the signal and overall "feel" consumers might perceive from listening to the signal (recordings). Of course, most of these "effects" are now generated within software programs. Commonly used generated effects include the following:

Compressions are used to reduce the amplitude (loudness) of a signal to record a proper signal on analog tape. Compression is also used to change the quality of the sound of instruments and vocalists. Settings include compression ratios and attack and release times used to fatten or tighten the quality of sound (the sound of a kick drum or bass guitar perhaps).

Echo is used to make the singer or instruments sound as if they were in a different size room than the actual recording studio. Long reflections of 50 milliseconds or greater are perceived as a repetition of a direct sound wave. Think about singing in the shower: the "echo" sound created makes everybody a singer… except me!

Gates are switches (set on a threshold) used to stop signals based on amplitude (loudness). Gates are used to block noise (other instruments) from leaking into microphones during the actual session. They are often used on drums and overdub vocals to "tighten" the quality of the sound.

Harmonizers offer hope for even me when it comes to singing. Along with changing or correcting the pitch, they can electronically double (with a slight delay) one vocalist or instrument to make it sound as if there were two. The delay settings can be varied between echo and reverberation, which differ in time settings.[482]

Limiters compress the dynamic range of a signal to its maximum compression. The amplitude is "limited" to the maximum settings, which tend to make the signal sound "thinner."

---

481 Personal interview with industry insiders and audio engineers including Jim Williamson, producer & audio engineer of Sound Emporium Studio, Nashville, TN (1978-2004).

482 Noiseaddicts.com, "First Ever Recording of Digital Music," Noiseaddicts.com, http://www.noiseaddicts.com/2008/08/first-ever-recording-of-digital-music/, (accessed August 5, 2010).

Slap is a delayed sound perceived as a distinct echo, usually set for a delay of 35-250 milliseconds. Think of the early "rockabilly" recordings of Elvis, Carl Perkins, and Johnny Cash, and you'll know how producers used it in the 1950s. It use to be created by recording a new vocal out of sync with some previously recorded vocals (the delay caused by the physical distance between the tracks coming off the playback heads and the new track being recorded on the record head).

Reverberations are a delay of 10 milliseconds or more after a direct sound wave. Engineers use it to make the vocalists or musician sound as if they are in a large auditorium instead of a small, acoustically controlled recording studio.[483]

Studio Schedules

In major recording cities like New York, Los Angeles, Nashville, Memphis, Miami, or Seattle, sessions are "booked" in three-hour blocks scheduled from 10 a.m., to 1 p.m., 2 to 5 p.m., 6 to 9 p.m., and 10 p.m. to 1 a,m. This allows producers, musicians, and vocalists to move from project to project during the day by going from one session to another as all the studios are working on the same hourly schedule. The hour between sessions is for tearing down the current session and setting up the next session.[484]

The Recording Process

It's time to create the magic in the studio that allows consumers to feel goose bumps. Producers are in charge of the recording processes, budget, and material "songs" the artist sings. They use their years of experience, musical knowledge, and opinions about "what" the public wants to hear to produce acts. In addition, producers often have a personal communicative talent that helps them encourage a maximum creative performance out of the singers and musicians individually and at the same time, together to create the magic or goose bumps we get when we hear the final recording. Not an easy thing to do! Producers have to select the perfect song for the perfect artist and somehow encourage all the musicians and singers to create a final master recording that is superior to the original demo. Creative people can be weird and are often very difficult to work with; so the producer also has to maintain control of the session or it may turn into something resembling of circus costing the label thousands of dollars per-hour. According to record producer *Jimmy Bowen* (1984),[485]

> *...If you're going to be a record producer, you must have an overall knowledge of the music industry. From a business standpoint you must, at all times, know where the industry stands. ...for example, if you're about to meet with a label head to discuss producing an act... if you know what's going on in the state of the industry, you're not going to blow yourself out of the deal by coming in too high (asking for too much money).*[486]

---

[483] Southside Glen, "The Difference between Delay and Reverb," Homerecording.com, http://homerecording.com/bbs/general-discussions/recording-techniques/difference-between-applying-delay-reverb-263441/, (accessed March 22, 2011).

[484] Personal interviews with industry sources (1984-2011).

[485] Jimmy Bowen (as quoted by Larry Wacholtz) *Inside Country Music*, Billboard Books, (New York: Watson-Guptil Publishers, 1986) & Larry Wacholtz, *Lights, Glitter and Business Sense*, Thumbs Up Publishing, (Washington: Cheney, 1984) 184-198

[486] Jimmy Bowen (as quoted by Larry Wacholtz) *Inside Country Music*, Billboard Books, (New York: Watson-Guptil Publishers, 1986) & Larry Wacholtz, *Lights, Glitter and Business Sense*, Thumbs Up Publishing, (Washington: Cheney, 1984) 184-198

Pre-Production

Bowen (1984) claims there are five basic steps in preproduction for recording an act, including (a) finding the artist, (b) researching the artist, (c) finding the material (songs), (d) hiring the musicians, and (e) setting up the session:[487]

> *You've got to have an artist to work with; that is the first thing. When you're first getting started you will probably work with artists who you wouldn't work with later on, but more than likely, you'll both be at the same stage. ...You'll produce some artists you probably shouldn't. You'll cause some marriages to happen that aren't the ideal marriages, but you must get some experience. When this happens, make sure you always do the very best job you can. If you realize that it's a super bad marriage, get out of it as gracefully as you can. Save the artist's time, save the artist's money, save your own reputation. You always want to maintain a business approach. If it doesn't work you're sorry it didn't work, but you'd rather not waste any more money.*[488]

Marrying the right song to the right artist is essential. The two must fit together in a way that allows the melody and lyrics to reinforce the perceptions consumers have of the artist's image. Bowen (1984) continues,

> *The first thing I suggest you do with an artist, when you first get involved with producing a specific artist, is to get a discography of that artist (a copy of all their recordings over their entire career, even the bad stuff). The artist has known themselves all of their life, you haven't! Don't try to come in after the artist has been singing for 12-14 years, working on their craft and hope you're going to jump on the train and ride a winner. Go at it seriously. ...There's so much you learn from researching the artist. You learn what not to do and you learn what to do. It's like anything else. A doctor wants an x-ray to try and figure out what's wrong before shooting medicine into you, at least a good doctor does. Some of them write prescriptions over the telephone. Beware of the doctor who does that. Beware of a producer who's ready to go to the studio a week or two after he's met the artist or gets the deal. He's looking for a miracle to happen; he's hoping it will all work out.*
>
> *...Being a producer, you've got to be a psychologist, not a psychiatrist, but a psychologist. You've got to dig into the artist's head. You've got to find out what makes an artist tick, what makes him give 100% sometimes, 80% sometimes, and 20% sometimes, or your going to be looking for luck, hoping the night you booked the studio you're going to get 100% and you may not get it. ...Have a deep relaxed discussion with the artist, read your artist and find out what environment will let them open up, relax, and have the best place to have a rap with you. If it's in a bar over a beer or at his house, go do it. If it's at your house, do it. If it's at the studio late at night go do it. Wherever. Find a place where that artist is more comfortable, where he'll open up to you, so he or she will talk to you, so you can start to read and understand them.*[489]

Producers are required to find and select the right songs for the artist to record. According to Bowen (1984),

> *You take a hit song if it comes from an ex-wife. You take a hit song if it comes from your biggest enemy. You owe that to the artist. Your job is to make hit records. He's paying you. It's his life and his money. Go out and hunt those songs. Anywhere you get a hit song is great. The obvious place to look is publishers and you need to have a good rapport with them. We look for material all the time. ...When I say the hunt is on, that's just what I mean. It's not going to come to you very often. You've got to create the relationships before the great songs are brought to you. You've got to go out and make yourself known. ...Thirty days before you're going to record an artist, put the word out. Then the songs flood in. The problem is that when you're going though songs (the last few weeks before a session) there's a tendency to take the best of the worst. So, have a big, long listening session for songs, cull out of 50 about 6 or 7. Get away from them until the next day and then go back and listen to those 6 or 7. You'll probably throw away 3 or 4 of them. ...Then play the songs for the artist. ...With the great songs, you'll both just light up. You'll light up, the artist' will light*

---

487 Jimmy Bowen (as quoted by Larry Wacholtz) *Inside Country Music*, Billboard Books, (New York: Watson-Guptil Publishers, 1986) & Larry Wacholtz, *Lights, Glitter and Business Sense,* Thumbs Up Publishing, (Washington: Cheney, 1984) 184-198

488 Jimmy Bowen (as quoted by Larry Wacholtz) *Inside Country Music*, Billboard Books, (New York: Watson-Guptil Publishers, 1986) & Larry Wacholtz, *Lights, Glitter and Business Sense,* Thumbs Up Publishing, (Washington: Cheney, 1984) 184-198

489 Jimmy Bowen (as quoted by Larry Wacholtz) *Inside Country Music*, Billboard Books, (New York: Watson-Guptil Publishers, 1986) & Larry Wacholtz, *Lights, Glitter and Business Sense,* Thumbs Up Publishing, (Washington: Cheney, 1984) 184-198

> *up. The great ones, you don't miss them. If you miss the great ones, then, I'd suggest plumbing or electrical work, because you aren't going to make it. …Also, when the hunt is on research old songs. Don't eliminate the possibility of 20 or 30 years of success.*[490]

The quality of the studio musicians, the recording artist's performances, the production, and engineering all contribute to the final *sound and feel* of the recording. Bowen (1984) claims that

> *It's like casting a movie if you put together a bad cast you're going to have a dog movie. …Talk to the artist about the musicians that he or she likes or doesn't like. Never cast a session and have a musician on it the artist has a bad vibe with. You're just putting a negative into your music that you don't need. … The whole trick is to figure out everything around the artist so when you go to tape, to make your record, you've got everything at max. You want the musicians at max; you want the artist at max. You want everything at its best. The ones that break through are the magical records that happen that way.*[491]

Basic Tracks

The first stage of a recording session in the studio is called *basic tracks* or *tracking*. The rhythm instruments and scratch (rough or practice) vocals lay the foundation for the rest of the instruments and vocals, which are cut later in their final versions. Session instruments can include drums, bass guitar, piano, and electric and acoustic guitars. The recording artist adds a reference or scratch vocal for the musicians to listen to while they play. It is re-sung and rerecorded later as a finished vocal. The session process involves the musicians and vocalists listening to the demo recording of the song, tuning up, and practicing the song at least a few times to prepare for the recording. Many of the studio musicians in the music centers of Los Angeles, New York, and Nashville learn, adept, and contribute their musical creative talents to the essence of the song in just a few minutes. Basic tracks are recorded once the musicians and vocalists are ready, the audio engineer has set the microphones, monitors, headphones, and equalization and effects levels, and the producer is satisfied with the quality of the sound and musical performance during practice.

Recording the right amount of signal on the tape is difficult. Too much signal will distort the tape. Too little signal will cause the playback to be noisy. Digital tape recorders and computer programs record a greater dynamic range, which solves some of the engineer's distortion and noise problems. If most of the musicians play poorly, the recording process is repeated. When the producer approves the basic musical tracks, the minor musical problems are usually fixed later. Logs are completed, which are written notes about the songs being recorded. Notes include length of the song, problems that need to be corrected in the overdub stage, and equalization and effects settings. Logs are stored in the box with the master tape. They are used in later recording sessions to alert the engineer and producers of necessary issues. Once the song has been recorded, everyone listens during tape playback for mistakes and opportunities to improve their performances. If recorded properly, the "take" becomes a "master."

Signal flow in basic tracks from the mics in the studio into the console is split and sent to the 24-track tape machine or hard disk drive (computer); the monitors in the control room (speakers); the musicians' headsets (earphones); the effects (add echo, reverb, pitch control to signals); and the two-track master tape machine or computer. Playback (to listen to the recording) reverses the signal flow from the tape machines or computer hard disk drive and allows the producer, audio engineer, musicians, and vocalists a chance to check their creative work.

---

490 Jimmy Bowen (as quoted by Larry Wacholtz) *Inside Country Music*, Billboard Books, (New York: Watson-Guptil Publishers, 1986) & Larry Wacholtz, *Lights, Glitter and Business Sense*, Thumbs Up Publishing, (Washington: Cheney, 1984) 184-198

491 Jimmy Bowen (as quoted by Larry Wacholtz) *Inside Country Music*, Billboard Books, (New York: Watson-Guptil Publishers, 1986) & Larry Wacholtz, *Lights, Glitter and Business Sense*, Thumbs Up Publishing, (Washington: Cheney, 1984) 184-198

Overdubbing

Adding instrumental parts and vocals to the previously recorded master tape is called overdubbing. The prior tracks are saved and the tape machine is placed into sel-sync (short for selective synchronization). Invented by guitarist *Les Paul* in the late 1940s, sel-sync turns the record heads on the previously recorded tracks into playback heads.[492] This allows the new instruments and vocals to be recorded in time with the instruments and vocals that were first recorded.

Signal flow in overdubbing is a combination of basic tracks and playback. The signal is played off the record head in playback and sent to the console where it is split and sent to the monitors, effects, 2-track/DAT, and through the cue system to the musicians' and recording artists' headsets (the signal is converted from an analog or binary magnet signal into an electronic signal by the playback heads and then sent to the console). Once the musicians and singers hear the signal (their previously recorded tracks), they play or sing their new tracks. The originals recorded in basic tracks are saved and the new tracks are added in sync with the previous tracks (microphones convert the artist's music into electrical signals, which travel back to the console to be split and sent to the monitors, effects, 2-track/DAT and are recorded as new tracks on the 24-or 32-track tape machine). "In sync" means that the record heads (on tape machines) are turned into playback heads, so that all tracks are played back, and the new tracks are recorded at the same time. Thus, the overdub stage is a combination of playback and recording at the same time.

Mix Down

The last stage in the recording process is mix down. After all the instruments and vocals have been recorded and overdubbed, the 24, 32, or whatever number tracks are mixed down to 2 tracks (stereo): left and right. Producers and audio engineers mix the tracks according to the "style" of the music genre (rock, hip hop, blues, jazz), create stereo images (using pan pots, which are switches and faders on the console that move the signal from left to right or anywhere in between), and create 3D depth (by acoustic positioning and pre-echo signals correlated to a dry signal). Of course, the mix down process is highly creative, and often depends on the perspective of the producers. Some labels use different producers to mix the same track, and then select the one they want to release.[493] Album cuts and dance mixes are sometimes different from the version of the song released to radio. Producers may even change the amount of compression on vocals and instruments for an AM radio release compared to an FM or digital release, as AM radio is primarily midrange, missing much of the bass and higher treble. Digital radio solves these problems because the signal is a binary code, and the music is generated by the computer chip in the receiver.

"Signal flow" is the converting of the magnetic signal stored on the tape of the analog or digital tape machine or hard drive into an electrical signal. It is sent (op amps) to the console where the producers and audio engineers may redirect it to effects equipment (reverb, echo, pitch, slap) and will finish by equalizing the signal (change the frequency response, bass, treble as examples), panning (stereo positioning), editing, and mixing.

Mastering

If the recording team of musicians, recording artists, audio engineers, and producers has done its job, the creativity of the recording session has been "captured" on tape or computers. The final mix stored as an

---

[492] Joe Cellini, "Les Paul Invented Here," Apple Pro, http://www.apple.com/pro/profiles/lespaul/, (accessed March 22, 2011).

[493] Personal interviews with industry professionals (1978-2011).

email attachment, 2-track analog or digital tape (DAT), or on a flash drive is sent to the mastering lab to be processed, and then pressed into CDs or released for digital downloads. *The Moving Picture Experts Group* developed compression systems to move digital video (movies and video) and digital audio data (the audio for the movies and video) quickly by reducing (compressing) the amount of digital information. Over time, the *sub-audio layer 3* has been abbreviated and has become known as *mp3.*[494] The music industry adopted this format to digitally download recorded songs. It has been very controversial, to say the least, as it provides a way for many consumes to illegally "share" tracks with anyone. In addition, the quality of mp3's is not as good as CDs because some of the digital information has been reduced to make the file easily transmittable. However, most of what has been taken out we would not hear anyway. According to Marshall Brain (2010),

> *...Some audiophiles – people who seek out the best ways to experience music – look down on the MP3 format. They argue that even at the highest bit rate settings, MP3 files are inferior to CDs and vinyl records. But other people argue that it's impossible for the human ear to detect the difference between an uncompressed CD file and an MP3 encoded with a 320 Kbps bit rate. ...In addition, some musicians and audio engineers say that the MP3 format is changing the way music studios mix recordings. They say that the MP3 format "flattens" out the dynamics – the differences in pitch and volume – in a song. As a result, much of the new music coming out of the industry has a similar sound, and there's not as much of a focus on creating a dynamic listening experience.*[495]

The mastering process for CDs is different from mp3s, as described in an article by Harris (2010):

> *In conventional CDs, these 1s and 0s are represented by millions of tiny bumps and flat areas on the disc's reflective surface. The bumps and flats are arranged in a continuous track that measures about 0.5 microns (millionths of a meter) across and 3.5 miles (5 km) long... To read this information, the CD player passes a laser beam over the track. When the laser passes over a flat area in the track, the beam is reflected directly to an optical sensor on the laser assembly. The CD player interprets this as a 1. When the beam passes over a bump, the light is bounced away from the optical sensor. The CD player recognizes this as a 0.*[496] *... CD-recordable discs, or CD-Rs, don't have any bumps or flat areas at all. Instead, they have a smooth reflective metal layer, which rests on top of a layer of photosensitive dye. When the disc is blank, the dye is translucent: Light can shine through and reflect off the metal surface. But when you heat the dye layer with concentrated light of a particular frequency and intensity, the dye turns opaque: It darkens to the point that light can't pass through.*[497]

Computer Programs

To the detriment of the recording studio business, many artists now forgo the cost of major recording studio sessions in favor of computer-based software. Great tracks are great tracks, and most consumers do not care if they were created in traditional studio sessions, costing hundreds of thousands of dollars or in a dorm room for a couple of pizzas. Years ago, the only way to record great artists and end up with goose bump-inducing tracks were in recording studios. Not today, as computers and software technology have provided almost anyone with the tools they need to create great tracks without the previously required studio sessions. Some major artists are recording only basic tracks in studios, reserving the overdub and mixing stages to be edited with computer programs at their leisure. They can even email their vocal recording to producers who remix the final tracks.

Technology has caused financial problems for many studios, musicians, and recording artists. However, it has also launched many creative opportunities for artists who, before this technology, could not afford the major

---

[494] Marshall Brain, "How Mp3 Files Work," Howstuffworks.com, http://computer.howstuffworks.com/mp32.htm, (accessed March 22, 2011).

[495] Marshall Brain, "How Mp3 Files Work," Howstuffworks.com, http://computer.howstuffworks.com/mp32.htm, (accessed March 22, 2011).

[496] Tom Harris, "How CD Burner Work," Howstuffworks.com, http://computer.howstuffworks.com/cd-burner1.htm, (accessed March 22, 2011).

[497] Tom Harris, "How CD Burner Work," Howstuffworks.com, http://computer.howstuffworks.com/cd-burner1.htm, (accessed March 22, 2011).

studios, musicians, and singers. Software has leveled the playing field, and almost anyone can create tracks consumers might enjoy. However, once great recordings have been created (in a studio or on a computer), consumers still have to "discover" them before they know if they like them. Who can accomplish that? The answer is *you* if you know how the industry works, and of course, the experts at the music companies and labels whose business it is to make recordings and acts profitable. Just because you can create great-sounding tracks on a computer does not mean that you can sell them. Consumers usually want more – an artist with an image, live shows, merchandise, physical copies, and things they can hear, see, dream about, associate with, get emotionally excited about, and hopefully spend money on. Therefore, creating tracks in a studio or on a computer is only one of the ingredients required for success in the business.

Super Producers

Because of the financial problems caused by P2P and consumer behavior, some of the artists and their labels are hiring super producers. These are the guys who wear about five hats at once as they produce the tracks using software programs in their own home studios, play the instruments (sometimes all of them on Midis), sing background harmonies, audio engineer, mix, and sometimes even develop the business plan and budgets. Labels save the cost of renting studios, hiring musicians and singers, and they often find that the tracks sound great and are delivered faster and at great financial savings.

Unions

There are several unions in the entertainment and music business that represent the creative artists and workers. Unions are organizations formed by individuals in the same or similar profession who band together for increased representation with employers.

The Screen Actors-American Federation of Television and Radio Artists

SAG and AFTRA joined together on March 30 of 2012, when more than 80% of both union's membership voted in favor of the merger.[498] According to the SAG-AFTRA website (2013):

> *This formed the most powerful union ever for more than 160,000 actors, announcers, broadcasters, journalists, dancers, DJs, news writers, editors, hosts, puppeteers, recording artist, singers, stunt performers, voiceover artist and other media professionals.*[499]

The American Federation of Television and Radio Artists had represented recording artists in studio sessions, television productions, and live performances since the late 1930s.[500] It also represented actors, announcers, sound effects artists, and other personalities working in radio and television. Representation was focused in five areas: sound recordings, broadcast news, commercials, industries, new technologies (non-broadcast industry films), and entertainment programs (television).[501] About 1,200 companies (including all the major

---

498 Nikki Finke, Deadline Hollywood, "Sag/AFTRA Merger Approved," http://www.deadline.com/2012/03/sag-aftra-merger-approved-screen-actors-guild-american-federation-television-radio-arts/, (accessed July 15, 2013).

499 SAG-AFTRA, "History," http://www.sagaftra.org/history, (accessed July 15, 2013).

500 AFTRA, "History: The People who Entertain and Inform America have been Moving Forward for 70 Years," AFTRA, http://www.aftra.org/history.htm, (accessed March 22, 2011).

501 AFTRA, "About AFTRA." AFTRA, http://www.aftra.org/aboutaftra.htm, (accessed March 22, 2011).

labels and music companies) had signed *The Code of Fair Practice for Phonograph Records.*[502] Accordingly, AFTRA's homepage stated (2010),

> *The American Federation of Television and Radio Artists (AFTRA) is a national labor union representing over 70,000 performers, journalists and other artists working in the entertainment and news media. …Representation covers broadcast, public and cable television (news, sports and weather; drama and comedy, soaps, talk and variety shows, documentaries, children's programming, reality and game shows); radio (news, commercials, hosted programs); sound recordings (CDs, singles, Broadway cast albums, audio books); "non-broadcast" and industrial material as well as Internet and digital programming.*[503]
>
> *…Membership includes an array of artists who bring pop, rock, country, classical, folk, jazz, comedy, Latin, hip hop, rap and R&B to the world. …Members perform in television and radio advertising, non-broadcast video, audio books and messaging, and provide their skills for developing technologies such as interactive games and Internet material.*[504]

The Screen Actors Guild had represented the superstars of Hollywood's film and television industry. According to the SAG-AFTRA website (2013) by merging together into one union they are:

> *...committed to organizing all work done under our jurisdictions; negotiating the best wages, working conditions, and health and pension benefits; preserving and expanding members' work opportunities; vigorously enforcing our contracts; and protecting members against unauthorized use of their work... (and as)... a proud member of the AFT-CIO, SAG-AFTRA partners with our fellow unions in the U.S. and internationally to seek the strongest protections for media artists throughout the world. We work with government at the international, federal, state, and local levels to expand protections for American media professional both at home and abroad.*[505]

The American Federation of Musicians

The American Federation of Musicians represents about 90,000 musicians in the United States and Canada for recordings and live performances in negotiated agreements for studio and other recordings, TV, films, jingles, concerts, stage shows, symphony, opera, and ballet.[506] Major record labels are signatories to The American Federation of Musicians *Sound Recording Labor Agreement* (formerly the Phonograph Record Label Agreement) that governs the wages, benefits, and working conditions of all its members, including studio musicians.[507] According to information posted on their homepage, *www.afm.org* (2010),

> *In the mid-1800s musicians in the United States began exploring ways to improve their professional lives. They formed Mutual Aid Societies to provide members with loans, financial assistance during illness or extended unemployment and death benefits. A number of these organizations became early unions serving various constituencies, but problems arose between them due to competition. In 1896, delegates from these organizations gathered at the invitation of American Federation of Labor (AFL) President Samuel Gompers to organize and charter a musicians' trade union. … They resolved: "That any musician who receives pay for his musical services, shall be considered a professional musician."*[508]

---

[502] AFTRA, "Code at a Glance," AFTRA, http://www.aftra.org/documents/03_02_SoundRecordingsGlance.pdf, (accessed March 22, 2011).

[503] AFTRA, "About AFTRA." AFTRA, http://www.aftra.org/aboutaftra.htm, (accessed March 22, 2011).

[504] AFTRA, "About AFTRA." AFTRA, http://www.aftra.org/aboutaftra.htm, (accessed March 22, 2011).

[505] SAG-AFTRA, "History," http://www.sagaftra.org/history, (accessed July 15, 2013).

[506] AF of M, "Why Join," AF of M, http://www.afm.org/why-join, (accessed March 22, 2011).

[507] AF of M, "Sound Recording Label Agreement," AF of M, http://www.afm.org/uploads/image, (accessed March 22, 2011).

[508] AF of M, "History of the AF of M (by years)," AF of M, http://www.afm.org/about/our-history, (accessed March 22, 2011).

Membership advantages include a retirement fund, health insurance, and AFL-CIO benefits.[509] The AF of M uses franchised booking agents who usually work for 10% commission to connect union musicians with people who want to hire them. Most of the agents represent musicians and recording artists locally and nationally.[510] If you are a musician playing gigs and do not want to get stiffed (play the gig and not get paid), representation by an AF of M licensed agent will usually prevent those types of problems. According to *www.afm.org* (2010),

> *AFM-Franchised Booking Agents are signatories to the AFM's Booking Agents Agreement. These booking agents act as the "sales force" for AFM members in the US and Canada. Purchasers are provided with legitimate agreements, members are provided with protection of their earnings, and the booking agents earn commissions for their sales. These agreements are comprehensive contracts which stand up in court, if need be, and obligate the parties – the purchaser is obligated to pay the stipulated price, and the musician(s) are obligated to perform the services described in the agreement.*[511]

Types of Recording Sessions (Scales and Rates)

There are several types of actual recording sessions, with the differences being based on union or nonunion agreements and if you live in a right-to-work state. The amount of money the recording team members receive is based on their fame, track record, contacts, and the kind of sessions the label authorizes. Record budgets are usually determined in advance by the label or whoever owns the copyright. Budgets are based on many factors such as the royalty artists, union agreements, the purpose of the recordings, and the marketing plan.

Master Session Rates

AF of M musicians are hired "by the session call" (3 hours, except for demo sessions) and AFTRA vocalists are hired by "the hour or number of songs recorded per-hour" with a two-hour minimum (whichever is greater).[512] Producers are usually hired "by the side" (one song) and paid half up front (when they agree to do the project) and the other half when the label accepts the final master tape.[513] Some also receive "producer points" (often between 1% and 3%) out of the royalty artist's points.[514] Audio engineers may be hired "by the hour, session, day, or project." Studios many be rented by the hour, session, day or project.

Typically, only the very best studio musicians and vocalists receive master session calls. A traditional master recording session is a three-hour call with a maximum length of 15 minutes of actual saved recorded time, four sides (songs) and a limited number of overdubs for corrections and sweetening.[515] However, there are

---

509 AF of M, "Why Join," AF of M, http://www.afm.org/why-join, (accessed March 22, 2011).

510 AF of M, "Book Agent Search," AF of M, http://www.afm.org/resources/booking-agent-search, (accessed March 22, 2011).

511 AF of M, "Book Agent Search," AF of M, http://www.afm.org/resources/booking-agent-search, (accessed March 22, 2011).

512 AF of M, "Sound Recording Label Agreement," AF of M, http://www.afm.org/uploads/image, (accessed March 22, 2011) and AFTRA, "Record Rates 2007-2010," AFTRA, http://www.aftra.org/146F6D705A314AA8980FE63A05C17E3A.htm, (accessed March 22, 2011).

513 Private interview with industry insiders (1978-2010).

514 Private interview with industry insiders (1978-2010).

515 AF of M, "Sound Recording Label Agreement," AF of M, http://www.afm.org/uploads/image, (accessed March 22, 2011).

also 3.5-hour scales, 4-hour scales, and overtime rates. One of the musicians must be declared "the leader" for the musicians and a "the contractor" for the singers.[516] AF of M leaders are paid double scale and act as the main communication link between the other musicians and the producer. The leader also provides the "card" that is signed by the musicians and turned into the union, who then bills the label for the musicians' work.[517] All session players (AF of M) are paid a scale plus $22.50 for the first service call or session except for (Low Budget and), $17.00 per additional services per-day for their health and welfare insurance, and an additional 11% of the total scale for contributions to their pension (EP) funds.[518]

The AFTRA contractor (leader) is paid about a 48% over scale (for a group of 3-8 singers or $95.5 per song or hour plus $46 extra per song or hour) and more for larger groups.[519] They are the main communication link between the other background singers and the producer. The AFTRA contractor provides the "card" and other paperwork that must be submitted to the union. AFTRA's payment scale is determined differently than the AF of M scale. Payments depend on the "number of sides" or "actual master takes," the number of overdubs, also called a side and the length of the actual recording in minutes and seconds, which is used as a multiplier. Thus, one side (or take) is limited to 4 minutes, 30 seconds. Four minutes and thirty-one seconds (4:31) to 9:00 minutes is considered double or two sides, and 9:01 or 13:30 is triple scale or 3 sides.[520] Overdubbing adds sides to the total. A new recording or side in each multitrack is an additional side.[521] So, to calculate the number of sides, take the original track, add any overdubs or additional tracks recorded, and multiply by the corresponding multiplier based on the actual length of the recording. As an example, a five-minute song with two overdubs is considered six sides. The original track is one side, plus two overdubs (two additional sides) times two as the multiplier (because the song is over four minutes and thirty-one seconds in length).[522]

Labels and music companies commonly pay their AFTRA royalty artists a maximum of triple scale.[523] However, that's a label decision not an AFTRA requirement. Contingency royalties are paid to non-label royalty singers for their performances on recordings that sell over 157,000 units. As an example, AFTRA non-royalty singers receive 50% of scale payments on recordings that sell over 157,500 and 75% additional

---

[516] AF of M, "Sound Recording Label Agreement," AF of M, http://www.afm.org/uploads/image, (accessed March 22, 2011)

[517] AF of M, "Sound Recording Label Agreement," AF of M, http://www.afm.org/uploads/image, (accessed March 22, 2011)

[518] AF of M, "Sound Recording Label Agreement," AF of M, http://www.afm.org/uploads/image, (accessed March 22, 2011)

[519] AFTRA, "Record Rates 2007-2010," AFTRA, http://www.aftra.org/146F6D705A314AA8980FE63A05C17E3A.htm, (accessed March 22, 2011).

[520] AFTRA, "Record Rates 2007-2010," AFTRA, http://www.aftra.org/146F6D705A314AA8980FE63A05C17E3A.htm, (accessed March 22, 2011).

[521] AFTRA, "Record Rates 2007-2010," AFTRA, http://www.aftra.org/146F6D705A314AA8980FE63A05C17E3A.htm, (accessed March 22, 2011).

[522] AFTRA, "Record Rates 2007-2010," AFTRA, http://www.aftra.org/146F6D705A314AA8980FE63A05C17E3A.htm, (accessed March 22, 2011).

[523] AFTRA, "Record Rates 2007-2010," AFTRA, http://www.aftra.org/146F6D705A314AA8980FE63A05C17E3A.htm, (accessed March 22, 2011).

scale payments for recordings that sell over 1,250,000 units.[524] For non-royalty artists, the labels also kick in an additional 11.5% payment (of total scale) for health and pension payments.[525]

Low Budget Rates/Side Letter

In the last few years, the musician's union has encouraged labels and producers to hire more studio musicians and vocalists by offering a special low budget scale (salaries). According to *AF of M's Low Budget Side Letter Agreement* (revised January 30, 2009),

> *Budgets computed for each full-length album shall include all costs customarily considered recording costs by the recording industry in this country, including (1) studio charges, (2) engineering, (3) tape (4) mixing costs, (5) payments to musicians (including their travel expenses), (6) equipment rental, and (7) cartage ...but excluding the producer and artist advances, art work, travel for the artists and producers and mastering costs.*[526]

Additionally, the *Low Budget Side Letter Agreement* sets the budget limits:

> *...To $99,000 for Tier 1 wages (regular recordings), $40,000 Tier 2 wages (experimental projects) and Tier 3 wages limited to $99,000 for choral recording (companion music for printed works) and $40,000 for concept pieces (primary focus is on concept, not a featured artists). If the maximum is exceeded... the Low Budget Side Letter will not apply and the provisions of the SRLA will apply.*[527]

AF of M scales are significantly reduced for low budget projects. A leader (at double scale) is required unless three or less members are called. Low budget scale for "regular" (royalty artist) sessions is almost 45% less than master scale. Musicians are paid $213.48 for a 3-hour call (for 15 minutes of maximum recorded time), pension fund contributions are still 11.44%, but health and welfare fund contributions are lowered to $15.50.[528] AFTRA vocalist scales are the same as master scales.

Limited Pressing Rates/Limited Pressing Agreement

Producers and labels may also decide to use a "Limited Pressing" session rate to reduce the cost and risks of independent productions and releases. Producers must agree to sign a *Limited Pressing Agreement* at one of the few union "locals" that still offer the rate.[529] The copyright owners (labels or producers on independent projects) are limited to 10,000 units to sell (hard copies and digital downloads), and if they sell more, they are required to pay the musicians (who played on the sessions) the differences between the limited pressing scales and master scales.[530]

---

524 AFTRA, "Record Rates 2007-2010," AFTRA, http://www.aftra.org/146F6D705A314AA8980FE63A05C17E3A.htm, (accessed March 22, 2011).

525 AFTRA, "Record Rates 2007-2010," AFTRA, http://www.aftra.org/146F6D705A314AA8980FE63A05C17E3A.htm, (accessed March 22, 2011).

526 Af of M, "Sound Recording Labor Agreement Low Budget Side Letter Summary," http://local1000.com/wordpress/wp-content/uploads/2010/10/Low-Budget-Scales.pdf, (accessed March 22, 2011).

527 Af of M, "Sound Recording Labor Agreement Low Budget Side Letter Summary," http://local1000.com/wordpress/wp-content/uploads/2010/10/Low-Budget-Scales.pdf, (accessed March 22, 2011).

528 Af of M, "Sound Recording Labor Agreement Low Budget Side Letter Summary," http://local1000.com/wordpress/wp-content/uploads/2010/10/Low-Budget-Scales.pdf, (accessed March 22, 2011).

529 AF of M, "Limited Pressing Rates," AF of M, http://www.rmanashville.com/index.php?p=afm%20scales, (accessed March 22, 2011).

530 AF of M, "Limited Pressing Rates," AF of M, http://www.rmanashville.com/index.php?p=afm%20scales, (accessed March 22, 2011).

Limited pressing sessions can reduce the cost of musicians for a project to $65.50 per hour and a two-hour minimum call (plus insurance and retirement). For musicians, this is a 52% reduction from master scale, yet it does provide an opportunity for work. So if you're recording a live session (all the musicians at once) or have a simple production to record, you can save money. The leader is paid 200% of the call rate. Health and welfare is an addition 22.50%, and pension is an addition 11.44% of basic rates.[531] AFTRA vocalist scales remain the same as master scales.

Demo Session Rates

If you want to record a song or vocalists to demonstrate the quality of the song (that you'll be pitching to publishers or labels) or the star potential of an artist (that you'll be pitching to the label's A&R department), then most professional producers use AF of M demo session rates. Calls are for a minimum of one hour, with the leader receiving the same scale as the side musicians of $104 per-hour, plus the $22.50 for H&W and 11.44% of scale for pension. However, on a two-hour call, the per-hour scales for side musicians are reduced to $52 per-hour, plus the $22.50 for H&W and 11.44% of scale for pension. The AF of M leader receives double scale plus the usual $22.50 for H&W and 11.44% of scale for pension.[532] AFTRA vocalist scales remain the same as master scales, yet the rate can depend on if the artist is a royalty or non-royalty artist. However, demos cannot be pressed or downloaded for sale. According to *The Sound Recording Scale Summary* posted by AF of M local 47 (2010),

> *A Demonstration Recording… is to be used exclusively for the purpose of recording a composition, an arrangement, and/or and artist or ensemble for personal use and study and/or for presentation to producers, employers, contractors, agents, purchasers, or institutions for the purpose of: 1) promoting the composition(s) or arrangement(s) recorded; and/or 2) obtaining employment for the performer(s) or other advancement (e.g., for admission to an educational institution, or for a scholarship or award).*[533]

Non-Union Session & Right to Work States

Anybody can record talent without using union members. Yet, most nonunion sessions are by nonprofessional artists, engineers, and producers who are in the process of developing their creative abilities. In addition, many states have right-to-work laws that allow for nonunion recordings. The best musicians and vocalists are usually union members and most likely (but are not supposed to) work for less than union scale. Unions help protect their members from unscrupulous producers, scam artists, and financially shaky record labels that promise payments but rarely deliver. Additionally, most nonunion recordings are used only for pitching songs and showcasing potentially new recording artists. If a label signs a nonunion act, it will usually (as they are signatories to union agreements) recut the tracks with union musicians or pay the difference between what the musicians were paid and union scale. Additional nonunion sessions by bands and other acts who create their own labels can give the recordings away on social websites or sell them off live performances, appearances, or on CD Baby and iTunes.

---

[531] AF of M, "Limited Pressing Rates," AF of M, http://www.rmanashville.com/index.php?p=afm%20scales, (accessed March 22, 2011).

[532] AF of M, Demonstration Recording Scale," AF of M, http://www.nashvillemusicians.org/documents/Demo72210.pdf, (accessed March 22, 2011).

[533] AF of M, Demonstration Recording Scale," AF of M, http://www.nashvillemusicians.org/documents/Demo72210.pdf, (accessed March 22, 2011).

Recording Budgets

Most artists never really think about what it is going to cost the label to create the recordings and, almost as importantly, what it will cost to promote, publicize, and distribute the final master recording. Having the artist submit the budget gives them an opportunity to understand the label's financial commitment to the recordings and to selling the album. *Some of the newer recording contracts require the artist to submit a budget for the label's approval.*[534] The process helps establish in the artist's mind that this is a business and the label expects their "best efforts" in the studio and on the road trying to sell the recordings at specific costs to the label.

From the previous information, you can see that artists, labels, music companies, and producers have many options when establishing recording budgets. Artists usually want everything, including many musicians (horn sections, strings, etc.), famous producers, and more time. Budgets put realistic constraints on the creative process. Too high a budget and the artist and label may never make any profits; too little money and the quality of the album may suffer. Although the artist is often responsible for submitting the budget, it's usually the manager or producer who writes it. Still, the process gets everyone in the same ballpark and establishes realistic and solid financial figures. It also puts the artist "on notice" that there are financial limits to their creative demands.

Recording Budget Expenses

Using the following chart, you can roughly determine the cost of one song recorded in a studio, and then multiply that figure by the number of songs on your album. By figuring the cost of an average song, you can calculate and predict the cost of a typical 10-12-song album at master, low budget, limited pressing, or demo rates. For the recording of one song, price out a studio, AFTRA singers, AF of M musicians, royalty artist payments (at triple scale), a producer, and an audio engineer for basic tracks, overdubbing, and mix down. The following recording budget forms combines three main factors: hiring and rental expenses, the types of sessions (master, limited pressing, etc.), and the stages of recording (tracking, overdubbing, and mix down).

---

[534] Industry contracts reviewed by author (2000-2011).

Recording Team	Responsibilities	Union	Basic Tracks 10am-1pm	Overdubbing 2-5pm 6pm-9pm	Mix Down 10pm-1am	Totals
Producer						
Audio Engineer						
Musicians						
Artist (vocal)						
BGVs						
Studio						
Misc	**Cartage** **Per-diem** **Tape/disc**					
Totals						

Type of Session	Master (3 Hour Call)	Low Budget (3 Hour Call)	Limited Pressing (3 Hour Call)	Demo (3 Hour Call)
Producer	$1-5,000 per side	$500-3,000 per side	$500-3,000 per side	$50-250 per side
Engineer	$100-150 per hour	$50-100 per hour	$50-100 per hour	$25-50 per hour
AF of M Musicians "Session Call"	$866.14 Leader ($760.04 for 3 hour call, plus $22.50 H&W, Plus 11% EP Fund) $444.32 Side Musician ($380.02 for 3-hour call, plus $22.50 H&W, Plus EP Fund of 11%)	$489.42 Leader ($426.96 for 3 hour call plus $15.50 H&W, Plus 11%) $252.46 Side Musician ($213.48 for 3-hour call, plus $15.50 H&W, Plus EP Fund of 11%)	$458.73 Leader ($393.00 for 3 hour call plus $22.50 H&W, Plus 11%) $262.76 Side Musician ($196.50 for 3-hour call plus, $22.50 H&W, Plus EP Fund of 11%)	$368.82 Leader ($312.00 for 3 hour call plus $22.50 H&W, Plus 11%) $195.66 Side Musician ($156.00 for 3-hour call. plus $22.50 H&W, Plus EP Fund of 11%)
Royalty Artist "By the hour or # of songs recorded per hour" 1-2 singers	$2,095.38 Label triple scale $698.46 Non-label ($209.75 Per-song or hour x 3 hour call), plus -11% royalty artist Health & Retirement, times triple label multiplier	$698.46 Non-label ($209.75 Per-song or hour x 3 hour call), plus -11% royalty artist Health & Retirement	$698.46 Non-label ($209.75 Per-song or hour x 3 hour call), plus -11% royalty artist Health & Retirement,	$698.46 Non-label ($209.75 Per-song or hour x 3 hour call), plus -11% royalty artist Health & Retirement,
BGVs "By the hour or # of songs recorded per hour" Group with 3-8 Singers	$322.31 Non-label per singer $477.56 *Contractor* (1 of the 3) @ an additional $46.00 x 3 for an extra $138 ($95.50 Per-song or hour x 3 hour call), plus -12.5% royalty artist Health & Retirement	$322.31 Non-label per singer $477.56 *Contractor* (1 of the 3) @ an additional $46.00 x 3 for an extra $138 ($95.50 Per-song or hour x 3 hour call), plus -12.5% royalty artist Health & Retirement,	$322.31 Non-label per singer $477.56 *Contractor* (1 of the 3) @ an additional $46.00 x 3 for an extra $138 ($95.50 Per-song or hour x 3 hour call), plus -12.5% royalty artist Health & Retirement	$322.31 Non-label per singer $477.56 *Contractor* (1 of the 3) @ an additional $46.00 x 3 for an extra $138 ($95.50 Per-song or hour x 3 hour call), plus -12.5% royalty artist Health & Retirement
Studio Day Rate	$1,200-2,400 Per day rates	$500-1,000 Per day rates	$500-1,000 Per day rates	$50-500 Per day rates

Recording Team	Duties	Union Guild	Basic Tracks 10 am-1pm	Overdubs 2pm-5pm	Overdubs 6pm-9pm	Mix Down 10pm-1am	Totals
Producer	Budget, Songs or Material and session production	None	5,000 per side	----------------	----------------	------------	$5,000
Audio Engineer	Quality of Sound on the Session, plus mix down	Audio Engineering Society (AES) guild	$1,200 Day rate @ $100 per hour	----------------	----------------	------------	$1.200
Musicians	5 Musicians at Master Scale Cut great tracks	American Federation of Musicians	$2,643.42	$2,643.42 Five new musicians with new call	----------------	------------	$5,286.84
Artist (vocal)	Services to Label, budget, cut tracks, promotion and Publicity	American Federation of Radio & Television Artists	$2,095.38 Scratch Vocals	----------------	$2,095.38 Master Vocals	------------	$4,190.76
BGVs	Provide harmonies to support royalty act	American Federation of Radio & Television Artists	-------------	----------------	$2,244.36 2 non-royalty BGV's at $322.21, plus contractor @ $477.56 sung twice (6 voices)	------------	$2,244.36
Studio	Master Studio with many extra effects and equipment	None	$1,200 Day rate @ $100 per hour	----------------	----------------	------------	$1,200.00
Other	Cartage (instruments) Per-diem (per-day expenses-act Tape/discs	None	$1.000	----------------	----------------	------------	$1,000.00
Totals	---------------	-------------	$13,138.80	$2,643.42	$4,339.74	Zero (Pre Paid)	$20,121.96

For example, if we hire five union musicians at *master scale* (meaning unlimited pressings) at $444.32 per musician (three-hour call of $380.02, plus $22.50 H&W, plus 11% of the base scale), plus $866.14 for the fifth who is the "leader" ($760.04 for base, plus $22.50, plus 11% of the base scale), the total cost of the five players is $2,643.42 for a one three-hour call. At the other end of the scale are the nonunion musician sessions where you can hire anyone who wants the experience of working in the industry for free. The problem is that the difference in sound and artistic quality is everything, and you get what you pay for. Great union musicians are a deal at twice the price, and that is why many major labels live by the union agreements. Remember that you've got many options such as low budget sessions (for recording budgets limited to $99,000) and limited pressing scales that are even lower. Union demos are for demonstration purposes only, such as song plugging or potential vocal pitches to labels or established artists managers. If that's your goal, then select the demo rates, and save the extra money.

Royalty artists receive triple scale multiplied by the three-hour call, plus health and welfare payments.[535] Thus, many royalty artists are paid around $2,000 on master sessions just to sing a scratch vocal (during the basic tracks) that will probably not be used in the final mix. Singing vocals during the basic tracks allows the producer and musicians to make sure they are getting the right rhythm and "feel of the song" recorded. Later, the royalty artist will return for an overdub session, sing the song again (for the master vocal take), and get paid again.

Recording Budget Scales and Prices

After figuring all the expenses (based on your decisions about the type of sessions, cost of players, etc.), use the one song total to determine the projected cost of the album. At master scale with five musicians for basic tracks and five more for overdubs plus royalty artist(s) cutting both a scratch and master vocal and paying for decent producers, engineers, and a studio rental, we'll probably be looking spending around $18,000-20,000 on one song in one day. Multiply the one song total by the number of songs for your album (usually 10-12), and you'll have your finished recording budget. In the following example, the total of the one-day, one song budget totaled $20,121.96. Thus, a ten-song recording budget would be about $200,000, which was not uncommon before the days of Logic and Pro Tools. However, this also allows us to understand why many labels are now using Pro Tools productions and accepting some of the recordings without the use and cost of live musicians.[536]

The All In's Budget

After the process of converting the master tape into CDs and formatting digital downloads into mp3, additional expenses now face the label. Call out the accountants to project the total number of units that might be sold (physical and digital). The label now has to press CDs (about $1.00 per CD with artwork, shrink wrap, mechanicals and digital download storage on server sites).[537] Of course, this is a base figure with the final cost per CD or digital download depending on the number of songs, complexity of the artwork, photography, booklet, and other marketing ideas. As an example, that $1.00 total consist of the 75% of the 9.1¢ statutory rate, or $0.06825 multiplied by 12 songs, for a total of 82¢ per album. If the label or music company presses 200,000 CDs, pays the controlled composition mechanicals, ($164,000 for the mechanical licenses, 5¢ for each CD, and $26,000 for the jewel cases, simple artwork, and shrink wrap) add another

535 Personal interviews with industry insiders (2000-2011).

536 Personal interviews with industry insiders (2008-2011).

537 Personal interviews with industry insiders (2005-2011).

$200,000 to the artist's recoupment debt. Add that to the recording cost of about $200,000 and we're already spending around $400,000 just to record the act, press CDs and digital storage and to pay the mechanicals. This is starting to look like real money!

Depending on the status of the act, the size of the marketing plan, and the street date launch, labels and music companies often budget between $150,000 and 300,000 for the "all in's," or the recording, mechanicals, and pressing or digital storage.[538] The all in's budget become the *baseline* for figuring the cost of promotion and publicity. Thus, the recording budget, including any advances, the mechanical license (usually at the controlled composition clause rate), and the cost of the pressings or digital storage are related to the size of the financial commitment of the marketing plan.

Promotion and Publicity Budgets

Promotion budgets are often based within a range of 100-200% of the all-in's budget (recordings mechanicals, advances, and production pressing, etc.), depending on the act and projected units sales.[539] *Publicity* is usually in a range of 50-100% of the all-in's recording and production budget, once again depending on the act and projected sales figures.[540] Thus, the publicity and promotion in the marketing plan may cost 150%-300% (or higher) of the recording and other all in's.[541] Famous acts may or may not fit into these estimates depending on the marketing plan; however, superstar acts often receive much larger advances, and lower tour support because they are already famous and so the marketing plan is based on information about new products instead of trying to launch an entirely new act.[542] New act budgets are often limited to a figure just high enough to see if products (albums, concert tickets and merchandise on 360 deals) sell once the album has been launched. Everything is negotiable! Also, second and additional album releases are often tied to an expected percentage increase in sales that hopefully indicates a positive skew line in expected and potential profits.

The International Federation of the Phonographic Industry claims that labels spend about "$5 billion investing in act."[543] In their publication *Investing In Music* (2010), they say that

> *The investment made by music companies will vary widely from one artist to another. A typical example of the breakdown of the costs of breaking a new pop act in major markets is (about $1,000,000) …This illustrates the very substantial costs involved in developing an artist."*[544]

---

538 Personal interviews with industry insiders (2005-2011).

539 Personal interviews with industry insiders (2005-2011).

540 Personal interviews with industry insiders (2005-2011).

541 Personal interviews with industry insiders (2005-2011).

542 IFPI, "New Report Show How Much Money Record Companies are 'Investing in Music'," IFPI (International Federation of the Phonographic Industry), http://www.ifpi.org/content/section_news/investing_in_music.html, (accessed March 24, 2011).

543 IFPI, "New Report Show How Much Money Record Companies are 'Investing in Music'," IFPI (International Federation of the Phonographic Industry), http://www.ifpi.org/content/section_news/investing_in_music.html, (accessed March 24, 2011).

544 IFPI, "New Report Show How Much Money Record Companies are 'Investing in Music'," IFPI (International Federation of the Phonographic Industry), http://www.ifpi.org/content/section_news/investing_in_music.html, (accessed March 24, 2011).

The following table and percentages have been created from the financials figures stated in the IFPI article *Investing in Music* (2010).[545]

Developing Act	Percent of Total	Label Expenses	Percent of Total	Super Sta Act
$200,000	20%	Advances	32%	$1,500,000
$200,000	20%	Recording Budget	8.6%	$400,000
$200,000	20%	3 Music Videos	9.7%	$450,000
$300,000	30%	Promotion & Marketing	49.4%	$2,300,000
$100,000	10%	Tour Support	Zero	None
$1,000,000		Totals		$4,650,000

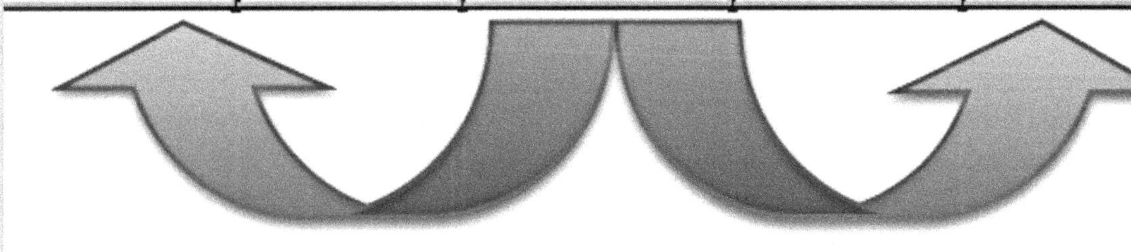

Now that the budget for the artist has been determined (recording budget, production budget, marketing, promotion, and publicity), break-even points are based on the number of units sold to recoup (pay back) all expenses. The formula for this recoupable debt account (in the artist's name, but the label has to repay itself) is the *suggested retail list price* (SRLP), minus the packaging fee (which establishes the new royalty base), multiplied by the artist's points (minus the producer points). Let's take a closer look.

The actual royalties an artist is paid is based on each unit sold (which for an album is usually between $1.00 and 2.35). *Remember, almost everything is negotiable!* Divide the unit royalty base (the $1.00-2.35) into the total debt to determine the total number of units that need to be sold before the artist's account breaks even. The label takes the royalties and applies them to the recoupable debt. As an example, if the recoupable artist account is $1.2 million and the artist royalty per unit sold is $2.00, then you divide the $1.2 million dollar debt by the $2.00 royalty to determine that **600,000 units** (albums) need to be sold before the artist will receive any money. It is easy to see why most recording artists rarely make any money from their record label deals.[546]

---

[545] IFPI, "New Report Show How Much Money Record Companies are 'Investing in Music'," IFPI (International Federation of the Phonographic Industry), http://www.ifpi.org/content/section_news/investing_in_music.html, (accessed March 24, 2011).

[546] Personal interviews with industry sources (2005-2011).

The record label is a different story. They receive about 40% of their SRLP or about \$6.78 on a \$16.95 album and about 70% of the \$10.00 album offered on Internet sites. Even if the album is sold for \$11.95 at Target or for \$9.95 as a digital download from iTunes, the original SRLP (\$16.95) is still used to determine royalties and break-even points. The label's formula is to subtract the artists' royalty per unit (\$1.00-2.35) from the 40% of the SRLP (\$16.95), or \$6.78 minus \$2.00 (using the same figure as before). With these figures, the label will receive \$4.78 per unit. Divide the \$4.78 into the total debt of \$1.2 million, and you'll see that the label only has to sell about **251,046 units** to break even. The difference of 600,000 units (artist break-even point) minus the label's break-even point of 251,046 units equal a difference of **348,954 units**. If the label sold those units, they would gain a profit of \$1,668,000 *before* the artist receives any additional money. *Welcome to music business economics!* However, remember the label *risked* over a million dollars to exploit the artist's creativity, betting that the act would become profitable. Unless you have a very rich uncle, who else is going to do that? An on top of the money the label has invested, if they artist or label do not make any money, it's the label who is saddled with the debt, as the artist is not required to repay any money as long as they have fulfilled their contractual obligations. It's the label who has to pay back it's own debt (to itself) though units sold. The 360 deals simple expand the labels ability to pay the debt by securing additional funds from the acts' merchandise, ticket and endorsement revenues.[547]

Picking Up Contract Options

It is important to understand that time plays an important part of the label's decision to pick up an artist's option. As an example, a fast-selling album with a sharp upward skew line (representing units and merchandise sold) may indicate a huge profit for the label, while an upward 10-15 degree angle skew line may indicate a good-selling act over a much longer time. A flat skew line reveals the act's record sales may have softened, and the budgets should be curtailed accordingly. It may also indicate that it is time to drop the act. The difficult part is trying to figure out which act (once the album has been recorded and released) will deliver the biggest profits. It depends on the original budget, money spent on the recordings, promotion, and publicity, and the profits on the number of units sold and not stolen. It's a business, and an artist's potential success is unknown until the public has a chance to hear and see the act to determine what they like and want to buy. In 360 deals, this philosophy is broadened to the other revenue streams associated with touring and image branding. Thus, the label accountants have to also project potential revenues from monetizing personal appearances, merchandise sales, and secondary products such as clothing lines, consumer goods, and other revenue sources. Thus, the industry today is morphing toward using recordings to break new acts and to sustain established acts to monetize the consumers' emotional connections by selling them anything they can connect to their feelings about the artist and their music. In the following example, you can see that *artist A* is highly profitable, *artist B* is taking a long time to develop, and *artist C* had what looked like a promising start to their career that faded fast. Labels and music companies are looking for the one-of-a-kind *A artists* and usually will not take the time to develop the *B artists* (except Disney), and the *C artist* is the one-hit wonder (maybe) dropped from their deal.

---

[547] Personal interviews with industry sources (2005-2011).

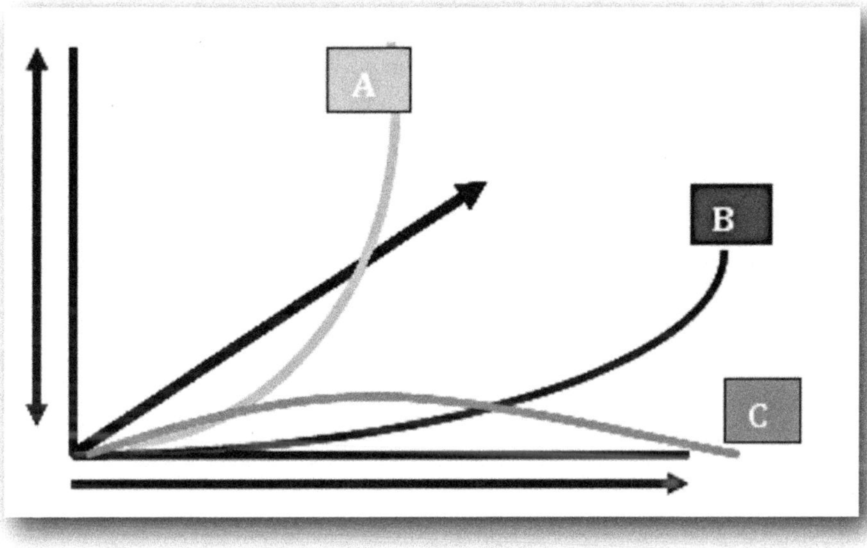

Computer-Based Recording Budgets

Most consumers do not care if tracks are created in a studio or on computers. They usually can't even tell the difference. As already discussed, the three principle factors to consider are the cost of (a) the recording team/studio, (b) the type of session (union/non-union), and (c) the cost of each stage of the recording for one day and one song. If you cut out the recording team players, unions, and other studio costs, the total cost of the recording may be reduced to almost nothing and if you are talented enough, the final product's sound quality will be similar to or better than the studio master recording that costs about $200,000.

Computer software programs such as Pro Tools, Logic Pro, and even GarageBand are revolutionary to the industry's bottom line. Many label and music company albums of famous artists are created on computer-based programs. Inexpensive Mac and PCs, together with innovative software, are replacing the studio rentals in many million-dollar major label budgets. In some albums, only the basic tracks are studio based. Computers with Pro Tools and Logic Pro are capable of providing recordings as good as (and in some cases better) than the very best professional studios. The savings in recording costs for the labels and music companies are significant. At the same time, the recording expenses to new and emerging artists are also reduced which allows them to record, showcase their talent, and in effect "enter the game" and compete with the major labels and their rooster. The advantage to the labels (both major and independent) is the saving of hundreds of thousands of dollars in recording costs; the advantage to the semiprofessional musicians and vocalists is that they can now record demos and albums on their home computers, saving thousands in the cost of studio time, producers, union musicians, audio engineers, and BGVs.

The Human Element

Computer-based programs that replace the need for acoustic studios with their expensive equipment and rental bills *do not replace the need for brilliant producers and audio/computer engineers.* Recording artists (musicians and vocalists) still want the direction, guidance, encouragement, and production insights experienced producers and audio engineers provide. Computer software can only record and "fix" the performance and audio imperfections tracked. However, to start with the best possible recordings, actual producers and engineers are still usually required to "get" the best human performance out of the live singers and musicians cutting the tracks. The software simply creates great sounding recordings, fixes the pitch problems, overdubbing, glitches, effects, and other recording situations that could usually be accomplished in a real recording studio. The computer can't tell an artist how to sing better or a group of musicians how to play a track better together. Thus, albums created with software programs are much cheaper and quicker than the traditional studio process, lowering the break-even point of unit sales and increasing the labels and music companies profits, but the human performance factors of quality and greatness are still only as good as the original tracks that need the creative guidance of an experience producer and audio/computer engineer.[548]

The Music Performance Fund

The Music Performance Fund (formally called The Recording Industry Music Performance Trust Fund) is the largest single sponsor of live music performances in the world (over 10,000 in 2009). Created in 1948, the fund is part of an agreement among AF of M, record labels, and additional sponsors. The fund is also based on record sales. The MPF website, *musicpf.org*, states (2010) that

> *The Fund was established in 1948 by the recording companies of North America and the American Federation of Musicians as part of their collective bargaining agreement. A small royalty on the sale of some recorded music is contributed to the Fund by signatory recording companies ...supplemented by co-sponsoring organizations. There is never an admission charge for MPF performances, and its performances cannot be used to raise money, sell merchandise, or promote political or religious events.*[549]

The Film Musicians Secondary Market Fund

Not all the musicians on recording sessions are label royalty artists. The backup musicians (called side musicians) are still "recording artists" and their musical recordings are often used in film soundtracks. The *Film Musicians Secondary Markets Fund* was established in 1972 as *The Theatrical and Television Motion Picture Special Payments Fund.*[550] According to FMSMF.org (2007),

> *The Fund functions as an agent of the Producers and exists as an entity formed through a collective Bargaining Agreement, whose terms are negotiated every three years, between the Alliance of Motion Picture & Television Producers (AMPTP) and the American Federations of Musicians (AF). The sole purpose of the Fund is to sere all those who are eligible to receive residual wage payments, including musicians who are participating members of the American Federation of Musicians, through its Local Unions.*[551]

The Alliance of Artist and Recording Companies (AARC)

The Alliance of Artists and Recording Companies (AARC) represents featured artists, music companies, and labels in the worldwide collection of royalties for the sale of blank CDs and digital recording devices as required by the Home Recording Act of 1992. According to aarcroyalties.com (2011),

> *The Alliance of Artists and Recording Companies, Inc. (AARC) is the leading organization representing featured artists and recording companies, both domestically and abroad, in the areas of home taping/private copy royalties and rental royalties. AARC, a non-profit organization, was formed to collect and distribute Audio Home Recording Act of 1992 (AHRA) royalties to featured recording artists and sound recording copyright owners (usually record companies.) However, based on its success in administering the AHRA royalties, AARC's mandate was expanded to include foreign home taping/private copy and rental royalties. ...AHRA*

---

548 Personal interviews with industry sources (2009-2011).

549 Music Performance Fund, "About Us: Enriching Lives Through Music," MPF, http://www.musicpf.org/AboutUs2.html, (accessed March 22, 2011).

550 The Film Musicians Secondary Markets Fund, "Our Mission," Fmsmf.org, http://www.fmsmf.org/aboutus/fundstatement.html, (accessed March 26, 2011).

551 The Film Musicians Secondary Markets Fund, "Our Mission," Fmsmf.org, http://www.fmsmf.org/aboutus/fundstatement.html, (accessed March 26, 2011).

> *royalties are generated from the sales of certain blank CDs and specific digital recording devices for non-commercial use. AARC is the sole administrator of this royalty in the US to featured artists and sound recording copyright owners.*[552]

The AFM & AFTRA Intellectual Property Rights Distribution Fund

The American Federation of Radio and Television Artists (AFTRA) and *The American Federation of Musicians* (AF of M) together formed *The AFM & AFTRA Intellectual Property Rights Distribution Fund* to collect and distribute royalties to non-featured singers and musicians for the rental, home copying, and digital broadcasting of sound recordings in foreign countries required by the 1995 Digital Millennium Copyright Act (signed into United States law in 1998).[553] According to AHRA.org (2011),

> *The Fund distributes money to non-featured vocalists and non-featured musicians for the rental in Japan of U.S. and Japanese produced sound recordings, Japanese Private Home Copying, Dutch royalties received from SENA in the Netherlands for Private Home Copying and certain broadcast royalties, Audio Home Recording Act (AHRA) monies, and statutory license royalties for the digital broadcast of sound recordings in the U.S pursuant to the DPRA (Digital Performance Rights in Sound Recordings Act of 1995) and DMCA (Digital Millennium Copyright Act of 1998). ...The Fund receives home taping money from Japan and the Netherlands, and is just now finalizing discussions with the applicable organization in Spain for the payment of audio visual royalties from that country. In addition, rates and fees have been established for Webcasting, and these monies are now being added to The Digital Performance Royalties (DPR) portion of the distributions. ...Distribution of these royalties are made to union and non-union performers alike. The Fund distributes to entitled singers and musicians without regard to union membership.*[554]

Additional Sources of Revenue

Every recording embodies at least two copyrights: the song, usually owned by the music publisher, and the recording of the song, usually owned by a record label or music company. They generate billions in sales, advertisements, and performance royalties. Once you're famous (usually because of a recording deal and the exposure it provides), many additional revenues streams are generated. According to the *Future of Music Coalition* (2009)[555] and other resources,[556] the following is a short example of other sources of revenue for royalty and non-royalty creative musicians, singers, and other artists.

---

[552] The Alliance of Artist and Recording Companies (AARC), "What is AARC?," aarecroyalties.com, https://www.aarcroyalties.com/2008/home.php?nav=whatis, (accessed March 26, 2011).

[553] The AFM & AFTRA Intellectual Property Rights Distribution Fund, "About Us," RARoyalties.org, http://www.ahra.org/aboutus.html, (accessed March 26, 2011).

[554] The AFM & AFTRA Intellectual Property Rights Distribution Fund, "About Us," RARoyalties.org, http://www.ahra.org/aboutus.html, (accessed March 26, 2011).

[555] The Future of Music Coalition, "29 Streams," Futureofmusic.org, http://futureofmusic.org/blog/2009/10/14/29-streams, (accessed March).

[556] Personal interviews with industry sources (1978-2011).

Musical Compositions	Source of Revenues	Agency/Source
Retail (Platform/CD) Sales	Mechanical Royalties (sale of the recording in stores and concerts).	Harry Fox Agency
Digital Sales	Digital Mechanical Royalties from online sources.	Harry Fox Agency
Sheet Music	Sales of printed music at music stores.	Direct negotiations required
PRO Royalties	ASCAP, BMI, SESAC collected royalties for live performances, foreign royalties, and radio and TV broadcasts.	ASCAP, BMI, SESAC
Advances	From music publishing deals	Music Publishing Company
Legal Settlements	Payments from litigation	Court Action
Commissions	Work for hire commission work (including commercials, and advertisements.	Hiring Company-such as advertisement firm

Performing Artist	Sources of Revenue	Agency/Source
Digital Performance Royalties	Digital streaming of satellite radio, webcasts and cable TV music	SoundExchange
Advances	Recording Deals	Labels or Music Companies
Tour Support	Recording Deals	Labels or Music Companies
Recording Budget Expenses	Recording Deals	Labels or Music Companies
Legal Settlements	Payments form litigation	Court Action
Consumer/Businesses rental and copying	Private copy and rental rights	AARC
Musicians Recording Session Work	Recording used in TV and Secondary markets	FMSMF.org
Musicians Recording Session Work	Sound Recording Special Payments Fund	AF of M
Musicians Record Session Work	Recording musicians for session calls for label session work	AF of M
Vocalist Recording Session Work	Recording vocalist for session calls for label session	AFTRA
Musicians and Vocalists Recording Session Work	Distribution of recording and performance royalties to non-featured artist in the United States and foreign territories as recorded by law-AFM/ AFTRA Intellectual Property Rights Distribution Fund.	AFTRA and AF of M.

Licensing of Music Compositions	Licenses	Agency/Source
Ringtones	Mechanical	Harry Fox
Songs in Visual Media-(in the production of) Movies, TV shows, Video Games, Commercials	Synchronization often called a Sync Licenses	Direct negotiations required
Sampling of another's acts recording	Sampling Licenses	Direct negotiations required

Performing Artist	Source of Revenues	Agency/Source
Live shows	Promoter, owner of venue, sponsoring organization	Direct negotiations required
Branding	Monetizing image through consumer products such as clothing lines, health drinks	Direct negotiations required
Sponsorships	Monetizing image to product and company names for tours and events	Direct negotiations required
Endorsements	Monetizing image by endorsements of consumer products through advertisements.	Direct negotiations required
Fan Clubs	Monetizing fan's emotional connection through direct fan club memberships, newsletters, websites.	Direct negotiations required
Commissions	Book commissions	Direct negotiations required
Acting	Monetizing fan emotional connections through media productions	AFTRA and SGA
Persona Licenses	Licensing of computer generated image in video games and other sources	Direct negotiations required

Knowledge & Experience	Source of Revenues	Agency/Source
Speaking engagements	Keynote speeches, master of ceremonies.	Talent Agency representation
Producing	Labels or from independent artist	Direct negotiations required
Teaching	Institution	Direct negotiations required
Grants	Government and nonprofit organizations	Direct negotiations required

Summary

Studios and computer software are an integral part of the music business. When the musicians play their instruments and the recording artists sing their songs, the universal language of music is being produced, captured, and converted into sellable recordings. In the studio, teams of people work together under time and money constraints to create their final musical products. Recording artists (also the musicians and singers) work together to create musical art with their vocals and musical instruments. Audio engineers are responsible for the quality of the technical recording. Producers are in charge of sessions, budgets, the musicians' and vocalists' performance, and the quality of the final master tape, which will eventually be turned into CDs and digital downloads.

Yet, it takes the business side of the industry to fund and develop the acts and recordings, distribute them for sale, and then provide the final marketing mix of promotion and publicity. Artists, labels, music companies, and independent producers have many options when developing budgets. Thus, the final recording may cost anywhere from just a few bucks to hundreds of thousands of dollars, depending on the three variables: (a) the recording teams consisting of the royalty artist(s), BGVs (background vocals), musicians, producer, and audio engineer; (b) the types of sessions including union master, limited pressing, low budget, and demo and nonunion recordings, which can be almost any type of session; and (c) the stage of the recording sessions which include basic tracks, overdubbing, and mix down. Preproduction is before the actual sessions (selection of songs, establishment of budgets, and practice sessions). Post-production includes converting the digital or analog master tape to a CD matrix and pressings and digital conversion to the mp3 and mp4 formats.

Key Website Resources

http://www.actorsequity.org/

http://www.afm.org/

http://www.aftra.org/

15

Managers

Representation
Management Team
Agents and Budgets

"A personal manager receives a percentage of what an artist earns. If the artist makes money, so does the manager. If the artist doesn't make money, the manager can still make money. What? You must understand that as an artist you sign an exclusive personal contract, which means the artist can work with NO other manager. On the other hand, a manager has NO exclusivity to the artist. He can manage as many acts as he can sign and that is why he can be making money while you might be waiting for your royalty check to get you out of trouble. Also if one of his other acts is dong well he might be, could be, probably is spending more time with the act doing well at the time. I have heard a great manager who handled many acts say that management is like spinning plates. You try to keep them all in the air so that none of the plates slow down so much that they stop spinning, fall and break. You must keep them all spinning, albeit, some might be spinning faster than others and one might really come close to falling, you must keep them all spinning for everyone to survive."

— Mark Volman, The Turtles[557]

"I want to shake off the dust of this one-horse town. I want to explore the world. I want to watch TV in a different time zone. I want to visit strange, exotic malls... I want to live..."

— Homer Simpson[558]

"Eighty percent of success is showing up."

— Woody Allen[559]

"My major (Music Business) gave me an overview of all the different aspects of the business, so when I tried to make a name for myself, I knew what questions to ask."

— Trisha Yearwood, MCA Recording Artist[560]

---

557 Mark Volman, "Survey of Music Business MBU 1110," (Nashville: TN, Belmont University Course Pack, 2008).

558 Homer Simpson, "Homer Simpson Quotes," Artquotes.net, http://www.artquotes.net/entertainment-quotes/famous-actors, (accessed March 24, 2011).

559 Woody Allen, "Woody Allen Quotes," Artquotes.net, http://www.artquotes.net/entertainment-quotes/woody-allen.htm, (accessed March 24, 2011).

560 Trisha Yearwood, "Yearwood is Singer/Businesswoman," The Tennessean, September 16, 1994.

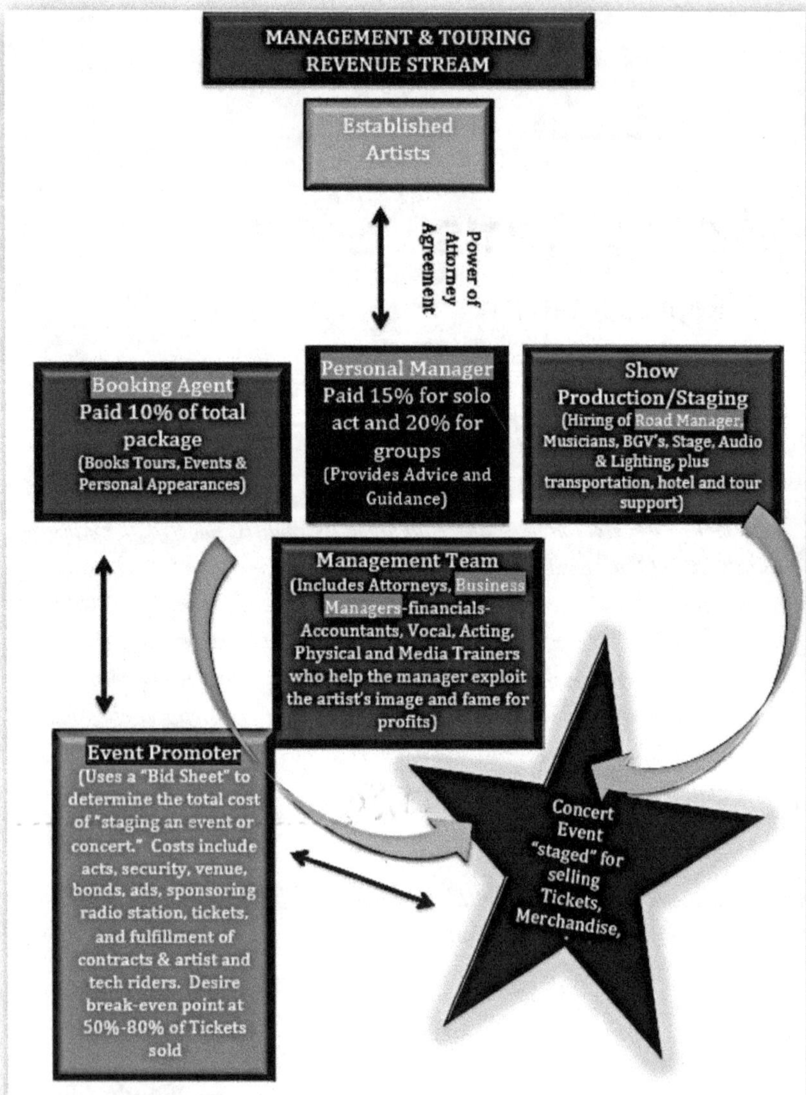

Talent Agencies

Talent agencies control entertainment promotion, publicity, and employment opportunities for many of the most famous acts, authors, public personalities, and artists. They frequently represent the superstars of music and films for productions, tours, appearances, advertisements, and any other type of events or work that benefits the iconic images of the artists. They provide worldwide representation and in doing so, provide talent to world markets. The four largest talent agencies are CAA, ICM, UTA, and WME$_2$.

Creative Artists Agency (CAA)

CAA was formed in 1975 and is noted for its powerful list of actors and entertainment personalities, including famous directors, sports, business, and celebrity motivational speakers.[561] According to *Answers.com & Hoover's Company Profile*, (2010), CAA is

> *Arguably the most powerful talent agency in the business. …Represents clients working in film, music, television, theater, sports, and literature. The firm's client list reads like a who's who of A-list stars, including such luminaries as Steven Spielberg, Tom Cruise, Brad Pitt, George Clooney, LeBron James, Simon Cowell, David Beckham, Will Ferrell, and Sandra Bullock. It has also works with commercial clients such as Coca-Cola and toymaker Mattel. Supplemental services include strategic counsel, financing, and consulting. Its Intelligence Group/Youth Intelligence unit tracks and conducts behavior research for consumers from ages 8 to 39.*[562]

---

561 Creative Artist Agency (CAA), "Creative Artist Agency LLC." Hoover's Company Profiles, http://www.answers.com/topic/creative-artists-agency, (accessed August 24, 2010).

562 Creative Artist Agency (CAA), "Creative Artist Agency LLC." Hoover's Company Profiles, http://www.answers.com/topic/creative-artists-agency, (accessed August 24, 2010).

International Creative Management (ICM)

ICM was formed in 1975 by the merger of Creative Management Associates and The International Famous Agency.[563] According to *Hoovers* (2010),

> *…The agency represents film and television actors and directors, as well as artists in theater, music, publishing, and new media. A major "ten percent" (along with CAA and William Morris Endeavor), ICM represents such A-list clients as Halle Berry, Rosario Dawson, Robert Duvall, Beyonce Knowles, and Chris Rock, as well as emerging performers. It has offices in Los Angeles, New York, and London.*[564]

United Talent Agency (UTA)

UTA represents major stars and the behind-the-scenes creative artists in the entertainment industry who *make* the entertainment products we love to watch.[565] According to *Hoovers* (2010),

> *Started in 1991 and different in Hollywood as some of its best agents own part of the company, clients include Harrison Ford, Miley Cyrus, Rachel McAdams, and Johnny Depp, as well as a client list of directors, producers, and screenwriters… Beyond the celluloid, the company represents literary authors, journalists, musicians, and creators of mobile, online, and gaming content. It also provides branding, licensing, and marketing services.*[566]

UTA also represents many of the behind-the-scenes workers in the film and production business. According to *UTAproductions.com* (2004), they

> *…Represent famous producers, directors of photography, production designers, costume designers, film editors, first and second directors, stunt coordinators, visual effects supervisors, production service providers, (including animatronics) and the Mediapro Studios in Romania which includes 19 fully equipped film and TV stages (four of which have water tanks, various workshops, approximately 100 acres of property on the shore of a lake, a park, and satellite uplink equipment).*[567]

William Morris Endeavor Entertainment (WME2)

WME$_2$ takes a different niche, as it represents talent, public personalities (speakers), and authors. It was formed in 1898 to represent vaudeville acts and currently has offices in New York, Beverly Hills, Nashville, London, Miami Beach, and Shanghai.[568] According to *Bloombergbusinessweek.com* (2010),

> *…It provides commercials and endorsements in the areas of print, on-camera, voiceovers, animation, video games, licensing and merchandising, infomercials, PR campaigns and satellite media tours, and non-performing personal appearances; and offers lecturers in the fields of national and global affairs, media, business and economics, health and science, humor, and sport and motivation. The company represents clients for music and personal appearances in various musical genres, including rock, pop, urban contemporary, country, comedy, Latin, Christian/gospel, and adult contemporary; and secures endorsement, sponsorship, commercial, marketing, licensing, motion picture, television, digital, publishing, and broadcasting opportunities. It provides screenwriters, producers, directors, and actors for motion pictures; represents reporters and anchors on network and cable outlets, covering news, sports, weather, and*

---

[563] International Creative Management Agency, (ICM) Answers.com, http://www.answers.com/topic/international-creative-management-inc, (accessed March 29, 2011).

[564] International Creative Management Agency, (ICM) "International Creative Agency," Hoovers Company Profiles, http://www.hoovers.com/company/International_Creative_Management_Inc/ccycji-1.html, (accessed August 24, 2010).

[565] United Talent Agency, (UTA), "Production Department," http://www.utaproduction.com/, (accessed August 24, 2010).

[566] United Talent Agency, (UTA), "United Talent Agency," Hoover's Company Profiles, http://www.hoovers.com/company/United_Talent_Agency_Inc/hytrxi-1.html, (accessed August 24, 2010).

[567] United Talent Agency, "Mediaprostudio," United Talent Agency, http://www.mediaprostudios.com/, (accessed March 29, 2011).

[568] Willaim Morris Endeavor Agency "Locations," http://www.wmeentertainment.com/, (accessed August 24, 2010).

entertainment, as well as television and talk show hosts, and producers in the news arena; provides writers, composers, lyricists, directors, choreographers, actors, and producers for theaters.[569]

Talent Agents

Talent agents own or work for agencies licenses by the unions to represent creative artists. They may provide some career advice and guidance just as personal managers in the music business, but their main job is to seek and acquire employment for their acts. However in today's music world the talent agent job descriptions are blending with some of the personal mangers. Usually, an artist's manager hires *AF of M licensed booking agents* to set up tours for their acts. However, talent agents working at the major agencies (CAA, ICM, UTA, and WME_2) also establish tours and provide "some management advice" to representative artists. AFTRA/SAG and the AF of M are unions while CAA, ICM, UTA, and WME_2 are talent agencies or businesses licenses by the unions to represent the union members (creative artists) by seeking employment opportunities (cattle calls for film, tour for musical acts, speaker engagement for personalities). Talent agents may seek many entertainment based employment opportunities (for examples, endorsements, acting, and commercials) for the creative acts they represent while AF of M booking agents are usually limited to musical tours and other types of musical performances. Thus, AFTRA and Equity "talent agents" have the same *title* as talent agents at CAA, ICM, UTA, and WME_2, but their *duties and responsibilities* are somewhat limited by the unions their clients represent. Some AFTRA and Equity agents also provide advice and guidance similar to music business personal managers on a limited bases.

Personal Managers

While most talent agencies are responsible for the worldwide employment of creative authors, artists, and production talent, personal managers are usually responsible for the "day-to-day career development and personal advice and guidance of iconic artists."[570] Personal managers are there to guide and provide advice to newer artists about their career decisions. Therefore, whomever the artist hires better know the business, have major industry contacts, understand business principles, maintain a positive attitude, and have the artist's best interests at heart. The manager is responsible for creating a team to take advantage of every possible positive opportunity to make money on the artist's fame, talent, and noteworthy publicity. *Ask yourself a question: what can a manager do for you that you can't do yourself?* The answers should be very clear now. Thus, the first step of a prospective artist is to find the perfect manager!

However, since managers are not talent agents seeking employment for the acts they represent, their job is to approve work "pitched" to them by booking agents (for concert tours), publicists (for articles and radio, personal, and TV appearances), record labels (for approval of recording issues and promotional ideas, etc.), and other business offers. Managers are *not* song pluggers, record producers, or record label executives, so their main job is to build the artist's career though contacts, wisdom, and solid career-based decisions.

---

[569] William Morris Endeavor Agency "William Morris Agency, Inc," Bloomberg Businessweek, http://investing.businessweek.com/research/stocks/private/snapshot.asp?privcapId=872395, (accessed August 24, 2010).

[570] M. William Krasilovsky, and Sydney Shemel, *This Business of Music*, 10th ed. (New York, NY: Billboard Books, 2007), 333.

Representation	Industry	Job Description	Who They Represent	How They are Paid
Talent Agent	Film & Visual Media; Tour Music industry	Advice; Find employment	Actors; Recording Artist Personalities; Writers; Film production	Percentage
Booking Agent AF of M	Music - for American Federation of Musicians	Advice; Tours, Musical Performances	Musicians for tours and performances	Percentage 10%
Personal Manager	Music Industry; Tours, Image, Promotion, Publicity, Song Selection (Advice)	Advise	Major Recording Artist; Touring Musicians	Percentage 15-20%
Performance Union Agent AFTRA SAG Equity	Video - American Federation of Television Radio Artists; SAG for Actors in Film; Equity in Stage	Advice; Find employment	Film, Video, and Stage Actors	Percentage 10%
Business Manager	Music, Film, and Stage	Control money and financial investments, plus taxes	All	Hourly, Salary or retainer
Attorney	Music, Film, and Stage	Negotiate, write Contracts, advise artist and managers.	All	Hourly, Salary or retainer

Trust

The artist usually hires the manager, but signs with the management company. The artist management relationship is built on trust in this emotionally high-strung industry. The artist has to trust the manager to make the right decisions, give the very best advice, and build the artist's career, sometimes over their own. The manager has to trust the artist to follow the advice given, stay healthy physically and mentally, work, work, work, and always exploit every opportunity to make use of shameless self-promotion.

It is the artist's responsibility to pick the right manager, someone who will make a great impression, be well respected by record label executives and talent agents, and be able to work and communicate well with the key industry figures. Don't hire a friend or relative because their lack of experience and poor decisions will affect your career and income forever! As an artist, you *have* to be able to say "no" to friends and family. If you can't, the manger will act as a gatekeeper and say *"no"* loudly to friends and family and others who are not the right people to be connected with or supportive of your career goals.

Timing

There are several types of personal managers in the business, and their success is generally based on their ability to help artists become rich and famous. Timing is everything, as the act's position in their career (new, established, superstar, etc.) usually determines the types of managers they can employ. If you are a new artist without label or music company support, securing a major or "heavy hitter" manager is unlikely. If you're an established artist with a career buzz and consumer momentum, then there is the possibility of gaining an established management company for representation. Superstars are often represented by only a handful of the most highly established personal managers who have earned respect based on their track record (the successes of major artists they have helped in the past).

Timing is also important from the perspective of when does an artist really needs a manager. The answer, of course, is only when the manager can do things for the act that they *cannot do for themselves*. The other side of the question is when does a manager need a specific act? The answer is when is the act ready (creatively, mentally) to dedicate their time and talents to growing their career as large as possible. They can't do it by themselves, but the right manager might be able to help them get it done. Therefore the artist and manager relationship is a partnership, similar to the emotional commitment of a marriage, based on trust, for the purpose of achieving business goals (making money) that each could not have attained without the other.

Types of Personal Managers

Personal managers usually fall into three categories, similar to professional boxing weight classes: heavyweight (or heavy hitters), middleweight, and lightweight. In the case of artist managers, the reference is to what can they accomplish (toughness is based on a the successful track record). It shows just how difficult the profession is and how hard managers have to work sometimes for the success of their acts. According to Volman (2010),

> *Heavyweight/Heavy Hitter managers are usually those who represent the biggest stars who make the most money. Most of the heavyweight managers are shareholders or partners in their artist's management companies. These managers have tremendous clout in the business, and when they call the president of the record company, the president takes his call. This is the sure sign of a heavyweight manager in the music business. On average, they have offices in Nashville, New York, or Los Angeles.*
>
> *Middleweight managers are the ones working hardest at their profession. I like this type of manager the best. They have not become totally jaded with the business, and they work hard at keeping up on all the possibilities and changes going on everyday. They command respect because they might not have a superstar artist yet, but they always seem on the verge of having a monster act on their hands.*
>
> *Lightweights or want-to-be managers might be a good friend who has worked for the band, doing everything they need. From loading the gear to loading the pipe, he sells the T-shirts and gets the towels and the drinks. He loves the music but usually doesn't know what he's talking about. They have no experience, and they make very little effort to further themselves. They call themselves a manager, but they don't know the job.*[571]

Duties

In general, the role of the personal manager is to counsel, assist, and supervise the development of the artist as a professional act. Obviously, to be able to successfully accomplish this mission, the manager needs

---

571 Mark Volman, "Survey of Music Business Course Pack," Belmont University, Nashville, TN: Belmont University, 2008).

experience, contacts, wisdom, specific industry knowledge (not often found in books), and good old common sense. They need to understand and love business! They should value the power of entertainment and monetizing consumers' emotional connections to entertainment. Managers should also help artists focus on their career direction by working with the artist to establish one-, three-, and five-year goals. Krasilosky and Shemel (2007) suggest additional responsibilities, including:

> *Choosing literary, artistic, and musical materials;*
>
> *Supervising publicity, public relations, and advertising campaigns;*
>
> *Adopting the proper format for the best presentation of the artist's talents;*
>
> *Selection booking agents to secure engagements for the artists;*
>
> *Determining (in conjunction with the booking agent) the types of employment most beneficial to the artist's career;*
>
> *Selecting and supervising the artist's accountants and attorneys; and*
>
> *Overseeing the design and maintenance of the artist's website.*[572]

Selecting a Personal Manager

Because we live in the digital world, opportunities for artists to succeed without a manager have increased. Still, someone has to do the work, take the time to market the act and their products, and build a plan based on a strategic business management model. Select a manager who can help you as an artist create, manage, and accomplish it.

A manager is a gatekeeper, keeping all the people, hangers on, fans, negative family, friends, and others away by saying, "no, no, no." Time really *is* money in this business, and so is the artist's name and image, which if connected to bad products or merchandise, bad news stories, rumors, politicians, etc., can be destroyed beyond repair. It is the manager's responsibility to fend off all the negative stuff and approve only people, products, and connections that are in the artist's best interest. Also, if you are singing a recording deal, the label will want to make sure you select a manager they approve of and support. They want to make sure their investment in you as an artist is going to have a better chance of success by encouraging you to select an establish, respected manager.

Power of Attorney

Artist managers bring order to the daily chaos caused by success in the music industry. Managers legally represent artists through a power-of-attorney agreement. It provides managers with the legal privilege and obligation of controlling the business and career decisions of the artist. Examples include record label agreements, music publishing, music producer selections, mass media promotion and publicity through a hired or label publicist, concert appearances supervised by the road manager and arranged by a talent agent through a concert promoter, merchandising, corporate sponsorship, endorsements, charity, and community service.[573] The power-of-attorney agreement permits the manager to lawfully represent (to the very best of their ability) the artist(s) in either specific or all business decisions (depending on how much the artist wants to remain involved in daily decisions).

---

[572] M. William Krasilovsky, and Sydney Shemel, *This Business of Music*, 10th ed. (New York, NY: Billboard Books, 2007), 333.

[573] Personal interviews with industry insiders (2000-2011).

Commission Base and Rates

Managers are typically paid 15-20% of an artist's royalty base, which includes income from record deals, concert tours, movie appearances, and corporate sponsorships. The standard is 15% for single artist representation and 20% for groups or bands.[574] However, the rates may be more or less depending on what is negotiated based on precedent, reputation, and the type of genre (rock managers are often paid 5-10% more, Christian acts are sometimes paid less, and hip-hop and rap acts' managers are paid whatever they can get). Management payment rates are based on the gross income of all or part of whatever the act earns. This too is negotiable, but the more powerful the manager, the less likely they are going to negotiate down the percentage of what they are paid or which types of incomes they are to be paid on. In addition, most managers will not agree to work for net, which is the amount of money an act is paid *after all expenses* (touring, recording, agent fees, taxes, etc.) are deducted. Also, the manager's typical business expenses (in the name of the artist) are paid out of the artist's gross income, not by the manager. Business office expenses, travel, payments to business managers, road managers, and booking agents, who are hired by the manager in the name of the artist (remember the power-of-attorney), are paid by the artist, not the manager.

Management Team

Artist managers bring representation, administrative supervision, and surrogate control to an artist's complex image and long-term career. A developed *strategic management plan* links the business and creative systems of the artist's career together. Career goals are established based on the perceived commercialization "branding" of the artist's image and talents. Managers act as gatekeepers selecting only the recording deals, concert appearances, and staff members that can best enhance the artist's long-term goals. Managers supervise everything connected with the business of the act. *Booking agents* are hired to establish contacts with promoters who create concert appearances. *Business managers* are added to the team to control the revenues and take care of the accounting, taxes and investments. *Road or tour managers* hire security, roadies, and everyone else needed to control all aspects of the tour. *Attorneys* are hired for legal opinions and representation. *Publicists* and *marketing experts* provide artist interviews to retail stores and the mass media to promote the act.

Business Managers

Business managers are the financial experts who provide the accounting, tax planning, and investment advice for the acts.[575] In good management situations all the money earned by the act goes first to the business manager who then pays everyone. By putting the business manager in charge of the money, it is easier to control the accounting, taxes, and long-term investments for the act. Business managers should be paid a flat or hourly rate for the amount of work they accomplish and for the success of their financial investments. Some are paid a small percentage of the gross income (2-6%), but this is rarely in the artist's best interest. It is desirable for a business manager to have a degree in finance, plus a successful track record in investments and money market funds and experience with industry professionals.

---

[574] Personal interviews with industry sources (2005-2011).

[575] M. William Krasilovsky, and Sydney Shemel, *This Business of Music*, 10th ed. (New York, NY: Billboard Books, 2007), 334.

Tour or Road Managers

Road managers are responsible for all the daily business decisions dealing with concerts and personal appearances on tour. As a result, road managers handle the local press as well as questions and concerns from promoters, local radio stations, and record retail promotions. In addition, they make hotel and restaurant reservations and handle any issues of concern among the recording artist(s), band members, roadies, and tour support. Road managers report directly to the artist and personal manager, and they are the local communication link between the artist, the promoter, and the manager of the venue. Great road managers often use the road and concert tours for networking, in hopes of starting their own artist management company later.

Booking Agents

Booking agents commissioned by the AF of M represent musicians employed as recording artists, session musicians, and concert performers. Equity union licensed agents represent actors and performers pursuing employment in any type of unionized live theater. AFTRA approves of agents who represent their members seeking employment as vocalists in recording sessions and as newscasters and TV personalities. The Screen Actors Guild (SAG) represents actors and performers in any type of film and visual media (as opposed to video, which is covered by AFTRA). Union-franchised booking agents are ordinarily limited to 10% commission rates, although some may charge more.[576] The unions, of course, bring the power of collective bargaining and legally supported contracts to encourage businesses that hire union musicians, vocalists, actors, and others to fulfill their financial and contractual obligations as originally stated in the deal. The agent holding the license commissioned by the AF of M or AFTRA may employ subagents. They are paid between 25-50% of the 10% gross income the acts receive when "booked" and paid to perform.[577] Film agents franchised by AFTRA represent acts to be hired by producers, film companies, and of course, directors (who are the real power behind visual media productions). Royalty artists, vocalists, musicians, and bands are represented by AF of M (musicians) and AFTRA (vocalists) to bar owners, restaurants, venues, and concert promoters who create, promote, and sometimes profit from concert events and tours.

Management Gatekeeper Duties

Artist managers rarely give a "yes" to anything unless it is something that is in the best interest of the artist. They often seek out only those industry insiders who can benefit the artist's image and career.

Termination of the Deal

Sometimes the breakup of an artist and manager is similar to a divorce as lawsuits and counter lawsuits are not uncommon, with the manager claiming commissions on the artists' future royalties. Unless there has been some kind of criminal conduct by the manager, he or she usually wins, gaining partial royalty payment for a limited time. Also, at the end of some deals, the manager may continue to receive a part of their commissions based on the idea that the acts future success is based on decisions the management team made during their tenure.[578]

---

576 Personal interviews with industry insiders (2000-2011).

577 Personal interviews with industry insiders (2005-2011).

578 Personal interviews with industry insiders (2000-2011).

Promoters

Promoters hire talent through the agents, rent venues for concerts, and then promote and advertise the event. Facility managers and their staff of event coordinators keep the arenas, theaters, and clubs in top shape for the concerts. Stagehand union members commonly provide the lighting and sound. Record labels provide free recordings to radio stations and in-store promotional items (free goods) to retail outlets.[579]

Talent Buyers

Talent buyers are usually an independent people who don't work for a theatre or club but can book shows there. Often they either work for or are promoters.

Attorneys

Managers hire attorneys to structure deals for artist tours, merchandise sales (through fulfillment companies), corporate sponsorships, label deals, appearances, and any other type of business opportunity. Accordingly, some attorneys become very powerful and can act as personal managers after they have established themselves in the business. Attorneys charge hourly rates ($250-1,000 per hour) or are placed on a retainer, which is a monthly minimum fee based on a negotiated number of hours of work per month or part of the artist's gross income. It is preferable to pay an attorney's hourly rate (as opposed to a retainer fee) to guarantee the productivity of the attorney.

Promotion – Artist Perspective

In the past, radio station airplay has been the most important type of exposure for new artists and their recordings. In addition, radio acted as a natural filter to expose only the potentially successful artists and recordings. However, large corporations such as Clear Channel (which owns close to 10% of all the radio stations in the United States) have made it very difficult to break new acts on radio. Also, Generation Y (the current 18-24 year old consumers) has changed the rules of the game by not reading newspapers, watching TV, or listening to radio. Instead, they download their music and listen to what they want when they want it through their computers, iPods, mp3 players, and cell phones. Artist managers and promoters are in the same situation as labels, struggling to find ways to make consumers pay for recordings instead of illegally downloading them and attempting to find better ways to exploit their acts and concert events through social networks and consumer technology.

Publicity – Artist Perspective

Artist managers, record labels, professional musicians, and event specialists hire publicists from public relations firms as part-time or full-time employees to plant stories and articles featuring their clients (the artist) in the professional trades and consumer mass media. The publicist assimilates images that have been created, molded, or enhanced by the artist's manager and label representatives into stores, news articles, and press releases. Then the publicist alerts the media to cover the events (which are often created by the management and label representatives) as news or entertainment stories. The stories are then released to the print and mass media with the hope of stimulating a positive correlation between the artist's name and public perceptions. Increase in the public's awareness of an artist and acknowledgment of an artist's creative talents often turn into record sales and record label profits. *Fahrenheit Media Group* is one of the largest firms

---

[579] Personal interviews with industry insiders (1978-2011).

connecting the dots between the personae of the act to image "branding" in media. According to *Fahrenheit's* website (2011),

> *Headquartered in New York, with a Nashville and Los Angeles Division, Fahrenheit Media Group is the go-to publicity firm for creative and maximum impact press campaigns. As a leading full-service press, promotions, branding, marketing, television, product development, talent placement, and consulting firm …We create campaigns that increase the engagement factor for our clients' brand resulting in increased brand awareness, enhanced brand loyalty, and increased sales and revenue both on and offline. …We understand the media and entertainment industries from all sides. It's not about getting just any media, It's about getting the right media. We are experts at image control and media negotiations. The key is not what you say about yourself, but what others say about you.*[580]

Public Relations

Public relations, which is usually provided by a hired publicist, is the process or act of providing material (stories, press releases, etc.) to the mass media so that once it is aired or printed consumers will develop a favorable public image for an artist. The process occurs whenever there is contact with the public or whenever an act has to counter bad publicity. Positive aspects of the act are provided to spin the truth or to let consumers choose for themselves what they want to believe about an artist. Bad publicity or negative news can hinder record and ticket sales, so management will often provide the artist's best side to enhance the artist's image with the public.

Electronic Press Kits (EPK's)

Press kits help establish authenticity of new and established artists. Publicists assemble press kits to alert the press and mass media of new recordings, acts, and newsworthy events. A press kit usually includes a black & white photograph (publicity photo), a one-page bio of demographic information, artistic and creative accomplishments, and copies of previous press releases to the trade and consumer press. Most artists are now releasing their press kits on CDs and DVDs with videos and soundtracks. Some are sent by email to fans and still others are voice recordings sent as a message to consumers over cell phones. In addition, artists and their managers offer websites and fan club home pages to keep the industry and fans updated.

TV Appearances

Broadcast television is still used to market recording artists and musicians. Variety, late night, and morning talk shows promote artists and their sellable products. Publicists are again hired to help "place" stories about the artists in the trade and consumer press. They also help generate interest in the artist's stories, which is publicity that can be used by the label and the artist's manager to "book" an act on a television variety/talk show. Appearances on popular TV shows reinforce the status of the act and inform the public of new recordings being released.[581]

Publicity Budget

The amount of money record labels spend on publicity varies greatly. The artist manager commonly meets with label representatives to coordinate publicity. The amount of money (budget) to be spent on publicity often depends on the star factor (name and image equals the strength of the artist based on past units sold

---

[580] Fahrenheit Media Group, "About Us," Fahrenheit Media Group, http://www.fahrenheitmediagroup.com/, (accessed April 3, 2011).

[581] Personal interviews with industry insiders (2005-2011).

and sales projections). Maximum publicity budgets are often limited to 50-100% of the creative production budget.

Stage Names

Artists often pick a stage name (other than their actual birth name) to perform or create an image. According to digitaldreamdoor.com[582] (2011), examples include:

Real Name	Stage Name
Stefani Joanne Angelina Germanotta	Lady Gaga
Ray Charles Robinson	Ray Charles
Tracy Morrow	Ice-T
Robert Zimmerman	Bob Dylan
Madonna Louise Ciccone	Madonna
Marco Antonio Muniz	Marc Anthony
Audrey Faith Perry	Faith Hill
Eleanora Fagan Gough	Billie Holliday
Curtis Jackson	50 Cent
John Francis Bongiovi Jr.	Jon Bon Jovi
Anthony Benedetto	Tony Bennett
Gloria Maria Fajardo	Gloria Estefan
Reginald Kenneth Dwight	Elton John
Born Steveland Hardaway Judkins; later renamed Steveland Hardaway Morris	Stevie Wonder
Declan Patrick McManus	Elvis Costello
Virginia Patterson Hensley	Patsy Cline
Riley B. King	B.B. King
Farrokh Bulsara	Freddie Mercury
Yorgos Panayiotou	George Michael
Barry Alan Pincus	Barry Manilow
Destiny Hope "Miley" Cyrus	Hannah Montana
Carlos Ray	Chuck Norris
Prince Rogers Nelson	Prince
Paul David Hewson	Bono (U2)
Henry Olusegun Olumide Samuel	Seal
Eileen Regina Edwards	Shania Twain

Tour Support

Record labels want their artists out on the road as a promotional tool to stir up record sales and profits. In addition, recording artists need to generate revenues to pay for their management team, supporting

582 Digitaldreamdoor.com "Music Stars Real Names," digitaldreamdoor.com, http://www.digitaldreamdoor.com/pages/realname.html, (accessed April 2, 2011).

musicians, stage crew, roadies, etc. Record sales provide royalties after recoupment of all related label expenses. As a result, most active recording artists need to be on the road performing to pay their bills.

Summary

Great managers can open the doors to success in the business. The artist-manager relationship must be built on trust, as the artist hires the manager but the manager signs the act to the company. Managers supervise a team consisting of an attorney, a talent or booking agent (who is franchised by the AF of M and commonly receives 10% of the gross income from arranged concert appearances), a business manager (to invest and account for revenue), a publicist (who will arrange opportunities for the act to use shameless self-promotion), media trainers, and of course, musicians, BGVs, road crews, and others to complete a concert tour.

If you just want to sing and skip the business of being a popular culture icon, then find employment as a musician, a soloist in choral group, an opera singer, or a BGV (background vocalists), or all the above at the same time. The world is waiting to be entertained, so go for it, and get paid in the process. It is helpful, even in a local market, to know sight reading and have quick memorization skills, a positive personality, knowledge of the copyright law, music publishing, accounting, marketing, publicity, business management, promotion, and a basic understanding of the music business. It's even better if you can sing in tune, love contributing to the group, and have fun helping others.

Everyone can't become the "next big thing," but almost everyone can connect locally to the creative arts scene, either as an artist or performer or as an organizer and entrepreneur. In today's world, you can also accomplish both at the same time; be an entrepreneurial artist! Start locally. If you're a hit and want to grow your artistry as a business, attempt regional success. If your act is regionally, financially, and creatively successful, you're probably going to get noticed by the industry! Then the question becomes, do you want to stay at a level below the national radar and enjoy what you're doing with your life, or do you want to jump off the cliff and attempt to become famous?

16

The Personal Management Agreement[583]

This AGREEMENT (the "Agreement") made and entered into the _______ day of _____, 2008 by and between ______________________________ (referred to as "Artist" or "your"), whose address is __________________ and

_________________ ("Manager"), whose address is _____________________________.

WHEREAS, Artist wishes to obtain Manager's exclusive advice, guidance, counsel, and direction to promote and develop Artist's Career as defined herein; and

WHEREAS, Manager wishes to provide such services on the terms and conditions set forth herein.

NOW, THEREFORE IN CONSIDERATION of the mutual covenants and agreements set forth below, and other good and valuable consideration, the receipt and sufficiency of which are hereby acknowledged, the parties agree as follows:

1. Term

The initial term of this Agreement (the "Initial Term") shall be for a period of two (2) years commencing on the date first written above, and terminating as of the end of the last day of the second year thereafter. Artist hereby grants to Manager three (3) additional one-year option periods (each year referred to as the "Option Period") automatically exercisable by Manager unless Manager on or before the end of the preceding Initial Term and/or Option Period, whichever is applicable, notifies the Artist in writing of its desire to terminate this Agreement.

2. Manager's Services

Throughout the Term of this Agreement, Manager agrees

- To advise, guide, direct and counsel Artist in any and all matters pertaining to employment, publicity, public relations, advertising, the selection of musical material, and all other matters pertaining to Artist's Career which are not specifically excepted herein.
- To advise, guide, direct and counsel Artist with relation to the adoption of the proper format for presentation of Artist's talents in the determination of proper style, mood, setting, and characterization in keeping with Artist's talent and best interest.

---

[583] Rich Hicks, "The Personal Management Agreement," by (Rush Hicks Esq.,: TN, Nashville, 2009).

- To advise, guide, direct and counsel Artist in the selection of artistic talents to assist, accompany, or embellish Artist's artistic presentation.
- To advise, guide, direct and counsel Artist concerning compensation and privileges for his talent and similar artistic talent.
- To advise, guide, direct and counsel Artist concerning the selection of booking agencies, artists' agents, artists' managers, and persons, firms and corporations who will counsel, advise, seek, and procure employment and engagements for Artist.
- As pertinent to Artist's Career, to advise, guide, direct and counsel with regard to general practices in the entertainment, music and recording fields and with respect to compensation and terms of contracts related thereto.
- To advise, guide, direct and counsel Artist regarding hiring publicists, marketing consultants, advertising agencies, and similar consultants and service providers hired to further Artist's Career.
- To meet with Artist when reasonably requested by Artist.

For purposes of this Agreement, "Artist's Career" shall mean and refer to Artist's career worldwide in the entertainment and related businesses, including without limitation, work done by Artist in the recording, acting, literary, theatrical, music publishing, music composing, personal appearance, advertising, entertainment, amusement, music, music performance, music video, television, radio, motion picture, motion picture sound track, commercials, endorsements, video, internet and merchandising fields and otherwise related to Artist's career in the entertainment field, as now known or hereinafter devised in which Artist's artistic talents and/or name, voice, likeness, and/or public image are developed and exploited.

3. Non-Exclusivity and Territory

Manager's services under this Agreement are non-exclusive. Manager shall at all times have the right to render the same or similar services to others whose talents may be similar to or may be in competition with Artist, as well as engage in any and all other business activities, however, Manager agrees to be reasonably available to render the services to Artist hereunder. Artist's engagement of Manager under this Agreement is exclusive throughout the world.

4. Agencies and Publicity

Artist may from time to time enter into agreements with talent agencies, theatrical agencies and employment agencies whose function and obligation shall be to procure employment and engagements for Artist. Any compensation (which Artist may be required to pay to these agencies) shall be at the sole cost and expense of Artist. If requested by Artist, Manager agrees to supervise and screen the selection and activity of such agency. All expenses of persons of companies specifically retained by Artist to do publicity, public relations or other work on behalf of Artist shall be at the sole cost and expense of Artist.

5. Manager's Authority

Consistent with the services Manager is engaged to provide as set forth herein, and subject to any specific limitations set forth in this Agreement:

Artist hereby grants to Manager the right to approve and permit any and all publicity and advertising and to approve and permit the use of Artist's name, pre-approved photograph(s), pre-approved likeness(es), pre-approved voice, pre-approved sound effects, pre-approved caricature(s), and pre-approved artistic and musical materials, for purposes of advertising and publicity in the promotion and advertising of Artist's products and services. Manager agrees to consult with Artist about tour plans and other activities on a regular basis. To the extent the foregoing requires Artist's signature or written approval, Manager shall reasonably attempt to obtain Artist's signature directly or via facsimile (considering Artist's actual availability and the turnaround time with respect to the particular matter concerned), or Manager shall attempt to obtain Artist's written approval via email which, solely if granted by Artist, shall confer in Manager the limited power of attorney to render the corresponding approval on behalf of Artist in respect of the particular matter concerned. In the event Manager makes any such decision with which Artist disagrees, then Artist's decision controls and the parties agree to use their best efforts to implement Artist's preference, as may be practical and reasonable under the circumstances then existing. Notwithstanding any other provision contained in this Agreement, Manager does not have the authority to execute or approve, and shall not execute or approve (pursuant to the authority granted to Manager in this paragraph 5 or otherwise) on behalf of Artist any recording, music, or book publishing, booking agency, video, endorsement, merchandising, or any other contract or agreement of any kind whatsoever, whether written or oral. Any such contract or agreement so executed or approved by Manager shall be null and void, and Manager indemnifies Artist with respect thereto. The authority granted to Manager pursuant to this paragraph 5 above is coupled with an interest and shall be irrevocable during the Term of this Agreement.

6. Receipt of Artist's Compensation

Artist shall engage at its expense a business manager or appropriate bookkeeping personnel to receive all Gross Income for Artist and shall account and remit to Manager in each month when there is either Compensation or expenses due Manager out of Gross Income including the period provided for in Section 7(c) below. Such business manager or bookkeeping personnel shall be available to Manager during regular business hours to confirm the receipt of monies and the payment of expenses. At the request of Artist, Manager shall assist Artist in the selection of a business manager or bookkeeping personnel. Manager and Artist (or Artist's business manager or appropriate bookkeeping personnel, as the case maybe) shall keep accurate and complete books of account and records with respect to all amounts received by Artist and Manager in connection with Artist's Career, which books may be inspected during regular business hours, by a certified public accountant designated either by Artist or Manager, upon reasonable notice to the other. Both Artist and Manager may audit up to three years at a time but may audit any given year only once. Each quarter during the Active Term and the period provided for in Section 7(c) below, Artist shall cause to be delivered to Manager a full statement of account showing the monthly Gross Income accruing to and received by Artist and any compensation and expense reimbursement due to Manager along with a payment for any additional amount due, if any, Manager may request, during the Active Term, monthly internal statements from Artist's business manager or appropriate bookkeeping personnel and other information upon reasonable request.

7. Manager's Compensation

Since the nature and extent of the success or failure of Artist's Career cannot be predetermined the parties desire that Manager's compensation be determined in such manner as will permit Manager to accept the risk of failure and to benefit from Artist's success. Therefore, as compensation for Manager's services, Artist agrees to pay Manager during and through the Term of this Agreement (and any modifications, extensions, replacements, renewals, or substitutions of this Agreement), the following in consideration of all of Manager's services hereunder ("Fee"): a sum equal to fifteen percent (15%) of all Gross Income (as defined herein in the attached and incorporated Glossary) received or accrued (as of the last day of the Term) directly or indirectly by Artist or by any other person or entity on Artist's behalf, including without limitation, Artist's heirs, executors, administrators, and assigns, regarding Artist's Career.

(a) For purposes of this Agreement, "Gross Income" shall include, without limitation but subject to the exclusions stated in paragraph 7 of the Agreement, all of the following relating to Artist's Career: salaries, earnings, fees, royalties, advances against royalties, merchandise, gifts (excluding bona fide gifts as defined by the Internal Revenue Code), bonuses, shares of profits, shares of stock, residuals, repeats or return fees, partnership interests, share of profits, percentages, percentages and the total amount paid for a package television or radio program (live or recorded) or other entertainment package, received directly or indirectly by Artist or by any other person or entity on Artist's behalf, including the aggregate amount paid to bands led by Artist (but only for Artist's services in connection therewith). It is understood that, for purposes hereof, no expense, cost or disbursement paid or incurred by Artist in connection with the receipt or earning of "Gross Income" (including salaries, shares of profits or other sums paid to individuals participating in Artist's presentations, recordings, videos or other forms of performances), shall be deducted therefrom prior to the calculation of Manager's compensation hereunder except only for the items excepted in paragraph 7(b) above. In the event that Artist receives, as all or part of his compensation for activities within Artist's Career, stock or other equity interests, or the right to buy stock or other equity interests, in any corporation or entity or that Artist becomes the packager or owner of all or part of an entertainment property, whether as an individual proprietor, stockholder, partner, joint venture or otherwise, Manager's Compensation shall apply to said stock or equity, right to buy stock or equity, individual proprietorship, partnership, joint venture or other forms of interest, and Manager shall be entitled to Manager's Compensation thereof. Should Artist be required to make any payment for such interest, Manager will pay his percentage share of such payment, except if Manager does not want his Fee thereof, the reasonable value of such interest (taking into account Artist's payment therefore) shall be deemed to be Gross Income for the purposes of this Agreement.

(b) The following are specifically excluded from Gross Income: (i) tour support funds to the extent such funds cover reasonably incurred actual tour losses (or any tour support funds to the extent actually paid for or incurred on behalf of Artist by any record company or tour/live performances sponsor to cover tour/live performance losses); (ii) funds or other considerations, which are received by Artist or on Artist's behalf and which are subsequently refunded to the payee (example: deposits received by booking agencies on live engagements which are not subsequently performed by Artist, and therefore the deposit must be refunded); (iii) funds which are paid by Artist or by third parties on Artist's behalf to third parties which are expended on actual video cost, recording costs (including, but not limited to, those costs, expenditures, and advances remitted or defined as recording costs or the equivalent thereof in any recording agreement entered into by Artist), and production costs, writers and publishers, producer, mixers, engineers, studio facilities, and salaried musicians; (iv) sound and light, opening acts, support acts, each with respect to live performances or other personal appearances by Artist, (v) actual publisher, sub-publisher and administrator fees under agreements related to music publishing income; (vi) the expenses of Artist for engaging musical groups other than Artist in the entertainment industry to the extent Artist is a "packager" of an entertainment property but such expense shall not reduce Gross Income by more then the Gross Income created by such entertainment package unless Manager has approved such package arrangement in advance in writing (such approval not to be unreasonably withheld); (vii) union pension and welfare plan benefits paid to Artist and on Artist's behalf with respect to recording sessions; (ix) verifiable reimbursed expenses; (x) monies earned by Artist from passive investments; (xi) gifts received by Artist to the extent not in lieu of compensation; and (xiv) loans to Artist.

(c) After the Term, Manager shall be paid, in lieu of the Fee, a sum (the "Post-Term Commission") equal to fifteen (15%) percent of all Gross Income (except for items excluded under the paragraph 7 above) received or accrued by Artist for the first five (5) years after the Term has ended, which Post-Term Commission shall be reduced to ten (10%) percent for the five (5) years thereafter, and then further reduced to five (5%)

percent for the next five years. For purposes of clarity, Manager shall not be entitled to any Post-Term Commission (or other compensation of any kind) beyond fifteen (15) years after the termination of this Agreement.

8. Manager's Expenses

In addition to the compensation provided in paragraph 7 above, Artist shall reimburse Manager for all reasonable expenses necessarily and actually incurred on Artist's behalf directly in connection with Manager's rendition of services under this Agreement during the Term including, but not limited to, overnight, certified or registered mail postage long distance telephone calls, facsimile transmissions, and travel expenses, but excluding office expenses and overhead. No Individual expense in excess of $500 shall be incurred by Manager without first having obtained Artist's prior written consent. Reimbursable expenses in any month shall not exceed an aggregate of $1,000 without Manager having first obtained Artist's prior written consent. Expenses shall only be reimbursed out of Gross Income actually earned by Artist from Artist's Career. Artist agrees that, in the event that Manager renders any services under this Agreement to Artist outside of the metropolitan area in which Manager's office is located, Manager shall be entitled to reimbursement from Artist for reasonable travel expenses (subject to applicable pre-approval hereunder). In the event that Manager must travel by air, Manager agrees to purchase airline tickets at the lowest fare available at the time of booking and, when applicable, for the same "class" that Artist travels (further subject to applicable pre-approval hereunder). All expenses charged or incurred by Manager shall be pro-rated with respect to Artist if Manager is simultaneously rendering services for or on behalf of other clients or parties. Subject to the foregoing, reimbursement of expenses shall be due Manager within thirty (30) days after receipt of itemized statements setting forth the nature and amount of each expense. During the Term of this Agreement and for a period of (3) years following, Manager agrees to keep and maintain reasonable documentation of each expense from which he requested reimbursement by Artist and all documentation shall be provided to Artist or his representative promptly after Artist's reasonable request.

9. Expenses, Loans, and Advances

Except as otherwise stated herein, Artist shall be solely responsible for the payment of all expenses which may arise in connection with Artist's Career, including, without limitation the cost of material, equipment, facilities, transportation, lodging and living expenses, costumes, make-up, promotion, publicity, accounting and legal fees, and Manager shall not have any liability whatsoever in such connection and therefore, such expense shall not reduce Gross Income subject to Manager's commission hereunder except only as set forth in paragraph 7 above. Manager shall not be obligated to lend to or advance money to Artist, but if it does so, Artist shall repay such amount(s) promptly from Gross Income (and only from Gross Income); Manager agrees to provide Artist a written tabulation of any such loan or advance actually made upon request by Artist. .

10. Offers of Employment

Artist shall advise Manager of all offers of employment related to Artist's Career submitted to Artist and will refer all inquiries concerning Artist's Career to Manager, so that Manager m ay advise Artist whether they are compatible with Artist's Career. Reciprocally, Manager shall inform Artist of any offers or prospective employment opportunities of or concerning Artist's Career which Manager receives.

11. Career

Artist agrees at all times to attend to Artist's Career, and to do all things reasonably necessary and desirable and consistent with this Agreement to promote Artist's Career and earnings. With Manager's advice, guidance, direction and counsel, Artist shall at all times endeavor to engage and utilize proper theatrical agents and booking agents to obtain engagements and employment for Artist.

12. Notice of Breach

In order to eliminate misunderstandings between the Artist and Manager, Artist and Manager agree to advise each other in writing of the specific nature of any claimed breach of this Agreement. The party receiving such notice shall have thirty (30) days after the receipt of the notice in which to cure the claimed breach. The written notice shall be deemed a condition precedent to the commencement of any arbitration and shall be sent by certified mail, return receipt requested. Notice to Artist shall be given to the address set forth in the first paragraph of this Agreement, with a copy to Artist's legal counsel, ____________________. Notice to Manager shall be given to the address set forth in the first paragraph of this Agreement, with a copy (which shall not constitute notice) to Manager's legal counsel, ____________________.

13. Business Entities

Artist's Career may be developed and exploited primarily through certain corporate, limited liability company or similar entities. Therefore, references herein to Artist, such as, without limitation, reference to income earned by Artist or received by Artist, shall be deemed to include the income earned or received by these entities. However, there shall be no double compensation hereunder, and therefore any distributions to Artist from such entities, including without limitation, dividends and salaries which are derived from gross revenues that have already been compensated hereunder, shall not he commissioned again upon payment to Artist.

14. Manager's Other Businesses

Artist acknowledges that from time to time during the Term, either alone or with others, Manager or individuals or entities affiliated with Manager may act as promoter of an event at which Artist shall perform. Manager agrees that in any such arrangements Artist will be compensated in the same manner as if Manager or such individuals or entities affiliated with Manager were not involved in the promotion and after full and adequate disclosure of the circumstances; however, Manager agrees to waive the Fee and Post-Term Commissions in respect of any such events to avoid a conflict of interest hereunder.

15. Parties Free to Enter into Agreement

Manager and Artist warrant that: they are under no disability restriction or prohibition with respect to their right to execute this Agreement and form its terms and conditions; no act or omission by either hereunder will violate any right or interest of any person or firm, or will subject either party to any liability, or claim of liability to any person or firm; and Artist warrants that he has the right to and shall collect any and all Gross Income derived from Artist's Career. Manager and Artist agree to indemnify the other and to hold the other harmless against any damages, cost, expenses, fees (including reasonable attorneys' fees) incurred by the other party in any third party claim, suit or proceeding instituted against the other party in which any assertion is made which is inconsistent with any warranty, representation or covenant of them provided such claim is finally adjudicated or settled with their consent (which consent shall not be unreasonably withheld).

16. Assignment

Manager shall not have the right to assign Manager's rights or responsibilities under this Agreement to any entity without Artist's prior written approval, which approval shall not be unreasonably withheld.

17. Reviews by Counsel

The Artist and Manager acknowledge that they have had an opportunity to retain independent counsel of their own choosing to review this Agreement and advise them regarding its terms and conditions.

18. Age

Artist represents and warrants that Artist has attained the age of eighteen (18) years.

19. Binding Effect

This Agreement shall be binding upon Artist and Manager, and, to the extent applicable, shall also be binding upon their heirs, executors, permitted successors, and permitted assigns.

20. Controlling Law

This Agreement shall be deemed to be executed in the State of Tennessee and shall be construed in accordance with the internal laws of the State of Tennessee.

21. Status of Parties

This Agreement shall not be construed to create a partnership or joint venture between Manager and Artist. Manager is an independent contractor hereunder.

22. Modification

No modification or alteration of this Agreement shall be valid unless it is made in writing and signed by both parties.

IN WITNESS WHEREOF, the parties hereto have executed this Agreement as of the day and date first written above.

ARTIST:	MANAGER:
______________________________	______________________________
Date Signed	Date Signed

17

The Concert Business

Promoters, Types of Deals
Bid Sheets and Riders

"I had learned throughout my life as a composer chiefly through my mistakes and pursuits of false assumptions, not by my exposure to the founts of wisdom and knowledge."

— Igor Stravinsky[584]

"Don't try to explain it, just sell it."

— Colonel Tom Parker[585]

"We didn't know this was a business, we just thought it was a rock & roll party."

— Vince Neil, Motley Crüe[586]

"A live concert to me is exciting because of all the electricity that is generated in the crowd and on stage. It's my favorite part of the business."

— Elvis Presley[587]

Promoters

Concert promoters use to work independently from the record labels to create their own entrepreneurial businesses. They still exist, but 360 companies such as Live Nation and AEG Live (which provide everything from tours to venues and everything in between including recordings, merchandise, and sponsorship deals), have joined the circuit. The entrepreneurial promoters and the 360s are the high-stakes money rollers in the music and entertainment industry who often make or lose hundreds of thousands of dollars in one night. They provide the expertise, money, social and business connections to stage concerts (events) that help generate the positive cash flow opportunities needed by many performing artists and music companies. Promoters are the individuals and companies who hire the bands through booking agents (with

[584] Igor Stravinsky, "Igor Stravinsky Quotes," Brainyquote.com, http://www.brainyquote.com/quotes/authors/i/igor_stravinsky.html, (April 3, 2011).

[585] Colonel Tom Parker, "Colonel Tom Parker Quotes," Brainyquote.com, http://www.brainyquote.com/quotes/quotes/c/coloneltom185469.html, April 3, 2011).

[586] Vince Neil of Motley Crüe, "Behind the Music," VH-1, (Intermedia Cable, transmission, Nashville, TN, December 14, 1998).

[587] Elvis Presley, "Elvis Presley Quotes," Artquote.com, http://www.artquotes.net/entertainment-quotes/famous-singers, (accessed April 3, 2011).

the managers approval) to tour territories of the country and world. The acts usually provide a live performance at the staged "events" organized, funded, and promoted by the promoters who are risking capital to monetize consumers' emotional connection to the artists' personae. Remember that the music business is really the emotion business and thus, the concert business is really a created "event" in a special "place in time and location" for the sole purpose of generating money based on the ticket buyers emotional connection to the acts performing.

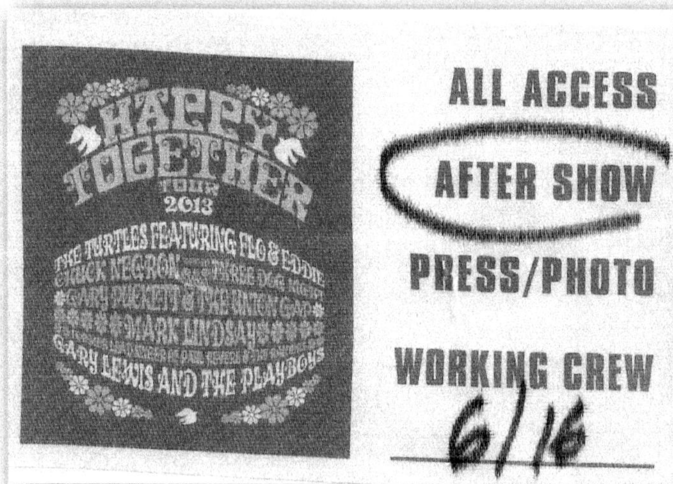

However, in the last year touring has seen a slight decrease from the previous years profits. According to *Pollstar* (2011) the leading trade magazine for the concert business,

> *… Combined ticket sales for the Top 50 North American tours generated $1.69 billion in 2010, down 15 percent from $1.99 billion in 2009. The Top 50 worldwide tours generated $2.93 billion in 2010, a drop of 12 percent from $3.34 billion the previous year. The total number of tickets sold to North American concerts dipped to 26.2 million, a 12 percent drop from 29.9 million in 2009. In addition, the show count was also less at 2,114, a 3 percent decrease, and the average cost of a show fell by $1.55, or 2 percent, primarily due to heavy discounting by Live Nation and others in an 11th-hour attempt to move slow-selling tickets. At the worldwide level, the total number of tickets sold decreased 15 percent to 38.3 million in 2010, down from 45.3 million in 2009. The show count dropped 8 percent to 2,650, but unlike in North America, worldwide average ticket prices rose by $2.86 or 4 percent.*[588]

IEBA

Promoters use IEBA and NACA and other showcase opportunities to discover, arrange, and set up concert tours. Basically, the organizations hold annual events that bring the buyers of talent (promoters) and the managers and acts together. *The International Entertainment Buyers Association* (IEBA) is the top nonprofit organization in the nation that annually sponsors a conference for buyers to view acts and buy tours. According to IEBA.org (2011),

> *IEBA was founded in 1970 as a non-profit trade organization for talent buyers, concert promoters, agents, managers, artists and other related entertainment professionals. IEBA provides networking, showcasing and educational opportunities to strengthen relationships, foster growth and increase revenue for the live entertainment industry. IEBA is known for showcasing the best and brightest talent in all genres of music and all fields of entertainment—exposing buyers to the freshest acts for the buying season. IEBA is an intimate organization that makes a huge impact.*[589]

NACA

The National Association of Campus Activities is a nonprofit organization that sponsors national and regional conferences for college representatives to view and book entertainment tours. According to naca.org (2011),

> *NACA hosts a National Convention each February. This … event provides networking opportunities with other professionals, students and associate members. Attracting more than 2,000 delegates from nearly 450 member schools, NACA's National*

---

[588] International Entertainment buyers Association, (IEBA), "2010 Ticket Sales Drop Due to Economy and Fickle Audiences," http://ieba.org/node/2646, (accessed April 4, 2011).

[589] International Entertainment buyers Association, (IEBA), "Welcome to IEBA," ieba.org, http://ieba.org/, (accessed April 4, 2011).

Convention is the nation's largest campus activities marketplace. During the Convention, delegates can view more than 80 live performances ranging from music and comedy to lecture and interactive programs.[590]

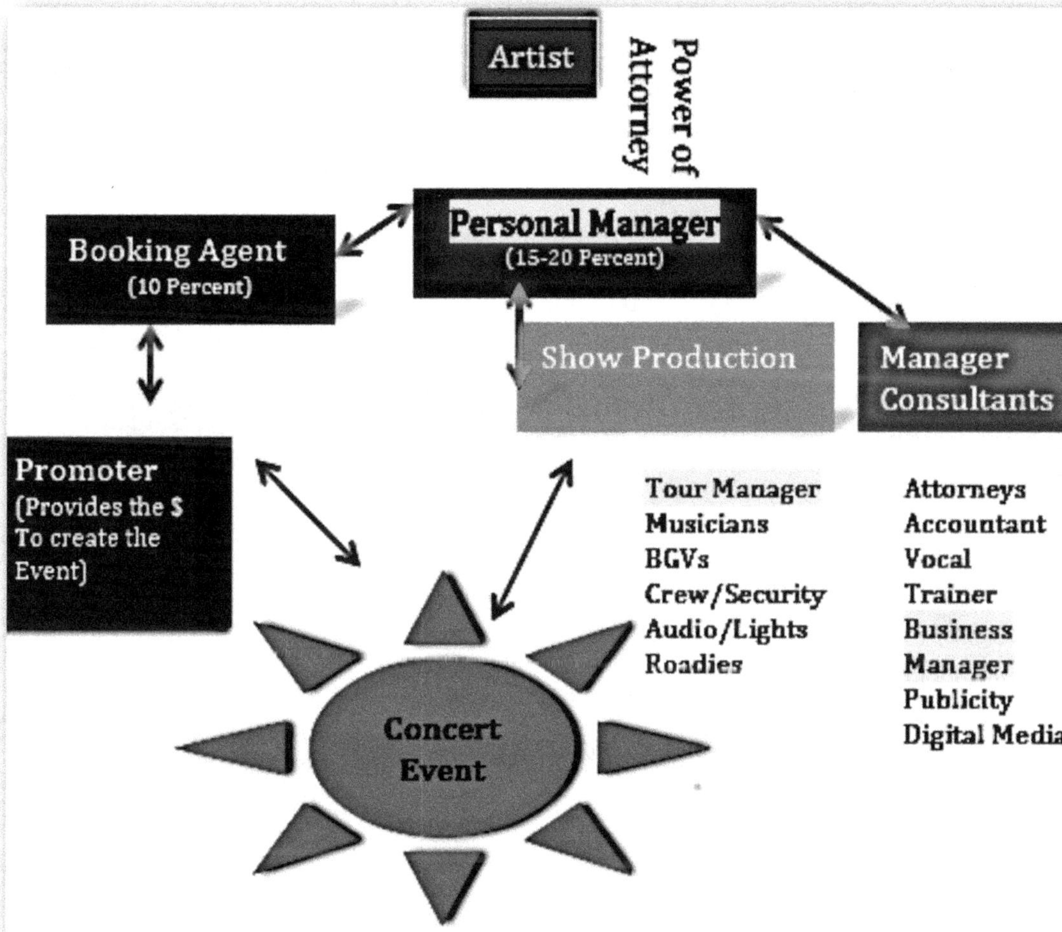

Bid Sheets

Promoters use bid sheets to determine their break-even points and projected expenses. Clearly, the concert business is very risky. Promoters often negotiate a guaranteed price plus a split of the profits to reduce the gamble. Superstar acts may require 80-95% of tickets to be sold before profit margins are achieved or they may just produce and promote the concert tour themselves to keep all the profits. In addition, concerts are sometimes scheduled in smaller cities between major concert venues. These concerts (called pick-ups) help pay expenses between the more profitable concerts in larger markets. But it is up to the promoter to take the risk with their money, so the bid sheet is a handy tool to use before the promoter and booking agent agree on a final price. Some agencies, such as *The Creative Artists Agency* (CAA), require the

CONCERTS/TOURS = HUGE. the money maker
promoters.
HOW YOU GET DISCOVERED.

[590] NACA (National Association of Campus Activities), "Events," Naca.org, http://www.naca.org/Events/Pages/default.aspx, (accessed April 4, 2011).

promoter to fill out a *bit sheet online* before they submit their request to the agency. According to the *Creative Artist Agency* (2011)[591] and others,[592] items and cost factors on a bid sheet often include the following:

Bid Sheet General Information	
Name of the Artists (you want to hire)	
Agent (who represents the act)	
Date of Show Beginning & Ending Time of Performance Public or Private Show Billing	1. 2. 3. Private [] Public [] Other [] 4. Headliner [] Other []
Note: The General Information is the raw information required by the booking agent to determine the basic information of dates times and acts the promoter is seeking to hire.	
Promoter (company buying services of talent)	
Promoter/Company	Website Address Phone Number Email Address
Signatory (person signing contract):	Print Name:
Note: Anyone can "claim" to be a promoter. Thus, the promoter part of the Bid Sheet provides information to the booking agent and manager to help them determine the financial solvency, history, key people, and general information about company before they even consider an offer.	
Venue (Place where the Concert is to be staged)	
Name of Venue	Website Address Phone Number Email Address
Contact Name (Manager of Venue & Events	Print Name:
Note: Where the act performs needs to "fit" the image and perceived "status" of the act. Also important are security, sound and light quality, dates, the reputation of the venue management, and other performances in (by the same act) nearby venues, that are or may be booked in the near future.	
Production Company (Production of Show)	
Name of Production Company	Website Address Phone Number Email Address
Contact Name (Manager of Production)	Print Name:
Note: Production companies are often hired to "put on the show" even if the venue is an IATSE crew for load in and out, sound and lighting. The production also needs to "fit" the image and perceived "status" of the act. Security, sound and light quality, and production company reputation, personal and management are important. Managers prefer to work with productions companies that have provided excellent show productions in the past with their acts.	

---

591 Creative Artists Agency (CAA), "Touring," CAA.com, CAA%20Creative%20Artists%20Agency.webarchive, (accessed April 7, 2011).

592 Personal interview with industry experts (1979-2011).

Bid Sheet Projected Expenses (Cost of Show)

Pre-Show Expenses	Show Expenses	Production Expenses	Post-Show Expenses
Advertising $ __________	Major Artist $ __________	Piano Rental $ __________	Stage Manager $ __________
Sponsoring Station (Ads & Comp Tickets) $ __________	Opening Act $ __________	Piano Tuner $ __________	Rider $ __________
IATSE Crew Load In $ __________	Security- [] Police [] T-shirt [] Private $ __________	Catering $ __________	IATSE Crew Load Out $ __________
Ticketmaster $ __________	Ticket Takers (show) $ __________	Chair Rental $ __________	Clean-Up $ __________
Ticket Printing $ __________	Ushers (show) $ __________	Electrician & Power $ __________	Credit Card Fees $ __________
Ticket Sellers $ __________	Box Office $ __________	Riggers $ __________	Housing (Acts) $ __________
Promoter Business Legal: Administration: $ __________	Dressing Room $ __________	Forklift Operator $ __________	Limo: Other: $ __________
Damage Deposit $ __________	Medical (on Standby) $ __________	Equipment Rental $ __________	Transportation $ __________
Insurance $ __________	IATSE Crew Operation of Super Troopers & Audio $ __________	Barricade Rental $ __________	Personal Bond $ __________
Licenses & Permits ASCAP/BMI & SESAC: City: State: $ __________	Fireman (As required by Codes) $ __________	Rental of Super Troopers & Lighting $ __________	Taxes: Federal: State: Local: $ __________
Total $	Total $	Total $	Total $

Projected Expenses	Total Projected Expenses
Pre-Show $ __________ Show $ __________ Production $ __________ Post Show $ __________ Total cost $ __________	$

The actual bid sheet helps the promoter project the total cost of the putting on the show (talent, venue, advertisement, insurance, bond, IATSE crew, riders expenses, etc., and then the information gathered helps the promoter and booking agent project a realistic "deal" for both based on projected expenses and revenue. Everything is negotiable, yet instead of trying to "score a huge profit by shafting the other guy," wise booking agents and promoters will attempt to establish long-term relationships that will provide future profitable events and opportunities.

Bid Sheet Projected Ticket Sales (Revenue)			
Type of Ticket # 1	Type of Ticket # 2	Type of Ticket # 3	Type of Ticket # 4
% Of Venue ______	% Of Venue ______	% Of Venue ______	% Of Venue ______
Advanced [] Premium [] Group [] Day of Show [] Student Discount [] Comp (Free) [] Other [] Number of Seats ______________ Ticket Price $______________ 100% gross $ _______ 80 % gross $ _______ 50% gross $ _______	Advanced [] Premium [] Group [] Day of Show [] Student Discount [] Comp (Free) [] Other [] Number of Seats ______________ Ticket Price $______________ 100% gross $ _______ 80% gross $ _______ 50% gross $ _______	Advanced [] Premium [] Group [] Day of Show [] Student Discount [] Comp (Free) [] Other [] Number of Seats ______________ Ticket Price $______________ 100% gross $ _______ 80% gross $ _______ 50% gross $ _______	Advanced [] Premium [] Group [] Day of Show [] Student Discount [] Comp (Free) [] Other [] Number of Seats ______________ Ticket Price $______________ 100% gross $ _______ 80% gross $ _______ 50% gross $ _______

Projected Revenue From Ticket Sales		
Revenue Tickets @ 100% Sold	Revenue Tickets 80% Sold	Revenue Tickets 50% Sold
Ticket # 1 $_________ Ticket # 2 $_________ Ticket # 3 $_________ Ticket # 4 $_________ Gross $ ____________	Ticket # 1 $_________ Ticket # 2 $_________ Ticket # 3 $_________ Ticket # 4 $_________ Gross $ ____________	Ticket # 1 $_________ Ticket # 2 $_________ Ticket # 3 $_________ Ticket # 4 $_________ Gross $ ____________
Projected Gross from Ticket Sales @ 100% Sold	Total Gross (100%) $	
Projected Gross from Ticket Sales @ 80% Sold	Total Gross (80%) $	
Projected Gross from Ticket Sales @ 50% Sold	Total Gross (50%) $	

The projected ticket sales part of the bid sheet is the responsibility of the promoter. Smart promoters research the act using BDS for radio airplay, SoundScan for actual unit sales in their specific markets, Big Champaign for legal and P2P downloads (a sign of how popular the act might be), and other mass media and new media sources. Then, they scale of the house (ticket prices for various sections of venue seating) base on their perception of how "hot the act is" (emotional connection of the fans to the artist).

Bid Sheet Project Revenue Food Commissions & Merchandise

Food Commissions	Split Percentages	Totals	Soft Drinks [] Hard Drinks []
[] Venue receives 100%	Price (- Cost) ____________		Popcorn [] Candy [], Hot Dogs []
[] Promoter receives 100%	% Promoter ___= _____ per Tic	$_____	Pizza [] Other []
[] Artist receives 100%	% Artist ___= ____ per Tic	$_____	
[] Splits	% Venue ___= ____ per Tic	$_____	

Merchandise/Other	Split Percentages	Totals	T-shirts []
[] Venue receives 100%	Price (- Cost) ____________		Posters [] Cloths [] CD's [] Hats
[] Promoter receives 100%	% Promoter ___= _____ per Tic	$_____	[]
[] Artist receives 100%	% Artist ___= _____ per Tic	$_____	Other []
[] Splits	% Venue ___= _____ per Tic	$_____	

Projected Revenue From Other Sources (if any)

Food Commissions (If any)	$ ___________	Added Gross at 100% ___________ Added Gross at 80 % ___________ Added Gross at 50 % ___________
Merchandise (If any)	$ ___________	Added Gross at 100% ___________ Added Gross at 80 % ___________ Added Gross at 50 % ___________

Projected Gross from Food Commissions & Merchandise @ 100% of tickets sold	Total Gross (100%) $
Projected Gross from Food Commissions & Merchandise @ 80% of tickets sold	Total Gross (80%) $
Projected Gross from Food Commissions & Merchandise @ 50% of tickets sold	Total Gross (50%) $

Promoters usually negotiate additional revenue sources (money) from food commissions (hot dogs, soft drinks, etc.), the rights and processes for fulfillment companies to sell merchandise, and the acts obligated requirement to hang branding advertisements from corporate sponsorship deals (posters and signs behind the performing act or in the venues). Promoters negotiate between the act, venue, and themselves for some portion of the additional revenue. Often the food revenues go to the venue and most or all of the merchandise goes to the act. However, a powerful promoter can negotiate a better deal, if they are establishing a tour instead of single date and yet it still depends on the power of the act, booking agent, and manager.

Profit & Loss Projections		
100% Sold Out Revenue Tickets $_________ Other $_________	Total $_________ (Minus) Expenses -$_________	$
80% Sold Out Revenue Tickets $_________ Other $_________	Total $_________ (Minus) Expenses -$_________	$
50% Sold Out Revenue Tickets $_________ Other $_________	Total $_________ (Minus) Expenses -$_________	$
The profit and loss part of the bid sheet shows the promoter their projected profits (or losses) based on the total revenues minus the total expenses based on the number of ticket buyers tied to the prices consumers paid at 100% sellout, 80% of venue, and 50%. Let the negotiation with the booking agent begin!		

Scaling the House/Ticket Prices

Scaling the house is the process of determining the ticket prices for various seats (in a variety of locations) in the arena or venue. Festivals often bypass the process by simply charging one ticket price for the entire festival, which may include many acts over a period of days or weeks. Fans will pay more money the closer they are to the acts or stage. Once the promoter has estimated the total projected cost of "putting on the show" by using the bid sheet, then they have to determine "how much money" they can make by estimating how much consumers will pay for tickets. The "hotter" the act, the higher the ticket prices!

A simple formula is to divide the total cost of the show by 50% of the seats. The idea is that by selling half of the venue seating the promoter should financially break even. Those ticket prices become the "average" ticket price for seats in the middle of the venue. Then, the promoter will sell the back of the house in either one or two levels of "cheaper tickets" depending on the size of the venue and the total number of seats available. As an example, the promoter may reduce seat ticket prices behind the middle of the "average" seats by 25% and then reduce the really distant or "bad" seats 35-50% off the average ticket price. To determine the "best seat" ticket prices, promoters simple add the average, poor, and bad ticket prices together to determine a premium ticket price. Sometimes super premium ticket prices are offered on first and second row seats or standing room areas next to the stage. Of course, this is a simple method, and in reality, actual ticket pricing may be more complex depending on the act, booking agent, venue, sponsorship contractual obligations, and other variables.

Scaling of the house for a concert with a bid sheet expense of $100,000 and a venue with 5,000 seats.

Type of Tickets	Seats	Percentage of Total Seats	Percent above or below Average	Ticket Price	Revenue Generated
Average Ticket Price	2,500	50%	-----------	$40.00	$100,000
"Poor" Seat Ticket	1,000	20%	(-) 25%	$30.00	$30,000
"Bad" Seat Ticket	500	10%	(-) 40%	$16.00	$ 8,000
Premium Seat Ticket	900	18%	(+) 216%	$86.00	$77,400
Super Premium (First row tickets)	100	2%	(+) 300%	$120.00	$12,000
Gross Totals	5,000	100%	-----------	----------	$227,400
Cost of Show (Bid Sheet)	-------	-----------	-----------	----------	(-)$100,000
Net Totals	-------	-----------	-----------	----------	$127,400
Federal, State & Local Taxes, about 50%	-------	-----------	-----------	----------	(-)$67,700
Estimated Profits after taxes	-------	-----------	-----------	----------	$67,700

Types of Deals

Concert promotion is a very risky business, so there are many types of deals that can be often structured. However, according to Mark Volman (2008),[593] the following four types of deals are the basic foundations for all the various scenarios that may be negotiated:

Straight Guarantee

> *The act receives a guaranteed amount of money regardless of the success or failure of the promoter to generate an audience. The straight guarantee deal provides the promoter with an opportunity to lock in the act at a fixed cost and therefore increase his or her potential profit based on the success of the event.*

---

[593] Mark Volman, "Types of Concert Tour Deals," Survey of Music Business Course Pace, (Belmont University, Nashville, TN, 2008).

Guarantee Plus a Percentage of the Net (Gate)

The act receives the guarantee plus a certain percentage of the net after the break-even point (all expenses have been paid). The percentage of the net becomes a negotiation point for the band to receive additional income on a very successful event and increases the negotiation leverage for the promoter to land or sign a more successful act for the event.

Guarantee Versus a Percentage of the Net

The act receives either the fixed guarantee or a percentage of the net whichever is greater. This type of deal is a mixture of the straight guarantee deal and the guarantee plus a percentage of the net deal and provides a little more financial security to the act. If the event is poorly attended or loses money for the promoter, the act is still paid the guarantee. If the event is very successful then the act is paid an amount that is better than just the guarantee. It also puts additional pressure on the promoter to control the bid sheet expenses and negotiate a correct percentage of the net (profit).

Guarantee Plus a Bonus

The act receives a guarantee amount plus a negotiated amount or bonus based on the number of tickets sold. The bonus is a variable amount that increases as the number of seats sold hit various level. This type of deal provides more security to the promoter and act as both receive payments based on the success of the event.[594]

Concert Promotion Process

Once the promoter determines which acts to book (employ), they match the artists (who are on tour and available) with the venues that have open dates. At the same time, booking agents who represent the artists call regional promoters, corporations and venture capitalists (who may act as promoters) to generate concert dates for their artists. It's a huge gamble. Bad weather, an artist's poor health, or some other uncontrollable situation can negatively determine the final concert attendance. A low turnout may cost independent promoters thousands of dollars. Conversely, successful concerts can profit hundreds of thousands of dollars in one evening. It's easy to see why the concert promotion business is considered a very risky business.

Deposits

The artist's manager must approve bookings (scheduling) of tour dates by the booking agent. A deposit or guarantee of 50-100% of the agreed upon price for the act is generally required from the promoter to complete the deal.[595] The money is placed into an interest-bearing account. During the concert, the road manager, tour accountant, and promoter tabulate the concert receipts in the back office. The down payment is subtracted from the money owed to the band. Full payment for the band's/artist's performance is required at closing. Successful promoters are known by industry insiders and are often hired for entire national tours, regions, or clusters of cities to reduce the band's risk of working with amateur promoters.

---

594 Mark Volman, "Types of Concert Tour Deals," Survey of Music Business Course Pace, (Belmont University, Nashville, TN, 2008).

595 Personal Interview with industry insiders (2000-2011).

Profit Margins

Promoters subtract their total projected expenses from their projected gross ticket sales revenues to determine their break-even points and profit margins. Knowing their profit margins helps the promoter to be familiar with how many tickets they can sell at various prices. That total becomes the projected gross ticket revenues (income). Then using a bid sheet, promoters determine their projected expenses (total cost of creating the event), subtract the projected expenses (debt) from the projected gross income (revenue), and determine profitability. Profit margins are based on how many seats must be sold to break even or make a profit. Many concerts require 50-80% of all tickets to be sold to break even financially. Promoters hope the profits will be much greater than the 20% depending on the act booked, promotion, and publicity. However, other types of margins are common depending on what is negotiated on the front end and of course, the type of deal and the number of tickets sold.

Sponsoring Radio Stations

Labels want their artists' touring to promote their latest recordings. Promoters and labels often work together to select a local radio station to sponsor the concert. The promoter receives a break on advertisements and the station is allowed to claim it is sponsoring the concert.

TIming

What if it rains or snows? What if there is another concert by another promoter the same week as yours? What if a band member gets sick? What if the artist makes a negative public statement or is caught by the press doing something illegal? The concert may still have to be played and the attendance may suffer, which means the promoter gambled and lost money.

Merchandising

Merchandising is an integral part of the concert industry. Companies such as EMI, Brockum, FMI, Nice Man, Winterland, and Missing Link, create a huge revenue stream by providing and selling merchandise for their artist(s).[596] The artists receive between 15-35% of the gross income from merchandise, while the providing company pays for all the merchandise, shipment, sales personnel, booths, tables, and advertisements.[597] Artists approve the design of the merchandise and receive quarterly checks for their percentage of each piece of stock sold. In addition, the concert venue usually receives part of the total merchandise profits for providing space, tables, and advertisement opportunities to the merchandising company. T-shirts, hats, records, CDs, and other types of merchandise endorsed by the artists are considered merchandise. Soft drinks, food, and candy are considered concessions that are sold by the venue with all profits remaining with the venue. Concession sales locations and commissions are negotiated by the booking agent and approved by the artist's manager before the final contracts are signed.[598]

---

596 Missing Link, "Who We Are," Missinglink.com, http://www.missingink.com/who_we_are, (accessed April 7, 2011).

597 Private interviews with industry insiders, (2008).

598 Private interviews with industry insiders, (2010-2008).

Artist Rider

A rider is an additional set of instructions for the promoter regarding specific artist's requirements. Riders usually include the size of the stage, lighting, etc., security and may even include the type of food, drinks, or other necessities the artist wants supplied in their dressing room.[599]

Production or Tech Rider

The production rider is sometimes included with the artist rider. It covers the specific technological processes and steps that promoters are required to follow for putting on the show. IATSE crews use the tech or production riders for setting up the stage, lighting, sound and other show processes. Items include the size and height of the stage, where all the instruments are to be placed, the number of super troopers (spot lights) and even when and where the lights are to be used during the show.[600]

I.A.T.S.E.

The International Alliance of Theatrical and Stage Employees or IATSE as it's called in the business, represents audio engineers, lighting technicians, set designers and builders, and stagehands for live shows.[601] A union house is a venue, studio, etc., that has signed an agreement with the performance unions (AFTRA, AF of M, etc.) to allow only union members to be employed during the creation of various entertainment productions. Most Broadway venues, sports complexes, and movies made in Hollywood, are considered union jobs made or performed in union houses. Exceptions include the production facilities in right-to-work states that often allow for nonunion productions.[602]

Roadies

The roadies are members of the touring acts who drive the trucks to each venue, load and unload and often setup, operate, and breakdown the musical instruments, lighting, and sound equipment. The amount and type of work roadies can accomplish depends on: (a) the I.A.T.S.E union agreements with each venue, (b) the contractual agreements made with the promoter and artist's manager, and (c) specific items listed in the artist's rider.[603]

---

599 Joe Sullivan, interview and class at Belmont University (1984) and Personal interviews with industry insiders (2010).

600 International Alliance of Theatrical Stage Employees, Moving Picture Technicians, Artists and Allied Crafts of the United States, Its Territories and Canada, (IATSE), "Welcome to IATSE," "http://www.iatse-intl.org/about/welcome.html, (accessed April 7, 2011).

601 International Alliance of Theatrical Stage Employees, Moving Picture Technicians, Artists and Allied Crafts of the United States, Its Territories and Canada, (IATSE), "Welcome to IATSE," "http://www.iatse-intl.org/about/welcome.html, (accessed April 7, 2011).

602 International Alliance of Theatrical Stage Employees, Moving Picture Technicians, Artists and Allied Crafts of the United States, Its Territories and Canada, (IATSE), "Welcome to IATSE," "http://www.iatse-intl.org/about/welcome.html, (accessed April 7, 2011).

603 International Alliance of Theatrical Stage Employees, Moving Picture Technicians, Artists and Allied Crafts of the United States, Its Territories and Canada, (IATSE), "Welcome to IATSE," "http://www.iatse-intl.org/about/welcome.html, (accessed April 7, 2011).

Ticketmaster

Ticketmaster started in 1976 by Albert Leffler and Peter Gadwa (two college staffers) and Phoenix executive Gordon Gunn.[604] Today the company controls almost all tickets sold at over 3,000 U.S. venues including those of more than 50 professional sports teams. It grew its business by offering many of the venues front money (in some cases millions of dollars) for the exclusive right to sell tickets to all the events scheduled at the venues.[605] In 2010 the company merged with Live Nation.[606] According to Live Nation website (2011),

> *...Ticketmaster is the global event ticketing leader and one of the world's top five eCommerce sites, with over 26 million monthly unique visitors. Live Nation Concerts produces over 20,000 shows annually for more than 2,000 artists globally. Front Line is the world's top artist management company, representing over 250 artists. These businesses power Live Nation Network, the leading provider of entertainment marketing solutions, enabling over 800 advertisers to tap into the 200 million consumers Live Nation delivers annually through its live event and digital platforms.*[607]

Ticketmaster, in the past, has bought most of its competitors through mergers and buyouts. In addition, Ticketmaster is currently offering services over the web and through many other ticketing venues. Now that it is part of Live Nation it combines the venues, ticketing, production, marketing and concert promotion process under one roof.

Ticket Scalping

In some states, it is legal to buy a large number of tickets and then resell them at a higher price to consumers before the show, concert, or sporting event. In other states, you'll end up in jail! Ticket scalping cost consumers as fewer tickets are available at the suggested retail list price, and many will buy a ticket from a scalper at a higher price than the original ticket. The process also makes it appear the event is "sold out" which is good publicity for the acts. However, if the event is not "in demand," then the promoters benefit as the scalpers bought tickets that may not have sold. The reality is that in 2010 there was a 15% decrease in concert revenues based on a gross of $1.7 billion.[608] Ticket prices may have to be reduced both at the original sources and from scalpers before gross incomes increase.

Digital Solutions for Ticketing

Bigscore.com is now offering unsold tickets to concerts and sporting events through the business model used by hotels.com, expedia.com, and priceline.com. Ticket prices for unsold seats (40% in some events) are "bid on" and the prices get lower as the starting time gets closer.[609]

---

604 Ticketmaster, "Our History" ticketmaster.com, http://www.ticketmaster.com/history/index.html?tm_link=abouttm_history, (accessed April 7, 2011).

605 Personal interviews with industry insiders (1978-2011).

606 Ticketmaster, "Our History" ticketmaster.com, http://www.ticketmaster.com/history/index.html?tm_link=abouttm_history, (accessed April 7, 2011).

607 Ticketmaster, "About Us," Live Nation, http://www.ticketmaster.com/h/about_us.html?tm_link=tm_homeA_i_abouttm, (accessed April 7, 2011).

608 Alan Pham, "Online Ticketing Service let's Fans Name Price," L.A. Times, as reported in the Nashville Tennessean, February 11, 2011; found online at http://www.tennessean.com/article/20110219/BUSINESS06/102190329/Online-ticketing-service-lets-fans-name-price-?odyssey=mod|newswell|img|FRONTPAGE|p, (February 19, 2011).

609 Alan Pham, "Online Ticketing Service let's Fans Name Price," L.A. Times, as reported in the Nashville Tennessean, February 11, 2011; found online at http://www.tennessean.com/article/20110219/BUSINESS06/102190329/Online-ticketing-service-lets-fans-name-price-?odyssey=mod|newswell|img|FRONTPAGE|p, (February 19, 2011).

Serious Music Market

The serious nonprofit music markets of symphony orchestras, opera, Broadway and dance companies contribute billions annually to the United States economy. Many opportunities are available for classically trained, consummate musicians and vocalists. Private and public organizations, churches, universities, public and private grants, donations, businesses, and local volunteer organizations often finance orchestras and various types of choral groups. Many serious music organizations are dependent on these political, social, and music-supporting groups to provide financial support for local musicians. Local symphonies, operas, etc., are marketed through the mass media by using their public service spots on radio and TV to announce performances and provide stories and photographs to the print media.

Concert Industry Trade Magazines

Billboard Magazine is the most power weekly publication covering all aspects of the music industry. Industry insiders however, use *Pollstar Magazine* to make concert business decisions. Promoters use the agency rosters to select and locate the artists they want to book. Venues use the trades to publicize their auditoriums for acts, managers and promoters. Domestic and international news stories detail the artists' lifestyles and their successful enterprises. To make business decisions, *Pollstar* provides a summary of radio charts, stations' play (by formats); a listing of recent concert revenues (by the average gross); the number of shows per week and per act; a summary of album sales (by artist, title, and label); and a listing of touring acts' scheduled concerts.[610]

Live Nation

Live Nation is the largest 360 company providing promotion, event production, act management, and concert promotion. According to Hoovers Company Profiles (2010),

> *Live Nation Entertainment holds center stage as the world's largest ticket seller and promoter of live entertainment. In 2010 the company significantly expanded its ticketing services with the purchase of Ticketmaster Entertainment. The deal, worth some $889 million, created a powerful live-music conglomerate. The firm also owns or operates more than 140 venues in North America and Europe. Annually, more than 52 million people attend some 22,000 Live Nation events. Live Nation also owns House of Blues venues through HOB Entertainment. In addition, through deals with pop stars such as Madonna and U2, Live Nation owns a stake in various artists' music, including albums, tours, and merchandise.*[611]

AEG Live

In addition to Live Nation, there's AEG Live, which stages about 4500 concerts annually out of 15 offices worldwide. It operates exclusively within books clubs, theaters, and large arenas with acts ranging from Lady Antebellum to Bon Jovi. Additionally, it provides many of the top shows in Las Vegas and festivals, live satellite feeds of concerts, and events in 3D, broadband, digital cinema, cable/satellite, VOD, wireless, and HDTV to theaters and other sources, and owns the fulfillment company BandMerch to deliver quality products and services to artists and their fans.[612] According their website AEGlive.com (2011),

---

[610] Pollstar "Boxoffice Reporting Policies," Pollstar.com, .pollstarpro.com/opencontent.aspx?ArticleID=1804&id=home, (accessed April 7, 2011).

[611] Live Nation Entertainment, "Live Nation Entertainment; Company Description," Hoovers.com, http://www.hoovers.com/company/Live_Nation_Entertainment_Inc/hhhkji-1.html, (accessed April 3, 2011).

[612] AEG Live, "Events, Artist & Festivals," AEG Live, http://www.aeglive.com/overview, (accessed April, 11).

> *AEG Live, the live-entertainment division of Los Angeles-based AEG, is dedicated to all aspects of live contemporary music performance. AEG Live is comprised of touring, festival, exhibition, broadcast, merchandise and special event divisions, fifteen regional offices and owns, operates or exclusively books thirty-five state-of-the-art venues. …AEG Lives' touring divisions are Concerts West, The Messina Group, New York Touring, Atlanta Worldwide Touring, Comedy and Latin. Internationally, AEG Live's touring divisions consist of London Touring and Marshall Arts LTD. … AEG's Goldenvoice created and operates … the Coachella Valley Music & Arts Festival …New Orleans Jazz & Heritage Festival, Bayou Country Superfest in Baton Rouge, Toronto's Edgefest, Rock on the Range, Rockfest and Rocklahoma in the Midwestern US, SunFest in Naples, FL, RockNess in the UK, and many more. …Kilamanjaro Live Unlimited specializes in contemporary rock and independent festivals, such as Wakestock and Sonisphere and … culturetainment" such as … King Tut: "Tutankhamun and the Golden Age of the Pharaohs," which has attracted more than 7 million visitors since 2005.*[613]

Virtual Corporations

Virtual Corporations are sole-purpose companies set up to run the tour, ticketing, and merchandising. Promoters run the businesses out of their hotel rooms using multiple phone lines, cell phones, fax machines and email. These corporations often gross millions of dollars during the tour, and when the tour is finished, the companies are closed and "out-of-business."[614]

Awards Shows

There's nothing better than hearing your name called as they open the envelope for the Grammy, Oscar, Tony, Emmy, ACM, Country Music, Golden Globe, or any other type of award. It really means you've hit the *jackpot of success* in your niche of the industry, and it also means MONEY! Winning a prestigious award usually increases profits from sales of your albums, movies, books, tour tickets, merchandise, whatever. Voting for some of the awards are by members only, other are by consumers who phone or email their votes into a central location. The best awards that include songs, music, or some form of music production include:

- The *Grammys* presented by the *National Academy of Record Arts and Sciences* (NARAS). The *Grammys* are the ultimate award for excellence in the recording arts. The founding nonprofit organization (NARAS) is located in Los Angeles with chapter offices in Atlanta, Chicago, Florida (Miami Beach-area office), L.A., Memphis, Nashville, New York, the Pacific Northwest (Seattle-area office), Philadelphia, San Francisco, Texas (Austin-area office) and Washington D.C. Voting members including singers, musicians, producers, songwriters, engineers, managers, and business professionals who work at the highest level in the industry. Associate and student members are connected with the business and creative industry but not at the same level as voting members.[615] According to Grammy 365 (2011),

> *…The GRAMMYs are the only peer-presented award to honor artistic achievement, technical proficiency and overall excellence in the recording industry, without regard to album sales or chart position. …Over the last decade particularly, The Academy has expanded its goals from the important work of recognizing the best in music through the GRAMMY Awards to establishing itself as the preeminent arts advocacy and outreach organization in the country. The Academy's mission statement is simple, but represents the heart and soul of the organization's efforts: to positively impact the lives of musicians, industry members and our society at large.*[616]

---

613 AEG Live, "Events, Artist & Festivals," AEG Live, http://www.aeglive.com/overview, (accessed April, 11).

614 Private interviews with industry sources (1998-2011).

615 Grammy Awards, (National Academy of Recording Arts and Sciences), "About Us," NARAS, http://www.grammy365.com/about, (accessed April 19, 2011).

616 Grammy 365, "About Us," NARAS, http://www.grammy365.com/about, (accessed April 19, 2011).

- The *Emmys* are the ultimate award in the television industry presented by the *National Academy of Television Arts and Sciences* (NATAS), and its sister organization the *Academy of Television Arts & Sciences* (ATAS). *Emmys* and *Global Media Awards* are presented for excellence in news, documentary, sports, daytime programming, creative and digital entertainment, public and community service, technology, engineering, business, and primetime programs.[617]

- The *Oscars* are presented by the *Academy of Motion Pictures Arts and Sciences.* They're the definitive award for filmmakers, producers, actors, scriptwriters, editors, songwriters, musicians, technical operators of cameras, lights, audio, effects, and of course, the directors. Awards are also provided by the Academy to prestigious contributors in the creative arts and business through the Governor's, Sci-Tech's, Student Academy Awards, and the Nicholl Foundation Award for scriptwriting.[618]

Summary

Concerts provide record labels with another way to publicize their artists and recordings. However, the concert business is really a separate industry with its own set of entrepreneurial executives and women. Concert promoters risk their own money on the public's interest to attend a staged event (a concert). Booking agents represent various acts. Their job is to call on the promoters to "book" the act into various tours and venues. The serious money in the industry is now in the event or concert business. While most artists never make any money from their label deals, (due to recoupment), they often become "famous" or "known" through their deals. That opens an opportunity for them to exploit their fame and talent though the third revenue stream, concerts. This is where most artists make very good to fabulous livings as performers. It also provides other opportunities including corporate sponsorships and merchandise sales to boost their bank accounts. Most concert promoters work independently from the record labels to create their own entrepreneurial businesses, however companies such as Live Nation and AEG Live are changing that perspective. Promoters are the high-stakes money rollers in the music and entertainment industry as they often make or lose hundreds of thousands of dollars in one night. They provide their expertise, money, social and business connections to stage concerts (events) that help generate the positive cash flow opportunities needed by many performing artists and labels (through increased unit sales due to the live appearance of the act). Concert tours and events are very important to the artist, (don't want to disappoint the fans), thus they need to ask many questions about the type of person and deal promoters are offering.

Consumers may change their buying habits more toward listening to music streaming services instead of buying or even stealing the recordings they love. This is still the emotion business based on a creative systems of writers, musicians, performing artists and other and a business systems based on the labels' money, production, publicity, distribution, sales and marketing. How the two systems work together and share the profits may be changing and evolving, yet the consumers desire to be entertainment will always remain a growing profitable business. This is the best time in many years to become a part of the industry. Go for it.

---

617 The Emmy Awards, (National Academy of Television Arts and Sciences), "History," NATAS, http://www.emmyonline.org/academy.html, (accessed April 19, 2011).

618 Oscar Awards, (Academy of Motion Picture Arts and Sciences), "History and Organization," AMPAS, http://www.oscars.org/awards/governors/index.html, (accessed April 19, 2011).

18

Entertainment Economics

So You Want to Be a Super Star: What's Economics Got to Do with It?

"Money is like a sixth sense without which you cannot make a complete use of the other five."

— W. Somerset Maugham[619]

"For I don't care too much for money, for money can't buy me love."

— The Beatles[620]

"But it is a pretty thing to see what money will do!"

— Lucius Annaeus Seneca[621]

Introduction

Have you ever wondered why superstars such as Elton John and the Rolling Stones give a limited number of concerts per year while newcomers like Taylor Swift travel all year long? Why there are a variety of prices for each concert – floor, mezzanine, backstage? Economics provides the key to answering these questions. The purpose of this chapter is to provide you with basic economic terminology and concepts to help you better understand the entertainment world around you.

Did you know that Mick Jagger, lead singer and band manager of the Rolling Stones, majored in economics at the London School of Economics? What about Young M.C.? He majored in economics at the University of Southern California. Other high profile entertainers and athletes such as Tiger Woods, Arnold Schwartzenegger, and Cate Blanchett also majored in economics.[622] Evidently creative individuals are drawn to the study of economics. What is economics, and why does it matter?

Choice Tradeoffs

Economics is the study of how and why we allocate our scarce resources among unlimited wants. Resources in this context can mean many things: time, money, natural resources, and other types of goods and services.

---

619 W. Somerset Maugham, "Money," Proverbia.net, http://en.proverbia.net/citastema.asp?tematica=780&page=4, (accessed March 9, 2011).

620 The Beatles, "The Beatles Quotes," ThinkExist.com, http://thinkexist.com/quotes/the_beatles, (accessed March 9, 2011).

621 Lucius Annaeus Seneca, "Money," Proverbia.net, http://en.proverbia.net/citastema.asp?tematica=780&page=4, (accessed March 9, 2011).

622 Economics Club, "Famous Economic Majors," Georgia State University Economics Club, http://www2.gsu.edu/~wwwecc/FamousEcMajors.htm, (accessed March 9, 2011).

The reason resources are scarce is because they are limited. Time is limited to 24 hours in a day. Our income is limited (even for multimillions), and other resources are limited too. Given these limitations, firms must make choices in the way they produce goods and services and we must make choices between the things we want. In economics we call these choices **tradeoffs.**

Opportunity Cost

Another idea associated with economic choice and tradeoffs is opportunity cost. **Opportunity cost** is what we give up to get something. For example, what would you be doing right now if you weren't reading this chapter – out with friends, working, sleeping, texting, or eating? When you chose to read this chapter, you gave up doing the other things. So the opportunity cost of reading this material is not hanging out with your friends, or not working and earning income, or not getting to take a nap. Notice that cost in this context can be money related, but it does not have to be. Time pursuing the things you enjoy is a valuable resource.

So you can see why artists might be drawn to the study of economics. Besides offering answers for business choices – why the Rolling Stones offer few tours now and pricing behavior of concert promoters – it is also at the heart of why individuals do the things they do. One only has to peruse music lyrics to see that they are about the choices – good and bad – people make and the opportunity costs associated with those choices. Economics is not just for eggheads; it is for people like you and me who want to better understand the world around us. So let's get started!

Markets

Two terms that economists use most often are **demand** and **supply**. If you want to understand how our economy works, it is essential that you understand how markets work. Markets are simply places where buyers and sellers come together to make an exchange, whether a physical location such as a store or a digital location like iTunes. Demand and supply are the catalysts behind markets. Together they determine the **price** and **quantity** of goods and services produced and sold in our economy. The following sections provide a glimpse into how buyers and sellers interact in the market place to determine quantity and price and in turn help to allocate our scarce resources.

Buyers Equal Demand

According to data from the Bureau of Economic Analysis, personal consumption spending on entertainment and recreation[623]is a large part of the U.S. economy representing $928 billion dollars in 2008. This is approximately 6% of our $14.3 trillion dollar U.S. economy as measured by the Gross Domestic Product (GDP).[624&625] During the same time, the Recording Industry Association of America (RIAA) reports that the music industry accounts for $8.8 billion dollars or about 1 percent (0.06%) of the U.S. economy.[626] To be a

---

623 *The Bureau of Economic Analysis (BEA) breaks the recreation function into eight sub-categories: (1) video and audio equipment, computers and related services, (2) sports and recreation goods and related services, (3) memberships clubs, sports centers, parks, theaters, and museums, (4) magazines, newspapers, books and stationary, (5) gambling, (6) pets, pet products and related services, (7) photographic goods and services, and (8) package tours.*

624 *Gross domestic product (GDP) is defined as the market value of all final goods and services produced within a country annually.*

625 Gregory N. Mankiw, *Principles of Economics*, 4th ed, (Thompson-Southwestern: Mason, Ohio).

626 Recording Industry Association of America (RIAA), "Facts and Figures," http://www.riaa.com/keystatistics.php, (accessed March 9, 2011).

part of the entertainment sector is an exciting opportunity but where do these numbers come from? The answer is consumers like you and me., represent the demand side of the economy and are made up of individuals, businesses, governments, and buyers from abroad.

A recent example of how consumers have an impact on the marketplace relates to the untimely death of pop star Michael Jackson. Between his death on June 25th and July 16th 2009 (not even a full month), he sold 2.3 million albums worldwide. One year later, the number has risen to approximately 9 million albums in the United States alone![627] Through music sales, film and television, music publishing, licensing and touring, and a new record deal, it is estimated that Michael Jackson generated approximately $1 billion in revenue only one year after his death.[628] This reflects an aspect of demand called **tastes** and **preferences**. When he died, consumers' tastes and preferences for his music increased so much that even old songs from previous albums were mixed and released on a new album called *The Stripped Mixes* released on July 7th, 2009.[629] Through the new recording contract with Sony Music Entertainment, it is expected that 10 albums will be released through 2017.[630]

One method of selling his songs is through the digital market, especially iTunes. Until recently, Apple charged the same price for all songs on iTunes, 99 cents for DRM songs and $1.29 for DRM-free songs. In April 2009, Apple shifted to a three-tier pricing strategy of $0.69, $0.99, and $1.29 per download, all DRM-free. Given that Apple accounts for more than 80% of the digital downloading market[631] and recently passed $6 billion in download sales,[632] how will this new pricing scheme have an impact on their digital sales? Economic theory would predict that raising the price of downloads from $0.99 to $1.29, although now DRM-free, will reduce the quantity demanded. This is exactly what Glenn Peoples reported on April 10, 2009, just 3 days after the launch of the price changes[633] and later by Ed Christman on July 8, 2010.[634]

The Law of Demand

Are you surprised that consumers will buy less when the price of a product is raised? You shouldn't be. In fact this is so prevalent in the market place that economists call this the **law of demand**. The law states that as the price of a product rises the quantity demanded falls (and vice versa), holding all else constant. To

---

627 Gil Kaufman, "Michael Jackson's Posthumous Global Record Sales Reach 9 Million," http://www.mtv.com/news/articles/1616358/michael-jackson-sells-9-million-worldwide-since-death.jhtml, (accessed March 9, 2011).

628 Ed Christman, Ann Donahue, Gail Mitchell, Glenn Peoples, and Ray Waddell, Profit and Loss: Michael Jackson One Year After, Billboard Magazine, *Billboard Magazine*, (June 26, 2010) 19.

629 Michael Jackson, "The Stripped Mixes," iTunes, http://itunes.apple.com/us/artist, (accessed March 9, 2011).

630 Ed Christman, Ann Donahue, Gail Mitchell, Glenn Peoples, and Ray Waddell, Profit and Loss: Michael Jackson One Year After, Billboard Magazine, *Billboard Magazine*, (June 26, 2010) 19.

631 Greg Sandova, "Amazon Finds Niche in iTunes-dominated Market, http://news.cnet.com/8301-1023_3-10213149-93, (accessed September 25, 2010).

632 Erick Schonfeld, "iTunes Sells 6 Billion Songs and Other Fun Stats from the Philnote," TechChrunch.com, http://techcrunch.com/2009/01/06/itunes-sells-6-billion-songs-and-other-fun-stats-from-the-philnote/, (accessed March 10, 2011).

633 Glen Peoples, "iTunes Price Changes Hurt Some Rankings," Billboard.biz, http://www.billboard.biz/bbbiz/content_display/industry/e3i7917210cb575a9b9adc60840c7d7f16e, (accessed September 25, 2010).

634 Ed Christman, "First Held 2010 Sales Recap: Lady Antebellum, UMG Leads the Way," Billboard.biz, http://www.billboard.biz/billboardbiz/photos/pdf/current.pdf, (accessed September, 25, 2010).

illustrate this, let's use a couple of tools: a demand schedule and a demand curve. A demand schedule is a table of different prices for a product and the accompanying quantity demanded associated with each price. A demand curve is a graphic illustration of the demand schedule. Let's use iTunes as the example.

Law of Demand

iTunes Price	Quantity of a Hit Single from iTunes (per week)
$0.39	25,000
$0.69	20,000
$0.99	15,000
$1.29	10,000
$1.59	5,000

Table 18.1 identifies different prices and quantities for a hit song downloaded from iTunes (the quantities are made up and I include additional prices).

The Demand Curve

Notice the inverse relationship between price and quantity demanded. *As price falls, quantity demanded rises and as price rises, quantity demanded falls.* This makes perfect sense. As the product becomes less expensive, we buy more of it.

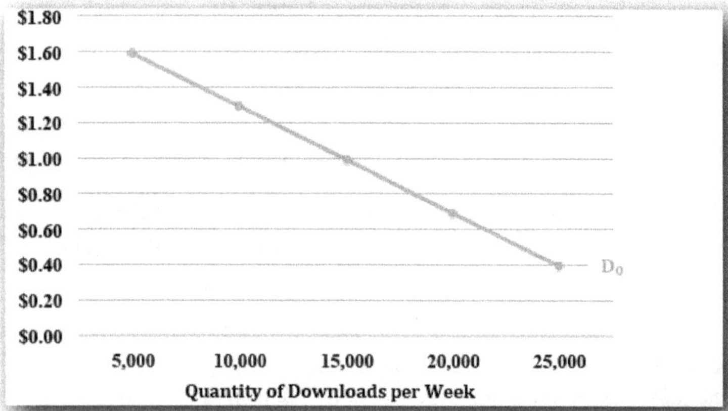

Table/Figure represents the demand curve – the demand schedule in graphic form. The demand curve is downward sloping, illustrating the inverse relationship between price and quantity demanded. As price changes, we move along the demand curve. This is known as a change in quantity demanded. For example, at $1.59 only 5,000 downloads are demanded, but as the price falls to $0.99 quantity demanded increases to 15,000 downloads (we move down and to the right of the demand curve). It also works in reverse. At $0.99 per download 15,000 are demanded, but as the price rises to $1.29 the quantity demanded falls to 10,000 (we move up and to the left of the demand curve).

The Determinants of Demand

At this point the only things changing are the product's price and the quantity demanded (the variables on the graph). Aren't there other things that come into play when someone decides to buy a product? You betcha! In economics, we call these other things the **determinants of demand**. Recall the definition of the law of demand – as the price of a good rises, the quantity demanded falls, holding all else constant. The determinants of demand are the "all else" that we hold constant. They include *tastes and preferences, income, number of buyers, prices of related goods*, and *expectations of future prices*. The entire graph shifts to the right (increase in demand) or to the left (decrease in demand) if any of the determinants of demand changes. This is known as a *change in demand.*

Let's see what this would look like in our demand schedule and on our graph. Assume that the number of buyers increases by 2,000 at each price, a small example of what took place when Michael Jackson died.

iTunes Price	Quantity of Hit Singles Demanded from iTunes (per week)	Quantity of Hit Singles Demanded from iTunes When # Buyers Increases
$0.39	25,000	27,000
$0.69	20,000	22,000
$0.99	15,000	17,000
$1.29	10,000	12,000
$1.59	5,000	7,000

Increase in the Determinant	Effect on Demand	Effect on Demand Curve
Number of Buyers	Increase	Shifts Right
Tastes and Preferences	Increase	Shifts Right
Expectations of Future Prices	Increase	Shifts Right
Income: Normal Good	Increase	Shifts Right
Income: Inferior Good	Decrease	Shifts Left
Price of Related Good: Substitute Good	Increase	Shifts Right
Price of Related Good: Complementary Good	Decrease	Shifts Left

Decrease in the Determinant	Effect on Demand	Effect on Demand Curve
Number of Buyers	Decrease	Shifts Left
Tastes and Preferences	Decrease	Shifts Left
Expectations of Future Prices	Decrease	Shifts Left
Income: Normal Good	Decrease	Shifts Left
Income: Inferior Good	Increase	Shifts Right
Price of Related Good: Substitute Good	Decrease	Shifts Left
Price of Related Good: Complementary Good	Increase	Shifts Right

Income as Related to Goods

Income is unique because there are some goods that we buy more of when our income rises (normal goods) and some goods that we buy less of when our income rises (inferior goods). If you don't believe me, how many Ramen noodles are you going to buy when you graduate and start making more money? Thus when our income rises, we buy more normal goods increasing demand and shifting the demand curve to the right. However, when our income rises we buy less inferior goods decreasing demand and shifting the demand curve to the right. The opposite will occur for a decrease in income.

Finally, there exist two types of goods that are related to the one we are considering buying. One good we use in place of the good we are considering buying. This is called a **substitute good**. Let's assume that John Mayer and Katy Perry are both playing in Nashville on the same night, and we like both equally. As such, they are substitutes for each other. So if the price of a John Mayer ticket goes up (leading to a decrease in quantity demanded for Mayer tickets), we will buy Katy Perry tickets instead, leading to an increase in demand for the Katy Perry tickets and shifting her demand curve to the right. On the other hand, if John Mayer decreases his ticket prices (highly unlikely), demand for Katy Perry tickets will fall shifting the demand curve to the left. Notice that in one case, it is a *change in quantity demanded* while in the other it is a *change in demand.* Regarding John Mayer tickets, we simply move along the demand curve because it is the price of his ticket that is changing. However, since his ticket is a substitute for Katy Perry tickets, it will have an impact on the demand for Katy Perry tickets and shift the demand curve for her tickets. The second type of good we use *along with* the good we are considering buying. This is called a **complementary good**. In this case, consider iPods and digital downloads. If we can't afford to buy the iPod, we certainly aren't going to buy downloads. As such, if the price of iPods increases, the demand for digital downloads decreases, shifting the demand curve to the left. On the other hand, if the price of iPods falls, the demand for digital downloads increases, leading to a rightward shift in the demand curve.

Whew! I know that was a lot to take in, but if you understand these concepts, you are on your way to thinking like an economist!

Test Your Knowledge!

Now that you've become more knowledgeable about demand and its determinants, consider the following questions. How do consumer tastes and preferences help explain why Susan Boyle's recordings are typically sold as CDs while Lady Gaga's sales are typically digital downloads? What is the difference between a change in quantity demanded and a change in demand? Explain and illustrate.

Economics and 360 Deals

One common form of consumption we see in the music industry is digital downloading. Whether it is legal or illegal, it has forever changed the way consumers buy music and labels do business in the music industry. What once was an industry built around the sale of physical units of recorded music (CDs) is no longer the primary revenue generator for labels. As such, the labels have had to adapt to make up for the falling sales in physical units. Thus, the creation of the "360 deal," whereby the labels sign an act with a contract that includes label revenue shares not only in unit sales but also in income from touring, songwriting, merchandising, fan clubs, sponsorships, acting, and other revenue generators.[635] While digital downloading is not the focus of this chapter, it is important to note that it has created economic implications that are being felt throughout the entire entertainment industry.

Figure 3 depicts the trend associated with the rise in the total value of digital shipments and its impact on CD shipments. As reported by the RIAA, the graph illustrates that digital shipments have increased from 1.54% of total shipment value in 2004 to approximately 41% in 2009. Thus, the total dollar value of physical unit shipments was nearly 100% in 2004 and by 2009 had declined to roughly 59%.[636] It's no wonder labels are seeking new ways to generate revenue![637]

---

[635] Donald Passman, *All You Need to Know About the Music Business*, 7th ed. (7th ed. (New York, NY: Free Press, 2009).

[636] Joshua P. Friedlander, "2009 Year-End Shipment Statistics, Recording Industry Association of America (RIAA), http://76.74.24.142/A200B8A7-6BBF-EF15-3038-582014919F78.pdf, (accessed September, 26, 2010).

[637] Friedlander, Joshua P. (2010). 2009 Year-End Shipment Statistics. Retrieved from http://76.74.24.142/A200B8A7-6BBF-EF15-3038-582014919F78.pdf

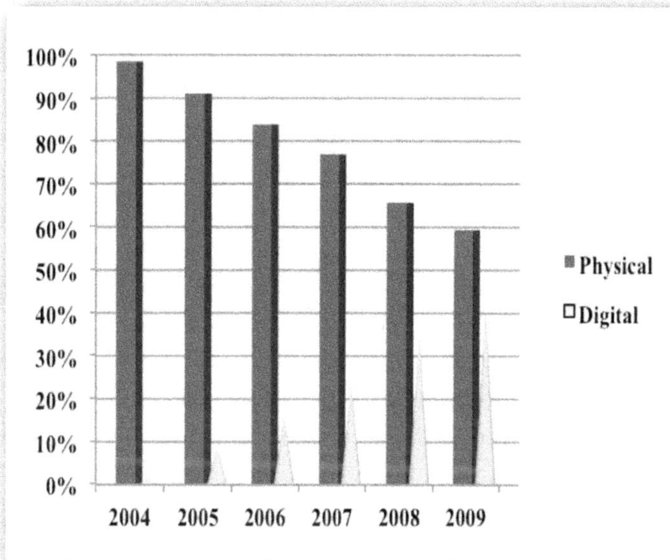

The graph illustrates the power of consumer demand in the marketplace. Consumers considered the tradeoff between buying a 10-song physical CD or downloading just the songs they want and have changed the way the marketplace works! This is an example of consumer sovereignty in economics. **Consumer sovereignty** is simply the idea that consumers are the best judges of their own preferences.

The graph helps to explain why firms are interested in consumer decision-making in the marketplace. Changes in consumer tastes and preferences enable companies to see where product innovation is taking place and where it is needed. Another reason firms are interested in consumer choice is *profits*. One goal of a firm is to maximize profits. If a business can figure out how to entice consumers to buy and become loyal to their product, then they can generate more profit. This is where the concept of price elasticity of demand comes into play.

Price Elasticity

Price elasticity of demand is a measure of the consumer's responsiveness to a change in a product's price.[638] There are three ways to describe the price elasticity of demand: *elastic*, *inelastic*, and *unit elastic*. One way to think about elasticity is to pinch the skin on your hand (or your grandparent's skin). If it goes back in place quickly (young skin), it is elastic. If it doesn't (older skin), it is inelastic. Another way to think about elasticity is with a rubber band. New rubber bands spring back quickly (elastic) while old rubber bands don't (inelastic). In both examples, the more responsive effect is elastic while the less responsive effect is inelastic.

When consumers are responsive to price changes, the price elasticity of demand is elastic. Consider an increase in price as an example. If consumers are elastic in demand, an increase in price of 5% leads to a decrease in quantity demanded of more than 5%. This typically occurs when the product someone is buying has many substitutes or is expensive. An example might be season tickets to the theater. They are expensive, and there are many other entertainment options available. When consumers are less responsive to a change in price, the price elasticity of demand is inelastic. This implies an increase in price of 5% leads to a decrease in quantity demanded of less than 5%. This often occurs when consumers are loyal to a brand, such as Apple products v. Dell products, or the product is inexpensive. The last way to describe the price elasticity of demand is unit elastic. This implies that a 5% increase in price will lead to exactly a 5% decrease in quantity demanded, leaving revenues and profits unchanged. Most products will fall into the elastic or inelastic categories. Firms care about the price elasticity of demand because consumer behavior will have an impact on their bottom line. In other words, the firms' profits will increase or decrease depending on whether consumers are elastic or inelastic with respect to demand. Let's look at this a little more closely.

---

[638] Price elasticity of demand is calculated as the percentage change in quantity demanded divided by the percentage change in price.

When consumers are elastic in their demand for a product, an increase in the price of the product means that firms will lose more consumers proportionately than the price increase. Given that revenues are the product of price times quantity sold, the loss in sales leads to lower revenues and lower profits. When demand is elastic and the firm raises its price, quantity demanded goes down by more than price goes up. As a result, revenue falls. This is where labels have forgotten about economics! In the case of CDs, there are better music alternatives – one song for 99 cents v. one CD for $12 – so the price elasticity of demand for CDs is elastic. Guess what? The more alternatives there are for a product, the more elastic the demand will be! When consumer demand is elastic, the best pricing policy for a company is to lower prices to increase revenue (this is because they will gain proportionately more customers than the price decrease). How often have you heard a business say that they will lower prices to increase revenue and profit? Not often – music labels included! Until the labels realize that consumer sovereignty holds and come up with a better alternative to buying one song at a time, they will continue to see their revenues and profit margins decline. This helps to explain why labels are now pushing the 360 deals to generate more revenue.

Does every firm face elastic demand? No! In many instances consumer demand is inelastic, and a price increase can ultimately lead to an increase in profits. When demand is inelastic, price goes up by more than quantity demanded goes down leading to an increase in revenue. Let's see how. Think about Apple and their advertising campaign explaining why Apple computers are better than PCs. This is a great advertising piece created to generate brand loyalty and thus create inelastic demand for their products. This way when Apple products have higher prices than others, they won't lose as many customers. They can increase their price by 5% and lose less than 5% of their customers, which means that overall their revenues go up. When revenues increase, profits typically follow. Thus, the best pricing policy for a product with inelastic demand is to increase price.

Previously, I mentioned that there are other alternatives to CDs, namely digital downloads, creating more elastic demand for CDs. This is just one of the determinants of price elasticity of demand – *availability of close substitutes*. There are other determinants that have an impact on the elasticity of demand: *amount of dollars it takes from your budget*, *necessities v. luxuries*, and *time*. The more income it takes to buy the product, the more elastic demand will be. You will think long and hard before spending a lot of money! The less income it takes to buy the product, the more inelastic demand will be. A 99 cent song is much easier to buy on a small budget than a $12 CD. Necessities will typically have inelastic demand – think about gas for your car – because you have to have them. However, luxury goods are more elastic in demand. Finally, time matters! The more *time* you have to consider the purchase, the more elastic your demand will be. This is because you will be able to find other substitutes over time. The less time you have, the more inelastic demand will be.

Recall the Apple example of three-tier pricing? Apple was able to price based upon the elasticity of demand. The higher price was set for those with the most inelastic demand – buyers who have to have the hit songs. The lower prices reflect the fact that as songs lose their favor in the market, the price elasticity of demand becomes more elastic. To generate more revenue, Apple must lower their price to entice consumers to buy the product. We also see this form of pricing at concerts. Those that want to sit closest to the stage are charged a higher price, because they are inelastic in demand. Those in the nosebleed section have a much more elastic demand and pay lower ticket prices because they wouldn't be there if they had to pay a higher price. This form of pricing enables firms to earn as much revenue as possible.

Test Your Knowledge!

Now that you've become more knowledgeable about the price elasticity of demand and its determinants, consider the following questions. Does Apple consider consumer demand to be elastic or inelastic for their product? Explain. Which product is more elastic in demand: a new car or a dime store novel? Why? Which product is more inelastic in demand: a single download of Katy Perry or a ticket to a Katy Perry concert? Why?

The Supply Side

In the previous section, we learned about how consumers make up the demand side of the market. Now we want to turn to the **supply side of the market** where firms participate in the production of goods and services for the industry. Many of you hope to make your living from this side of the market, so it is important that you have a good understanding of firm behavior.

The goal of the firm is to maximize profit just like your goal of being an artist, songwriter, or producer is to generate as much income as possible. That doesn't make firms or you greedy; it is just a fact of life. Just like you and I have to make choices between differing wants, firms have to choose how to allocate their resources between hiring workers, buying equipment, and reinvesting in their firms. They too experience opportunity costs!

The Supply Side and You

Since most of us have never owned our own company, it is often difficult to understand the supply side of the market. To help bring the ideas into perspective, I want to use a very simple model – you. You supply labor to the firms that means you sell your services just like a firm would sell its products. Let's assume you work by the hour. The job is the same regardless of how much you make per hour. How many hours would you be willing to work for $2 per hour, $5 per hour, $10 per hour, $15 per hour, or $20 per hour? Most people wouldn't want to get off of the couch for $2 per hour, which by the way, is well below the federal minimum wage! As the hourly wage goes up however, I suspect that people would be willing to work more hours. Let's put this in a supply schedule and create a supply curve just like we did when we were discussing demand. A supply schedule is a table of different prices for a product or service and the accompanying quantity supplied associated with each price. A supply curve is a picture of the supply table.

Hourly Wage	Quantity of Hours of Work Supplied (per week)
$2	0
$5	15
$10	25
$15	35
$20	40

Do you see a relationship between price and quantity? As the hourly wage (price of labor) goes up, the quantity of labor supplied also goes up. Firms work the same way. They are willing to sell increasingly product as the price of their product goes up. We see this so often in the marketplace that economists call this the **law of supply**. The law states that as the price of the good or service increases, quantity supplied increases, holding all else constant. Let's graph it and see what happens.

Notice that the supply curve is upward sloping. This illustrates the positive relationship between price and quantity supplied. As price rises, so does quantity supplied. Similarly, as price falls so does quantity supplied.

As the wage changes, the amount of hours you are willing to work also changes, and we move along the supply curve. This is called a *change in quantity supplied.* For example, at a wage of $10 per hour you are willing to work 25 hours per week. As your hourly wage increases to $20 per hour, you are willing to work 40 hours per week. In this case, you move up the supply curve. It also works in reverse. You will move down the supply curve if your wage falls.

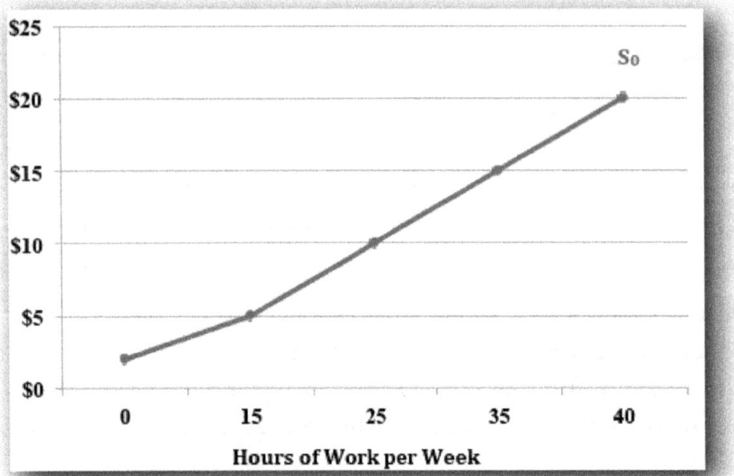

Once again, the only things changing at this point are the wage and the quantity of hours supplied. Are there other things that would aid your decision in how much to work? Yes! The other things are the determinants of supply, and they include: *the cost of inputs, number of sellers in the market, technology*, and *expectations of future prices.* The entire supply curve shifts to the left (decrease in supply) or to the right (increase in supply) when one of the determinants changes. This is known as a *change in supply.* For example, if you expect to receive a raise in a month, you might choose to work more hours today (increase supply) to give them good cause to give you a raise.

The Supply Side and the Number of Workers

Another example of an increase in supply seen often is an increase in the number of workers. They are sellers in the labor market, so the determinant *number of sellers* has increased. Let's see what this would look like in our supply schedule and on our graph. Assume that the number of sellers or workers increases by 5,000 at each wage.

Hourly Wage	Quantity of Workers Supplying Labor (per week)	Quantity of Workers Supplying Labor When # Sellers Increases
$5	10,000	15,000
$10	15,000	20,000
$15	20,000	25,000
$20	25,000	30,000
$25	30,000	35,000

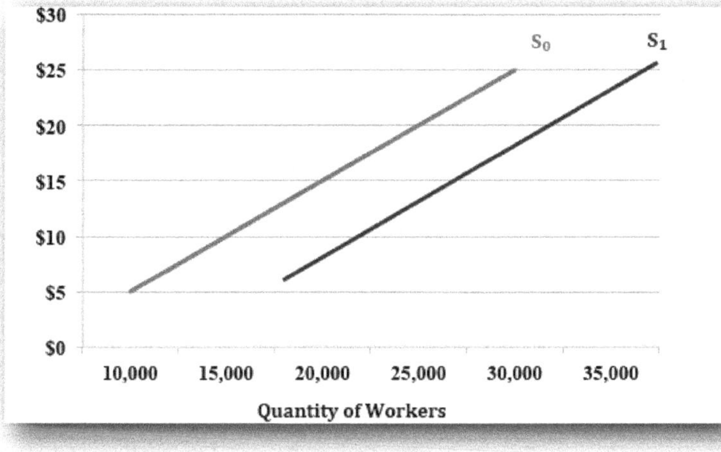

The Quality of Workers

Notice that when the number of sellers increases, the supply curve shifts to the right. This is known as an increase in supply. A decrease in supply would cause the entire supply curve to shift to the left.

Just as we did on the demand side, we need to discuss each of the determinants of supply. Table 10.11 highlights the effects of an increase and decrease in each determinant of supply on supply and its corresponding supply curve.

Impact of a Change in One of the Determinants of Supply on Supply

Increase in the Determinant	Effect on Supply	Effect on Supply Curve
Number of Sellers	Increase	Shifts Right
Technology	Increase	Shifts Right
Cost of Inputs	Decrease	Shifts Left
Expectations of Future Prices	Decrease	Shifts Left

Decrease in the Determinant	Effect on Supply	Effect on Supply Curve
Number of Sellers	Decrease	Shifts Left
Technology	Decrease	Shifts Left
Cost of Inputs	Increase	Shifts Right
Expectations of Future Prices	Increase	Shifts Right

We just provided an example using the number of sellers, so let's pick up with technology. Regarding firms, technology refers to the ability to take inputs (labor, raw materials, equipment, etc.) and create output (goods and services). Improvements in technology enable firms to produce more goods and services with the same inputs, leading to an increase in supply and a corresponding rightward shift of the supply curve. A decrease in technology, though rare, would have the opposite effect. The cost of inputs is vital to firm behavior since payroll often makes up a large portion of costs for a business. As the cost of inputs rises, it becomes more expensive for the firm to produce the same amount of goods and services. Thus, supply decreases leading to a leftward shift in the supply curve. A decrease in the cost of inputs will have the opposite effect. Finally if firms expect future prices to rise, they will cut back on supply today to sell it when the prices rise. This results in a decrease in supply and a resulting leftward shift of the supply curve. If they expect prices to fall in the future, they will try to sell as much as they can today leading to an increase in supply and a rightward shift of the supply curve.

The supply curves we have drawn so far have been upward sloping because for most industries firms are willing to sell more of their product as the price increases. The entertainment industry has a couple of exceptions to the upward sloping supply curve. First is the vertical supply curve. This occurs when supply is capped such as the number of tickets available for a concert or sporting event. The firms *would* be willing to sell more tickets as the price increases, but they are unable to do so because there are a limited number available. The second exception is known as a *backward bending supply curve, which illustrates the substitution and income effects of an individual.*

This occurs in the labor market, and we typically see this with superstars. When they first start out they are willing to work a lot, but as they become better known and earn larger and larger salaries for their work, they prefer more leisure. This is known as the **income effect**. For most of us, the **substitution effect** holds – as our salaries increase we tend to work more and leisure less (we substitute work for leisure). However, superstars' income increases so much that the additional income is not as important as the additional leisure. This helps to explain why many pop stars party more than they work, why major recording artists cut back on tours over time, and why major film stars only do a film or two per year. Table/Figure 10.12 illustrates a backward bending supply curve with the associated substitution and income effects.

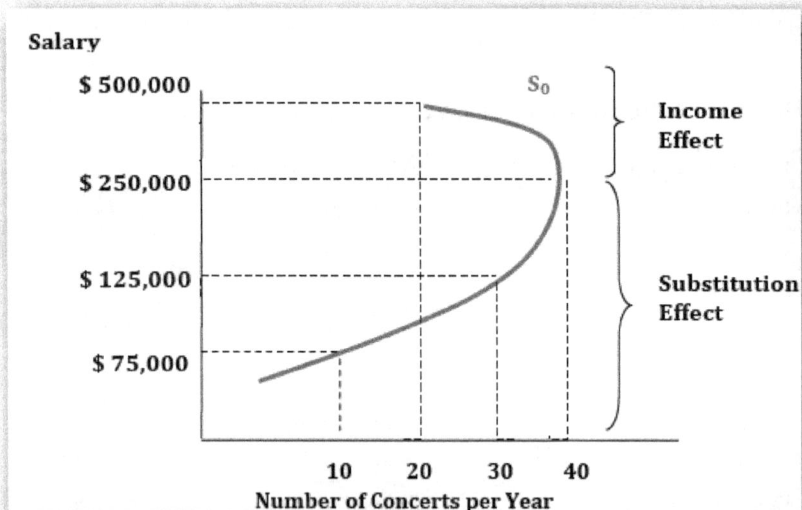

The Substitution and Income Effects

Notice that a newcomer to the touring industry may make a salary of $75,000 with 10 concerts. As they build more of a fan base, their earnings rise to $250,000, and they increase the number of concerts per year to 40. However, once they are superstars and their income rises to $500,000 per year, they reduce the number of concerts to 20 per year. The *substitution effect* is represented by a salary of $250,000 (or less) as the artist increases the number of concerts per year. They are substituting work in place of leisure. The *income effect* is represented by a salary above $250,000 since the artist reduces the number of concerts per year. They are now making so much income that they can substitute leisure in place of work.

Test Your Knowledge!

Now that you've become more knowledgeable about supply and its determinants, consider the following questions. How do the concepts of supply help to explain why Tom Cruise only makes one film per year or Kenny Chesney tours six months out of the year while Ke$ha tours all year long? What is the difference between a change in quantity supplied and a change in supply? Explain and illustrate.

Putting Demand and Supply Together + Equilibrium

Understanding demand and supply separately is good, but we do not get a complete picture of the market until we put the two together. Once we combine demand and supply, we are able to determine the price and quantity in the market. Additionally, we can answer questions like, why are older mp3 players so much cheaper today than when Apple introduced the iPod?

For simplicity, we are going to use the standard downward sloping demand and upward sloping supply curves. While simplistic, this model is very powerful. It will enable us to determine what happens to price and quantity when demand changes holding supply constant or when supply changes holding demand constant.

What is equilibrium, and why does it matter? **Equilibrium** is the point at which quantity demanded equals quantity supplied for a given price. This implies that the amount that consumers want to buy and the amount that firms want to sell is the same. It occurs where the demand and supply curves intersect. Equilibrium is important because it provides price information to buyers and sellers as well as identifies the amount of goods and services to be exchanged at a given price enabling firms to better allocate our scarce resources. The pricing information is provided by the **equilibrium price (P_e)**, *which is the price at which quantity demanded equals quantity supplied.* Similarly, *equilibrium quantity (Q_e) is the amount of goods and services exchanged at the equilibrium price.*

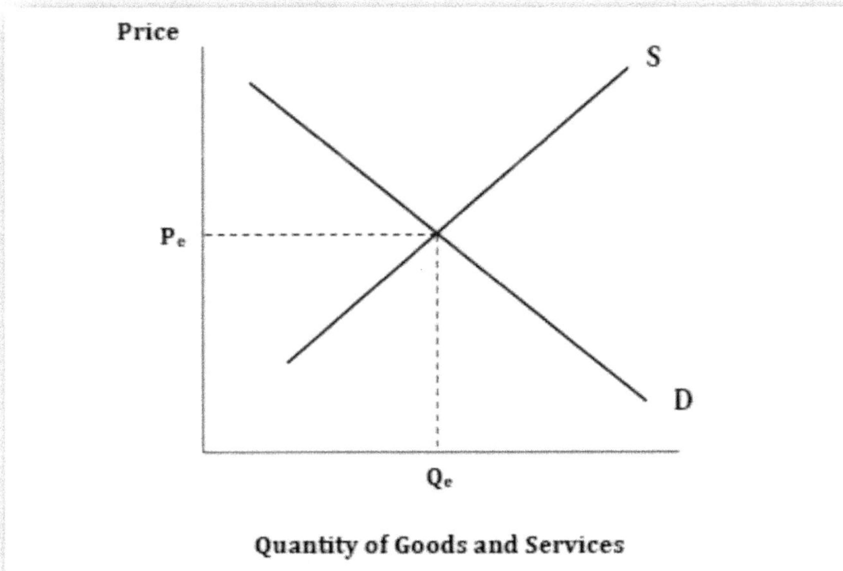

Table illustrates the idea of equilibrium in the demand and supply model.

Now that we know what the basic demand and supply model looks like, let's see what happens to price and quantity when either demand or supply changes. This is when things get really interesting, and what we see in the real world begins to make sense! Recall, that in order for the entire demand curve to shift, one of the determinants of demand must change – *tastes and preferences, income, number of buyers, prices of related goods*, or *expectations of future prices*. Similarly, for the supply curve to shift, one of the determinants of supply must change – *number of sellers, technology, cost of inputs*, or *expectations of future prices*.

Let's start with an increase in demand, holding supply constant. Assume that tastes and preferences increase for Apple's new product the iPad. What would economics say should happen to equilibrium price and quantity in the market for iPads? Let's see! Table/Figure 10.14 illustrates the impact of an increase in tastes and preferences on demand, supply, equilibrium price, and equilibrium quantity in the market for iPads.

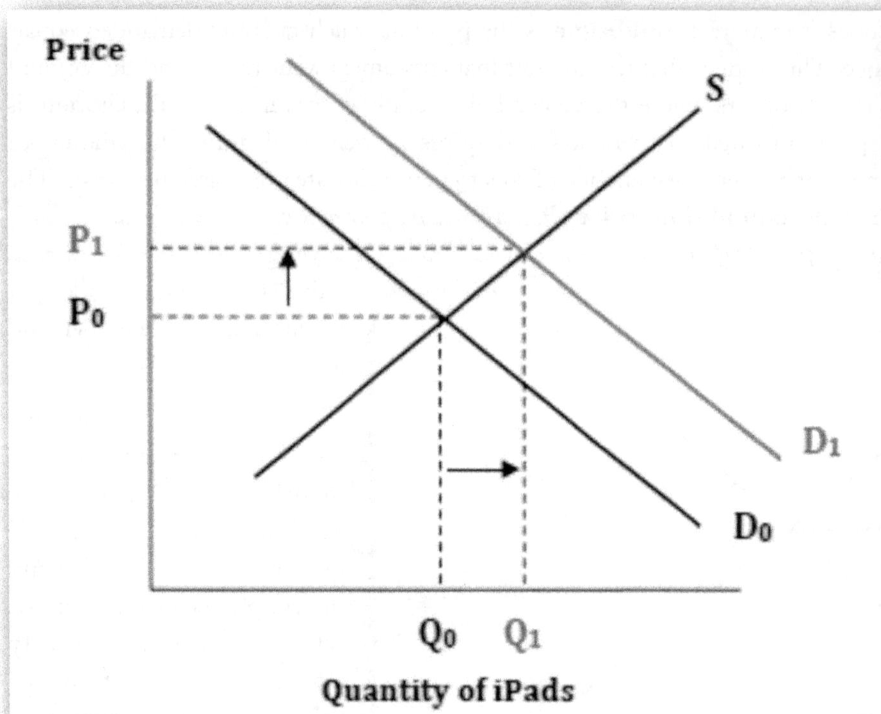

In this example, many things happen. The increase in tastes and preferences results in an increase in demand from D_0 to D_1 as indicated by the rightward shift in the demand curve. Did any of the determinants of supply change? No! Since no determinants of supply changed, the supply curve remains constant. As a result of the increase in demand and no change in supply, a new equilibrium is reached (from P_0Q_0 to P_1Q_1). As a result, the equilibrium price of iPads rises from P_0 to P_1. Equilibrium quantity increases from Q_0 to Q_1 for two reasons: one demand related and one supply related. The quantity of iPads demanded increases at each price because tastes and preferences has caused demand to increase. Quantity supplied increases because price has risen. Apple will move up along the fixed supply curve since they now receive a higher price for the iPad (remember the law of supply). Both the increase in quantity demanded and quantity supplied lead to an overall increase in the equilibrium quantity of iPads from Q_0 to Q_1. Thus, an increase in demand with no change in supply leads to higher equilibrium prices and quantities in the market. This helps to explain why Apple has been able to increase its prices and still sell a lot of product. It is driven by demand.

Now let's see what happens when supply changes while demand remains constant. In this example, we are going to let the number of sellers increase in the mp3 player market. What would economics predict about equilibrium prices and quantities in this case?

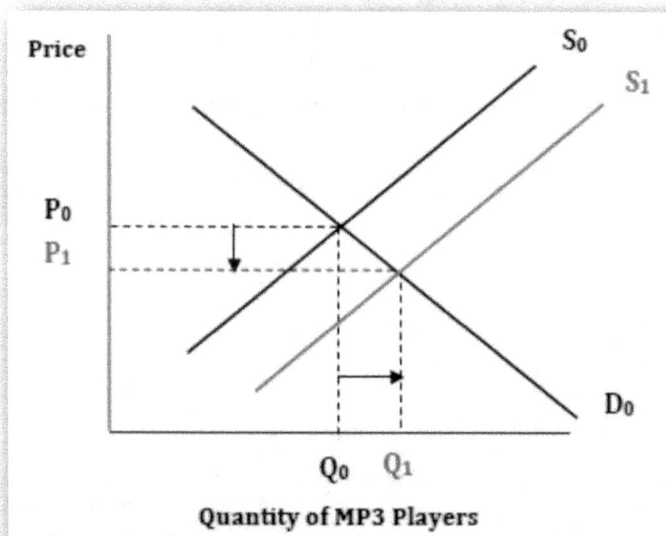

Here we see different things happening. Since the number of sellers has increased, the supply curve shifts right as a result of an increase in supply. Given that no determinants of demand changed, the demand curve remains constant. With an increase in supply and no change in demand, a new equilibrium is reached (from P_0Q_0 to P_1Q_1). As a result, equilibrium price falls from P_0 to P_1. The equilibrium quantity of mp3 players increases from Q_0 to Q_1 for two reasons: supply side and demand side. Quantity supplied increases because more firms are making mp3 players (increase in number of sellers increases supply). Quantity demanded increases because the price of mp3 players has fallen, and buyers move down the fixed demand curve. The combined effect of increases in quantity supplied and quantity demanded results in an overall increase in equilibrium quantity from Q_0 to Q_1. Thus, an increase in supply with no change in demand leads to lower equilibrium prices and higher equilibrium quantities. Think about it. After Apple introduced the iPod did other competitors introduce mp3 players? Yes, indeed, and what happened to prices? They fell. Similarly, we see the same impact on wages when the number of graduates increases, and the demand for workers remains the same. Economic theory does work!

Hopefully, you now have a better understanding of how the basic model of supply and demand works. Table synthesizes the effects of changes in demand and changes in supply on equilibrium price and quantity.

Effects of Changes in Supply and Demand on Equilibrium Prices and Quantities

Increase in	Equilibrium Price, P_0	Equilibrium Quantity, Q_0
Demand with Supply Constant	Rises	Rises
Supply with Demand Constant	Falls	Rises

Decrease in	Equilibrium Price, P_0	Equilibrium Quantity, Q_0
Demand with Supply Constant	Falls	Falls
Supply with Demand Constant	Rises	Falls

Although we know that reality is more complicated than the basic model, understanding the basic model enables one to see the world around them a little more clearly. Developing more complicated models is beyond the scope of this chapter. I know that's a relief!

Test Your Knowledge!

Now that you've become more knowledgeable about the basic model of demand and supply, consider the following questions. How would a decrease in income impact equilibrium prices and quantities in the iPod market (assume iPods are a normal good)? Illustrate and explain. How would an increase in wages impact equilibrium prices and quantities in the iPod market? Illustrate and explain. Hint: remember your determinants!

Summary

One goal of this chapter was to introduce you to basic terminology and concepts of economics to help you better understand the world around you. Hopefully, mission accomplished. You should no longer be surprised that salaries will be lower in fields that have many graduates (number of sellers) or that gasoline prices will rise during the summer (tastes and preferences increase for travel). The basic model of demand and supply provides the answers. While most of you do not intend on majoring in economics, it is important for you to know that it is all around you in the choices you make each day. The ideas of tradeoffs and opportunity cost explain those choices.

Finally, I wanted to answer questions posed throughout the chapter. If you haven't already figured them out. Have you ever wondered why superstars such as Elton John and The Rolling Stones give a limited number of concerts per year while newcomers like Taylor Swift travel all year long? Economics tells us that Elton John and The Rolling Stones are superstars and operate at the upper portion of a backward bending supply curve where the income effect dominates the substitution effect. Taylor Swift, on the other hand, is relatively new to the industry and is working her way up the backward bending supply curve. Will she reach the top? Only time will answer that question. Why did Apple recently change their pricing scheme for downloading iTunes songs? As you learned it was to take advantage of the price elasticity of demand of their customers and increase their revenues. Those that have to have the "big hits" pay a higher price because they are inelastic with respect to demand, while those that do not have to have the big hits pay a lower price because they are elastic with respect to demand. Price elasticity of demand also explains why there are a multiple prices for each concert, airline flight, or football game. Finally, economic theory explains why Michael Jackson sold millions of songs and records after his death and why labels created new mixes to sell after his death. It's no longer surprising that all of his songs that were selling at $0.99 quickly sold for $1.29, or why more of his music was made available.

While economics might not be a sexy science, it is also not so dismal. People and businesses apply it every day to their decision-making. In fact, a recent student of mine who was working in the music business pointed out this fact. He stated that although he did not formally draw graphs or use terms such as price elasticity of demand, he responded to increases in consumer demand by raising the price of hit CDs. He was able to associate the increase in consumer demand to his revenues. Over time as the demand fell, he lowered the CD price to entice more sales. He stated that taking a course in economics enabled him to better understand why his decisions worked they way they did. It is my hope that you too will apply the concepts and tools learned in this chapter!

19

Action Pack Building Your Career

Trends

Where do you "fit" in

Creating your own Niche

"A career is wonderful, but you can't curl up with it on a cold night."

— Marilyn Monroe[639]

"iCloud keeps your important information and content up to date across all your devices. All of this happens automatically and wirelessly, and because it's integrated into our apps you don't even need to think about it—it all just works."

— Steve Jobs[640]

"Creativity is the basis of all of our businesses and the core of our value creation. We therefore continue to invest in our creative businesses and expand them."

— Thomas Rabe, Chairman & CEO of Bertelsmann[641]

On December 31, 1999, my publishing contract with Warner-Chappell expired, thus emancipating the name I was given at birth, Prince, from all long-term restrictive documents."

— The artist formerly known as and again known as Prince

---

639 Marilyn Monroe, "Marilyn Monroe Quotes," Artquotes.net, http://www.artquotes.net/entertainment-quotes/famous-actresses/marilyn-monroe.htm, (accessed March 15, 2011).

640 Steve Jobs, "Apple Introduces iCloud," From the press release iCloud Images, http://www.apple.com/pr/library/2011/06/06icloud.html, (accessed June 9, 2011).

641 Thomas Rabe, Bertelsman's 2013 Annual Report, Strengthening the Core, "The Power of Creativity," http://reports2.equitystory.com/reports/bertelsmann/annual/2012/gb/English/0.html, (accessed July 7, 2013).

The Benchmark

Elvis Presley made it happen by having the talent to sing, the passion to entertain, the initiative to learn from others through listening, watching, and asking questions, and most importantly, by being in the right place at the right time. Elvis didn't, however, become a world-famous recording artist by himself. He used his vocal talents, good looks, and assertiveness to get his foot in the door of the music business. It was also the music business, or more precisely, the people in the business that helped *Elvis* become the *King of Rock and Roll.*

If you do not have the talent or desire to be an artist or write a song, there are still many entrepreneurial opportunities available in the entertainment business. Artists need studio and tour musicians, record producers, audio engineers, managers, attorneys, booking agents, promotion agents, publicists, radio announcers, sales, and financial managers to help them build their careers. Entrepreneurs who are not label or mega entertainment corporation employees fill most supportive careers. *Elvis Presley*'s talent, combined with *Sam Phillips*' producing skills and *Colonel Parker*'s managerial expertise, created one of the most successful *businesses* in history. This is a stellar example of how entrepreneurship (*Elvis, Sam Phillips,* and *Colonel Parker*) and the industry (RCA Records) embraced numerous entertainment opportunities to generate huge profits. There are many other examples like this, of course: *The Beatles, Madonna, My Chemical Romance, Garth Brooks, The Eagles, Michael Jackson, Shania Twain, Elton John, Metallica, Prince, Pearl Jam, Aerosmith, Eminem, Billy Joel, Red Hot Chili Peppers,* and newer ones, including *Taylor Swift, Lady Gaga, Brad Paisley,* and *Jay-Z*. Also, we should not forget all of the artists and business people behind the iconic stars who have helped them become so successful such as the songwriters, producers, managers, labels, promoters, etc.

The Brain Rush

It is easy to dream about someday being discovered as the next superstar artist, songwriter, producer, manager, concert promoter, scriptwriter, dancer, actor, or music video director. My point is simple: if you want to be in the business of music or entertainment, you have to move past the brain rush of possibilities and take some risks. You've got to get the ball rolling, not some unknown entity who may or may not exist! Have you got the talent, ability, personality, and business skills to make money (a career) in the business? If you think you do, find out if you have what it takes to be successful by taking the first step. Start doing what you want to do even if you're dreading it! Everyone has to start somewhere, and *nobody* starts on top.

"It: The X Factor"

Nobody is coming to discover you, so stop dreaming about it. However, once you have something that clearly may be sellable, you've got to turn *it* into a product that can be monetized! Then, you've got to prove to yourself and others that *it* is worthy of their time, money, and personal investment *before* established industry managers, labels, music companies, songwriters, publishers, etc., gain interest in working with you. So, form your band, write songs, create music, gig, draw, act, dance, get weird, write books and film scripts, shoot a movie, develop whatever your creative talent is and try to monetize it locally.

Unit Sales Levels of Success

The big surprise is how few cd's or digital downloads artists need to sell to be considered successful. A *gold record* is 500,000 units sold which is only .16% of the United Stated population. A *Platinum award* is only .3 percent![642] In other words, if you sell far less then one percent of the United States population you may still be consider a superstar!. However, the exposure required to convince the masses they "need" your music is not easy. So, remember, according to *Kelly's Theory of Personality* consumer select who and what they listen to

---

[642] Rolston, Clyde, as suggested by him in personal interview. (February 28, 2012).

based on psychological wants and needs of mental self-definition and elaboration used to subconsciously construct their mental self value and world view. Of course, consumers also may perceive your music and your branded image emotionally out of their subconscious mind. Thus your creative recording or performance is actually a communicative message selected for use by consumers who need to understand or celebrate who and what they are by using the message they perceive in your image and songs.

The "No Starving Artist" Rule

Artist and teacher *Lisa Canning* has established the "no starving artist" rule.[643] It's brilliant! Can you sell your artistic products to 1,000 consumers out of the several billion consumers on the planet? If you can't, then either you're not an artist whose talent is "monitizable" or you're not doing your part trying to market your talent. Learn about entrepreneurship and the corresponding business processes and how to use technology to sell your "*it*" to the planet! It's your responsibility as an artist to *not only create some artistic talent or product*, but to *sell it* by creating a *fan base* that may lead to consumers discussing your talent, which may *create a buzz* and a *consumer market* for your products. A thousand consumers at 10 bucks a shot totals $10,000 annually. Can you (as an artist) sell anything connected to your artistry monthly, such as subscription to your fans base of 1,000 (a T-shirt, a newsletter, a recording, free downloads, a live show ticket, whatever)? That's $10 a month times 1,000 consumers times 12 months, which equals $120,000 annually. That's a great living with only 1,000 fans out of billions of potential consumers. It's important to understand that it is up to you (the artist) not only to create but to sell whatever your talent is and the corresponding products!

Creating a Local Buzz

Create a *local buzz*, and you'll capture the attention of someone in the business or someone who knows someone in the business. It doesn't matter if you want to produce sessions or be a session player or a touring musician. Get noticed! In other words, in the beginning, your first step is just to *get noticed*, and in most cases, that means making money for someone else. Performing in a small bar or club will hopefully make the owner money and at the same time, you'll be noticed by other establishments and consumers. Build a fan base, and get their email addresses. Being able to draw a small audience is a reason for a bar or small venue to hire you to perform. Need a demo? Get on your Mac or PC, or find a producer in a studio or a classmate or friend with Pro Tools or GarageBand.

However, do not forget to educate yourself about how the business works and meet the local important players, such as promoters, mangers and media experts. Befriend the right people locally and avoid the *slugs*; the "self proclaimed" experts who claim to know it all and have all the connections you'll need to make it in the biz. Most of them do not have a clue, so be careful!

If you are in a band, record a simple, yet honest demo, give it to the local radio station, put it on sale at the local record store, set up a website on one of the social networks, include a bio, tracks, and tour dates, and try to create some local excitement. Develop an *electronic press kit* with sample songs, video interviews, news clips, and contact information. If you can get a buzz going, then invite local insiders to a showcase. If you're terrific, people connected to industry personalities *will help you* meet the right people. A *referral* about a band that is selling product and getting local airplay by a local radio personality will get the attention of an A&R department, as they are always looking for the next big thing.

---

643 Lisa Canning, "The No Starving Artist Rule," www.entrepreneurTheArts.com (as discussed at the Self-Employment in the Arts Conference, Chicago, 2011).

Social Network Postings

Sadly, do not expect to get discover by just posting your name and picture and giving away your recordings on a social network. You'll have to actively work at the exposure. *Facebook* has over 500 million active users (that visited the site in the last 30 days).[644] Use social networks to build a fan base and then announce events and opportunities where the fans can attend your shows, buy your merchandise, and get to know you better. However, it's easy to get lost in the crowd and very difficult to drive potential fans to your site. Word of mouth is the best advertisement. As you get started, without it, selling albums is almost impossible. According to *Ariel Hyatt* of Ariel Cyber PR, who used a *pyramid graph* to explain social network album sales at *The Future of Music Summit* (2009),

> *...There are 5 million bands on MySpace as a way to have a figure representing the huge number of bands out there. Out of those bands, 105,575 released albums last year. There were only 110 bands, which sold 250,000 or more copies of their album. There were 1,515 bands who sold over 10,000 albums and 5,945 bands who sold 1000 albums or less. ...If you remove the major label artists from those numbers how many are left? That is the reality of the digital marketplace.*[645]

Liz Kennedy, Deputy Director of Communications for the RIAA (2011), adds that

> *...In a world where there are 2.5 million hip-hop and 1.8 million rock acts on MySpace alone, more often than not, the addition of a music label is usually the difference between a band that offers songs to a few devoted fans online, and one who embarks on a multi-city tour, whose music is featured on a hit TV show or commercial and who goes on to earn Gold and Platinum plaques. In a noisy digital music market, it takes a label to help acts stand out in the crowd.*[646]

So, getting discovered is up to the artist, and (as an artist) you'll have to do more than give away your music on Facebook or MySpace pages. Start by building your fan base playing gigs, selling recordings, networking, and committing shameless self-promotion. If you're good enough, you're on you way! Once you've created a buzz and the potential for greater success, then find the right industry connections. Many club and concert promoters know the insiders you need to know. After all, they often started their career as assistants working on the road, interning with established management companies, or even in the mailroom at *The William Morris Agency*.[647] Most have learned the business from the bottom up. Only the smartest and best survive in this industry, so experience speaks for itself. Connect with the right music business insiders, be a one-of-a-kind artists, with a proven track record and following (fan base) and the industry moguls will take notice.

Branding – Culture Icons

The music business is an ever-changing, high-pressure, competitive business where millions of dollars change hands every day based on how successful the industry's creative and business systems work together. However, most consumers are interested in the public image of the artist, not the intimate details and legalities of the business. They are most excited by the artists, their music, and how it makes them feel (of course, we really know that consumers use the music and thoughts about an act to express their own emotions). The music industry and most of the artists themselves use their public images as marketing icons

---

[644] Facebook, "Statistics," Facebook.com, http://www.facebook.com/press/info.php?statistics, (accessed March 26, 2011).

[645] Ariel Hyatt, (in an article by Scott Macaulay), "Five Million Bands on MySpace at the Future of Music Summit," FilmMaker.com, http://www.filmmakermagazine.com/news/2009/10/5-million-bands-on-myspace-at-the-future-of-music-summit/, (accessed March 26, 2011).

[646] Liz Kennedy, "Why Being Signed to a Music Label Rocks," RIAA.org, http://www.riaa.org/blog.php?content_selector=Why-Being-Signed-, (April 2, 2011).

[647] Personal interviews with industry professional (2005-2011).

to motivate concert ticket and recorded music unit sales. Non-label artists and musicians can build a great career from personal performances as a member of an orchestra, a nightclub band, playing at weddings and parties, being a jam band on festival tours, and by providing entertainment at a number of unique events.

If you've created a local buzz and gotten the attention of the industry, then you may have proven (in effect, test-marketed yourself) that you or your act have the potential for much greater success if you could just reach a larger market share. *The bottom line is that having a record deal with a street release, promotion, publicity, distribution, and financial advances places the artist into a powerful position.* It allows the artist to use their notoriety and the label's power of distribution and marketing plan to exploit their image for profit. If, and it's a big "if," the act's recordings and appearances connect with a worldwide consumer base, the profits can be huge for both sides (the label and artist) depending on the specifics in the deal.

Exposure – The Grand Canyon

There are many wonderful artists and acts that never receive the exposure need to be "discovered" by consumers. They get it! Somehow they have to jump the Grand Canyon of silence from being unknown and unheard to reach the ears of the world's six billion potential consumers to become famous! Record labels and music companies are still the best way to achieve fame. Singers and musicians either have to build their local support and buzz to a level of success where the labels "are interested" or they have to build and control their own business careers (entrepreneurship) through many years of self-advertisement, promotion, publicity, and then (once they have the gigs) performance after performance. Thus, many artists are rediscovering the value of record labels and music company deals. In a recent survey of over 2,000 unsigned bands conducted by ReverbNation and Digital Music News (2011),

> *...Over 75% of indie artists said that it was one of their goals to get signed to a record label. The exact percentage varied from genre to genre; including a high of 81% of hip hop artists wanting a deal, and a low of 63% of alternative artists wanting to get signed. When asked which labels were at the top of their wish lists, artists surveyed consistently listed Sony, Universal, Atlantic, Warner, Columbia, Epic, Capitol, and Interscope.*[648]

The Cash Machine

Recording artists generally make the greatest share of their annual income from the billion-dollar concert industry, which includes merchandise sales and corporate sponsorships. Even major recording royalty artists rarely sell enough CDs to cover their recording and marketing expenses (recoupment). Hence, paid live appearances usually provide the cash flow most artists need to sustain the economic side of their careers. Record label and music company promotion and publicity give consumers an opportunity to "discover" what they like or dislike about acts. Thus, if you're either a small local act or a famous superstar, someone has to manage the whole mess, excuse me..., business.

Building the Artist's Business

Moving past the local community usually requires a manager and booking agent as well as a team of attorneys, consultants, business accountants financial experts, and media trainers. Building this team of experts to help exploit an artist's image through promotion, publicity, recordings, and tours is the artist's responsibility and the next step toward a successful and profitable career. In the film business, scripts have plot points where the direction of the film changes. The decision by an artist to accept creativity and artistry as a business and set up a management organization as a means for making money is a real life plot point in

---

[648] ReverbNation, (article posting by Ferol) "Reverbnations' Facebook app My Band gets a name (Band Profile) new features, and it's still 100% Free," ReverbNation & Digital Music News, http://blog.reverbnation.com/, (accessed April 2, 2011).

an act's career. The creation of an event such as a concert or nightclub appearance, gives the artist an opportunity to be paid for a performance. In addition, it gives the artist another opportunity to become an entrepreneur by selling merchandise, corporate sponsorships, endorsements, recordings, and other products to consumers.

Image

What are you trying to say? It doesn't matter if you are an artist, producer, musician, or an accountant; it is important to have a professional image. If you are starting as an artist, think about what your image says about you – what the songs you sing, play, produce, or write represent. Then, try to figure out who will buy into the image you're portraying. Remember, success as an artist is based on more than the ability to sing in tune. Listen to the artists who are not the best singers: they have very successful careers because their *image* represents some emotion to consumers. In todays music business an artist's image that is tied to a career breaking song (radio airplay) can lead to product branding. That's where the profits for the labels in 360 deals can be huge as most of the recordings are not paid for, yet consumers will buy into clothing lines, soft, booze, and water drink endorsements. In the old days the business was about selling disks, today it's about getting famous and then selling branding endorsements, tours, and merchandise.

Musicians, promoters, managers, booking agents, and film people, have the ability and image to accomplish for an artist what the artist cannot accomplish for themselves. Songwriters write the perfect songs for artists who can't. Screenwriters write the stories for actors, directors, and production technicians who can't. Studio musicians often play in recording sessions because they are better musicians than the actual stars. Managers manage the business of an artist who can't, and booking agents acquire concert tours for the manager and the artists who either can't or don't want to. Stage managers oversee the production and presentation of the live shows, and the list goes on and on. Gain experience locally, and then move up to regional and later, national positions working for the superstars.

Industry Networking

Success takes more than talent; it takes drive, passion, and courage to achieve it. In the entertainment business, everyone promotes himself or herself to be hired for sessions, tours, publicity campaigns, promotion, and other industry-related jobs. Students and prospective industry professionals attend professional seminars and meetings and work in jobs that will create career opportunities. However, networking is a refined skill. It has to be done with confidence, humor, and a sense of respect for the boss, the artists, and their positions in the industry. Blatantly shoving CDs at producers to prove your songwriting skills, audio engineering session work, or singing ability is not advisable. If you want their help, get to know them first and learn all you can about the business. All major recording artists, producers, label executives, booking agents, and concert promoters constantly network with each other to find songs, acts, musicians, singers, and business-educated executives to help their careers. It is amazing to watch a huge superstar approach a well-known industry songwriter. Both know they need each other: the artist needs a great song to sing and record to get airplay, sell concert tickets and record sales; the writer needs someone famous to record their song to receive music publishing royalties from mechanicals, sync, and performance royalties. This networking dance takes place everyday at all levels of the entertainment business. *It's whom you know and what you can contribute to the industry that will help you get your first break.* Learn all you can about how to present yourself in a professional manner and how to network by using shameless self-promotion. It will put you years ahead of the competition.

Conceivable "Value"

Artists who have achieved local fame and financial success are often perceived as having a conceivable or thinkable value. What if they got a record deal with a great producer? Wouldn't they now need a great manager? The decision for representation or artist management is usually based on the perceived financial potential of the artists. If they have a label deal, then they should get the exposure needed to jump the Grand Canyon of Silence and be "discovered." That could lead to an emotional communicative connection between the act's image, recordings, and live performances, which could lead to endorsements, merchandise deals, and corporate sponsorships. The goal, of course, is to become a culture icon representing whatever constructs the consumer base is most passionately excited about. If the potential is perceived correctly, brilliant management decisions at the right time and place are needed for success.

Representation

A simple word, yet it means many different things to different people in the entertainment industry. The term personal representation is often use to define the jobs of both agents and managers.[649] Yet, agents in the film industry are different (and can receive a different percentage for commission) than booking agents in the music industry. Can we make this even more confusing? Sure. Personal managers are different from personal representation, depending upon if we are talking about the film or music business. *In this respect, talent agents in the film and theater business are quite different from personal managers in the music business, who are usually entrepreneurs in small businesses who provide advice and guidance for their acts but do not seek employment for their acts.* Also, agents for *The Screen Actors Guild-The American Federation of Television and Radio Artists* (AFTRA) often acquire employment opportunities for their singers and actors, while personal managers in the music business provide advice and guidance and then suggest a booking agent the artist should hire to find gigs.[650] Acts in the past were usually represented by film agents in media entertainment and by another agent for a music career. Today representation talent agencies are blending where even the CAA's of the world may now represent top musical artists as well as film and media personalities.[651]

Not everyone is going to become a superstar artist. Yet, as you've probably noticed by now, the music and entertainment business is really many industries that survive and work together to make each other financially successful. Entrepreneurship is also a major part of the "game" and because of technology in audio and film production software the real question is "are you good enough to create sellable products?" In other words, you can compete with the "big boys," "the suits," etc., and if you're good enough they will be chasing you. Here's the news you want to hear... the established industry now usually wait until you (the creative artists, promotor, producer, whatever), do something that causes a buzz, stir, emotional explosion, (whatever), that gets you "noticed" by the establishment (the major labels, producers, etc.). Then, they throw money at you to acquire whatever you've got in order to "blow it up" (distribute and sell it worldwide) and profit from it. Sticking your tracks on youtube with a sucky video or joining a social network simple isn't enough. It's just too hard to be discovered when millions are doing the same thing.

Reality

If you create a buzz (consumers are excited, talking about you or your creative products) then, be proactive

---

649 M. William Krasilovsky, and Sydney Shemel, *This Business of Music*, 10th ed. (New York, NY: Billboard Books, 2007), 332.

650 Personal interviews with industry insiders (2008-2011).

651 Personal interviews with industry insiders (2011).

by "getting to know" the people and established industry "insiders" who can help you. They will want to get involved! The "establishment" can also help you because they know each other (the major players in the business) and have true knowledge (street smarts) that only success and failure can bring. I believe we learn more from our failures than successes. The key is yours, so slide it into the industry's door and unlock all the opportunities it can provide.

Unions & Guilds

There are several unions in the entertainment and music business who represent the creative artists and workers. Unions are "trade organizations" formed by individuals in the same or similar profession who band together for increased representation with employers. According to the *Merriam-Webster Dictionary* (2013) unions are, "an organization of workers formed for the purpose of advancing its members' interests in respect to wages, benefits, and working conditions."[652] Remember that each "union" usually represents one type of creative performance, so a superstar who is a musician, singer, and actor may actually belong to three different unions, the AF of M for musicians, SAG-AFTRA for singing and acting and Equity for stage performances. Guilds are different than unions as they are "associations" that do not always represent their members for employment. Still in the music industry their are several "guilds" that require their members to use specific contracts. Guilds are important as they offer representation and business opportunities. According to *The Merriam-Webster Dictionary* (2013) guilds are an:

> *...Association of craftsmen or merchants formed for mutual aid and for the advancement of their professional interests. Guilds flourished in Europe between the 11th and 16th century and were of two types: merchant guilds, including all the merchants of a particular town or city; and craft guilds, including all the craftsmen in a particular branch of industry (e.g., weavers, painters, goldsmiths). Their functions included establishing trade monopolies, setting standards for quality of goods, maintaining stable prices, and gaining leverage in local governments in order to further the interests of the guild. Craft guilds also established hierarchies of craftsmen based on level of training (e.g., masters, journeymen, and apprentices).*[653]

Industry Related Unions

The most important "unions" in the music and entertainment industry are *The American Federation of Musicians* often called the AF of M, *The Screen Actors Guild* which merged recently with *The American Federation of Television and Radio Artists* to form SAG/AFTRA and *Equity*. Other unions include the *International Alliance of Theatrical Stage Employees (and Moving Picture Machine Operators of the U.S. and Canada)* better known as I.A.S.T.E., *The National Association of Broadcast Employees and Technicians-Communications Workers of America* often known as NABET.

The American Federation of Musicians

The American Federation of Musicians represents about 90,000 musicians in the United States and Canada for recordings and live performances in negotiated agreements for studio and other recordings, TV, films,

---

652 Merriam-Webster Dictionary, "Unions," http://www.merriam-webster.com/dictionary/labor%20union, (accessed July 15, 2013).

653 Merriam-Webster Dictionary, "Guilds," http://www.merriam-webster.com/dictionary/guild, (accessed July 15, 2013).

jingles, concerts, stage shows, symphony, opera, and ballet.[654] Major record labels are signatories to *The American Federation of Musicians Sound Recording Labor Agreement* (formerly the Phonograph Record Label Agreement) that governs the wages, benefits, and working conditions of all its members, including studio musicians.[655] According to information posted on their homepage, www.afm.org (2010),

> *In the mid-1800s musicians in the United States began exploring ways to improve their professional lives. They formed Mutual Aid Societies to provide members with loans, financial assistance during illness or extended unemployment and death benefits. A number of these organizations became early unions serving various constituencies, but problems arose between them due to competition. In 1896, delegates from these organizations gathered at the invitation of American Federation of Labor (AFL) President Samuel Gompers to organize and charter a musicians' trade union. … They resolved: "That any musician who receives pay for his musical services, shall be considered a professional musician."*[656]

Membership advantages include a retirement fund, health insurance, and AFL-CIO benefits.[657] The AF of M uses franchised booking agents who usually work for 10% commission to connect union musicians with people who want to hire them. Most of the agents represent musicians and recording artists locally and nationally.[658] Thus the AF of M has many local offices and a national office. If you are a musician playing gigs and do not want to get stiffed (play the gig and not getting paid), representation by an AF of M licensed agent will usually prevent these and other types of problems. According to www.afm.org (2010),

> *AFM-Franchised Booking Agents are signatories to the AFM's Booking Agents Agreement. These booking agents act as the "sales force" for AFM members in the US and Canada. Purchasers are provided with legitimate agreements, members are provided with protection of their earnings, and the booking agents earn commissions for their sales. These agreements are comprehensive contracts which stand up in court, if need be, and obligate the parties – the purchaser is obligated to pay the stipulated price, and the musician(s) are obligated to perform the services described in the agreement.*[659]

Technology in software has given producers, musicians, and other creative artists the opportunity to create great sounding musical tracks without using a formal recording studio and even musicians. We should all support live musician recordings but the reality is they cost more for the label to use and the labels are having a difficult time financially surviving peer to peer downloading and legal streaming sites. Also, many consumers can't tell the difference between live recorded musical tracks and those created by *pro-tool* or *logic pro*-software. The future is here and many labels have started to reduce their use of AF of M musicians even though they are still signed to the union agreement. They simply hire super producers who can producer, write songs, play many of the instruments themselves, and record tracks on their home studio computers. They also sign distribution deals with artists who have already produced their own recordings that have created a local buzz fan base. As frustrating as this is, the "live performance" world is starting to increase musicians opportunity to work and perform. Consumers are starting to demand the real deal when they go to clubs and shows. So, things are starting to improve, yet, Baskerville (2006) claims their are six reasons for

---

[654] AF of M, "Why Join," AF of M, http://www.afm.org/why-join, (accessed March 22, 2011).

[655] AF of M, "Sound Recording Label Agreement," AF of M, http://www.afm.org/uploads/image, (accessed March 22, 2011).

[656] AF of M, "History of the AF of M (by years)," AF of M, http://www.afm.org/about/our-history, (accessed March 22, 2011).

[657] AF of M, "Why Join," AF of M, http://www.afm.org/why-join, (accessed March 22, 2011).

[658] AF of M, "Book Agent Search," AF of M, http://www.afm.org/resources/booking-agent-search, (accessed March 22, 2011).

[659] AF of M, "Book Agent Search," AF of M, http://www.afm.org/resources/booking-agent-search, (accessed March 22, 2011).

reduced AF of M membership:

Difficulty in attracting many of the new, young professionals

State and national laws restricting certain kinds of collective bargaining,

Continuing displacement of live performances with recorded music,

Increasing displacement of live musicians by electronic instruments

Importance of music recorded abroad, and

Increasing prevalence of nonunion performances live and recorded.[660]

The AF of M offers its members many benefits in health, retirement, and professional connections, plus it's popular monthly magazine *International Musician.* According to the AF of M website the magazine offers it members "...news and information you need, industry employment and audition advertisements, and useful career advice."[661]

The Screen Actors-American Federation of Television and Radio Artists

SAG and AFTRA joined together on March 30 of 2012, when more than 80% of both union's membership voted in favor of the merger.[662] According to the SAG-AFTRA website (2013):

> *This formed the most powerful union ever for more than 160,000 actors, announcers, broadcasters, journalists, dancers, DJs, news writers, editors, hosts, puppeteers, recording artist, singers, stunt performers, voiceover artist and other media professionals.*[663]

The American Federation of Television and Radio Artists had represented recording artists in studio sessions, television productions, and live performances since the late 1930s.[664] It also represented actors, announcers, sound effects artists, and other personalities working in radio and television. Representation was focused in five areas: sound recordings, broadcast news, commercials, industries, new technologies (non-broadcast industry films), and entertainment programs (television).[665] About 1,200 companies (including all the major labels and music companies) had signed *The Code of Fair Practice for Phonograph Records.*[666] Accordingly, AFTRA's homepage stated (2010),

> *The American Federation of Television and Radio Artists (AFTRA) is a national labor union representing over 70,000 performers, journalists and other artists working in the entertainment and news media. ...Representation covers broadcast, public and cable television (news, sports and weather; drama and comedy, soaps, talk and variety shows, documentaries, children's programming, reality and game shows); radio (news, commercials, hosted programs); sound recordings (CDs, singles, Broadway cast albums, audio*

---

[660] Baskerville, *Unions and Guilds*, Music Business Handbook and Career Guide (8th edition), 9, 182.

[661] AF of M, Who Join, "Subscription to International Musician." http://www.afm.org/why-join, (accessed July 15, 2013).

[662] Nikki Finke, Deadline Hollywood, "Sag/AFTRA Merger Approved," http://www.deadline.com/2012/03/sag-aftra-merger-approved-screen-actors-guild-american-federation-television-radio-arts/, (accessed July 15, 2013).

[663] SAG-AFTRA, "History," http://www.sagaftra.org/history, (accessed July 15, 2013).

[664] AFTRA, "History: The People who Entertain and Inform America have been Moving Forward for 70 Years," AFTRA, http://www.aftra.org/history.htm, (accessed March 22, 2011).

[665] AFTRA, "About AFTRA." AFTRA, http://www.aftra.org/aboutaftra.htm, (accessed March 22, 2011).

[666] AFTRA, "Code at a Glance," AFTRA, http://www.aftra.org/documents/03_02_SoundRecordingsGlance.pdf, (accessed March 22, 2011).

> *books); "non-broadcast" and industrial material as well as Internet and digital programming.*[667]
>
> *…Membership includes an array of artists who bring pop, rock, country, classical, folk, jazz, comedy, Latin, hip hop, rap and R&B to the world. …Members perform in television and radio advertising, non-broadcast video, audio books and messaging, and provide their skills for developing technologies such as interactive games and Internet material.*[668]

The Screen Actors Guild had represented the superstars of Hollywood's film and television industry. According to the SAG-AFTRA website (2013) by merging together into one union they are:

> *...committed to organizing all work done under our jurisdictions; negotiating the best wages, working conditions, and health and pension benefits; preserving and expanding members' work opportunities; vigorously enforcing our contracts; and protecting members against unauthorized use of their work... (and as)... a proud member of the AFT-CIO, SAG-AFTRA partners with our fellow unions in the U.S. and internationally to seek the strongest protections for media artists throughout the world. We work with government at the international, federal, state, and local levels to expand protections for American media professional both at home and abroad.*[669]

To join SAG-AFTRA you need to become eligible. According to the SAG-AFTRA website (2013);

> *...A performer becomes eligible for SAG-AFTRA membership under one of the following two conditions: (1) Proof of SAG or AFTRA employment ... those who work in a position covered by a SAG-AFTRA collective bargaining agreement, provided that any person qualifying though work ... completed three days of work as a under a SAG-AFTRA collective bargaining agreement. (2) ...may join SAG-AFTRA if the applicant is a paid-up member of an affiliated performers union (ACTRA, AEA, AGMA or AGVA for a period of one year and has worked and been paid.*[670]

The SAG AFTRA (2013) website also states that:

> *...membership requires members to follow three basic rules including the Global Rule Number One and the No Contract/No Work Rule. And, ...never accept work during a Union strike."*[671]

Also according to SAG-AFTRA (2013), The Global Rule Number One is

> *...no member shall work as a performer or make an agreement to work as a performer for any producer who has not executed a basic minimum agreement with the guild which is in full force and effect."*[672]

Actors Equity Association

Actors Equity Association was formed in 1913 and currently represents almost 48,000 performers in national and international tours and theater productions.[673] It is also a member of the *Associated Actors and Artists of America*, an alliance of AFTRA (*American Federation of Television and Radio Artists*), AGMA (*American Guild of Musical Artists*), AGVA (*American Guild of Variety Artists*), SAG-AFTRA, (Screen Actors' Guild-American

---

667 AFTRA, "About AFTRA." AFTRA, http://www.aftra.org/aboutaftra.htm, (accessed March 22, 2011).

668 AFTRA, "About AFTRA." AFTRA, http://www.aftra.org/aboutaftra.htm, (accessed March 22, 2011).

669 SAG-AFTRA, "History," http://www.sagaftra.org/history, (accessed July 15, 2013).

670 SAG-AFTRA "Steps to Join." http://www.sagaftra.org/content/steps-join, (accessed July 15, 2013).

671 SAG-AFTRA "Join," http://www.sagaftra.org/join, (accessed July 15, 2013).

672 SAG-AFTRA "Global Rule One." http://www.sagaftra.org/production-center/globalruleone, (accessed July 15, 2013).

673 Actors' Equity, "About Equity," Actors' Equity, http://www.actorsequity.org/AboutEquity/aboutequityhome.asp, (accessed March 22, 2011).

Federation of Television and Recording Artists), and the *Italian Actors'* Union.[674] According to an Equity news release (May 14, 2010), they work together to "recognize, respect and support each others' efforts to organize and negotiate fair and equitable contracts."[675] Actors may join *Equity* whenever they are cast (employed) under an equity contract, which usually allows them to earn their "equity card." According to the Equity Handbook (2010) you have to have the card to work in:

> ... *"Broadway touring productions, stock theatre, resident theatre, business theatre, and ... many regional and local theatre such as ... Disney World, dinner theatre, western civic light opera, off Broadway, Chicago, San Francisco, and Hollywood area theatre."*[676]

There is also a "white contract" and a "pink contract."[677] According to an *Equity* article, *All about Contracts and Codes* (2010),

> *Equity contracts cover jobs in three categories: Principal, Chorus and Stage Manager. The Principal contract (sometimes referred to as a "white" contract) is used for all principal actors and most stage managers. The Chorus contract (sometimes referred to as the "pink" contract) is used for those actors who are primarily performing chorus work. Each individual employment contract is referenced to a specific rulebook and incorporates all of its terms.*[678]

Actors Equity also supports a series of "codes," which are not contracts. According to the About Equity Handbook (May 2010),

> *Theatrical codes are not standard Equity agreements. Most are "showcase-type" codes where professional services are rendered without pay, there is no obligation to remain in a production for any specific period of time, and none of the regular benefits of standard agreements exists. Theatrical showcase codes were developed at the specific requests of members and are designed primarily to provide a theatrical environment where members may hone their skills and "showcase" themselves in the hopes of securing future employment. Most showcase-type codes provide some limited protections, including Future Rights guarantees (also referred to as Subsidiary Rights) should the production move to a standard agreement.*[679]

I.A.T.S.E.

The International Alliance of Theatrical and Stage Employees or IATSE as it's called in the business, represents audio engineers, lighting technicians, set designers and builders, and stagehands for live shows.[680] A union house is a venue, studio, etc., that has signed an agreement with the performance unions (AFTRA, AF of M, etc.) to allow only union members to be employed during the creation of various entertainment productions. Most Broadway venues, sports complexes, and movies made in Hollywood, are considered union jobs made or

---

674 Actors' Equity, "About Equity," Actors' Equity, http://www.actorsequity.org/AboutEquity/aboutequityhome.asp, (accessed March 22, 2011).

675 Actors' Equity, "NewsMedia: How to Work or Not to Work," Actor's Equity, http://www.actorsequity.org/docs/about/aboutequity_WebMay2010.pdf, (accessed August 7, 2010).

676 Actors' Equity, "Contracts and Codes, (Agreements & Codes)," Actors' Equity, http://www.actorsequity.org/AboutEquity/contracts, (accessed August 7, 2010).

677 Actors' Equity, "Contracts and Codes, (Agreements & Codes)," Actors' Equity, http://www.actorsequity.org/AboutEquity/contracts, (accessed August 7, 2010).

678 Actors' Equity, "Contracts and Codes, (Agreements & Codes)," Actors' Equity, http://www.actorsequity.org/AboutEquity/contracts, (accessed August 7, 2010).

679 Actors' Equity, (Handbook-called About Equity), "About Equity," Actors' Equity, http://www.actorsequity.org/docs/about/aboutequity_booklet_06.pdf, (accessed March 22, 2011).

680 International Alliance of Theatrical Stage Employees, Moving Picture Technicians, Artists and Allied Crafts of the United States, Its Territories and Canada, (IATSE), "Welcome to IATSE," "http://www.iatse-intl.org/about/welcome.html, (accessed April 7, 2011).

performed in union houses.[681] Exceptions include the production facilities in right-to-work states that often allow for nonunion productions.

Industry Related Guilds

The American Guild of Variety Artists (AGVA) "is an AFL-CIO affiliated union that represents performing artists and stage managers for live performances (including singers, and dancers) in theme parks, skaters, circus performers, comedians, comics, cabaret and club artist, variety performers, and lecturers."[682] According to www.agvausa.com (2013):

> *AGVA is a branch of The Associated Actors and Artistes of America (commonly referred to as "The 4 A's"), which is the parent union to AGVA, as well as to other performer unions such as Actors' Equity Association (AEA), Screen Actors Guild (SAG), American Federation of Television and Radio Artists (AFTRA), American Guild of Musical Artists (AGMA), and Guild of Italian American Actors (GIAA, formerly Italian Actors Union, IAU). These are our sister unions,and we are all branches under the same parent union - "The 4 A's.*[683]

The American Guild of Musical Artists (AGMA) is also affiliated with the AFL-CIO as it represents the classic arts of live opera, dance, concert, and production staff.[684] According to AGMA.org (2013):

> *...Performing artists live to perform. But their talents, their skill and the beauty they create won't necessarily pay the rent, put food on the table or guarantee the necessities of life. Without forceful advocacy and defense of their rights, artists may be vulnerable to exploitation or illegal discrimination. They need protection. They can find it by joining AGMA, the American Guild of Musical Artists.*[685]

Arts Administration

There are artist managers and then management of the "arts." *Arts Administration* has grown over the last 50 years to become an important and vital part of the entertainment and music industry. Arts Administration is the business of managing the classic arts such as musical theater, opera, orchestras, Broadway and off Broadway productions, dance, ballet, museums, and other forms of "serious" artistic expression. Classic arts are defined by many different types of art and various genre of musical expression. Accordingly, each may have it's own union, guild, or government representation. Most operate as non-profit organizations surviving on their membership and donations from major national and local corporate citizens. Few musicians have the talent to perform in both the popular culture world of rock, hip hop, etc., recordings and performances and the serious world of classic music and opera.

Sadly few consumers financially support (or emotionally need) both; thus the money is in the popular culture side while the very talented performers are often in the "non-profit" serious music performance occupation of opera and classical music. The popular culture of rock, etc., is not expense to produce compared to the massive performance groups required to provide live symphony orchestra performances of the classics. With

---

[681] International Alliance of Theatrical Stage Employees, Moving Picture Technicians, Artists and Allied Crafts of the United States, Its Territories and Canada, (IATSE), "Welcome to IATSE," "http://www.iatse-intl.org/about/welcome.html, (accessed April 7, 2011).

[682] The American Guild of Variety Artists, "About AGVA," http://www.agvausa.com/aboutagva.html, (accessed July 29, 2013).

[683] The American Guild of Variety Artists, "About AGVA," http://www.agvausa.com/aboutagva.html, (accessed July 29, 2013).

[684] The American Guild of Musical Artists, "Auditions," http://www.musicalartists.org/index.html, (July 29, 2013).

[685] The American Guild of Musical Artists, "Auditions," http://www.musicalartists.org/index.html, (July 29, 2013).

the advancement in computer software, live orchestra and opera performances should be cherished. They are expensive, yet vital to humanity compare to a computer generated sound produced at random by a creative operator. Both are important to our human expression, yet a real performance by live, talented performers is a treasure to humanity.

Interest in the serious arts appears to be circular as what started as private performances in honor of a King or Royal Family became more popular to private citizens. World war two caused the development of arts management in England. Chong (2012) states;

> *...the creation of the Arts Council of Great Britain (ACGB) ...was incorporated in 1946 as an outgrowth of the Committee for the Encouragement of Music and the Arts, which formed in 1939 as a wartime program to bolster moral. Prominent features of the ACGB, included an arm's length relationship with government and peer review as a method of adjudication of r awarding funds, served as a model for arts councils that emerged in other industrialized Commonwealth countries...and the USA. ...The ACGV played a leading role in initiating arts management courses and encouraging greater business involvement in the arts.*[686]

Arts management as a profession expended in the United States due to the increased popularity of classical arts performances in the 1960s. According to Baskerville (2006):

> *The quarter century from the early 1960s to the mid-1980 saw an unprecedented growth in the arts in America. The number of professional symphony orchestras and opera or music theater companies nearly doubled in the 1960s, and in the 15 years preceding 1985, ballet and modern dance companies burgeoned from 30 to more than 150. In those 15 years, there was also a dramatic increase in arts performances, employment of artist, and arts administrators and attendance at art events. ...But that encouraging picture was changing by the end of the 1980s ...as a number of orchestras experienced severe financial problems, some to the point of canceling seasons or declaring bankruptcy. ...caused in part by government and foundation cutbacks and a new toughness in contract negotiations between orchestra musicians and management.*[687]

Marketing to the middle class and the graying population with money and morphing some of their presentation to a more contemporary theme has increased popularity of the classical arts. Some use direct mail marketing tools, while others brought in pop artists to perform with the orchestra. Today, arts management is about marketing with social media and corporate contacts as much as it is about managing financial accounts and union contracts. The following are important representative union and guilds who work with arts management personal to increase the success of the classical arts.

League of American Orchestras

The League of American is a non-profit organization that provides strong support for youth orchestras and music education. According to it's website americanorchestras.org (2013):

> *...The League of American Orchestras leads, supports, and champions America's orchestras and the vitality of the music they perform. Its diverse membership of more than 800 orchestras across North America runs the gamut from world-renowned symphonies to community groups, from summer festivals to student and youth ensembles. The only national organization dedicated solely to the orchestral experience, the League is a nexus of knowledge and innovation, advocacy, and leadership advancement for managers, musicians, volunteers, and boards. Its conferences and events, award-winning Symphony magazine, website, and other publications inform music lovers around the world about orchestral activity and developments. Founded in 1942 and chartered by Congress in 1962, the League links a national network of thousands of instrumentalists, conductors, managers and administrators, board members, volunteers, and business partners.*[688]

---

686 Derrick Chang, Arts Managment (2nd Edition), "Foundation of Arts Managment" 1, 22.

687 David Baskerville, Music Career Handbook and Career Guide, (8th edition), "Arts Administration," 13, 264.

688 League of American Orchestras "About the League," http://www.americanorchestras.org/about-the-league.html, (accessed July 30, 2013).

American Guild of Organists

Professional organist, choir directors, teachers technicians and others are organized under the AGO membership. According to AGOhq.org (2013):

> *...The mission of the American Guid of Organists is to enrick lives othrough organ and choral music. To achieve this, we:*
>
> - *Encourage excellence in the performance of organ and choral music;*
> - *Inspire, educate, and offer certification for organists and choral conductors;*
> - *Provide networking, fellowship, and mutual support;*
> - *Nurture future generations of organists;*
> - *Promote the organ in its historic and evolving roles; and*
> - *Engage wider audiences with organ and choral music.*[689]

American Composers Alliance

ACA is a special alliance of composers and performers and offers it members publishing and affiliation with the performance rights organization Broadcast Music Inc. (BMI). According to the website composers.com;

> *ACA is a non-profit, alternative American concert music publisher in New York City (BMI affiliated). With a history dating to 1937, ACA distributes printed and electronic scores for orchestras, performing artists, chamber ensembles, libraries and other users of sheet music, as well as licenses its works for academic and commercial uses. The ACA catalog of music is one of the most interesting and diverse collections of American music in the world and includes compositions from the early 1900s to the present day by such composers as Robert Evett, Miriam Gideon, Robert Helps, Otto Luening, Daniel Pinkham, Dane Rudhyar, Halsey Stevens, Joan Tower, Vladimir Ussachevsky, and many others.*[690]

National Music Council

According to musiccouncil.org (2013) the National Music Council is an umbrella arts organization ..."formed in 1940 and chartered by Congress to represent the United States to the International Music Council/ UNESCO" (Part of the United Nations) and "...to act as a clearing house for the opinions and decision of its members who are dedicated to strengthening the importance of music in our life and culture."[691] The website (2013) also states their mission as:

> *Through the cooperative work of its member organizations, the National Music Council promotes and supports music and music education as an integral part of the curricula in the schools of our nation, and in the lives of its citizens. ...The Council provides for the exchange of information and coordination of efforts between its member organizations and speaks with one voice for the music community whenever an authoritative expression of opinion is desirable.*

National Endowment for the Arts

The National Endowment for the Arts is our governments way of supporting artistic expressions. Nea.gov (2013) states:

> *The National Endowment for the Arts was established by Congress in 1965 as an independent agency of the federal government. To date, the NEA has awarded more than $4 billion to support artistic excellence, creativity, and innovation for the benefit of*

---

689 American Guild of Organists, About, "AGO Mission Statement," http://www.agohq.org/about/index.html, (accessed July 30, 2013).

690 American Composers Alliance http://composers.com, (accessed july 30, 2013).

691 National Music Council, "Welcome," http://www.musiccouncil.org/home-page/, (accessed July 30, 2013).

individuals and communities. The NEA extends its work through partnerships with state arts agencies, local leaders, other federal agencies, and the philanthropic sector.[692]

The NEA offers grants to artists for the creation and display of their artistic expressions through a selection process judged by the National Council on the Arts, The nea.gov website (2013) claims

> *The National Foundation on the Arts and Humanities Act of 1965 established the National Endowment for the Arts and provided for 26 citizens to serve as advisors to the agency as members of the National Council on the Arts. Members are appointed by the President and approved by the Senate for six-year, staggered terms. Congress has since enacted legislation that reduced the membership of the Council. Currently, there are 18 members of the National Council on the Arts and an additional six members of Congress to serve in an ex officio,non-voting capacity for two-year terms. ...The Presidential appointments, by law, are selected for their widely recognized knowledge of the arts or their expertise or profound interest in the arts. They have records of distinguished service or achieved eminence in the arts and are appointed so as to represent equitably all geographical areas of the country. Congressional members are appointed in the following manner: two by the Speaker of the House, one by the Minority Leader of the House, two by the Majority Leader of the Senate, and one by the Minority Leader of the Senate.*

OPERA American

The National Opera American Center better know as OPERA American is a very cool "service" organization for opera company members. According to operaamerica.com (2013):

> *Founded in 1970, OPERA America has an international membership that includes nearly 150 Professional Company Members, 300 Associate and Business Members, 2,000 Individual Members and over 16,000 subscribers to its electronic news service. ...The association provides members with an array of publications and online resources, regional workshops, an annual conference and network-specific services such as conference calls, listservs and direct contact with staff with expertise in opera production, administration and education. OPERA America provides members with tools to maximize the effectiveness of financial and human resources, expand the scope of repertoire and programs, and extend their reach to new and diverse audiences.*[693]

The Association of Performing Arts Presenters

The APAP represents administrators, professionals, and educators in connection with the above organizations to resources and connections to the serious performance arts industry. Apap365,org states:

The Association of Performing Arts Presenters (APAP), based in Washington, D.C., is the national service and advocacy organization with more than 1,500 members worldwide, dedicated to developing and supporting a robust performing arts presenting field and the professionals who work within it. Our members represent the nation's leading performing arts centers, municipal and university performance facilities, nonprofit performing arts centers, culturally specific organizations, foreign governments, as well as artist agencies, managers, touring companies, and national consulting practices that serve the field, and a growing roster of self-presenting artists. As a leader in the field, APAP works to effect change through advocacy, professional development, resource sharing, and civic engagement. ...APAP is a non-profit 501(c)(3) organization, governed by a volunteer board of directors. In addition to presenting the annual APAP|NYC – the world's leading forum and marketplace for the performing arts – APAP continues to be the industry's leading resource, knowledge and networking destination for the advancement of performing arts presenting.[694]

Trends

Industry gross revenues are shifting from labels to tours, merchandise, and new media. The trends in the industry caused by P2P are moving away from traditional CD sales and toward digital downloads, clouds, and sadly, free or non-paid acquisition of recordings. Consumers often use the Internet instead of traditional radio airplay to discover new acts. However, this also gives artists (without radio station

---

[692] National Endowment for the Arts, "About Us/" http://www.nea.gov/about/index.html, (accessed July 30, 2013).

[693] National Opera American Center, "About," http://www.operaamerica.org/content/about/, (accessed July 30, 2013).

[694] Association of Performing Arts Presenters, About APAP, http://www.apap365.org/About/Pages/default.aspx, (accessed July 30, 2013).

airplay) exposure, and some are being discovered by younger generations. Thus, the curse of technology and P2P file sharing, which has caused the financial destruction of many traditional record labels, is also empowering talented new entrepreneurial artists and managers. Therefore, the combination of digital technology and consumer's failure to pay for entertainment products is causing the industry to invent new business models. Some of the trends include the following:

Music Companies are Replacing Record Labels.

As the shakeout from P2P file sharing has destroyed labels financial investments on most of their recording artists, labels have morphed into broader umbrella companies. Thus, traditional labels are reinventing themselves as "music companies" offering 180, 270, 360, and partnership deals to corner, control, and market new exciting acts through touring, merchandise, branding, and new media exposure.[695]

Superstars Artists are Creating Labels/Music Companies

As they are being dropped (due to unit sales under 100,000) or their current label or music company demand they sign a 360 multiple rights deal, artists are instead forming their own labels.[696] The artists are already famous, so it's easy for them to hire former label executives, record their own albums with Pro Tools or Logic Pro, establish a distribution deal with a mega conglomerate, stage or tie into touring, merchandise, and corporate sponsorships, and laugh all the way to the bank.

Business Moguls are Reinventing the Business System

As the industry returns to the 1950s business models of strong individual entrepreneurial businesspersons and women making and controlling their own career as well as their artists,' smart entrepreneurial artists are also becoming rich executives. Former artists such as *Shawn "Jay-Z" Carter, Sean "Diddy" Combs, Curtis "50 Cent" Jackson,*[697] and entrepreneurs such as *Simon Fuller*[698] and *Simon Cowell*[699] are making history by controlling almost every business aspect of their acts' careers and in some cases, the actual media production, distribution, and content.

Creative Moguls are Reinventing the Creative System

As the labels need to reduce their recording budgets to break-even financially producers are reinventing the recording process. By hiring one "super producer" who uses Pro Tools, Logic Pro, Midi, and music software to record, produce, and create all the musical tracks, sing backup, file the business plan, and control the recording budget, music companies save hundreds of thousands of dollars on each album project. Many of newer artists' albums including *Taylor Swift's*, are created in this fashion.[700] According to Taylor's producer Nathan Chapman (2011),

> *Taylor and I made the demos for the first album at my then studio, … with me playing all the instruments. …we took these demos*

---

[695] Private interviews with industry experts (2010-2011).

[696] Private interviews with industry insiders (2010-2011).

[697] Zack O' Malley Greenburg, "You Want to Be a Billionaire: How Bad," Forbes, March 28, 2011, 28.

[698] Simon Fuller, "Big Pay Day for American Idol's Simon Fuller,' American Idol, http://www.footnoted.com/my-big-fat-deal/big-payday-for-american-idols-simon-fuller/, (accessed April 7, 2011).

[699] Simon Cowell, "American Idol: Bio," American Idol, http://www.americanidol.com/bio/simon_cowell/, (accessed April 7, 2011).

[700] Personal interviews with industry insiders (2010-2011), & Nathan Chapman, "Insiders View" (Interviewed at Belmont University, by Harry Chapman, Nashville, TN, April 6, 2011).

> *into a few professional studios and tracked them there with a small band. …The second album was easier because we were coming off the momentum of the first album, and we simply continued the artistic track that we were on. …Taylor came to my studio and I played all the instruments on the demos, and because I have a good vocal booth, her demo vocals ended up being the vocals you hear on the record. After finishing the demos, we went out to different studios, and tried different combinations of engineers and musicians to replace some of the elements of my demos, mostly the programmed drums, and to do additional overdubs.*[701]

Tingen (2011) claims that

> *Chapman's contribution (on Taylor Swift's demos and albums) is equally impressive, given that he says that he's responsible for playing "probably 60 percent of the music on the album, including 90 percent of the guitars." He also turns out to be a very quick engineer and arranger, playing, arranging, and recording the demos for each song in just a few hours at his Pain In The Art Studio in Nashville. The demo for 'Mine' apparently took less than five hours to record, and sounded, according to Chapman, "almost identical to the record."*

Artist Branding

Branding is becoming as important to the labels or music company as their actual recordings. They know that the majority of the recordings in which they have invested money, creativity, promotion, and publicity (marketing campaigns) will not generate profits because too many consumers just steal the stuff over illegal sites and P2P. The 360 deals help labels or music companies reduce their financial risks by receiving some of the acts' profits from tours, merchandise, sponsorships, and endorsements. After all, without the labels' investment, the acts usually never get "heard" by potential consumers. The trend is to use the recordings to help the act get "discovered" by consumer so that both the act and the label or music company can "cash in" on the acts' emotional connections to the fans by selling them recordings (hopefully), concert tickets, clothing lines, soft drink endorsements, and other profit-generating events and products.

Consumers Discover New Acts Digitally

Instead of discovering new acts through traditional radio station airplay, many consumers download music free to see if they enjoy it. The use of social media and P2P has presented consumers with the ability to search for new and evolving acts that do not receive traditional radio station airplay. It's about time! There are many very talented acts that never got airplay and therefore never got discovered. At least now with digital technology, if a great song or recording is heard and consumers start to talk about it, there is a very good chance the act can (if they understand the business) make money.

New Acts are Using Technology

New acts create their own entrepreneurial business models by using every digital trick in the book. Bands are starting to questions if they really need a major record deal to become successful. Most wish they could get a major deal, yet many are not waiting for it to happen. Instead, bands and acts are using *Pro Tools* or *Logic Pro* to record themselves, internet sites such as *topspin.com* for promotion, *TuneCore.com* for distribution, *Vevo.com* for video streams, and *Bandcamp.com* for selling their music and merchandise directly to fans.

CDs are Disappearing Quickly

It is predicted that within 3 to 5 years all hard platform sales (except some niche items such as vinyl) will disappear from traditional brick-and-mortar stores.[702] Digital distribution is quicker, cheaper, and considered the wave of the future, as consumers have already stopped buying entertainment products. The big challenge is to get them to pay for it instead of stealing it though P2P. The solution may be cloud servers such as *iCloud,*

---

[701] Nathan Chapman, (in the article by Paul Tingen), "Secrets of the Mix Engineers: Nathan Chapman & Justin Niebank: Taylor Swift's Speak Now," Soundonsound.com, http://www.soundonsound.com/sos/feb11/articles/it-0211.htm, (accessed April 7, 2011).

[702] Private interview with industry sources (2011).

Spotify, Mog.com, and *Amazon.com* who store entertainment products and then supply them to you anytime, anyplace, for just a few pennies.

Festivals are becoming the Tour Circuit

Instead of amphitheaters, arenas, and venues many acts are bypassing the traditional venues and label deals to build their fan base through festival appearances. Many consumers view *festivals* as a better entertainment value than the major tours often staged in football or basketball arenas and amphitheaters. For about the same price as a two-hour superstar concert (including the price of the tickets and merchandise), festivals such as *Coachella, Bonnaroo, Lollapalooza, Austin City Limits,* and many others provide a week of entertainment from both major and lesser-known acts. Festivals provide consumers with a "bonding opportunity" with other like-minded music lovers and entrepreneurial business opportunities for venders. Additionally, Europe has always been a festival-based business. According to *Billboard.biz* (2008), "Festivals have long been the driving force of the summer live business in Europe, where no structured amphitheater network exists. During the summer in Europe, the festival is king."[703]

Future Business Model Opportunities

Technology is changing the way the entertainment industry conducts business. So, how might it be used to morph the traditional business models into new entertainment and music industry financial opportunities? It's all about the songs and the music, so the question becomes, "How can the industry grow more successful by using the tech tools of today?" Onlookers suggest the industry should consider the following (2010):[704]

- Make money not from selling CDs or digital downloads, but from all the other opportunities created when consumers "discover" new acts by P2P and hearing CDs and digital downloads.
- Work with technology, not against it. The cost of everything decreases when everyone in the industry uses digital technology to create recordings, network with consumers through social networks instead of traditional media, and operate their actual businesses virtually.
- Support touring for independent, local, and regional acts and fewer national acts. The Rolling Stones are old enough to be grandparents, and it is very cool they are still rocking the planet. Yet, the future is in the new, local, independent, and regional acts that need established industry experts, management, production, financial support, distribution, promotion, and publicity to develop into a national talent.
- Labels/music companies should be consultants and more subservient to the artists and their businesses, and acts should be more realistic and respectful of the distribution, promotion, and publicity power major labels and music companies quickly supply to their careers.
- Acts need to be "heard and seen" before anyone knows if consumers will spend any money on them. Labels/music companies provide the best opportunity for the acts to reach consumers and should therefore be considered as valuable partners in business.
- Labels/music companies should consider dropping recoupment deals with artists who contribute venture capital by restructuring "the deal" as a true partnership, by combining debt payoff first and splits of profits thereafter.
- Music companies should be the vital umbrella company for the act, bundling all goods and services in a partnership to pay off debt in exchange for a percentage of the profits.

---

[703] Billboard, "The Summer Preview," (Billboard Magazine, May 17, 2008), 42.

[704] Private interviews with industry insiders (2010-2011) and students in the fall MBU 4015 class at Belmont University (2010).

- Acts should forget the "artistic ego" and approach their creativity as a marketable product that may generate a profit depending on how well they expand the rules of traditional business models into entrepreneurial opportunities using digital recording and media technology.
- Radio airplay is too expensive and probably does not work well in breaking new acts. Labels/music companies and artists should take advantage of new media and other inexpensive marketing tools, such as blogs, to further exposure and careers. Some examples include a surprise appearance on Conan, self-mixing contests, fan involvement and investments, ISP addresses on Google and Apple, and videophone and video and audio Internet feeds of small local concerts.
- Make concerts an interactive virtual reality event for specific fan club members who can request songs while watching the concert on their computer, cell phone, iPad, etc.

Your Niche

To be successful in the digital world, sometimes it is wise to focus on dominating a niche (a specific type of consumer demand or preference). How much money can be made from a product (a film or album)? How much *additional money* can be made from merchandise sales such as toys in stores or products sold at concerts? In the music business, the total amount of money that may be generated is negotiated as part of a *360 deal* (which includes not only album, gross and net, but also merchandise, touring income, and other possible revenues).

Controlling Your Destiny

Take control of your own creativity by embracing business knowledge and digital technologies. Take a look at *Madonna* or even *Lady Gaga,* and you'll start to realize they are laughing all the way to the bank. Even *The Rolling Stones*, who are old enough to be your grandparents, are rolling in millions annually. Also, realize "great" and "talented" are defined two ways in the business. One way is the creative definition of quality, and the second is the amount of money made. Turn on the radio, and you'll realize that some acts signed to deals can barely sing. Still, a great act and recording (plus a great song) that consumers love will usually become successful. The problem is getting it recorded right (magic in the production) and the marketing, promotion, and publicity required (it costs money) to get the song "heard" by potential consumers.

The solution is digital technology, as it is providing start up acts with an opportunity to *launch their talent as a business.* Using computer programs to record your act, the Internet and social media to build a fan base and to network, and many available marketing sites, you can now build your own careers, bypassing the traditional labels and industry touring companies. According to a recent article by Panay (2011),

> *… The music business is not so much imploding as — like any other industry that has been around for more than a dozen years — it is evolving. Consumer tastes are changing, and record labels and radio are no longer the cultural arbitrators they once were. Music listeners are moving away from the mass-produced music consumption habits of the broadcast media to the more tailored and personalized experiences of the social media age. Just as importantly, artists are migrating away from the mass-market revenue model of the broadcast era to the mass of niches model of the new, Internet era. …Perhaps what's been most amazing has been the way that the music performer community has adjusted to all of these changes both by seizing opportunities that did not exist a few years ago as well as by adapting to the new landscape of the industry — and by adopting and co-opting revenue generating ideas from other industries and applying them to their trade. Far from dying, the music business is alive and ever resourceful in finding new ways of making money and evolving. …Last year (2010) nearly 80,000 gigs were booked between artists and promoters that would traditionally fall "under the radar." (Internal estimates put the total number of U.S. live gigs at close to 8 million). …This includes bars, coffee houses, art galleries, cruise ships, wineries, amusement parks, breweries, restaurants, cinema lobbies, ski resorts, corporate retreats, museums, colleges, street fairs, and countless others. It's a nearly $10 billion market that's expanding at a rate of 11% a*

year.[705]

Step One: Think like a Beatle

Artists are responsible for their own success. If you're hanging around waiting to be discovered, forget it! Instead think like a *Beatle*! According to Richard Courtney and George Cassidy in their book *Come Together: The Business Wisdom of the Beatles* (2011),

> *If you wish to achieve Beatle-level success in your field, you must first learn to think like a Beatle. Because the Beatles were no accident. They wanted to be big. Bigger than Elvis. Bigger than anyone who went before or came after. …If you truly think like a Beatle, take heart. You are in a very small minority. Few aspire to greatness even fewer to be the greatest. Most around you are comfortable with mediocrity. Others may achieve success, even set records and receive awards with their performances. Many others want to be big enough to receive a regular paycheck. You however, will not be satisfied until you have taken a shot at the top.*[706]

Step Two: Have a Vision

What is it going to take to become successful? Fans! You've got to create a local buzz or (a better way of saying it) a solid fan base through live performances, radio (if possible), Internet hits, record and digital download sales. Millions of artists *can't* give away their recordings on social websites because very few know they exist, and the consumers who have found them are not usually interested in what they see or hear. There's no emotional connection! So you've got to perform and find out what works for the *consumers*! Success really is based on how well consumers dig, feel, love, dance to, etc. your recordings, performances, or whatever. Have a clear vision of *who you are* and *what you represent* emotionally through your music, image, and persona. Hear it in you head, find others *who get it, share it, and can play it*, and create the magic (music) that lets consumers find joy in their life by enjoying it anywhere and everywhere. Richard Courtney and George Cassidy (2011) say,

> *Begin. And be strong. To enjoy the success you seek, you must have the courage and fortitude to beat a different path from that of anyone you know. …Somewhere deep down Lennon knew he would form … a band. Lennon began his musical career playing a cheap guitar tuned like a banjo. Paul McCartney first learned music on a trumpet before switching to guitar. George Harrison worked his way though guitar manuals. Ringo Starr, taught himself to play on a drum kit his mother purchased for him.*[707]

Step Three: Work like a Dog

Consumers have to see and hear you before they can decide if they like you. Therefore, if you want to be a singer, band, or some other type of artist, you have to take a deep breath, cut tracks, play live, write songs, play, perform, believe in yourself, and thrive on rejection. Very cheesy, I know, but true, so go for it. Occasionally, artists are discovered locally or on the Internet because someone likes what they see or hear – and guess what! They start talking about it. The buzz begins. However, to stand out from all the other millions of acts that post their average recordings on social networks, you've got to become great and that usually takes talent and thousands of hours of practice and work. Courtney and Cassidy (2011) tell us what the *Beatles* did:

> *In 1960, the group, …were booked to play in Hamburg, Germany. Once there, they played eight hours a day, seven days a week – sets at 3pm, 11pm, 2am, and 4am. Playing in a sleazy club located in the red-light district of a town filled with prostitutes, strippers, and drunken sailors, the Beatles learned to Beatle. They learned to Mach Shau, German for make show. They learned to*

---

705 Panos Panay, "Rethinking Music: The Future of Making Money as a Performing Musicians," The Berkman Center for Internet & Society at Harvard University, Harvard University, http://cyber.law.harvard.edu/publications/2011/Rethinking_Music, (accessed May 2, 2011).

706 Richard Courtney & George Cassidy, *Come Together: The Business Wisdom of The Beatles*, (New York, NY: Turner Publishing, 2011) 3-4.

707 Richard Courtney & George Cassidy, *Come Together: The Business Wisdom of The Beatles*, (New York, NY: Turner Publishing, 2011) 8-22.

> *and performed reams of material under duress, on-the-job. ...They underwent a remarkable transformation, returning from a total of two trips to Hamburg with a distinctive style that would soon earn them a spot as one of the top two or three bands in Liverpool. ... Work a hard day's night. Work like a dog. Eight days a week, if possible. It's the only want to find out if you have the appetite for success. And you'll find out if the world has an appetite for you.*[708]

Step Four: Become a Business/Entrepreneur

If you're in a band, start a business by creating your own label using computer software. Record a demo, give it to the local college radio station; hope perspective fans steal it online (a sign they might like it and start talking about the band); put it on sale at the local record shop (if you can find one), and play many live shows to get famous locally. Play showcases; link to websites. If you've got a business mind, educate yourself, learn how the business works, and network to meet the key successful current industry insiders. The fact is that the music and entertainment industry is a wonderful business and can be a great life. Build a fan base; every fan means more money in your pocket. If you get really successful locally, exploit yourself through digital technology and the new media. Then the major labels and music companies, managers, producers and concert promoters will usually find you! Don't chase the money; let the money (industry) chase you!

Step Five: Surround Yourself with Experts

If you've got a buzz going, then it's time to consider forming a team of experts who can help you reach the next level. Passman, in his book *All You Need to Know About the Music Business* (2009), states that

> *The way you pick your professional team will either set up you career and finances for life, or assure you a place on the next Electric Prunes tour. So be very careful and pay attention personally to the process of assembling them... If you pick the right people, you can set your life on automatic pilot and just check up on it periodically. If you pick the wrong people and set it on automatic pilot you'll smash into a mountain before you know what happened.*[709]

Surround yourself with people who can really help. Passman (2009) claims your team should include a "personal manager, business manager, booking agent, and attorney."[710] However, none of them will be interested in you as a client until you've shown potential to become a successful artist. Personal managers and booking agents usually make a percentage of what the artist earns, and business managers are expensive to hire. Attorneys will take your money anytime, and yet finding one who knows the business and has industry contacts is very difficult. So be careful. Sadly, there is blood in the water and many sharks posing as successful industry executives who will promise the world. You need to avoid the sharks, and educate yourself about what it takes to make it in the business.

Most people do not know it, but there are reference directories available from solid industry sources. They are expensive, yet worth the money. *Billboard* magazine is considered the "bible" of the business. Created in 1894, it helps the creative and business people in the entertainment industry connect. In the weekly magazine, *Billboard* reports charts, concerts, airplay, recording figures, touring sales, and other related business news. In their source directories, they have the actual email addresses, phone numbers, and other contact information of most of the industry's managers, labels, and promoters. *Pollstar* magazine and *Pollstar.com* cover the touring world and have excellent related directories. *Variety* magazine and *variety.com* report the film and TV production business in a similar manner.

---

[708] Richard Courtney & George Cassidy, *Come Together: The Business Wisdom of The Beatles*, (New York, NY: Turner Publishing, 2011) 8-22.

[709] Donald Passman, *All you need to know about the music business*, 7th ed. (New York, NY: Free Press, 2009),

[710] Donald Passman, *All you need to know about the music business*, 7th ed. (New York, NY: Free Press, 2009),

Step Six: Learn Shameless Self-Promotion

Build your tribe through the fans' emotional connection to your recordings, songs, performances, and image. *Shameless self-promotion* is telling your story (who you are, tied to your image) in the press, on local TV, at concerts, on your website, and by talking to fans after the concerts, one fan at a time. Use *YouTube, Twitter,* and every technology you can think of to expose your creativity to potential fans. Build the connection between yourself as an artist and the emotions fans have for you. It's what's in their heads and hearts (the emotional connection) that make you financially successful as an artist. Post videos of your shows (legally, of course), work and play at every opportunity, small to large, to give others an opportunity to "discover" you. Then, *monetize it* by selling recordings, concert tickets, merchandise, and by seeking corporate sponsorships.

Step Seven: Arrive!

Plug into the established industry! Now, if you've got a proven track record, fan base, and the potential to become a cash machine, you'll probably need to alert the industry professionals at labels and management companies. Honestly, they probably already know about you if you've been successful at building your fan base. Send them a one page "pitch memo" email requesting a short meeting. Explain the purpose of the meeting by detailing your accomplishments (number of units sold, concerts, the number of web hits and song downloads (paid for or stolen), and the size of your fan base or club) as an indication of how successfully you've connected with consumers. Provide links to your recordings, photos, videos, and your website. Request a meeting!

Step Eight: Thrive on Rejection

Of course, you'll get many rejections. Turn failure into success. According to Richard Courtney and George Cassidy in their book *Come Together: The Business Wisdom of the Beatles* (2011), even the Beatles had to deal with failure and rejections:

> *Brian Epstein, secure in his role as manager, dedicated his life to the pursuit of a recording contract for "the boys"... His efforts were rewarded when Dick Rowe at Decca Records agreed to an audition for the Beatles. The Beatles were excited. This was it! They had made it. They knew they were good... not great. Once Decca heard their sound, they'd flip. But it turned out, Rowe rejected them believing (as he famously told Epstein) that guitar groups were somewhat old hat. ...The Beatles felt their years of work, playing in the worst and the best of venues, all the cleaning up, the new clothes, and everything else-all flushed down the toilet. They were devastated. Brian felt as if he had failed them. ...Brian went straight to working the phones. The lads went back to the Cavern to work even harder. John and Paul decided they would write better songs. Six months later, they would have their record contract.*[711]

Don't give up! Nowadays, you'll also be able to use technology (from computer software for recordings, distribution, promotion, and publicity to selling your stuff online) to make a living without plugging into the established business systems. Therefore, if you're wise, educated, and talented enough, you'll have to opportunity to choose between doing it all yourself or plugging into the established business systems. You can be a financial success or failure either way, based on your knowledge of this business and whom you decide to put on your team. There are schools that teach the industry, books you can read (besides this one), and people who can really help you, and that adds up to a great life creating music.

Blogs

There are many blogs and Internet related sources you can use to "catch up" on daily industry news, events, and opinions. *The Dean's List* (J Fred Knobloch jfred@comcast.net) is quickly becoming one of the best

---

[711] Richard Courtney & George Cassidy, *Come Together: The Business Wisdom of The Beatles*, (New York, NY: Turner Publishing, 2011) 15-16.

places to find stories, thoughts, and opinions posted daily. In addition, review *Billboard.com, Billboard.biz, Pollstar.com,* and *Variety.com* for other related information.

20

Action Pack Learn the Language

If you want to be in the music business, then you need to listen to what's being played on the radio and television to see what you're going to be competing against. Surviving in the music business demands a new terminology. These are the words used by all the entities that will help you sound professional and experienced.

Common Terms [712 & 713]

2-D barcode is one that a scanner reads both horizontally and vertically. A 2-D barcode is generated when an applicant completes Form, CO on the Office's website. The 2-D barcode is unique for each work registered. It contains information that the applicant has entered on the blank form, but in encrypted format.

A & B Schedules are terms found on the forms sent to AFTRA by record labels, detailing the total scale payments made to label recording artists (designated as "A" vocalists/artists) and to non-royalty artists (designated as "B" vocalists/artists).

A collective work is a work, such as a periodical issue, anthology, or encyclopedia, in which a number of contributions (which are separate and independent by themselves) have been assembled into a new collective work.

A compilation is a work formed by the collection and assembling of preexisting materials or of data that are selected, coordinated, or arranged in such a way that the resulting work as a whole constitutes an original work of authorship. Compilations include collective works.

A derivative work is a work based upon one or more preexisting works, such as a translation, musical arrangement, dramatization, fictionalization, motion picture version, sound recording, art reproduction, abridgment, condensation, or any other form in which a work may be recast, transformed, or adapted. A work consisting of editorial revision, annotations, elaboration, or other modifications, which, as a whole, represent an original work of authorship, is a derivative work.

---

712 Library of Congress, "Definitions," http://www.copyright, (July 12, 2010).

713 Library of Congress, "Definitions," http://www.copyright, (July 12, 2010).

A digital transmission is a transmission, in whole or in part, in a digital or other non-analog format.

To display a work means to show a copy of it either directly or by means of a film, slide, television image, or any other device or process, or in the case of motion picture or other audiovisual work, to show individual images non-sequentially.

A food service or drinking establishment is a restaurant, inn, bar, tavern, or any other similar place of business, in which the public or patrons assemble for the primary purpose of being served food or drink, in which the majority of the gross square feet of space, that is nonresidential is used for that purpose.

A performing rights society is an association, corporation, or other entity that licenses the public performance of non-dramatic musical works on behalf of copyright owners of such works. The three American PROs are the American Society of Composers, Authors and Publishers (ASCAP), Broadcast Music, Inc. (BMI), and SESAC, Inc.

A transfer of copyright ownership is an assignment, mortgage, exclusive license, or any other legal conveyance, of a copyright or any of the exclusive rights comprised in a copyright, whether or not it is limited in time or place of effect, not including a non-exclusive license.[714]

Accounting statements are provided by music publisher's quarterly or semiannually. The accounting statement that lists the money the publisher paid the songwriter in advance, plus chargeable expenses against the money credited or due to the songwriter from the royalties.

Acoustics can make or break the quality of a recording. All the talents of the recording artists, studio musicians, audio engineer, and producer are only as good as the studio's acoustics. Poor acoustics can destroy the best creative efforts of world-class musicians. Floating walls, ceilings, and floors are used to isolate sound from room to room in a performance studio and control room. Grooves are cut in the floors, walls are mounted on rubber tubes, and ceilings are often spring-loaded. Windows between the performance studios and control room are made of thick, double-pane glass with 5.5 inches of air space between each panel. Soundproof doors complete the package.

Advances are technically all monies advanced for the recordings, marketing, promotion, and publicity of an artist. However, actual money is often provided at the time an artist signs a contract to help the artist with living expenses for a short period of time (usually during recording sessions). The financial advances are 50-100% recoupable paid out of the artist's royalties (based on each unit sold) to pay the total debt to the label before the artist is paid for units sold.

Administrative rights determine who controls the potential revenue-generating assets of a song. Administrative rights include the right to assign or transfer the copyright at any time, the right to control licensing and the right to collect royalties for the use of the song.

Ambiance is the "feel" or "sound" of a room that is created by its mixture of hard and soft walls, floors, ceiling, etc.

Amps or Amplifiers increase the loudness of a sound wave or the amplitude (volume) of an electronic signal. Examples include guitar amps, monitor speakers, and operational amps inside the console.

Amplitude is "how loud" a sound wave is and is measured in decibels (dBs).

Analog Tape Machines record both the amplitude (loudness) and frequency (number of vibrations) of the electronic signal sent by the mics to the tape recorder through the console.

---

[714] Library of Congress, "Definitions," http://www.copyright, (July 12, 2010).

Application forms refer to those provided by The Office for use in applying for registration of a claim to copyright. Registration makes a public record of the basic facts of a particular copyright.

Artist accounts or in-house accounts are set up in the artist's name by the record label to fund all approved projects including recordings, advances, and tour support that are recoupable at 100%. The marketing, promotion, and publicity is recoupable at 50%; however, most labels run them through tour support so that all expenses will become 100% recoupable. *Audiovisual works* consist of a series of related images (pictures, etc.), which are intrinsically viewed, or shown by machines or devices, such as projectors, viewers, or electronics equipment, together with accompanying sounds. Mediums include films or tapes in which the works themselves are embodied.

Assignment means the appointment of the manager to represent an artist. Also, the assignment of the exclusive rights and copyright to a music publisher in a single songwriter deal.

Audits are something labels hate, but they are a reality of doing business with creative artists. Labels usually grant the artist's accountant the right to audit the books (account of the artist only) to determine if the label has failed to pay any royalties received through record sales and publishing agreements. Because money is coming into the label at different times from different sources it is not unusual to find some royalties that need to be paid. A 30- to 60-day notice in writing is usually required before the accountant may examine the books. Audits are often allowed only once a year.

Authority artists often turn all authority for performing, interviews, etc., over to the manager who will determine which offer is in the best long-term interest of the artist. This also means that the artist may not accept movies, concert opportunities, or record deals without the advice of the manager.

Authorship refers to "who wrote or owns" the song. If the songwriter is a work-for-hire employee, then the publisher is usually considered the "author" of a song. If the songwriter is an independent contractor, staff writer, or owns a publishing company (as in co-or sub-publishing), then he/she is usually considered the author of a song. A work-for-hire songwriter may also retain authorship and ownership if he/she has a signed agreement stating that the authorship and ownership will remain with the original songwriter(s).

Automated Consoles are included in the standard recording technology today. Some of the older boards were computer-assisted, using VCAs (Voltage Control Amplifiers) to scan the settings on the console and record their positions onto one of the tape machine tracks or a computer hard disk. Most of these functions are now part of Pro Tools and Logic Pro software.

Berne Convention is an international treaty, the "Convention for the Protection of Literary and Artistic Works, signed at Berne, Switzerland, on September 9, 1886, and all acts, protocols, and revisions thereto." The United States acceded to the Berne Convention effective March 1, 1989.

Best efforts is used here in the context of the Publisher agreeing to use their best efforts to exploit the copyright to all forms of music users in the music and entertainment industry including artists, labels, film and television production companies, advertisement agencies, digital media, mass media, and other companies that use music in their forms of business.

Bidirectional Pickup Patterns allow sound waves from the front and back of the mic and cancel out sound waves on the sides of the mic.

Bonuses are negotiated non-recoupable monies paid to songwriters (and often recording artists and producers) for albums that reach various sales levels, usually gold (500,000 units), platinum (1,000,000 units), or multi-platinum.

Break-even point is the point in financial statements where the income (monies gained) from the event (concert, recording contract, etc.) equals the cost or total expenses for the event (or cost of recording, promotion, marketing, etc., of the recording).

Cardioid Pickup Patterns cancel the sound from the sides and rear of the mics. They sense sound waves that are only directly in front of the mic. Most mics in the recording studio use cardioid pickup patterns to avoid instruments' music from leaking into other instruments' mics.

Cartage is an extra payment (paid by the session producer) for musicians (or a private company) to haul instruments and amplifiers to and from the recording sessions. Insurance coverage is provided on harp, timpani, string bass, accordion, tuba, drums, baritone saxophone, bass saxophone, cello, contra bassoon, contra bass, and the clarinet.

Catalog is a collection of the songs (copyrights) and recordings (usually demos) a music publisher owns and controls.

Certificate of registration is an official paper denoting that a particular copyright has been registered with the Copyright Office. Provided the claim is registered within 5 years of the date on which the work is first published, the facts on a certificate of registration and the validity of the copyright are accepted by courts of law as self-evident unless later shown to be false.

Certificate of Recordation is the official filing in the Copyright Office of a document having to do with copyright, such as a transfer of ownership or a grant of a security interest. The purpose of recordation is to make a public record of the facts in the document. The document must bear the actual signature of the person who executed it, or it must be accompanied by a sworn or official certification that it is a true copy of the original signed document.

Circulars are informational brochures published by the Copyright Office for distribution to the public. Each circular deals with an aspect of the copyright law, e.g. duration of copyright, copyright registration of musical compositions, and copyright notice.

Copies are material objects other than phonorecords, in which a work is fixed by any method now known or later developed, and from which the work can be perceived, reproduced, or otherwise communicated, either directly or with the aid of a machine or device.

Collaboration happens when two or more people work together to create a song, recording, etc. It is suggested that all the specific items of the agreement be in writing, including exceptions of the traditional royalty splits, permission to change each other's lyrics, and a listing of who will pay demo recording, legal, and promotion expenses. However, once the working arrangement is decided, a written agreement concerning the actual copyright is not required. The Copyright Law calls the songs written by more than one individual a "joint work."

Commission Base **is** the negotiated artist's revenue sources that will earn the manager a commission.

Commission Rate is the percentage of the commission base that is paid to the manager for his or her service.

Commitment Album is the only album that the label is committed to financing. Labels may offer a seven-year, seven-album deal, but they only have to pay for the recording, marketing, and promotion of the first album during the initial period (usually one year), and then each additional album *if* they pick up the corresponding option (usually based on album sales figures from the previously released recording).

Comp Ticket or complementary ticket to a concert is often provided to radio stations and local important music insiders to promote an event. The number of tickets is usually supplied by the promoter and approved by the artist's manager.

Compensation – the manager's percentage of income should be stated in the contract. The percentage often ranges from 15-20% of all money resulting from all direct and indirect artist's activities in the entertainment industry to very specific percentages based on defined revenue sources.

Compression is used to reduce the amplitude (amount of volume) of a signal to record a proper signal on the tape track. Compression is also used to change the quality of the sound of an instrument or vocalist. Most consoles have four compression ratios, various attack times, and release from compression times. It is often used to "fatten up" the sound of a kick drum or bass guitar.

Computers are now used to store recorded signals as often as tape machines. Software with virtual reality consoles, tape machines, 64/128 digital tracks, and special effects allows master-session-quality recordings into your home as well as the best professional recording studios.

Compressors are outboard equipment used to reduce the amplitude (loudness) of a signal. They allow the audio engineer to record the proper amount of signal and to also change the quality of the sound. They are often used on bass guitars and kick drums to make them sound "punchier" and on singers to help the engineer "catch" increases in amplitude.

Condenser Mics have two plates that hold a static electronic charge: one is a permanent plate, and the other is a moveable plate. Sound waves vibrate the moveable plate, changing the distance between the two plates, which generates the electrical output of the mic. Condenser mics need batteries or phantom power supplied from the console.

Consoles or "boards," act as electronic traffic lights, dividing and directing the microphone and electrical instrument signals to various destinations.

Contingency Scale Payments are made to AFTRA non-royalty artist members (who recorded the album). These payments are 50% of original scale, are made by record labels after the album unit sales have reached levels of 157,000.[715]

Contractors are in charge of union members and are required by those unions to be hired. AFTRA requires for one of the singers to be designated as the contractor when more than three singers are hired, and that this contractor is paid an additional 50%. The AF of M requires a contractor to be paid double scale to the leader when more than 12 musicians are called for a session.

Control Room Speakers (Monitors) are used in the control room to convert microphone signals back into sound waves. To insure the speakers and control room acoustics are providing a correct sound (flat frequency response), room equalizers are used to compensate for the "hype of the sound" created by the speakers and control room acoustics. "Hype of the sound" refers to the change in the sound of the monitors caused by the acoustics of the control room. Reflective sound from the acoustics can phase add, causing the speakers to sound as if they are reproducing more bass or treble.

---

[715] AFTRA, "Record Rates 2007-2010," AFTRA, http://www.aftra.org/146F6D705A314AA8980FE63A05C17E3A.htm, (accessed March 22, 2011).

Creative Representation – artists grant a power of attorney to managers, and managers accept it as a mutual agreement to exhibit common interest in the development of the artist's creative talents, recording, performing, and professional career.

Crossover Networks are in speakers to separate the frequencies (bass, midrange, and treble) and send them to the proper speakers.

Controlled composition clause refers to the fact that since labels habitually want to save money on album projects, they've developed a way to do this by paying only 75% of the statutory rate for mechanical licenses. As stated earlier, if the main artist owns, controls, or has written all or part of the composition, then the label can declare the song a controlled composition. Sadly, in contracts, songs that are not owned, controlled, or written by the label or recording artists are usually required to share label publishing or songwriter credits with the main recording artist. The actual songwriter(s) receives reduced songwriting share royalties, the publisher (if not part of the label) receives reduced publishing share royalties, and the label's publishing company or recording artists receive shares of royalties for songs they did not publish or write. The label also saves on the bottom line as it pays 25% less of the statutory rate for the mechanical licenses. It does not seem fair, yet it is an industry standard, and it does provide a way for the label to share the fundamental financial risk of recording an unknown tune.

Copyright is a form of protection provided by the laws of the United States and most democracies for "original works of authorship" including literary, dramatic, musical, architectural, cartographic, choreographic, pantomimic, pictorial, graphic, sculptural, and audiovisual creations. "Copyright" literally means the right to copy, but has come to mean the body of exclusive rights granted by law to copyright owners for protection of their work. Copyright protection does not extend to any idea, procedure, process, system, title, principle, or discovery. Similarly, names, titles, short phrases, slogans, familiar symbols, mere variations of typographic ornamentation, lettering, coloring, and listings of contents or ingredients are not subject to copyright.

Copyright notice consists of three elements. They are the "c" in a circle (©), the year of first publication, and the name of the owner of copyright. A copyright notice is no longer legally required to secure copyright on works first published on or after March 1, 1989, but it does provide legal benefits.

Copyright owner of a recording is the record label (who pays for all the bills). Most recording artists are signed as work-for-hire to the label, so that they will only be able to recapture their copyrights between the 35th and 40th years of ownership. The value of the label's equity is tied to ownership of their very successful recording products. They can sell stock in the company based on the recordings' value (they own) and the artists they have under long-term contract.

Copyright owner of a song is either the creator of the song or the music publisher if it meets specific work-for-hire requirements. The duration of ownership depends on when it was written and which act it falls under. Most songwriters are able to recapture their copyrights between the 35th and 40th years of ownership. The value of the song's equity is tied to ownership and use of the song in various products such as recordings and films which is then tied to consumer acceptance.

Cross Collateralization is a process when the labels/music companies recoup past debts (on previous releases) by transferring income from currently profitable projects to cover previous debts. Labels cross collateralize record sales while music companies cross collateralize record sales, concert tickets grosses, merchandise, and sometimes corporate sponsorships in their 360 deals.

Cue System allows the musicians and recording artists to hear themselves in their headphones. The mic signals sent to the console are simply mixed and returned to the artists and musicians through the cue systems and their headphones. Headset boxes allow the musicians and artists to control the amplitude (loudness) of their own headphones. Most consoles have a minimum of two stereo or four mono cue systems.

DART is an acronym for Digital Audio Recording Technology. Refers to digital audio recording devices and media covered by the Audio Home Recording Act of 1992 (P.L.102-563), the first statutory license to grant royalties to copyright owners for home copying.

Delivery date is the actual date the artist is to present an acceptable digital master of their recording to the label (usually the Vice President of A&R).

Demo recordings are often the music publisher's obligation: to record a song for presentation to a major recording artist, the A&R Department at record labels, record producers, and artist managers. Expenses for the quick recording are often recoupable out of the songwriter's future royalties. The quality of the recording (number of musicians, tracks, etc.), ownership of the master tape, and a share of the expenses are rarely negotiable, depending on the level and status of the songwriter based on the number of hits and money generated by the songs written.

Deposit **(noun)** refers to the copy, copies, or phonorecords of an original work of authorship that are placed in the Copyright Office to support the claim to copyright in the work or to meet the mandatory deposit requirement of the 1976 Copyright Act. Deposits become part of the public record and may be selected by the Library of Congress for its collections.

Deposit **(verb)** is to send to the Copyright Office a copy, copies, or phonorecords of an original work of authorship to support a claim to copyright or to meet the mandatory deposit requirement of the 1976 Copyright Act.

Deposit account refers to money kept in a special account set up in the Copyright Office by individuals or firms and from which copyright fees are deducted.

Digital Machines are computers that convert microphone electronic signals into magnetic binary codes of 1s and 0s (pulses and no pulses of voltage), which are then recorded onto the computer disc or recording tape as a magnetic signal. When the codes are played back, the computer reconverts the magnetic signal or lack of signal into ls and 0s, which are then converted back into music.

Direct Boxes may be used instead of mics to convert the high impedance signal of the musical instruments into a low impedance signal acceptable to the console when musicians connect their guitars and keyboards directly to the console. Direct boxes eliminate the sound of one electrical musical instrument leaking into another open mic. However, they also limit the musician's ability to control their own instrument's sound quality as the guitar amp's tone controls are also removed from the signal flow.

Billing is a term that refers to the location or placement of the act or artist's name (logo) on tickets, advertisements, and press releases. Top billing means that the name of the artist will be on top of the venue's billboard or marquee and appear in larger print than other acts' or artists' names on tickets, and first mention on radio promotion spots.

Document, in copyright terms, is a paper relating to the ownership of a copyright or to any other matter involving a copyright. Documents may be recorded in the Copyright Office for the public record.

Dry/Wet refers to recording a signal on the tape with or without reverb or "effects" while listening to the signal in the control room monitor speakers and musicians' and recording artists' headsets. Dry is no effect; wet is when you are recording with the effect.

Dynamic Mics have a coil of wire in the element (or top) of the mic. Sound waves vibrate a plastic diaphragm, which moves the coil in and out of a permanent magnetic field. This movement converts the sound waves into an electronic signal.

Dynamic Range is the increase or decrease in amplitude of a sound wave. As an example, the dynamic range (loudness) of music is 120 dB.

eCO is the "electronic Copyright Office." eCO has two parts: eCO Service, a system for inputting and processing copyright information, and eCO Search, the Copyright Office records search system that provides access to Copyright Office records.

Editing in the old days was the process of removing unwanted sounds or musical notes by cutting the analog tape with a razor blade and then taping the parts back together. Now it is usually done on computer software programs.

Effects usually called outboard equipment (not located on the console), are "patched" into the console to change the quality of the signal. Examples include digital reverb, echo and delay units, noise gates (which cut off the signal at various amplitude levels used to prevent noise), compressors and limiters (which reduce the amplitude or loudness of the signal), and harmonizers (which are used to change the pitch).

Effect Sends and Returns are controls on each module of the console that are used to send a signal to the effects equipment to change the quality of the sound.

EQ or Equalization refers to the bass, midrange, and treble controls on the console used to change the quality of the sound. Similar examples include the tone controls on your home stereo or car radio.

eSearch is the online computer system that allows users to search Copyright Office registration and recordation records from 1978 to the present.

eService is the online computer system that receives applications for copyright registration, records and tracks all service requests, and supports all Copyright Office business requirements.[716]

Exceptions to Mic Rules include using condenser mics when you would normally use dynamic mics if you use a pad. A pad reduces the output of the mic and protects the inner electronics from high sound pressure levels (distortion).

Economic Business Terms Economics, tradeoffs, opportunity costs, markets, law of demand, demand schedule, demand curve, change in quantity demanded, determinants of demand, change in demand, normal good, inferior good, substitute good, complementary good, consumer sovereignty, price elasticity of demand, revenue, supply schedule, supply curve, law of supply, change in quantity supplied, change in supply, technology, backward bending supply curve, income effect, substitution effect, equilibrium, equilibrium price, equilibrium quantity.

Exclusivity means to the exclusion of all others. You cannot record for another record company, assign songs to another music publisher, or use another manager.

Expense accounts are usually controlled by business managers who pay all the bills, as stated in the contract. This is also the location in the contract where the manager will state if they will lend the act money.

Faders are an amplitude control on the console that moved up and down (instead of left to right like the volume control on your car radio). One hand can manipulate several faders at the same time. Faders control

[716] Library of Congress, "Definitions," http://www.copyright, (July 12, 2010).

the monitor speakers, cue, the signal being sent to the recording artists' and musicians' headsets, and the amount of signal being sent to the tape recorder.

Favored Nations Clause is mostly used in film soundtracks and compilation albums. Mainly used as a negotiating tool, it states that the newest artist or lesser-paid artist negotiates to get paid the same amount of money as the highest paid artist being featured.

Financial gain includes receipt, or expectation of receipt, of anything of value, including the receipt of other copyrighted works.

Firm offer is a signed contracted agreement which includes the concert dates, time of appearance, negotiated price for the act's performance, and a deposit consisting of a cashier's check or money order that will be placed into a secured account.

Float is a term used in when a writer assigns performance royalties to be paid through a music publisher (performance royalties are usually paid directly to the songwriter by the Performance Rights Organization). The publisher will often "float" the payment in order to earn interest off of the monies. This is a practice that is not supported by songwriter organizations as the music publisher may recoup expenses from the writers royalties and may also make interest from the writers royalties before they are paid.

Formula is usually a predetermined percentage of the profits or losses that will determine the artist's cash advances for the next album if the label picks up the "option." If the artist is to receive an advantage of 20% of profitable sales of, let's say, $1 million, then the advance would be $200,000. Formulas are often based on a series of issues, however the key is for the artists to know the actual amount will have a floor (guaranteed low amount and a possible high ceiling) which create a range for the advance to fall within. An example is a range of $50,000-$200,000. If the record looses money the artist is guaranteed to receive at least the bottom floor of $50,000 on their next album advance. However, let's say that the artist is to receive 30% of a million dollar profit. The ceiling is $200,000, so the artist will only receive the $200,000 ceiling figure instead of the higher $300,000.

Four walls are the most basic levels of service a venue has available to the concert promoter and act are listed under the term "four walls" or "four walling." The amount of electricity available (amps), heating, air conditioning, lights, and personnel, including house security, are listed on the contractual agreement between the venue and concert promoter.

Free goods are new recordings labels provide to retail outlets in order to "encourage them to stock" new and unknown artists. A percentage of the albums or singles (free downloads) are given to a retail outlet with an order. Retail may sell or give away the free good units and try to sell the extra ones they purchased at wholesale. If the product does not sell, then the free goods given to retail remain with the store and the purchased units are exchanged "sellable" product.

Frequency is the number of complete cycles (sound waves or vibrations) per second, measured in "Hz" (or Hertz, after the inventor of the concept). We hear 20 to 320 Hz as bass, 320 to 5,120 Hz as midrange, and 5,120 Hz to 20 Khz as treble. High end is treble.

Gates are electronic switches (thresholds) used to eliminate a signal based on the amplitude. Gates are used to "block" tape hiss heard between musical notes as well as ambiance, rumble, and leakage from other microphones. They are regularly used on drums and overdub vocals to "tighten" the sound.

Gross Monthly Earnings is the gross monthly earnings are usually the total monies made by the artists from recording royalty points, bonuses or salaries, profits from concerts and merchandise sales, music publishing and songwriting royalties, commercial endorsements, movie and television performances, and profits from shares in capital ventures.

Gross potential or GP is the maximum amount of money that will be generated by the concert if all tickets are sold.

Guarantee is the minimum amount of money the artist or act will earn for the performance. Often, artists will accept a guarantee plus an additional split of the profits. The bigger name acts demand a larger guarantee and a percentage of the promoter's profits.

Harmonizing offers a variety of special effects including the doubling of an input signal, delay of signal, and changing of the pitch. Doubling allows the engineer to make one instrument or vocalist sound like two. Delay provides echo or reverberation. Changing the pitch allows the engineer to detune or tune instruments and vocalists.

Headliner is the main attraction or most famous act to perform at the concert. Headliners are paid more money to perform than supporting acts.

"In the Mud" is a term that refers to recording an analog signal too low, causing the playback to have too much noise.

"In the Red" is a term that refers to recording an analog signal too "hot" on the tape machine, causing distortion.

Independent contractor is a term used to mean writers who uses their own musical instruments, don't have to meet a publisher song quota, have their own demo-recording studio, or pay for their own recordings.

Key Person Clause refers to a contract clause (verbal or written) that states a singer or group can negotiate to leave a management company or record company if the one key person who the artist has designated at the management company or record company ceases to be with the contracting company. It can be a manager or record company executive you believe is essential to your career.

Limitations of the power-of-attorney agreement is usually limited to matters reasonably related to the artist's career as the hiring and paying of musician, songwriter, publisher, and performing artists.

Limiter is a compressor at maximum compression. The amplitude of the output is "limited" to the manually adjusted level of the threshold.

Literary works are works, other than audiovisual works, expressed in words, numbers, or other verbal or numerical symbols or indicia, regardless of the nature of the material objects, such as books, periodicals, manuscripts, phonorecords, film, tapes, disks, or cards, in which they are embodied.

Loudspeakers are one of the several types of performance studio monitors that are used in the control room to determine the quality of the sound through large to small speakers.

Power of Attorney, also known as an Authority Clause or an Attorney in fact clause, gives the power to sign contracts on behalf of the artist. He can also sign checks, and he can hire or fire people on the artist's behalf. The artist should try to put a limit on this. The contract terms should say, "with our prior approval." In essence, this would be creating a "limited" power of attorney.

Mandatory deposit is a requirement of the 1976 Copyright Act that copies or phonorecords of every work published in the United States be sent to the Copyright Office within 3 month of publication whether or not copyright registration is sought. In general, two copies are required. Deposits are made available to the

Library of Congress for its collections or for exchange or transfer to any other library. Works deposited under the mandatory deposit requirement may also be used for copyright registration.

Mechanical Royalties come from the sale of all things mechanical – that is, audio records, compact discs and more recently, videos and DVDs sold to the general public.

Microphone Pickup Patterns are areas where they are most sensitive to sound.

Microphones convert sound waves into electronic signals. Knowing which one to select, where to place it in the performance studio, and in what proximity to the talent is extremely important. Proper selection and usage is the difference between a "great" sounding session and a mediocre one.

Mixer is the name for both the console and the audio engineer or producer who are mixing the final recording into a two-track master tape.

Modules allow for quick repairs and smaller and lighter consoles. They are another benefit of the space race: specifically, the design of plug-in modules.

Moral rights concern the protection of the reputation of the author. According to Stephanie C. Ardito of InformationToday (2002);

> *"Moral rights" is the English translation of the French phrase droit moral. Moral rights differ from copyright. Copyright protects property rights, which entitles authors to publish and economically benefit from their published works. Moral rights safeguard personal and reputational rights, which permit authors to defend both the integrity of their works and the use of their names. In countries that legally recognize moral rights, authors have redress to protect any distortion, misrepresentation, or interference of their works that could negatively affect their honor. Moral rights are often described as "inalienable." French law recognizes perpetual moral rights. In Germany, moral rights end when the author's copyright expires (70 years after he or she dies), while in other countries, moral rights terminate with the author's death.*[717]

Multi-Track Tape Recorders/Computers are used to store the recorded signals of the musicians, singers, and vocalists.

Multiple Tracking (tracking) is the process of the multiple-track recording process. The requirement of AFTRA and AF of M is that musicians and singers must be paid a new call when recording multiple parts or the same parts to additional tracks (depending on the type of session).

Music Publishing Advance is the money that the publisher "advances and does not "lend" to you. It is a paid sum publishers charge against the royalties earned. However, it is not a loan and is usually paid back only through recoupment. based on licenses. If the company doesn't make enough to pay back the "advance" the *artist is not required* to personally repay the the remainder.. Thus, "advances" are money paid to the writer from the music publisher for the right to exploit their song(s). Advances are not considered a salary. They include a one-time payment for a song, the cost of the demo recording, hiring of an independent songplugger, legal cost, and sometimes travel expenses, including per diem. Advances are repaid to the publisher by the publisher themselves from collected song royalties.

Name and likeness means that artists grant to the label the rights to use their professional name, image, likeness, and biographical information to market and promote their recordings. The same is often in a songwriter/music publishing deal.

Negotiation Period for an artist with a management agreement may include a performance clause (such as a requirement for the manager to secure a major recording contract) for the act. If the manager fails to achieve

---

717 Stephanie C. Ardito, "Moral Rights for Authors and Artists: In light of the Tasini ruling, is the next step to advocate for legislation?", InformationToday, http://www.infotoday.com/it/jan02/ardito.htm (accessed May 11, 2013).

the stated performance clause within a certain time (often 12-24 months), the artist may cancel the agreement by sending a written statement to the manager. The agreement is usually concluded within 30 days after the manager receives the cancellation notice. These can also be considered "goals" for the manager and thus are not usually found in a artist/manager agreement.

Originality in a song contract means the writer has to state that a "creative work" is original and not plagiarized from another person's creative efforts. This statement provides legal "proof" the publisher can use to protect itself (sometimes against the writer) if sued by other writers who claim authorship.

Omnidirectional Pickup Patterns allow sound waves to enter from all directions into the mic at approximately the same loudness level.

Op Amps are the many small operational (op) amplifiers that power a console, instead of one large, powerful amplifier. This technology was developed by the space race when it was determined that many small one-watt amplifiers were lighter to lift into outer space than one huge amp. The additional benefits to the audio recording business include a more compact size as well as less noise in the final recording.

Oscillator is a frequency or tone generator that was used to record signals on the tape, align tape machines, and provide special effects when mixed with musical instruments in the old days.

Ownership of a copyright may be transferred, in whole or in part, including any or all the exclusive rights.

Pan Pots are controls on the console that place a signal into the left side or right side monitor speaker or in the center of the mix.

Patch Bays allow an audio engineer to reroute the signal to a different module, special effect, or other equipment.

Payment of Services all monies from the artist's performances, record sales, and commercial endorsements are paid to the business manager or the artist's accountant as approved by the manager. The manager usually collects his or her negotiated percentage of the commission base and then has the business manager invest or place the remaining portion of the monies collected into the artist's accounts or businesses.

Peer-to-peer (P2P) networking is a type of network where computers communicate directly with each other, rather than through a central server. Often referred to simply as peer-to-peer, or abbreviated P2P, a type of network in which each workstation has equivalent capabilities and responsibilities in contrast to client/server architectures, in which some computers are dedicated to serving the other computers. A "network" is a group of two or more computer systems linked together by various methods. In recent usage, peer-to-peer has come to describe applications in which users can use the Internet to exchange files with each other directly or through a mediating server.

Performing Rights Organizations like BMI, ASCAP, and SESAC collect money for songwriters for performance royalties.

Performance Royalties are a major source of income for a writer. These are the Royalties that the copyright owner and songwriter receive when the song is performed publicly. The most common uses are radio, network and local TV, jukeboxes, Muzak, and live performances.

Phonorecord refers to the material object in which sounds are fixed and from which the sounds can be perceived, reproduced, or otherwise communicated, either directly or with the aid of a machine or device. A phonorecord may include a cassette tape, an LP vinyl disk, a compact disk, or other means of fixing sounds. A phonorecord does not include those sounds accompanying a motion picture or other audiovisual work.

Print Royalties are royalties made every time music is printed for Sheet Music, Songbooks, album folios, compilation folios, or educational purposes, i.e. chorus, marching band, jazz band, and orchestra arrangements.

Recoupment is the term for paying back the advance that the record company gave you. When a record company or publisher gives you an advance, they can recoup it, or get it back, from any future royalties.

Representation refers to the provision that if both the Publisher and Writer agree to a contract, it shall be subject to any existing agreements between the parties hereto and their following performance rights organizations (ASCAP, BMI, SESAC), mechanical rights organization (The Harry Fox Agency), and digital rights management agency (SoundExchange). Representation is also a term used by recording artists to refer to management and booking agencies. Actors also are represented by agents representing unions (such as the AFTRA and Sag and musicians are represented by the AF of M.

Reverberation is sound reflections from many sources (several hard surfaces) heard more than 10 milliseconds after a direct sound wave. Reverb is an effect that makes the vocalists or musicians sound as if they were in a large auditorium (a hard-surfaced, empty acoustic room) instead of the smaller, acoustically correct recording studio.

Reversion clause is a provision in the songwriter music publisher's contract that states if the publisher does not obtain a commercial sound recording (or some other form of written performance) then they return your song's copyright within a specified time.

Ribbon Mics operate on the same principle as dynamic mics, except they have flexible, metallic ribbons. Sound waves vibrate in and out of the permanent, magnetic force field. Because the ribbon is flexible, the quality of sound generated is often considered "warmer" and "smoother."

Rooms in a recording studio have many different names and functions. The recording artists and musicians perform in rooms that are collectively called "the studio." Producers and audio engineers supervise and record the artists' and musicians' performances from the control room. An equipment room isolates the noise of the tape machines from the control and performance studios, and a storage area is used for keeping microphones, music stands, headsets, cords, direct boxes, and other recording equipment that is not in use. The studio's acoustics are used to emphasize and match the feel of the song to the image and vocal characteristics of the recording artist. Placement of the performers and their microphones in the studio add the final acoustics for the recording.

Seeking Employment is not alway allowed by artist Managers as in some states they are not allowed to seek employment for the acts they represent. They usually limit their role to negotiating with agents and labels for various types of deals, and consulting the artists on hiring, firing, and employment opportunities.

Suspension of artists in the music industry can be from label deals and artist management agreements if they become sick, refuse to perform, breach any part of their legal contracts, or break written moral clauses or social norms by committing a criminal act.

Sound recording is a work that results from the fixation of a series of musical, spoken, or other sounds, regardless of the nature of the material objects in which they are embodied. A sound recording does not include the sounds accompanying a motion picture or other audiovisual work. Copyright in a sound recording protects the particular series of sounds embodied in the sound recording. Copyright registration for a sound recording alone is not the same as registration for the musical, dramatic, or literary work recorded. The underlying work may be registered in its own right apart from any recording of the performance.[718]

Splits are a percentage (PC) of the profits or money collected from the gate (entry) after the concert expenses have reached the break-even point.

Statements either monthly or quarterly are provided by the business manager to the personal manager and artist(s) concerning financial matters.

Synchronization Royalties are another important area for writers and publishers. Sync Royalties are the money due based on the licensing of the right to record music or song timed to the pictures in a film or TV movie. This is always negotiable and depends on the popularity of the song and the way it is used.

Street date is the actual date the recording is to be released for sale to retail outlets.

Term is the actual length of the initial period of an agreement (usually 1 year) followed by 6 one-year options. In a songwriting agreement it includes a period of time and number of required acceptable songs. In a reading deal its usually a period of time and number of recordings, and in a management agreement it often refers to the initial period being between 2-3 years and then 4-5 one-year options.

The best edition of a work is the edition published (distributed) in the United States at any time before the date of deposit, which the Library of Congress determines to be most suitable for its purposes.

The Copyright Office provides the following definitions and additional information at this site: *http://www.copyright.gov/help/faq/definitions.html*. You will find them helpful in understanding copyright language and terminology.

The copyright owner is the person or company who created the original work or who purchased the work from the person who created the work as a work-for-hire.

To display a work means to show a copy of it either directly or by means of a film, slide, television image, or any other device or process, or in the case of motion picture or other audiovisual work, to show individual images non-sequentially.

Ticket manifest is a computerized list of every seat (and ticket price) in a venue for a specific act or artists for each concert date.

To perform a work means to recite, render, play, dance, or act it, either directly or by means of any device, or in the case of a motion picture or other audiovisual work, to show its images in any sequence or to make the words accompanying it audible.

To Publish a work is to distribute copies or phonorecords of the work to the public by sale or other transfer of ownership, or by rental, lease, or lending. Publication also includes offering to distribute copies or phonorecords to a group of persons for purposes of further distribution, public performance, or public display. A public performance or display of a work does not of itself constitute publication.

Transfer of copyright and all exclusive rights happens when the Writer assigns, transfers, and delivers to the Publisher an original musical composition written and/or composed by the named songwriter(s). The Writer also assigns to the Publisher the title, words and music thereof, and the right to secure the copyright ownership registration throughout the world.

---

[718] Library of Congress, "Definitions," http://www.copyright, (July 12, 2010).

Two-Track Tape Machines are used to mix the 24-or 32-track tape to 2-track stereo. Accepted master tapes are usually sent to a mastering lab to be converted into a matrix that can be used to make CDs and stereo audio for DVDs.

Unions are "groups of people who band together to demand better pay and working conditions." They bargain for wages and set scales for different types of employment. There are two unions that affect the music business:

> *AF of M*, or American Federation of Musicians, is a union for musician's that assures that they are paid a minimum amount of money for recordings and live concerts. They also provide for health insurance and retirement benefits.
>
> *AFTRA,* or American Federation of Television and Radio Artists, represents vocalists and recording artists in studio sessions, television productions, and live performances. They also represent actors, announcers, sound effect artists, and other personalities working in radio and TV. They also provide for health insurance and retirement benefits.

Warrants and rights refer to when the Writer "warrants" the composition is his(s)/her(s) sole, exclusive, and original work; that he or she has the legal "right" to complete this contract (they are not signed with anyone else), and that there is no known adverse claim to the above stated or listed composition.

Work-for-Hire is a "one-time job." These musicians are paid for a specific one-time job when they are needed. They are usually paid a flat fee. This can also be for a songwriter hired for a specific piece of music for film, TV, jingle, or commercial. The songwriter receives no royalties. The company that they work would owns all of the copyrights involved. However, the creative person being "hired" may retain ownership of the copyright if they meet specific written qualifications including having the person or company hiring them to sign a document stating that they (the creative person being hired) with retain ownership of the copyright of whatever they are being hired to create.

Bibliography

AEG Live, "Events, Artist & Festivals," AEG Live, http://www.aeglive.com/overview, (accessed April, 11).

———, "Events, Artist & Festivals," AEG Live, http://www.aeglive.com/overview, (accessed April, 11).

A&M Records v. Napster, "The Ninth Circuit Decision, February 9, 2001," http://gseis.ucla.edu/iclp/napster.htm, (accessed January 3, 2011).

———, "The Ninth Circuit Decision, February 9, 2001," http://gseis.ucla.edu/iclp/napster.htm, (accessed January 3, 2011).

Actors' Equity, "About Equity," Actors' Equity, http://www.actorsequity.org/AboutEquity/aboutequityhome.asp, (accessed March 22, 2011).

———, "About Equity," Actors' Equity, http://www.actorsequity.org/AboutEquity/aboutequityhome.asp, (accessed March 22, 2011).

———, "Contracts and Codes, (Agreements & Codes)," Actors' Equity, http://www.actorsequity.org/AboutEquity/contracts, (accessed August 7, 2010).

———, "Contracts and Codes, (Agreements & Codes)," Actors' Equity, http://www.actorsequity.org/AboutEquity/contracts, (accessed August 7, 2010).

———, "Contracts and Codes, (Agreements & Codes)," Actors' Equity, http://www.actorsequity.org/AboutEquity/contracts, (accessed August 7, 2010).

———, "NewsMedia: How to Work or Not to Work," Actor's Equity, http://www.actorsequity.org/docs/about/aboutequity_WebMay2010.pdf, (accessed August 7, 2010).

———, (Handbook-called About Equity), "About Equity," Actors' Equity, http://www.actorsequity.org/docs/about/aboutequity_booklet_06.pdf, (accessed March 22, 2011).

AF of M "Demonstration Recording Rates," AF of M, http://www.nashvillemusicians.org/documents/Demo72210.pdf, (accessed March 22, 2011).

———, "Limited Pressing Recording Rates," AF of M, http://www.nashvillemusicians.org/documents/lpnew2.pdf, (accessed March 22, 2011).

———, "Low Budget Recording Rates," Af of M, http://www.nashvillemusicians.org/documents/LB72210.pdf, (accessed March 22, 2011).

———, "Sound Recording Master Scale," AF of M, http://www.nashvillemusicians.org/documents/masternew2.pdf, (accessed March 22, 2011).

———, "Book Agent Search," AF of M, http://www.afm.org/resources/booking-agent-search, (accessed March 22, 2011).

———, "Book Agent Search," AF of M, http://www.afm.org/resources/booking-agent-search, (accessed March 22, 2011).

———, "History of the AF of M (by years)," AF of M, http://www.afm.org/about/our-history, (accessed March 22, 2011).

———, "Limited Pressing Rates," AF of M, http://www.rmanashville.com/index.php?p=afm%20scales, (accessed March 22, 2011).

———, "Limited Pressing Rates," AF of M, http://www.rmanashville.com/index.php?p=afm%20scales, (accessed March 22, 2011).

———, "Limited Pressing Rates," AF of M, http://www.rmanashville.com/index.php?p=afm%20scales, (accessed March 22, 2011).

———, "Sound Recording Label Agreement," AF of M, http://www.afm.org/uploads/image, (accessed March 22, 2011).

———, "Sound Recording Label Agreement," AF of M, http://www.afm.org/uploads/image, (accessed March 22, 2011) and AFTRA, "Record Rates 2007-2010," AFTRA, http://www.aftra.org/146F6D705A314AA8980FE63A05C17E3A.htm, (accessed March 22, 2011).

———, "Sound Recording Label Agreement," AF of M, http://www.afm.org/uploads/image, (accessed March 22, 2011).

———, "Sound Recording Label Agreement," AF of M, http://www.afm.org/uploads/image, (accessed March 22, 2011)

———, "Sound Recording Label Agreement," AF of M, http://www.afm.org/uploads/image, (accessed March 22, 2011)

———, "Sound Recording Label Agreement," AF of M, http://www.afm.org/uploads/image, (accessed March 22, 2011)

———, "Sound Recording Labor Agreement Low Budget Side Letter Summary," http://local1000.com/wordpress/wp-content/uploads/2010/10/Low-Budget-Scales.pdf, (accessed March 22, 2011).

———, "Sound Recording Labor Agreement Low Budget Side Letter Summary," http://local1000.com/wordpress/wp-content/uploads/2010/10/Low-Budget-Scales.pdf, (accessed March 22, 2011).

———, "Sound Recording Labor Agreement Low Budget Side Letter Summary," http://local1000.com/wordpress/wp-content/uploads/2010/10/Low-Budget-Scales.pdf, (accessed March 22, 2011).

———, "Why Join," AF of M, http://www.afm.org/why-join, (accessed March 22, 2011).

———, "Why Join," AF of M, http://www.afm.org/why-join, (accessed March 22, 2011).

———, Demonstration Recording Scale," AF of M, http://www.nashvillemusicians.org/documents/Demo72210.pdf, (accessed March 22, 2011).

———, Demonstration Recording Scale," AF of M, http://www.nashvillemusicians.org/documents/Demo72210.pdf, (accessed March 22, 2011).

AFM & AFTRA Intellectual Property Rights Distribution Fund, "About Us," RARoyalties.org, http://www.ahra.org/aboutus.html, (accessed March 26, 2011).

———, Intellectual Property Rights Distribution Fund, "About Us," RARoyalties.org, http://www.ahra.org/aboutus.html, (accessed March 26, 2011).

AFTRA, "About AFTRA." AFTRA, http://www.aftra.org/aboutaftra.htm, (accessed March 22, 2011).

———, "About AFTRA." AFTRA, http://www.aftra.org/aboutaftra.htm, (accessed March 22, 2011).

———, "About AFTRA." AFTRA, http://www.aftra.org/aboutaftra.htm, (accessed March 22, 2011).

———, "Code at a Glance, AFTRA, http://www.aftra.org/contracts, (accessed March 22, 2011).

———, "Code at a Glance," AFTRA, http://www.aftra.org/documents/03_02_SoundRecordingsGlance.pdf, (accessed March 22, 2011).

———, "History: The People who Entertain and Inform America have been Moving Forward for 70 Years," AFTRA, http://www.aftra.org/history.htm, (accessed March 22, 2011).

———, "Record Rates 2007-2010," AFTRA, http://www.aftra.org/146F6D705A314AA8980FE63A05C17E3A.htm, (accessed March 22, 2011).

———, "Record Rates 2007-2010," AFTRA, http://www.aftra.org/146F6D705A314AA8980FE63A05C17E3A.htm, (accessed March 22, 2011).

———, "Record Rates 2007-2010," AFTRA, http://www.aftra.org/146F6D705A314AA8980FE63A05C17E3A.htm, (accessed March 22, 2011).

———, "Record Rates 2007-2010," AFTRA, http://www.aftra.org/146F6D705A314AA8980FE63A05C17E3A.htm, (accessed March 22, 2011).

———, "Record Rates 2007-2010," AFTRA, http://www.aftra.org/146F6D705A314AA8980FE63A05C17E3A.htm, (accessed March 22, 2011).

———, "Record Rates 2007-2010," AFTRA, http://www.aftra.org/146F6D705A314AA8980FE63A05C17E3A.htm, (accessed March 22, 2011).

———, "Record Rates 2007-2010," AFTRA, http://www.aftra.org/146F6D705A314AA8980FE63A05C17E3A.htm, (accessed March 22, 2011).

———, "Record Rates 2007-2010," AFTRA, http://www.aftra.org/146F6D705A314AA8980FE63A05C17E3A.htm, (accessed March 22, 2011).

Allen, Katie. "Never Ends for Peter Pan: JM Barrie bequeathed all rights to Peter Pan to Great Ormond Street hospital. Its imminent expiry is set to revive the debate over copyright term," The Guardian, http://www.guardian.co.uk/business/2007/dec/28/gtormondst (accessed January 1, 2011).

Allen, Woody. "Woody Allen Quotes," Artquotes.net, http://www.artquotes.net/entertainment-quotes/woody-allen.htm, (accessed March 24, 2011).

Alliance of Artist and Recording Companies (AARC), "What is AARC?," aarecroyalties.com, https://www.aarcroyalties.com/2008/home.php?nav=whatis, (accessed March 26, 2011).

———, (AARC), "What is AARC?," aarecroyalties.com, https://www.aarcroyalties.com/2008/home.php?nav=whatis, (accessed March 26, 2011).

Answers.com, "BMI: Some Industry Background," http://www.answers.com/topic/broadcast-music-inc, (accessed July 19, 2010).

Answers.encyclopedia.com, "How Dynamic Microphones Work," Answers.encyclopedia.com, http://answers.encyclopedia.com/question/do-dynamic-microphones, (accessed August 5, 2010).

———, "How Dynamic Microphones Work," Answers.encyclopedia.com, http://answers.encyclopedia.com/question/do-dynamic-microphones, (accessed August 5, 2010).

———, "How is Sound Recorded on an Audio Recorder," Answers.encyclopedia.com, http://answers.encyclopedia.com/question/sound-recorded-audio-recorder-105145.html, (accessed March 19, 2011).

———, "What is an Electrostatic Microphones," Answers.encyclopedia.com, http://answers.encyclopedia.com/question/electret-microphones-96543.html, (accessed March 19, 2011).

———, "What is the Definition of a Binary Code," Answers.encyclopedia.com, http://answers.encyclopedia.com/

question/definition-binary-code-747599.html, (accessed March 19, 2011).
———, "Who Invented Microphones," Answers.encyclopedia.com, http://answers.encyclopedia.com/question/do-dynamic-microphones, (accessed March 19, 2011).

Arrington, Michael. "360 Music Deals Become Mandatory as Labels Prepare for Free Music," Techcrunch.com, http://techcrunch.com/2008/11/08/360-music-deals-become-mandatory-as-labels, (accessed March 17, 2011).

ASACP, "Customer Licenses," http://www.ascap.com/licensing/licensingfaq.html, (accessed July 19, 2010).

———, "Music and Money, The Controlled Composition Clause," http://.ascap.com/musicbiz/money-clauses.html, (July 18, 2010).

———, "Annual Report 2009," http://www.ascap.com/about/annualReport/annual_2009.pdf, (accessed January 30, 2011).

———, "Annual Report 2009," http://www.ascap.com/about/annualReport/annual_2009.pdf, (accessed January 30, 2011).

———, "Annual Report 2009," http://www.ascap.com/about/annualReport/annual_2009.pdf, (accessed January 30, 2011).

———, "ASCAP News: ASCAP"s MediaGuide has Become the New Standard in Broadcast Monitoring," http://www.ascap.com/press/2005/090705_mediaguide.html, (accessed July 19, 2010).

———, "ASCAP's Governing Documents," http://www.ascap.com/members/governingDocuments/, (accessed July 19, 2010).

———, "ASCAP's Governing Documents," http://www.ascap.com/members/governingDocuments/, (accessed July 19, 2010).

———, "Common Licensing Terms," http://www.ascap.com/licensing/termsdefined.html, (accessed January 30, 2011).

———, "Fairness in Music Licensing Legislation," http://www.ascap.com/legislation/legis_qa.aspx, (accessed January 2, 2011).

———, "Playback: Rapidcue," http://www.ascap.com/playback/2007/summer/action/rapidcue.html, (accessed July 20, 2010).

———, "The History of ASCAP: The Birth of BMI," http://www.fundinguniverse.com/company-histories/The-American-Society-of-Composers-Authors-and-Publishers-ASCAP-Company-History.html, (accessed January 30, 2011).

Ask Yahoo, "Does Michael Jackson Still Own the Publishing Rights to the Beatles Song Catalog?" Yahoo!, http://ask.yahoo.com/20031210.html, (accessed July16, 2010).

Author Unknown, "Quotations about Music, " The Quote Garden.com, http://www.quotegarden.com/music.html (accessed December 31, 2010).

Baskerville, David. *The Music Business Handbook & Career Guide* 6th ed. Thousand Oaks: Sherwood Publication Partners, 1990.

———, *The Music Business Handbook & Career Guide*, Thousand Oaks: Sherwood Publication Partners, 1979.

Beck Robert & Tysver, Dan. "Welcome to Bitlaw: Joint Ownership" http://www.bitlaw.com/copyright, (accessed July 12, 2010).

———, "Welcome to Bitlaw: Joint Ownership" http://www.bitlaw.com/copyright, (accessed July 12, 2010).

———, "Welcome to Bitlaw: Works Made for Hire, Why is it Important," http://www.bitlaw.com/copyright, (accessed July 12, 2011).

———, "Works Made for Hire-the Standard," BitLaw, http://www.bitlaw.com/copyright, (accessed July 12, 2010).

———, "Welcome to Bitlaw: Copyright Duration" http://www.bitlaw.com/copyright (accessed July 12, 2010).

Beethoven, Ludwig Van. "Favorite Quotes About Music & Songwriting," http://www.songwritersresourcenetwork.com/quotes.html, (accessed July 13, 2010).

Begley, Sharon. "Science and Technology." Newsweek.msnbc.com, http://www.brams.umontreal.ca/plab/research/dossiers_vulgarisation/newsweek_musicmind/newsweek_musicmind. "Music on the Mind," Newsweek, July 24, 2000,

———, "Music on the Mind," Newsweek, July 24, 2000,

Berkman Center for Internet & Society at Harvard University, "*Rethinking Music: A Framing Paper,*" Harvard University,
http://cyber.law.harvard.edu/publications/2011/Rethinking_Music, (accessed May 2, 2011).

———, "*Rethinking Music: A Framing Paper,*" Harvard University,
http://cyber.law.harvard.edu/publications/2011/Rethinking_Music, (accessed May 2, 2011).

———, "*Rethinking Music: A Framing Paper,*" Harvard University,
http://cyber.law.harvard.edu/publications/2011/Rethinking_Music, (accessed May 2, 2011).

———, "*Rethinking Music: A Framing Paper,*" Harvard University,
http://cyber.law.harvard.edu/publications/2011/Rethinking_Music, (accessed May 2, 2011).

———, *"Rethinking Music: A Framing Paper,"* Harvard University, http://cyber.law.harvard.edu/publications/2011/Rethinking_Music, (accessed May 2, 2011).

Berman, Anthony, "Multi-Media Law Online News: Foreign Publishing Royalties," http://beatblog.typepad.com/melon/2007/06/music-law-forei.html, (July 18, 2010).

Berne Convention Implementation Act of 1988, ""Section 4, Subject Matter and Scope of Copyrights," The Coalition for Networked Information, http://www.cni.org/docs/infopols/US.Berne.Convention.html, (January 1, 2011).

———, "Berne Convention for the Protection of Literary and Creative Works," http://www.wipo.int/treaties/en/ip/berne/trtdocs_wo001.html, (accessed January 1, 2011).

Bertelsmann, "Corporate Report 2009," Bertelsmann A.G. Carl-Bertelsmann-Strasse, 270, D-333111 Gutersloh, Germany Phone:+49-52-41-80-1362, http://www.bertelsmann.com and Yahoo.com, http://biz.yahoo.com/ic/40/40661.html (July 21, 2010).

———, "Corporate Report 2009," Bertelsmann A.G. Carl-Bertelsmann-Strasse, 270, D-333111 Gutersloh, Germany Phone:+49-52-41-80-1362, http://www.bertelsmann.com and Yahoo.com, Company Profile, http://biz.yahoo.com/ic/40/40661.html (July 21, 2010).

———, "Corporate Report 2009," Bertelsmann A.G. Carl-Bertelsmann-Strasse, 270, D-333111 Gutersloh, Germany Phone:+49-52-41-80-1362, http://www.bertelsmann.com and Yahoo.com, http://biz.yahoo.com/ic/40/40661.html (July 21, 2010).

Big Champagne, "About," http://bcdash.bigchampagne.com/who, (accessed March 17, 2011).

Billboard Magazine, "About Us," Billboard.com, http://www.billboard.com/#/footer/about-us, (accessed April 8, 2011).

———, "About Us," http://www.billboard.com/#/footer/about-us, (accessed March 17, 2011).

———, "The Summer Preview," Billboard Magazine, May 17, 2008, 42.

BMI, "BMI Digital Initiatives' Project to Set Benchmarks for 21st Century Copyright Administration," http://www.bmi.com/news/entry/234045, (accessed July 19, 2010).

———, "Tradition," http://www.bmi.com/about/entry/533105, (accessed July 19, 2011).

———, "Annual Report 2009-10," http://www.bmi.com/pdfs/publications/2010/annual_review_0910.pdf, (accessed January 30, 2011).

———, "Annual Report 2009-10," http://www.bmi.com/pdfs/publications/2010/annual_review_0910.pdf, (accessed January 30, 2011).

Boerre, George. "Personality Theories, George Kelly," http://webspace.ship.edu/cgboer/kelly.html, (accessed July 14, 2010).

Bowen, Jimmy, (as quoted by Larry Wacholtz) *Inside Country Music*, Billboard Books, New York: Watson-Guptil Publishers, 1986

———, (as quoted by Larry Wacholtz) *Inside Country Music*, Billboard Books, New York: Watson-Guptil Publishers, 1986 & Wacholtz, Larry, *Lights, Glitter and Business Sense*, Thumbs Up Publishing, (Washington: Cheney, 1984) 184-198.

———, (as quoted by Larry Wacholtz) *Inside Country Music*, Billboard Books, New York: Watson-Guptil Publishers, 1986 & Wacholtz, Larry, *Lights, Glitter and Business Sense*, Thumbs Up Publishing, (Washington: Cheney, 1984) 184-198.

———, (as quoted by Larry Wacholtz) *Inside Country Music*, Billboard Books, New York: Watson-Guptil Publishers, 1986 & Wacholtz, Larry, *Lights, Glitter and Business Sense*, Thumbs Up Publishing, (Washington: Cheney, 1984) 184-198.

———, (as quoted by Larry Wacholtz) *Inside Country Music*, Billboard Books, New York: Watson-Guptil Publishers, 1986 & Wacholtz, Larry, *Lights, Glitter and Business Sense*, Thumbs Up Publishing, (Washington: Cheney, 1984) 184-198.

———, (as quoted by Larry Wacholtz) *Inside Country Music*, Billboard Books, New York: Watson-Guptil Publishers, 1986 & Wacholtz, Larry, *Lights, Glitter and Business Sense*, Thumbs Up Publishing, (Washington: Cheney, 1984) 184-198.

———, (as quoted by Larry Wacholtz) *Inside Country Music*, Billboard Books, New York: Watson-Guptil Publishers, 1986 & Wacholtz, Larry, *Lights, Glitter and Business Sense*, Thumbs Up Publishing, (Washington: Cheney, 1984) 184-198.

———, (as quoted by Larry Wacholtz) *Inside Country Music*, Billboard Books, New York: Watson-Guptil Publishers, 1986 & Wacholtz, Larry, *Lights, Glitter and Business Sense*, Thumbs Up Publishing, (Washington: Cheney, 1984) 184-198.

BPI, "About Us," http://www.bpi.co.uk/category/about-us.aspx, (accessed July 18, 2010).

Brain, Marshall. "How Mp3 Files Work," Howstuffworks.com, http://computer.howstuffworks.com/mp32.htm, (accessed March 22, 2011).

———, "How Mp3 Files Work," Howstuffworks.com, http://computer.howstuffworks.com/mp32.htm, (accessed March 22, 2011).

Bransford, John. *How People Learn,* (reprint, National Academy Press, 2000), and at http://www.nap.edu/openbook.php?isbn=0309070368 (accessed April 10, 2011).

———, *How People Learn,* (reprint, National Academy Press, 2000), and at http://www.nap.edu/openbook.php?isbn=0309070368 (accessed April 10, 2011).

———, John. *How People Learn,* (reprint, National Academy Press, 2000), and at http://www.nap.edu/openbook.php?isbn=0309070368 (accessed April 10, 2011).

Bronfman, Edgar "Chairman of the Board and Chief Executive Officer, Warner Music Group Corporation," Forbes.com, http://people.forbes.com/profile/edgar-j-bronfman/42366, (accessed July 16, 2010).

———, "Edgar Bronfman," Forbes.com, http://people.forbes.com/profile/edgar-j-bronfman/42366, (accessed March 17, 2011).

Butt, Trevor, "The Choice Corollary," The Internet Encyclopedia of Personal Construct Psychology. http://www.pcp-net.org/encyclopaedia/choice.html, (accessed July 15, 2010).

Canning, Lisa. "The No Starving Artist Rule," www.entrepreneurTheArts.com (as discussed at the Self-Employment in the Arts Conference, Chicago, 2011).

Caparro, Jim. "Music Business Quotes," Barryrudolph.com. http://www.barryrudolph.com/utilities/quotes.html (accessed December 31, 2010).

CCLI, "Who We Are," http://www.ccli.com/WhoWeAre/CompanyProfile.aspx, (accessed January 27, 2011).

Cellini, Joe. "Les Paul Invented Here," Apple Pro, http://www.apple.com/pro/profiles/lespaul/, (accessed March 22, 2011).

Chaffin, Joshua. "By Promoting Gigs, Record Labels Get in on Bigger Acts," The Financial Times, http://www.ft.com/cms/s/0/6e362eee-4204-11dd-a5e8-0000779fd2ac.html#axzz1GgKEQk46, (accessed March 15, 2011).

———, "By Promotion Gigs, Record Labels Get in on Bigger Acts," Financial Times, http://us.ft.com/ftgateway/superpage.ft?news_id=fto062420081450546621, (accessed March 17, 2011).

Chapman, Nathan (in the article by Paul Tingen), "Secrets of the Mix Engineers: Nathan Chapman & Justin Niebank: Taylor Swift's Speak Now," Soundonsound.com, http://www.soundonsound.com/sos/feb11/articles/it-0211.htm, (accessed April 7, 2011).

Christman, Ed. "First Held 2010 Sales Recap: Lady Antebellum, UMG Leads the Way," Billboard.biz, http://www.billboard.biz/billboardbiz/photos/pdf/current.pdf, (accessed September, 25, 2010).

———, "Profit and Loss: Michael Jackson One Year After," Billboard Magazine, (June 26, 2010) 19.

———, "Profit and Loss: Michael Jackson One Year After," Billboard Magazine, (June 26, 2010) 19.

Clark, Dick. "Music Industry Quotes to Live By," Christopher Knob-Fourfront Media & Music, http://www.musicbizacademy.com/knab/articles/musicquotes.htm, (accessed July 16,2010).

Clear Channel, "Clear Chanel Fact Sheet," http://www.clearchannel.com/Corporate/PressRelease.aspx?PressReleaseID=1564&p=hidden, (accessed March 17, 2011).

Cobain, Kurk. "Music Business Quotes," Barryrudolph.com. http://www.barryrudolph.com/utilities/quotes.html (accessed December 31, 2010).

———, "Music Business Quotes," Barryrudolph.com.http://www.barryrudolph.com/utilities/quotes.html (accessed December 31, 2010).

Comcast Corporation, "Corporate Report 2010" http://apps, (accessed March 11, 2011).

Courtney, Richard & Cassidy, George, *Come Together: The Business Wisdom of The Beatles*, (New York, NY: Turner Publishing, 2011) 3-4.

———, *Come Together: The Business Wisdom of The Beatles*, (New York, NY: Turner Publishing, 2011) 8-22.

———, *Come Together: The Business Wisdom of The Beatles*, (New York, NY: Turner Publishing, 2011) 8-22.

———, *Come Together: The Business Wisdom of The Beatles*, (New York, NY: Turner Publishing, 2011) 33-34.

———, *Come Together: The Business Wisdom of The Beatles*, (New York, NY: Turner Publishing, 2011) 71

———, *Come Together: The Business Wisdom of The Beatles*, (New York, NY: Turner Publishing, 2011) 101.

Cowell, Simon. "American Idol:Bio," Amerian Idol, http://www.americanidol.com/bio/simon_cowell/, (accessed April 7, 2011).

Cox Radio, "Company Overview," http://coxradio.com/company/profile.html, (accessed March 17, 2011).

Creative Artist Agency (CAA), "Creative Artist Agency LLC." Hoover's Company Profiles, http://www.answers.com/topic/creative-artists-agency, (accessed August 24, 2010).

———, (CAA), "Creative Artist Agency LLC." Hoover's Company Profiles, http://www.answers.com/topic/creative-artists-agency, (accessed August 24, 2010).

———, (CAA), "Touring," CAA.com, CAA%20Creative%20Artists%20Agency.webarchive, (accessed April 7, 2011).

Crum, Chris. "Pandora Reaches 69 Million Milestone," Webpronews.com, http://www.webpronews.com/pandora-reaches-60-million-user-milestone-2010-07, (accessed July 21, 2010).

Cuban, David., as referenced in Fred Goodmans' book *Fortune's Fool, Edgar Brofnman Jr., Warner Music, and an Industry in Crisis,* New York, NY: Simon & Schuster, 2010, p.231.

Curb, Mike. forward to *Moser on Music Copyright*, Boston, MA: Course Technology/Cenage Learning, 2006.

D. Chuck. (Rapper), in an article by Richard Gehr, "Steal This Industry," Time Media Kit, http://www.time.com/time/digital/reports/mp3/artists.html (accessed 2010).

Damain, Bill. "The History of the Major Labels," *Performing Songwriter Magazine*, July/August, 2003.

———, "The History of the Major Labels," *Performing Songwriter Magazine*, July/August, 2003.

———, "The History of the Major Labels," *Performing Songwriter Magazine*, July/August, 2003.

———, "The History of the Major Labels," *Performing Songwriter Magazine*, July/August, 2003.

———, "The History of the Major Labels," *Performing Songwriter Magazine*, July/August, 2003.

———, "The History of the Major Labels," *Performing Songwriter Magazine*, July/August, 2003.

Digital Media Conference at Belmont University, 2007.

Digital Summit 2007 "RIAA Presentation," Belmont University, (2007).

Digitaldreamdoor.com "Music Stars Real Names," digitaldreamdoor.com, http://www.digitaldreamdoor.com/pages/realname.html, (accessed April 2, 2011).

Disserens, Charles. *Influences of Music on Behavior* (1926) as quoted in Langer on pages 212-213.

Dobbis, Rick. "By Promoting Gigs, Record Labels Get in on Bigger Acts," The Financial Times, http://www.ft.com/cms/s/0/6e362eee-4204-11dd-a5e8-0000779fd2ac.html#axzz1GgKEQk46, (accessed March 15, 2011).

Donnelly, Bob, Esq., "Why Artists Should "Do a 180" on "360 Deals," Lommen, Abdo, Cole, King & Stageberg, http://www.lommen.com/pdf/Bob-Donnelly-360-Article.aspx, (accessed April 23, 2011).

———, "Why Artists Should "Do a 180" on "360 Deals," Lommen, Abdo, Cole, King & Stageberg, http://www.lommen.com/pdf/Bob-Donnelly-360-Article.aspx, (accessed April 23, 2011).

Economics Club, "Famous Economic Majors," Georgia State University Economics Club, http://www2.gsu.edu/~wwwecc/FamousEcMajors.htm, (accessed March 9, 2011).

Einstein, Albert. "Favorite Quotes about Music & Songwriting" Songwriters Resource Network, http://www.songwritersresourcenetwork.com/quotes.html (accessed July 13, 2010).

Electronic Frontier Foundation, "Fair Use Frequently Asked Questions (and Answers)," http://w2.eff.org/IP/eff_fair_use_faq.php, (January 1, 2011).

EMI, "History of EMI," Emigroup.com, http://www.emimusic.com/, (accessed 1998).

Emmy Awards, (National Academy of Television Arts and Sciences), "History," NATAS, http://www.emmyonline.org/academy.html, (accessed April 19, 2011).

Facebook, "Statistics," Facebook.com, http://www.facebook.com/press/info.php?statistics, (accessed March 26, 2011).

Fahrenheit Media Group, "About Us," Fahrenheit Media Group, http://www.fahrenheitmediagroup.com/, (accessed April 3, 2011).

Farhi, Paul "Matsushita to Acquire MCA for $7.5 Billion; Deal is Largest Japanese Buyout of U.S. Firm," The Washington Post, accessed at HighBeam.com, http://www.highbeam.com/doc/1P2-1160780.html, (accessed July 22, 2010).

Farro, Josh, (as quoted in) "The New Deal, Band as Brand," The New York Times, http://musicrowlawyer.typepad.com/music_row_lawyer/360, (accessed July 21, 2010).

Faxon, Roger., as reported by David M. Ross, "Faxon's Note to EMI Staff," http://www.musicrow.com/2011/02/citigroup-acquires-emi/, (accessed February 4, 2011).

Film Musicians Secondary Markets Fund, "Our Mission," Fmsmf.org, http://www.fmsmf.org/aboutus/fundstatement.html, (accessed March 26, 2011).

———, "Our Mission," Fmsmf.org, http://www.fmsmf.org/aboutus/fundstatement.html, (accessed March 26, 2011).

Fintage House "Our Businesses," Fintage.com, http://www.fintagehouse.com/basic.php?sid=12&ptid=2, (accessed June 9, 2011), and personal interview with Bruce Lampcov, Los Angles, CA (June 1, 2011).

Friedlander, P., Joshua. "2009 Year-End Shipment Statistics, Recording Industry Association of America (RIAA), http://76.74.24.142/A200B8A7-6BBF-EF15-3038-582014919F78.pdf, (accessed September, 26, 2010).

Fuller, Simon. "Big Pay Day for American Idol's Simon Fuller,' American Idol, http://www.footnoted.com/my-big-fat-deal/big-payday-for-american-idols-simon-fuller/, (accessed April 7, 2011).

Future of Music Coalition, "29 Streams," Futureofmusic.org, http://futureofmusic.org/blog/2009/10/14/29-streams, (accessed March).

———, "29 Streams," Futureofmusic.org, http://futureofmusic.org/blog/2009/10/14/29-streams, (accessed

March).

Grammy Awards, (National Academy of Recording Arts and Sciences), "About Us," NARAS, http://www.grammy365.com/about, (accessed April 19, 2011).

Grammy 365, "About Us," NARAS, http://www.grammy365.com/about, (accessed April 19, 2011).

Goodman, Fred. *Fortune's Fool, Edgar Brofnman Jr., Warner Music, and an Industry in Crisis*, New York, NY: Simon & Schuster, 2010, p247.

———, *Fortune's Fool: Edgar Bronfman Jr., Warner Music and an Industry in Crisis*, New York: Simon & Schuster, 2010 7.

Greenberg, Sue. *Artist as a Bookkeeper*, 2nd ed. St. Louis, MO: St. Louis Volunteer Lawyers and Accountants for the Arts, 2011, 14.

———, *Artist as a Bookkeeper*, 2nd ed. St. Louis, MO: St. Louis Volunteer Lawyers and Accountants for the Arts, 2011, 17.

———, *Artist as a Bookkeeper*, 2nd ed. St. Louis, MO: St. Louis Volunteer Lawyers and Accountants for the Arts, 2011, 16.

———, *Artist as a Bookkeeper*, 2nd ed. St. Louis, MO: St. Louis Volunteer Lawyers and Accountants for the Arts, 2011, 16.

———, *Artist as a Bookkeeper*, 2nd ed. St. Louis, MO: St. Louis Volunteer Lawyers and Accountants for the Arts, 2011, 18.

———, *Artist as a Bookkeeper*, 2nd ed. St. Louis, MO: St. Louis Volunteer Lawyers and Accountants for the Arts, 2011, 18.

Hall, Tia. "Music Piracy and the Audio Home Recording Act," Duke law and Technology Review, http://www.law.duke.edu/journals/dltr/articles/2002dltr0023.html (accessed July 20, 2010).

———, "Music Piracy and the Audio Home Recording Act," Duke law and Technology Review, http://www.law.duke.edu/journals/dltr/articles/2002dltr0023.html (accessed July 20, 2010), & http://everything2.com/title/Audio+Home+Recording+Act, (accessed June 26, 2010).

———, "Music Piracy and the Audio Home Recording Act," Duke law and Technology Review, http://www.law.duke.edu/journals/dltr/articles/2002dltr0023.html (accessed July 20, 2010), & http://everything2.com/title/Audio+Home+Recording+Act, (accessed June 26, 2010).http://www.copyright (accessed July 12, 2010)

Harris, Tom. "How CD Burner Work." Howstuffworks.com, http://computer.howstuffworks.com/cd-burner1.htm, (accessed March 22, 2011).

———, "How CD Burner Work." Howstuffworks.com, http://computer.howstuffworks.com/cd-burner1.htm, (accessed March 22, 2011).

Harry Fox Agency, "General Information," http://www.harryfox.com/public/FAQ.jsp#12, (accessed July 17, 2010).

———, "General Information," https://www.harryfox.com/public/FAQ.jsp#12, (accessed July 18, 2010).

———, "HFA Produces Industry's Highly Anticipated Publisher Airplay Charts," http://www.harryfox.com/public/userfiles/file/PressReleases/PublisherCharts3rdquarterFinal20101112.pdf, (accessed January 30, 2011).

———, "HFA Ready to Implement the New Digital Era Mechanical Royalty Rates," http://www.harryfox.com/public/userfiles/file/Licensee/HFARoyaltyRatePR10-2-08.pdf, (accessed July 18, 2010).

———, "HFA Ready to Implement the New Digital Era Mechanical Royalty Rates," http://www.harryfox.com/public/userfiles/file/Licensee/HFARoyaltyRatePR10-2-08.pdf, (accessed July 18, 2010).

———, "HFA Ready to Implement the New Digital Era Mechanical Royalty Rates," http://www.harryfox.com/public/userfiles/file/Licensee/HFARoyaltyRatePR10-2-08.pdf, (accessed July 18, 2010).

———, "Mechanical Licensing," http://www.harryfox.com/public/MechanicalLicenseslic.jsp, (January 1, 2011).

———, "Songfile Licensing," http://www.harryfox.com/public/moreSongfile.jsp, (accessed July 18, 2010).

Hedges, Chris. "Mobilizing Against Pop Music and Other Horrors" The New York Times International, July 21, 1993.

Hicks, Rush, *The Personal Management Agreement*, by (Rush Hicks Esq.,: TN, Nashville, 2009).

———, *The Recording Deal/Contract*, provided by attorney Rush Hicks, Nashville, TN, (2010).

———, *The Single Song Agreement*, by (Rush Hicks Esq.,: TN, Nashville, 2009).

Hillsidemusic.com, "License Types," http://www.hillsongmusic.com/publishing/types, (accessed March 9, 2011).

Hipgrave, Dave. (by Mark Anstead), "Toploader's Dave Hipgrave: We Sold Over 2Million Records, But Didn't Walk Away with a Penny." Telegraph.com, http://www.telegraph.co.uk/finance/personalfinance/fameandfortune/8184741/Toploaders-Dan-Hipgrave-We-sold-over-2m-records-but-didnt-walk-away-with-a-penny.html, (accessed March 17, 2011).

History of Rock & Roll (Part One), Video Series: Warner Home Video, 1995.

Holloran, Mark. *The Musicians Business & Legal Guide*, Prentice Hall Publishing, Upper Sadle River: NJ, 1991, 335.

Horowitz, Leonard M., Banner, James & Cannon, H.C. *The Elements of Learning*, New Haven: Yale, 1999.
———, *The Elements of Learning*, New Haven: Yale, 1999.
———, *The Elements of Learning*, New Haven: Yale, 1999.
Hyatt, Ariel, (in an article by Scott Macaulay), "Five Million Bands on MySpace at the Future of Music Summit," FilmMaker.com, http://www.filmmakermagazine.com/news/2009/10/5-million-bands-on-myspace-at-the-future-of-music-summit/, (accessed March 26, 2011).
Hyman, David. "MOG Announces Premium digital Music Service Coming Soon," Reuters.com, http://www.reuters.com/article/2009/10/14/idUS109142+14-Oct-2009+PRN20091014, (accessed March 17, 2011).
I.A.T.S.E., "Welcome to IATSE," http://www.iatse-intl.org/about/about.html (accessed July 1, 2010).
I.F.P.I, "New Report Shows How Much Record Companies are 'Investing in Music,' http://www.ifpi.org/content/section_news/investing_in_music.html (accessed July 3, 2010).
———, Recording Industry in Numbers 2009, International Federation of the Phonographic Industry: "The Broader Music Industry in 2008," (London: IFPI 2009) 23.
———, "New Report Show How Much Money Record Companies are 'Investing in Music'," IFPI (International Federation of the Phonographic Industry), http://www.ifpi.org/content/section_news/investing_in_music.html, (accessed March 24, 2011).
———, "New Report Show How Much Money Record Companies are 'Investing in Music'," IFPI (International Federation of the Phonographic Industry), http://www.ifpi.org/content/section_news/investing_in_music.html, (accessed March 24, 2011).
———, "New Report Show How Much Money Record Companies are 'Investing in Music'," IFPI (International Federation of the Phonographic Industry), http://www.ifpi.org/content/section_news/investing_in_music.html, (accessed March 24, 2011).
———, "New Report Show How Much Money Record Companies are 'Investing in Music'," IFPI (International Federation of the Phonographic Industry), http://www.ifpi.org/content/section_news/investing_in_music.html, (accessed March 24, 2011).
International Alliance of Theatrical Stage Employees, Moving Picture Technicians, Artists and Allied Crafts of the United States, Its Territories and Canada, (IATSE), "Welcome to IATSE," "http://www.iatse-intl.org/about/welcome.html, (accessed April 7, 2011).
———, (IATSE), "Welcome to IATSE," "http://www.iatse-intl.org/about/welcome.html, (accessed April 7, 2011).
———, (IATSE), "Welcome to IATSE," "http://www.iatse-intl.org/about/welcome.html, (accessed April 7, 2011).
———, (IATSE), "Welcome to IATSE," "http://www.iatse-intl.org/about/welcome.html, (accessed April 7, 2011).
International Creative Management Agency, (ICM) "International Creative Agency," Hoovers Company Profiles, http://www.hoovers.com/company/International_Creative_Management_Inc/ccycji-1.html, (accessed August 24, 2010).
———, (ICM) Answers.com, http://www.answers.com/topic/international-creative-management-inc, (accessed March 29, 2011).
International Entertainment Buyers Association, (IEBA), "2010 Ticket Sales Drop Due to Economy and Fickle Audiences," http://ieba.org/node/2646, (accessed April 4, 2011).
———, (IEBA), "Welcome to IEBA," ieba.org, http://ieba.org/, (accessed April 4, 2011).
International Federation of the Phonographic Industry, "What is a Copyright?" by the IFPI, ifpi.org, http://www.ifpi.org/content/section_views/what_is_copyright.html (accessed 07/06/2000).
———, (IFPI), "IFPI's Mission," http://www.ifpi.org/content/section_about/index.html, (accessed March 17, 2011).
International Revenue Service (IRS), "Employee Id Numbers," IRS.gov, http://www.irs.gov/businesses/small/article/0,,id=98350,00.html, (accessed April 5, 2011).
Jackson, Michael. "The Stripped Mixes," iTunes, http://itunes.apple.com/us/artist, (accessed March 9, 2011).
Jassin, Lloyd. "Copyright Termination: How Authors (and their Heirs) can Recapture their Pre-1978 Copyrights," CopyLaw.com, (accessed March 9, 2011).
JCN Newswire, "Sony to Purchase Berteslmann's 50% Stake in Sony BG: Music Company to Become Wholly Owned Subsidiary of Sony Corporation of America," 50 BMG, http://wn.com/50_BMG, (accessed 2008).
Jobs, Steve, "Apple Introduces iCloud," From the press release iCloud Images, http://www.apple.com/pr/library/2011/06/06icloud.html, (accessed June 9, 2011).
———, "Thoughts on Music," Apple.com, http://www.apple.com/hotnews/thoughsonmusic/, (accessed August 1, 2010).
———, (as quoted in the article by Meir P. Pugatch), "The Ecomonics of DRM in Capitalist Markets," Ifpi.org, http://www.ifpi.org/content/section_views/view027.html, (accessed March 17, 2011).
John, Elton. "Elton John Quotes," Artquotes.net, http://www.artquotes.net/entertainment-quotes/famous-singers, (accessed March 15, 2011).

Johnson, Tom. "Internet Leader and Entertainment Firm to Join Forces; New Company worth $350 Billion," CNN Money, http://money.cnn.com/2000/01/10/deals/aol_warner/, (March 11, 2011).

———, "Internet Leader and Entertainment Firm to Join Forces; New Company worth $350 Billion," CNN Money, http://money.cnn.com/2000/01/10/deals/aol_warner/, (March 11, 2011).

Jones, Quincy. *The Recording Industry Career Handbook*, NARAS Foundations (NARAS: Los Angeles, CA) 1995.

Kallman, Craig. "The New Deal, Band as Brand," The New York Times, http://musicrowlawyer.typepad.com/music_row_lawyer/360, (accessed July 21, 2010).

Kaufman, Gil. "Michael Jackson's Posthumous Global Record Sales Reach 9 Million," http://www.mtv.com/news/articles/1616358/michael-jackson-sells-9-million-worldwide-since-death.jhtml, (accessed March 9, 2011).

Kelly, George. "Personality Synopsis: Cognitive Theory-The Beginning of Cognitivism," http://allpsych.com/personalitysynopsis/kelly.html (accessed July 13, 2010.

———, *Personal Construct Psychology*, found at Learning and Teaching info," http://www.learningandteaching.info/learning/personal.htm (accessed July 14, 2010).

Kennedy, John & Wenham, Alison. "Investing in Music," IFPI.org, http://www.ifpi.org/content/library/investing_in_music.pdf, (accessed March 17, 2011).

———, "Investing in Music: How Music Companies Discover Promote Talent," IFPI.org, http://www.ifpi.org/content/library/investing_in_music.pdf, (accessed March 19, 2011).

Kennedy, Liz. "Why Being Signed to a Music Label Rocks," RIAA.org, http://www.riaa.org/blog.php?content_selector=Why-Being-Signed-, (April 2, 2011).

King, B.B. "Brainy Quotes," Brainyquotes.com. http://www.brainyquote.com/quotes/quotes/b/bbking173521.html, (accessed January 7, 2011).

Kirkpatrick, David. "Time Warner Sell Music Unit for $2.6d Billion," New York Times, http://www.nytimes.com/2003/11/25/business, (accessed March 17, 2011).

———, "Time Warner Sells Music Unit for $2.6 Billion," New York Times, http://www.nytimes.com/2003/11/25/business, (July 22, 2010).

Knopfler, Mark. "Brainy Quotes: Songwriting Quotes," http://www.brainyquote.com/quotes/keywords/songwriting.html, (accessed July 13, 2010).

Kohn, Al. & Kohn, Bob. *Kohn on Music Licensing*, Google Books: Radio Transcription Licensing, http://books.google.com/books?id=rMFSUTNWRzgC&pg=PT429&lpg=PT429&dq=radio+transcription+licenses&source=bl&ots=RIZktgfMmy&sig=bxyFiuAi1GlRSJ4Epkalai5I2iE&hl=en&ei=GxFjTN7ZJ8OclgeDrOStCg&sa=X&oi=book_result&ct=result&resnum=1&ved=0CBgQ6AEwAA%2522%20%255Cl%20%2522v=onepage&q=rad#v=onepage&q=rad&f=false

———, *Kohn on Music Licensing*, Google Books: Transcription Licensing, http://books.google.com/books?id=rMFSUTNWRzgC&pg=PT431&lpg=PT431&dq=TRANSCRIPTION+LICENSE&source=bl&ots=RIYsuflJlw&sig=0g0dBQGBvMtoAFQ4f6BJZnZUP88&hl=en&ei=YwJGTIizIcKqlAfsrvmPBA&sa=X&oi=book_result&ct=result&resnum=8&ved=0CDkQ6AEwBw%2522%20%255Cl%20%2522v=onepage&q=TRANSCRIPT#v=onepage&q=TRANSCRIPT&f=false, (accessed March 9, 2011).

Kosslyn, Stephen. "Imaginagion" as stated in the World Book, and at http://www.scribd.com/doc/15745675/Academic-Readings-Ok-2, (accessed July1 2006) and January 17, 2011).

Krasilovsky, William, M. & Shemel, Sydney. *This Business of Music*, 10th ed. New York, NY: Billboard Books, 2007, 157.

———, *This Business of Music*, 10th ed. New York, NY: Billboard Books, 2007, 102.

———, *This Business of Music*, 10th ed. New York, NY: Billboard Books, 2007, 116.

———, *This Business of Music*, 10th ed. New York, NY: Billboard Books, 2007, 123.

———, *This Business of Music*, 10th ed. New York, NY: Billboard Books, 2007, 123.

———, *This Business of Music*, 10th ed. New York, NY: Billboard Books, 207, 211-216

———, *This Business of Music*, 10th ed. New York, NY: Billboard Books, 168.

———, *This Business of Music*, 10th ed. (New York, NY: Billboard Books, 168.

———, *This Business of Music*, 10th ed. (New York, NY: Billboard Books, 238).

———, *This Business of Music*, 10th ed. (New York, NY: Billboard Books, 142).

———, *This Business of Music*, 10th ed. New York, NY: Billboard Books, 143.

———, *This Business of Music*, 10th ed. New York, NY: Billboard Books, 2007, 332.

———, *This Business of Music*, 10th ed. New York, NY: Billboard Books, 2007, 333.

———, *This Business of Music*, 10th ed. New York, NY: Billboard Books, 2007, 333.

———, *This Business of Music*, New York, NY: Billboard Books, 2007, 334.

Langer, Susanne. *Philosophy in a New Key*, 2nd ed. Cambridge: Harvard University Press, 1951, 625-630.

———, *Philosophy in a New Key*, 2nd ed. Cambridge: Harvard University Press, 1951, 212-213

———, *Philosophy in a New Key*, 2nd ed. Cambridge: Harvard University Press, 1951, 201-215.

———, *Philosophy in a New Key*, 2nd ed. Cambridge: Harvard University Press, 1951, 625-630.

Lauder, Thomas Suh. "Spending on Entertainment," Los Angeles Times, http://latimes.com/business, (accessed January 17, 2011).

Leaffer, Marshall. *Understanding Copyright Law*, 4th ed. New York, NY: Matthew Bender, 1989.

———, *Understanding Copyright Law*, 4th ed. New York, NY: Matthew Bender, 1989.

———, *Understanding Copyright Law*, 4th ed. New York, NY: Matthew Bender, 1989.

———, *Understanding Copyright Law*, 4th ed. New York, NY: Matthew Bender, 1989.

———, *Mind at a Time* New York: Simon & Schuster, 2002.

———, *Mind at a Time* New York: Simon & Schuster, 2002.

———, *Mind at a Time* New York: Simon & Schuster, 2002.

Levitin, Daniel. *The World in Six Songs: How the Musical Brain Created Human Nature*, New York: Penguin Books: 2008.

———, *The World in Six Songs: How the Musical Brain Created Human Nature*, New York: Penguin Books: 2008, 3-4.

Library of Congress, "Notice of Termination," http://www.copyright (accessed July 6, 2010).

———, "Notice of Termination," http://www.copyright (accessed July 6, 2010).

———, "Announcements: Notice with Requests for Comments as Containment for Controversy for 1992 and 1993 Digital Audio Recording Royalty Funds http://www.copyright.gov/history/mls/ML-475.pdf (accessed July 8, 2010).

———, "Code of Federal Regulations: section 201.18:Notice of intent to obtain a compulsory license for making and distributing phonorecords of non dramatic musical works, http://www.loc.gov/cgi-bin/formprocessor/copyright, (accessed September 18, 2010).

———, "Code of Federal Regulations: section 201.18:Notice of intent to obtain a compulsory license for making and distributing phonorecords of non dramatic musical works, http://www.loc.gov/cgi-bin/formprocessor/copyright, (accessed January 30, 2011).

———, "Copyright Act of 1909," http://www.copyright, (accessed January 1, 2011).

———, "Copyright Act of 1909," http://www.copyright, (accessed January 1, 2011).

———, "Copyright Arbitration Royalty Panels (CARP)," http://www.copyright (accessed July 7, 2010)

———, "Copyright Basic: What is a Copyright," http://www.copyright.gov/circs/circ1.pdf, (accessed June 25, 2010).

———, "Copyright Basic: What is a Copyright," http://www.copyright.gov/circs/circ1.pdf, (accessed June 25, 2010).

———, "Copyright Basics: Termination of Transfers," http://www.copyright (accessed July 6, 2010).

———, "Copyright in General: When is My Work Protected?" http://www.copyright, (accessed January 1, 2011).

———, "Copyright Law of the United States of America and Related Laws Contained in Title 17 of the United States Code: 405 Notice of Copyright: Omission of Notice on Certain Copies and Phonorecords," http://www.copyright, (accessed January 1, 2011).

———, "Copyright Law of the United States of America and Related Laws Contained in Title 17 of the United States Code: 405 Notice of Copyright: Omission of Notice on Certain Copies and Phonorecords," http://www.copyright, (accessed January 1, 2011).

———, "Copyright Law Revision, Section 19: Certificate of Recordation," http://www.copyright, (accessed, January 30, 2011).

———, "Copyright Law: Chapter One: 106A. Rights of certain authors to attribution and integrity," http://www.copyright, (accessed January 1, 2011).

———, "Copyright Notice," http://www.copyright, (accessed January 1, 2011).

———, "Copyright Notice," http://www.copyright, (accessed January 1, 2011).

———, "Copyright Notice," http://www.copyright, (accessed January 1, 2011).

———, "Copyright Office, Notice of Intent of Obtain a Compulsory License," http://www.copright.gov/circs/circ73.pdf, (accessed July 6, 2010).

———, "Copyright Office: Copyright Basics-How Long Copyright Protections Endures," http://www.copyright, (accessed July 12, 2010).

———, "Copyright Office: Copyright Basics-How Long Copyright Protections Endures," http://www.copyright, (accessed July 12, 2010).

———, "Copyright Office: eCO online system," http://www.copyright, (accessed July 12. 2-10).

———, "Copyright Office: eCO online system," http://www.copyright, (accessed July 12. 2-10).

———, "Copyright Office: eCO online system," http://www.copyright, (accessed July 12. 2-10).

———, "Copyright Office: eCO online system," http://www.copyright, (accessed July 12. 2-10).

———, "Copyright Office: eCO online system," http://www.copyright, (accessed July 12. 2-10).
———, "Copyright Office: Memorandum Opinion-In the Manner of Mechanical and Digital Phonorecords Delivery Rate Adjustment Proceedings," http://www.copyright, (accessed January 30, 2011).
———, "Copyright Office: Memorandum Opinion-In the Manner of Mechanical and Digital Phonorecords Delivery Rate Adjustment Proceedings," http://www.copyright, (accessed January 30, 2011).
———, "Copyright Royalty and Distribution Reform Act of 2004," http://www.copyright (accessed July 8, 2010) & Statement of Marybeth Peters, Register of the Copyrights, before the Sub Committee on the Courts and the Internet, and Intellectual Property Committee on the Judiciary," http://www.copyright.gov/docs/regstat040103.html, (accessed January 3, 2011)
———, "Definitions," http://www.copyright, (July 12, 2010).
———, "Definitions," http://www.copyright, (July 12, 2010).
———, "Definitions," http://www.copyright, (July 12, 2010).
———, "Definitions," http://www.copyright, (July 12, 2010).
———, "Digital Performance Right in Sound Recording Act of 1995," http://www.google.com/#hl=en&expIds=17259,17315,23628,23670, (accessed January 2, 2011).
———, "Digital Performance Right in Sound Recording Act of 1995," http://www.copyright (accessed July 7, 2010).
———, "Duration of a Copyright: Effect of 1976 Act on Length of Subsisting Copyrights," http://www.copyright, (accessed January 1, 2011).
———, "http://www.copyright.gov/wipo/, (accessed January 3, 2011).
———, "No Electronic Theft Act (NET ACT), http://www.justice.gov/criminal/cybercrime/17-18red.htm (January 2, 2011)
———, "No Electronic Theft Act (NET ACT)," "http://www.copyright (accessed September 5, 2010)
———, "Notable Dates in United States Copyrights," http://www.copyright.gov/circs/circ1a.html, (accessed June 25, 2010).
———, "Sonny Bono Copyright Term Extension Act of 1998: Chapter 3, Duration of Copyright," http://www.copyright, (accessed January 2, 2011).
———, "The Digital Millennium Copyright Act of 1998," http://cryptome.org/dmca/dmca-index.htm#DMCA, (accessed January, 2, 2011)
———, "The United States Copyright Office: A Brief Introduction and History," http://www.copyright.gov/circs/circ1a.html, (accessed June 25, 2010).
———, "The United States Copyright Office: A Brief Introduction and History," http://www.copyright.gov/circs/circ1a.html, (accessed June 25, 2010).
———, "The United States Copyright Office: A Brief Introduction and History," http://www.copyright.gov/circs/circ1a.html, (accessed June 25, 2010).
———, "The United States Copyright Office: A Brief Introduction and History," http://www.copyright.gov/circs/circ1a.html, (accessed June 25, 2010).
———, "The United States Copyright Office: A Brief Introduction and History," http://www.copyright, (accessed February 24, 2011).
———, "Transfer of Copyright," http://www.copyright, (accessed January 30, 2011).
———, "Transfer of Copyright," http://www.copyright, (accessed January 30, 2011).
———, "United States Copyright Office: Compulsory License for Making and Distributing Phonorecords," http://www.copyright.gov/circs/circ73.pdf (accessed July 6, 2010).
———, "United States Public Laws 102-563-The Home Recording Act of 1992," http://www.brouhaha.com/~eric/bad_laws/ahra.html (accessed January 1, 2011).
———, "Welcome to the eCO tutorial," http://www.copyright, (accessed January 30, 2011).
———, "What Does Copyright Protect?" http://www.copyright, (January 3, 2011).
———, "What Does Copyright Protect?" http://www.copyright, (January 3, 2011).
———, "Works Made for Hire Under the 1976 Copyright Act," http://www.copyright, (accessed January 1, 2011).
———, Copyright Law of the United States of America, The Copyright Royalty and Distribution Reform Act of 2004," http://www.copyright, (accessed January 2, 2011)
———, Mechanical and Digital Phonorecord Delivery Compulsory License," http://www.copyright, (accessed January 30, 2011).
———, Title 37: Patents, Trademarks, and Copyrights, "The Code of Federal Regulations: 201.18 Notice of Intent to Obtain a Compulsory License for Making and Distributing Records of Nondramatic Musical Works," http://www.loc.gov/cgi-bin/formprocessor/copyright (accessed July 6, 2010).
Lipman, Monte. (as quoted by Joshua Chaffin), "By Promoting Gigs, Record Labels Get in on Bigger Acts," The

Financial Times, http://www.ft.com/cms/s/0/6e362eee-4204-11dd-a5e8-0000779fd2ac.html#axzz1GgKEQk46, (accessed March 15, 2011).

Live Nation Entertainment, "Live Nation Entertainment; Company Description," Hoovers.com, http://www.hoovers.com/company/Live_Nation_Entertainment_Inc/hhhkji-1.html, (accessed April 3, 2011).

Lopes, Gabriela. "The Broader Music Industry," International Federation of the Phonographic Industry, http://www.ifpi.org/content/library/the-broader-music-industry.pdf as reported from PriceWaterhouseCoppers (accessed July 8, 2010).

Love, Courtney. "Courtney Love does the Math," Salon.com, http://www.salon.com/technology/feature/2000/06/14/love, (accessed March 15, 2011).

Mankiw, N., Gregory. *Principles of Economics*, 4th ed, Thompson-Southwestern: Mason, Ohio.

Marcus, David, Adam. *The Celestial Jukebox Revisited: Best Practices and Copyright Law Revisions for Subscription-Based Online Music Services*. A Thesis submitted to the Faculty of the Graduate School of Arts and Sciences of Georgetown University in partial fulfillment of the requirements for the degree of Master of Arts in Communication, Culture and Technology, http://www8.georgetown.edu/cct/thesis/AdamMarcus.pdf, (accessed March 9, 2011).

Marley, Bob. "Bob Marley Quotes," Artnotes.net, http://www.artquotes.net/entertainment-quotes/bob-marley.htm, (accessed March 19, 2011).

Marquis, Don. "Publishing Quotes," Brainy Quote, http://www.brainyquote.com/quotes/keywords/publishing_3.html, (accessed July 17, 2010).

Maugham, Somerset, W. "Money," Proverbia.net, http://en.proverbia.net/citastema.asp?tematica=780&page=4, (accessed March 9, 2011).

MC Marketing Charts, "Email Drives Social Networking," Marketingcharts.com, http://www.marketingcharts.com/direct/email-drives-social-networking-13448/, (accessed August 1, 2010).

MC Marketing Charts, "Email Drives Social Networking," Marketingcharts.com, http://www.marketingcharts.com/direct/email-drives-social-networking-13448/, (accessed August 1, 2010).

MCA, "MCA, Seagram and Universal Group," Ketupa.com, http://ketupa.net/universal.htm, (accessed July 22, 2010).

McCracken, Sandra. "Music's Foreign Royalties bring Welcome Windfall," The Tennessean, http://www.tennessean.com/article/20100724/BUSINESS01/7240308/Music+s+foreign+royalties (accessed July 24, 2010).

McCready, Michael. "Copyright Law, Treaties and Advice: The Law Regarding Music Sampling ," http://www.copynot.org/Pages/Music%20sampling.htm, (January 17, 2011).

McDonald, Macy. "History of MCA Records," Ehow.com, http://www.ehow.com/facts_5122069_history-mca-records.html, (accessed July 22, 2010).

Missing Link, "Who We Are," Missinglink.com, http://www.missingink.com/who_we_are, (accessed April 7, 2011).

Monroe, Marilyn. "Marilyn Monroe Quotes," Artquotes.net, http://www.artquotes.net/entertainment-quotes/famous-actresses/marilyn-monroe.htm, (accessed March 15, 2011).

Morrison, Van. "Top 50 Music Quotations," John Pawlett, http://afgen.com/top50.html, (accessed January 7, 2011).

Moser, David, *Moser on Music Copyrights*, Boston, MA: Course Technology/Cenage Learning, 2006, 2.

———, *Moser on Music Copyrights*, Boston, MA: Course Technology/Cenage Learning, 2006, 3.

———, *Moser on Music Copyrights*, Boston, MA: Course Technology/Cenage Learning, 2006, 15.

———, *Moser on Music Copyrights*, Boston, MA: Course Technology/Cenage Learning, 2006, 15.

———, *Moser on Music Copyrights*, Boston, MA: Course Technology/Cenage Learning, 2006, 16-17.

———, *Moser on Music Copyrights*, Boston, MA: Course Technology/Cenage Learning, 2006, 23.

———, *Moser on Music Copyrights*, Boston, MA: Course Technology/Cenage Learning, 2006, 66.

———, *Moser on Music Copyrights*, Boston, MA: Course Technology/Cenage Learning, 2006, 19.

———, *Moser on Music Copyrights*, Boston, MA: Course Technology/Cenage Learning, 2006, 192-3.

Music Performance Fund, "About Us: Enriching Lives Through Music," MPF, http://www.musicpf.org/AboutUs2.html, (accessed March 22, 2011).

NACA (National Association of Campus Activities), "Events," Naca.org, http://www.naca.org/Events/Pages/default.aspx, (accessed April 4, 2011).

NAKASHIMA, R. "MOG, Radio New Entrants to $10-a-Month Mobile Music," The Associated Press, http://www.rgj.com/article/20100704/BIZ15/7040316/MOG-Rdio-new-entrants-to-10-a-month-mobile-music (accessed 2010 July 5).

———, "MOG, Radio New Entrants to $10-a-Month Mobile Music," The Associated Press, http://www.rgj.com/article/20100704/BIZ15/7040316/MOG-Rdio-new-entrants-to-10-a-month-mobile-music (accessed 2010 July 5).

National Music Publishers Association (NMPA), "About the NMPA," http://www.nmpa.org/home/index.asp, (accessed July 20, 2010).

———, (NMPA), "About the NMPA," http://www.nmpa.org/home/index.asp, (accessed July 20, 2010).

———, (NMPA), "About the NMPA," http://www.nmpa.org/home/index.asp, (accessed July 20, 2010).

Neil, Vince, (of Motley Crüe), "Behind the Music," VH-1, (Intermedia Cable, transmission, Nashville, TN, December 14, 1998).

NewsCorp, "Executives and Contacts," http://www.newscorp.com/management/index.html, (accessed March 11, 2011).

Nielsen, "Fact Sheet," http://en-us.nielsen.com/content/dam/nielsen/en_us/documents/pdf/Fact%20Sheets/Nielsen%20SoundScan%20One%20Sheet.pdf, (accessed July 18, 2010).

———, "Nielsen's U.S. Soundscan Venue Sales Procedures," http://www.nielsen.com/content/dam/corporate/us/en/public%20factsheets/Soundscan/SoundScan, (accessed March 9, 2011).

Noiseaddicts.com, "First Ever Recording of Digital Music," Noiseaddicts.com, http://www.noiseaddicts.com/2008/08/first-ever-recording-of-digital-music/, (accessed August 5, 2010).

———, "First Ever Recording of Digital Music," Noiseaddicts.com, http://www.noiseaddicts.com/2008/08/first-ever-recording-of-digital-music/, (accessed August 5, 2010).

Norris, Chuck. "Biography for Chuck Norris," IMDB.com (The Internet Movie Database), http://www.imdb.com/name/nm0001569/bio, (accessed April 2, 2011).

NPR (National Public Radio), "About." www.npr.org/about, (accessed March 17, 2011).

NSAI (The Nashville Songwriters Association International), "It all Begins with a Song," http://members.nashvillesongwriters.com/news.php?NewsSectionId=87, (accessed July 15, 2010).

O. Yale Lewis, Jr. for Hendricks & Lewis PLLC, "Publicity Rights Revisited," http://hllaw.com/images/78222PublicityRights.pdf, (accessed January 3, 2011).

O' Malley-Greenburg, Zack. "You Want to Be a Billionair: How Bad," Forbes, March 28, 2011, 28.

———, "You Want to Be a Billionaire: How Bad," Forbes, March 28, 2011, 28

Obringer, Ann, Lee. "How Music royalties Work," http://entertainment.howstuffworks.com/music-royalties4.htm (accessed July, 20, 2010).

Oscar Awards, (Academy of Motion Picture Arts and Sciences), "History and Organization," AMPAS, http://www.oscars.org/awards/governors/index.html, (accessed April 19, 2011).

Ostrowski, Hartmut. "Press Release: "Sony to Purchase Berteslmann's 50% Stake in Sony BG: Music Company to Become Wholly Owned Subsidiary of Sony Corporation of America," Sony Corporation of America, http://www.sony.com/SCA/press/080805.shtml, (accessed March 15, 2011).

Oxenford, David. "Department of Commerce Seeks Comments on The Relationship of Protecting Copyrighted Content and Innovation in the Internet Economy," http://www.broadcastlawblog.com/tags/digital-millennium-copyright (accessed January 2, 2011).

Palmer, James. "Brain Works More Like Internet than 'Top Down' Company," BBC, News Science & Environment. http://www.bbc.co.uk/news/science-environment-10925841, (accessed August, 10, 2010).

Panos Panay, "Rethinking Music: The Future of Making Money as a Performing Musicians," The Berkman Center for Internet & Society at Harvard University, Harvard University, http://cyber.law.harvard.edu/publications/2011/Rethinking_Music, (accessed May 2, 2011).

———, "Rethinking Music: The Future of Making Money as a Performing Musicians," The Berkman Center for Internet & Society at Harvard University, Harvard University, http://cyber.law.harvard.edu/publications/2011/Rethinking_Music, (accessed May 2, 2011).

Parker, Charley. "Charley Parker Quotes," Thinkexist.com, http://thinkexist.com/quotation/music_is_your_own_experience-your_own_thoughts/202273.html, (accessed March 19, 2011).

———, "Colonel Tom Parker Quotes," Brainyquote.com, http://www.brainyquote.com/quotes/quotes/c/coloneltom185469.html, April 3, 2011).

Passman, Donald. *All you need to know about the music business*, 7th ed. New York, NY: Free Press, 2009.

———, *All you need to know about the music business*, 7th ed. New York, NY: Free Press, 2009.

———, *All You Need to Know About the Music Business*, 7th ed. 7th ed. (New York, NY: Free Press, 2009.

———, *All You Need to Know About the Music Business,* 7th ed. (New York: Freepress, 2009) 163.

———, *All You Need to Know About the Music Business,* 7th ed. (New York: Freepress, 2009) 163.

———, *All You Need to Know About the Music Business,* 7th ed. (New York: Freepress, 2009) 163.

Peoples, Glen "iTunes Price Changes Hurt Some Rankings," Billboard.biz, http://www.billboard.biz/bbbiz/content_display/industry/e3i7917210cb575a9b9adc60840c7d7f16e, (accessed September 25, 2010).

Peters, Marybeth. "Statement of Marybeth Peters
The Register of Copyrights
before the

Subcommittee on Courts,
The Internet and Intellectual Property
of the House Committee on the Judiciary," http://www.copyright, (accessed July 18, 2010).

———, "Statement of Marybeth Peters
The Register of Copyrights
before the
Subcommittee on Courts,
The Internet and Intellectual Property
of the House Committee on the Judiciary," http://www.copyright, (accessed July 18, 2010).

———, "Statement of Marybeth Peters
The Register of Copyrights
before the
Subcommittee on Courts,
The Internet and Intellectual Property
of the House Committee on the Judiciary," http://www.copyright, (accessed July 18, 2010).

———, "Statement of Marybeth Peters
The Register of Copyrights
before the
Subcommittee on Courts,
The Internet and Intellectual Property
of the House Committee on the Judiciary," http://www.copyright, (accessed July 18, 2010).

———, "Statement of Marybeth Peters, The Register of Copyrights before the Subcommittee on Courts, The International and Intellectual Property of the House Committee on the Judiciary," http://www.copyright (accessed September 5, 2010).

———, "Statement of Marybeth Peters, The Register of Copyrights before the Subcommittee on Courts, The International and Intellectual Property of the House Committee on the Judiciary," http://www.copyright (accessed September 5, 2010).

———, "Statement of Marybeth Peters, The Register of Copyrights before the Subcommittee on Courts, The International and Intellectual Property of the House Committee on the Judiciary," http://www.copyright (accessed September 5, 2010).

———, "Statement of Marybeth Peters, The Register of Copyrights before the Subcommittee on Courts, The International and Intellectual Property of the House Committee on the Judiciary," http://www.copyright (accessed September 5, 2010).

———, "Statement of Marybeth Peters, The Register of Copyrights before the Subcommittee on Courts, The International and Intellectual Property of the House Committee on the Judiciary," http://www.copyright (accessed September 5, 2010).

———, "Statement of Marybeth Peters: The Register of Copyrights Before the Subcommittee on Courts and Intellectual Property Committee on the Judiciary," Sound Recordings As Works Made for Hire. http://www.copyright, (accessed January 18, 2011).

———, "Statement of Marybeth Peters: The Register of Copyrights Before the Subcommittee on Courts and Intellectual Property Committee on the Judiciary," Sound Recordings As Works Made for Hire. http://www.copyright, (accessed January 18, 2011).

———, The Register of Copyrights
before the
Subcommittee on Courts and Intellectual Property
Committee on the Judiciary," "Sound Recordings as Works Made for Hire," http://www.copyright, (accessed January 7, 2011).

Petrecca, Laura. "Sony Nearer Control of Beatles' Songs," USA Today, http://www.usatoday.com/money/media, (accessed July 16, 2010).

———, "Sony Nearer Control of Beatles' Songs," USA Today, http://www.usatoday.com/money/media, (accessed July 16, 2010).

Pham, Alan. "Online Ticketing Service let's Fans Name Price," L.A. Times, as reported in the Nashville Tennessean, February 11, 2011; found online at http://www.tennessean.com/article/20110219/BUSINESS06/102190329/Online-ticketing-service-lets-fans-name-price-?odyssey=mod|newswell|img|FRONTPAGE|p, (February 19, 2011).

———, "Online Ticketing Service let's Fans Name Price," L.A. Times, as reported in the Nashville Tennessean, February 11, 2011; found online at http://www.tennessean.com/article/20110219/BUSINESS06/102190329/Online-ticketing-service-lets-fans-name-price-?odyssey=mod|newswell|img|FRONTPAGE|p, (February 19,

2011). Chapter 24-No Citations
Plato, "Favorite Quotes About Music & Songwriting," http://www.songwritersresourcenetwork.com/quotes.html, (accessed July 13, 2010).
Poe, Randy. *Music Publishing: A Songwriters Guide*. Cincinnati, OH: Writers Digest Books, 1997.
Pollstar "Boxoffice Reporting Policies," Pollstar.com, .pollstarpro.com/opencontent.aspx?ArticleID=1804&id=home, (accessed April 7, 2011).
———, "Store," Pollstar.com, http://www.pollstar.com/reviews.aspx, (accessed April 8, 2011).
Presley, Elvis. "Elvis Presley Quotes," Artquote.com, http://www.artquotes.net/entertainment-quotes/famous-singers, (accessed April 3, 2011).
———, "Elvis Presley Quotes," How Stuff Works, A Discovery Company, http://entertainment.howstuffworks.com/elvis-presley-quotes.htm, (accessed July 13, 2010).
Prince, "The Artist Formerly Known as Prince Say He will use the Name Prince Once Again," Bnet.com, http://findarticles.com/p/articles/mi_m1355/is_26_97/ai_62685485/, (accessed March 24, 2011).
Radiomagonline.com, "Copyright Office Post NAB, Sound Exchange Streaming Rates in Federal Register," http://radiomagonline.com/IT_technology/streaming/copyright-office-posts-nab-sound-exchanage-streaming-federal-register-0305/ (accessed March 9, 2011).
———, "Copyright Office Post NAB, Sound Exchange Streaming Rates in Federal Register," http://radiomagonline.com/IT_technology/streaming/copyright-office-posts-nab-sound-exchanage-streaming-federal-register-0305/ (accessed March 9, 2011).
———, "Copyright Office Post NAB, Sound Exchange Streaming Rates in Federal Register," http://radiomagonline.com/IT_technology/streaming/copyright-office-posts-nab-sound-exchanage-streaming-federal-register-0305/ (accessed March 9, 2011).
Recording History, "The History of Recording," Recording-history.org, http://www.recording-history.org/HTML/musicbiz1.php, (accessed March 15, 2011).
Recording Industry Association of America (RIAA), "Facts and Figures," http://www.riaa.com/keystatistics.php, (accessed March 9, 2011).
———, (RIAA), "Piracy Online and on the Street," http://www.riaa.org/physicalpiracy.php, (accessed January 2, 2011).
———, "2008-2009 U.S. Shipment Numbers," "http://www.riaa.org/keystatistics.php?content_selector=2008-2009-U.S-Shipment-Numbers (accessed July 3, 2010).
———, (RIAA), "About Us," http://www.riaa.com/aboutus.php, (accessed March 17, 2011).
———, (RIAA) "Gold and Platinum," RIAA.org, http://www.riaa.com/goldandplatinum.php?content_selector=digital_sales_award, (accessed April 2, 2011).
ReverbNation, (article posting by Ferol) "Reverbnations' Facebook app My Band gets a name (Band Profile) new features, and it's still 100% Free," ReverbNation & Digital Music News, http://blog.reverbnation.com/, (accessed April 2, 2011).
———, (article posting by Ferol) "Reverbnations' Facebook app My Band gets a name (Band Profile) new features, and it's still 100% Free," ReverbNation & Digital Music News, http://blog.reverbnation.com/, (accessed April 2, 2011).
RIAA, "Piracy: Online and On the Streets," http://www.riaa.org/physicalpiracy.php, (accessed March 29, 2011).
———, Recording Industry Association of American (R.I.A.A.), (NPD Digital Music Study 2009 as Reported in "Let the Music Play," RIAA 2010) 11.
———, Recording Industry Association of American (R.I.A.A.), (NPD Digital Music Study 2009 as Reported in "Let the Music Play," RIAA 2010) 11.
Ricketson, Samuel. "The Birth of the Berne Union, 11 Colum-VLAJ.L. & Arts," http://www.peteryu.com/intip/class2.pdf, (January 1, 2011).
Robinson, Smokey. "Great-Quotes.com." Gledhill Enterprises, 2011, http://www.great-quotes.com/quote/1460494, (accessed July 16, 2010).
Rudd, Benjamin. (At the Library of Congress), "Notable Dates in American Copyrights 1783-1969" http://www.copyright, (accessed January 1, 2011).
Sandova, Greg. "Amazon Finds Niche in iTunes-dominated Market, http://news.cnet.com/8301-1023_3-10213149-93, (accessed September 25, 2010).
Sara Edelman, "Death Pays: The Fight Over Marilyn Monroe's Publicity Rights," http://www.metrocorpcounsel.com/current.php?artType=view&artMonth=July&artYear=2007&EntryNo=6903, (accessed January 3, 2011).
Schneider, Stephen. *Iced: The Story of Organized Crime in Canada*, http://books.google.com/books?id=ZO8jKSn25DAC&pg=PA200&lpg=PA200&dq=Bonaventure+Liquor+Store+Company.&source=bl&ots=rZnXslgXrj&sig=nk3YfFaOmeVaP0JYxA9nYdA-

ozM&hl=en&ei=SHpITMOoJIGClAfj0dnkDA&sa=X&oi=book_result&ct=result&resnum=2&ved=0CBYQ6AEwAQ#v=onepage&q=Bonaventure%20Liquor%20Store%20Company.&f=false (July 22, 2010).

Schonfeld, Erick. "iTunes Sells 6 Billion Songs and Other Fun Stats from the Philnote," TechChrunch.com, http://techcrunch.com/2009/01/06/itunes-sells-6-billion-songs-and-other-fun-stats-from-the-philnote/, (accessed March 10, 2011).

Schulenberg, Richard. *Legal Aspects of the Music Industry: An Insider's View of the Legal and Practical Aspects of the Music Business* New York, NY: Billboard Books 1999.

Schumpeter, Joseph A. "Creative Destruction" From the book, *Capitalism, Socialism and Democracy*, New York, NY: Harper, 1975 [orig. pub. 1942], 82-85 & found at http://transcriptions.english.ucsb.edu/archive/courses/liu/english25/materials/schumpeter.html, (accessed April 7, 2011).

———, "Creative Destruction," From the book, *Capitalism, Socialism and Democracy*, Harper: New York: NY, 1942 82-85.

Schwartz, Evan, (as quoted in an article by Ken Bruno), "Music in the Cloud," Forbes.com, http://www.forbes.com/2010/07/21/music-cloud-computing-technology-thumbplay.html?boxes=techchanneltopstories, (accessed March 17, 2011).

———, (as quoted in an article by Ken Bruno), "Music in the Cloud," Forbes.com, http://www.forbes.com/2010/07/21/music-cloud-computing-technology-thumbplay.html?boxes=techchanneltopstories, (accessed March 17, 2011).

Science and Technology." Newsweek.msnbc.com, http://www.brams.umontreal.ca/plab/research/dossiers_vulgarisation/newsweek_musicmind/newsweek_musicmind.

Seneca, Annaeus, Lucius, "Money," Proverbia.net, http://en.proverbia.net/citastema.asp?tematica=780&page=4, (accessed March 9, 2011).

SESAC, "About SESAC: How Does SESAC Differ from ASCAP and BMI," http://www.sesac.com/EDU/faqs.aspx, (July 19, 2010).

———, "About SESAC: SESAC was Established in 1930, Built on Tradition, Service and Innovation," http://www.sesac.com/About/History.aspx, (Accessed July 19, 2010).

———, "About SESAC: SESAC was Established in 1930, Built on Tradition, Service and Innovation," http://www.sesac.com/About/History.aspx, (Accessed July 19, 2010).

———, "SESAC Selects TuneSet to Monitor Performance in Television Broadcasts," http://www.sesac.com/News/News_Details.aspx?id=1129, (accessed July 19, 2010).

———, "SESAC Selects TuneSet to Monitor Performance in Television Broadcasts," http://www.sesac.com/News/News_Details.aspx?id=1129, (accessed July 19, 2010).

Silverman, Tommy. & Garland, Eric. "Warning, Some of these Stats are really, really Scary," Digitalmusicnews.com, http://www.digitalmusicnews.com/stories/072110nmsstats#sm_FMtJUSBV5-9voXkkYLQ, (accessed March 17, 2011).

———, "Warning, Some of these Stats are really, really Scary," Digitalmusicnews.com, http://www.digitalmusicnews.com/stories/072110nmsstats#sm_FMtJUSBV5-9voXkkYLQ, (accessed March 17, 2011).

Simpson, Homer. "Homer Simpson Quotes," Artquotes.net, http://www.artquotes.net/entertainment-quotes/famous-actors, (accessed March 24, 2011).

Siwek, Stephen. "Copyright Industries in the U.S: Songwriters Resource Network, Economy: The 2003-2007 Report," Economists Incorporated, prepared for the International Intellectual Property Alliance (IIPA), June 2009, available at www.iipa.com, (accessed June 26, 2010).

Siwek, Stephen. "The True Cost of Sound Recording Piracy in the Uninted States," The United States Institute for Policy Innovation, http://www.ipi.org/IPI/IPIHome.nsf?OpenDatabase, (Accessed May 13, 2011).

Songwriter's Guild of America, "SGA Provides 75 Years of Advocacy, Education to Songwriters," http://www.songwritersguild.com/history.htm, (accessed July 15, 2010).

———, "SGA Provides 75 Years of Advocacy, Education to Songwriters," http://www.songwritersguild.com/history.htm, (accessed July 15, 2010).

Sony Corporation of America, "jobs at Sony," Sony Corporation of America, http://www.sony.com/SCA/jobs.shtml & Warner Music Group, "Jobs," Warner Music Group, http://www.wmg.com/jobsoverview, (accessed April 3, 2011), & Personal interviews with industry insiders (2011).

———, "Make.Believe," Sony Corporation Annual Report 2011, http://www.sony.net/SonyInfo/IR/financial/ar/8ido18000003dkyy-att/8ido18000003dl0u.pdf, (accessed March 11, 2011).

———, "Make.Believe," Sony Corporation Annual Report 2011, http://www.sony.net/SonyInfo/IR/financial/ar/8ido18000003dkyy-att/8ido18000003dl0u.pdf, (accessed March 11, 2011).

———, "Make.Believe," Sony Corporation Annual Report 2011, http://www.sony.net/SonyInfo/IR/financial/ar/8ido18000003dkyy-att/8ido18000003dl0u.pdf, (accessed March 11, 2011).

———, "Remembering Masaru Ibuka," Sony Corporation Annual Report 1998, "Do You Dream in Sony?" http://www.sony.net/SonyInfo/IR/financial/ar/qfhh7c000000g7ry-att/ar_sony_1998.pdf, (accessed March 11, 2011).

———, "Remembering Masaru Ibuka," Sony Corporation Annual Report 1998, "Do You Dream in Sony?" http://www.sony.net/SonyInfo/IR/financial/ar/qfhh7c000000g7ry-att/ar_sony_1998.pdf, (accessed March 11, 2011).

———, "Remembering Masaru Ibuka," Sony Corporation Annual Report 1998, "Do You Dream in Sony?" http://www.sony.net/SonyInfo/IR/financial/ar/qfhh7c000000g7ry-att/ar_sony_1998.pdf, (accessed March 11, 2011).

Sony Music Holdings, Hoovers, http://www.hoovers.com/company/Sony_Music_Holdings_Inc/ryhctsi-1.html, (accessed July 16, 2010).

SoundExchange, "I'm Not Sure, Help Me Figure this Out," http://soundexchange.com/service-provider/service-category/im-not-sure-help-me-figure-it-out/, (accessed February 8, 2011).

———, "SoundExchange Is," http://www.soundexchange.com/, (accessed January 30, 2011).

Southside Glen, "The Difference between Delay and Reverb," Homerecording.com, http://homerecording.com/bbs/general-discussions/recording-techniques/difference-between-applying-delay-reverb-263441/, (accessed March 22, 2011).

Sparks, Nicholas. "Publishing Quotes," Brainy Quote, http://www.brainyquote.com/quotes/keywords/publishing_3.html, (accessed July 17, 2010).

Stewart, Valerie. "Enquire Within, Understanding Personal Construct Theory and George Kelly: Man is a Scientist," http://www.enquirewithin.co.nz/HINTS/skills2.htm, (accessed July 15, 2010).

———, "Enquire Within, Understanding Personal Construct Theory and George Kelly: Man is a Scientist," http://www.enquirewithin.co.nz/HINTS/skills2.htm, (accessed July 15, 2010).

———, "Enquire Within, Understanding Personal Construct Theory and George Kelly: Man is a Scientist," http://www.enquirewithin.co.nz/HINTS/skills2.htm, (accessed July 15, 2010).

Stravinsky, Igor. "Igor Stravinsky Quotes," Brainyquote.com, http://www.brainyquote.com/quotes/authors/i/igor_stravinsky.html, (April 3, 2011).

Stringer, Howard Sir. "Entertaining the Future," (Speech presented at the 2006 International Consumer Electronics Show, Las Vegas, NV, January 5, 2006) and at http://www.sony.com/SCA/speeches/060105_stringer.shtml, (accessed April 3, 2011).

———, "Entertaining the Future," (Speech presented at the 2006 International Consumer Electronics Show, Las Vegas, NV, January 5, 2006) and at http://www.sony.com/SCA/speeches/060105_stringer.shtml, (accessed April 3, 2011).

———, (as quoted in an article by Eliot Van Buskirk), "Sony Buys Out Bertelsmann Sony's BMG Stake for $1.2 Billion, Wired: Listening Post, http://www.wired.com/listening_post/2008/08/bertelsmann-bai/, (accessed March 15, 2011).

Strong, William. *The Copyright Book: A Practical Guide*, 5th ed. Cambridge, MA: The MIT Press, 1999, 2.

Swanekamp, Kelsey. "RealNetworks Spins off Rhapsody," http://www.forbes.com/2010/02/10/realnetworks-rhapsody-music-markets-equities-closer.html (July 25, 2010).

Terrafirma, "Terrafirma Annual Review 2009," http://www.terrafirma.com/ar09/AR09.pdf, (accessed July 21, 2010).

The 100 Greatest Songs of All Times, Squidoo, http://www.squidoo.com/100songs, (accessed July 15, 2010).

The AFM & AFTRA Intellectual Property Rights Distribution Fund, "About Us," RARoyalties.org, http://www.ahra.org/aboutus.html, (accessed March 26, 2011).

The Beatles, "The Beatles Quotes," ThinkExist.com, http://thinkexist.com/quotes/the_beatles, (accessed March 9, 2011).

Thompson, Hunter. "Music Business Quotes," Barryrudolph.com. http://www.barryrudolph.com/utilities/quotes.html (accessed December 31, 2010).

Ticketmaster, "About Us," Live Nation, http://www.ticketmaster.com/h/about_us.html?tm_link=tm_homeA_i_abouttm, (accessed April 7, 2011).

———, "Our History" ticketmaster.com, http://www.ticketmaster.com/history/index.html?tm_link=abouttm_history, (accessed April 7, 2011).

———, "Our History" ticketmaster.com, http://www.ticketmaster.com/history/index.html?tm_link=abouttm_history, (accessed April 7, 2011).

Time Archive, "History of Time," http://www.time.com/time/archive/collections/0,21428,c_time_history,00.shtml (July 22, 2010).

Time Warner, "Corporate Report," http://phx.corporate-ir.net/External.File?item=UGFyZW50SUQ9MzkxNTR8Q2hpbGRJRD0tMXxUeXBlPTM=&t=1 (July 21, 2010)

———, "The CBS-Viacom Merger: World of the Media Giants," http://www.time.com/time/magazine/article/0,9171,992008,00.html, July 22, 2010).

———, Annual Report 2009, http://phx.corporate-ir.net/External.File?

item=UGFyZW50SUQ9MzkxNTR8Q2hpbGRJRD0tMXxUeXBlPTM=&t=1, (accessed July 22, 2010).
———, Annual Report 2009, http://phx.corporate-ir.net/External.File?item=UGFyZW50SUQ9MzkxNTR8Q2hpbGRJRD0tMXxUeXBlPTM=&t=1, (accessed July 22, 2010).
———, Annual Report 2009, http://phx.corporate-ir.net/External.File?item=UGFyZW50SUQ9MzkxNTR8Q2hpbGRJRD0tMXxUeXBlPTM=&t=1, (accessed July 22, 2010).
———, Annual Report 2009, http://phx.corporate-ir.net/External.File?item=UGFyZW50SUQ9MzkxNTR8Q2hpbGRJRD0tMXxUeXBlPTM=&t=1, (accessed July 22, 2010).

Tuck, Paul. "Broadcast Data Systems," Music Media, http://www.musicmedianetwork.com/diy-bds.html, (accessed July 19,2010).

Turabian, Kate L. A Manual for Writers of Research Papers, Theses, and Dissertations, 7th ed. Chicago: The University of Chicago Press, 2007, 133-215.

U.S. Library of Congress, "Copyright: Fair Use Rights, http://www.copyright, (accessed January 1, 2011).
———, "Copyright: Stopping Copyright Infringements," http://www.copyright, (accessed January 1, 2011).
———, "Copyright Basics: Duration of a Copyright," http://www.copyright (accessed July 4, 2010) §
———, "Copyright Basics: How to Secure a Copyright," http://www.copyright.gov/circs/circ1.pdf, (accessed July 4, 2010).
———, "Copyright Basics: What is a Copyright," http://www.copyright.gov/circs/circ1.pdf, (accessed June 25, 2010).
———, "Copyright Basics: What Works are Protected," http://www.copyright.gov/circs/circ1.pdf, (accessed June 25, 2010).
———, "Copyright Basics: What Works are Protected," http://www.copyright.gov/circs/circ1.pdf, (accessed June 25, 2010).
———, "Copyright Basics: Who Can Claim a Copyright," http://www.copyright.gov/circs/circ1.pdf, (accessed July 4, 2010).
———, "Copyright in General: When is my Work Protected," http://www.copyright, (July 12, 2010).
———, "Title 17, U.S. Code", http://www.copyright (accessed October 2, 2010).
———, "Title 17, U.S. Code", http://www.copyright (accessed October 2, 2010).
———, "U.S. Copyright Definitions", http://www.copyright (accessed July 12, 2010).
———, "United States Copyright Office, Copyrights in General," http://www.copyright.gov/help/faq/faq-general.html, (accessed January 7, 2011)
———, "Sony Corp. v. Universal City Studios, Inc., 464 U.S. 417,"http://caselaw.lp.findlaw.com/scripts/getcase.pl?court=us&vol=464&invol=417 (accessed July 7, 2010)
———, "Sony Corp. v. Universal City Studios, Inc., 464 U.S. 417,"http://caselaw.lp.findlaw.com/scripts/getcase.pl?court=us&vol=464&invol=417 (accessed July 7, 2010)

Ulrich, Lars. as quoted by Fred Goodman, *Fortune's Fool: Edgar Bronfman Jr., Warner Music and an Industry in Crisis*, New York: Simon & Schuster, 2010, 133.

United States Constitution, "Art.1, sec.8" http://www.usconstitution.net/xconst_A1Sec8.html, (accessed June 25, 2010).
———, "Art.1, sec.8" http://www.usconstitution.net/xconst_A1Sec8.html, (accessed June 25, 2010).

United States Supreme Court, "GM Studios, Inc. v. Grokster, Ltd.," http://lawschool.courtroomview.com/acf_cases/9263-mgm-studios-inc-v-grokster-ltd- (accessed July 7, 2010).
———, "Metro-Goldwyn-Mayer Studios v. Grokster Ltd," http://www.oyez.org/cases/2000-2009/2004/2004_04_480, & http://scholar.google.com/scholar_case?case=8647956476676426155&hl=en&as_sdt=2&as_vis=1&oi=scholarr (accessed January 3, 2011).
———, "Metro-Goldwyn-Mayer Studios v. Grokster Ltd," http://www.oyez.org/cases/2000-2009/2004/2004_04_480, & http://scholar.google.com/scholar_case?case=8647956476676426155&hl=en&as_sdt=2&as_vis=1&oi=scholarr (accessed January 3, 2011).

United Talent Agency, "Mediaprostudio," United Talent Agency, http://www.mediaprostudios.com/, (accessed March 29, 2011).
———, (UTA), "Production Department," http://www.utaproduction.com/, (accessed August 24, 2010).
———, (UTA), "United Talent Agency," Hoover's Company Profiles, http://www.hoovers.com/company/United_Talent_Agency_Inc/hytrxi-1.html, (accessed August 24, 2010).

Universal Music Group, "History, Polygram and Universal," http://www.universalmusic.com/history#year1996, (July 22, 2010).
———, "History, Polygram and Universal," http://www.universalmusic.com/history#year1996, (July 22, 2010).
———, "History, Polygram and Universal," http://www.universalmusic.com/history#year1996, (July 22, 2010).
———, "History," http://new.umusic.com/history.aspx, (accessed March 17, 2011).
———, "History," http://new.umusic.com/history.aspx, (accessed March 17, 2011).

———, "History," http://new.umusic.com/history.aspx, (accessed March 17, 2011).

———, "Overview," http://new.umusic.com/Overview.aspx, (accessed March 17, 2011).

Unknown Author, "The Entertainment Glut," Business Week Magazine, (09/11/1998).

Vevendi/Universal, "Corporate Information," Vivendi.com, 42, Avenue de Friedland, 75380 Paris Tel: 33 1 71 7110 00, Fax: 33 1 71 7111 79, www.vivendi.com

———, "Viacom Annual Report 2009." http://www.viacom.com/news/Pages/newstext.aspx?RID=1312788, (accessed March 11, 2011).

———, "Vivendi: Favorable US Supreme Court Judgement," http://www.vivendi.com/vivendi/Vivendi-Favorable-US-Supreme-Court (July 22, 2010).

Volman, Mark. "Types of Concert Tour Deals," *Survey of Music Business Course Pack*, (Belmont University, Nashville, TN, 2008).

———, "Types of Concert Tour Deals," *Survey of Music Business Course Pack*, (Belmont University, Nashville, TN, 2008).

———, *All Access Pass* (Course Pack-Belmont University, 2008).

———, *All Access Pass* (Course Pack-Belmont University, 2008).

———, *Survey of Music Business Course Pack*, Belmont University, Nashville, TN: Belmont University, 2008).

———, *Survey of Music Business MBU 1110*, (Nashville: TN, Belmont University Course Pack, 2008).

W.I.P.O., World Intellectual Property Organization Handbook, W.I.P.O., http://www.wipo.int/export/sites/www/about-ip/en/iprm/pdf/ch2.pdf (accessed July 3, 2010).

———, World Intellectual Property Organization Handbook, W.I.P.O., http://www.wipo.int/export/sites/www/about-ip/en/iprm/pdf/ch2.pdf (accessed July 3, 2010).

———, World Intellectual Property Organization Handbook, W.I.P.O., http://www.wipo.int/export/sites/www/about-ip/en/iprm/pdf/ch2.pdf (accessed July 3, 2010).

Wacholtz, Larry *Lights, Glitter and Business Sense*, Thumbs Up Publishing, Washington: Cheney, 1984, 184-198.

Walt Disney Company, "Corporate Report 2009" http://corporate.disney.go.com/corporate/overview.html (July 21, 2010).

———, "Corporate Report 2009" http://corporate.disney.go.com/corporate/overview.html (July 21, 2010).

———, "Corporate Report 2009" http://corporate.disney.go.com/corporate/overview.html (July 21, 2010).

———, "Corporate Report 2009" http://corporate.disney.go.com/corporate/overview.html (July 21, 2010).

———, "Corporate Report 2009" http://corporate.disney.go.com/corporate/overview.html (July 21, 2010).

———, "Corporate Report 2009" http://corporate.disney.go.com/corporate/overview.html (July 21, 2010).

Wayne, Gary. "Seeing Stars: The Movie Studios," http://www.seeing-stars.com/Studios/warnerBrosStudios.shtml, (July 22, 2010).

We Are Listening, "Expose Your Music: Sync Licensing," http://www.wearelistening.org/sync_license.php, (accessed July 18, 2010).

Weaver, Steven. "Music Row Lawyer", http://musicrowlawyer.typepad.com/music_row_lawyer/360, (accessed March 10, 2011).

Weber, Bruce. "Jerry Wexler, A Behind-the-Scenes Force in Black Music is Dead at 91," New York Times, http://www.nytimes.com/2008/08/16/arts/music/16wexler.html?_r=2&hp=&pagewanted=all, (accessed March 19, 2011).

Webster's New World Dictionary, 11th ed., 894.

William Morris Endeavor Agency "Locations," http://www.wmeentertainment.com/, (accessed August 24, 2010).

———, "William Morris Agency, Inc," Bloomberg Businessweek, http://investing.businessweek.com/research/stocks/private/snapshot.asp?privcapId=872395, (accessed August 24, 2010).

Willis, Barry. "Seagram Buys Polygram," Stereophile.com, http://www.stereophile.com/news/10176/, (accessed July 22, 2010).

———, "Seagram Buys Polygram," Stereophile.com, http://www.stereophile.com/news/10176/, (accessed March 17, 2011).

Wollenberg, Skip. "Dream Deal Still Faces Many Hurdles," The Associated Press, as reported in The Tennessean, "Business Section," (page IE, 9/23/1995).

World Book Encyclopedia, CD-ROM, Windows XP, Chicago: World Book Inc., 2006.

World Intellectual Property Organization, "WIPO Performances and Phonograms Treaty," International Copyrights Relations of the United States, Cirular 38A, http://www.copyright.gov/circs/circ38a.pdf (accessed 07/26/2000).

World Trade Organization, "Marrakech Agreement." http://www.wipo.int/treaties/en/ip/wppt/trtdocs_wo034.html (accessed July 9, 2010)

Wortham, Jenna. "Facebook Tops 500 Million Users," New York Times, http://www.nytimes.com/2010/07/22/technology/22facebook.html?_r=1, (accessed July 22, 2010).

Yearwood, Trisha. "Yearwood is Singer/Businesswoman," The Tennessean, September 16, 1994.
Young, Scott. "Music Industry Quotes to live by," The musicbizacademy.com., http://wwwmusicbizacademy.com/knab/articles/musicquotes.htm (accessed July 16, 2010)

① 1 5 1

② 1 4 1

③ 1 4 5 1

④ 1 3 2 5 1

⑤ 1 1

⑥

GBD

100% of THIS is CRAZY

hannah lane

I love you!

1.) P5
2.) M3
3.) m2
4.) P4
5.) M7
6.) M6
7.) aug 4th
8.) m7
9.) m6
10.) M3

1.) 1 4 5 1
2.) 1 5 1
3.) 1 5 6 4 1
4.) 1 2 4 5 1
5.) 1 4 1
6.) 1 5 4 2 1
7.) 1 4 2 5 1
8.)
9.)
10.)

SPEND money

HANNAH
Lane

CPSIA information can be obtained
at www.ICGtesting.com
Printed in the USA
LVHW10s0116110918
589768LV00001B/4/P

9 780984 057245